Preface

I. N. I.

THE LUTHERAN HYMNAL is intended for use in church, school, and home. The committee entrusted with the task of compiling and editing has earnestly endeavored to produce a hymnal containing the best of the hymnodical treasures of the Church, both as to texts and tunes, in accord with the highest standards of Christian worship. It is our sincere prayer that these treasures may be cherished by God's people wherever the English tongue is used in public or private worship. We have freely used whatever we found of value and, by way of acknowledgment, have carefully indicated all sources. In turn, we freely offer for the use of others all original contributions or translations made by the committee as such or by its individual members.

"Unto Him that loved us and washed us from our sins in His own blood and hath made us kings and priests unto God and His Father: to Him be glory and dominion forever and ever! Amen."

THE INTERSYNODICAL COMMITTEE ON HYMNOLOGY AND
LITURGICS FOR THE EV. LUTH. SYNODICAL CONFERENCE
OF NORTH AMERICA

Copyright 1941
CONCORDIA PUBLISHING HOUSE
This copyright is held by Concordia Publishing House in trust for the four synods
now constituting the Evangelical Lutheran Synodical Conference of North America

PRINTED IN U. S. A.

The
Lutheran Hymnal

Authorized by the Synods Constituting

The

Evangelical Lutheran Synodical Conference
of North America

"And He hath put a new song in my
mouth, even praise unto our God"
Ps. 40:3

Publishing House
St. Louis   London

The Calendar

Advent Sunday
>The Advent Season — four weeks

St. Thomas — Apostle — December 21

CHRISTMAS DAY — The Feast of the Nativity of Our Lord — December 25

St. Stephen — Martyr — December 26

St. John — Apostle, Evangelist — December 27

The Holy Innocents — December 28

The Circumcision and the Name of Jesus (New Year's Day) — January 1

The Epiphany of Our Lord — January 6
>The Epiphany Season — one to six weeks

The Transfiguration of Our Lord — The Last Sunday
>after the Epiphany

Septuagesima Sunday

Sexagesima Sunday

Quinquagesima Sunday

The Conversion of St. Paul — January 25

The Presentation of Our Lord and The Purification of Mary — February 2

St. Matthias — Apostle — February 24

Ash Wednesday — The First Day of Lent
>The Lententide — forty-six days

Invocavit — First Sunday in Lent

Reminiscere — Second Sunday in Lent

Oculi — Third Sunday in Lent

Laetare — Fourth Sunday in Lent

Judica — Passion Sunday — Fifth Sunday in Lent

Palmarum — Sixth Sunday in Lent

Monday of Holy Week

Tuesday of Holy Week

Wednesday of Holy Week

Maundy Thursday

Good Friday

Holy Saturday — Easter Eve

EASTER DAY — The Feast of the Resurrection of Our Lord
>The Easter Season — forty days

Easter Monday

Easter Tuesday

The Annunciation — March 25

Quasimodogeniti — First Sunday after Easter

Misericordias Domini — Second Sunday after Easter

Jubilate — Third Sunday after Easter

Cantate — Fourth Sunday after Easter

Rogate — Fifth Sunday after Easter

The Ascension of Our Lord

Exaudi — The Sunday after the Ascension

St. Mark — Evangelist — April 25

St. Philip and St. James — Apostles — May 1

WHITSUNDAY — The Feast of Pentecost

Monday of Whitsun Week

Tuesday of Whitsun Week

The Feast of the Holy Trinity
>The Trinity Season — from 22 to 27 weeks

The Nativity of St. John the Baptist — June 24

St. Peter and St. Paul — Apostles — June 29

The Visitation — July 2

St. Mary Magdalene — July 22

St. James the Elder — Apostle — July 25

St. Bartholomew — Apostle — August 24

St. Matthew — Apostle, Evangelist — September 21

St. Michael and All Angels — September 29

St. Luke — Evangelist — October 18

St. Simon and St. Jude — Apostles — October 28

The Festival of the Reformation — October 31

All Saints' Day — November 1

St. Andrew — Apostle — November 30

Short Prayers

A Prayer upon Entering Church

Almighty, ever-living God, grant that I may gladly hear Thy Word and that all my worship may be acceptable unto Thee; through Jesus Christ, my Lord. Amen.

A Prayer at the Close of the Service

Grant, I beseech Thee, Almighty God, that the Word which I have heard this day may through Thy grace be so engrafted in my heart that I may bring forth the fruit of the Spirit; through Jesus Christ, my Lord. Amen.

A Prayer before Communion

Dear Savior, upon Thy gracious invitation I come to Thine altar. Let me find favor in Thine eyes that I may approach Thy Table in true faith and receive the Sacrament to the salvation of my soul. Amen.

A Prayer after Communion

O Thou blessed Savior Jesus Christ, who hast given Thyself to me in this holy Sacrament, keep me in Thy faith and favor; as Thou livest in me, let me also live in Thee. May Thy body and blood preserve me in the true faith unto everlasting life! Amen.

General Rubrics

The word "shall" in the Rubrics makes the part of the Service so designated obligatory, while the word "may" leaves it optional.

If the Confessional Service immediately precedes the Communion Service, the latter shall begin with the Trinitarian Invocation, followed by the Introit.

Good usage permits speaking the Preparatory Service.

The sign of the cross may be made at the Trinitarian Invocation and at the words of the Nicene Creed "and the life of the world to come."

℣ stands for Versicle, said by the Minister; ℟ designates the Response by the Congregation.

Instead of the Introit, a Psalm may be used. The Introit consists of Antiphon, Psalm, and Gloria Patri. When also the Gloria Patri is sung by the choir, the Antiphon is repeated.

Other Collects may be used with the Collect for the Day; the Congregation shall say or chant "Amen" after each Collect.

In the Service other Scripture lessons may be read before the Epistle. The Epistle and the Gospel shall always be read.

The Introit, Collect, Epistle, Gradual, and Gospel for the Transfiguration of our Lord shall be used on the last Sunday after the Epiphany in each year, except when there is only one Sunday after the Epiphany.

Choir selections may be sung immediately after the Gradual or after the Hallelujah.

On Trinity Sunday, at Matins, the Athanasian Creed may be used instead of the Psalmody.

Silent prayer should be offered upon entering the church and after the Benediction.

All necessary announcements which are not part of the Special Intercessions and Thanksgivings should be made after the close of the Service.

Matins and Vespers end with the Benedicamus if the Minister is not conducting the Service. If the Minister is the Officiant, he shall pronounce the Benediction, and the Benedicamus may be omitted.

Congregations are urged to let the basic structure of the Service remain intact. The wide choice permitted in the Rubrics makes it possible to have the Service as simple or as elaborate as the circumstances of each congregation may indicate.

The Hymnal is intended for use not only in the church service and in the school, but it may serve profitably also for family and private devotions. The prayers and the tables for Bible reading will be an aid for these uses.

The Order of Morning Service

Without Communion

A Hymn of Invocation of the Holy Ghost or another Hymn shall be sung

The Congregation shall rise, and the Minister shall say:

In the name of the Father and of the Son and of the Holy Ghost.

The Congregation shall say or chant:

A — — — men.

Then shall be said

The Confession of Sins

Minister: Beloved in the Lord! Let us draw near with a true heart and confess our sins unto God, our Father, beseeching Him in the name of our Lord Jesus Christ to grant us forgiveness.

All may kneel

℣: Our help is in the name of the Lord.

℟: Who made heaven and earth.

℣: I said, I will confess my transgressions unto the Lord.

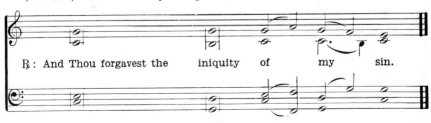

℟: And Thou forgavest the iniquity of my sin.

Minister: Almighty God, our Maker and Redeemer, we poor sinners confess unto Thee that we are by nature sinful and unclean and that we have sinned against Thee by thought, word, and deed. Wherefore we flee for refuge to Thine infinite mercy, seeking and imploring Thy grace for the sake of our Lord Jesus Christ.

Congregation and Minister: O most merciful God, who hast given Thine only-begotten Son to die for us, have mercy upon us and for His sake grant us remission of all our sins; and by Thy Holy Spirit increase in us true knowledge of Thee and of Thy will and true obedience to Thy Word, to the end that by Thy grace we may come to everlasting life; through Jesus Christ, our Lord. Amen.

Minister: Almighty God, our heavenly Father, hath had mercy upon us and hath given His only Son to die for us and for His sake forgiveth us all our sins. To them that believe on His name He giveth power to become the sons of God and hath promised them His Holy Spirit. He that believeth and is baptized shall be saved. Grant this, Lord, unto us all.

Congregation:

Then all may stand to the close of the Collect. Then shall be said or chanted

The Introit

The Introit (page 54) may be chanted by the Choir. If the Antiphon and Psalm are said by the Minister, the Gloria Patri shall be said or chanted by the Congregation

GLORIA PATRI

Glo - ry be to the Fa-ther and to the Son and to the Ho - ly Ghost;

As it was in the beginning, is now, and ever shall be, world without end. Amen.

The Kyrie

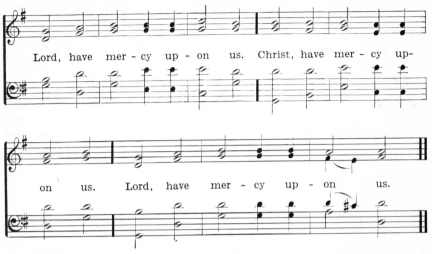

Lord, have mer - cy up - on us. Christ, have mer - cy up-

on us. Lord, have mer - cy up - on us.

Then may be said or chanted

The Gloria in Excelsis

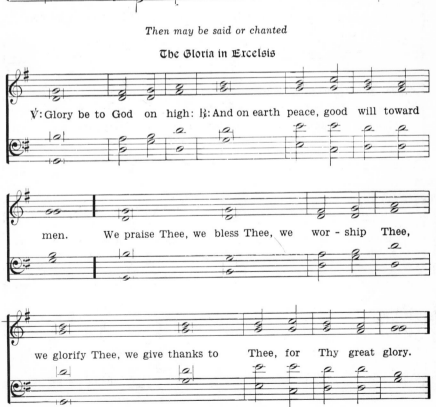

℣: Glory be to God on high: ℟: And on earth peace, good will toward

men. We praise Thee, we bless Thee, we wor - ship Thee,

we glorify Thee, we give thanks to Thee, for Thy great glory.

O Lord God, heav'n-ly King, God the Fa-ther Al - mighty.

O Lord, the only-begotten Son, Je - sus Christ;

O Lord God, Lamb of God, Son of the Father,

That takest away the sin of the world, have mercy up - on us.

Thou that takest away the sin of the world, re - ceive our prayer.

Thou that sittest at the right hand of God the Father, have mercy up-on us.

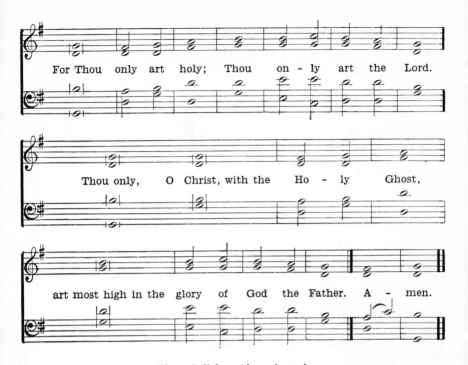

For Thou only art holy; Thou on-ly art the Lord. Thou only, O Christ, with the Ho-ly Ghost, art most high in the glory of God the Father. A - men.

Then shall be said or chanted

The Salutation

℣: The Lord be with you.

℞: And with thy spir - it.

℣: Let us pray:

Then shall the Minister say or chant

The Collect for the Day

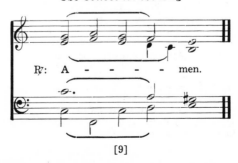

℞: A - - - - men.

[9]

Then shall the Minister read

The Epistle

Minister: The Epistle for .... is written in the .... chapter of
........................, beginning at the .... verse:

The Epistle ended, the Minister shall say: Here endeth the Epistle.

The Gradual

*may be chanted by the Choir. If the Gradual be read by the Minister, the Hallelujah
may be said or chanted by the Congregation, or the Sentence for the Season, or
a Sequence Hymn may be sung.*

The Hallelujah

Congregation:

Hal - le - lu - - - jah!

Or:

The Triple Hallelujah

Hal - le - lu - jah! Hal - le - lu - jah! Hal - le - lu - jah!

Or:

Hal - le - lu - jah! Hal - le - lu - jah! Hal - le - lu - jah!

Sentences for the Seasons

FOR ADVENT

Hallelujah! Remember, O Lord, Thy tender mercies: for they have been ever
of old. Hallelujah!

FOR CHRISTMAS

Hallelujah! Let the heavens rejoice, and let the earth be glad before the Lord:
for He hath made known His salvation. Hallelujah!

FOR THE EPIPHANY SEASON

Hallelujah! Oh, praise the Lord, all ye nations, and laud Him, all ye people. For His merciful kindness is great toward us: and the truth of the Lord endureth forever. Hallelujah!

FOR THE PASSION SEASON

Christ hath humbled Himself and become obedient unto death: even the death of the cross.

FOR THE EASTER SEASON

Hallelujah! Christ, our Passover, is sacrificed for us. Hallelujah!

FOR WHITSUNTIDE

Hallelujah! Thou sendest forth Thy Spirit, they are created: and Thou renewest the face of the earth. Hallelujah!

FROM TRINITY TO ADVENT

Hallelujah! O Lord, deal with Thy servant according unto Thy mercy and teach me Thy statutes. I am Thy servant, give me understanding: that I may know Thy testimonies. Hallelujah!

Or:

Hallelujah! Blessed be the Lord God of our fathers: praise Him and highly exalt Him forever. Hallelujah!

The Gospel

The Minister shall announce the Gospel for the Day:

The Holy Gospel is written in the .... chapter of St. ...., beginning at the .... verse:

The Congregation shall rise, unless it has stood during the reading of the Epistle, and shall say or chant:

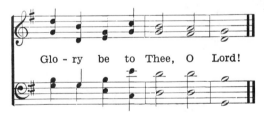

Glo - ry be to Thee, O Lord!

The Minister shall read the Gospel for the Day

The Gospel ended, the Minister shall say:

Here endeth the Gospel.

Congregation:

Praise be to Thee, O Christ!

Then shall be said or chanted

The Apostles' Creed

I believe in God the Father Almighty, Maker of heaven and earth.

And in Jesus Christ, His only Son, our Lord; Who was conceived by the Holy Ghost, Born of the Virgin Mary; Suffered under Pontius Pilate, Was crucified, dead, and buried; He descended into hell; The third day He rose again from the dead; He ascended into heaven And sitteth on the right hand of God the Father Almighty; From thence He shall come to judge the quick and the dead.

I believe in the Holy Ghost; The holy Christian Church, the communion of saints; The forgiveness of sins; The resurrection of the body; And the life everlasting. Amen.

Then shall a Hymn be sung. Then shall follow

The Sermon

The Sermon ended, the Congregation shall rise, and the Minister shall say:

The peace of God, which passeth all understanding, keep your hearts and minds through Christ Jesus.

The Offertory shall then be said or chanted, at the close of which the Congregation shall be seated

The Offertory

Cre-ate in me a clean heart, O God, and re-new a right spir-it with-in me. Cast me not a-way from Thy pres-ence; and take not Thy Ho-ly Spir-it from me. Re-store un-to me the

joy of Thy sal-va-tion; and up-hold me with Thy free spir - it. A-men.

Then shall the Offerings be gathered. They may be brought to the altar

Then shall follow

The General Prayer

Almighty and everlasting God, who art worthy to be had in reverence by all the children of men, we give Thee most humble and hearty thanks for the innumerable blessings, both temporal and spiritual, which, without any merit or worthiness on our part, Thou hast bestowed upon us.

We praise Thee especially that Thou hast preserved unto us in their purity Thy saving Word and the sacred ordinances of Thy house. And we beseech Thee, O Lord, to preserve and extend Thy Kingdom of Grace and to grant unto Thy holy Church throughout the world purity of doctrine and faithful pastors, who shall preach Thy Word with power; and help all who hear rightly to understand and truly to believe it. Send forth laborers into Thy harvest, and open the door of faith unto all the heathen and unto the people of Israel. In mercy remember the enemies of Thy Church, and grant unto them repentance unto life. Be Thou the Protector and Defender of Thy people in all time of tribulation and danger; and may we, in communion with Thy Church and in brotherly unity with all our fellow Christians, fight the good fight of faith and in the end receive the salvation of our souls.

Bestow Thy grace upon all the nations of the earth. Especially do we entreat Thee to bless our land and all its inhabitants and all who are in authority. Cause Thy glory to dwell among us and let mercy and truth, righteousness and peace, everywhere prevail. To this end we commend to Thy care all our schools and pray Thee to make them nurseries of useful knowledge and Christian virtues, that they may bring forth the wholesome fruits of life.

Graciously defend us from all calamities by fire and water, from war and pestilence, from scarcity and famine. Protect and prosper everyone in his appropriate calling, and cause all useful arts to flourish among us. Be Thou the God and Father of the widow and the fatherless children, the Helper of the sick and the needy, and the Comforter of the forsaken and distressed.

Accept, we beseech Thee, our bodies and souls, our hearts and minds, our talents and powers, together with the offerings we bring before Thee, which is our reasonable service.

Here special Supplications, Intercessions, and Prayers may be made

And as we are strangers and pilgrims on earth, help us by true faith and a godly life to prepare for the world to come; doing the work Thou hast given us to do while it is day; before the night cometh when no man can work. And when our last hour shall come, support us by Thy power and receive us into Thine everlasting kingdom; through Jesus Christ, Thy Son, our Lord, who liveth and reigneth with Thee and the Holy Ghost forever and ever.

[13]

Then shall be said by all

The Lord's Prayer

Our Father who art in heaven, Hallowed be Thy name; Thy kingdom come; Thy will be done on earth as it is in heaven; Give us this day our daily bread; And forgive us our trespasses, as we forgive those who trespass against us; And lead us not into temptation; But deliver us from evil; For Thine is the kingdom and the power and the glory forever and ever. **Amen.**

Then may a Hymn be sung

Then may be said or chanted

The Collect for the Word

Blessed Lord, who hast caused all Holy Scriptures to be written for our learning, grant that we may in such wise hear them, read, mark, learn, and inwardly digest them, that by patience and comfort of Thy holy Word we may embrace, and ever hold fast, the blessed hope of everlasting life, which Thou hast given us in our Savior Jesus Christ, who liveth and reigneth with Thee and the Holy Ghost, ever one God, world without end.

Or:

The Collect for the Church

Grant, we beseech Thee, Almighty God, unto Thy Church Thy Holy Spirit and the wisdom which cometh down from above, that Thy Word, as becometh it, may not be bound, but have free course and be preached to the joy and edifying of Christ's holy people, that in steadfast faith we may serve Thee and in the confession of Thy name abide unto the end; through Jesus Christ, our Lord, who liveth and reigneth with Thee and the Holy Ghost, ever one God, world without end.

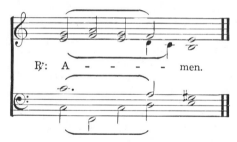

Then shall the Minister say or chant

The Benediction

Minister: The Lord bless thee and keep thee.
The Lord make His face shine upon thee and be gracious unto thee.
The Lord lift up His countenance upon thee and give thee peace.

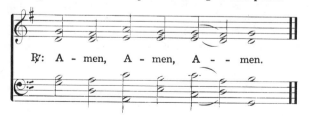

Silent Prayer

The Order of the Holy Communion

A Hymn of Invocation of the Holy Ghost or another Hymn shall be sung

The Congregation shall rise, and the Minister shall say:

In the name of the Father and of the Son and of the Holy Ghost.

The Congregation shall say or chant:

A - - - men.

Then shall be said

The Confession of Sins

Minister: Beloved in the Lord! Let us draw near with a true heart and confess our sins unto God, our Father, beseeching Him in the name of our Lord Jesus Christ to grant us forgiveness.

All may kneel

℣: Our help is in the name of the Lord.

℟: Who made heaven and earth.

℣: I said, I will confess my transgressions unto the Lord.

℟: And Thou forgavest the iniquity of my sin.

Then the Minister and the Congregation shall say:

O almighty God, merciful Father, I, a poor, miserable sinner, confess unto Thee all my sins and iniquities with which I have ever offended Thee and justly deserved Thy temporal and eternal punishment. But I am heartily sorry for them and sincerely repent of them, and I pray Thee of Thy boundless mercy and for the sake of the holy, innocent, bitter sufferings and death of Thy beloved Son, Jesus Christ, to be gracious and merciful to me, a poor, sinful being.

Then the Minister shall pronounce the Absolution:

Upon this your confession, I, by virtue of my office, as a called and ordained servant of the Word, announce the grace of God unto all of you, and in the stead and by the command of my Lord Jesus Christ I forgive you all your sins in the name of the Father and of the Son and of the Holy Ghost.

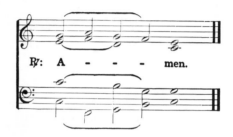

Then all may stand to the close of the Collect. Then shall be said or chanted

The Introit

The Introit (page 54) may be chanted by the Choir. If the Antiphon and Psalm are said by the Minister, the Gloria Patri shall be said or chanted by the Congregation

GLORIA PATRI

[16]

Then shall be said or chanted by the Minister and the Congregation

The Kyrie

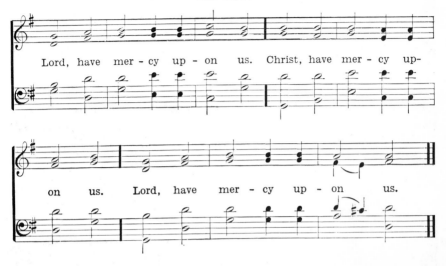

Lord, have mer - cy up - on us. Christ, have mer - cy up-

on us. Lord, have mer - cy up - on us.

Then shall be said or chanted

The Gloria in Excelsis

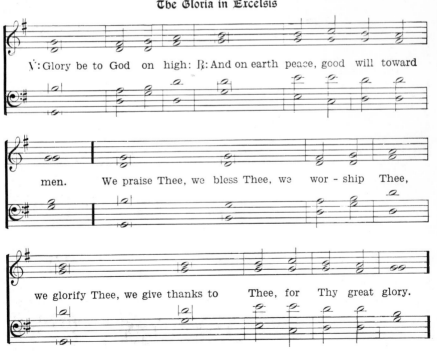

V: Glory be to God on high: R: And on earth peace, good will toward

men. We praise Thee, we bless Thee, we wor - ship Thee,

we glorify Thee, we give thanks to Thee, for Thy great glory.

O Lord God, heav'n-ly King, God the Fa - ther Al - mighty.

O Lord, the only-begotten Son, Je - sus Christ;

O Lord God, Lamb of God, Son of the Father,

That takest away the sin of the world, have mercy up - on us.

Thou that takest away the sin of the world, re - ceive our prayer.

Thou that sittest at the right hand of God the Father, have mercy up-on us.

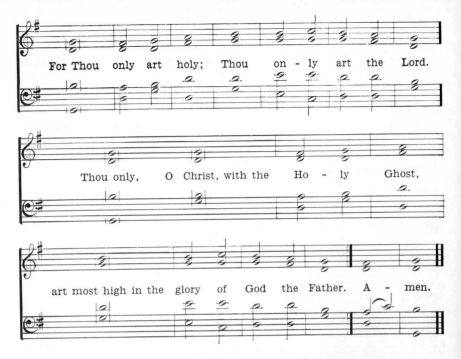

For Thou only art holy; Thou on-ly art the Lord.

Thou only, O Christ, with the Ho-ly Ghost,

art most high in the glory of God the Father. A - men.

Then shall be said or chanted

The Salutation

℣: The Lord be with you.

℟: And with thy spir - it.

℣: Let us pray.

Then shall the Minister say or chant

The Collect for the Day

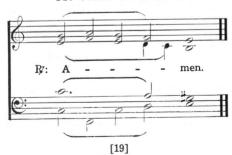

℟: A - - - - men.

[19]

Then shall the Minister read

The Epistle

Minister: The Epistle for .... is written in the .... chapter of
................, beginning at the .... verse:

The Epistle ended, the Minister shall say: Here endeth the Epistle.

The Gradual

*may be chanted by the Choir. If the Gradual be read by the Minister, the Hallelujah
may be said or chanted by the Congregation, or the Sentence for the Season, or
a Sequence Hymn may be sung.*

The Hallelujah

Congregation:

Or:

The Triple Hallelujah

Or:

Sentences for the Seasons

FOR ADVENT

Hallelujah! Remember, O Lord, Thy tender mercies: for they have been ever
of old. Hallelujah!

FOR CHRISTMAS

Hallelujah! Let the heavens rejoice, and let the earth be glad before the Lord:
for He hath made known His salvation. Hallelujah!

FOR THE EPIPHANY SEASON

Hallelujah! Oh, praise the Lord, all ye nations, and laud Him, all ye people. For His merciful kindness is great toward us: and the truth of the Lord endureth forever. Hallelujah!

FOR THE PASSION SEASON

Christ hath humbled Himself and become obedient unto death: even the death of the cross.

FOR THE EASTER SEASON

Hallelujah! Christ, our Passover, is sacrificed for us. Hallelujah!

FOR WHITSUNTIDE

Hallelujah! Thou sendest forth Thy Spirit, they are created: and Thou renewest the face of the earth. Hallelujah!

FROM TRINITY TO ADVENT

Hallelujah! O Lord, deal with Thy servant according unto Thy mercy and teach me Thy statutes. I am Thy servant, give me understanding: that I may know Thy testimonies. Hallelujah!

Or:

Hallelujah! Blessed be the Lord God of our fathers: praise Him and highly exalt Him forever. Hallelujah!

The Gospel

The Minister shall announce the Gospel for the Day:

The Holy Gospel is written in the .... chapter of St. ...., beginning at the .... verse:

The Congregation shall rise, unless it has stood during the reading of the Epistle, and shall say or chant:

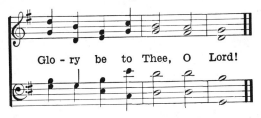

Glo - ry be to Thee, O Lord!

The Minister shall read the Gospel for the Day

The Gospel ended, the Minister shall say:

Here endeth the Gospel.

Congregation:

Praise be to Thee, O Christ!

[21]

The Nicene Creed

I believe in one God, the Father Almighty, Maker of heaven and earth and of all things visible and invisible.

And in one Lord Jesus Christ, the only-begotten Son of God, begotten of His Father before all worlds, God of God, Light of Light, Very God of Very God, Begotten, not made, Being of one substance with the Father, By whom all things were made; Who for us men and for our salvation came down from heaven And was incarnate by the Holy Ghost of the Virgin Mary And was made man; And was crucified also for us under Pontius Pilate. He suffered and was buried; And the third day He rose again according to the Scriptures; And ascended into heaven, And sitteth on the right hand of the Father; And He shall come again with glory to judge both the quick and the dead; Whose kingdom shall have no end.

And I believe in the Holy Ghost, The Lord and Giver of Life, Who proceedeth from the Father and the Son, Who with the Father and the Son together is worshiped and glorified, Who spake by the Prophets. And I believe one holy Christian and Apostolic Church. I acknowledge one Baptism for the remission of sins, And I look for the resurrection of the dead, And the life of the world to come. Amen.

Then shall a Hymn be sung. Then shall follow

The Sermon

The Sermon ended, the Congregation shall rise, and the Minister shall say:

The peace of God, which passeth all understanding, keep your hearts and minds through Christ Jesus.

The Offertory shall then be said or chanted, at the close of which the Congregation shall be seated

The Offertory

Cre-ate in me a clean heart, O God, and re-new a right spir-it with-in me. Cast me not a-way from Thy pres-ence, and

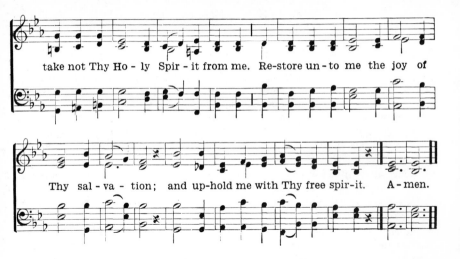

take not Thy Ho - ly Spir - it from me. Re-store un - to me the joy of Thy sal - va - tion; and up-hold me with Thy free spir-it. A - men.

Then shall the Offerings be gathered. They may be brought to the altar

Then shall follow

The General Prayer

Almighty and most merciful God, the Father of our Lord Jesus Christ, we give Thee thanks for all Thy goodness and tender mercies, especially for the gift of Thy dear Son and for the revelation of Thy will and grace; and we beseech Thee so to implant Thy Word in us that in good and honest hearts we may keep it and bring forth fruit by patient continuance in welldoing.

Most heartily we beseech Thee so to rule and govern Thy Church Universal, with all its pastors and ministers, that we may be preserved in the pure doctrine of Thy saving Word, whereby faith toward Thee may be strengthened, charity increased in us toward all mankind, and Thy kingdom extended. Send forth laborers into Thy harvest, and sustain those whom Thou hast sent, that the Word of Reconciliation may be proclaimed to all people and the Gospel preached in all the world.

Grant also health and prosperity to all that are in authority, especially to * the President and Congress of the United States, the Governor and Legislature of this commonwealth, and to all our Judges and Magistrates,

For Use in the British Empire { * Her Majesty the Queen of the British Commonwealth of Nations, the Governor-general and the Prime Minister of our Dominion, as well as the Premier of our Province, and all Governments and Parliaments, and all Judges and Magistrates,

and endue them with grace to rule after Thy good pleasure, to the maintenance of righteousness and to the hindrance and punishment of wickedness, that we may lead a quiet and peaceable life in all godliness and honesty.

May it please Thee also to turn the hearts of our enemies and adversaries that they may cease their enmity and be inclined to walk with us in meekness and in peace.

All who are in trouble, want, sickness, anguish of labor, peril of death, or any other adversity, especially those who are in suffering for Thy name's and for Thy truth's sake, comfort, O God, with Thy Holy Spirit, that they may receive and acknowledge their afflictions as the manifestation of Thy fatherly will.

And although we have deserved Thy righteous wrath and manifold punishments, yet, we entreat Thee, O most merciful Father, remember not the sins of our youth nor our many transgressions, but out of Thine unspeakable goodness, grace, and mercy defend us from all harm and danger of body and soul. Preserve us from false and pernicious doctrine, from war and bloodshed, from plague and pestilence, from all calamity by fire and water, from hail and tempest, from failure of harvest and from famine, from anguish of heart and despair of Thy mercy, and from an evil death. And in every time of trouble show Thyself a very present Help, the Savior of all men, and especially of them that believe.

Cause all needful fruits of the earth to prosper, that we may enjoy them in due season. Give success to the Christian training of the young, to all lawful occupations on land and sea, and to all pure arts and useful knowledge; and crown them with Thy blessing.

Receive, O God, our bodies and souls and all our talents, together with the offerings we bring before Thee, for Thou hast purchased us to be Thine own, that we may live unto Thee.

Here special Supplications, Intercessions, and Prayers may be made

These and whatsoever other things Thou wouldst have us ask of Thee, O God, grant unto us for the sake of the bitter sufferings and death of Jesus Christ, Thine only Son, our Lord and Savior, who liveth and reigneth with Thee and the Holy Ghost, ever one God, world without end. Amen.

Then may a Hymn be sung

The Hymn ended, the Congregation shall rise and stand to the end of the Agnus Dei

The Preface

℣: The Lord be with you.

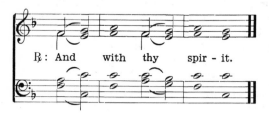

℣: Lift up your hearts.

[24]

℣: Let us give thanks unto the Lord, our God.

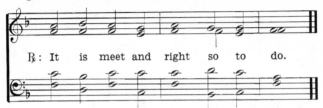

R̥: It is meet and right so to do.

Minister: It is truly meet, right, and salutary that we should at all times and in all places give thanks unto Thee, O Lord, holy Father, almighty, everlasting God:

Here shall follow the Proper Preface

Proper Prefaces

Advent: Through Jesus Christ, our Lord, whose way John the Baptist prepared, proclaiming Him the Messiah, the very Lamb of God, and calling sinners to repentance, that they might escape from the wrath to be revealed when He cometh again in glory. Therefore —

Christmas: For in the mystery of the Word made flesh Thou hast given us a new revelation of Thy glory, that, seeing Thee in the person of Thy Son, we may be drawn to the love of those things which are not seen. Therefore —

Epiphany: And now do we praise Thee that Thou didst send unto us Thine only-begotten Son and that in Him, being found in fashion as a man, Thou didst manifest the fullness of Thy glory. Therefore —

Lent: Who on the tree of the cross didst give salvation unto mankind that, whence death arose, thence Life also might rise again; and that he who by a tree once overcame might likewise by a tree be overcome, through Christ, our Lord; through whom with angels —

Easter: But chiefly are we bound to praise Thee for the glorious resurrection of Thy Son, Jesus Christ, our Lord; for He is the very Paschal Lamb which was offered for us and hath taken away the sins of the world; who by His death hath destroyed death and by His rising to life again hath restored to us everlasting life. Therefore —

Ascension Day: Through Jesus Christ, our Lord, who after His resurrection appeared openly to all His disciples and in their sight was taken up into heaven that He might make us partakers of His divine nature. Therefore —

Whitsunday: Through Jesus Christ, our Lord, who ascended above the heavens and, sitting on Thy right hand, poured out on this day the Holy Spirit, as He had promised, upon the chosen disciples; whereat the whole earth rejoices with exceeding joy. Therefore —

Trinity: Who with Thine only-begotten Son and the Holy Ghost art one God, one Lord. And in the confession of the only true God we worship the Trinity in Person and the Unity in Substance, of Majesty coequal. Therefore —

Days of the Apostles and Evangelists: Because Thou didst mightily govern and protect Thy holy Church, which the blessed Apostles and Evangelists instructed in Thy divine and saving truth, through Jesus Christ, our Lord. Therefore —

Then shall follow immediately:

Therefore with angels and archangels and with all the company of heaven we laud and magnify Thy glorious name, evermore praising Thee and saying:

Then shall be said or chanted

The Sanctus

Ho - ly, ho - ly, ho - ly, Lord God of Sab - a - oth;

Heav'n and earth are full of Thy glo - ry; Ho - san - na, Ho -

san - na, Ho - san - na in the high - est. Bless - ed is He,

Bless - ed is He, Bless - ed is He that com - eth in the name of the Lord.

Ho - san - na, Ho - san - na, Ho - san - na in the high - est.

The Lord's Prayer

Minister: Our Father who art in heaven, Hallowed be Thy name; Thy kingdom come; Thy will be done on earth as it is in heaven; Give us this day our daily bread; And forgive us our trespasses, as we forgive those who trespass against us; And lead us not into temptation; But deliver us from evil;

Then shall the Minister say or chant

The Words of Institution

Our Lord Jesus Christ, the same night in which He was betrayed, took bread; and when He had given thanks, He brake it and gave it to His disciples, saying, "Take, eat; this is My body, which is given for you. This do in remembrance of Me."

After the same manner also He took the cup when He had supped, and when He had given thanks, He gave it to them, saying, "Drink ye all of it; this cup is the New Testament in My blood, which is shed for you for the remission of sins. This do, as oft as ye drink it, in remembrance of Me."

The Pax Domini

℣: The peace of the Lord be with you alway!

The Agnus Dei

O Christ, Thou Lamb of God, that tak-est a-way the sin of the

world, have mer-cy up-on us. O Christ, Thou Lamb of God, that

tak-est a-way the sin of the world, have mer-cy up-on us.

O Christ, Thou Lamb of God, that tak-est a-way the sin of the

world, grant us Thy peace. . . A - - - - men.

The Distribution

During the Distribution the Congregation may sing one or more hymns

When the Minister giveth the bread, he shall say:

Take, eat; this is the true body of our Lord and Savior Jesus Christ, given into death for your sins. May this strengthen and preserve you in the true faith unto life everlasting!

When he giveth the cup, he shall say:

Take, drink; this is the true blood of our Lord and Savior Jesus Christ, shed for the remission of your sins. May this strengthen and preserve you in the true faith unto life everlasting!

In dismissing the Communicants, the Minister may say:

Depart in peace.

The Distribution ended, all shall rise and say or chant

The Nunc Dimittis

Lord, now lettest Thou Thy servant de - part in peace ac-cord-ing to Thy word, For mine eyes have seen Thy Salvation: which Thou hast pre - pared be - fore the face of all people, a Light to light - en the Gen - tiles and the Glo - ry of Thy

[29]

peo-ple Is - - - - ra-el. Glo-ry be to the Father and to the Son and to the Ho-ly Ghost; As it was in the be-ginning, is now, and ev-er shall be, world with-out end. A-men.

Then shall be said or chanted

The Thanksgiving

℣: Oh, give thanks unto the Lord, for He is good.

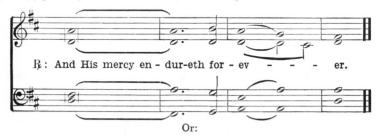

℞: And His mercy en-dur-eth for-ev - - - er.

Or:

℣: As often as ye eat this bread and drink this cup:

℞: **Ye do show the Lord's death till He come.**

Minister: We give thanks to Thee, Almighty God, that Thou hast refreshed us through this salutary gift; and we beseech Thee that of Thy mercy Thou wouldst strengthen us through the same in faith toward Thee and in fervent love toward one another; through Jesus Christ, our Lord, who liveth and reigneth with Thee and the Holy Ghost, ever one God, world without end.

Or:

O God the Father, Fount and Source of all goodness, who in loving-kindness didst send Thine only-begotten Son into the flesh, we thank Thee that for His sake Thou hast given us pardon and peace in this Sacrament; and we beseech Thee not to forsake Thy children, but evermore to rule our hearts and minds by Thy Holy Spirit, that we may be enabled constantly to serve Thee; through Jesus Christ, our Lord, who liveth and reigneth with Thee and the Holy Ghost, ever one God, world without end.

℟: A - - - - - men.

Then may a post-Communion Hymn be sung

Then may be said or chanted the Salutation and the Benedicamus

℣: The Lord be with you.

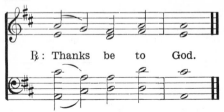

℟: And with thy spir - it.

℣: Bless we the Lord.

℟: Thanks be to God.

Then shall the Minister say or chant

The Benediction

Minister: The Lord bless thee and keep thee.
The Lord make His face shine upon thee and be gracious unto thee.
The Lord lift up His countenance upon thee and give thee peace.

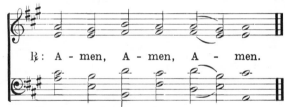

℟: A - men, A - men, A - men.

Silent Prayer

[31]

The Order of Matins

A Hymn of Invocation of the Holy Ghost or another Hymn may be sung

The Congregation shall rise

Then shall be said or chanted the Versicles here following. During the Penitential Seasons the Hallelujah shall be omitted. All shall stand to the end of the Venite

℣: O Lord, open Thou my lips.

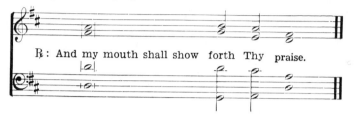

℟: And my mouth shall show forth Thy praise.

℣: Make haste, O God, to deliver me.

℟: Make haste to help me, O Lord.

Glory be to the Father and to the Son and to the Ho - ly Ghost; As it was in the beginning, is now, and ev - er shall be, world with - out end. A - men. Hal - le - lu - jah!

[32]

Then shall follow the Invitatory with the Venite or on Feast Days the special Invitatory

The Invitatory

℣: Oh, come, let us worship the Lord:

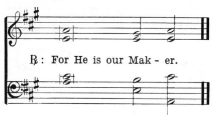

℟ : For He is our Mak - er.

The Venite

1 Oh, come, let us sing - - - - - | unto the | Lord:
3 For the Lord is a - - - - - - | great | God:
5 The sea is His, and He - - - - | made | it:
Glory be to the Father and - - - - | to the | Son:

1 let us make a joyful noise to the Rock of | our sal- | va- | tion.
3 and a great - - - - - - | King a- | bove all | gods.
5 and His hands - - - - - | form-ed | the dry | land.
and - - - - - - - | to the | Ho-ly | Ghost;

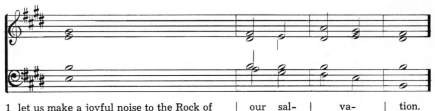

2 Let us come before His presence with thanks- | giv- | ing:
4 In His hand are the deep places - - - | of the | earth:
6 Oh, come, let us worship and - - - - | bow | down:
7 For He - - - - - - - | is our | God:
As it was in the beginning, is now, and - - | ever shall | be,

2 and make a joyful - - - -	noise unto	Him with	psalms.
4 the strength of the hills is - - -	His	al-	so.
6 let us kneel before the - - -	Lord, our	Mak-	er.
7 and we are the people of His pasture and the	sheep of	His	hand.
world - - - - - - -	with-out	end. A-	men.

Then shall be sung

The Hymn

Then shall follow

The Psalmody

One or more Psalms shall be said or chanted. At the end of each Psalm or at the end of the Psalmody the Gloria Patri shall be said or chanted. The Congregation may be seated during the Psalmody and rise at the last Gloria Patri. Instead of one of the Psalms, the Athanasian Creed (page 53) may be used on Trinity Sunday. An Antiphon may be used with each Psalm

The Lection

The Lesson or Lessons shall then be read, and after each Lesson may be said or chanted:

℣: But Thou, O Lord, have mercy upon us.

℟: Thanks be to Thee, O Lord!

After the Lesson or Lessons a Responsory may be said or chanted
Then may follow a brief Exhortation or

The Sermon

The Offerings may then be gathered
The Congregation shall rise and say or chant

The Canticle

The Te Deum Laudamus or the Benedictus may be used on Sundays
Other Canticles may be used on other days

[34]

THE TE DEUM LAUDAMUS

1 We praise Thee, O God; we acknowledge Thee to - | be the | Lord.
3 Holy, holy, holy, Lord God of - - - - - | Sab-a- | oth!
5 The noble army of martyrs - - - - - | praise | Thee;

1 All the earth doth worship Thee, the Father | ev-er- | last- | ing.
3 Heaven and earth are full of the majesty | of Thy | glo- | ry.
5 the holy Church throughout all the world | doth ac- | knowl-edge | Thee:

2 To Thee all angels cry aloud, the heavens and
  all the - - - - - - - - | powers there- | in;
4 The glorious company of the Apostles - - | praise | Thee;
6 The Father of an infinite majesty; Thine ador-
  able true and - - - - - - - | on-ly | Son,
7 Thou art the King of Glory, - - - - | O | Christ.

2 To Thee cherubim and seraphim con- - | tin-ual- | ly do | cry:
4 The goodly fellowship of the - - | proph-ets | praise | Thee;
6 also the Holy - - - - - | Ghost, the | Com-fort- | er.
7 Thou art the everlasting Son - - | of the | Fa- | ther.

[35]

8 When Thou tookest upon Thee to de- - - | liv-er | man,
10 Thou sittest at the right - - - - - | hand of | God
12 We therefore pray Thee, help Thy - - - | serv- | ants,

8 Thou didst humble Thyself to be born - | of a | vir- | gin.
10 in the glory - - - - - - | of the | Fa- | ther.
12 whom Thou hast redeem-ed - - - | with Thy | pre-cious | blood.

9 When Thou hadst overcome the - - - | sharp-ness of | death,
11 We believe that - - - - - - | Thou shalt | come
13 Make them to be number-ed - - - | with Thy | saints

9 Thou didst open the kingdom of heaven to | all be- | liev- | ers.
11 to - - - - - - - - - | be | our | Judge.
13 in glory - - - - - - - - | ever- | last- | ing.

14 O Lord, save Thy people and bless Thine   - | her-i- | tage.
16 Vouchsafe, O Lord, to keep us this day with- | out | sin.

14 Govern them and lift them - - - | up for- | ev- | er.
16 O Lord, have mercy upon us, have - - | mercy up- | on | us.

15 Day by day we - - - - - - - | magni-fy | Thee.
17 O Lord, let Thy mercy be upon us, as our trust - | is in | Thee.

15 And we worship Thy name ever, - - | world with- | out | end.
17 O Lord, in Thee have I trusted; let me never | be con- | found- | ed.

Or:

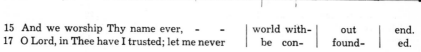

[37]

THE BENEDICTUS

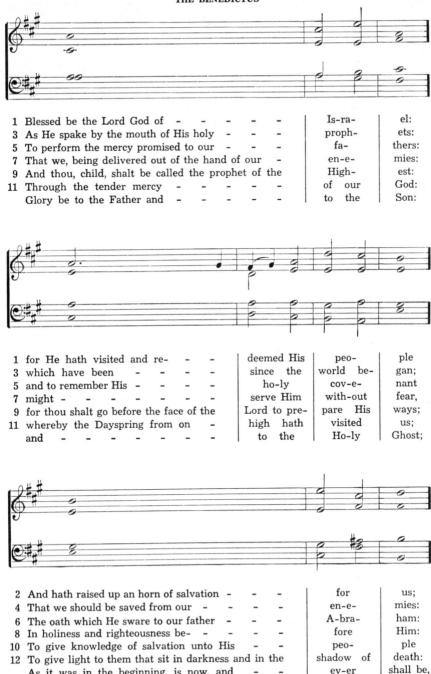

1	Blessed be the Lord God of - - - - -	Is-ra-	el:
3	As He spake by the mouth of His holy - - -	proph-	ets:
5	To perform the mercy promised to our - - -	fa-	thers:
7	That we, being delivered out of the hand of our -	en-e-	mies:
9	And thou, child, shalt be called the prophet of the	High-	est:
11	Through the tender mercy - - - - -	of our	God:
	Glory be to the Father and - - - - -	to the	Son:

1	for He hath visited and re- - - -	deemed His	peo-	ple
3	which have been - - - - -	since the	world be-	gan;
5	and to remember His - - - -	ho-ly	cov-e-	nant
7	might - - - - - - -	serve Him	with-out	fear,
9	for thou shalt go before the face of the	Lord to pre-	pare His	ways;
11	whereby the Dayspring from on -	high hath	visited	us;
	and - - - - - - -	to the	Ho-ly	Ghost;

2	And hath raised up an horn of salvation - - -	for	us;
4	That we should be saved from our - - - -	en-e-	mies:
6	The oath which He sware to our father - - -	A-bra-	ham:
8	In holiness and righteousness be- - - - -	fore	Him:
10	To give knowledge of salvation unto His - -	peo-	ple
12	To give light to them that sit in darkness and in the	shadow of	death:
	As it was in the beginning, is now, and - -	ev-er	shall be,

[38]

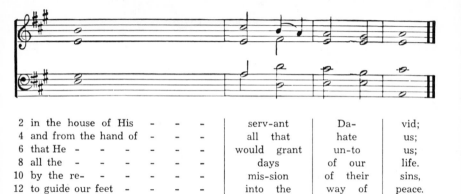

2 in the house of His - - -	serv-ant	Da-	vid;
4 and from the hand of - - -	all that	hate	us;
6 that He - - - - - -	would grant	un-to	us;
8 all the - - - - -	days	of our	life.
10 by the re- - - - -	mis-sion	of their	sins,
12 to guide our feet - - -	into the	way of	peace.
world - - - - -	with-out	end. A-	men.

The Prayers

Then shall be said the Prayers here following or the Suffrages (p. 113), the Litany (p. 110), or other Prayers. All shall say or chant

THE KYRIE

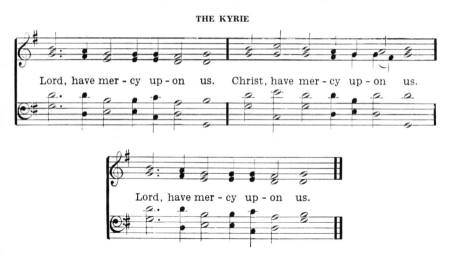

Lord, have mer - cy up - on us. Christ, have mer - cy up - on us.

Lord, have mer - cy up - on us.

Then all shall say or chant

THE LORD'S PRAYER

Our Father who art in heaven, Hallowed be Thy name; Thy kingdom come; Thy will be done on earth as it is in heaven; Give us this day our daily bread; And forgive us our trespasses, as we forgive those who trespass against us; And lead us not into temptation; But deliver us from evil; For Thine is the kingdom and the power and the glory forever and ever. Amen.

Then shall be said or chanted the Salutation, the Collect for the Day or other Collects, and the Collect for Grace. Each Collect may be preceded by a Versicle. After each Collect the Congregation shall say or chant: Amen

℣: The Lord be with you.

℟: And with thy spir - it.

THE COLLECT FOR GRACE

O Lord, our heavenly Father, almighty and everlasting God, who hast safely brought us to the beginning of this day, defend us in the same with Thy mighty power and grant that this day we fall into no sin, neither run into any kind of danger, but that all our doings, being ordered by Thy governance, may be righteous in Thy sight; through Jesus Christ, Thy Son, our Lord, who liveth and reigneth with Thee and the Holy Ghost, ever one God, world without end.

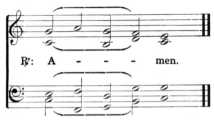

℟: A - - - men.

The Benedicamus

℣: Bless we the Lord.

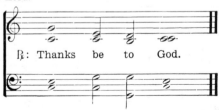

℟: Thanks be to God.

The Benediction

℣: The grace of our Lord Jesus Christ and the love of God and the communion of the Holy Ghost be with you all.

℟: A - - - men.

Silent Prayer

[40]

The Order of Vespers

A Hymn of Invocation of the Holy Ghost or another Hymn may be sung

The Congregation shall rise
Then shall be said or chanted the Versicles here following. During the Penitential Seasons the Hallelujah shall be omitted

℣: O Lord, open Thou my lips.

℟: And my mouth shall show forth Thy praise.

℣: Make haste, O God, to deliver me.

℟: Make haste to help me, O Lord.

Glory be to the Father and to the Son and to the Ho-ly Ghost: As it was in the beginning, is now, and ev-er shall be: world with-out end. A-men. Hal-le-lu-jah!

[41]

The Psalmody

One or more Psalms may be said or chanted. At the end of each Psalm or at the end of the Psalmody the Gloria Patri shall be said or chanted. The Congregation may be seated during the Psalmody and rise at the last Gloria Patri. An Antiphon may be used with each Psalm

The Lection

The Lesson or Lessons shall then be read, and after each Lesson may be said or chanted:

℣: But Thou, O Lord, have mercy upon us.

℞: Thanks be to Thee, O Lord!

After the Lesson or Lessons a Responsory may be said or chanted

Then a Hymn may be sung

Then may follow

The Sermon

The Offerings may then be gathered

Then shall be sung

The Hymn

*Then, all standing, may be said or chanted this Versicle
On Feast Days a special Versicle may be used*

℣: Let my prayer be set forth before Thee as incense:

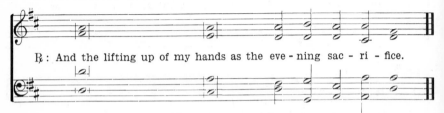

℞: And the lifting up of my hands as the eve - ning sac - ri - fice.

Then shall be said or chanted

The Canticle

An Antiphon may be said or chanted with the Canticle

[42]

THE MAGNIFICAT

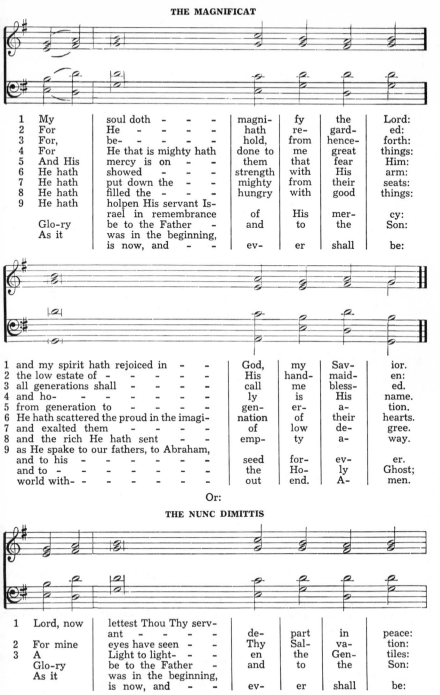

1	My	soul doth - - -	magni-	fy	the	Lord:
2	For	He - - - -	hath	re-	gard-	ed:
3	For,	be- - - - -	hold,	from	hence-	forth:
4	For	He that is mighty hath	done to	me	great	things:
5	And His	mercy is on - -	them	that	fear	Him:
6	He hath	showed - - -	strength	with	His	arm:
7	He hath	put down the - -	mighty	from	their	seats:
8	He hath	filled the - - -	hungry	with	good	things:
9	He hath	holpen His servant Is-rael in remembrance	of	His	mer-	cy:
	Glo-ry	be to the Father -	and	to	the	Son:
	As it	was in the beginning, is now, and - -	ev-	er	shall	be:

1	and my spirit hath rejoiced in - -	God,	my	Sav-	ior.
2	the low estate of - - - - -	His	hand-	maid-	en:
3	all generations shall - - - -	call	me	bless-	ed.
4	and ho- - - - - -	ly	is	His	name.
5	from generation to - - -	gen-	er-	a-	tion.
6	He hath scattered the proud in the imagi-	nation	of	their	hearts.
7	and exalted them - - - -	of	low	de-	gree.
8	and the rich He hath sent - -	emp-	ty	a-	way.
9	as He spake to our fathers, to Abraham, and to his - - - - - -	seed	for-	ev-	er.
	and to - - - - - - -	the	Ho-	ly	Ghost;
	world with- - - - - -	out	end.	A-	men.

Or:

THE NUNC DIMITTIS

1	Lord, now	lettest Thou Thy serv-ant - - - -	de-	part	in	peace:
2	For mine	eyes have seen - -	Thy	Sal-	va-	tion:
3	A	Light to light- - -	en	the	Gen-	tiles:
	Glo-ry	be to the Father -	and	to	the	Son:
	As it	was in the beginning, is now, and - -	ev-	er	shall	be:

[43]

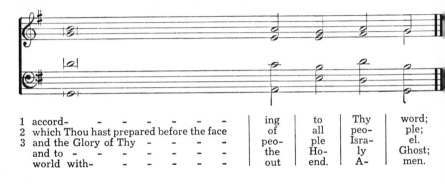

1 accord- - - - - - -	ing	to	Thy	word;
2 which Thou hast prepared before the face	of	all	peo-	ple;
3 and the Glory of Thy - - - -	peo-	ple	Isra-	el.
and to - - - - - - -	the	Ho-	ly	Ghost;
world with- - - - - -	out	end.	A-	men.

The Prayers

Then shall be said or chanted the Prayers here following or the Suffrages (p. 113), the Litany (p. 110), or other Prayers. All shall say or chant

THE KYRIE

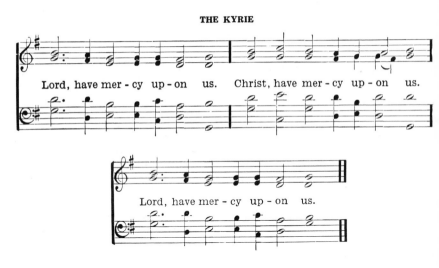

Then all shall say or chant

THE LORD'S PRAYER

Our Father who art in heaven, Hallowed be Thy name; Thy kingdom come Thy will be done on earth as it is in heaven; Give us this day our daily bread And forgive us our trespasses, as we forgive those who trespass against us; And lead us not into temptation; But deliver us from evil; For Thine is the kingdom and the power and the glory forever and ever. Amen.

Then shall be said or chanted the Salutation, the Collect for the Day, or other Collects and the Collect for Peace. Each Collect may be preceded by a Versicle. After each Collect the Congregation shall say or chant: Amen

THE SALUTATION

℣: The Lord be with you.

℞: And with thy spir - it.

THE COLLECT FOR PEACE

O God, from whom all holy desires, all good counsels, and all just works do proceed, give unto Thy servants that peace which the world cannot give, that our hearts may be set to obey Thy commandments, and also that we, being defended by Thee from the fear of our enemies, may pass our time in rest and quietness; through the merits of Jesus Christ, our Savior, who liveth and reigneth with Thee and the Holy Ghost, ever one God, world without end.

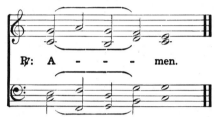

℞: A - - men.

The Benedicamus

℣: Bless we the Lord.

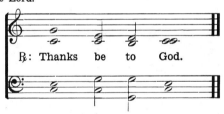

℞: Thanks be to God.

The Benediction

℣: The grace of our Lord Jesus Christ and the love of God and the communion of the Holy Ghost be with you all.

℞: A - - men.

Silent Prayer

[45]

The Order of the Confessional Service

A Hymn of Repentance or another Hymn may be sung

Minister: In the name of the Father and of the Son and of the Holy Ghost.

The Congregation shall say or chant:

A - - - men.

℣: Make haste, O God, to deliver me.

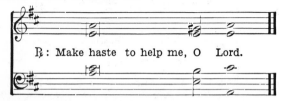

℞: Make haste to help me, O Lord.

℣: The sacrifices of God are a broken spirit.

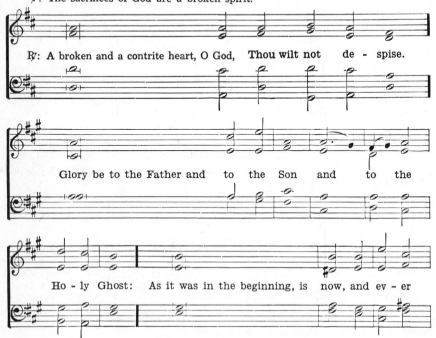

℞: A broken and a contrite heart, O God, **Thou wilt not de - spise.**

Glory be to the Father and to the Son and to the

Ho - ly Ghost: As it was in the beginning, is now, and ev - er

[46]

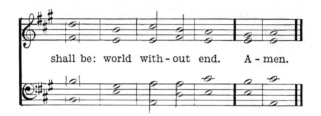

shall be: world with-out end. A-men.

Then shall the Minister read Psalm 51 or another Psalm

Then may be read

The Scripture Lesson

Then may follow

The Confessional Address

Or, if time does not permit, the Minister may read

The Exhortation

Dearly beloved: Forasmuch as we purpose to come to the Holy Supper of our Lord Jesus Christ, it becometh us diligently to examine ourselves, as St. Paul exhorteth us. For this holy Sacrament hath been instituted for the special comfort and strengthening of those who humbly confess their sins and hunger and thirst after righteousness.

But if we thus examine ourselves, we shall find nothing in us but sin and death, from which we can in no wise set ourselves free. Therefore our Lord Jesus Christ hath had mercy upon us and hath taken upon Himself our nature, that so He might fulfill for us the whole will and Law of God and for us and for our deliverance suffer death and all that we by our sins have deserved. And to the end that we should the more confidently believe this and be strengthened by our faith in a cheerful obedience to His holy will, He hath instituted the holy Sacrament of His supper, in which He feedeth us with His body and giveth us to drink of His blood.

Therefore, whoso eateth of this bread and drinketh of this cup, firmly believing the words of Christ, dwelleth in Christ, and Christ in him, and hath eternal life.

We should do this also in remembrance of Him, showing His death, that He was delivered for our offenses and raised again for our justification, and rendering unto Him most hearty thanks for the same, take up our cross and follow Him, and, according to His commandment, love one another even as He hath loved us. For we are all one bread and one body, even as we are all partakers of this one bread and drink of this one cup.

Then the Minister shall say: Having now heard the Word of God, let us kneel and make confession of our sins:

O almighty God, merciful Father, I, a poor, miserable sinner, confess unto Thee all my sins and iniquities with which I have ever offended Thee and justly deserved Thy temporal and eternal punishment. But I am heartily sorry for them and sincerely repent of them, and I pray Thee of Thy boundless mercy and for the sake of the holy, innocent, bitter sufferings and death of Thy beloved Son, Jesus Christ, to be gracious and merciful to me, a poor, sinful being.

Then the Minister shall rise and say:

I now ask you before God, Is this your sincere confession, that you heartily repent of your sins, believe on Jesus Christ, and sincerely and earnestly purpose, by the assistance of God the Holy Ghost, henceforth to amend your sinful life? Then declare so by saying: Yes.

℟: **Yes.**

Then shall the Minister pronounce

𝕿𝖍𝖊 𝕬𝖇𝖘𝖔𝖑𝖚𝖙𝖎𝖔𝖓

Upon this your confession, I, by virtue of my office, as a called and ordained servant of the Word, announce the grace of God unto all of you, and in the stead and by the command of my Lord Jesus Christ I forgive you all your sins in the name of the Father and of the Son and of the Holy Ghost.

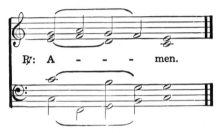

Or the following form may be used:

And now I ask you before God, who searcheth the heart:

1. Do you sincerely confess that you have sinned against God and deserved His wrath and punishment? — Then declare so by saying: I do confess.

Verily, you should confess; for Holy Scripture declares: "If we say that we have no sin, we deceive ourselves, and the truth is not in us."

2. Do you heartily repent of all your sins committed in thought, word, and deed? Then declare so by saying: I do repent.

Verily, you should repent, as did the penitent sinners: King David, who prayed for a contrite heart; Peter, who wept bitterly; the sinful woman; the prodigal son; and others.

3. Do you sincerely believe that God, by grace, for Jesus' sake, will forgive you all your sins? Then declare so by saying: I do believe.

Verily, you should so believe, for Holy Scripture declares: "God so loved the world that He gave His only-begotten Son, that whosoever believeth in Him should not perish, but have everlasting life."

4. Do you promise that with the aid of the Holy Ghost you will henceforth amend your sinful life? Then declare so by saying: I do promise.

Verily, you should so promise, for Christ, the Lord, says: "Let your light so shine before men that they may see your good works and glorify your Father which is in heaven."

5. Finally, do you believe that through me, a called servant of God, you will receive the forgiveness of all your sins? Then declare so by saying: I do believe.

As you believe, even so may it be unto you.

Upon this your confession, I, by virtue of my office, as a called and ordained servant of the Word, announce the grace of God unto all of you, and in the stead and by the command of my Lord Jesus Christ I forgive you all your sins in the name of the Father and of the Son and of the Holy Ghost. Amen.

[48]

The Collect

Then shall be said or chanted the Collect for the Day, or other Collects, and the Collect for Peace

℣: The Lord will give strength unto His people.

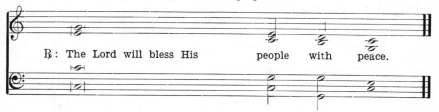

℟: The Lord will bless His people with peace.

The Collect for Peace

O God, from whom all holy desires, all good counsels, and all just works do proceed, give unto Thy servants that peace which the world cannot give, that our hearts may be set to obey Thy commandments, and also that we, being defended by Thee from the fear of our enemies, may pass our time in rest and quietness; through the merits of Jesus Christ, our Savior, who liveth and reigneth with Thee and the Holy Ghost, ever one God, world without end.

℟: A — — men.

The Benediction

℣: The grace of our Lord Jesus Christ and the love of God and the communion of the Holy Ghost be with you all.

℟: A — — men.

Silent Prayer

[49]

A Form for Opening and Closing Christian Schools

A Hymn of Invocation of the Holy Ghost or another Hymn may be sung

Then shall be said or chanted:

℣: O Lord, open Thou my lips.

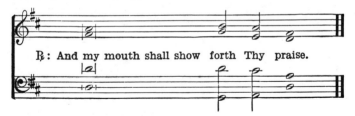

℟: And my mouth shall show forth Thy praise.

℣: Make haste, O God, to deliver me.

℟: Make haste to help me, O Lord.

Glory be to the Father and to the Son and to the

Ho - ly Ghost: As it was in the beginning, is now, and ev - er

shall be: world with - out end. A - men. Hal - le - lu - jah!

Then shall be said

The Psalm

At the end of the Psalm the Gloria Patri shall be said or chanted. Then shall follow

The Collect for the Day

Then shall be said one of the principal parts of

The Catechism

Then may be sung

A Hymn

*If this Form is used for Sessions of the Sunday School,
there shall follow, after the Hymn,*

The Instruction for the Day

The Instruction ended, Announcements and Reports may be made. Then may be sung

A Hymn

Then may be said

The Apostles' Creed

I believe in God the Father Almighty, Maker of heaven and earth.

And in Jesus Christ, His only Son, our Lord; Who was conceived by the Holy Ghost, Born of the Virgin Mary; Suffered under Pontius Pilate, Was crucified, dead, and buried; He descended into hell; The third day He rose again from the dead; He ascended into heaven and sitteth on the right hand of God the Father Almighty; From thence He shall come to judge the quick and the dead.

I believe in the Holy Ghost; the holy Christian Church, the communion of saints; The forgiveness of sins; The resurrection of the body; And the life everlasting. Amen.

Then may be said

A Closing Prayer

and all shall say

The Lord's Prayer

Our Father who art in heaven, Hallowed be Thy name; Thy kingdom come; Thy will be done on earth as it is in heaven; Give us this day our daily bread; And forgive us our trespasses, as we forgive those who trespass against us; And lead us not into temptation; But deliver us from evil; For Thine is the kingdom and the power and the glory forever and ever. Amen.

Then may be said

The Benedicamus

℣: Bless we the Lord.

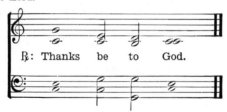

℟: Thanks be to God.

or, if the Minister be in charge,

The Benediction

℣: The grace of our Lord Jesus Christ and the love of God and the communion of the Holy Ghost be with you all.

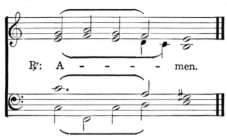

℟: A — — — men.

Silent Prayer

Whosoever will be saved, before all things it is necessary that he hold the catholic [*i. e.*, universal, Christian] faith.

Which faith except everyone do keep whole and undefiled, without doubt he shall perish everlastingly.

And the catholic faith is this, that we worship one God in Trinity and Trinity in Unity.

Neither confounding the Persons nor dividing the Substance.

For there is one Person of the Father, another of the Son, and another of the Holy Ghost.

But the Godhead of the Father, of the Son, and of the Holy Ghost is all one: the glory equal, the majesty coeternal.

Such as the Father is, such is the Son, and such is the Holy Ghost.

The Father uncreate, the Son uncreate, and the Holy Ghost uncreate.

The Father incomprehensible, the Son incomprehensible, and the Holy Ghost incomprehensible.

The Father eternal, the Son eternal, and the Holy Ghost eternal.

And yet they are not three Eternals, but one Eternal.

As there are not three Uncreated nor three Incomprehensibles, but one Uncreated and one Incomprehensible.

So likewise the Father is almighty, the Son almighty, and the Holy Ghost almighty.

And yet they are not three Almighties, but one Almighty.

So the Father is God, the Son is God, and the Holy Ghost is God.

And yet they are not three Gods, but one God.

So likewise the Father is Lord, the Son Lord, and the Holy Ghost Lord.

And yet not three Lords, but one Lord.

For like as we are compelled by the Christian verity to acknowledge every Person by Himself to be God and Lord,

So are we forbidden by the catholic religion to say, There be three Gods or three Lords.

The Father is made of none, neither created nor begotten.

The Son is of the Father alone, not made nor created, but begotten.

The Holy Ghost is of the Father and of the Son, neither made nor created nor begotten, but proceeding.

So there is one Father, not three Fathers; one Son, not three Sons; one Holy Ghost, not three Holy Ghosts.

And in this Trinity none is before or after other; none is greater or less than another;

But the whole three Persons are coeternal together and coequal, so that in all things, as is aforesaid, the Unity in Trinity and the Trinity in Unity is to be worshiped.

He, therefore, that will be saved must thus think of the Trinity.

Furthermore, it is necessary to everlasting salvation that he also believe faithfully the incarnation of our Lord Jesus Christ.

For the right faith is that we believe and confess that our Lord Jesus Christ, the Son of God, is God and Man;

God of the Substance of the Father, begotten before the worlds; and Man of the substance of His mother, born in the world;

Perfect God and perfect Man, of a reasonable soul and human flesh subsisting.

Equal to the Father as touching His Godhead and inferior to the Father as touching His manhood;

Who, although He be God and Man, yet He is not two, but one Christ:

One, not by conversion of the Godhead into flesh, but by taking the manhood into God;

One altogether; not by confusion of Substance, but by unity of Person.

For as the reasonable soul and flesh is one man, so God and Man is one Christ;

Who suffered for our salvation; descended into hell; rose again the third day from the dead;

He ascended into heaven; He sitteth on the right hand of the Father, God Almighty; from whence He shall come to judge the quick and the dead.

At whose coming all men shall rise again with their bodies and shall give an account of their own works.

And they that have done good shall go into life everlasting; and they that have done evil, into everlasting fire.

This is the catholic faith; which except a man believe faithfully and firmly, he cannot be saved.

FIRST SUNDAY IN ADVENT

INTROIT

Unto Thee, O Lord, do I lift up my soul: O my God, I trust in Thee.

Let me not be ashamed: let not mine enemies triumph over me.

Yea, let none that wait on Thee: be ashamed.

Psalm. Show me Thy ways, O Lord: teach me Thy paths.

Glory be to the Father and to the Son and to the Holy Ghost; as it was in the beginning, is now, and ever shall be, world without end. Amen.

COLLECT

Stir up, we beseech Thee, Thy power, O Lord, and come, that by Thy protection we may be rescued from the threatening perils of our sins and saved by Thy mighty deliverance; who livest and reignest with the Father and the Holy Ghost, ever one God, world without end.

Epistle, Rom. 13:11-14

GRADUAL

All they that wait on Thee shall not be ashamed, O Lord.

Verse. Show me Thy ways, O Lord: teach me Thy paths. Hallelujah! Hallelujah!

V. Show us Thy mercy, O Lord: and grant us Thy salvation. Hallelujah!

Gospel, Matt. 21:1-9

SECOND SUNDAY IN ADVENT

INTROIT

Daughter of Zion: behold, thy Salvation cometh.

The Lord shall cause His glorious voice to be heard: and ye shall have gladness of heart.

Ps. Give ear, O Shepherd of Israel: Thou that leadest Joseph like a flock.

Glory be to the Father, etc.

COLLECT

Stir up our hearts, O Lord, to make ready the way of Thine only-begotten Son, so that by His coming we may be enabled to serve Thee with pure minds; through the same Jesus Christ, Thy Son, our Lord, who liveth, etc.

Epistle, Rom. 15:4-13

GRADUAL

Out of Zion, the perfection of beauty, God hath shined: our God shall come.

V. Gather My saints together unto Me: those that have made a covenant with Me by sacrifice. Hallelujah! Hallelujah!

V. The powers of heaven shall be shaken: and then shall they see the Son of Man coming in a cloud with power and great glory. Hallelujah!

Gospel, Luke 21:25-36

THIRD SUNDAY IN ADVENT

INTROIT

Rejoice in the Lord alway: and again I say, Rejoice.

Let your moderation be known unto all men: the Lord is at hand.

Be careful for nothing: but in everything, by prayer and supplication with thanksgiving, let your requests be made known unto God.

Ps. Lord, Thou hast been favorable unto Thy land: Thou hast brought back the captivity of Jacob.

Glory be to the Father, etc.

COLLECT

Lord, we beseech Thee, give ear to our prayers and lighten the darkness of our hearts by Thy gracious visitation; who livest, etc.

Epistle 1 Cor. 4:1-5

GRADUAL

Thou that dwellest between the cherubim, shine forth: stir up Thy strength and come.

V. Give ear, O Shepherd of Israel: Thou that leadest Joseph like a flock. Hallelujah! Hallelujah!

V. Stir up Thy strength: and come and save us. Hallelujah!

Gospel, Matt. 11:2-10

FOURTH SUNDAY IN ADVENT

INTROIT

Drop down, ye heavens, from above: and let the skies pour down righteousness. Let the earth open: and bring forth salvation.

Ps. The heavens declare the glory of God: and the firmament showeth His handiwork.

Glory be to the Father, etc.

COLLECT

Stir up, O Lord, we beseech Thee, Thy power, and come and help us with Thy great might, that by Thy grace whatsoever is hindered by our sins may be speedily accomplished through Thy mercy and satisfaction; who livest, etc.

Epistle, Phil. 4:4-7

GRADUAL

The Lord is nigh unto all them that call upon Him: to all that call upon Him in truth.

V. My mouth shall speak the praise of the Lord: and let all flesh bless His holy name. Hallelujah! Hallelujah!

V. Thou art my Help and my Deliverer: make no tarrying, O my God. Hallelujah!

Gospel, John 1:19-28

OTHER COLLECTS FOR THE SEASON OF ADVENT

Mercifully hear, O Lord, the prayers of Thy people, that, as they rejoice in the advent of Thine only-begotten Son according to the flesh, so when He cometh a second time in His majesty, they may receive the reward of eternal life; through the same Jesus Christ, Thy Son, our Lord, who liveth, etc.

O God, who dost gladden us with the yearly anticipation of our redemption, grant that we who now joyfully receive Thine only-begotten Son as our Redeemer may also behold Him without fear when He cometh as our Judge; who liveth, etc.

Most merciful God, who hast given Thine eternal Word to be made incarnate of the pure Virgin, grant unto Thy people grace to put away fleshly lusts that so they may be ready for Thy visitation; through the same Jesus Christ, Thy Son, our Lord, who liveth, etc.

CHRISTMAS DAY, THE FEAST OF THE NATIVITY OF OUR LORD

INTROIT

Unto us a Child is born, unto us a Son is given: and the government shall be upon His shoulder.

And His name shall be called Wonderful, Counselor, the Mighty God: the Everlasting Father, the Prince of Peace.

Ps. Oh, sing unto the Lord a new song: for He hath done marvelous things.

Glory be to the Father, etc.   Or:

The Lord hath said unto Me: Thou art My Son, this day have I begotten Thee.

Ps. The Lord reigneth, He is clothed with majesty: the Lord is clothed with strength, wherewith He hath girded Himself.

Glory be to the Father, etc.

COLLECT FOR CHRISTMAS NIGHT

O God, who hast made this most holy night to shine with the brightness of the true Light, grant, we beseech Thee, that, as we have known on earth the mysteries of that Light, we may also come to the fullness of its joys in heaven; through the same Jesus Christ, Thy Son, our Lord, who liveth, etc.

COLLECT FOR CHRISTMAS DAY

Grant, we beseech Thee, Almighty God, that the new birth of Thine only-begotten Son in the flesh may set us free, who are held in the old bondage under the yoke of sin; through the same Jesus Christ, Thy Son, our Lord, who liveth, etc.

Epistle, Titus 2:11-14 or Is. 9:2-7

GRADUAL

Thy people shall be willing in the day of Thy power: in the beauties of holiness from the womb of the morning.

V. The Lord said unto my Lord, Sit Thou at My right hand: until I make Thine enemies Thy footstool. Hallelujah! Hallelujah!

V. The Lord hath said unto Me, Thou art My Son: this day have I begotten Thee. Hallelujah!

GRADUAL

All the ends of the earth have seen the salvation of our God: make a joyful noise unto the Lord, all the earth.

V. The Lord hath made known His salvation: His righteousness hath He openly showed in the sight of the heathen. Hallelujah! Hallelujah!

V. Oh, come, let us sing unto the Lord: let us worship and bow down before Him. Hallelujah!

Gospel, Luke 2:1-14

SECOND CHRISTMAS DAY

(The Introit and Collect are the same as for Christmas Day)
Epistle, Titus 3:4-7

GRADUAL

Blessed is He that cometh in the name of the Lord: God is the Lord which hath showed us light.

V. This is the Lord's doing: it is marvelous in our eyes. Hallelujah! Hallelujah!

V. The Lord reigneth, He is clothed with majesty: the Lord is clothed with strength, wherewith He hath girded Himself. Hallelujah!

Gospel, Luke 2:15-20

SUNDAY AFTER CHRISTMAS

INTROIT

Thy testimonies are very sure: holiness becometh Thine house, O Lord, forever. Thy throne is established of old: Thou art from everlasting.

Ps. The Lord reigneth, He is clothed with majesty: the Lord is clothed with strength, wherewith He hath girded Himself.

Glory be to the Father, etc.   Or:

When all was still, and it was midnight: Thine almighty Word, O Lord, descended from the royal throne.

Ps. The Lord reigneth, He is clothed with majesty: the Lord is clothed with strength, wherewith He hath girded Himself.

Glory be to the Father, etc.

Almighty and everlasting God, direct our actions according to Thy good pleasure, that in the name of Thy beloved Son we may be made to abound in good works; through the same Jesus Christ, Thy Son, our Lord, who liveth, etc.

Epistle, Gal. 4:1-7

GRADUAL

Thou art fairer than the children of men: grace is poured into Thy lips.

V. My heart is inditing a good matter, I speak of the things which I have made touching the King: my tongue is the pen of a ready writer. Hallelujah! Hallelujah!

V. The Lord reigneth, He is clothed with majesty: the Lord is clothed with strength, wherewith He hath girded Himself. Hallelujah!

Gospel, Luke 2:33-40

THE CIRCUMCISION AND THE NAME OF JESUS

(New Year's Day)

INTROIT

O Lord, our Lord, how excellent is Thy name in all the earth: who hast set Thy glory above the heavens.

What is man that Thou art mindful of him: and the Son of Man that Thou visitest Him?

Ps. Thou, O Lord, art our Father and our Redeemer: Thy name is from everlasting.

Glory be to the Father, etc.   Or:

At the name of Jesus every knee should bow of things in heaven and things in earth and things under the earth: and every tongue should confess that Jesus Christ is Lord, to the glory of God the Father.

Ps. O Lord, our Lord: how excellent is Thy name in all the earth.

Glory be to the Father, etc.

COLLECTS

O Lord God, who for our sakes hast made Thy blessed Son, our Savior, subject to the Law and caused Him to endure the circumcision of the flesh, grant us the true circumcision of the Spirit that our hearts may be pure from all sinful desires and lusts; through the same Jesus Christ, Thy Son, our Lord, who liveth, etc.

Almighty God, whose only-begotten Son, lest He break the Law which He had come to fulfill, was this day circumcised, grant that He may ever defend our minds against all allurements of the flesh by the power of His grace; through the same Jesus Christ, Thy Son, our Lord, who liveth, etc.

God, who hast made Thine only-begotten Son the Savior of mankind and didst give Him the name of Jesus, mercifully grant that we who worship His name on earth may joyfully behold Him in heaven; through the same, etc.

Almighty and everlasting God, from whom cometh down every good and perfect gift, we give Thee thanks for all Thy benefits, temporal and spiritual, bestowed upon us in the year past, and we beseech Thee of Thy goodness, grant us a favorable and joyful year, defend us from all dangers and adversities, and send upon us the fullness of Thy blessing; through Jesus Christ, Thy Son, our Lord, who liveth, etc.

Epistle, Gal. 3:23-29

GRADUAL

All the ends of the earth have seen the salvation of our God: make a joyful noise unto the Lord, all the earth.

V. The Lord hath made known His salvation: His righteousness hath He openly showed in the sight of the heathen. Hallelujah! Hallelujah!

V. God, who at sundry times and in divers manners spake in times past unto the fathers by the prophets: hath in these last days spoken unto us by His Son. Hallelujah!

Gospel, Luke 2:21

SUNDAY AFTER NEW YEAR

(The Introit and Collect are the same as for the Sunday after Christmas)

Epistle, 1 Peter 4:12-19

GRADUAL

Save us, O Lord, our God, and gather us from among the heathen: to give thanks unto Thy holy name and to triumph in Thy praise.

V. Thou, O Lord, art our Father, our Redeemer: Thy name is from everlasting. Hallelujah! Hallelujah!

V. My mouth shall speak the praise of the Lord: and let all flesh bless His holy name forever. Hallelujah!

Gospel, Matt. 2:13-23

THE EPIPHANY OF OUR LORD

INTROIT

Behold, the Lord, the Ruler, hath come: and the kingdom and the power and the glory are in His hand.

Ps. Give the King Thy judgments, O God: and Thy righteousness unto the King's Son.

Glory be to the Father, etc.

COLLECT

O God, who by the leading of a star didst manifest Thine only-begotten Son to the Gentiles, mercifully grant that we, who know Thee now by faith, may after this life have the fruition of Thy glorious Godhead; through the same Jesus Christ, Thy Son, our Lord, who liveth, etc.

Epistle, Is. 60:1-6

GRADUAL

All they from Sheba shall come; they shall bring gold and incense: and they shall show forth the praises of the Lord.

V. Arise, shine, O Jerusalem: for the glory of the Lord is risen upon thee. Hallelujah! Hallelujah!

V. We have seen His star in the East: and are come with gifts to worship the Lord. Hallelujah!

Gospel, Matt. 2:1-12

FIRST SUNDAY AFTER THE EPIPHANY

INTROIT

I saw also the Lord sitting upon a throne: high and lifted up.

And I heard the voice of a great multitude, saying, Alleluia: for the Lord God Omnipotent reigneth.

Ps. Make a joyful noise unto the Lord, all ye lands: serve the Lord with gladness.

Glory be to the Father, etc.   Or:

On a throne, high and lifted up, I saw a Man sitting, whom the multitude of angels adores, singing together: Behold, His dominion endureth forever.

Ps. Make a joyful noise unto the Lord, all ye lands: serve the Lord with gladness.

COLLECT

O Lord, we beseech Thee mercifully to receive the prayers of Thy people who call upon Thee; and grant that they may both perceive and know what things they ought to do and also may have grace and power faithfully to fulfill the same; through Jesus Christ, Thy Son, our Lord, who liveth, etc.

Epistle, Rom. 12:1-5

[58]

Blessed be the Lord God, the God of Israel, who only doeth wondrous things: and blessed be His glorious name forever.

V. The mountains shall bring peace to Thy people: and the hills righteousness. Hallelujah! Hallelujah!

V. Make a joyful noise unto the Lord, all ye lands: serve the Lord with gladness. Hallelujah!

Gospel, Luke 2:41-52

SECOND SUNDAY AFTER THE EPIPHANY

(The Introit, Collect, Epistle, Gradual, and Gospel for the Transfiguration of our Lord, given under the Sixth Sunday after the Epiphany, p. 60, shall be used on the Last Sunday after the Epiphany in each year, except when there is only one Sunday after the Epiphany)

INTROIT

All the earth shall worship Thee: and shall sing unto Thee, O God.

They shall sing to Thy name: O Thou Most High.

Ps. Make a joyful noise unto God, all ye lands: sing forth the honor of His name, make His praise glorious.

Glory be to the Father, etc.

COLLECT

Almighty and everlasting God, who dost govern all things in heaven and earth, mercifully hear the supplications of Thy people and grant us Thy peace all the days of our life; through Jesus Christ, Thy Son, our Lord, who liveth, etc.

Epistle, Rom. 12:6-16

GRADUAL

The Lord sent His Word and healed them: and delivered them from their destructions.

V. Oh, that men would praise the Lord for His goodness: and for His wonderful works to the children of men! Hallelujah! Hallelujah!

V. Praise ye Him, all His angels: praise ye Him, all His hosts. Hallelujah!

Gospel, John 2:1-11

THIRD SUNDAY AFTER THE EPIPHANY

INTROIT

Worship Him, all ye His angels: Zion heard and was glad.

The daughters of Judah rejoiced: because of Thy judgments, O Lord.

Ps. The Lord reigneth, let the earth rejoice: let the multitude of isles be glad thereof.

Glory be to the Father, etc.

COLLECT

Almighty and everlasting God, mercifully look upon our infirmities, and in all our dangers and necessities stretch forth the right hand of Thy majesty to help and defend us; through Jesus Christ, Thy Son, our Lord, who liveth, etc.

Epistle, Rom. 12:16-21

GRADUAL

The heathen shall fear the name of the Lord: and all the kings of the earth Thy glory.

V. When the Lord shall build up Zion: He shall appear in His glory. Hallelujah! Hallelujah!

V. The Lord reigneth; let the earth rejoice: let the multitude of isles be glad thereof. Hallelujah!

Gospel, Matt. 8:1-13

FOURTH SUNDAY AFTER THE EPIPHANY

(The Introit and the Gradual are the same as for the Third Sunday after the Epiphany)

COLLECT

Almighty God, who knowest us to be set in the midst of so many and great dangers that by reason of the frailty of our nature we cannot always stand upright, grant to us such strength and protection as may support us in all dangers and carry us through all temptations; through Jesus Christ, Thy Son, our Lord, who liveth, etc.

Epistle, Rom. 13:8-10

Gospel, Matt. 8:23-27

FIFTH SUNDAY AFTER THE EPIPHANY

(The Introit and the Gradual are the same as for the Third Sunday after the Epiphany)

COLLECT

O Lord, we beseech Thee to keep Thy Church and household continually in Thy true religion that they who do lean upon the hope of Thy heavenly grace may evermore be defended by Thy mighty power; through Jesus Christ, Thy Son, our Lord, who liveth, etc.

Epistle, Col. 3:12-17

Gospel, Matt. 13:24-30

SIXTH SUNDAY AFTER THE EPIPHANY

(The Introit, Collect, Epistle, Gradual, and Gospel for the Transfiguration of our Lord shall be used on the last Sunday after the Epiphany in each year, except when there is only one Sunday after the Epiphany)

INTROIT

The lightnings lightened the world: the earth trembled and shook.

Ps. How amiable are Thy tabernacles, O Lord of hosts: my soul longeth, yea, even fainteth for the courts of the Lord.

Glory be to the Father, etc.

COLLECT

O God, who in the glorious transfiguration of Thine only-begotten Son hast confirmed the mysteries of the faith by the testimony of the fathers, and who, in the voice that came from the bright cloud, didst in a wonderful manner foreshow the adoption of sons, mercifully vouchsafe to make us coheirs with the King of His glory and bring us to the enjoyment of the same; through the same Jesus Christ, Thy Son, our Lord, who liveth, etc.

Epistle, 2 Peter 1:16-21

GRADUAL

Thou art fairer than the children of men: grace is poured into Thy lips.

V. The Lord said unto my Lord, Sit Thou at My right hand: until I make Thine enemies Thy footstool. Hallelujah! Hallelujah!

V. Sing unto the Lord, bless His name; show forth His salvation from day to day: Declare His glory among all people. Hallelujah!

Gospel, Matt. 17:1-9

SEPTUAGESIMA SUNDAY

INTROIT

The sorrows of death compassed me: the sorrows of hell compassed me about.

In my distress I called upon the Lord: and He heard my voice out of His temple.

Ps. I will love Thee, O Lord, my Strength: the Lord is my Rock and my Fortress.

Glory be to the Father, etc.

O Lord, we beseech Thee favorably to hear the prayers of Thy people that we, who are justly punished for our offenses, may be mercifully delivered by Thy goodness, for the glory of Thy name; through Jesus Christ, Thy Son, our Savior, who liveth, etc.

Epistle, 1 Cor. 9:24 to 10:5

GRADUAL

The Lord will be a Refuge for the oppressed, a Refuge in times of trouble: and they that know Thy name will put their trust in Thee; for Thou, Lord, hast not forsaken them that seek Thee.

V. For the needy shall not alway be forgotten: the expectation of the poor shall not perish forever. Arise, O Lord; let not man prevail.

Tract. Out of the depths have I cried unto Thee, O Lord: Lord, hear my voice.

V. Let Thine ears be attentive: to the voice of my supplications.

V. If Thou, Lord, shouldest mark iniquities: O Lord, who shall stand?

V. But there is forgiveness with Thee: that Thou mayest be feared.

Gospel, Matt. 20:1-16

SEXAGESIMA SUNDAY

INTROIT

Awake, why sleepest Thou, O Lord?: Arise, cast us not off forever.

Wherefore hidest Thou Thy face: and forgettest our affliction?

Our soul is bowed down to the dust: arise for our help and redeem us.

Ps. We have heard with our ears, O God: our fathers have told us what work Thou didst in their days.

Glory be to the Father, etc.

COLLECT

O God, who seest that we put not our trust in anything that we do, mercifully grant that by Thy power we may be defended against all adversity; through Jesus Christ, Thy Son, our Lord, who liveth, etc.

Epistle, 2 Cor. 11:19 to 12:9

GRADUAL

Let the nations know that Thy name is Jehovah: Thou alone art the Most High over all the earth.

V. O my God, make them like a wheel and like chaff before the wind.

Tract. Thou, O Lord, hast made the earth to tremble and hast broken it.

V. Heal the breaches thereof, for it shaketh.

V. That Thy beloved may be delivered, save with Thy right hand.

Gospel, Luke 8:4-15

QUINQUAGESIMA SUNDAY

INTROIT

Be Thou my strong Rock: for an house of defense to save me.

Thou art my Rock and my Fortress: therefore for Thy name's sake lead me and guide me.

Ps. In Thee, O Lord, do I put my trust; let me never be ashamed: deliver me in Thy righteousness.

Glory be to the Father, etc.

COLLECT

O Lord, we beseech Thee, mercifully hear our prayers and, having set us free from the bonds of sin, defend us from all evil; through Jesus Christ, Thy Son, our Lord, who liveth, etc.

Epistle, 1 Cor. 13:1-13

Thou art the God that doest wonders: Thou hast declared Thy strength among the people.

V. Thou hast with Thine arm redeemed Thy people: the sons of Jacob and Joseph.

Tract. Make a joyful noise unto the Lord, all ye lands: serve the Lord with gladness.

V. Enter into His gates with thanksgiving.

V. Know ye that the Lord, He is God.

V. It is He that hath made us and not we ourselves: we are His people and the sheep of His pasture. *Gospel, Luke 18:31-43*

ASH WEDNESDAY, THE FIRST DAY OF LENT

INTROIT

I will cry unto God Most High: unto God that performeth all things for me.

Yea, in the shadow of Thy wings will I make my refuge: until these calamities be overpast.

Ps. Be merciful unto me, O God, be merciful unto me: for my soul trusteth in Thee.

Glory be to the Father, etc. COLLECT

Almighty and everlasting God, who hatest nothing that Thou hast made and dost forgive the sins of all those who are penitent, create and make in us new and contrite hearts, that we, worthily lamenting our sins and acknowledging our wretchedness, may obtain of Thee, the God of all mercy, perfect remission and forgiveness; through Jesus Christ, Thy Son, our Lord, who liveth, etc.

Epistle, Joel 2:12-19

GRADUAL

Be merciful unto me, O God, be merciful unto me: for my soul trusteth in Thee.

V. He shall send from heaven: and save me from the reproach of him that would swallow me up.

Tract. O Lord, deal not with us after our sins: nor reward us according to our iniquities.

V. O Lord, remember not against us former iniquities: let Thy tender mercies speedily come to us, for we are brought very low.

V. Help us, O God of our salvation: for the glory of Thy name.

Gospel, Matt. 6:16-21

INVOCAVIT, THE FIRST SUNDAY IN LENT

INTROIT

He shall call upon Me, and I will answer Him: I will deliver him and honor him. With long life will I satisfy him: and show him My salvation.

Ps. He that dwelleth in the secret place of the Most High: shall abide under the shadow of the Almighty.

Glory be to the Father, etc. COLLECT

O Lord, mercifully hear our prayer and stretch forth the right hand of Thy majesty to defend us from them that rise up against us; through Jesus Christ, Thy Son, our Lord, who liveth, etc. *Epistle, 2 Cor. 6:1-10*

GRADUAL

For He shall give His angels charge over thee: to keep thee in all thy ways.

V. They shall bear thee up in their hands: lest thou dash thy foot against a stone.

Tract. He that dwelleth in the secret place of the Most High: shall abide under the shadow of the Almighty.

V. I will say of the Lord, He is my Refuge and my Fortress, my God: in Him will I trust.

V. He shall cover thee with His feathers: and under His wings shalt thou trust.

Gospel, Matt. 4:1-11

[62]

REMINISCERE, THE SECOND SUNDAY IN LENT

Remember, O Lord, Thy tender mercies and Thy loving-kindnesses: for they have been ever of old.

Let not mine enemies triumph over me: God of Israel, deliver us out of all our troubles.

Ps. Unto Thee, O Lord, do I lift up my soul: O my God, I trust in Thee; let me not be ashamed.

Glory be to the Father, etc.

COLLECT

O God, who seest that of ourselves we have no strength, keep us both outwardly and inwardly that we may be defended from all adversities which may happen to the body and from all evil thoughts which may assault and hurt the soul; through Jesus Christ, Thy Son, our Lord, who liveth, etc.

Epistle, 1 Thess. 4:1-7

GRADUAL

The troubles of my heart are enlarged: oh, bring Thou me out of my distresses.

V. Look upon mine affliction and my pain: and forgive all my sins.

Tract. Oh, give thanks unto the Lord; for He is good: for His mercy endureth forever.

V. Who can utter the mighty acts of the Lord? Who can show forth His praise?

V. Blessed are they that keep judgment: and he that doeth righteousness at all times.

V. Remember me, O Lord, with the favor that Thou bearest unto Thy people: Oh, visit me with Thy salvation.

Gospel, Matt. 15:21-28

OCULI, THE THIRD SUNDAY IN LENT

INTROIT

Mine eyes are ever toward the Lord: for He shall pluck my feet out of the net.

Turn Thee unto me and have mercy upon me: for I am desolate and afflicted.

Ps. Unto Thee, O Lord, do I lift up my soul: O my God, I trust in Thee; let me not be ashamed.

Glory be to the Father, etc.

COLLECT

We beseech Thee, Almighty God, look upon the hearty desires of Thy humble servants and stretch forth the right hand of Thy majesty to be our defense against all our enemies; through Jesus Christ, Thy Son, our Lord, who liveth, etc.

Epistle, Eph. 5:1-9

GRADUAL

Arise, O Lord; let not man prevail: let the heathen be judged in Thy sight.

V. When mine enemies are turned back: they shall fall and perish at Thy presence.

Tract. Unto Thee lift I up mine eyes, O Thou that dwellest in the heavens: have mercy upon us, O Lord, have mercy upon us.

Gospel, Luke 11:14-28

LAETARE, THE FOURTH SUNDAY IN LENT

INTROIT

Rejoice ye with Jerusalem and be glad with her: all ye that love her.

Rejoice for joy with her: all ye that mourn for her.

Ps. I was glad when they said unto me: Let us go into the house of the Lord.

Glory be to the Father, etc.

Grant, we beseech Thee, Almighty God, that we, who for our evil deeds do worthily deserve to be punished, by the comfort of Thy grace may mercifully be relieved; through Jesus Christ, Thy Son, our Lord, who liveth, etc.

Epistle, Gal. 4:21-31

GRADUAL

I was glad when they said unto me: Let us go into the house of the Lord.

V. Peace be within thy walls: and prosperity within thy palaces.

Tract. They that trust in the Lord shall be as Mount Zion: which cannot be removed, but abideth forever.

V. As the mountains are round about Jerusalem: so the Lord is round about His people from henceforth even forever.

Gospel, John 6:1-15

JUDICA, THE FIFTH SUNDAY IN LENT (PASSION SUNDAY)

INTROIT

Judge me, O God: and plead my cause against an ungodly nation.

Oh, deliver me from the deceitful and unjust man: for Thou art the God of my strength.

Ps. Oh, send out Thy light and Thy truth: let them lead me; let them bring me unto Thy holy hill.

Glory be to the Father, etc.

COLLECT

We beseech Thee, Almighty God, mercifully to look upon Thy people, that by Thy great goodness they may be governed and preserved evermore both in body and soul; through Jesus Christ, Thy Son, our Lord, who liveth, etc.

Epistle, Heb. 9:11-15

GRADUAL

Deliver me, O Lord, from mine enemies: teach me to do Thy will.

V. He delivereth me from mine enemies: yea, Thou liftest me up above those that rise up against me: Thou hast delivered me from the violent man.

Tract. Many a time have they afflicted me from my youth.

V. May Israel now say: many a time have they afflicted me from my youth.

V. Yet they have not prevailed against me.

Gospel, John 8:46-59

PALMARUM, THE SIXTH SUNDAY IN LENT

INTROIT

Be not Thou far from me, O Lord: O my Strength, haste Thee to help me.

Save me from the lion's mouth: and deliver me from the horns of the unicorns.

Ps. My God, My God, why hast Thou forsaken Me?: Why art Thou so far from helping Me?

Glory be to the Father, etc.

COLLECT

Almighty and everlasting God, who hast sent Thy Son, our Savior Jesus Christ, to take upon Him our flesh and to suffer death upon the cross that all mankind should follow the example of His great humility, mercifully grant that we may both follow the example of His patience and also be made partakers of His resurrection; through the same Jesus Christ, Thy Son, our Lord, who liveth, etc.

Epistle, Phil. 2:5-11

Thou hast holden me by my right hand: Thou shalt guide me with Thy counsel and afterward receive me to glory.

V. Truly, God is good to Israel, even to such as are of a clean heart: but as for me, my feet were almost gone, my steps had well-nigh slipped; for I was grieved at the ungodly.

Tract. My God, My God, why hast Thou forsaken Me?

V. Why art Thou so far from helping Me: and from the words of My roaring?

V. I am a worm and no man: a reproach of men and despised of the people.

V. Be not Thou far from Me, O Lord; O My Strength, haste Thee to help Me.

V. I will declare Thy name unto My brethren: in the midst of the congregation will I praise Thee.

V. They shall come and shall declare His righteousness unto a people that shall be born: that He hath done this.

Gospel, Matt. 21:1-9

MONDAY OF HOLY WEEK

INTROIT

Plead my cause, O Lord, with them that strive with me: fight against them that fight against me.

Take hold of shield and buckler: and stand up for mine help.

Ps. Draw out also the spear and stop the way against them that persecute me: say unto my soul, I am thy Salvation.

Glory be to the Father, etc.

COLLECT

Grant, we beseech Thee, Almighty God, that we, who amid so many adversities do fail through our own infirmities, may be restored through the Passion and intercession of Thine only-begotten Son; who liveth, etc.

Epistle, Is. 50:5-10

GRADUAL

Stir up Thyself and awake to my judgment: even unto my cause, my God and my Lord.

V. Draw out also the spear: and stop the way against them that persecute me.

Tract. Help us, O God of our salvation, for the glory of Thy name: and deliver us and purge away our sins for Thy name's sake.

Gospel, John 12:1-23, or The Passion History

TUESDAY OF HOLY WEEK

INTROIT

God forbid that I should glory: save in the Cross of our Lord Jesus Christ.

In Him is salvation, life, and resurrection from the dead: by Him we are redeemed and set at liberty.

Ps. God be merciful unto us and bless us: and cause His face to shine upon us.

Glory be to the Father, etc.

COLLECT

Almighty and everlasting God, grant us grace so to pass through this holy time of our Lord's Passion that we may obtain the pardon of our sins; through the same Jesus Christ, Thy Son, our Lord, who liveth, etc.

Epistle, Jer. 11:18-20

As for me, my clothing was sackcloth: I humbled my soul with fasting; and my prayer returned into mine own bosom.

V. Plead my cause, O Lord, with them that strive with me: Take hold of shield and buckler and stand up for mine help.

Gospel, John 12:24-43, or The Passion History

WEDNESDAY OF HOLY WEEK

INTROIT

At the name of Jesus every knee shall bow: of things in heaven and things in earth and things under the earth.

For He became obedient unto death, even the death of the cross: wherefore He is Lord, to the glory of God the Father.

Ps. Hear my prayer, O Lord: and let my cry come unto Thee.

Glory be to the Father, etc.

COLLECT

Grant, we beseech Thee, Almighty God, that we, who for our evil deeds are continually afflicted, may mercifully be relieved by the Passion of Thine only-begotten Son, who liveth, etc. *Epistle, Is. 62:11 to 63:7*

GRADUAL

Hide not Thy face from Thy Servant; for I am in trouble: hear Me speedily.

V. Save Me, O God: for the waters are come in unto My soul; I sink in deep mire, where there is no standing.

Tract. Hear my prayer, O Lord: and let my cry come unto Thee.

V. Thou shalt arise and have mercy upon Zion: for the time is come to favor her, yea, the set time is come.

Gospel, Luke 22:1 to 23:43, or The Passion History

MAUNDY THURSDAY

INTROIT

God forbid that I should glory: save in the Cross of our Lord Jesus Christ.

In Him is salvation, life, and resurrection from the dead: by Him we are redeemed and set at liberty.

Ps. God be merciful unto us and bless us: and cause His face to shine upon us.

Glory be to the Father, etc.

COLLECT

O Lord God, who hast left unto us in a wonderful Sacrament a memorial of Thy Passion, grant, we beseech Thee, that we may so use this Sacrament of Thy body and blood that the fruits of Thy redemption may continually be manifest in us; Thou, who livest, etc. *Epistle, 1 Cor. 11:23-32*

GRADUAL

Christ hath humbled Himself and become obedient unto death: even the death of the cross.

V. Wherefore God also hath highly exalted Him: and given Him a name which is above every name. Or:

He hath made His wonderful works to be remembered: the Lord is gracious and full of compassion.

V. He hath given meat unto them that fear Him: He will ever be mindful of His covenant.

V. My flesh is meat indeed, and My blood is drink indeed: he that eateth My flesh and drinketh My blood dwelleth in Me and I in him.

Gospel, John 13:1-15, or The Passion History

[66]

GOOD FRIDAY

INTROIT

Surely He hath borne our griefs and carried our sorrows: He was wounded for our transgressions, He was bruised for our iniquities.

All we like sheep have gone astray: and the Lord hath laid on Him the iniquity of us all.

Ps. Hear my prayer, O Lord: and let my cry come unto Thee.

Glory be to the Father, etc.

(Or the Introit for Tuesday of Holy Week may be used)

COLLECTS

Almighty God, we beseech Thee graciously to behold this Thy family, for which our Lord Jesus Christ was contented to be betrayed and given up into the hands of wicked men and to suffer death upon the cross; through the same Jesus Christ, Thy Son, our Lord, who liveth, etc.

Merciful and everlasting God, who hast not spared Thine only Son, but delivered Him up for us all that He might bear our sins upon the cross, grant that our hearts may be so fixed with steadfast faith in Him that we may not fear the power of any adversaries; through the same Jesus Christ, Thy Son, our Lord, who liveth, etc.

Almighty and everlasting God, who hast willed that Thy Son should bear for us the pains of the cross that Thou mightest remove from us the power of the adversary, help us so to remember and give thanks for our Lord's Passion that we may obtain remission of sins and redemption from everlasting death; through the same Jesus Christ, Thy Son, our Lord, who liveth, etc.

Epistle, Is. 52:13 to 53:12

GRADUAL

Tract. Reproach hath broken My heart, and I am full of heaviness: and I looked for some to take pity, but there was none, and for comforters, but I found none.

V. Is it nothing to you, all ye that pass by?: Behold and see if there be any sorrow like unto My sorrow, which is done unto Me, wherewith the Lord hath afflicted Me in the day of His fierce anger.

V. He was wounded for our transgressions, He was bruised for our iniquities: the chastisement of our peace was upon Him, and with His stripes we are healed.

Gospel, John 18:1 to 19:42, or The Passion History

HOLY SATURDAY, EASTER EVE

COLLECT

O God, who didst enlighten this most holy night with the glory of the Lord's resurrection, preserve in all Thy people the spirit of adoption which Thou hast given, so that, renewed in body and soul, they may perform unto Thee a pure service; through the same Jesus Christ, Thy Son, our Lord, who liveth, etc.

Epistle, 1 Peter 3:17-22

Gospel, Matt. 27:57-66

EASTER DAY, THE FEAST OF THE RESURRECTION OF OUR LORD

INTROIT

When I awake, I am still with Thee. Hallelujah!: Thou hast laid Thine hand upon me. Hallelujah!

Such knowledge is too wonderful for me: it is high, I cannot attain unto it. Hallelujah! Hallelujah!

Ps. O Lord, Thou hast searched me and known me: Thou knowest my downsitting and mine uprising.

Glory be to the Father, etc.   Or:

He is risen, Hallelujah!: Why seek ye the Living among the dead? Hallelujah!

Remember how He spake unto you, Hallelujah!: the Son of Man must be crucified and the third day rise again. Hallelujah! Hallelujah!

Ps. Thou crownedst Him with glory and honor: Thou madest Him to have dominion over the works of Thy hands.

Glory be to the Father, etc.

COLLECTS

Almighty God, who through Thine only-begotten Son, Jesus Christ, hast overcome death and opened unto us the gate of everlasting life, we humbly beseech Thee that, as Thou dost put into our minds good desires, so by Thy continual help we may bring the same to good effect; through the same Jesus Christ, Thy Son, our Lord, who liveth, etc.

Grant, we beseech Thee, Almighty God, that we who celebrate Thy Paschal Feast, kindled with heavenly desires, may ever thirst for the Fountain of Life, Jesus Christ, Thy Son, our Lord, who liveth, etc.

Grant, we beseech Thee, Almighty God, that we who celebrate the solemnities of the Lord's resurrection may by the renewal of Thy Holy Spirit rise again from the death of the soul; through the same Jesus Christ, Thy Son, our Lord, who liveth, etc.

Epistle, 1 Cor. 5:6-8

GRADUAL

This is the day which the Lord hath made: we will rejoice and be glad in it.

V. Oh, give thanks unto the Lord, for He is good: for His mercy endureth forever. Hallelujah! Hallelujah!

V. Christ, our Passover, is sacrificed for us.

V. Let us keep the feast with the unleavened bread of sincerity and truth. Hallelujah!

Gospel, Mark 16:1-8

EASTER MONDAY

INTROIT

The Lord hath brought you into a land flowing with milk and honey, Hallelujah!: that His Law might be continually in your mouth. Hallelujah! Hallelujah!

Ps. Oh, give thanks unto the Lord; call upon His name: make known His deeds among the people.

Glory be to the Father, etc.

COLLECTS

O God, who in the Paschal Feast hast bestowed restoration upon the world, continue unto Thy people Thy heavenly gift that they may both attain unto perfect freedom and advance unto life eternal; through Jesus Christ, Thy Son, our Lord, who liveth, etc.

O God, who through the resurrection of Thy Son didst bestow life and freedom upon the world, continue, we beseech Thee, these Thy gifts unto Thy people that they both walk in perfect freedom and attain unto life eternal; through the same Jesus Christ, Thy Son, our Lord, who liveth, etc.

Epistle, Acts 10:34-41

GRADUAL

This is the day which the Lord hath made: we will rejoice and be glad in it.

V. Let Israel now say: that His mercy endureth forever. Hallelujah! Hallelujah!

V. Did not our hearts burn within us while He talked with us by the way: and while He opened to us the Scriptures? Hallelujah!

Gospel, Luke 24:13-35

EASTER TUESDAY

INTROIT

He gave them to drink of the water of wisdom, and they will be strengthened thereby, and they shall not be moved, Hallelujah!: and it will exalt them forever. Hallelujah! Hallelujah!

Ps. Oh, give thanks unto the Lord; call upon His name: make known His deeds among the people.

Glory be to the Father, etc.

COLLECTS

Almighty God, who through the resurrection of Thy Son didst secure peace for our troubled conscience, grant unto us evermore this peace, that, trusting in the merit of Thy Son, we at length come unto the perfect peace of heaven through the same Jesus Christ, Thy Son, our Lord, who liveth, etc.

O almighty and eternal God, who hast bestowed on us the paschal mysteries in the token of the covenant of man's redemption, give us the will to show forth in our lives that which we profess with our lips; through Jesus Christ, Thy Son, our Lord, who liveth, etc.

O almighty and eternal God, who through the resurrection of Thy Son hast sealed the covenant of man's reconciliation, grant unto us who joy in this Thy covenant grace to show forth in our lives that which we profess with our lips; through the same Jesus Christ, Thy Son, our Lord, who liveth, etc.

Epistle, Acts 13:26-33

GRADUAL

(The same as for Easter Monday)

Gospel, Luke 24:36-48

QUASIMODOGENITI, THE FIRST SUNDAY AFTER EASTER

INTROIT

As newborn babes: desire the sincere milk of the Word.

Hear, O My people, and I will testify unto thee: O Israel, if thou wilt hearken unto Me.

Ps. Sing aloud unto God, our Strength: make a joyful noise unto the God of Jacob.

Glory be to the Father, etc.

COLLECT

Grant, we beseech Thee, Almighty God, that we who have celebrated the solemnities of the Lord's resurrection may, by the help of Thy grace, bring forth the fruits thereof in our life and conversation; through the same Jesus Christ, Thy Son, our Lord, who liveth, etc.

Epistle, 1 John 5:4-10

GRADUAL

Hallelujah! Hallelujah!

V. Christ, our Passover, is sacrificed for us. Hallelujah!

V. The angel of the Lord descended from heaven: and came and rolled back the stone from the door and sat upon it. Hallelujah!

Gospel, John 20:19-31

MISERICORDIAS DOMINI, THE SECOND SUNDAY AFTER EASTER

INTROIT

The earth is full of the goodness of the Lord: by the word of the Lord were the heavens made.

Ps. Rejoice in the Lord, O ye righteous: for praise is comely for the upright.

Glory be to the Father, etc.

God, who by the humiliation of Thy Son didst raise up the fallen world, grant unto Thy faithful ones perpetual gladness, and those whom Thou hast delivered from the danger of everlasting death do Thou make partakers of eternal joys; through the same Jesus Christ, Thy Son, our Lord, who liveth, etc.

Epistle, 1 Peter 2:21-25

GRADUAL

Hallelujah! Hallelujah!

V. Then was the Lord Jesus known of the disciples: in the breaking of bread. Hallelujah!

V. I am the Good Shepherd: and know My sheep and am known of Mine. Hallelujah!

Gospel, John 10:11-16

JUBILATE, THE THIRD SUNDAY AFTER EASTER

INTROIT

Make a joyful noise unto God, all ye lands: sing forth the honor of His name; make His praise glorious.

Ps. Say unto God, How terrible art Thou in Thy works: through the greatness of Thy power shall Thine enemies submit themselves unto Thee.

Glory be to the Father, etc.

COLLECT

Almighty God, who showest to them that be in error the light of Thy truth to the intent that they may return into the way of righteousness, grant unto all them that are admitted into the fellowship of Christ's religion that they may avoid those things that are contrary to their profession and follow all such things as are agreeable to the same; through Jesus Christ, Thy Son, our Lord, who liveth, etc.

Epistle, 1 Peter 2:11-20

GRADUAL

Hallelujah! Hallelujah!

V. The Lord hath sent redemption unto His people. Hallelujah!

V. It behooved Christ to suffer and to rise from the dead: and thus to enter into His glory. Hallelujah!

Gospel, John 16:16-23

CANTATE, THE FOURTH SUNDAY AFTER EASTER

INTROIT

Oh, sing unto the Lord a new song: for He hath done marvelous things.

The Lord hath made known His salvation: His righteousness hath He openly showed in the sight of the heathen.

Ps. His right hand and His holy arm: hath gotten Him the victory.

Glory be to the Father, etc.

COLLECT

O God, who makest the minds of the faithful to be of one will, grant unto Thy people that they may love what Thou commandest and desire what Thou dost promise, that among the manifold changes of this world our hearts may there be fixed where true joys are to be found; through Jesus Christ, Thy Son, our Lord, who liveth, etc.

Epistle, James 1:16-21

GRADUAL

Hallelujah! Hallelujah!

V. The right hand of the Lord is exalted: the right hand of the Lord doeth valiantly. Hallelujah!

V. Christ, being raised from the dead, dieth no more: death hath no more dominion over Him. Hallelujah!

Gospel, John 16:5-15

ROGATE, THE FIFTH SUNDAY AFTER EASTER

INTROIT

With the voice of singing declare ye and tell this: utter it even to the end of the earth. Hallelujah!

The Lord hath redeemed His servant Jacob: Hallelujah! Hallelujah!

Ps. Make a joyful noise unto God, all ye lands: sing forth the honor of His name; make His praise glorious.

Glory be to the Father, etc.

COLLECT

O God, from whom all good things do come, grant to us, Thy humble servants, that by Thy holy inspiration we may think those things that be right and by Thy merciful guiding may perform the same; through Jesus Christ, Thy Son, our Lord, who liveth, etc. *Epistle, James 1:22-27*

GRADUAL

Hallelujah! Hallelujah!

V. Christ, who hath redeemed us with His blood: is risen and hath appeared unto us. Hallelujah!

V. I came forth from the Father and am come into the world: again, I leave the world and go to the Father. Hallelujah!

Gospel, John 16:23-30

THE ASCENSION OF OUR LORD

INTROIT

Ye men of Galilee, why stand ye gazing up into heaven?: Hallelujah!

This same Jesus which is taken up from you into heaven shall so come in like manner as ye have seen Him go into heaven: Hallelujah! Hallelujah!

Ps. Oh, clap your hands, all ye people: shout unto God with the voice of triumph.

Glory be to the Father, etc.

COLLECTS

Grant, we beseech Thee, Almighty God, that like as we do believe Thine only-begotten Son, our Lord Jesus Christ, to have ascended into the heavens, so may we also in heart and mind thither ascend and with Him continually dwell; who liveth, etc.

O King of Glory, Lord of hosts, who didst this day ascend in triumph far above all heavens, we beseech Thee, leave us not comfortless, but send to us the Spirit of Truth, promised of the Father; O Thou who with the Father and the Holy Ghost livest, etc. *Epistle, Acts 1:1-11*

GRADUAL

Hallelujah! Hallelujah!

V. God is gone up with a shout: the Lord with the sound of a trumpet. Hallelujah!

V. Thou hast ascended on high: Thou hast led captivity captive. Hallelujah!

Gospel, Mark 16:14-20

EXAUDI, THE SUNDAY AFTER THE ASCENSION

INTROIT

Hear, O Lord, when I cry with my voice: Hallelujah!

When Thou saidst, Seek ye My face, my heart said unto Thee, Thy face, Lord, will I seek: Hide not Thy face from me. Hallelujah! Hallelujah!

Ps. The Lord is my Light and my Salvation: whom shall I fear?

Glory be to the Father, etc.

COLLECT

Almighty, everlasting God, make us to have always a devout will toward Thee and to serve Thy Majesty with a pure heart; through Jesus ·Christ, Thy Son, our Lord, who liveth, etc.

Epistle, 1 Peter 4:7-11

GRADUAL

Hallelujah! Hallelujah!

V. God reigneth over the heathen: God sitteth upon the throne of His holiness. Hallelujah!

V. I will not leave you comfortless: I go, and I will come again to you, and your heart shall rejoice. Hallelujah!

Gospel, John 15:26 to 16:4

WHITSUNDAY, THE FEAST OF PENTECOST

INTROIT

The Spirit of the Lord filleth the world: Hallelujah!

Let the righteous be glad; let them rejoice before God: yea, let them exceedingly rejoice. Hallelujah! Hallelujah!

Ps. Let God arise; let His enemies be scattered: let them also that hate Him flee before Him.

Glory be to the Father, etc.

COLLECT

O God, who didst teach the hearts of Thy faithful pecple by sending to them the light of Thy Holy Spirit, grant us by the same Spirit to have a right judgment in all things and evermore to rejoice in His holy comfort; through Jesus Christ, Thy Son, our Lord, who with Thee and the Holy Ghost liveth, etc.

Epistle, Acts 2:1-13

GRADUAL

Hallelujah! Hallelujah!

V. Thou sendest forth Thy Spirit, they are created: and Thou renewest the face of the earth. Hallelujah!

V. Come, Holy Spirit, fill the hearts of the faithful: and kindle in them the fire of Thy love. Hallelujah!

Gospel, John 14:23-31

MONDAY OF WHITSUN WEEK

INTROIT

He fed them with the finest of the wheat, Hallelujah!: and with honey out of the rock He satisfied them. Hallelujah! Hallelujah!

Ps. Sing aloud unto God, our Strength: make a joyful noise unto the God of Jacob.

Glory be to the Father, etc.

COLLECT

O God, who didst give Thy Holy Spirit to Thine Apostles, grant unto Thy people the performance of their petitions, so that on us, to whom Thou hast given faith, Thou mayest bestow also peace; through Jesus Christ, Thy Son, our Lord, who liveth, etc.

Epistle, Acts 10:42-48

GRADUAL

Hallelujah! Hallelujah!

V. The Apostles spake with other tongues the wonderful works of God. Hallelujah!

V. Come, Holy Spirit, fill the hearts of the faithful: and kindle in them the fire of Thy love. Hallelujah!

Gospel, John 3:16-21

[72]

TUESDAY OF WHITSUN WEEK

INTROIT

Receive the joy of your glory, Hallelujah! giving thanks to God, Hallelujah!: who has called you to His heavenly kingdom. Hallelujah! Hallelujah!

Ps. Give ear, O My people, to My Law: incline your ears to the words of My mouth.

Glory be to the Father, etc.

(The Collect for Tuesday of Whitsun week is the same as for Whitsunday)

Epistle, Acts 8:14-17

(The Gradual is the same as for Monday of Whitsun week)

Gospel, John 10:1-10

THE FEAST OF THE HOLY TRINITY

INTROIT

Blessed be the Holy Trinity and the undivided Unity: let us give glory to Him because He hath shown His mercy to us.

Ps. O Lord, our Lord: how excellent is Thy name in all the earth!

Glory be to the Father, etc.   Or:

Holy, holy, holy, is the Lord of hosts: of Him and through Him and to Him are all things.

Ps. O Lord, our Lord: how excellent is Thy name in all the earth!

Glory be to the Father, etc.

COLLECT

Almighty and everlasting God, who hast given unto us, Thy servants, grace, by the confession of a true faith, to acknowledge the glory of the eternal Trinity and in the power of the Divine Majesty to worship the Unity, we beseech Thee that Thou wouldst keep us steadfast in this faith and evermore defend us from all adversities; who livest, etc.   *Epistle, Rom. 11:33-36*

GRADUAL

Blessed art Thou, O Lord, who beholdest the deep; and who dwellest between the cherubim.

V. Blessed art Thou, O Lord, in the firmament of heaven: and greatly to be praised forever. Hallelujah! Hallelujah!

V. Blessed art Thou, O Lord God of our fathers: and greatly to be praised and glorified forever. Hallelujah!   *Gospel, John 3:1-15*

THE FIRST SUNDAY AFTER TRINITY

INTROIT

O Lord, I have trusted in Thy mercy: my heart shall rejoice in Thy salvation.

I will sing unto the Lord: because He hath dealt bountifully with me.

Ps. How long wilt Thou forget me, O Lord?: How long wilt Thou hide Thy face from me?

Glory be to the Father, etc.

COLLECT

O God, the Strength of all them that put their trust in Thee, mercifully accept our prayers; and because through the weakness of our mortal nature we can do no good thing without Thee, grant us the help of Thy grace that in keeping Thy commandments we may please Thee both in will and deed; through Jesus Christ, Thy Son, our Lord, who liveth, etc.   *Epistle, 1 John 4:16-21*

[73]

I said, Lord, be merciful unto me: heal my soul, for I have sinned against Thee.

V. Blessed is he that considereth the poor: the Lord will deliver him in time of trouble. Hallelujah! Hallelujah!

V. Give ear to my words, O Lord: consider my meditation. Hallelujah!

Gospel, Luke 16:19-31

THE SECOND SUNDAY AFTER TRINITY

INTROIT

The Lord was my Stay: He brought me forth also into a large place.

He delivered me: because He delighted in me.

Ps. I will love Thee, O Lord, my Strength: The Lord is my Rock and my Fortress.

Glory be to the Father, etc.

COLLECT

O Lord, who never failest to help and govern those whom Thou dost bring up in Thy steadfast fear and love, make us to have a perpetual fear and love of Thy holy name; through Jesus Christ, Thy Son, our Lord, who liveth, etc.

Epistle, 1 John 3:13-18

GRADUAL

In my distress I cried unto the Lord: and He heard me.

V. Deliver my soul, O Lord, from lying lips: and from a deceitful tongue. Hallelujah! Hallelujah!

V. God judgeth the righteous: and God is angry with the wicked every day. Hallelujah!

Gospel, Luke 14:16-24

THE THIRD SUNDAY AFTER TRINITY

INTROIT

Turn Thee unto me and have mercy upon me: for I am desolate and afflicted.

Look upon mine affliction and my pain: and forgive all my sins.

Ps. Unto Thee, O Lord, do I lift up my soul: O my God, I trust in Thee, let me not be ashamed.

Glory be to the Father, etc.

COLLECT

O God, the Protector of all that trust in Thee, without whom nothing is strong, nothing is holy, increase and multiply upon us Thy mercy that, Thou being our Ruler and Guide, we may so pass through things temporal that we finally lose not the things eternal; through Jesus Christ, Thy Son, our Lord, who liveth, etc.

Epistle, 1 Peter 5:6-11

GRADUAL

Cast thy burden upon the Lord: and He shall sustain thee.

V. I will call upon God; and the Lord shall save me: He hath delivered my soul in peace. Hallelujah! Hallelujah!

V. I will love Thee, O Lord, my Strength: the Lord is my Rock and my Fortress and my Deliverer. Hallelujah!

Gospel, Luke 15:1-10

THE FOURTH SUNDAY AFTER TRINITY

INTROIT

The Lord is my Light and my Salvation; whom shall I fear?: The Lord is the Strength of my life; of whom shall I be afraid?

When the wicked, even mine enemies and my foes, came upon me: they stumbled and fell.

Ps. Though an host should encamp against me: my heart shall not fear.

Glory be to the Father, etc.

Grant, O Lord, we beseech Thee, that the course of this world may be so peaceably ordered by Thy governance that Thy Church may joyfully serve Thee in all godly quietness; through Jesus Christ, Thy Son, our Lord, who liveth, etc.

Epistle, Rom. 8:18-23

Forgive our sins, O Lord: lest the heathen say, Where is their God?

V. Help us, O God of our salvation: and for the glory of Thy name deliver us. Hallelujah! Hallelujah!

V. O God, Thou sittest in the throne, judging right: be a Refuge for the oppressed in times of trouble. Hallelujah! *Gospel, Luke 6:36-42*

THE FIFTH SUNDAY AFTER TRINITY

Hear, O Lord, when I cry with my voice: Thou hast been my Help.

Leave me not, neither forsake me: O God of my salvation.

Ps. The Lord is my Light and my Salvation: whom shall I fear?

Glory be to the Father, etc.

O God, who hast prepared for them that love Thee such good things as pass man's understanding, pour into our hearts such love toward Thee that we, loving Thee above all things, may obtain Thy promises, which exceed all that we can desire; through Jesus Christ, Thy Son, our Lord, who liveth, etc.

Epistle, 1 Peter 3:8-15

Behold, O God, our Shield: and look upon Thy servants.

V. O Lord God of hosts: hear our prayer. Hallelujah! Hallelujah!

V. The king shall joy in Thy strength: and in Thy salvation, how greatly shall he rejoice! Hallelujah! *Gospel, Luke 5:1-11*

THE SIXTH SUNDAY AFTER TRINITY

The Lord is the Strength of His people: He is the saving Strength of His anointed.

Save Thy people and bless Thine inheritance: feed them also and lift them up forever.

Ps. Unto Thee will I cry, O Lord, my Rock; be not silent unto me: lest, if Thou be silent to me, I become like them that go down into the pit.

Glory be to the Father, etc.

Lord of all power and might, who art the Author and Giver of all good things, graft in our hearts the love of Thy name, increase in us true religion, nourish us with all goodness, and of Thy great mercy keep us in the same; through Jesus Christ, Thy Son, our Lord, who liveth, etc. *Epistle, Rom. 6:3-11*

Return, O Lord, how long?: And let it repent Thee concerning Thy servants.

V. Lord, Thou hast been our Dwelling Place in all generations. Hallelujah! Hallelujah!

V. In Thee, O Lord, do I put my trust; let me never be ashamed: deliver me in Thy righteousness; bow down Thine ear to me, deliver me speedily. Hallelujah!

Gospel, Matt. 5:20-26

THE SEVENTH SUNDAY AFTER TRINITY

INTROIT

Oh, clap your hands, all ye people!: Shout unto God with the voice of triumph.

Ps. He shall subdue the people under us: and the nations under our feet.

Glory be to the Father, etc.

COLLECT

O God, whose never-failing providence ordereth all things both in heaven and earth, we humbly beseech Thee to put away from us all hurtful things and to give us those things which be profitable for us; through Jesus Christ, Thy Son, our Lord, who liveth, etc.

Epistle, Rom. 6:19-23

GRADUAL

Come, ye children, hearken unto me: I will teach you the fear of the Lord.

V. Look unto Him and be lightened: and let your faces not be ashamed. Hallelujah! Hallelujah!

V. Oh, clap your hands, all ye people: shout unto God with the voice of triumph. Hallelujah!

Gospel, Mark 8:1-9

THE EIGHTH SUNDAY AFTER TRINITY

INTROIT

We have thought of Thy loving-kindness, O God: in the midst of Thy Temple.

According to Thy name, O God, so is Thy praise unto the ends of the earth: Thy right hand is full of righteousness.

Ps. Great is the Lord and greatly to be praised: in the city of our God, in the mountain of His holiness.

Glory be to the Father, etc.

COLLECT

Grant to us, Lord, we beseech Thee, the Spirit to think and do always such things as are right, that we, who cannot do anything that is good without Thee, may by Thee be enabled to live according to Thy will; through Jesus Christ, Thy Son, our Lord, who liveth, etc.

Epistle, Rom. 8:12-17

GRADUAL

Be Thou my strong Rock: for an house of defense to save me.

V. In Thee, O Lord, do I put my trust: let me never be ashamed. Hallelujah! Hallelujah!

V. Give ear, O My people, to My Law: incline your ears to the words of My mouth. Hallelujah!

Gospel, Matt. 7:15-23

THE NINTH SUNDAY AFTER TRINITY

INTROIT

Behold, God is mine Helper: the Lord is with them that uphold my soul.

He shall reward evil unto mine enemies: cut them off in Thy truth, O Lord.

Ps. Save me, O God, by Thy name: and judge me by Thy strength.

Glory be to the Father, etc.

COLLECT

Let Thy merciful ears, O Lord, be open to the prayers of Thy humble servants; and that they may obtain their petitions, make them to ask such things as shall please Thee; through Jesus Christ, Thy Son, our Lord, who liveth, etc.

Epistle, 1 Cor. 10:6-13

O Lord, our Lord, how excellent is Thy name in all the earth: who hast set Thy glory above the heavens. Hallelujah! Hallelujah!

V. Blessed is the man that feareth the Lord: that delighteth greatly in His commandments. Hallelujah!

Gospel, Luke 16:1-9

THE TENTH SUNDAY AFTER TRINITY

INTROIT

As for me, I will call upon God; and He shall hear my voice: He hath delivered my soul in peace from the battle that was against me.

God shall hear and afflict them, even He that abideth of old: Cast thy burden upon the Lord, and He shall sustain thee.

Ps. Give ear to my prayer, O God: and hide not Thyself from my supplication.

Glory be to the Father, etc.

COLLECT

O God, who declarest Thine almighty power chiefly in showing mercy and pity, mercifully grant unto us such a measure of Thy grace that we, running the way of Thy commandments, may obtain Thy gracious promises and be made partakers of Thy heavenly treasure; through Jesus Christ, Thy Son, our Lord, who liveth, etc.

Epistle, 1 Cor. 12:1-11

GRADUAL

Keep me, O Lord, as the apple of the eye: hide me under the shadow of Thy wings.

V. Let my sentence come forth from Thy presence: let Thine eyes behold the things that are equal. Hallelujah! Hallelujah!

V. O Lord God of my salvation, I have cried day and night before Thee. Hallelujah!

Gospel, Luke 19:41-48

THE ELEVENTH SUNDAY AFTER TRINITY

INTROIT

God is in His holy habitation: He is God who setteth the solitary in families.

The God of Israel is He that giveth strength: and power unto His people.

Ps. Let God arise, let His enemies be scattered: let them also that hate Him flee before Him.

Glory be to the Father, etc.

COLLECT

Almighty and everlasting God, who art always more ready to hear than we to pray and art wont to give more than either we desire or deserve, pour down upon us the abundance of Thy mercy, forgiving us those things whereof our conscience is afraid, and giving us those good things which we are not worthy to ask but through the merits and mediation of Jesus Christ, Thy Son, our Lord, who liveth, etc.

Epistle, 1 Cor. 15:1-10

GRADUAL

My heart trusteth in God, and I am helped: therefore my heart greatly rejoiceth; and with my song will I praise Him.

V. Unto Thee will I cry, O Lord, my Rock: be not silent to me; hear the voice of my supplications. Hallelujah! Hallelujah!

V. Lord, Thou hast been our Dwelling Place in all generations. Hallelujah!

Gospel, Luke 18:9-14

THE TWELFTH SUNDAY AFTER TRINITY

Make haste, O God, to deliver me: make haste to help me, O Lord.

Let them be ashamed and confounded: that seek after my soul.

Ps. Let them be turned backward and put to confusion: that desire my hurt.

Glory be to the Father, etc.

COLLECT

Almighty and merciful God, of whose only gift it cometh that Thy faithful people do unto Thee true and laudable service, grant, we beseech Thee, that we may so faithfully serve Thee in this life that we fail not finally to attain Thy heavenly promises; through Jesus Christ, Thy Son, our Lord, who liveth, etc.

Epistle, 2 Cor. 3:4-11

GRADUAL

I will bless the Lord at all times: His praise shall continually be in my mouth.

V. My soul shall make her boast in the Lord: the humble shall hear thereof and be glad. Hallelujah! Hallelujah!

V. Sing aloud unto God, our Strength: make a joyful noise unto the God of Jacob. Hallelujah!

Gospel, Mark 7:31-37

THE THIRTEENTH SUNDAY AFTER TRINITY

INTROIT

Have respect, O Lord, unto Thy covenant: oh, let not the oppressed return ashamed!

Arise, O God, plead Thine own cause: and forget not the voice of Thine enemies.

Ps. O God, why hast Thou cast us off forever?: Why doth Thine anger smoke against the sheep of Thy pasture?

Glory be to the Father, etc.

COLLECT

Almighty and everlasting God, give unto us the increase of faith, hope, and charity; and that we may obtain that which Thou dost promise, make us to love that which Thou dost command; through Jesus Christ, Thy Son, our Lord, who liveth, etc.

Epistle, Gal. 3:15-22

GRADUAL

Have respect, O Lord, unto Thy covenant: oh, let not the oppressed return ashamed!

V. Arise, O God, plead Thine own cause: and forget not the voice of Thine enemies. Hallelujah! Hallelujah!

V. O Lord God of my salvation: I have cried day and night before Thee. Hallelujah!

Gospel, Luke 10:23-37

THE FOURTEENTH SUNDAY AFTER TRINITY

INTROIT

Behold, O God, our Shield, and look upon the face of Thine anointed: for a day in Thy courts is better than a thousand.

Ps. How amiable are Thy tabernacles, O Lord of hosts!: My soul longeth, yea, even fainteth, for the courts of the Lord.

Glory be to the Father, etc.

COLLECT

Keep, we beseech Thee, O Lord, Thy Church with Thy perpetual mercy; and because the frailty of man without Thee cannot but fall, keep us ever by Thy help from all things hurtful and lead us to all things profitable to our salvation; through Jesus Christ, Thy Son, our Lord, who liveth, etc.

Epistle, Gal. 5:16-24

It is a good thing to give thanks unto the Lord: and to sing praises unto Thy name, O Most High.

V. To show forth Thy loving-kindness in the morning: and Thy faithfulness every night. Hallelujah! Hallelujah!

V. Praise waiteth for Thee, O God, in Zion: and unto Thee shall the vow be performed. Hallelujah! *Gospel, Luke 17:11-19*

THE FIFTEENTH SUNDAY AFTER TRINITY

INTROIT

Bow down Thine ear, O Lord, hear me: O Thou, my God, save Thy servant that trusteth in Thee.

Be merciful to me, O Lord: for I cry unto Thee daily.

Ps. Rejoice the soul of Thy servant: for unto Thee, O Lord, do I lift up my soul.

Glory be to the Father, etc. ### COLLECT

O Lord, we beseech Thee, let Thy continual pity cleanse and defend Thy Church; and because it cannot continue in safety without Thy help, preserve it evermore by Thy help and goodness; through Jesus Christ, Thy Son, our Lord, who liveth, etc.

Epistle, Gal. 5:25 to 6:10

GRADUAL

It is better to trust in the Lord: than to put confidence in man.

V. It is better to trust in the Lord: than to put confidence in princes. Hallelujah! Hallelujah!

V. O God, my heart is fixed: I will sing and give praise, even with my glory. Hallelujah! *Gospel, Matt. 6:24-34*

THE SIXTEENTH SUNDAY AFTER TRINITY

INTROIT

Be merciful unto me, O Lord: for I cry unto Thee daily.

For Thou, Lord, art good and ready to forgive: and plenteous in mercy unto all them that call upon Thee.

Ps. Bow down Thine ear, O Lord, hear me: for I am poor and needy.

Glory be to the Father, etc. ### COLLECT

Lord, we pray Thee that Thy grace may always go before and follow after us and make us continually to be given to all good works; through Jesus Christ, Thy Son, our Lord, who liveth, etc. *Epistle, Eph. 3:13-21*

GRADUAL

The heathen shall fear the name of the Lord: and all the kings of the earth Thy glory.

V. When the Lord shall build up Zion: He shall appear in His glory. Hallelujah! Hallelujah!

V. Ye that fear the Lord, trust in the Lord: He is their Help and their Shield. Hallelujah! *Gospel, Luke 7:11-17*

THE SEVENTEENTH SUNDAY AFTER TRINITY

INTROIT

Righteous art Thou, O Lord: and upright are Thy judgments.

Deal with Thy servant: according to Thy mercy.

Ps. Blessed are the undefiled in the way: who walk in the Law of the Lord.

Glory be to the Father, etc.

Lord, we beseech Thee, grant Thy people grace to withstand the temptations of the devil and with pure hearts and minds to follow Thee, the only God; through Jesus Christ, Thy Son, our Lord, who liveth, etc.

Epistle, Eph. 4:1-6

GRADUAL

Blessed is the nation whose God is the Lord: and the people whom He hath chosen for His own inheritance.

V. By the Word of the Lord were the heavens made: and all the host of them by the Breath of His mouth. Hallelujah! Hallelujah!

V. The right hand of the Lord is exalted: the right hand of the Lord doeth valiantly. Hallelujah!

Gospel, Luke 14:1-11

THE EIGHTEENTH SUNDAY AFTER TRINITY

INTROIT

Reward them that wait for Thee, O Lord: and let Thy prophets be found faithful.

Hear the prayer of Thy servants: and of Thy people Israel.

Ps. I was glad when they said unto me: Let us go into the house of the Lord.

Glory be to the Father, etc.

COLLECT

O God, forasmuch as without Thee we are not able to please Thee, mercifully grant that Thy Holy Spirit may in all things direct and rule our hearts; through Jesus Christ, Thy Son, our Lord, who liveth, etc.

Epistle, 1 Cor. 1:4-9

GRADUAL

I was glad when they said unto me: Let us go into the house of the Lord.

V. Peace be within thy walls: and prosperity within thy palaces. Hallelujah! Hallelujah!

V. Oh, praise the Lord, all ye nations: praise Him, all ye people. Hallelujah!

Gospel, Matt. 22:34-46

THE NINETEENTH SUNDAY AFTER TRINITY

INTROIT

Say unto my soul, I am thy Salvation: The righteous cry, and the Lord heareth.

He delivereth them out of their troubles: He is their God forever and ever.

Ps. Give ear, O My people, to My Law: incline your ears to the words of My mouth.

Glory be to the Father, etc.

COLLECT

O almighty and most merciful God, of Thy bountiful goodness keep us, we beseech Thee, from all things that may hurt us, that we, being ready, both in body and soul, may cheerfully accomplish those things that Thou wouldst have done; through Jesus Christ, Thy Son, our Lord, who liveth, etc.

Epistle, Eph. 4:22-28

GRADUAL

Let my prayer be set forth before Thee as incense: and the lifting up of my hands as the evening sacrifice. Hallelujah! Hallelujah!

V. Oh, sing unto the Lord a new song: for He hath done marvelous things. Hallelujah!

Gospel, Matt. 9:1-8

THE TWENTIETH SUNDAY AFTER TRINITY

INTROIT

The Lord, our God, is righteous in all His works which He doeth: for we obeyed not His voice.

Give glory to Thy name, O Lord: and deal with us according to the multitude of Thy mercies.

Ps. Great is the Lord and greatly to be praised: in the city of our God, in the mountain of His holiness.

Glory be to the Father, etc.

COLLECT

Grant, we beseech Thee, merciful Lord, to Thy faithful people pardon and peace, that they may be cleansed from all their sins and serve Thee with a quiet mind; through Jesus Christ, Thy Son, our Lord, who liveth, etc.

Epistle, Eph. 5:15-21

GRADUAL

The eyes of all wait upon Thee, O Lord: and Thou givest them their meat in due season.

V. Thou openest Thine hand: and satisfiest the desire of every living thing. Hallelujah! Hallelujah!

V. Out of the depths have I cried unto Thee, O Lord: Lord, hear my voice. Hallelujah!

Gospel, Matt. 22:1-14

THE TWENTY-FIRST SUNDAY AFTER TRINITY

INTROIT

The whole world is in Thy power, O Lord, King Almighty: there is no man that can gainsay Thee.

For Thou hast made heaven and earth and all the wondrous things under the heaven: Thou art Lord of all.

Ps. Blessed are the undefiled in the way: who walk in the Law of the Lord.

Glory be to the Father, etc.

COLLECT

Lord, we beseech Thee to keep Thy household, the Church, in continual godliness, that through Thy protection it may be free from all adversities and devoutly given to serve Thee in good works, to the glory of Thy name; through Jesus Christ, Thy Son, our Lord, who liveth, etc.

Epistle, Eph. 6:10-17

GRADUAL

Lord, Thou hast been our Dwelling Place: in all generations.

V. Before the mountains were brought forth or ever Thou hadst formed the earth and the world: even from everlasting to everlasting, Thou art God. Hallelujah! Hallelujah!

V. They that trust in the Lord shall be as Mount Zion: which cannot be removed, but abideth forever. Hallelujah!

Gospel, John 4:46-54

THE TWENTY-SECOND SUNDAY AFTER TRINITY

(The Introit and Collect for the Twenty-third Sunday after Trinity, p. 82, and the Epistle, Gradual, and Gospel for the Twenty-seventh Sunday after Trinity, p. 83, shall be used on the last Sunday after Trinity in each year)

INTROIT

If Thou, Lord, shouldest mark iniquities: O Lord, who shall stand?

But there is forgiveness with Thee: that Thou mayest be feared, O God of Israel.

Ps. Out of the depths have I cried unto Thee, O Lord: Lord, hear my voice.

Glory be to the Father, etc.

O God, our Refuge and Strength, who art the Author of all godliness, be ready, we beseech Thee, to hear the devout prayers of Thy Church, and grant that those things which we ask faithfully we may obtain effectually; through Jesus Christ, Thy Son, our Lord, who liveth, etc.

Epistle, Phil. 1:3-11

GRADUAL

Behold how good and how pleasant it is: for brethren to dwell together in unity!

V. The Lord commanded blessing: even life forevermore. Hallelujah! Hallelujah!

V. The Lord healeth the broken in heart: and bindeth up their wounds. Hallelujah!

Gospel, Matt. 18:23-35

THE TWENTY-THIRD SUNDAY AFTER TRINITY

INTROIT

I know the thoughts that I think toward you, saith the Lord: thoughts of peace and not of evil.

Then shall ye call upon Me and pray unto Me, and I will hearken unto you: and I will turn your captivity and gather you from all nations and from all places.

Ps. Lord, Thou hast been favorable unto Thy land: Thou hast brought back the captivity of Jacob.

Glory be to the Father, etc.

COLLECT

Absolve, we beseech Thee, O Lord, Thy people from their offenses, that from the bonds of our sins which by reason of our frailty we have brought upon us we may be delivered by Thy bountiful goodness; through Jesus Christ, Thy Son, our Lord, who liveth, etc.

Epistle, Phil. 3:17-21

GRADUAL

Thou hast saved us from our enemies: and hast put them to shame that hated us.

V. In God we boast all the day long: and praise Thy name forever. Hallelujah! Hallelujah!

V. Ye that fear the Lord, trust in the Lord: He is their Help and their Shield. Hallelujah!

Gospel, Matt. 22:15-22

THE TWENTY-FOURTH SUNDAY AFTER TRINITY

INTROIT

Oh, come, let us worship and bow down: let us kneel before the Lord, our Maker.

For He is our God: and we are the people of His pasture and the sheep of His hand.

Ps. Oh, come, let us sing unto the Lord: let us make a joyful noise to the Rock of our salvation.

Glory be to the Father, etc.

COLLECT

Stir up, we beseech Thee, O Lord, the wills of Thy faithful people that they, plenteously bringing forth the fruit of good works, may of Thee be plenteously rewarded; through Jesus Christ, Thy Son, our Lord, who liveth, etc.

Epistle, Col. 1:9-14

GRADUAL

Thou hast delivered my soul from death: mine eyes from tears, and my feet from falling.

V. I love the Lord: because He hath heard my voice and my supplication. Hallelujah! Hallelujah!

V. With Thee is the fountain of life: in Thy light shall we see light. Hallelujah!

Gospel, Matt. 9:18-26

THE TWENTY-FIFTH SUNDAY AFTER TRINITY

INTROIT

Have mercy upon me, O Lord, for I am in trouble: deliver me from the hand of mine enemies and from them that persecute me.

Let me not be ashamed, O Lord: for I have called upon Thee.

Ps. In Thee, O Lord, do I put my trust: let me never be ashamed.

Glory be to the Father, etc.

COLLECT

Almighty God, we beseech Thee, show Thy mercy unto Thy humble servants, that we who put no trust in our own merits may not be dealt with after the severity of Thy judgment, but according to Thy mercy; through Jesus Christ, Thy Son, our Lord, who liveth, etc.

Epistle, 1 Thess. 4:13-18

GRADUAL

Thine enemies roar in the midst of Thy congregations: they set up their ensigns for signs.

V. Remember Thy congregation which Thou hast purchased of old: the rod of Thine inheritance, which Thou hast redeemed. Hallelujah! Hallelujah!

V. There is a river the streams whereof shall make glad the city of God: God is in the midst of her, she shall not be moved. Hallelujah!

Gospel, Matt. 24:15-28

THE TWENTY-SIXTH SUNDAY AFTER TRINITY

INTROIT

Save me, O God, by Thy name: and judge me by Thy strength.

Hear my prayer, O God: give ear to the words of my mouth.

Ps. He shall reward evil to mine enemies: cut them off in Thy truth.

Glory be to the Father, etc.

COLLECT

O God, so rule and govern our hearts and minds by Thy Holy Spirit that, being ever mindful of the end of all things and the day of Thy just judgment, we may be stirred up to holiness of living here and dwell with Thee forever hereafter; through Jesus Christ, Thy Son, our Lord, who liveth, etc.

Epistle, 2 Peter 3:3-14   or   2 Thess. 1:3-10

GRADUAL

He shall call to the heavens from above: and to the earth that He may judge His people.

V. The heavens shall declare His righteousness: for God is Judge Himself. Hallelujah! Hallelujah!

V. The ransomed of the Lord shall come to Zion with everlasting joy upon their heads: they shall obtain joy and gladness, and sorrow and weeping shall fly away. Hallelujah!

Gospel, Matt. 25:31-46

THE TWENTY-SEVENTH SUNDAY AFTER TRINITY

(The Introit and Collect for the Twenty-third Sunday after Trinity shall be used on the last Sunday after Trinity in each year)

Epistle, 1 Thess. 5:1-11

GRADUAL

The King's daughter shall be brought unto the King: the virgins, her companions that follow her, shall be brought unto Thee.

V. With gladness and rejoicing shall they be brought: they shall enter into the King's palace. Hallelujah! Hallelujah!

V. I saw the holy city, New Jerusalem, coming down from God out of heaven: prepared as a bride adorned for her husband. Hallelujah!

Gospel, Matt. 25:1-13

THE FESTIVAL OF HARVEST

INTROIT

O Lord, Thou crownest the year with Thy goodness: and Thy paths drop fatness. Thou visitest the earth and waterest it: Thou blessest the springing thereof.

Ps. Praise waiteth for Thee, O God, in Zion: and unto Thee shall the vow be performed.

Glory be to the Father, etc.

COLLECT

Almighty God, most merciful Father, who openest Thine hand and satisfiest the desire of every living thing, we give Thee most humble and hearty thanks that Thou hast crowned the fields with Thy blessing and hast permitted us once more to gather in the fruits of the earth; and we beseech Thee to bless and protect the living seed of Thy Word sown in our hearts that in the plenteous fruits of righteousness we may always present to Thee an acceptable thankoffering; through Jesus Christ, Thy Son, our Lord, who liveth, etc.

Epistle, Deut. 26:1-11

GRADUAL

The eyes of all wait upon Thee: and Thou givest them their meat in due season.

V. Thou openest Thine hand: and satisfiest the desire of every living thing. Hallelujah! Hallelujah!

V. Bless the Lord, O my soul, and all that is within me, bless His holy name: Bless the Lord, O my soul, and forget not all His benefits. Hallelujah!

Gospel, Luke 12:13-21

THE FESTIVAL OF THE REFORMATION

INTROIT

The Lord of hosts is with us: the God of Jacob is our Refuge.

Therefore will not we fear though the earth be removed: and though the mountains be carried into the midst of the sea.

Ps. God is our Refuge and Strength: a very present Help in trouble.

Glory be to the Father, etc.

COLLECT

O Lord God, heavenly Father, pour out, we beseech Thee, Thy Holy Spirit upon Thy faithful people, keep them steadfast in Thy grace and truth, protect and comfort them in all temptations, defend them against all enemies of Thy Word, and bestow upon Christ's Church Militant Thy saving peace; through the same Jesus Christ, Thy Son, our Lord, who liveth, etc.

Epistle, Rev. 14:6, 7

GRADUAL

Great is the Lord and greatly to be praised: in the city of our God, in the mountain of His holiness.

V. Walk about Zion; tell the towers thereof; mark well her bulwarks; consider her palaces: that ye may tell it to the generation following. Hallelujah! Hallelujah!

V. For this God is our God forever and ever: He will be our Guide even unto death. Hallelujah!

Gospel, Matt. 11:12-15

A DAY OF HUMILIATION AND PRAYER

INTROIT

Hear, O heavens, and give ear, O earth, for the Lord hath spoken: I have nourished and brought up children, and they have rebelled against Me.

They have forsaken the Lord, they have provoked the Holy One of Israel unto anger: they are gone away backward.

Ps. If Thou, Lord, shouldest mark iniquities: O Lord, who shall stand?

(On this day the Gloria Patri is omitted)

COLLECT

Almighty and most merciful God, our heavenly Father, of whose compassion there is no end, who art long-suffering, gracious, and plenteous in goodness and truth, forgiving iniquity, transgression, and sin, we have sinned and done perversely, we have forsaken and grievously offended Thee; against Thee, Thee only, have we sinned and done evil in Thy sight. But we beseech Thee, O Lord, remember not against us former iniquities; let Thy tender mercies speedily come to us, for we are brought very low; help us, O God of our salvation, and purge away our sins for the glory of Thy holy name and for the sake of Thy dear Son, Jesus Christ, our Savior, who liveth, etc.

Epistle, Joel 2:12-19

GRADUAL

Seek ye the Lord while He may be found: call ye upon Him while He is near.

V. Let the wicked forsake his way: and the unrighteous man his thoughts.

V. And let him return unto the Lord, and He will have mercy upon him: and to our God, for He will abundantly pardon.

Gospel, Matt. 6:16-21

A DAY OF GENERAL OR SPECIAL THANKSGIVING

INTROIT

Let everything that hath breath praise the Lord: praise ye the Lord.

Praise Him for His mighty acts: praise Him according to His excellent greatness.

Ps. Praise ye the Lord; praise God in His sanctuary: praise Him in the firmament of His power.

Glory be to the Father, etc.

COLLECT

Almighty God, our heavenly Father, whose mercies are new unto us every morning and who, though we have in no wise deserved Thy goodness, dost abundantly provide for all our wants of body and soul, give us, we pray Thee, Thy Holy Spirit that we may heartily acknowledge Thy merciful goodness toward us, give thanks for all Thy benefits, and serve Thee in willing obedience; through Jesus Christ, Thy Son, our Lord, who liveth, etc.

Epistle, 1 Tim. 2:1-8

GRADUAL

The eyes of all wait upon Thee: and Thou givest them their meat in due season.

V. Thou openest Thine hand: and satisfiest the desire of every living thing. Hallelujah! Hallelujah!

V. Bless the Lord, O my soul, and all that is within me, bless His holy name: Bless the Lord, O my soul, and forget not all His benefits. Hallelujah!

Gospel, Luke 17:11-19

THE PRESENTATION OF OUR LORD AND THE PURIFICATION OF MARY

(The Introit is the same as for the Eighth Sunday after Trinity)

COLLECTS

Almighty and ever-living God, we humbly beseech Thy Majesty that, as Thine only-begotten Son was this day presented in the Temple in the substance of our flesh, so we may be presented unto Thee with pure and clean hearts; by the same Jesus Christ, Thy Son, our Lord, who liveth, etc.

Lord God, Heavenly Father, who hast given Thy Son to be our Savior, a Light to lighten the Gentiles, and the Glory of Thy people Israel, we beseech Thee, enlighten our hearts, that we may know Thy grace and fatherly will in Him toward us, and obtain everlasting life; through the same Thy Son, Jesus Christ, our Lord, who liveth, etc.

Epistle, Mal. 3:1-4

[85]

We have thought of Thy loving-kindness, O God, in the midst of Thy Temple. according to Thy name, O God, so is Thy praise unto the ends of the earth.

V. As we have heard, so have we seen in the city of our God: in the mountain of His holiness. Hallelujah! Hallelujah!

V. I will worship toward Thy holy Temple: and will praise Thy name. Hallelujah!

(If this day comes after Septuagesima, the Hallelujah and Verse of the Gradual are omitted, and the Nunc Dimittis is used as Tract.)

Tract. Lord, now lettest Thou Thy servant depart in peace, according to Thy word.

V. For mine eyes have seen: Thy Salvation.

V. Which Thou hast prepared: before the face of all people.

V. A Light to lighten the Gentiles: and the Glory of Thy people Israel.

Gospel, Luke 2:22-32

THE ANNUNCIATION

INTROIT

All the rich among the people shall entreat Thy favor: She shall be brought unto the King in raiment of needlework.

Her companions shall be brought unto Thee: with gladness and rejoicing.

Ps. My heart is inditing a good matter: I speak of the things which I have made touching the King.

Glory be to the Father, etc.   Or:

Drop down, ye heavens, from above: and let the skies pour down righteousness.

Let the earth open: and bring forth salvation.

Ps. My heart is inditing a good matter: I speak of the things which I have made touching the King.

Glory be to the Father, etc.

COLLECTS

We beseech Thee, O Lord, pour Thy grace into our hearts, that, as we have known the incarnation of Thy Son Jesus Christ by the message of an angel, so by His cross and Passion we may be brought unto the glory of His resurrection; through the same Jesus Christ, Thy Son, our Lord, who liveth, etc.

Almighty God, who didst will that agreeably to the angel's message Thy Son become incarnate of the Virgin Mary, mercifully grant that our sinful conception may be cleansed by His immaculate conception; through the same Jesus Christ, Thy Son, our Lord, who liveth, etc.

Epistle, Is. 7:10-16

GRADUAL

There shall come forth a Rod out of the stem of Jesse: and a Branch shall grow out of his roots.

V. Behold, a virgin shall conceive and bear a Son: and shall call His name Immanuel.

Tract. The angel of the Lord came in unto Mary and said, Hail, thou that art highly favored, the Lord is with thee: blessed art thou among women.

V. The Holy Ghost shall come upon thee: and the power of the Highest shall overshadow thee. Hallelujah! Hallelujah!

V. Therefore also that Holy Thing which shall be born of thee: shall be called the Son of God. Hallelujah!

Gospel, Luke 1:26-38

THE VISITATION

(The Introit is the same as for the Annunciation)

COLLECTS

Almighty God, who hast dealt wonderfully with Thy handmaiden, the Virgin Mary, and hast chosen her to be the mother of Thy Son and hast graciously made known that Thou regardest the poor and lowly and the despised, grant us grace in all humility and meekness to receive Thy Word with hearty faith and so to be made one with Jesus Christ, Thy Son, our Lord, who liveth, etc.

Grant, we beseech Thee, O Lord, unto Thy servants the gift of Thy heavenly grace, that, as the Son of the Virgin Mary hath made us partakers of salvation, we may daily grow in grace; through the same Jesus Christ, Thy Son, our Lord, who liveth, etc.

Almighty God, who didst exalt the lowly Virgin Mary by Thy grace, give us ever humble hearts that we may never fail of Thy grace; through the same Jesus Christ, Thy Son, our Lord, who liveth, etc.

Epistle, Is. 11:1-5

GRADUAL

There shall come forth a Rod out of the stem of Jesse: and a Branch shall grow out of his roots.

V. There shall be a Root of Jesse, which shall stand for an ensign to the people: to it shall the Gentiles seek. Hallelujah! Hallelujah!

V. Blessed art thou, O Mary, among women, and blessed is the fruit of thy womb: behold, there shall be a performance of those things which were told thee from the Lord. Hallelujah!

Gospel, Luke 1:39-56

EVANGELISTS', APOSTLES', AND MARTYRS' DAYS

INTROIT

I know whom I have believed: and am persuaded that He is able to keep that which I have committed unto Him against that Day.

There is laid up for me a crown of righteouness: which the Lord, the righteous Judge, shall give me.

Ps. O Lord, Thou hast searched me and known me: Thou knowest my downsitting and mine uprising.

Glory be to the Father, etc.

Apostles' Days

The Spirit of Truth will guide you into all truth: for He shall glorify Me.

Ye shall be My witnesses: because ye have been with Me from the beginning.

Blessed are ye when ye are persecuted for My sake: for the kingdom of heaven is yours.

Ps. The Lord is my Light and my Salvation: I will sing, yea, I will sing praises unto the Lord.

Glory be to the Father, etc.   Or:

They that be wise shall shine as the brightness of the firmament: and they that turn many to righteousness as the stars forever and ever.

Jesus said, Ye which have followed Me, in the regeneration: when the Son of Man shall sit in the throne of His glory, ye also shall sit upon twelve thrones.

Ps. I will bless the Lord at all times: His praise shall continually be in my mouth.

Glory be to the Father, etc.

Evangelists' Days

The Lord God said unto me: Write all the words that I have spoken unto thee into a book for a memorial.

Ps. His name shall endure forever: His name shall be continued as long as the sun.

Glory be to the Father, etc.

COLLECT

O almighty God, who hast built Thy Church upon the foundation of the Apostles and Prophets, Jesus Christ Himself being the Head Cornerstone, grant us to be joined together in unity of spirit by their doctrine that we may be made a holy temple acceptable unto Thee; through Jesus Christ, Thy Son, our Lord, who liveth, etc.

GRADUAL

Apostles' Days

Their sound is gone out into all the earth: and their words to the end of heaven.

V. The heavens declare the glory of God: and the firmament showeth forth His handiwork. Hallelujah! Hallelujah!

V. I have chosen you out of the world that ye should bring forth fruit: and your fruit should remain. Hallelujah!

Or:

Hallelujah! Hallelujah!

V. The Lord Jesus gave some, Apostles, and some Evangelists: for the edifying of the body of Christ. Hallelujah!

Or:

The mouth of the righteous speaketh of wisdom: and his tongue talketh of judgment.

V. The Law of his God is in his heart: none of his steps shall slide. Hallelujah! Hallelujah!

V. The righteous shall flourish like the palm tree: those that be planted in the house of the Lord shall flourish in the courts of our God. Hallelujah!

Evangelists' Days

Thou art fairer than the children of men: grace is poured into Thy lips.

V. My heart is inditing a good matter: I speak of the things which I have made touching the King. Hallelujah! Hallelujah!

V. The Lord Jesus gave some, Apostles, and some, Evangelists: for the edifying of the body of Christ. Hallelujah!

Or:

How beautiful are the good tidings of him that publisheth peace: that saith unto Zion, Thy God reigneth!

V. The Lord hath made bare His holy arm in the eyes of all nations: and all the ends of the earth shall see the salvation of our God. Hallelujah! Hallelujah!

V. The Word of the Lord endureth forever: this is the Word which by the Gospel is preached unto you. Hallelujah!

SAINT THOMAS THE APOSTLE'S DAY

*(The Introit and Gradual are the same as for Evangelists',
Apostles', and Martyrs' Days)*

COLLECT

Almighty and ever-living God, who through the Word of Thy Son didst mightily strengthen the faith of Thine Apostle Saint Thomas: by the same Word keep us ever steadfast in the faith unto our end; through Jesus Christ, Thy dear Son, our Lord, who liveth, etc.

Epistle, Eph. 1:3-6

Gospel, John 20:24-31

SAINT STEPHEN THE MARTYR'S DAY

INTROIT

Princes also did sit and speak against me: the wicked have waited for me to destroy me.

Help Thou me, Lord, my God: for I have kept Thy testimonies.

Ps. Blessed are the undefiled in the way: who walk in the Law of the Lord.

Glory be to the Father, etc.

Grant, O Lord, that in all our sufferings here upon earth for the testimony of Thy truth we may steadfastly look up to heaven and by faith behold the glory that shall be revealed; and, being filled with the Holy Ghost, may learn to love and bless our persecutors by the example of Thy first martyr, Saint Stephen, who prayed for his murderers to Thee, O blessed Jesus, who standest at the right hand of God to help all those that suffer for Thee, our only Mediator and Advocate; who livest, etc.

Epistle, Acts 6:8-15 and 7:54-60

Hallelujah! Hallelujah! **GRADUAL**

V. I see the heavens opened: and Jesus standing at the right hand of God. Hallelujah!

Gospel, Matt. 23:34-39

SAINT JOHN THE APOSTLE AND THE EVANGELIST'S DAY

INTROIT

In the midst of the congregation shall he open his mouth, and the Lord filled him with the spirit of wisdom and understanding: and clothed him with a robe of glory.

Ps. It is a good thing to give thanks unto the Lord: and to sing praise unto Thy name, O Thou Most High.

Glory be to the Father, etc. COLLECT

Merciful Lord, we beseech Thee to cast the bright beams of Thy light upon Thy Church that it, being instructed by the doctrines of Thy blessed Apostle and Evangelist Saint John, may attain to the light of everlasting life; through Jesus Christ, Thy Son, our Lord, who liveth, etc. *Epistle, 1 John 1:1-10*

GRADUAL

Then went this saying abroad among the brethren: that that disciple should not die.

V. But Jesus said, If I will that he tarry till I come, what is that to thee?: Follow thou Me. Hallelujah! Hallelujah!

V. This is the disciple which testifieth of these things: and we know that his testimony is true. Hallelujah! *Gospel, John 21:19-24*

THE HOLY INNOCENTS' DAY

INTROIT

Out of the mouth of babes and sucklings, O Lord: hast Thou ordained strength because of Thine enemies.

Ps. O Lord, our Lord: how excellent is Thy name in all the earth!

Glory be to the Father, etc. COLLECTS

O God, whose martyred innocents showed forth Thy praise not by speaking but by dying, mortify all vices within us that our lives may in deed confess Thy faith which our tongue uttereth; through Jesus Christ, Thy Son, our Lord, who liveth, etc.

O almighty God, who out of the mouths of babes and sucklings hast ordained strength and madest infants to glorify Thee by their deaths, mortify and kill all vices in us and so strengthen us by Thy grace that by the innocency of our lives and the constancy of our faith, even unto death, we may glorify Thy holy name; through Jesus Christ, Thy Son, our Lord, who liveth, etc.

Epistle, Rev. 14:1-5

GRADUAL

Our soul is escaped as a bird out of the snare of the fowlers.

V. The snare is broken, and we are escaped: our help is in the name of the Lord, who made heaven and earth. Hallelujah! Hallelujah!

V. Praise, O ye servants of the Lord: praise the name of the Lord. Hallelujah!

Gospel, Matt. 2:13-18

THE CONVERSION OF SAINT PAUL

(The Introit is the same as for Evangelists', Apostles', and Martyrs' Days)

COLLECT

O God, who through the preaching of the blessed Apostle Saint Paul hast caused the light of Thy Gospel to shine to the Gentile world, give us grace ever to joy in the saving light of Thy Gospel and to spread it to the uttermost parts of the earth; through the same Jesus Christ, Thy Son, our Lord, who liveth, etc.

Epistle, Acts 9:1-22

GRADUAL

He that wrought effectually in Peter to the apostleship of the circumcision, the same was mighty in me toward the Gentiles: and they glorified God in me.

V. By the grace of God I am what I am: and His grace which was bestowed upon me was not in vain. Hallelujah! Hallelujah!

V. The Lord said unto Paul, Thou art a chosen vessel unto Me: to bear My name before the Gentiles. Hallelujah!

Gospel, Matt. 19:27-30

SAINT MATTHIAS THE APOSTLE'S DAY

*(The Introit and Gradual are the same as for Evangelists',
Apostles', and Martyrs' Days)*

COLLECT

Almighty God, who into the place of the traitor Judas didst choose Thy faithful servant Matthias, grant that Thy Church, ever being preserved from false apostles, may continually abide in the doctrine of Thy true Apostles; through Jesus Christ, Thy Son, our Lord, who liveth, etc.

Epistle, Acts 1:15-26

Gospel, Matt. 11:25-30

SAINT MARK THE EVANGELIST'S DAY

*(The Introit and Gradual are the same as for Evangelists',
Apostles', and Martyrs' Days)*

COLLECT

O almighty God, who hast enriched Thy Church with the precious Gospel written by Thine Evangelist Saint Mark, give us grace that we may firmly believe Thy glad tidings of salvation and daily walk as it becometh the Gospel of Christ; through the same Jesus Christ, Thy Son, our Lord, who liveth, etc.

Epistle, Eph. 4:7-16

Gospel, Luke 10:1-9

SAINT PHILIP AND SAINT JAMES THE APOSTLES' DAY

*(The Introit and Gradual are the same as for Evangelists',
Apostles', and Martyrs' Days)*

COLLECT

Almighty God, whom to know is everlasting life, grant unto us that, as Thy Son gave knowledge of life eternal to Thine Apostles Philip and James by revealing Himself to them as the only Way to Thee, we may by a true and living faith ever know Him as our only Savior; through the same, Thy dear Son, Jesus Christ, our Lord, who liveth, etc.

Epistle, Eph. 2:19-22

Gospel, John 14:1-14

THE NATIVITY OF SAINT JOHN THE BAPTIST

INTROIT

The voice of him that crieth in the wilderness: Prepare ye the way of the Lord, make straight in the desert a highway for our God.

And the glory of the Lord: shall be revealed.

Ps. It is a good thing to give thanks unto the Lord: and to sing praises unto Thy name, O Most High.

Glory be to the Father, etc.

COLLECTS

O Lord God, heavenly Father, who through Thy servant John the Baptist didst bear witness that Jesus Christ is the Lamb of God, which taketh away the sin of the world, and that all who believe in Him shall inherit eternal life, we humbly pray Thee to enlighten us by Thy Holy Spirit that we may at all times find comfort and joy in this witness, continue steadfast in the true faith, and at last with all believers attain unto eternal life; through the same Jesus Christ, Thy Son, our Lord, who liveth, etc.

Almighty God, who through John the Baptist, the forerunner of Christ, didst proclaim salvation, grant that we may know this Thy salvation and serve Thee in holiness and righteousness all the days of our life; through Jesus Christ, Thy Son, our Lord who liveth, etc.

God, who didst honor this day through the birth of Saint John the Baptist, grant unto Thy people spiritual gladness and direct the minds of all Thy faithful into the way of everlasting life; through Jesus Christ, Thy Son, our Lord, who liveth, etc.

Epistle, Is. 40:1-5

GRADUAL

Before I formed thee, I knew thee: and before thou wast born, I sanctified thee.

V. The Lord put forth His hand and touched my mouth: and the Lord said unto me, Behold, I have put My words into thy mouth. Hallelujah! Hallelujah!

V. The voice of one crying: Prepare ye the way of the Lord. Hallelujah!

Gospel, Luke 1:57-80

SAINT PETER AND SAINT PAUL THE APOSTLES' DAY

(The Introit is the same as for Evangelists', Apostles', and Martyrs' Days)

COLLECT

O God, who didst give Thine Apostles Peter and Paul grace to lay down their lives for the sake of Thy dear Son, endow us, we beseech Thee, with like constancy that we may at all times be ready to lay down our lives for Him who laid down His life for us; through the same Jesus Christ, Thy Son, our Lord, who liveth, etc.

Epistle, Acts 12:1-11

GRADUAL

I am now ready to be offered: and the time of my departure is at hand.

V. I have fought a good fight, I have finished my course: I have kept the faith. Hallelujah! Hallelujah!

V. Thou comest to him with blessing and goodness: Thou settest a crown of pure gold on his head. Hallelujah!

Gospel, Matt. 16:13-20

SAINT MARY MAGDALENE'S DAY

INTROIT

The wicked have waited to destroy me: but I gave heed unto Thy testimonies.

I have seen an end of all perfection: but Thy commandment is exceeding broad.

Ps. Blessed are the undefiled in the way: who walk in the Law of the Lord.

Glory be to the Father, etc.

Almighty God, who hast given Thine only Son to be unto us both a Sacrifice for sin and also an Example of godly life, give us grace that we may always most thankfully receive this His inestimable benefit and also daily endeavor ourselves to follow the blessed steps of His most holy life; through the same Jesus Christ, Thy Son, our Lord, who liveth, etc. *Epistle, Prov. 31:10-31*

GRADUAL

Hearken, O daughter, incline thine ear: forget also thine own people and thy father's house.

V. So shall the King greatly desire thy beauty: for He is thy Lord, and worship thou Him. Hallelujah! Hallelujah!

V. Who can find a virtuous woman?: For her price is far above rubies. Hallelujah!

Gospel, Luke 7:36-50

SAINT JAMES THE ELDER THE APOSTLE'S DAY

(The Introit and Gradual are the same as for Evangelists',
Apostles', and Martyrs' Days)

COLLECT

Grant, O Lord, that, as Thine Apostle Saint James readily obeyed the calling of Thy Son Jesus Christ, we may by Thy grace be enabled to forsake all wordly and carnal affections and to follow Him alone; through the same Jesus Christ, Thy Son, our Lord, who liveth, etc. *Epistle, Rom. 8:28-39*

Gospel, Matt. 20:20-28

SAINT BARTHOLOMEW THE APOSTLE'S DAY

(The Introit and Gradual are the same as for Evangelists',
Apostles', and Martyrs' Days)

COLLECT

Almighty God, who through Thy Son Jesus Christ didst choose Saint Bartholomew to be an Apostle to preach the blessed Gospel, give unto Thy Church evermore faithful teachers to proclaim the glory of Thy name; through Jesus Christ, Thy Son, our Lord, who liveth, etc. *Epistle, 2 Cor. 4:7-10*

Gospel, Luke 22:24-30

SAINT MATTHEW THE APOSTLE AND THE EVANGELIST'S DAY

(The Introit and Gradual are the same as for Evangelists',
Apostles', and Martyrs' Days)

COLLECT

O almighty God, who by Thy blessed Son didst call Saint Matthew from the receipt of custom to be an Apostle and Evangelist, grant us grace to forsake all covetous desires and inordinate love of riches and to follow the same Jesus Christ, Thy Son, our Lord, who liveth, etc. *Epistle, Eph. 4:7-14*

Gospel, Matt. 9:9-13

SAINT MICHAEL'S AND ALL ANGELS' DAY

INTROIT

Bless the Lord, ye His angels, that excel in strength: that do His commandments, hearkening unto the voice of His Word.

Bless ye the Lord, all ye His hosts: ye ministers of His that do His pleasure.

Ps. Bless the Lord, O my soul: and all that is within me, bless His holy name.

Glory be to the Father, etc.

O everlasting God, who hast ordained and constituted the services of angels and men in a wonderful order, mercifully grant that, as Thy holy angels always do Thee service in heaven, so by Thine appointment they may help and defend us on earth; through Jesus Christ, Thy Son, our Lord, who liveth, etc.

Epistle, Rev. 12:7-12

GRADUAL

God hath given His angels charge over thee: to keep thee in all thy ways.

V. Bless the Lord, O my soul: and all that is within me, bless His holy name. Hallelujah! Hallelujah!

V. And one cried unto another and said, Holy, holy, holy, is the Lord of hosts: the whole earth is full of His glory. Hallelujah!

Gospel, Matt. 18:1-11

SAINT LUKE THE EVANGELIST'S DAY

(The Introit and Gradual are the same as for Evangelists',
Apostles', and Martyrs' Days)

COLLECT

Almighty God, who calledst Saint Luke the physician to be an Evangelist and physician of the soul, heal, we beseech Thee, all the diseases of our souls by the wholesome medicine of Thy Word; through Jesus Christ, Thy Son, our Lord, who liveth, etc.

Epistle, 2 Tim. 4:5-15

Gospel, Luke 10:1-9

SAINT SIMON AND SAINT JUDE THE APOSTLES' DAY

(The Introit, Collect, and Gradual are the same as for Evangelists',
Apostles', and Martyrs' Days)

Epistle, 1 Peter 1:3-9

Gospel, John 15:17-21

ALL SAINTS' DAY

INTROIT

A great multitude which no man could number stood before the throne and before the Lamb: clothed with white robes and with palms in their hands;

And cried with a loud voice, saying: Salvation to our God which sitteth upon the throne, and unto the Lamb.

Ps. Rejoice in the Lord, O ye righteous: for praise is comely for the upright.

Glory be to the Father, etc.

COLLECT

O almighty God, who hast knit together Thine elect in one communion and fellowship in the mystical body of Thy Son Jesus Christ, our Lord, grant us grace so to follow Thy blessed saints in all virtuous and godly living that we may come to those unspeakable joys which Thou hast prepared for those who unfeignedly love Thee; through Jesus Christ, Thy Son, our Lord, who liveth, etc.

Epistle, Rev. 7:2-17

GRADUAL

Oh, fear the Lord, ye His saints: for there is no want to them that fear Him.

V. They that seek the Lord: shall not want any good thing. Hallelujah! Hallelujah!

V. Come unto Me, all ye that labor and are heavy laden: and I will give you rest. Hallelujah!

Gospel, Matt. 5:1-12

SAINT ANDREW THE APOSTLE'S DAY

(The Introit and Gradual are the same as for Evangelists',
Apostles', and Martyrs' Days)

COLLECT

Almighty God, by whose grace Thine Apostle Saint Andrew obeyed the call of Thy Son Jesus Christ, grant unto us also grace to follow Him in heart and life; through the same Jesus Christ, Thy Son, our Lord, who liveth, etc.

Epistle, Rom. 10:8-18

Gospel, Matt. 4:18-22

DEDICATION OF A CHURCH

INTROIT

Surely the Lord is in this place: This is none other but the house of God, and this is the gate of heaven. Hallelujah!

Ps. The Lord reigneth, He is clothed with majesty: the Lord is clothed with strength, wherewith He hath girded Himself.

Glory be to the Father, etc.

COLLECT

Lord God, heavenly Father, the unfailing Giver of good gifts, we thank Thee that Thou this day didst enter into this house with Thy Word; and we heartily beseech Thee continually to dwell among us with Thy Word and Thy Sacraments, so that by Thy grace we poor sinners may be converted unto Thee and saved eternally; through Jesus Christ, Thy Son, our Lord, who liveth, etc.

Epistle, Rev. 21:1-5

GRADUAL

In all places where I record My name I will come unto thee: and bless thee, saith your God.

V. How amiable are Thy tabernacles: O Lord of hosts! Hallelujah! Hallelujah!

V. Yea, the sparrow hath found an house and the swallow a nest for herself, where she may lay her young: even Thine altars, O Lord of hosts, my King and my God. Hallelujah!

Gospel, Luke 19:1-10

MISSION FESTIVAL

INTROIT

All the earth shall worship Thee: and shall sing unto Thee, O God.

They shall sing to Thy name: O Thou Most High.

Ps. Make a joyful noise unto God, all ye lands: sing forth the honor of His name, make His praise glorious.

Glory be to the Father, etc.

COLLECT

O Lord God Almighty, mercifully grant that we, who know Thee now by faith may with our whole heart believe in Him, our only Savior, serve Him, and steadfastly confess and glorify Him before all men, making known Thy saving health among the nations, that He may see of the travail of His soul and be satisfied, to whom, with Thee and the Holy Ghost, be honor and glory, world without end.

Epistle, Rom. 10:8-18; or Is. 12:2-4; 42:1-12; 49:1-6

GRADUAL

The Graduals for the First, Second, or Third Sunday after the Epiphany may be used on this day.

Gospel, Matt. 9:35-38; Mark 4:26-32

Invitatories, Antiphons, Responsories, and Versicles for the Church Year

The *Invitatory* varies with the Season and is always used with *Psalm 95* at Matins. It is divided into two parts, separated by a colon. The first part, or the whole, of the *Invitatory* may be sung or said by the Minister or sung by a single voice or by the choir before the Psalm; and after the Psalm and *Gloria Patri* the whole *Invitatory* shall be sung.

An *Antiphon* is used at Matins and Vespers with the Psalms, the *Magnificat*, the *Nunc Dimittis*, and the *Benedictus*. It is used in the same manner as the *Invitatory*.

The *Responsory* varies with the Season and may be sung after the last *Lesson* at Vespers and Matins. At the end of the *Responsory* is sung *Glory be to the Father and to the Son and to the Holy Ghost* (but not "As it was in the beginning," etc.), followed by the repetition of the last sentence of the *Responsory*.

A *Versicle* may be used at Vespers after the *Hymn* and at Vespers and Matins before the closing *Collect*. A *Versicle* is used before the *Litany Collects*. The *first part* of the *Versicle* is said by the Minister and the second part sung or said by the people.

THE ADVENT SEASON

INVITATORY

Behold, the King cometh: Oh, come, let us worship Him.

ANTIPHONS

1. Behold, the name of the Lord cometh from far: and let the whole earth be filled with His glory.
2. Come, O Lord, and make no tarrying: loosen the bonds of Thy people Israel.
3. Rejoice greatly, O Jerusalem: behold, thy King cometh.
4. Behold, the Lord shall come and all His saints with Him: and in that day the light shall be great. Hallelujah!

RESPONSORY

Behold, the days come, saith the Lord, that I will raise unto David a righteous Branch, and a King shall reign and prosper and shall execute judgment and justice in the earth. And this is His name whereby He shall be called, The Lord Our Righteousness.

Verse. In His days shall Judah be saved, and Israel shall dwell safely.

And this is His name whereby He shall be called, The Lord Our Righteousness.

Glory be to the Father and to the Son and to the Holy Ghost.

And this is His name whereby He shall be called, The Lord Our Righteousness.

VERSICLES

1. ℣: Out of Zion, the perfection of beauty, God hath shined:
   ℟: **Our God shall come. Hallelujah!**
2. ℣: Prepare ye the way of the Lord. Hallelujah!
   ℟: **Make His paths straight. Hallelujah!**
3. ℣: Drop down, ye heavens, from above, and let the skies pour down righteousness:
   ℟: **Let the earth open and bring forth salvation.**

CHRISTMASTIDE

INVITATORY

Unto us the Christ is born: Oh, come, let us worship Him.

ANTIPHONS

1. The Lord hath said unto Me: Thou art My Son; this day have I begotten Thee.
2. The Lord hath sent redemption unto His people: He hath commanded His covenant forever.
3. Of the fruit of thy body: will I set upon thy throne.
4. Christ the Lord, our Savior, everlasting God and Mary's Son: we praise Thee evermore

[95]

The Word was made flesh and dwelt among us. And we beheld His glory, the glory as of the Only-begotten of the Father, full of grace and truth.

Verse. In the beginning was the Word, and the Word was with God, and the Word was God.

Full of grace and truth.

Glory be to the Father and to the Son and to the Holy Ghost.

Full of grace and truth.

VERSICLES

1. ℣: At even ye shall know that the Lord will come:
   ℟: **And in the morning, then shall ye see the glory of the Lord.**

2. ℣: As the bridegroom from his chamber:
   ℟: **Cometh forth the Lord to run His race.**

3. ℣: The Word was made flesh. Hallelujah!
   ℟: **And dwelt among us. Hallelujah!**

4. ℣: Blessed is He that cometh in the name of the Lord:
   ℟: **God is the Lord, which hath showed us light.**

5. ℣: Unto us a Child is born. Hallelujah!
   ℟: **Unto us a Son is given. Hallelujah!**

6. ℣: Unto you is born this day a Savior. Hallelujah!
   ℟: **Which is Christ the Lord. Hallelujah!**

THE EPIPHANY SEASON

INVITATORY

Christ hath appeared unto us: Oh, come, let us worship Him.

ANTIPHONS

1. Give unto the Lord glory and strength: worship the Lord in the beauty of holiness.

2. The Lord hath made known His Word. Hallelujah!: the Word of His salvation. Hallelujah! Hallelujah!

3. A Light to lighten the Gentiles: and the Glory of Thy people Israel.

4. We have seen His star in the East: and are come to worship Him.

RESPONSORY

Arise, shine, for thy Light is come, and the Glory of the Lord is risen upon thee.

Verse. And the Gentiles shall come to thy Light and kings to the brightness of thy rising.

And the Glory of the Lord is risen upon thee.

Glory be to the Father and to the Son and to the Holy Ghost.

And the Glory of the Lord is risen upon thee.

VERSICLES

1. ℣: The kings of Tarshish and of the isles shall bring presents. Hallelujah!
   ℟: **The kings of Sheba and Seba shall offer gifts. Hallelujah!**

2. ℣: All they from Sheba shall come. Hallelujah!
   ℟: **They shall bring gold and incense. Hallelujah!**

3. ℣: Oh, praise the Lord, all ye nations. Hallelujah!
   ℟: **Praise Him, all ye people. Hallelujah!**

THE PASSION SEASON

ANTIPHONS

1. Man shall not live by bread alone: but by every word that proceedeth out of the mouth of God.

2. Behold, now is the accepted time: behold, now is the day of salvation.

3. The kings of the earth set themselves, and the rulers take counsel together: against the Lord and against His Anointed.

4. He was oppressed, and He was afflicted, yet He opened not His mouth: and the Lord hath laid on Him the iniquity of us all.

RESPONSORY

He was brought as a lamb to the slaughter, He was oppressed, and He was afflicted, yet He opened not His mouth: He was delivered up to death that He might quicken His people.

Verse. In Salem also is His tabernacle and His dwelling place in Zion.

He was delivered up to death that He might quicken His people.

VERSICLES

1. ℣: Save me from the lion's mouth, O Lord:
   ℟: **And deliver me from the horns of the unicorns.**

2. ℣: Christ became obedient unto death:
   ℟: **Even the death of the cross.**

3. ℣: Christ was wounded for our transgressions:
   ℟: **He was bruised for our iniquities.**

EASTERTIDE

INVITATORY

The Lord is risen indeed: Hallelujah!

ANTIPHONS

1. Hallelujah!: Hallelujah! Hallelujah!

2. I laid me down and slept; I awaked: for the Lord sustained me. Hallelujah! Hallelujah!

3. Hallelujah! The Lord is risen. Hallelujah!: As He said unto you. Hallelujah! Hallelujah!

4. Hallelujah! Abide with us, for it is toward evening: and the day is far spent. Hallelujah! Hallelujah!

RESPONSORY

Christ, being raised from the dead, dieth no more; death hath no more dominion over Him.

In that He liveth, He liveth unto God. Hallelujah! Hallelujah!

Verse. Christ was delivered for our offenses and raised again for our justification.

In that He liveth, He liveth unto God. Hallelujah!

Glory be to the Father and to the Son and to the Holy Ghost.

In that He liveth, He liveth unto God. Hallelujah!

VERSICLES

1. ℣: The Lord is risen from the grave. Hallelujah!
   ℟: **Who hung for us upon the tree. Hallelujah!**

2. ℣: Then were the disciples glad. Hallelujah!
   ℟: **When they saw the Lord. Hallelujah!**

3. ℣: This is the day which the Lord hath made. Hallelujah!
   ℟: **We will rejoice and be glad in it. Hallelujah!**

4. ℣: The Lord is risen indeed. Hallelujah!
   ℟: **And hath appeared unto Simon. Hallelujah!**

ASCENSION DAY

INVITATORY

Hallelujah! The King ascendeth into heaven: Oh, come, let us worship Him. Hallelujah!

ANTIPHONS

1. If I go not away, the Comforter will not come unto you: but if I depart, I will send Him unto you. Hallelujah!

2. Hallelujah! Christ hath ascended up on high. Hallelujah!: And hath led captivity captive. Hallelujah! Hallelujah!

3. I ascend unto My Father and your Father: and to My God and your God. Hallelujah!

RESPONSORY

Go ye into all the world and preach the Gospel. Hallelujah!
He that believeth and is baptized shall be saved. Hallelujah! Hallelujah!
Verse. In the name of the Father and of the Son and of the Holy Ghost.
He that believeth and is baptized shall be saved.
Glory be to the Father and to the Son and to the Holy Ghost.
He that believeth and is baptized shall be saved.

VERSICLES

1. ℣: I will not leave you comfortless. Hallelujah!
   ℟: **I go away and come again unto you. Hallelujah!**

2. ℣: God is gone up with a shout. Hallelujah!
   ℟: **The Lord with the sound of a trumpet. Hallelujah!**

WHITSUNTIDE

INVITATORY

Hallelujah! The Spirit of the Lord filleth the world: Oh, come, let us worship Him. Hallelujah!

ANTIPHONS

1. Come, Holy Ghost, and fill the hearts of Thy faithful people, and kindle in them the fire of Thy love: Thou, who through divers tongues gatherest together the nations in the unity of the faith. Hallelujah! Hallelujah!

2. Thou sendest forth Thy Spirit, they are created: and Thou renewest the face of the earth. Hallelujah! Hallelujah!

3. I will not leave you comfortless. Hallelujah!: I will come to you, and your heart shall rejoice. Hallelujah!

RESPONSORY

And there appeared unto the Apostles cloven tongues like as of fire. Hallelujah!
And the Holy Ghost sat upon each of them. Hallelujah! Hallelujah!
Verse. And they began to speak with other tongues the wonderful works of God.
And the Holy Ghost sat upon each of them.
Glory be to the Father and to the Son and to the Holy Ghost.
And the Holy Ghost sat upon each of them.

VERSICLES

1. ℣: The Comforter, which is the Holy Ghost. Hallelujah!
   ℟: **He shall teach you all things. Hallelujah!**

2. ℣: And they were all filled with the Holy Ghost. Hallelujah!
   ℟: **And they began to speak. Hallelujah!**

3. ℣: Create in me a clean heart, O God! Hallelujah!
   ℟: **And renew a right spirit within me. Hallelujah!**

THE TRINITY SEASON

INVITATORY

The true God, One in Three and Three in One: Oh, come, let us worship Him.

ANTIPHONS

1. Unto Thee do we call, Thee do we praise, Thee do we worship: O blessed Trinity.
2. Glory be to Thee, coequal Trinity: one God before all worlds began, and now and forevermore.
3. Holy, holy, holy, Lord God Almighty: which was and is and is to come.

RESPONSORY

We bless the Father and the Son and the Holy Ghost. Praise Him and magnify Him forever.

Verse. Blessed art Thou, O Lord, in the firmament of heaven and above all to be praised and glorified forever.
Praise Him and magnify Him forever.
Glory be to the Father and to the Son and to the Holy Ghost.
Praise Him and magnify Him forever.

VERSICLE

℣: We bless the Father and the Son and the Holy Ghost.
℟: **Praise Him and magnify Him forever.**

THE FESTIVAL OF THE REFORMATION

ANTIPHON

I will speak of Thy testimonies also before kings: and will not be ashamed.

VERSICLES

1. ℣: Thy Word is a lamp unto my feet. Hallelujah!
   ℟: **And a light unto my path. Hallelujah!**
2. ℣: The Lord, our God, be with us. Hallelujah!
   ℟: **As He was with our fathers. Hallelujah!**
3. ℣: Do good in Thy good pleasure unto Zion. Hallelujah!
   ℟: **Build Thou the walls of Jerusalem. Hallelujah!**
4. ℣: Stand fast therefore in the liberty. Hallelujah!
   ℟: **Wherewith Christ hath made you free. Hallelujah!**

A DAY OF HUMILIATION AND PRAYER

ANTIPHON

Be merciful unto me, O Lord, for I cry unto Thee daily: Bow down Thine ear, O Lord, hear me, for I am poor and needy.

VERSICLES

1. ℣: Have mercy upon me, O God, according to Thy loving-kindness:
   ℟: **According unto the multitude of Thy tender mercies blot out my transgressions.**
2. ℣: Enter not into judgment with Thy servant, O Lord:
   ℟: **For in Thy sight shall no man living be justified.**
3. ℣: Lord, deal not with us after our sins:
   ℟: **Nor reward us according to our iniquities.**
4. ℣: Create in us a clean heart, O God:
   ℟: **And take not Thy Holy Spirit from us.**
5. ℣: We have sinned with our fathers:
   ℟: **We have committed iniquity, we have done wickedly.**

DEDICATION OF A CHURCH

ANTIPHON

The Lord is in His holy temple: the Lord's throne is in heaven.

VERSICLE

℣: Thy testimonies are very sure. Hallelujah!

℞: **Holiness becometh Thine house, O Lord, forever. Hallelujah!**

THE COMMEMORATION OF THE DEAD

ANTIPHONS

1. God shall wipe away all tears from their eyes: and there shall be no more death, neither sorrow nor crying, neither shall there be any more pain; for the former things are passed away.

2. Oh, how glorious is that kingdom: wherein all the saints do rejoice with Christ! They are clothed with white robes and follow the Lamb whithersoever He goeth.

VERSICLES

1. ℣: We have here no continuing city. Hallelujah!

   ℞: **But we seek one to come. Hallelujah!**

2. ℣: Blessed are the dead which die in the Lord. Hallelujah!

   ℞: **They rest from their labors, and their works do follow them. Hallelujah!**

FOR OTHER TIMES

ANTIPHONS

1. Out of the depths: have I cried unto Thee, O Lord.
2. Out of Zion, the perfection of beauty: God hath shined.
3. Commit thy way unto the Lord: trust also in Him.
4. Preserve my life: from the fear of the enemy.
5. It is good to sing praises: unto our God.
6. Forsake not the works: of Thine own hands.
7. The Lord: is the Strength of my life.
8. The Lord said unto my Lord: Sit Thou at My right hand.
9. Blessed be the Lord God: the God of Israel.
10. Blessed be the Lord out of Zion: which dwelleth at Jerusalem.
11. Blessed: be His glorious name forever.
12. I was glad when they said unto me: Let us go into the house of the Lord.
13. In the day of my trouble I will call upon Thee: for Thou wilt answer me.
14. I will praise Thy name: forever and ever.
15. Thou wilt show me: the path of life.
16. We praise the Lord: now, henceforth, and forever.
17. Blessed: is the man that feareth the Lord.

RESPONSORY

Forever, O Lord, Thy Word is settled in heaven.

Thy Word is a lamp unto my feet and a light unto my path.

Lord, I have loved the habitation of Thy house and the place where Thine honor dwelleth.

Verse. Blessed are they that hear the Word of God and keep it.

Lord, I have loved the habitation of Thy house and the place where Thine honor dwelleth.

Glory be to the Father and to the Son and to the Holy Ghost.

Lord, I have loved the habitation of Thy house and the place where Thine honor dwelleth.

1. ℣: The eyes of all wait upon Thee,
   ℟: **And Thou givest them their meat in due season.**

2. ℣: The Lord is merciful and gracious. Hallelujah!
   ℟: **Slow to anger and plenteous in mercy. Hallelujah!**

3. ℣: Pray ye therefore the Lord of the harvest
   ℟: **That He would send forth laborers into His harvest.**

4. ℣: Ask, and ye shall receive,
   ℟: **That your joy may be full.**

5. ℣: Oh, give thanks unto the Lord, for He is good. Hallelujah!
   ℟: **For His mercy endureth forever. Hallelujah!**

6. ℣: It is a good thing to give thanks unto the Lord
   ℟: **And to sing praises unto Thy name, O Most High.**

7. ℣: Lord, Thou hast heard the desire of the humble.
   ℟: **Thou wilt preserve their heart; Thou wilt cause Thine ear to hear.**

8. ℣: The Lord will give strength unto His people. Hallelujah!
   ℟: **The Lord will bless His people with peace. Hallelujah!**

9. ℣: They that be wise shall shine as the brightness of the firmament. Hallelujah!
   ℟: **And they that turn many to righteousness, as the stars forever and ever. Hallelujah!**

10. ℣: By Me kings reign and princes decree justice.
    ℟: **By Me princes rule and nobles, even all the judges of the earth.**

11. ℣: He shall give His angels charge over thee
    ℟: **To keep thee in all thy ways.**

12. ℣: The Lord God is a Sun and Shield; the Lord will give grace and glory. Hallelujah!
    ℟: **No good thing will He withhold from them that walk uprightly. Hallelujah!**

13. ℣: Sanctify us through Thy truth. Hallelujah!
    ℟: **Thy Word is truth. Hallelujah!**

14. ℣: Lord, teach me to do Thy will. Hallelujah!
    ℟: **Let Thy good Spirit lead me in the right way. Hallelujah!**

15. ℣: Show me Thy ways, O Lord. Hallelujah!
    ℟: **Teach me Thy paths. Hallelujah!**

16. ℣: Save Thy people and bless Thine inheritance;
    ℟: **Feed them also and lift them up forever.**

17. ℣: Help us, O God of our salvation, for the glory of Thy name.
    ℟: **Deliver us and purge away our sins for Thy name's sake.**

18. ℣: I have trusted in Thy mercy.
    ℟: **My heart shall rejoice in Thy salvation.**

19. ℣: Suffer the little children to come unto Me, and forbid them not;
    ℟: **For of such is the kingdom of heaven.**

20. ℣: Bless the Lord, O my soul; and all that is within me, bless His holy name. Hallelujah!
    ℟: **Bless the Lord, O my soul, and forget not all His benefits. Hallelujah!**

21. ℣: Call upon Me in the day of trouble.
    ℟: **I will deliver thee, and thou shalt glorify Me.**

22. ℣: Make me to understand the way of Thy precepts.
    ℟: **Strengthen Thou me according unto Thy Word.**

Prayers

Collects

GENERAL

1

Grant us, we beseech Thee, Almighty God, a steadfast faith in Jesus Christ, a cheerful hope in Thy mercy, and a sincere love to Thee and to all our fellow men; through Jesus Christ, Thy Son, our Lord.

2

O Lord God, heavenly Father, we give Thee thanks that of Thy great goodness and mercy Thou didst suffer Thine only-begotten Son to become incarnate and to redeem us from sin and everlasting death; and we beseech Thee, enlighten our hearts by Thy Holy Spirit that we may evermore yield Thee unfeigned thanks for this Thy grace and may comfort ourselves with the same in all time of tribulation and temptation; through the same Jesus Christ, Thy Son, our Lord.

3

Almighty God, who hast given us commandment to pray for the gift of the Holy Ghost, most heartily we beseech Thee through Jesus Christ, our Advocate, to grant us Thy Holy Spirit that He may quicken our hearts by Thy saving Word and lead us into all truth, that He may guide, instruct, enlighten, govern, comfort, and sanctify us unto everlasting life; through the same Jesus Christ, Thy Son, our Lord.

4

Send, we beseech Thee, Almighty God, Thy Holy Spirit into our hearts that He may rule and direct us according to Thy will, comfort us in all our temptations and afflictions, defend us from all error, and lead us into all truth, that we, being steadfast in the faith, may increase in love and in all good works and in the end obtain everlasting life; through Jesus Christ, Thy Son, our Lord.

5

Almighty God, our heavenly Father, who of Thy tender love toward us sinners hast given us Thy Son that, believing on Him, we might have everlasting life, grant us, we beseech Thee, Thy Holy Spirit that we may continue steadfast in this faith to the end and may come to everlasting life; through Jesus Christ, Thy Son, our Lord.

6

Almighty and everlasting God, who by Thy Son hast promised us forgiveness of sins and everlasting life, we beseech Thee so to rule and govern our hearts by Thy Holy Spirit that in our daily need, and especially in all time of temptation, we may seek help from Him and by a true and lively faith in Thy Word obtain the same; through Jesus Christ, Thy Son, our Lord.

7

O Lord God, heavenly Father, we beseech Thee, let Thy Holy Spirit dwell in us that He may enlighten and lead us into all truth and evermore defend us from all adversities; through Jesus Christ, Thy Son, our Lord.

8

O Lord God, heavenly Father, who hast given Thine only Son to die for our sins and to rise again for our justification, quicken us, we beseech Thee, by Thy Holy Spirit, unto newness of life that through the power of His resurrection we may dwell with Christ forever; through the same Jesus Christ, Thy Son, our Lord.

9

Almighty and ever-living God, who makest us both to will and to do those things which are good and acceptable unto Thy divine Majesty, let Thy fatherly hand, we beseech Thee, ever be over us; let Thy Holy Spirit ever be with us; and so lead us in the knowledge and obedience of Thy Word that in the end we may obtain everlasting life; through Jesus Christ, Thy Son, our Lord.

FOR THE CHURCH

10

Grant, we beseech Thee, Almighty God, unto Thy Church Thy Holy Spirit and the wisdom which cometh down from above that Thy Word, as becometh it, may not be bound, but have free course and be preached to the joy and edifying of Christ's holy people, that in steadfast faith we may serve Thee and in the confession of Thy name abide unto the end; through Jesus Christ, Thy Son, our Lord.

11

Merciful God, we beseech Thee to cast the bright beams of Thy light upon Thy Church that, being instructed by the doctrine of the blessed Apostles, it may so walk in the light of Thy truth that it may at length attain to the light of everlasting life; through Jesus Christ, Thy Son, our Lord.

12

O God, our Protector, behold, and look upon, the face of Thine Anointed, who hath given Himself for the redemption of all, and grant that from the rising of the sun to the going down thereof Thy name may be great among the Gentiles and that in every place sacrifice and a pure offering may be made unto Thy name; through Jesus Christ, Thy Son, our Lord.

13

O Lord, favorably receive the prayers of Thy Church, that, being delivered from all adversity and error, it may serve Thee in safety and freedom; and grant us Thy peace in our time; through Jesus Christ, Thy Son, our Lord.

14

FOR THE CHILDREN OF THE CHURCH

Almighty and everlasting God, who dost will that not one of these little ones should perish and hast sent Thine only Son to seek and to save that which was lost and through Him hast said, Suffer the little children to come unto Me and forbid them not; for of such is the kingdom of God, most heartily we beseech Thee so to bless and govern the children of Thy Church by Thy Holy Spirit that they may grow in grace and in the knowledge of Thy Word; protect and defend them against all danger and harm, giving Thy holy angels charge over them; through Jesus Christ, Thy Son, our Lord.

15

FOR THE MINISTERS OF THE WORD

Almighty and everlasting God, who alone doest great wonders, send down upon Thy ministers and upon the congregations committed to their charge the healthful Spirit of Thy grace; and that they may truly please Thee, pour upon them the continual dew of Thy blessing; through Jesus Christ, Thy Son, our Lord.

16

Almighty and gracious God, the Father of our Lord Jesus Christ, who hast commanded us to pray that Thou wouldest send forth laborers into Thy harvest, of Thine infinite mercy give us true teachers and ministers of Thy Word, and put Thy saving Gospel in their hearts and on their lips that they may truly fulfill Thy command and preach nothing contrary to Thy holy Word, that we, being warned, instructed, nurtured, comforted, and strengthened by Thy heavenly Word, may do those things which are well-pleasing to Thee and profitable to us; through Jesus Christ, Thy Son, our Lord.

17

O almighty God, who by Thy Son, Jesus Christ, didst give to Thy holy Apostles many excellent gifts and commandedst them earnestly to feed Thy flock, make, we beseech Thee, all pastors diligently to preach Thy holy Word and the people obediently to follow the same that they may receive the crown of everlasting glory; through Jesus Christ, Thy Son, our Lord.

18

FOR THE CHURCH IN ITS CONFLICTS

Almighty and everlasting God, who wilt have all men to be saved and to come to the knowledge of the truth, we beseech Thy glorious majesty, through Jesus Christ, our Lord and Savior, impart the grace and help of Thy Holy Spirit to all ministers of Thy Word that they may purely teach it to the saving of men. Bring to naught by Thine almighty power and unsearchable wisdom all the counsels of those who hate Thy Word and who, by corrupt teaching or with violent hands, would destroy it, and enlighten them with the knowledge of Thy glory, that we, leading a quiet and peaceable life, may by a pure faith learn the riches of Thy heavenly grace and in holiness and righteousness serve Thee, the only true God; through Jesus Christ, Thy Son, our Lord.

19

FOR THOSE WHO HAVE ERRED

Almighty God, our heavenly Father, whose property it is always to have mercy, we most earnestly beseech Thee to visit with Thy fatherly correction all such as have erred and gone astray from the truth of Thy holy Word and to bring them to a due sense of their error that they may again with hearty faith receive, and hold fast, Thine unchangeable truth; through Jesus Christ, Thy Son, our Lord.

20

Almighty, merciful, and gracious God and Father, with our whole heart we beseech Thee for all who have forsaken the Christian faith, all who have wandered from any portion thereof or are in doubt or temptation through the corrupters of Thy Word, that Thou wouldest visit them as a Father, reveal unto them their error, and bring them back from their wanderings, that they, in singleness of heart, taking pleasure alone in the pure truth of Thy Word, may be made wise thereby unto everlasting life through faith in Jesus Christ, Thy Son, our Lord.

21

FOR UNITY

O God, who restorest to the right way them that err, who gatherest them that are scattered, and preservest them that are gathered, of Thy tender mercy we beseech Thee, pour upon Thy Christian people the grace of unity, that, all schisms being healed, Thy flock, united to the true Shepherd of Thy Church, may worthily serve Thee; through Jesus Christ, Thy Son, our Lord.

22

FOR THE REMOVAL OF SCHISM

Bring to naught, O Christ, the schisms of heresy which seek to subvert Thy truth, that, as Thou art acknowledged in heaven and in earth as one and the same Lord, so Thy people, gathered from all nations, may serve Thee in unity of faith.

23

FOR THE JEWS

Almighty and everlasting God, who lovest to show mercy, hear the prayers which we offer unto Thee for Thine ancient people, that, acknowledging Jesus Christ, who is the Light of truth, they may be delivered from their darkness; through the same Jesus Christ, Thy Son, our Lord.

24

FOR THE HEATHEN

Almighty and everlasting God, who desirest not the death of a sinner, but wouldest have all men to repent and live, hear our prayers for the heathen, take away iniquity from their hearts, and turn them from their idols unto the living and true God and to Thine only Son; and gather them into Thy holy Church, to the glory of Thy name; through Jesus Christ, Thy Son, our Lord.

FOR THE CIVIL AUTHORITIES

25

O merciful Father in heaven, who holdest in Thy hand all the might of man and who hast ordained the powers that be for the punishment of evildoers and for the praise of them that do well, and of whom is all rule and authority in the kingdoms of the world, we humbly beseech Thee, graciously regard Thy servants,* the President of the United States, the Governor of this Commonwealth, our Judges and Magistrates,

For Use in the British Empire
{ * Her Majesty the Queen of the British Commonwealth of Nations, the Governor-general and the Prime Minister of our Dominion, as well as the Premier of our Province, and all Governments and Parliaments, and all Judges and Magistrates,

and all the rulers of the earth. May all that receive the sword as Thy ministers bear it according to Thy commandment. Enlighten and defend them by Thy name, O God. Grant them wisdom and understanding, that under their peaceable governance Thy people may be guarded and directed in righteousness, quietness, and unity. Protect and prolong their lives, O God of our salvation, that we with them may show forth the praise of Thy name; through Jesus Christ, Thy Son, our Lord.

26

FOR OUR ENEMIES

Forgive, we beseech Thee, O Lord, our enemies and them that despitefully use us, and so change their hearts that they may walk with us in meekness and peace; through Jesus Christ, Thy Son, our Lord.

27

O almighty, everlasting God, who through Thine only Son, our blessed Lord, hast commanded us to love our enemies, to do good to them that hate us, and to pray for them that persecute us, we earnestly beseech Thee that by Thy gracious visitation they may be led to true repentance and may have the same love and be of one accord and of one mind and heart with us and with Thy whole Church; through the same Jesus Christ, Thy Son, our Lord.

28

IN TIME OF NATIONAL CALAMITY

O Lord God, heavenly Father, we humbly confess unto Thee that by our evil-doing and continual disobedience we have deserved these Thy chastisements; yet we earnestly beseech Thee, for Thy name's sake, to spare us; restrain the harmful power of the enemy and help Thy suffering people that Thy Word may be declared faithfully and without hindrance and that we, amending our sinful lives, may walk obedient to Thy holy commandments; through Jesus Christ, Thy Son, our Lord.

29

Look mercifully, O Lord, we beseech Thee, on the affliction of Thy people, and let not our sin destroy us, but let Thine almighty mercy save us; through Jesus Christ, Thy Son, our Lord.

30

Most loving and gracious Lord God, who for our many grievous sins art pleased sorely to chasten us, we flee to Thy tender and fatherly compassion alone, beseeching Thee that, as a father pitieth his children, Thou wouldest pity us miserable sinners. Turn away Thy righteous wrath and give us not over to deserved death, but deliver us that we may now and evermore praise Thee, O gracious God and Father, who desirest not the death of a sinner, but rather that he may turn from his wickedness and live; through Jesus Christ, Thy Son, our Lord.

31

FOR PRISONERS

Almighty God, who didst bring the Apostle Peter forth out of prison, have mercy upon all who are suffering unjust imprisonment and set them free from their bonds that we may rejoice in their deliverance and continually give praise to Thee; through Jesus Christ, Thy Son, our Lord.

32

FOR PEACE AND QUIETNESS

O Lord, we beseech Thee mercifully to hear the prayers of Thy Church that we, being delivered from all adversities and serving Thee with a quiet mind, may enjoy Thy peace all the days of our life; through Jesus Christ, Thy Son, our Lord.

IN TIME OF AFFLICTION AND DISTRESS

33

Almighty and everlasting God, the Consolation of the sorrowful and the Strength of the weak, may the prayers of them that in any tribulation or distress cry unto Thee, graciously come before Thee, so that in all their necessities they may mark and receive Thy manifold help and comfort; through Jesus Christ, Thy Son, our Lord.

34

Almighty and most merciful God, who hast appointed us to endure sufferings and death with our Lord Jesus Christ before we enter with Him into eternal glory, grant us grace at all times to subject ourselves to Thy holy will and to continue steadfast in the true faith unto the end of our lives and at all times to find peace and joy in the blessed hope of the resurrection of the dead and of the glory of the world to come; through Jesus Christ, Thy Son, our Lord.

35

Almighty God, cast not away Thy people who cry unto Thee in their tribulation, but for the glory of Thy name be pleased to help the afflicted; through Jesus Christ, Thy Son, our Lord.

36

FOR THE SICK

Almighty, everlasting God, the eternal Salvation of them that believe, hear our prayers in behalf of Thy servants who are sick, for whom we implore the aid of Thy mercy, that, being restored to health, they may render thanks to Thee in Thy Church; through Jesus Christ, Thy Son, our Lord.

37

O Lord, look down from heaven, behold, visit, and relieve Thy servants for whom we offer our supplications; look upon them with the eyes of Thy mercy; give them comfort and sure confidence in Thee, defend them from the danger of the enemy, and keep them in perpetual peace and safety; through Jesus Christ, Thy Son, our Lord.

38

FOR MOTHERS

O almighty, everlasting God and Father, Creator of all things, who by Thy grace, through Thy Son, our Lord, who hath redeemed us from sin, makest the anguish of our human birth a holy and salutary cross, we pray Thee, O gracious Father, Lord, and God, that Thou wouldest preserve and guard the work of Thine own hand. Forsake not them who cry to Thee in sore travail, but deliver them out of all their pains, to their joy and to the glory of Thy goodness; through Jesus Christ, Thy Son, our Lord.

39

IN TIME OF GREAT SICKNESS

Almighty and most merciful God, our heavenly Father, we, Thine erring children, humbly confess unto Thee that we have justly deserved the chastening which for our sins Thou hast sent upon us; but we entreat Thee, of Thy boundless goodness to grant us true repentance, graciously to forgive our sins, to remove from us, or to lighten, our merited punishment, and so to strengthen us by Thy grace that as obedient children we may be subject to Thy will and bear our afflictions in patience; through Jesus Christ, Thy Son, our Lord.

40

IN TIME OF DROUGHT

O God, most merciful Father, we beseech Thee to open the windows of heaven and to send a fruitful rain upon us, to revive the earth, and to refresh the fruits thereof, for all things droop and wither. Graciously hear our prayer in this our necessity that we may praise and glorify Thy name forever and ever; through Jesus Christ, Thy Son, our Lord.

41

IN TIME OF UNSEASONABLE WEATHER

O Lord God, heavenly Father, who art gracious and merciful and hast promised that Thou wilt hear us when we call upon Thee in our troubles, we beseech Thee, look not upon our sins and evil-doings, but upon our necessities, and according to Thy mercy send us such seasonable weather that the earth may in due time yield her increase, that by Thy goodness we may receive our daily bread and learn to know Thee as a merciful God and evermore give thanks to Thee for Thy goodness; through Jesus Christ, Thy Son, our Lord.

THANKSGIVING

42

O Lord God, heavenly Father, from whom without ceasing we receive exceeding abundantly all good gifts and who daily of Thy pure grace guardest us against all evil, grant us, we beseech Thee, Thy Holy Spirit that, acknowledging with our whole heart all this Thy goodness, we may now and evermore thank and praise Thy loving-kindness and tender mercy; through Jesus Christ, Thy Son, our Lord.

43

Almighty God, our heavenly Father, whose mercies are new unto us every morning and who, though we have in no wise deserved Thy goodness, dost abundantly provide for all our wants of body and soul, give us, we pray Thee, Thy Holy Spirit that we may heartily acknowledge Thy merciful goodness toward us, give thanks for all Thy benefits, and serve Thee in willing obedience; through Jesus Christ, Thy Son, our Lord.

44

Almighty and most merciful God, who in Thy fatherly wisdom hast chastened us on account of our sins that we might not continue in impenitence and vain confidence and thus perish with the ungodly, in the midst of wrath Thou hast remembered mercy and hast graciously delivered us out of our affliction. We give Thee therefore most hearty thanks and praise that Thou hast turned away from us Thy just anger and shown Thyself favorable toward us, Thine unworthy servants. Bless the Lord, O my soul; and all that is within me, bless His holy name. Bless the Lord, O my soul, and forget not all His benefits. Thou, Lord, art merciful and gracious, slow to anger, and plenteous in mercy. Glory be to Thee, O God, forever; through Jesus Christ, Thy Son, our Lord.

45

Glory be to Thee, O God most holy. Glory be to Thee, O God most high. Glory be to Thee, O King of heaven and earth, who, as a father pitieth his children, pitiest us. Fill us with joy and gladness in the Holy Ghost that, when Thou shalt render to every man according to his works, we may be found acceptable before Thee; through Him who hath redeemed us from the shame and curse of sin, even Jesus Christ, Thy Son, our Lord.

FOR SPECIAL GIFTS AND GRACES

46

FOR PROTECTION DURING THE DAY

O Lord, our heavenly Father, almighty and everlasting God, who hast safely brought us to the beginning of this day, defend us in the same with Thy mighty power, and grant that this day we fall into no sin, neither run into any kind of danger, but that all our doings, being ordered by Thy governance, may be righteous in Thy sight; through Jesus Christ, Thy Son, our Lord.

47

FOR PROTECTION DURING THE NIGHT

Lighten our darkness, we beseech Thee, O Lord; and by Thy great mercy defend us from all perils and dangers of this night; for the love of Thine only Son, our Savior, Jesus Christ.

48

FOR GRACE TO USE OUR GIFTS

O Lord God Almighty, who dost endue Thy servants with divers and singular gifts of the Holy Ghost, leave us not, we beseech Thee, destitute of Thy manifold gifts nor yet of grace to use them always to Thine honor and glory; through Jesus Christ, Thy Son, our Lord.

49

FOR GRACE TO RECEIVE THE WORD

Blessed Lord, who hast caused all Holy Scriptures to be written for our learning, grant that we may in such wise hear them, read, mark, learn, and inwardly digest them that by patience and comfort of Thy holy Word we may embrace, and ever hold fast, the blessed hope of everlasting life which Thou hast given us in our Savior Jesus Christ.

50

FOR GRACE TO BE LED INTO ALL TRUTH

Enlighten our minds, we beseech Thee, O God, by the Spirit which proceedeth from Thee, that, as Thy Son hath promised, we may be led into all truth; through the same Jesus Christ, Thy Son, our Lord.

51

FOR SPIRITUAL RENEWAL

Almighty God, who hast given us Thine only-begotten Son to take our nature upon Him, grant that we, being regenerate and made Thy children by adoption and grace, may daily be renewed by Thy Holy Spirit; through the same Jesus Christ, Thy Son, our Lord.

52

FOR PENITENCE

Merciful Father, give us grace that we may never presume to sin; but if at any time we offend Thy divine majesty, may we truly repent and lament our offense and by a lively faith obtain remission of all our sins, solely through the merits of Thy Son, our Savior, Jesus Christ.

53

FOR PARDON

Hear, we beseech Thee, O Lord, the prayer of Thy suppliants and spare those who confess their sins unto Thee that Thou mayest bestow upon us both pardon and peace; through Jesus Christ, Thy Son, our Lord.

54

FOR DELIVERANCE FROM SIN

We beseech Thee, O Lord, in Thy clemency to show us Thine unspeakable mercy that Thou mayest both set us free from our sins and rescue us from the punishments which for our sins we deserve; through Jesus Christ, Thy Son, our Lord.

55

FOR GRACE TO DO GOD'S WILL

Almighty God, give us grace that we may cast away the works of darkness and put upon ourselves the armor of light, now in the time of this mortal life, in which Thy Son Jesus Christ came to visit us in great humility, that in the Last Day, when He shall come again in His glorious majesty to judge both the quick and the dead, we may rise to the life immortal; through Jesus Christ, Thy Son, our Lord.

56

FOR GRACE TO LOVE AND SERVE GOD

O God, who, through the grace of Thy Holy Spirit, dost pour the gifts of charity into the hearts of Thy faithful people, grant unto Thy servants health both of mind and body that they may love Thee with their whole strength and with their whole heart perform those things which are pleasing unto Thee; through Jesus Christ, Thy Son, our Lord.

57

FOR AID AGAINST TEMPTATION

O God, who justifiest the ungodly and who desirest not the death of the sinner, we humbly implore Thy majesty that Thou wouldest graciously assist by Thy heavenly aid, and evermore shield with Thy protection, Thy servants who trust in Thy mercy, that they may be separated by no temptations from Thee and without ceasing may serve Thee; through Jesus Christ, Thy Son, our Lord.

58

FOR FAITH

Almighty and ever-living God, who hast given to them that believe exceeding great and precious promises, grant us so perfectly and without all doubt to believe in Thy Son Jesus Christ that our faith in Thy sight may never be reproved. Hear us, O Lord, through the same Savior, Thy Son, Jesus Christ.

59

FOR DIVINE GUIDANCE AND HELP

Direct us, O Lord, in all our doings with Thy most gracious favor and further us with Thy continual help, that in all our works begun, continued, and ended in Thee we may glorify Thy holy name and finally, by Thy mercy, obtain everlasting life; through Jesus Christ, our Lord.

60

O almighty and everlasting God, vouchsafe, we beseech Thee, to direct, sanctify, and govern both our hearts and bodies in the ways of Thy laws and in the works of Thy commandments, that through Thy most mighty protection, both here and ever, we may be preserved in body and in soul; through our Lord and Savior Jesus Christ.

61

FOR SPIRITUAL ILLUMINATION

Grant, we beseech Thee, almighty God, that the brightness of Thy glory may shine forth upon us and that the light of Thy light, by the illumination of the Holy Spirit, may stablish the hearts of all that have been born anew by Thy grace; through Jesus Christ, Thy Son, our Lord.

62

FOR LIKENESS TO CHRIST

Almighty God, who hast given Thine only Son to be unto us both a Sacrifice for sin and also an Example of godly life, give us grace that we may always most thankfully receive this His inestimable benefit and also daily endeavor ourselves to follow the blessed steps of His most holy life; through the same Jesus Christ, Thy Son, our Lord.

63

FOR A RIGHT KNOWLEDGE OF CHRIST

O almighty God, whom to know is everlasting life, grant us perfectly to know Thy Son, Jesus Christ, to be the Way, the Truth, and the Life, that, following His steps, we may steadfastly walk in the way that leadeth to eternal life; through the same Jesus Christ, Thy Son, our Lord.

64

FOR THE HOLY SPIRIT

O Lord God, heavenly Father, who by the blessed light of Thy divine Word hast led us to the knowledge of Thy Son, we most heartily beseech Thee so to replenish us with the grace of Thy Holy Spirit that we may ever walk in the light of Thy truth and, rejoicing with sure confidence in Christ, our Savior, may in the end be brought unto everlasting salvation; through the same Jesus Christ, Thy Son, our Lord.

65

Almighty and everlasting God, who of Thy great mercy in Jesus Christ, Thy Son, dost grant us forgiveness of sin and all things pertaining to life and godliness, grant us, we beseech Thee, Thy Holy Spirit that He may so rule our hearts that we, being ever mindful of Thy fatherly mercy, may strive to mortify the flesh and to overcome the world and, serving Thee in holiness and pureness of living, may give Thee continual thanks for all Thy goodness; through Jesus Christ, Thy Son, our Lord.

66

FOR PURITY

Almighty God, unto whom all hearts are open, all desires known, and from whom no secrets are hid, cleanse the thoughts of our hearts by the inspiration of Thy Holy Spirit that we may perfectly love Thee and worthily magnify Thy holy name; through Jesus Christ, Thy Son, our Lord.

67

FOR INNOCENCY OF LIFE

O God, whose strength is made perfect in weakness, mortify and kill all vices in us and so strengthen us by Thy grace that by the innocency of our lives and the constancy of our faith, even unto death, we may glorify Thy holy name; through Jesus Christ, Thy Son, our Lord.

68

FOR LOVE TO GOD

O God, who makest all things to work together for good to them that love Thee, pour into our hearts such steadfast love toward Thee that the pure desires which by Thy Spirit have been stirred up in us may not be turned aside by any temptation; through Jesus Christ, Thy Son, our Lord.

69

FOR CHARITY

O Lord, who hast taught us that all our doings without charity are worth nothing, send Thy Holy Spirit and pour into our hearts that most excellent gift of charity, the very bond of peace, and all virtues, without which whosoever liveth is counted dead before Thee. Grant this for Thine only Son Jesus Christ's sake.

70

FOR HUMILITY

O God, who resistest the proud and givest grace to the humble, grant unto us true humility, after the likeness in which Thine only Son hath revealed it in Himself, that we may never be lifted up and provoke Thy wrath, but in all lowliness be made partakers of the gifts of Thy grace; through Jesus Christ, Thy Son, our Lord.

71

FOR PATIENCE

O God, who by the meek endurance of Thine only-begotten Son didst beat down the pride of the old enemy, help us, we beseech Thee, rightly to treasure in our hearts what our Lord hath of His goodness borne for our sakes, that after His example we may bear with patience whatsoever things are adverse to us; through Jesus Christ, Thy Son, our Lord.

72

FOR A HAPPY DEATH

Confirm, we beseech Thee, Almighty God, Thine unworthy servants in Thy grace that in the hour of our death the adversary may not prevail against us but that we may be found worthy of everlasting life; through Jesus Christ, Thy Son, our Lord.

73

FOR THE BLESSEDNESS OF HEAVEN

Almighty, everlasting God, who didst give Thine only Son to be a High Priest of good things to come, hereafter grant unto us, Thine unworthy servants, to have our share in the company of the blessed; through Jesus Christ, Thy Son, our Lord.

74

FOR PEACE

O God, who art the Author of peace and Lover of concord, in knowledge of whom standeth our eternal life, whose service is perfect freedom, defend us, Thy humble servants, in all assaults of our enemies, that we, surely trusting in Thy defense, may not fear the power of any adversaries; through the might of Jesus Christ, Thy Son, our Lord.

FOR AN ANSWER TO PRAYER

75

Almighty God, who hast given us grace at this time with one accord to make our common supplications unto Thee and dost promise that, when two or three are gathered together in Thy name, Thou wilt grant their requests, fulfill now, O Lord, the desires and petitions of Thy servants, as may be most expedient for them; granting us in this world knowledge of Thy truth and in the world to come life everlasting; through Jesus Christ, Thy Son, our Lord.

76

Almighty God, the Fountain of all wisdom, who knowest our necessities before we ask and our ignorance in asking, we beseech Thee to have compassion upon our infirmities; and those things which for our unworthiness we dare not, and for our blindness we cannot, ask vouchsafe to give us for the worthiness of Jesus Christ, Thy Son, our Lord.

77

Almighty God, who hast promised to hear the petitions of those who ask in Thy Son's name, we beseech Thee mercifully to incline Thine ears to us who have now made our prayers and supplications unto Thee; and grant that those things which we have faithfully asked according to Thy will may effectually be obtained to the relief of our necessity and to the setting forth of Thy glory; through Jesus Christ, Thy Son, our Lord.

I

Almighty God, our heavenly Father, we, Thine unworthy servants, do give Thee most humble and hearty thanks for all Thy goodness and loving-kindness to us and to all men. We praise Thee for our creation, preservation, and all the blessings of this life, but above all for Thine inestimable love in the redemption of the world by our Lord and Savior Jesus Christ, for the means of grace, and for the hope of glory. And we beseech Thee, give us that due sense of all Thy mercies that our hearts may be unfeignedly thankful and that we may show forth Thy praise, not only with our lips, but in our lives; that, walking before Thee in holiness and righteousness all our days, we may enjoy the testimony of a good conscience and the hope of Thy favor, be sustained and comforted under the troubles of this life, and finally be received into Thine everlasting kingdom; through Thine infinite mercy in Jesus Christ, our Lord.

We offer unto Thee our common supplications for the good estate of Thy Church throughout the world, that it may be so guided and governed by Thy good Spirit that all who profess themselves Christians may be led into the way of truth and hold the faith in unity of spirit, in the bond of peace, and in righteousness of life. Send down upon all ministers of the Gospel and upon all congregations committed to their charge the healthful spirit of Thy grace, and that they may truly please Thee, pour upon them the continual dew of Thy blessing.

Most heartily we beseech Thee with Thy favor to behold * the President and Congress of the United States and all others in authority

For Use in the British Empire { * Her Majesty the Queen of the British Commonwealth of Nations, the Governor-general and the Prime Minister of our Dominion, as well as the Premier of our Province, and all Governments and Parliaments, and all Judges and Magistrates

and so to replenish them with Thy grace that they may always incline to Thy will and walk in Thy way. Prosper all good counsels and all just works that peace and happiness, truth and righteousness, religion and piety, may be established among us throughout all generations.

We humbly entreat Thee also for all sorts and conditions of men, that Thou wouldst be pleased to make Thy ways known unto them, Thy saving health unto all nations.

May it please Thee to preserve all that travel by land or water, to help all that are in peril or need, and to satisfy the wants of all Thy creatures.

We also commend to Thy fatherly goodness all those who are in any way afflicted or distressed in mind, body, or estate, that it may please Thee to comfort and relieve them according to their several necessities, giving them patience under their sufferings and a happy issue out of all their afflictions.

(Here special Supplications, Intercessions, and Prayers may be made.)

Hear us, most merciful God, in these our humble requests, which we offer up unto Thee in the name of Jesus Christ, Thy Son, our Lord, to whom, with Thee and the Holy Ghost, be all honor and glory, world without end.

II

THE LITANY

(The Litany may be used at Vespers on Sundays, Wednesdays, and Fridays, on Days of Humiliation and Prayer, and at Matins on Sundays when there is no Communion. The Responses in boldface should be sung or said by the Congregation. [A musical setting is given at the end of the hymn section of this book.] The Responses may be repeated after each phrase or only at the end of each group, as here followeth:)

O Lord,
   Have mercy upon us.

O Christ,
   Have mercy upon us.

O Lord,
   Have mercy upon us.

O Christ,
   Hear Thou us.

O God the Father in heaven,
   Have mercy upon us.

O God the Son, Redeemer of the world,
   Have mercy upon us.

O God the Holy Ghost,
   Have mercy upon us.

Be gracious unto us.
   Spare us, good Lord.

Be gracious unto us.

Help us, good Lord.

From all sin;
From all error;
From all evil:

Good Lord, deliver us.

From the crafts and assaults of the devil;
From sudden and evil death;
From pestilence and famine;
From war and bloodshed;
From sedition and rebellion;
From lightning and tempest;
From all calamity by fire and water;
And from everlasting death:

Good Lord, deliver us.

By the mystery of Thy holy incarnation;
By Thy holy nativity;
By Thy baptism, fasting, and temptation;
By Thine agony and bloody sweat;
By Thy cross and Passion;
By Thy precious death and burial;
By Thy glorious resurrection and ascension;
And by the coming of the Holy Ghost, the Comforter:

Help us, good Lord.

In all time of our tribulation;
In all time of our prosperity;
In the hour of death;
And in the day of Judgment:

Help us, good Lord.

We poor sinners do beseech Thee

To hear us, O Lord God,

And to rule and govern Thy holy Christian Church;
To preserve all pastors and ministers of Thy Church in the true knowledge and understanding of Thy Word and in holiness of life;
To put an end to all schisms and causes of offense;
To bring into the way of truth all such as have erred and are deceived;
To beat down Satan under our feet;
To send faithful laborers into Thy harvest;
To accompany Thy Word with Thy Spirit and grace;
To raise up them that fall and to strengthen such as do stand;
And to comfort and help the weakhearted and the distressed:

We beseech Thee to hear us, good Lord.

To give to all nations peace and concord;
To preserve our country from discord and contention;
To give to our nation perpetual victory over all its enemies;
To direct and defend our President and all in authority;
And to bless and keep our magistrates and all our people:

We beseech Thee to hear us, good Lord.

To behold and help all who are in danger, necessity, and tribulation;
To protect all who travel by land or water;
To preserve all women in the perils of childbirth;
To strengthen and keep all sick persons and young children;
To set free all who are innocently imprisoned;
To defend and provide for all fatherless children and widows;
And to have mercy upon all men:

We beseech Thee to hear us, good Lord.

To forgive our enemies, persecutors, and slanderers, and to turn their hearts;
To give and preserve to our use the fruits of the earth;
And graciously to hear our prayers:

We beseech Thee to hear us, good Lord.

O Lord Jesus Christ, Son of God,

We beseech Thee to hear us.

O Lamb of God, that takest away the sin of the world,

Have mercy upon us.

O Lamb of God, that takest away the sin of the world,

Have mercy upon us.

O Lamb of God, that takest away the sin of the world,

Grant us Thy peace.

O Christ,

Hear Thou us.

O Lord,

Have mercy upon us.

O Christ,

Have mercy upon us.

Minister and Congregation: **Lord, have mercy upon us. Amen.**

(Then shall the Minister, and the Congregation with him, say the Lord's Prayer, after which may be said one or more of the Litany Collects here following.)

Our Father who art in heaven; Hallowed be Thy name; Thy kingdom come; Thy will be done on earth as it is in heaven; Give us this day our daily bread; And forgive us our trespasses, as we forgive those who trespass against us; And lead us not into temptation; But deliver us from evil; For Thine is the kingdom and the power and the glory forever and ever. Amen.

LITANY COLLECTS

1

℣: O Lord, deal not with us after our sins.

℞: **Neither reward us according to our iniquities.**

Almighty God, our heavenly Father, who desirest not the death of a sinner, but rather that he should turn from his evil way and live, we beseech Thee graciously to turn from us those punishments which we by our sins have deserved and to grant us grace ever hereafter to serve Thee in holiness and pureness of living; through Jesus Christ, Thy Son, our Lord.

2

℣: Help us, O God of our salvation, for the glory of Thy name.

℞: **Deliver us and purge away our sins for Thy name's sake.**

Almighty and everlasting God, who by Thy Holy Spirit dost govern and sanctify the whole Christian Church, hear our prayers for all members of the same and mercifully grant that by Thy grace they may serve Thee in true faith; through Jesus Christ, Thy Son, our Lord.

3

℣: O Lord, deal not with us after our sins.

℞: **Neither reward us according to our iniquities.**

O God, merciful Father, who despisest not the sighing of a contrite heart nor the desire of such as are sorrowful, mercifully assist our prayers which we make before Thee in all our troubles and adversities whensoever they oppress us, and graciously hear us that those evils which the craft and subtlety of the devil or man worketh against us may by Thy good providence be brought to naught, that we, Thy servants, being hurt by no persecutions, may evermore give thanks unto Thee in Thy holy Church; through Jesus Christ, Thy Son, our Lord.

4

℣: O Lord, enter not into judgment with Thy servant.

℞: **For in Thy sight shall no man living be justified.**

Almighty God, who knowest us to be set in the midst of so many and great dangers that by reason of the frailty of our nature we cannot always stand upright, grant us such strength and protection as may support us in all dangers and carry us through all temptations; through Jesus Christ, Thy Son, our Lord.

5

℣: Call upon Me in the day of trouble.

℞: **I will deliver thee, and thou shalt glorify Me.**

Spare us, O Lord, and mercifully forgive us our sins, and though by our continual transgressions we have merited Thy punishments, be gracious unto us and grant that all those evils which we have deserved may be turned from us and overruled to our everlasting good; through Jesus Christ, Thy Son, our Lord.

6

FOR PEACE

℣: The Lord will give strength unto His people.

℞: **The Lord will bless His people with peace.**

O God, from whom all holy desires, all good counsels, and all just works do proceed, give unto Thy servants that peace which the world cannot give, that our hearts may be set to obey Thy commandments, and also that we, being defended by Thee from the fear of our enemies, may pass our time in rest and quietness; through the merits of Jesus Christ, our Savior.

III

THE SUFFRAGES

(The Suffrages may be used at Matins or Vespers in the same manner as the Litany.)

O Lord,
Have mercy upon us.

O Christ,
Have mercy upon us.

O Lord,
Have mercy upon us.

Our Father who art in heaven; Hallowed be Thy name; Thy kingdom come; Thy will be done on earth as it is in heaven; Give us this day our daily bread; And forgive us our trespasses, as we forgive those who trespass against us; And lead us not into temptation;
But deliver us from evil.

I said, O Lord, be merciful unto me;
Heal my soul; for I have sinned against Thee.

Return, O Lord, how long?
And let it repent Thee concerning Thy servants.

Let Thy mercy, O Lord, be upon us,
According as we hope in Thee.

Let Thy priests be clothed with righteousness,
And let Thy saints shout for joy.

O Lord, save our rulers;
Let the King hear us when we call.

Save Thy people and bless Thine inheritance;
Feed them also and lift them up forever.

Remember Thy congregation,
Which Thou hast purchased of old.

Peace be within thy walls
And prosperity within thy palaces.

Let us pray for our absent brethren.
O Thou, our God, save Thy servants that trust in Thee.

Let us pray for the brokenhearted and the captives.
Redeem Israel, O God, out of all his troubles.

Send them help from the Sanctuary
And strengthen them out of Zion.

Hear my prayer, O Lord;
And let my cry come unto Thee.

(Then may be said responsively, by the Minister and Congregation, the Psalm De Profundis at Matins, and at Vespers the Psalm Miserere Mei.)

Ps. 130. De Profundis

Out of the depths have I cried:
Unto Thee, O Lord.

Lord, hear my voice:
Let Thine ears be attentive to the voice of my supplications.

If Thou, Lord, shouldest mark iniquities:
O Lord, who shall stand?

But there is forgiveness with Thee:
That Thou mayest be feared.

I wait for the Lord, my soul doth wait:
And in His Word do I hope.

My soul waiteth for the Lord more than they that watch for the morning:
I say, more than they that watch for the morning.

Let Israel hope in the Lord:
For with the Lord there is mercy, and with Him is plenteous redemption.

And He shall redeem Israel:
From all his iniquities.

Glory be to the Father and to the Son and to the Holy Ghost:
As it was in the beginning, is now, and ever shall be, world without end. Amen.

Or at Vespers

Ps. 51. Miserere Mei

Have mercy upon me, O God, according to Thy loving-kindness:
According unto the multitude of Thy tender mercies, blot out my transgressions.

Wash me thoroughly from mine iniquity:
And cleanse me from my sin.

For I acknowledge my transgressions:
And my sin is ever before me.

Against Thee, Thee only, have I sinned and done this evil in Thy sight:

That Thou mightest be justified when Thou speakest and be clear when Thou judgest.

Behold, I was shapen in iniquity:

And in sin did my mother conceive me.

Behold, Thou desirest truth in the inward parts:

And in the hidden part shalt Thou make me to know wisdom.

Purge me with hyssop, and I shall be clean:

Wash me, and I shall be whiter than snow.

Make me to hear joy and gladness:

That the bones which Thou hast broken may rejoice.

Hide Thy face from my sins:

And blot out all mine iniquities.

Create in me a clean heart, O God:

And renew a right spirit within me.

Cast me not away from Thy presence:

And take not Thy Holy Spirit from me.

Restore unto me the joy of Thy salvation:

And uphold me with Thy free Spirit.

Then will I teach transgressors Thy ways:

And sinners shall be converted unto Thee.

Deliver me from blood-guiltiness, O God, Thou God of my salvation:

And my tongue shall sing aloud of Thy righteousness.

O Lord, open Thou my lips:

And my mouth shall show forth Thy praise.

For Thou desirest not sacrifice, else would I give it:

Thou delightest not in burnt offering.

The sacrifices of God are a broken spirit:

A broken and a contrite heart, O God, Thou wilt not despise.

Do good in Thy good pleasure unto Zion:

Build Thou the walls of Jerusalem.

Then shalt Thou be pleased with the sacrifices of righteousness, with burnt offering and whole burnt offering:

Then shall they offer bullocks upon Thine altar.

Glory be to the Father and to the Son and to the Holy Ghost:

As it was in the beginning, is now, and ever shall be, world without end. Amen.

Then shall be said:

Turn us again, O God of hosts,

Cause Thy face to shine, and we shall be saved.

Arise, O Christ, for our help

And redeem us for Thy mercy's sake.

Hear my prayer, O Lord,

And let my cry come unto Thee.

The Lord be with you.

And with thy spirit.

Let us pray.

(Then may the Minister say a Collect for the Season and any other suitable Collects, and after that he may say this Collect for Peace:)

Give peace in our days, O Lord:

Because there is none other that fighteth for us except Thou, our God.

O Lord, let there be peace in Thy strength:

And abundance in Thy towers.

Let us pray:

O God, from whom all holy desires, all good counsels, and all just works do proceed, give unto Thy servants that peace which the world cannot give, that our hearts may be set to obey Thy commandments, and also that we, being defended by Thee from the fear of our enemies, may pass our time in rest and quietness; through the merits of Jesus Christ, our Savior. **Amen.**

Then may be said or chanted the

Benedicamus

Bless we the Lord:

Thanks be to God.

IV

THE MORNING SUFFRAGES

(To be said at Matins or in the Morning Prayer of the Household.)

O Lord,
> **Have mercy upon us.**

O Christ,
> **Have mercy upon us.**

O Lord,
> **Have mercy upon us.**

Then shall all say:

Our Father who art in heaven; Hallowed be Thy name; Thy kingdom come; Thy will be done on earth as it is in heaven; Give us this day our daily bread; And forgive us our trespasses, as we forgive those who trespass against us; And lead us not into temptation; But deliver us from evil. Amen.

I believe in God the Father Almighty, Maker of heaven and earth; And in Jesus Christ, His only Son, our Lord; Who was conceived by the Holy Ghost, Born of the Virgin Mary; Suffered under Pontius Pilate, Was crucified, dead, and buried; He descended into hell; The third day He rose again from the dead; He ascended into heaven, And sitteth on the right hand of God the Father Almighty; From thence He shall come to judge the quick and the dead.

I believe in the Holy Ghost; The holy Christian Church, the communion of saints; The forgiveness of sins; The resurrection of the body; And the life everlasting. Amen.

Unto Thee have I cried, O Lord:
> **And in the morning shall my prayer come before Thee.**

Let my mouth be filled with Thy praise:
> **And with Thine honor all the day.**

O Lord, hide Thy face from my sins:
> **And blot out all mine iniquities.**

Create in me a clean heart, O God:
> **And renew a right spirit within me.**

Cast me not away from Thy presence:
> **And take not Thy Holy Spirit from me.**

Restore unto me the joy of Thy salvation:
> **And uphold me with Thy free Spirit.**

Vouchsafe, O Lord, this day:
> **To keep us without sin.**

Have mercy upon us, O Lord:
> **Have mercy upon us.**

O Lord, let Thy mercy be upon us:
> **As our trust is in Thee.**

Hear my prayer, O Lord:
> **And let my cry come unto Thee.**

The Lord be with you:
> **And with thy spirit.**

Let us pray.

(Then shall be said the prayer here following or No. 46 or No. 60 of the Collects and Prayers or any other suitable prayer.)

We give thanks unto Thee, heavenly Father, through Jesus Christ, Thy dear Son, that Thou hast kept us this night from all harm and danger; and we pray Thee that Thou wouldst keep us this day also from sin and every evil, that all our doings and life may please Thee. For into Thy hands we commend ourselves, our bodies and souls, and all things. Let Thy holy angel be with us that the wicked Foe may have no power over us. **Amen.**

Then may be said or chanted the

Benedicamus

Bless we the Lord.
> **Thanks be to God.**

V

THE EVENING SUFFRAGES

(To be used at Vespers or at the Evening Prayer of the Household.)

O Lord,
> **Have mercy upon us.**

O Christ,
> **Have mercy upon us.**

O Lord,
> **Have mercy upon us.**

Then shall all say:

Our Father who art in heaven; Hallowed be Thy name; Thy kingdom come; Thy will be done on earth as it is in heaven; Give us this day our daily bread; And forgive us our trespasses, as we forgive those who trespass against us; And lead us not into temptation; But deliver us from evil. Amen.

I believe in God the Father Almighty, Maker of heaven and earth; And in Jesus Christ, His only Son, our Lord; Who was conceived by the Holy Ghost, Born of the Virgin Mary; Suffered under Pontius Pilate; Was crucified, dead, and buried; He descended into hell; The third day He rose again from the dead; He ascended into heaven; And sitteth on the right hand of God the Father Almighty; From thence He shall come to judge the quick and the dead.

I believe in the Holy Ghost; The holy Christian Church, the communion of saints; The forgiveness of sins; The resurrection of the body; And the life everlasting. Amen.

Blessed art Thou, O Lord God of our fathers:
> **And greatly to be praised and glorified forever.**

Bless we the Father and the Son and the Holy Ghost:
> **We praise and magnify Him forever.**

Blessed art Thou, O Lord, in the firmament of heaven:
> **And greatly to be praised and glorified and highly exalted forever.**

The almighty and merciful Lord bless and preserve us.
> **Amen.**

Vouchsafe, O Lord, this night:
> **To keep us without sin.**

O Lord, have mercy upon us:
> **Have mercy upon us.**

O Lord, let Thy mercy be upon us:
> **As our trust is in Thee.**

Hear my prayer, O Lord:
> **And let my cry come unto Thee.**

The Lord be with you.
> **And with thy spirit.**

Let us pray:

(Then shall be said the prayer here following or No. 47 of the Collects and Prayers or any other suitable prayer.)

We thank Thee, heavenly Father, through Jesus Christ, Thy dear Son, that Thou hast kept us this day; and we pray Thee that Thou wouldst graciously forgive us all our sins where we have done wrong, and graciously keep us this night.

For into Thy hands we commend ourselves, our bodies and souls, and all things. Let Thy holy angel be with us that the wicked Foe may have no power over us. **Amen.**

Then may be said or chanted the

Benedicamus

Bless we the Lord.
> **Thanks be to God.**

VI

THE BIDDING PRAYER

(By ancient usage this prayer was specially appointed for Good Friday.)

Brethren, let us pray for the whole *Christian Church,* that our Lord God would vouchsafe to defend it against all the assaults and temptations of the Adversary and to keep it perpetually upon the true foundation, Jesus Christ.

Almighty and everlasting God, who hast revealed Thy glory to all nations in Jesus Christ and the Word of His truth, keep, we beseech Thee, in safety the works of Thy mercy that so Thy Church, spread throughout all nations, may serve Thee in true faith and persevere in the confession of Thy name; through Jesus Christ, our Lord. **Amen.**

Let us pray for the *Ministers* of the Word, for all *Estates* of men in the Church, and for all the *people of God.*

Almighty and everlasting God, by whose Spirit the whole body of the Church is governed and sanctified, receive the supplications and prayers which we offer before Thee for all Estates of men in Thy holy Church, that every member of the same, in his vocation and ministry, may truly and godly serve Thee; through Christ, our Lord. **Amen.**

Let us pray for our *Catechumens,* that our Lord God would open their hearts and the door of His mercy, that, having received the remission of all their sins by the washing of regeneration, they may be mindful of their baptismal covenant and evermore be found in Christ Jesus, our Lord.

Almighty and everlasting God, who dost always multiply Thy Church and with Thy light and grace dost strengthen the hearts of those whom Thou hast regenerated, confirming unto them Thy covenant and faithfulness, grant unto our Catechumens increase both of faith and knowledge that they may rejoice in their baptism and really and heartily renew their covenant with Thee. **Amen.**

Let us pray for *All in Authority*, and especially for the Government * of the United States,

For Use in the { * of the British Empire,
British Empire {

that we may lead a quiet and peaceable life in all godliness and honesty.

O merciful Father in heaven, who holdest in Thy hand all the might of man and who hast ordained the powers that be for the punishment of evildoers and for the praise of them that do well, and of whom is all rule and authority in the kingdoms of the world, we humbly beseech Thee, graciously regard Thy servants,* the President of the United States,

For Use in the ⎰ * Her Majesty the Queen
British Empire ⎱ of the British Commonwealth and the Parliaments in the Empire,

the Governor of this Commonwealth, our judges and magistrates, and all the rulers of the earth, that all who receive the sword as Thy ministers may bear it according to Thy commandment; through Christ, our Lord. **Amen.**

Let us pray our Lord God Almighty that He would deliver the world from all *error,* take away *disease,* ward off *famine,* set free all those who are *in chains* and *bondage,* grant a safe return to the *wayfarers,* health to the *sick,* and to our *mariners* a harbor of security.

Almighty and everlasting God, the Consolation of the sorrowful and the Strength of the weak, may the prayers of them that in any tribulation or distress cry unto Thee graciously come before Thee, so that in all their necessities they may mark and receive Thy manifold help and comfort; through Christ, our Lord. **Amen.**

(Here may be offered prayers for schismatics, Jews, and heathen. See Collects and Prayers 19—24.)

Let us pray for *peace,* that we may come to the knowledge of God's holy Word and walk before Him as becometh Christians.

Almighty and everlasting God, King of Glory, and Lord of heaven and earth, by whose Spirit all things are governed, by whose providence all things are ordered, who art the God of peace and the Author of all concord, grant us, we beseech Thee, Thy heavenly peace and concord that we may serve Thee in true fear, to the praise and glory of Thy name; through Christ, our Lord. **Amen.**

Let us pray for our *enemies,* that God would remember them in mercy and graciously vouchsafe unto them such things as are both needful for them and profitable unto their salvation.

O almighty, everlasting God, who through Thine only Son, our blessed Lord, hast commanded us to love our enemies, to do good to them that hate us, and to pray for them that persecute us, we earnestly beseech Thee that by Thy gracious visitation all our enemies may be led to true repentance and may have the same love and be of one accord and of one mind and heart with us and with Thy whole Christian Church; through Christ, our Lord. **Amen.**

Let us pray for the *fruits of the earth,* that God would send down His blessing upon them and graciously dispose our hearts to enjoy them in submission to His holy will.

O Lord, Father Almighty, who by Thy Word hast created, and dost bless and uphold, all things, we pray Thee so to reveal unto us Thy Word, our Lord Jesus Christ, that, He dwelling in our hearts, we may by Thy grace be made meet to receive Thy blessing on all the fruits of the earth and whatsoever pertains to our bodily need; through Christ, our Lord. **Amen.**

Finally, let us pray for all those things for which our Lord would have us ask, saying:

Our Father who art in heaven; Hallowed be Thy name; Thy kingdom come; Thy will be done on earth as it is in heaven; Give us this day our daily bread; And forgive us our trespasses, as we forgive those who trespass against us; And lead us not into temptation; But deliver us from evil; For Thine is the kingdom and the power and the glory forever and ever. **Amen.**

Prayers for Various Occasions

MORNING PRAYER

In the name of God the Father, Son, and Holy Ghost. Amen.

I thank Thee, my heavenly Father, through Jesus Christ, Thy dear Son, that Thou hast kept me this night from all harm and danger; and I pray Thee that Thou wouldst keep me this day also from sin and every evil that all my doings and life may please Thee. For into Thy hands I commend myself, my body and soul, and all things. Let Thy holy angel be with me that the wicked Foe may have no power over me. Amen.

O Thou crucified Lord Jesus Christ, who, as the truly patient Lamb of God, didst suffer for me the most shameful death on the cross and with Thy precious blood didst redeem me from all sins, from death, and from the power of the devil, I pray Thee, give me the assurance of this redemption through Thy Word, govern my heart with Thy Holy Spirit, preserve me with Thy divine love, and hide me this day, both soul and body, in Thy holy wounds. Wash me clean from all my sins, teach me to live a life of good works, and finally lead me from this world of sorrows to Thine eternal joy and glory, Thou most faithful Savior, Jesus Christ, mine only Comfort, Hope, and Life. Amen.

EVENING PRAYER

In the name of God the Father, Son, and Holy Ghost. Amen.

I thank Thee, my heavenly Father, through Jesus Christ, Thy dear Son, that Thou hast graciously kept me this day; and I pray Thee that Thou wouldst forgive me all my sins where I have done wrong, and graciously keep me this night. For into Thy hands I commend myself, my body and soul, and all things. Let Thy holy angel be with me that the wicked Foe may have no power over me. Amen.

O Lord Jesus Christ, Thou patient Lamb of God, Thou holy Sacrificial Offering for all my sins, and not for mine only, but for the sins of the whole world, I most heartily thank Thee that Thou hast graciously kept both my body and soul under Thy protecting care this day; and I pray Thee that Thou wouldst graciously pardon and forgive all the sins which I have committed this day, both through the weakness of my old evil nature and the temptations of the Evil Spirit, all of which sorely oppress my heart and conscience. Cover me this night with the wings of Thy grace and grant that my body may sleep in safety while my soul watches for Thy glorious coming to Judgment, ready to enter Thy blessed Kingdom of Glory. Grant this, O Lord, for the sake of Thy suffering and death. Amen.

BEFORE MEALS

The eyes of all wait upon Thee, O Lord, and Thou givest them their meat in due season; Thou openest Thine hand and satisfiest the desire of every living thing. Amen.

Lord God, heavenly Father, bless us and these Thy gifts which we receive from Thy bountiful goodness; through Jesus Christ, our Lord. Amen.

AFTER MEALS

Oh, give thanks unto the Lord, for He is good; for His mercy endureth forever. He giveth food to all flesh: He giveth to the beast his food and to the young ravens which cry. He delighteth not in the strength of the horse. He taketh not pleasure in the legs of a man. The Lord taketh pleasure in them that fear Him, in those that hope in His mercy. Amen.

We thank Thee, Lord God, heavenly Father, through Jesus Christ, our Lord, for all Thy benefits, who livest and reignest forever and ever. Amen.

PRAYER BEFORE RECEIVING THE SACRAMENT

O God, who desirest not the death of a sinner, but rather that he turn from his evil way and live, I come to Thee although I have sinned and deserve only Thy wrath. But I flee to Thy mercy in Christ Jesus, my Lord, who gave His body and His blood for my redemption. Lord, grant that I may ever thus believe and never waver. Grant that in such faith I may worthily go to Thine altar to receive the very body and the true blood which Thy Son has given for my salvation, that I may duly praise, laud, and honor Thy love and Thy mercy all the days of my life. Hear me for the sake of Jesus Christ, Thy Son, my Redeemer and Savior. Amen.

PRAYER AFTER RECEIVING THE SACRAMENT

Thanks and praise to Thee, almighty, everlasting God, heavenly Father, for this Thy divine tenderness and love that Thou hast again given me grace to receive the holy body and the precious blood of Thine only Son, Jesus Christ, my Lord. I humbly beseech Thee, fill me with the power of Thy Holy Spirit that through this Sacrament which I have received with the mouth of my body I by faith may evermore retain the treasures of Thy grace imparted to me in this Sacrament, even the forgiveness of sins, oneness with Christ, and eternal life. Let this Thy grace enable me steadfastly to walk in the footsteps of my Lord Jesus Christ, nothing doubting that at the last Thou wilt give unto me and to all that bear the cross for His sake the crown of everlasting life. Hear me, heavenly Father, for the sake of Jesus Christ, my Lord and Savior. Amen.

FOR THE SICK AND THE DYING

O Lord Jesus, who hast made it my lot to bear the cross, give me also an obedient and submissive heart that I may willingly take Thy yoke upon me and follow Thee in every affliction. Amen.

Almighty God, who forgivest all our iniquities and healest all our diseases, who hast proclaimed Thy name to be the Lord that healeth us and hast sent Thy well-beloved Son to bear our sicknesses, look in mercy upon Thine unworthy servants, pardon and forgive us our transgressions, and of Thy lovingkindness remove the plague of sickness with which Thou hast visited us. This we ask according to Thy will, through Jesus Christ, our Lord. Amen.

O Christ, Thou Son of God, who didst bear for *him* the pain of the cross and hast died for *his* sins, have mercy upon *him*, forgive *him* all *his* trespasses, and suffer not *his* faith to fail. Amen.

O God the Holy Ghost, our true Comforter in all distress, uphold *him* in patience and right prayer, sanctify *him* with full assurance, and forsake *him* not in the last extremity. Lead *him* from this world of sorrow to the heavenly home. Amen.

Almighty, everlasting, and most merciful God, Thou who dost summon and take us out of this sinful and corrupt world to Thyself through death that we may not perish by continual sinning, but pass through death to life eternal, help us, we beseech Thee, to know and believe this with our whole heart, to the end that we may rejoice in our departure and at Thy call cheerfully enter into Thine everlasting kingdom; through Jesus Christ, Thy Son, our Lord. Amen.

Depart in peace, thou ransomed soul, in the name of God the Father Almighty, who created thee; in the name of Jesus Christ, the Son of the living God, who redeemed thee; in the name of the Holy Ghost, who sanctified thee. Enter now into Mount Zion, the city of the living God, the heavenly Jerusalem, to the innumerable company of angels, and to the general assembly and Church of the first-born which are written in heaven. The Lord preserve thy going out and thy coming in from this time forth and even forevermore. Amen.

Canticles

BENEDICITE OMNIA OPERA
(The Song of the Three Children)

O all ye works of the Lord, bless ye the Lord: praise Him and magnify Him forever.

O ye angels of the Lord, bless ye the Lord: O ye heavens, bless ye the Lord.

O ye waters that are above the firmament, bless ye the Lord: O ye powers of the Lord, bless ye the Lord.

O ye sun and moon, bless ye the Lord: O ye stars of heaven, bless ye the Lord.

O ye showers and dew, bless ye the Lord: O ye winds of God, bless ye the Lord.

O ye fire and heat, bless ye the Lord: O ye winter and summer, bless ye the Lord.

O ye dews and frost, bless ye the Lord: O ye frost and cold, bless ye the Lord.

O ye ice and snow, bless ye the Lord: O ye nights and days, bless ye the Lord.

O ye light and darkness, bless ye the Lord: O ye lightnings and clouds, bless ye the Lord.

Oh, let the earth bless the Lord: yea, let it praise Him and magnify Him forever.

O ye mountains and hills, bless ye the Lord: O all ye green things upon the earth, bless ye the Lord.

O ye wells, bless ye the Lord: O ye seas and floods, bless ye the Lord.

O ye whales and all that move in the waters, bless ye the Lord: O all ye fowls of the air, bless ye the Lord.

O all ye beasts and cattle, bless ye the Lord: O ye children of men, bless ye the Lord.

Oh, let Israel bless the Lord: praise Him and magnify Him forever.

O ye priests of the Lord, bless ye the Lord: O ye servants of the Lord, bless ye the Lord.

O ye spirits and souls of the righteous, bless ye the Lord: O ye holy and humble men of heart, bless ye the Lord.

Bless we the Father and the Son and the Holy Ghost: let us praise Him and magnify Him forever.

CONFITEBOR TIBI

O Lord, 1 will praise Thee: though Thou wast angry with me, Thine anger is turned away, and Thou comfortedst me.

Behold, God is my Salvation: I will trust and not be afraid.

For the Lord Jehovah is my Strength and my Song: He also is become my Salvation.

Therefore with joy shall ye draw water: out of the wells of salvation.

Praise the Lord, call upon His name, declare His doings among the people: make mention that His name is exalted.

Sing unto the Lord, for He hath done excellent things: this is known in all the earth.

Cry out and shout, thou inhabitant of Zion: for great is the Holy One of Israel in the midst of Thee.

Glory be to the Father, etc.

EXULTAVIT COR MEUM

My heart rejoiceth in the Lord: mine horn is exalted in the Lord.

My mouth is enlarged over mine enemies: because I rejoice in Thy salvation.

There is none holy as the Lord, for there is none beside Thee: neither is there any Rock like our God.

Talk no more so exceedingly proudly: let not arrogancy come out of your mouth.

For the Lord is a God of knowledge: and by Him actions are weighed.

The bows of the mighty men are broken: and they that stumbled are girded with strength.

The Lord killeth and maketh alive: He bringeth down to the grave and bringeth up.

The Lord maketh poor and maketh rich: He bringeth low and lifteth up.

He raiseth up the poor out of the dust and lifteth up the beggar from the dunghill: to set them among princes and to make them inherit the throne of glory.

For the pillars of the earth are the Lord's: and He hath set the world upon them.

He will keep the feet of His saints, and the wicked shall be silent in darkness: for by strength shall no man prevail.

The adversaries of the Lord shall be broken to pieces: out of heaven shall He thunder upon them.

The Lord shall judge the ends of the earth: and He shall give strength unto His King and exalt the horn of His Anointed.

Glory be to the Father, etc.

CANTEMUS DOMINO

I will sing unto the Lord, for He hath triumphed gloriously: the horse and his rider hath He thrown into the sea.

The Lord is my Strength and Song: and He is become my Salvation.

He is my God, and I will prepare Him an habitation: my father's God, and I will exalt Him.

Thy right hand, O Lord, is become glorious in power: Thy right hand, O Lord, hath dashed in pieces the enemy.

Who is like unto Thee, O Lord, among the gods?: who is like Thee, glorious in holiness, fearful in praises, doing wonders?

Thou in mercy hast led forth the people which Thou hast redeemed: Thou hast guided them in Thy strength unto Thy holy habitation.

Thou shalt bring them in and plant them in the mountain of Thine inheritance: in the place, O Lord, which Thou hast made for Thee to dwell in, in the Sanctuary, O Lord, which Thy hands have established.

The Lord shall reign: forever and ever.

Glory be to the Father, etc.

DOMINE, AUDIVI

O Lord, I have heard Thy speech and was afraid: O Lord, revive Thy work in the midst of the years.

In the midst of the years make known: in wrath remember mercy.

God came from Teman: and the Holy One from Mount Paran.

His glory covered the heavens: and the earth was full of His praise.

His brightness was as the light; He had horns coming out of His hand: and there was the hiding of His power.

Before Him went the pestilence: and burning coals went forth at His feet.

He stood and measured the earth: He beheld and drove asunder the nations.

And the everlasting mountains were scattered, the perpetual hills did bow: His ways are everlasting.

Thou wentest forth for the salvation of Thy people: even for salvation with Thine Anointed.

Thou woundedst the head out of the house of the wicked: by discovering the foundation unto the neck.

I will rejoice in the Lord: I will joy in the God of my salvation.

The Lord is my Strength: and He will make me to walk upon mine high places.

Glory be to the Father, etc.

AUDITE, COELI

Give ear, O ye heavens, and I will speak: and hear, O earth, the words of my mouth.

My doctrine shall drop as the rain, my speech shall distill as the dew: as the small rain upon the tender herb and as the showers upon the grass.

Because I will publish the name of the Lord: ascribe ye greatness unto our God.

He is the Rock, His work is perfect: for all His ways are judgment.

A God of truth and without iniquity: just and right is He.

The Lord's portion is His people: Jacob is the lot of His inheritance.

For the Lord shall judge His people and repent Himself for His servants: when He seeth that their power is gone and there is none shut up or left.

And He shall say, I lift up My hand to heaven: and say, I live forever.

Rejoice, O ye nations, with His people: for He will avenge the blood of His servants.

He will render vengeance to His adversaries: and will be merciful unto His land and to His people.

Glory be to the Father, etc.

EGO DIXI

I said in the cutting off of my days, I shall go to the gates of the grave: I am deprived of the residue of my years.

I said, I shall not see the Lord, even the Lord, in the land of the living: I shall behold man no more with the inhabitants of the world.

Mine age is departed and is removed from me as a shepherd's tent: I have cut off like a weaver my life; from day even to night wilt Thou make an end of me.

I reckoned till morning that, as a lion, so will He break all my bones: from day even to night wilt Thou make an end of me.

Like a crane or a swallow, so did I chatter; I did mourn as a dove: mine eyes fail with looking upward. O Lord, I am oppressed; undertake for me.

What shall I say? He hath both spoken unto me and Himself hath done it: I shall go softly all my years in the bitterness of my soul.

O Lord, by these things men live, and in all these things is the life of my spirit: so wilt Thou recover me and make me to live.

Behold, for peace I had great bitterness, but Thou hast in love to my soul delivered it from the pit of corruption: for Thou hast cast all my sins behind Thy back.

For the grave cannot praise Thee, death cannot celebrate Thee: they that go down into the pit cannot hope for Thy truth.

The living, the living, he shall praise Thee, as I do this day: the father to the children shall make known Thy truth.

The Lord was ready to save me: therefore we will sing my songs to the stringed instruments all the days of our life in the house of the Lord.

Glory be to the Father, etc.

BEATI PAUPERES
(The Beatitudes)

Blessed are the poor in spirit: for theirs is the kingdom of heaven.

Blessed are they that mourn: for they shall be comforted.

Blessed are the meek: for they shall inherit the earth.

Blessed are they which do hunger and thirst after righteousness: for they shall be filled.

Blessed are the merciful: for they shall obtain mercy.

Blessed are the pure in heart: for they shall see God.

Blessed are the peacemakers: for they shall be called the children of God.

Blessed are they which are persecuted for righteousness' sake: for theirs is the kingdom of heaven.

Blessed are ye when men shall revile you and persecute you and shall say all manner of evil against you falsely for My sake: rejoice and be exceeding glad, for great is your reward in heaven.

Glory be to the Father, etc.

DIGNUS EST AGNUS

Worthy is the Lamb that was slain to receive power and riches and wisdom: and strength and honor and glory and blessing.

Blessing and honor and glory and power be unto Him that sitteth upon the throne: and unto the Lamb forever and ever.

Great and marvelous are Thy works, Lord God Almighty: just and true are Thy ways, Thou King of saints.

Who shall not fear Thee, O Lord, and glorify Thy name?: for Thou only art holy.

Praise our God, all ye His servants: and ye that fear Him, both small and great.

Alleluia! for the Lord God Omnipotent reigneth: Alleluia, Alleluia! Amen.

Psalms

Psalm 1. Beatus vir

Blessed is the man that walketh not in the counsel of the ungodly: nor standeth in the way of sinners nor sitteth in the seat of the scornful;

But his delight is in the Law of the Lord: and in His Law doth he meditate day and night.

And he shall be like a tree planted by the rivers of water, that bringeth forth his fruit in his season: His leaf also shall not wither; and whatsoever he doeth shall prosper.

The ungodly are not so: but are like the chaff which the wind driveth away.

Therefore the ungodly shall not stand in the Judgment: nor sinners in the congregation of the righteous.

For the Lord knoweth the way of the righteous: but the way of the ungodly shall perish.

Psalm 2. Quare fremuerunt gentes

Why do the heathen rage: and the people imagine a vain thing?

The kings of the earth set themselves, and the rulers take counsel together: against the Lord and against His Anointed, saying,

Let us break their bands asunder: and cast away their cords from us.

He that sitteth in the heavens shall laugh: the Lord shall have them in derision.

Then shall He speak unto them in His wrath: and vex them in His sore displeasure.

Yet have I set My King: upon My holy hill of Zion.

I will declare the decree: the Lord hath said unto Me, Thou art My Son; this day have I begotten Thee.

Ask of Me, and I shall give Thee the heathen for Thine inheritance: and the uttermost parts of the earth for Thy possession.

Thou shalt break them with a rod of iron: thou shalt dash them in pieces like a potter's vessel.

Be wise now therefore, O ye kings: be instructed, ye judges of the earth.

Serve the Lord with fear: and rejoice with trembling.

Kiss the Son lest He be angry and ye perish from the way when His wrath is kindled but a little: blessed are all they that put their trust in Him.

Psalm 4. Cum invocarem, exaudivit

Hear me when I call, O God of my righteousness: Thou hast enlarged me when I was in distress; have mercy upon me and hear my prayer.

O ye sons of men, how long will ye turn my glory into shame? How long will ye love vanity and seek after leasing?

But know that the Lord hath set apart him that is godly for himself: the Lord will hear when I call unto Him.

Stand in awe and sin not: commune with your own heart upon your bed and be still.

Offer the sacrifices of righteousness: and put your trust in the Lord.

There be many that say, Who will show us any good?: Lord, lift Thou up the light of Thy countenance upon us.

Thou hast put gladness in my heart: more than in the time that their corn and their wine increased.

I will both lay me down in peace and sleep: for Thou, Lord, only makest me dwell in safety.

Psalm 5. Verba mea auribus

Give ear to my words, O Lord: consider my meditation.

Hearken unto the voice of my cry, my King and my God: for unto Thee will I pray.

My voice shalt Thou hear in the morning, O Lord: in the morning will I direct my prayer unto Thee and will look up.

For Thou art not a God that hath pleasure in wickedness: neither shall evil dwell with Thee.

The foolish shall not stand in Thy sight: Thou hatest all workers of iniquity.

Thou shalt destroy them that speak leasing: the Lord will abhor the bloody and deceitful man.

But as for me, I will come into Thy house in the multitude of Thy mercy: and in Thy fear will I worship toward Thy holy Temple.

Lead me, O Lord, in Thy righteousness because of mine enemies: make Thy way straight before my face.

For there is no faithfulness in their mouth; their inward part is very wickedness: their throat is an open sepulcher; they flatter with their tongue.

Destroy Thou them, O God; let them fall by their own counsels: cast them out in the multitude of their transgressions; for they have rebelled against Thee.

But let all those that put their trust

in Thee rejoice; let them ever shout for joy because Thou defendest them: let them also that love Thy name be joyful in Thee.

For Thou, LORD, wilt bless the righteous: with favor wilt Thou compass him as with a shield.

Psalm 6. Domine, ne in furore

O LORD, rebuke me not in Thine anger: neither chasten me in Thy hot displeasure.

Have mercy upon me, O LORD; for I am weak: O LORD, heal me; for my bones are vexed.

My soul is also sore vexed: but Thou, O LORD, how long?

Return, O LORD, deliver my soul: oh, save me for Thy mercy's sake.

For in death there is no remembrance of Thee: in the grave, who shall give Thee thanks?

I am weary with my groaning; all the night make I my bed to swim: I water my couch with my tears.

Mine eye is consumed because of grief: it waxeth old because of all mine enemies.

Depart from me, all ye workers of iniquity: for the LORD hath heard the voice of my weeping.

The LORD hath heard my supplication: the LORD will receive my prayer.

Let all mine enemies be ashamed and sore vexed: let them return and be ashamed suddenly.

Psalm 8. Domine, Dominus noster

O LORD, our Lord, how excellent is Thy name in all the earth: who hast set Thy glory above the heavens.

Out of the mouth of babes and sucklings hast Thou ordained strength because of Thine enemies: that Thou mightest still the enemy and the avenger.

When I consider Thy heavens, the work of Thy fingers: the moon and the stars which Thou hast ordained,

What is man that Thou art mindful of him: and the Son of Man that Thou visitest Him?

For Thou hast made Him a little lower than the angels: and hast crowned Him with glory and honor.

Thou madest Him to have dominion over the works of Thy hands: Thou hast put all things under His feet,

All sheep and oxen: yea, and the beasts of the field;

The fowl of the air and the fish of the sea: and whatsoever passeth through the paths of the seas.

O LORD, our Lord: how excellent is Thy name in all the earth!

Psalm 13
Usque quo, Domine, oblivisceris?

How long wilt Thou forget me, O LORD? Forever?: How long wilt Thou hide Thy face from me?

How long shall I take counsel in my soul, having sorrow in my heart daily?: How long shall mine enemy be exalted over me?

Consider and hear me, O LORD, my God: lighten mine eyes, lest I sleep the sleep of death,

Lest mine enemy say, I have prevailed against him: and those that trouble me rejoice when I am moved.

But I have trusted in Thy mercy: my heart shall rejoice in Thy salvation.

I will sing unto the LORD: because He hath dealt bountifully with me.

Psalm 14. Dixit insipiens in corde suo

The fool hath said in his heart, There is no God: They are corrupt; they have done abominable works; there is none that doeth good.

The LORD looked down from heaven upon the children of men: to see if there were any that did understand and seek God.

They are all gone aside, they are all together become filthy: there is none that doeth good, no, not one.

Have all the workers of iniquity no knowledge?: who eat up My people as they eat bread and call not upon the LORD.

There were they in great fear: for God is in the generation of the righteous.

Ye have shamed the counsel of the poor: because the LORD is his Refuge.

Oh, that the salvation of Israel were come out of Zion! When the LORD bringeth back the captivity of His people: Jacob shall rejoice and Israel shall be glad.

Psalm 15. Domine, quis habitabit?

LORD, who shall abide in Thy tabernacle?: Who shall dwell in Thy holy hill?

He that walketh uprightly and worketh righteousness: and speaketh the truth in his heart.

He that backbiteth not with his tongue nor doeth evil to his neighbor: nor taketh up a reproach against his neighbor.

In whose eyes a vile person is contemned; but he honoreth them that fear the LORD: He that sweareth to his own hurt and changeth not;

He that putteth not out his money to usury nor taketh reward against the innocent: he that doeth these things shall never be moved.

Psalm 16. Conserva me, Domine

Preserve Me, O God: for in Thee do I put My trust.

O My soul, Thou hast said unto the LORD, Thou art My Lord: My goodness extendeth not to Thee,

But to the saints that are in the earth and to the excellent: in whom is all My delight.

Their sorrows shall be multiplied that hasten after another god: Their drinkofferings of blood will I not offer nor take up their names into My lips.

The LORD is the Portion of Mine inheritance and of My cup: Thou maintainest My lot.

The lines are fallen unto Me in pleasant places: yea, I have a goodly heritage.

I will bless the LORD, who hath given Me counsel: My reins also instruct Me in the night seasons.

I have set the LORD always before Me: because He is at My right hand, I shall not be moved.

Therefore My heart is glad, and My glory rejoiceth: My flesh also shall rest in hope.

For Thou wilt not leave My soul in hell: neither wilt Thou suffer Thine Holy One to see corruption.

Thou wilt show Me the path of life: in Thy presence is fullness of joy; at Thy right hand there are pleasures forevermore.

Psalm 18. Diligam Te, Domine

I will love Thee: O LORD, my Strength.

The LORD is my Rock and my Fortress and my Deliverer: my God, my Strength, in whom I will trust; my Buckler, and the Horn of my salvation and my high Tower.

I will call upon the LORD, who is worthy to be praised: so shall I be saved from mine enemies.

The sorrows of death compassed me: and the floods of ungodly men made me afraid.

The sorrows of hell compassed me about: the snares of death prevented me.

In my distress I called upon the LORD and cried unto my God: He heard my voice out of His Temple, and my cry came before Him, even into His Ears.

Then the earth shook and trembled: the foundations also of the hills moved and were shaken because He was wroth.

There went up a smoke out of His nostrils, and fire out of His mouth devoured: coals were kindled by it.

He bowed the heavens also and came down: and darkness was under His feet.

And He rode upon a cherub and did fly: yea, He did fly upon the wings of the wind.

He made darkness His secret place: His pavilion round about Him were dark waters and thick clouds of the skies.

At the brightness that was before Him His thick clouds passed: hailstones and coals of fire.

The LORD also thundered in the heavens, and the Highest gave His voice: hailstones and coals of fire.

Yea, He sent out His arrows and scattered them: and He shot out lightnings and discomfited them.

Then the channels of waters were seen, and the foundations of the world were discovered: at Thy rebuke, O LORD, at the blast of the breath of Thy nostrils.

He sent from above, He took me: He drew me out of many waters.

He delivered me from my strong enemy and from them which hated me: for they were too strong for me.

They prevented me in the day of my calamity: but the LORD was my Stay.

He brought me forth also into a large place: He delivered me because He delighted in me.

The LORD rewarded me according to my righteousness: according to the cleanness of my hands hath He recompensed me.

For I have kept the ways of the LORD: and have not wickedly departed from my God.

For all His judgments were before me: and I did not put away His statutes from me.

I was also upright before Him: and I kept myself from mine iniquity.

Therefore hath the LORD recompensed me according to my righteousness: according to the cleanness of my hands in His eyesight.

With the merciful Thou wilt show Thyself merciful: with an upright man Thou wilt show Thyself upright;

With the pure Thou wilt show Thyself pure: and with the froward Thou wilt show Thyself froward.

For Thou wilt save the afflicted people: but wilt bring down high looks.

For Thou wilt light my candle: the LORD, my God, will enlighten my darkness.

For by Thee I have run through a troop: and by my God have I leaped over a wall.

As for God, His way is perfect: the Word of the LORD is tried; He is a Buckler to all those that trust in Him.

For who is God save the LORD?: Or who is a rock save our God?

It is God that girdeth me with strength: and maketh my way perfect.

He maketh my feet like hinds' feet: and setteth me upon my high places.

He teacheth my hands to war: so that a bow of steel is broken by mine arms.

Thou hast also given me the shield of Thy salvation: and Thy right hand hath holden me up, and Thy gentleness hath made me great.

Thou hast enlarged my steps under me: that my feet did not slip.

I have pursued mine enemies and overtaken them: neither did I turn again till they were consumed.

I have wounded them that they were not able to rise: they are fallen under my feet.

For Thou hast girded me with strength unto the battle: Thou hast subdued under me those that rose up against me.

Thou hast also given me the necks of mine enemies: that I might destroy them that hate me.

They cried, but there was none to save them: even unto the LORD, but He answered them not.

Then did I beat them small as the dust before the wind: I did cast them out as the dirt in the streets.

Thou hast delivered me from the strivings of the people; and Thou hast made me the head of the heathen: a people whom I have not known shall serve me.

As soon as they hear of me, they shall obey me: the strangers shall submit themselves unto me.

The strangers shall fade away: and be afraid out of their close places.

The LORD liveth, and blessed be my Rock: and let the God of my salvation be exalted.

It is God that avengeth me: and subdueth the people under me.

He delivereth me from mine enemies; yea, Thou liftest me up above those that rise up against me: Thou hast delivered me from the violent man.

Therefore will I give thanks unto Thee, O LORD, among the heathen: and sing praises unto Thy name.

Great deliverance giveth He to His king: and showeth mercy to His anointed, to David, and to his seed forevermore.

Psalm 19. Coeli enarrant

The heavens declare the glory of God: and the firmament showeth His handiwork.

Day unto day uttereth speech: and night unto night showeth knowledge.

There is no speech nor language: where their voice is not heard.

Their line is gone out through all the earth: and their words to the end of the world.

In them hath He set a tabernacle for the sun: which is as a bridegroom coming out of his chamber and rejoiceth as a strong man to run a race.

His going forth is from the end of the heaven and his circuit unto the ends of it: and there is nothing hid from the heat thereof.

The Law of the LORD is perfect, converting the soul: the testimony of the LORD is sure, making wise the simple.

The statutes of the LORD are right, rejoicing the heart: the commandment of the LORD is pure, enlightening the eyes.

The fear of the LORD is clean, enduring forever: the judgments of the LORD are true and righteous altogether.

More to be desired are they than gold, yea, than much fine gold: sweeter also than honey and the honeycomb.

Moreover, by them is Thy servant warned: and in keeping of them there is great reward.

Who can understand his errors?: Cleanse Thou me from secret faults.

Keep back Thy servant also from presumptuous sins; let them not have dominion over me: then shall I be upright, and I shall be innocent from the great transgression.

Let the words of my mouth and the meditation of my heart be acceptable in Thy sight: O LORD, my Strength and my Redeemer.

Psalm 20. Exaudiat te Dominus

The LORD hear thee in the day of trouble: the name of the God of Jacob defend thee;

Send thee help from the Sanctuary: and strengthen thee out of Zion;

Remember all thy offerings: and accept thy burnt sacrifice;

Grant thee according to thine own heart: and fulfill all thy counsel.

We will rejoice in thy salvation, and in the name of our God we will set up our banners: the LORD fulfill all thy petitions.

Now know I that the LORD saveth His anointed: He will hear him from His holy heaven with the saving strength of His right hand.

Some trust in chariots and some in horses: but we will remember the name of the LORD, our God.

They are brought down and fallen: but we are risen and stand upright.

Save, LORD: let the King hear us when we call.

Psalm 21. Domine, in virtute tua

The king shall joy in Thy strength, O Lord: and in Thy salvation how greatly shall he rejoice!

Thou hast given him his heart's desire: and hast not witholden the request of his lips.

For Thou preventest him with the blessings of goodness: Thou settest a crown of pure gold on his head.

He asked life of Thee, and Thou gavest it him: even length of days forever and ever.

His glory is great in Thy salvation: honor and majesty hast Thou laid upon him.

For Thou hast made him most blessed forever: Thou hast made him exceeding glad with Thy countenance.

For the king trusteth in the Lord: and through the mercy of the Most High he shall not be moved.

Thine hand shall find out all Thine enemies: Thy right hand shall find out those that hate Thee.

Thou shalt make them as a fiery oven in the time of Thine anger: the Lord shall swallow them up in His wrath, and the fire shall devour them.

Their fruit shalt Thou destroy from the earth: and their seed from among the children of men.

For they intended evil against Thee: they imagined a mischievous device, which they are not able to perform.

Therefore shalt Thou make them turn their back: when Thou shalt make ready Thine arrows upon Thy strings against the face of them.

Be Thou exalted, Lord, in Thine own strength: so will we sing and praise Thy power.

Psalm 22. Deus, Deus meus

My God, My God, why hast Thou forsaken Me?: Why art Thou so far from helping Me and from the words of My roaring?

O My God, I cry in the daytime, but Thou hearest not: and in the night season, and am not silent.

But Thou art holy: O Thou that inhabitest the praises of Israel.

Our fathers trusted in Thee: they trusted, and Thou didst deliver them.

They cried unto Thee and were delivered: they trusted in Thee and were not confounded.

But I am a worm and no man: a reproach of men and despised of the people.

All they that see Me laugh Me to scorn: they shoot out the lip, they shake the head, saying,

He trusted on the Lord that He would deliver Him: let Him deliver Him, seeing He delighted in Him.

But Thou art He that took Me out of the womb: Thou didst make Me hope when I was upon My mother's breasts.

I was cast upon Thee from the womb: Thou art My God from My mother's belly.

Be not far from Me; for trouble is near: for there is none to help.

Many bulls have compassed Me: strong bulls of Bashan have beset Me round.

They gaped upon Me with their mouths: as a ravening and a roaring lion.

I am poured out like water, and all My bones are out of joint: My heart is like wax; it is melted in the midst of My bowels.

My strength is dried up like a potsherd; and My tongue cleaveth to My jaws: and Thou hast brought Me into the dust of death.

For dogs have compassed Me; the assembly of the wicked have inclosed Me: they pierced My hands and My feet.

I may tell all My bones: they look and stare upon Me.

They part My garments among them: and cast lots upon My vesture.

But be not Thou far from Me, O Lord: O My Strength, haste Thee to help Me.

Deliver My soul from the sword: My darling from the power of the dog.

Save Me from the lion's mouth: for Thou hast heard Me from the horns of the unicorns.

I will declare Thy name unto My brethren: in the midst of the congregation will I praise Thee.

Ye that fear the Lord, praise Him; all ye, the seed of Jacob, glorify Him: and fear Him, all ye, the seed of Israel.

For He hath not despised nor abhorred the affliction of the afflicted: neither hath He hid His face from Him; but when He cried unto Him, He heard.

My praise shall be of Thee in the great congregation: I will pay My vows before them that fear Him.

The meek shall eat and be satisfied: they shall praise the Lord that seek Him; your heart shall live forever.

All the ends of the world shall remember and turn unto the Lord: and all the kindreds of the nations shall worship before Thee.

For the kingdom is the Lord's: and He is the Governor among the nations.

All they that be fat upon the earth shall eat and worship: All they that go down to the dust shall bow before Him; and none can keep alive his own soul.

A seed shall serve Him: it shall be accounted to the LORD for a generation.

They shall come and shall declare His righteousness unto a people that shall be born: that He hath done this.

Psalm 23. Dominus regit me

The LORD is my Shepherd: I shall not want.

He maketh me to lie down in green pastures: He leadeth me beside the still waters.

He restoreth my soul: He leadeth me in the paths of righteousness for His name's sake.

Yea, though I walk through the valley of the shadow of death, I will fear no evil: for Thou art with me; Thy rod and Thy staff, they comfort me.

Thou preparest a table before me in the presence of mine enemies: Thou anointest my head with oil; my cup runneth over.

Surely goodness and mercy shall follow me all the days of my life: and I will dwell in the house of the LORD forever.

Psalm 24. Domini est terra

The earth is the LORD'S and the fullness thereof: the world and they that dwell therein.

For He hath founded it upon the seas: and established it upon the floods.

Who shall ascend into the hill of the LORD: or who shall stand in His Holy Place?

He that hath clean hands and a pure heart: who hath not lifted up his soul unto vanity nor sworn deceitfully.

He shall receive the blessing from the LORD: and righteousness from the God of his salvation.

This is the generation of them that seek Him: that seek thy face, O Jacob.

Lift up your heads, O ye gates; and be ye lift up, ye everlasting doors: and the King of Glory shall come in.

Who is this King of Glory?: The LORD strong and mighty, the LORD mighty in battle.

Lift up your heads, O ye gates; even lift them up, ye everlasting doors: and the King of Glory shall come in.

Who is this King of Glory?: The LORD of hosts, He is the King of Glory.

Psalm 25. Ad te, Domine, levavi

Unto Thee, O LORD: do I lift up my soul.

O my God, I trust in Thee: let me not be ashamed, let not mine enemies triumph over me.

Yea, let none that wait on Thee be ashamed: let them be ashamed which transgress without cause.

Show me Thy ways, O LORD: teach me Thy paths.

Lead me in Thy truth and teach me: for Thou art the God of my salvation; on Thee do I wait all the day.

Remember, O LORD, Thy tender mercies and Thy loving-kindnesses: for they have been ever of old.

Remember not the sins of my youth nor my transgressions: according to Thy mercy remember Thou me for Thy goodness' sake, O LORD.

Good and upright is the LORD: therefore will He teach sinners in the way.

The meek will He guide in judgment: and the meek will He teach His way.

All the paths of the LORD are mercy and truth: unto such as keep His covenant and His testimonies.

For Thy name's sake, O LORD, pardon mine iniquity: for it is great.

What man is he that feareth the LORD?: Him shall He teach in the way that he shall choose.

His soul shall dwell at ease: and his seed shall inherit the earth.

The secret of the LORD is with them that fear Him: and He will show them His covenant.

Mine eyes are ever toward the LORD: for He shall pluck my feet out of the net.

Turn Thee unto me and have mercy upon me: for I am desolate and afflicted.

The troubles of my heart are enlarged: oh, bring Thou me out of my distresses.

Look upon mine affliction and my pain: and forgive all my sins.

Consider mine enemies, for they are many: and they hate me with cruel hatred.

Oh, keep my soul and deliver me: let me not be ashamed; for I put my trust in Thee.

Let integrity and uprightness preserve me: for I wait on Thee.

Redeem Israel, O God: out of all his troubles.

Psalm 26. Iudica me, Domine

Judge me, O LORD; for I have walked in mine integrity: I have trusted also in the LORD; therefore I shall not slide.

Examine me, O LORD, and prove me: try my reins and my heart.

For Thy loving-kindness is before mine eyes: and I have walked in Thy truth.

I have not sat with vain persons: neither will I go in with dissemblers.

I have hated the congregation of evil-doers: and will not sit with the wicked.

I will wash mine hands in innocency: so will I compass Thine altar, O Lord,

That I may publish with the voice of thanksgiving: and tell of all Thy wondrous works.

Lord, I have loved the habitation of Thy house: and the place where Thine honor dwelleth.

Gather not my soul with sinners: nor my life with bloody men;

In whose hands is mischief: and their right hand is full of bribes.

But as for me, I will walk in mine integrity: redeem me and be merciful unto me.

My foot standeth in an even place: in the congregations will I bless the Lord.

Psalm 27. Dominus illuminatio mea

The Lord is my Light and my Salvation; whom shall I fear?: The Lord is the Strength of my life; of whom shall I be afraid?

When the wicked, even mine enemies and my foes, came upon me to eat up my flesh: they stumbled and fell.

Though an host should encamp against me, my heart shall not fear: though war should rise against me, in this will I be confident.

One thing have I desired of the Lord, that will I seek after: that I may dwell in the house of the Lord all the days of my life to behold the beauty of the Lord and to inquire in His Temple.

For in the time of trouble He shall hide me in His pavilion: in the secret of His Tabernacle shall He hide me; He shall set me up upon a rock.

And now shall mine head be lifted up above mine enemies round about me: Therefore will I offer in His Tabernacle sacrifices of joy; I will sing, yea, I will sing praises unto the Lord.

Hear, O Lord, when I cry with my voice: have mercy also upon me and answer me.

When Thou saidst, Seek ye My face: my heart said unto Thee, Thy face, Lord, will I seek.

Hide not Thy face far from me; put not Thy servant away in anger: Thou hast been my Help; leave me not, neither forsake me, O God of my salvation.

When my father and my mother forsake me: then the Lord will take me up.

Teach me Thy way, O Lord: and lead me in a plain path because of mine enemies.

Deliver me not over unto the will of mine enemies: for false witnesses are risen up against me and such as breathe out cruelty.

I had fainted: unless I had believed to see the goodness of the Lord in the land of the living.

Wait on the Lord; be of good courage, and He shall strengthen thine heart: wait, I say, on the Lord.

Psalm 28. Ad Te, Domine, clamabo

Unto Thee will I cry, O Lord, my Rock. Be not silent to me: lest, if Thou be silent to me, I become like them that go down into the pit.

Hear the voice of my supplications when I cry unto Thee: when I lift up my hands toward Thy holy oracle.

Draw me not away with the wicked and with the workers of iniquity: which speak peace to their neighbors, but mischief is in their hearts.

Give them according to their deeds: and according to the wickedness of their endeavors: Give them after the work of their hands; render to them their desert.

Because they regard not the works of the Lord nor the operation of His hands: He shall destroy them and not build them up.

Blessed be the Lord: because He hath heard the voice of my supplications.

The Lord is my Strength and my Shield; my heart trusted in Him, and I am helped: therefore my heart greatly rejoiceth; and with my song will I praise Him.

The Lord is their Strength: and He is the saving Strength of His anointed.

Save Thy people and bless Thine inheritance: feed them also and lift them up forever.

Psalm 30. Exaltabo Te, Domine

I will extol Thee, O Lord; for Thou hast lifted me up: and hast not made my foes to rejoice over me.

O Lord, my God, I cried unto Thee: and Thou hast healed me.

O Lord, Thou hast brought up my soul from the grave: Thou hast kept me alive that I should not go down to the pit.

Sing unto the Lord, O ye saints of His: and give thanks at the remembrance of His holiness.

For His anger endureth but a moment; in His favor is life: weeping may endure for a night, but joy cometh in the morning.

And in my prosperity I said: I shall never be moved.

Lord, by Thy favor Thou hast made my mountain to stand strong: Thou didst hide Thy face, and I was troubled.

I cried to Thee, O Lord: and unto the Lord I made supplication.

What profit is there in my blood when I go down to the pit?: Shall the dust praise Thee? Shall it declare Thy truth?

Hear, O Lord, and have mercy upon me: Lord, be Thou my Helper.

Thou hast turned for me my mourning into dancing: Thou hast put off my sackcloth and girded me with gladness,

To the end that my glory may sing praise to Thee and not be silent: O Lord, my God, I will give thanks unto Thee forever.

Psalm 31. In Te, Domine, speravi

In Thee, O Lord, do I put my trust; let me never be ashamed: deliver me in Thy righteousness.

Bow down Thine ear to me; deliver me speedily: be Thou my strong Rock, for an house of defense to save me.

For Thou art my Rock and my Fortress; therefore for Thy name's sake lead me and guide me.

Pull me out of the net that they have laid privily for me: for Thou art my Strength.

Into Thine hand I commit my spirit: Thou hast redeemed me, O Lord God of truth.

I have hated them that regard lying vanities: but I trust in the Lord.

I will be glad and rejoice in Thy mercy: for Thou hast considered my trouble; Thou hast known my soul in adversities

And hast not shut me up into the hand of the enemy: Thou hast set my feet in a large room.

Have mercy upon me, O Lord, for I am in trouble: mine eye is consumed with grief, yea, my soul and my belly.

For my life is spent with grief and my years with sighing: my strength faileth because of mine iniquity, and my bones are consumed.

I was a reproach among all mine enemies, but especially among my neighbors, and a fear to mine acquaintance: they that did see me without fled from me.

I am forgotten as a dead man out of mind: I am like a broken vessel.

For I have heard the slander of many; fear was on every side: while they took counsel together against me, they devised to take away my life.

But I trusted in Thee, O Lord: I said, Thou art my God.

My times are in Thy hand: deliver me from the hand of mine enemies and from them that persecute me.

Make Thy face to shine upon Thy servant: save me for Thy mercies' sake.

Let me not be ashamed, O Lord; for I have called upon Thee: let the wicked be ashamed, and let them be silent in the grave.

Let the lying lips be put to silence: which speak grievous things proudly and contemptuously against the righteous.

Oh, how great is Thy goodness which Thou hast laid up for them that fear Thee: which Thou hast wrought for them that trust in Thee before the sons of men!

Thou shalt hide them in the secret of Thy presence from the pride of man: Thou shalt keep them secretly in a pavilion from the strife of tongues.

Blessed be the Lord: for He hath showed me His marvelous kindness in a strong city.

For I said in my haste, I am cut off from before Thine eyes: nevertheless Thou heardest the voice of my supplications when I cried unto Thee.

Oh, love the Lord, all ye His saints: for the Lord preserveth the faithful and plentifully rewardeth the proud doer.

Be of good courage, and He shall strengthen your heart: all ye that hope in the Lord.

Psalm 32. Beati, quorum

Blessed is he whose transgression is forgiven: whose sin is covered.

Blessed is the man unto whom the Lord imputeth not iniquity: and in whose spirit there is no guile.

When I kept silence: my bones waxed old through my roaring all the day long.

For day and night Thy hand was heavy upon me: my moisture is turned into the drought of summer.

I acknowledged my sin unto Thee, and mine iniquity have I not hid: I said, I will confess my transgressions unto the Lord; and Thou forgavest the iniquity of my sin.

For this shall everyone that is godly pray unto Thee in a time when Thou mayest be found: surely in the floods of great waters they shall not come nigh unto him.

Thou art my Hiding Place; Thou shalt preserve me from trouble: Thou shalt compass me about with songs of deliverance.

I will instruct thee and teach thee in the way which thou shalt go: I will guide thee with Mine eye.

Be ye not as the horse or as the mule, which have no understanding: whose mouth must be held in with bit and bridle lest they come near unto thee.

Many sorrows shall be to the wicked: but he that trusteth in the Lord, mercy shall compass him about.

Be glad in the Lord and rejoice, ye righteous: and shout for joy, all ye that are upright in heart.

Psalm 33. Exultate, iusti, in Domino

Rejoice in the Lord, O ye righteous: for praise is comely for the upright.

Praise the Lord with harp: sing unto Him with the psaltery and an instrument of ten strings.

Sing unto Him a new song: play skillfully with a loud noise.

For the Word of the Lord is right: and all His works are done in truth.

He loveth righteousness and judgment: the earth is full of the goodness of the Lord.

By the Word of the Lord were the heavens made: and all the host of them by the Breath of His mouth.

He gathereth the waters of the sea together as a heap: He layeth up the depth in storehouses.

Let all the earth fear the Lord: let all the inhabitants of the world stand in awe of Him.

For He spake, and it was done: He commanded, and it stood fast.

The Lord bringeth the counsel of the heathen to naught: He maketh the devices of the people of none effect.

The counsel of the Lord standeth forever: the thoughts of His heart to all generations.

Blessed is the nation whose God is the Lord: and the people whom He hath chosen for His own inheritance.

The Lord looketh from heaven: He beholdeth all the sons of men.

From the place of His habitation He looketh: upon all the inhabitants of the earth.

He fashioneth their hearts alike: He considereth all their works.

There is no king saved by the multitude of a host: a mighty man is not delivered by much strength.

An horse is a vain thing for safety: neither shall he deliver any by his great strength.

Behold, the eye of the Lord is upon them that fear Him: upon them that hope in His mercy.

To deliver their soul from death: and to keep them alive in famine.

Our soul waiteth for the Lord: He is our Help and our Shield.

For our heart shall rejoice in Him: because we have trusted in His holy name.

Let Thy mercy, O Lord, be upon us: according as we hope in Thee.

Psalm 34. Benedicam Dominum

I will bless the Lord at all times: His praise shall continually be in my mouth.

My soul shall make her boast in the Lord: the humble shall hear thereof and be glad.

Oh, magnify the Lord with me: and let us exalt His name together.

I sought the Lord, and He heard me: and delivered me from all my fears.

They looked unto Him and were lightened: and their faces were not ashamed.

This poor man cried, and the Lord heard him: and saved him out of all his troubles.

The angel of the Lord encampeth round about them that fear Him: and delivereth them.

Oh, taste and see that the Lord is good: blessed is the man that trusteth in Him.

Oh, fear the Lord, ye His saints: for there is no want to them that fear Him.

The young lions do lack and suffer hunger: but they that seek the Lord shall not want any good thing.

Come, ye children, hearken unto me: I will teach you the fear of the Lord.

What man is he that desireth life: and loveth many days that he may see good?

Keep thy tongue from evil: and thy lips from speaking guile.

Depart from evil and do good: seek peace and pursue it.

The eyes of the Lord are upon the righteous: and His ears are open unto their cry.

The face of the Lord is against them that do evil: to cut off the remembrance of them from the earth.

The righteous cry, and the Lord heareth: and delivereth them out of all their troubles.

The Lord is nigh unto them that are of a broken heart: and saveth such as be of a contrite spirit.

Many are the afflictions of the righteous: but the Lord delivereth him out of them all.

He keepeth all his bones: not one of them is broken.

Evil shall slay the wicked: and they that hate the righteous shall be desolate.

The Lord redeemeth the soul of His servants: and none of them that trust in Him shall be desolate.

Psalm 36. Dixit iniustus

The transgression of the wicked saith within my heart: that there is no fear of God before his eyes.

For he flattereth himself in his own eyes: until his iniquity be found to be hateful.

The words of his mouth are iniquity and deceit: he hath left off to be wise and to do good.

He deviseth mischief upon his bed: he setteth himself in a way that is not good; he abhorreth not evil.

Thy mercy, O Lord, is in the heavens: and Thy faithfulness reacheth unto the clouds.

Thy righteousness is like the great mountains; Thy judgments are a great deep: O Lord, Thou preservest man and beast.

How excellent is Thy loving-kindness, O God: therefore the children of men put their trust under the shadow of Thy wings.

They shall be abundantly satisfied with the fatness of Thy house: and Thou shalt make them drink of the river of Thy pleasures.

For with Thee is the fountain of life: in Thy light shall we see light.

Oh, continue Thy loving-kindness unto them that know Thee: and Thy righteousness to the upright in heart.

Let not the foot of pride come against me: and let not the hand of the wicked remove me.

There are the workers of iniquity fallen: they are cast down and shall not be able to rise.

Psalm 38. Domine, ne in furore

O Lord, rebuke me not in Thy wrath: neither chasten me in Thy hot displeasure.

For Thine arrows stick fast in me: and Thy hand presseth me sore.

There is no soundness in my flesh because of Thine anger: neither is there any rest in my bones because of my sin.

For mine iniquities are gone over mine head: as an heavy burden they are too heavy for me.

For in Thee, O Lord, do I hope: Thou wilt hear, O Lord, my God.

For I am ready to halt: and my sorrow is continually before me.

For I will declare mine iniquity: I will be sorry for my sin.

Forsake me not, O Lord: O my God, be not far from me.

Make haste to help me: O Lord, my Salvation.

Psalm 40

Exspectans exspectavi Dominum

I waited patiently for the Lord: and He inclined unto Me and heard My cry.

He brought Me up also out of a horrible pit, out of the miry clay: and set My feet upon a rock; and established My goings.

And He hath put a new song in My mouth, even praise unto our God: many shall see it and fear and shall trust in the Lord.

Blessed is that man that maketh the Lord his trust: and respecteth not the proud nor such as turn aside to lies.

Many, O Lord, My God, are Thy wonderful works which Thou hast done and Thy thoughts which are to us-ward; they cannot be reckoned up in order unto Thee: If I would declare and speak of them, they are more than can be numbered.

Sacrifice and offering Thou didst not desire; Mine ears hast Thou opened: burnt offering and sin-offering hast Thou not required.

Then said I, Lo, I come: in the Volume of the Book it is written of Me.

I delight to do Thy will, O My God: yea, Thy Law is within My heart.

I have preached righteousness in the great congregation: lo, I have not refrained My lips, O Lord, Thou knowest.

I have not hid Thy righteousness within My heart; I have declared Thy faithfulness and Thy salvation: I have not concealed Thy loving-kindness and Thy truth from the great congregation.

Withhold not Thou Thy tender mercies from Me, O Lord: let Thy loving-kindness and Thy truth continually preserve Me.

For innumerable evils have compassed Me about; Mine iniquities have taken hold upon Me, so that I am not able to look up: they are more than the hairs of Mine head; therefore My heart faileth Me.

Be pleased, O Lord, to deliver Me: O Lord, make haste to help Me.

Let them be ashamed and confounded together that seek after My soul to destroy it: let them be driven backward and put to shame that wish Me evil.

Let them be desolate for a reward of their shame: that say unto Me, Aha, aha!

Let all those that seek Thee rejoice and be glad in Thee: let such as love Thy salvation say continually, The Lord be magnified.

But I am poor and needy; yet the Lord thinketh upon Me: Thou art My Help and My Deliverer; make no tarrying, O My God.

Psalm 42
Quemadmodum desiderat cervus

As the hart panteth after the water-brooks: so panteth my soul after Thee, O God.

My soul thirsteth for God, for the living God: When shall I come and appear before God?

My tears have been my meat day and night: while they continually say unto me, Where is thy God?

When I remember these things, I pour out my soul in me; for I had gone with the multitude: I went with them to the house of God, with the voice of joy and praise, with a multitude that kept holy day.

Why art thou cast down, O my soul, and why art thou disquieted in me? Hope thou in God: for I shall yet praise Him for the help of His countenance.

O my God, my soul is cast down within me: therefore will I remember Thee from the land of Jordan, and of the Hermonites, from the hill Mizar.

Deep calleth unto deep at the noise of Thy waterspouts: all Thy waves and Thy billows are gone over me.

Yet the LORD will command His loving-kindness in the daytime: and in the night His song shall be with me and my prayer unto the God of my life.

I will say unto God, my Rock, Why hast Thou forgotten me?: Why go I mourning because of the oppression of the enemy?

As with a sword in my bones, mine enemies reproach me: while they say daily unto me, Where is thy God?

Why art Thou cast down, O my soul, and why art thou disquieted within me? Hope thou in God: for I shall yet praise Him, who is the Health of my countenance and my God.

Psalm 43. Iudica me, Deus

Judge me, O God, and plead my cause against an ungodly nation: oh, deliver me from the deceitful and unjust man.

For Thou art the God of my strength, why dost Thou cast me off?: Why go I mourning because of the oppression of the enemy?

Oh, send out Thy light and Thy truth, let them lead me: let them bring me unto Thy holy hill and to Thy Tabernacles.

Then will I go unto the altar of God, unto God, my exceeding Joy: yea, upon the harp will I praise Thee, O God, my God.

Why art thou cast down, O my soul, and why art thou disquieted within me? Hope in God: for I shall yet praise Him who is the Health of my countenance and my God.

Psalm 45. Eructavit cor meum

My heart is inditing a good matter; I speak of the things which I have made touching the King: My tongue is the pen of a ready writer.

Thou art fairer than the children of men: grace is poured into Thy lips; therefore God hath blessed Thee forever.

Gird Thy sword upon Thy thigh, O Most Mighty: with Thy glory and Thy majesty.

And in Thy majesty ride prosperously because of truth and meekness and righteousness: and Thy right hand shall teach Thee terrible things.

Thine arrows are sharp in the heart of the King's enemies: whereby the people fall under Thee.

Thy throne, O God, is forever and ever: the scepter of Thy kingdom is a right scepter.

Thou lovest righteousness and hatest wickedness: therefore God, Thy God, hath anointed Thee with the oil of gladness above Thy fellows.

All Thy garments smell of myrrh and aloes and cassia: out of the ivory palaces, whereby they have made Thee glad.

Kings' daughters were among Thy honorable women: upon Thy right hand did stand the queen in gold of Ophir.

Hearken, O daughter, and consider and incline thine ear: forget also thine own people and thy father's house.

So shall the King greatly desire thy beauty: for He is thy Lord, and worship thou Him.

And the daughter of Tyre shall be there with a gift: even the rich among the people shall intreat thy favor.

The King's daughter is all glorious within: her clothing is of wrought gold.

She shall be brought unto the King in raiment of needlework: the virgins, her companions that follow her, shall be brought unto thee.

With gladness and rejoicing shall they be brought: they shall enter into the King's palace.

Instead of Thy fathers shall be Thy children: whom Thou mayest make princes in all the earth.

I will make Thy name to be remembered in all generations: therefore shall the people praise Thee forever and ever.

Psalm 46. Deus noster refugium

God is our Refuge and Strength: a very present Help in trouble.

Therefore will not we fear though the earth be removed: and though the mountains be carried into the midst of the sea;

Though the waters thereof roar and be troubled: though the mountains shake with the swelling thereof.

There is a river the streams whereof shall make glad the city of God: the Holy Place of the Tabernacles of the Most High.

God is in the midst of her; she shall not be moved: God shall help her, and that right early.

The heathen raged, the kingdoms were moved: He uttered His voice, the earth melted.

The Lord of hosts is with us: the God of Jacob is our Refuge.

Come, behold the works of the Lord: what desolations He hath made in the earth.

He maketh wars to cease unto the end of the earth: He breaketh the bow and cutteth the spear in sunder; He burneth the chariot in the fire.

Be still and know that I am God: I will be exalted among the heathen, I will be exalted in the earth.

The Lord of hosts is with us: the God of Jacob is our Refuge.

Psalm 47. Omnes gentes, plaudite

Oh, clap your hands, all ye people: shout unto God with the voice of triumph.

For the Lord most high is terrible: He is a great King over all the earth.

He shall subdue the people under us: and the nations under our feet.

He shall choose our inheritance for us: the excellency of Jacob whom He loved.

God is gone up with a shout: the Lord with the sound of a trumpet.

Sing praises to God, sing praises: sing praises unto our King, sing praises.

For God is the King of all the earth: sing ye praises with understanding.

God reigneth over the heathen: God sitteth upon the throne of His holiness.

The princes of the people are gathered together, even the people of the God of Abraham: for the shields of the earth belong unto God; He is greatly exalted.

Psalm 48. Magnus Dominus

Great is the Lord and greatly to be praised: in the city of our God, in the mountain of His holiness.

Beautiful for situation, the joy of the whole earth, is Mount Zion: on the sides of the north, the city of the great King.

God is known in her palaces: for a refuge.

For, lo, the kings were assembled: they passed by together.

They saw it, and so they marveled: they were troubled and hastened away.

Fear took hold upon them there and pain: as of a woman in travail.

Thou breakest the ships of Tarshish: with an east wind.

As we have heard, so have we seen in the city of the Lord of hosts, in the city of our God: God will establish it forever.

We have thought of Thy loving-kindness, O God: in the midst of Thy Temple.

According to Thy name, O God, so is Thy praise unto the ends of the earth: Thy right hand is full of righteousness.

Let Mount Zion rejoice, let the daughters of Judah be glad: because of Thy judgments.

Walk about Zion and go round about her: tell the towers thereof.

Mark ye well her bulwarks, consider her palaces: that ye may tell it to the generation following.

For this God is our God forever and ever: He will be our Guide even unto death.

Psalm 51. Miserere mei, Deus, secundum

Have mercy upon me, O God, according to Thy loving-kindness: according unto the multitude of Thy tender mercies blot out my transgressions.

Wash me throughly from mine iniquity: and cleanse me from my sin.

For I acknowledge my transgressions: and my sin is ever before me.

Against Thee, Thee only, have I sinned and done this evil in Thy sight: that Thou mightest be justified when Thou speakest and be clear when Thou judgest.

Behold, I was shapen in iniquity: and in sin did my mother conceive me.

Behold, Thou desirest truth in the inward parts: and in the hidden part Thou shalt make me to know wisdom.

Purge me with hyssop, and I shall be clean: wash me, and I shall be whiter than snow.

Make me to hear joy and gladness: that the bones which Thou hast broken may rejoice.

Hide Thy face from my sins: and blot out all mine iniquities.

Create in me a clean heart, O God: and renew a right spirit within me.

Cast me not away from Thy presence: and take not Thy Holy Spirit from me.

Restore unto me the joy of Thy salvation: and uphold me with Thy free Spirit.

Then will I teach transgressors Thy ways: and sinners shall be converted unto Thee.

Deliver me from blood-guiltiness, O God, Thou God of my salvation: and my tongue shall sing aloud of Thy righteousness.

O Lord, open Thou my lips: and my mouth shall show forth Thy praise.

For Thou desirest not sacrifice, else would I give it: Thou delightest not in burnt offering.

The sacrifices of God are a broken spirit: a broken and a contrite heart, O God, Thou wilt not despise.

Do good in Thy good pleasure unto Zion: build Thou the walls of Jerusalem.

Then shalt Thou be pleased with the sacrifices of righteousness, with burnt offering, and whole burnt offering: then shall they offer bullocks upon Thine altar.

Psalm 54. Deus, in nomine

Save me, O God, by Thy name: and judge me by Thy strength.

Hear my prayer, O God: give ear to the words of my mouth.

For strangers are risen up against me, and oppressors seek after my soul: they have not set God before them.

Behold, God is mine Helper: the Lord is with them that uphold my soul.

He shall reward evil unto mine enemies: cut them off in Thy truth.

I will freely sacrifice unto Thee: I will praise Thy name, O Lord, for it is good.

For He hath delivered me out of all trouble: and mine eye hath seen his desire upon mine enemies.

Psalm 56. Miserere mei, Deus, quoniam

Be merciful unto me, O God; for man would swallow me up: he, fighting daily, oppresseth me.

Mine enemies would daily swallow me up: for they be many that fight against me, O Thou Most High.

What time I am afraid: I will trust in Thee.

In God I will praise His Word: in God I have put my trust; I will not fear what flesh can do unto me.

Every day they wrest my words: all their thoughts are against me for evil.

They gather themselves together, they hide themselves: they mark my steps when they wait for my soul.

Shall they escape by iniquity?: In Thine anger cast down the people, O God.

Thou tellest my wanderings; put Thou my tears into Thy bottle: are they not in Thy book?

When I cry unto Thee, then shall mine enemies turn back: This I know; for God is for me.

In God will I praise His Word: in the Lord will I praise His Word.

In God have I put my trust: I will not be afraid what man can do unto me.

Thy vows are upon me, O God: I will render praises unto Thee.

For Thou hast delivered my soul from death; wilt not Thou deliver my feet from falling: that I may walk before God in the light of the living?

Psalm 57. Miserere mei, Deus, miserere

Be merciful unto me, O God, be merciful unto me; for my soul trusteth in Thee: yea, in the shadow of Thy wings will I make my refuge, until these calamities be overpast.

I will cry unto God Most High: unto God that performeth all things for me.

He shall send from heaven and save me from the reproach of him that would swallow me up: God shall send forth His mercy and His truth.

My soul is among lions, and I lie even among them that are set on fire: even the sons of men, whose teeth are spears and arrows and their tongue a sharp sword.

Be Thou exalted, O God, above the heavens: let Thy glory be above all the earth.

They have prepared a net for my steps; my soul is bowed down: they have digged a pit before me, into the midst whereof they are fallen themselves.

My heart is fixed, O God, my heart is fixed: I will sing and give praise.

Awake up, my glory; awake, psaltery and harp: I myself will awake early.

I will praise Thee, O Lord, among the people: I will sing unto Thee among the nations.

For Thy mercy is great unto the heavens: and Thy truth unto the clouds.

Be Thou exalted, O God, above the heavens: let Thy glory be above all the earth.

Psalm 61. Exaudi, Deus, deprecationem

Hear my cry, O God: attend unto my prayer.

From the end of the earth will I cry unto Thee when my heart is overwhelmed: lead me to the rock that is higher than I.

For Thou hast been a Shelter for me: and a strong Tower from the enemy.

I will abide in Thy Tabernacle forever: I will trust in the covert of Thy wings.

For Thou, O God, hast heard my vows: Thou hast given me the heritage of those that fear Thy name.

Thou wilt prolong the king's life: and his years as many generations.

He shall abide before God forever: oh, prepare mercy and truth, which may preserve him.

So will I sing praise unto Thy name forever: that I may daily perform my vows.

Psalm 62. Nonne Deo subiecta

Truly my soul waiteth upon God: from Him cometh my salvation.

He only is my Rock and my Salvation; He is my Defense: I shall not be greatly moved.

How long will ye imagine mischief against a man? Ye shall be slain, all of you: as a bowing wall shall ye be and as a tottering fence.

They only consult to cast him down from his excellency; they delight in lies: they bless with their mouth, but they curse inwardly.

My soul, wait thou only upon God: for my expectation is from Him.

He only is my Rock and my Salvation; He is my Defense: I shall not be moved.

In God is my salvation and my glory: the rock of my strength and my refuge is in God.

Trust in Him at all times; ye people, pour out your heart before Him: God is a Refuge for us.

Surely men of low degree are vanity, and men of high degree are a lie: to be laid in the balance, they are altogether lighter than vanity.

Trust not in oppression and become not vain in robbery: if riches increase, set not your heart upon them.

God hath spoken once; twice have I heard this: that power belongeth unto God.

Also unto Thee, O Lord, belongeth mercy: for Thou renderest to every man according to his work.

Psalm 65. Te decet hymnus, Deus

Praise waiteth for Thee, O God, in Zion: and unto Thee shall the vow be performed.

O Thou that hearest prayer: unto Thee shall all flesh come.

Iniquities prevail against me: as for our transgressions, Thou shalt purge them away.

Blessed is the man whom Thou choosest and causest to approach unto Thee that he may dwell in Thy courts: we shall be satisfied with the goodness of Thy house, even of Thy holy Temple.

By terrible things in righteousness wilt Thou answer us, O God of our salvation: who art the Confidence of all the ends of the earth and of them that are afar off upon the sea,

Which by His strength setteth fast the mountains: being girded with power;

Which stilleth the noise of the seas: the noise of their waves, and the tumult of the people.

They also that dwell in the uttermost parts are afraid at Thy tokens: Thou makest the outgoings of the morning and evening to rejoice.

Thou visitest the earth and waterest it; Thou greatly enrichest it with the river of God, which is full of water: Thou preparest them corn, when Thou hast so provided for it.

Thou waterest the ridges thereof abundantly; Thou settlest the furrows thereof: Thou makest it soft with showers; Thou blessest the springing thereof.

Thou crownest the year with Thy goodness: and Thy paths drop fatness.

They drop upon the pastures of the wilderness: and the little hills rejoice on every side.

The pastures are clothed with flocks; the valleys also are covered over with corn: they shout for joy, they also sing.

Psalm 66. Iubilate Deo, omnis terra

Make a joyful noise unto God, all ye lands: sing forth the honor of His name; make His praise glorious.

Say unto God, How terrible art Thou in Thy works: through the greatness of Thy power shall Thine enemies submit themselves unto Thee.

All the earth shall worship Thee and shall sing unto Thee: they shall sing to Thy name.

Come and see the works of God: He is terrible in His doing toward the children of men.

He turned the sea into dry land:

they went through the flood on foot; there did we rejoice in Him.

He ruleth by His power forever; His eyes behold the nations: let not the rebellious exalt themselves.

Oh, bless our God, ye people: and make the voice of His praise to be heard,

Which holdeth our soul in life: and suffereth not our feet to be moved.

For Thou, O God, hast proved us: Thou hast tried us as silver is tried.

Thou broughtest us into the net: Thou laidst affliction upon our loins.

Thou hast caused men to ride over our heads: we went through fire and through water; but Thou broughtest us out into a wealthy place.

I will go into Thy house with burnt offerings: I will pay Thee my vows,

Which my lips have uttered and my mouth hath spoken: when I was in trouble.

I will offer unto Thee burnt sacrifices of fatlings with the incense of rams: I will offer bullocks with goats.

Come and hear, all ye that fear God: and I will declare what He hath done for my soul.

I cried unto Him with my mouth: and He was extolled with my tongue.

If I regard iniquity in my heart: the LORD will not hear me.

But, verily, God hath heard me: He hath attended to the voice of my prayer.

Blessed be God, which hath not turned away my prayer: nor His mercy from me.

Psalm 67. Deus misereatur nostri

God be merciful unto us and bless us: and cause His face to shine upon us.

That Thy way may be known upon earth: Thy saving health among all nations.

Let the people praise Thee, O God: let all the people praise Thee.

Oh, let the nations be glad and sing for joy: for Thou shalt judge the people righteously and govern the nations upon earth.

Let the people praise Thee, O God: let all the people praise Thee.

Then shall the earth yield her increase: and God, even our own God, shall bless us.

God shall bless us: and all the ends of the earth shall fear Him.

Psalm 68. Exsurgat Deus

Let God arise, let His enemies be scattered: let them also that hate Him flee before Him.

As smoke is driven away, so drive them away: as wax melteth before the fire, so let the wicked perish at the presence of God.

But let the righteous be glad; let them rejoice before God: yea, let them exceedingly rejoice.

Sing unto God, sing praises to His name: extol Him that rideth upon the heavens by His name JAH, and rejoice before Him.

A Father of the fatherless and a Judge of the widows: is God in His holy habitation.

God setteth the solitary in families; He bringeth out those which are bound with chains: but the rebellious dwell in a dry land.

O God, when Thou wentest forth before Thy people: when Thou didst march through the wilderness,

The earth shook, the heavens also dropped at the presence of God: even Sinai itself was moved at the presence of God, the God of Israel.

Thou, O God, didst send a plentiful rain: whereby Thou didst confirm Thine inheritance, when it was weary.

Thy congregation hath dwelt therein: Thou, O God, hast prepared of Thy goodness for the poor.

The LORD gave the Word: great was the company of those that published it.

Kings of armies did flee apace: and she that tarried at home divided the spoil.

Though ye have lien among the pots, yet shall ye be as the wings of a dove: covered with silver and her feathers with yellow gold.

When the Almighty scattered kings in it: it was white as snow in Salmon.

The hill of God is as the hill of Bashan: a high hill as the hill of Bashan.

Why leap ye, ye high hills? This is the hill which God desireth to dwell in: yea, the LORD will dwell in it forever.

The chariots of God are twenty thousand, even thousands of angels: the LORD is among them, as in Sinai, in the Holy Place.

Thou hast ascended on high, Thou hast led captivity captive, Thou hast received gifts for men: yea, for the rebellious also, that the LORD God might dwell among them.

Blessed be the LORD, who daily loadeth us with benefits: even the God of our salvation.

He that is our God is the God of salvation: and unto God the LORD belong the issues from death.

But God shall wound the head of His

enemies: and the hairy scalp of such an one as goeth on still in his trespasses.

The LORD said, I will bring again from Bashan: I will bring My people again from the depths of the sea.

That thy foot may be dipped in the blood of thine enemies: and the tongue of thy dogs in the same.

They have seen Thy goings, O God: even the goings of my God, my King, in the Sanctuary.

The singers went before, the players on instruments followed after: among them were the damsels playing with timbrels.

Bless ye God in the congregations: even the LORD, from the fountain of Israel.

There is little Benjamin with their ruler, the princes of Judah and their council: the princes of Zebulun and the princes of Naphtali.

Thy God hath commanded Thy strength: strengthen, O God, that which Thou hast wrought for us.

Because of Thy Temple at Jerusalem: shall kings bring presents unto Thee.

Rebuke the company of spearmen, the multitude of the bulls, with the calves of the people, till everyone submit himself with pieces of silver: scatter Thou the people that delight in war.

Princes shall come out of Egypt: Ethiopia shall soon stretch out her hands unto God.

Sing unto God, ye kingdoms of the earth: O sing praises unto the Lord.

To Him that rideth upon the heavens of heavens, which were of old: lo, He doth send out His voice, and that a mighty voice.

Ascribe ye strength unto God; His excellency is over Israel: and His strength is in the clouds.

O God, Thou art terrible out of Thy holy places: the God of Israel is He that giveth strength and power unto His people. Blessed be God.

Psalm 70. Deus, in adiutorium

Make haste, O God, to deliver me: make haste to help me, O LORD.

Let them be ashamed and confounded that seek after my soul: let them be turned backward and put to confusion that desire my hurt.

Let them be turned back for a reward of their shame that say: Aha, aha!

Let all those that seek Thee rejoice and be glad in Thee: and let such as love Thy salvation say continually, Let God be magnified.

But I am poor and needy; make haste unto me, O God: Thou art my Help and my Deliverer; O LORD, make no tarrying.

Psalm 72. Deus, iudicium

Give the King Thy judgments, O God: and Thy righteousness unto the King's Son.

He shall judge Thy people with righteousness: and Thy poor with judgment.

The mountains shall bring peace to the people: and the little hills, by righteousness.

He shall judge the poor of the people, He shall save the children of the needy: and shall break in pieces the oppressor.

They shall fear Thee as long as the sun and moon endure: throughout all generations.

He shall come down like rain upon the mown grass: as showers that water the earth.

In His days shall the righteous flourish: and abundance of peace so long as the moon endureth.

He shall have dominion also from sea to sea: and from the river unto the ends of the earth.

They that dwell in the wilderness shall bow before Him: and His enemies shall lick the dust.

The kings of Tarshish and of the isles shall bring presents: the kings of Sheba and Seba shall offer gifts.

Yea, all kings shall fall down before Him: all nations shall serve Him.

For He shall deliver the needy when he crieth: the poor also, and him that hath no helper.

He shall spare the poor and needy: and shall save the souls of the needy.

He shall redeem their soul from deceit and violence: and precious shall their blood be in His sight.

And He shall live, and to Him shall be given of the gold of Sheba: prayer also shall be made for Him continually; and daily shall He be praised.

There shall be an handful of corn in the earth upon the top of the mountains: the fruit thereof shall shake like Lebanon; and they of the city shall flourish like grass of the earth.

His name shall endure forever; His name shall be continued as long as the sun: and men shall be blessed in Him; all nations shall call Him blessed.

Blessed be the LORD God, the God of Israel: who only doeth wondrous things.

And blessed be His glorious name forever: and let the whole earth be filled with His glory. Amen, and Amen.

Psalm 75. Confitebimur tibi

Unto Thee, O God, do we give thanks, unto Thee do we give thanks: for that Thy name is near, Thy wondrous works declare.

When I shall receive the congregation: I will judge uprightly.

The earth and all the inhabitants thereof are dissolved: I bear up the pillars of it.

I said unto the fools, Deal not foolishly: and to the wicked, Lift not up the horn.

Lift not up your horn on high: speak not with a stiff neck.

For promotion cometh neither from the east: nor from the west nor from the south;

But God is the Judge: He putteth down one and setteth up another.

For in the hand of the LORD there is a cup, and the wine is red; it is full of mixture, and He poureth out of the same: but the dregs thereof, all the wicked of the earth shall wring them out and drink them.

But I will declare forever: I will sing praises to the God of Jacob.

All the horns of the wicked also will I cut off: but the horns of the righteous shall be exalted.

Psalm 77
Voce mea ad Dominum clamavi

I cried unto God with my voice: even unto God with my voice, and He gave ear unto me.

In the day of my trouble I sought the LORD: my sore ran in the night and ceased not; my soul refused to be comforted.

I remembered God and was troubled: I complained, and my spirit was overwhelmed.

Thou holdest mine eyes waking: I am so troubled that I cannot speak.

I have considered the days of old: the years of ancient times.

I call to remembrance my song in the night: I commune with mine own heart, and my spirit made diligent search.

Will the Lord cast off forever: and will He be favorable no more?

Is His mercy clean gone forever?: Doth His promise fail forevermore?

Hath God forgotten to be gracious?: Hath He in anger shut up His tender mercies?

And I said, This is my infirmity: but I will remember the years of the right hand of the Most High.

I will remember the works of the LORD: surely I will remember Thy wonders of old.

I will meditate also of all Thy work: and talk of Thy doings.

Thy way, O God, is in the Sanctuary: who is so great a God as our God?

Thou art the God that doest wonders: Thou hast declared Thy strength among the people.

Thou hast with Thine arm redeemed Thy people: the sons of Jacob and Joseph.

The waters saw Thee, O God, the waters saw Thee; they were afraid: the depths also were troubled.

The clouds poured out water; the skies sent out a sound: Thine arrows also went abroad.

The voice of Thy thunder was in the heaven: the lightnings lightened the world; the earth trembled and shook.

Thy way is in the sea and Thy path in the great waters: and Thy footsteps are not known.

Thou leddest Thy people like a flock: by the hand of Moses and Aaron.

Psalm 82. Deus stetit

God standeth in the congregation of the mighty: He judgeth among the gods.

How long will ye judge unjustly: and accept the persons of the wicked?

Defend the poor and fatherless: do justice to the afflicted and needy.

Deliver the poor and needy: rid them out of the hand of the wicked.

They know not, neither will they understand; they walk on in darkness: all the foundations of the earth are out of course.

I have said, Ye are gods: and all of you are the children of the Most High.

But ye shall die like men: and fall like one of the princes.

Arise, O God, judge the earth: for Thou shalt inherit all nations.

Psalm 84. Quam dilecta tabernacula!

How amiable are Thy tabernacles: O LORD of hosts!

My soul longeth, yea, even fainteth, for the courts of the LORD: my heart and my flesh crieth out for the living God.

Yea, the sparrow hath found an house: and the swallow a nest for herself where she may lay her young, even Thine altars, O LORD of hosts, my King and my God.

Blessed are they that dwell in Thy house: they will be still praising Thee.

Blessed is the man whose strength is in Thee: in whose heart are the ways of them;

Who, passing through the Valley of

Baca, make it a well: the rain also filleth the pools.

They go from strength to strength: every one of them in Zion appeareth before God.

O Lord God of hosts, hear my prayer: give ear, O God of Jacob.

Behold, O God, our Shield: and look upon the face of Thine anointed.

For a day in Thy courts is better than a thousand: I had rather be a doorkeeper in the house of my God than to dwell in the tents of wickedness.

For the Lord God is a Sun and Shield; the Lord will give grace and glory: no good thing will He withhold from them that walk uprightly.

O Lord of hosts: blessed is the man that trusteth in Thee.

Psalm 85. Benedixisti, Domine

Lord, Thou hast been favorable unto Thy land: Thou hast brought back the captivity of Jacob.

Thou hast forgiven the iniquity of Thy people: Thou hast covered all their sin.

Thou has taken away all Thy wrath: Thou hast turned Thyself from the fierceness of Thine anger.

Turn us, O God of our salvation: and cause Thine anger toward us to cease.

Wilt Thou be angry with us forever?: Wilt Thou draw out Thine anger to all generations?

Wilt Thou not revive us again: that Thy people may rejoice in Thee?

Show us Thy mercy, O Lord: and grant us Thy salvation.

I will hear what God the Lord will speak: for He will speak peace unto His people and to His saints; but let them not again turn to folly.

Surely His salvation is nigh them that fear Him: that glory may dwell in our land.

Mercy and truth are met together: righteousness and peace have kissed each other.

Truth shall spring out of the earth: and righteousness shall look down from heaven.

Yea, the Lord shall give that which is good: and our land shall yield her increase.

Righteousness shall go before Him: and shall set us in the way of His steps.

Psalm 86. Inclina, Domine

Bow down Thine ear, O Lord, hear me: for I am poor and needy.

Preserve my soul; for I am holy:

O Thou my God, save Thy servant that trusteth in Thee.

Be merciful unto me, O Lord: for I cry unto Thee daily.

Rejoice the soul of Thy servant: for unto Thee, O Lord, do I lift up my soul.

For Thou, Lord, art good and ready to forgive: and plenteous in mercy unto all them that call upon Thee.

Give ear, O Lord, unto my prayer: and attend to the voice of my supplications.

In the day of my trouble I will call upon Thee: for Thou wilt answer me.

Among the gods there is none like unto Thee, O Lord: neither are there any works like unto Thy works.

All nations whom Thou hast made shall come and worship before Thee, O Lord: and shall glorify Thy name.

For Thou art great and doest wondrous things: Thou art God alone.

Teach me Thy way, O Lord; I will walk in Thy truth: unite my heart to fear Thy name.

I will praise Thee, O Lord, my God, with all my heart: and I will glorify Thy name forevermore.

For great is Thy mercy toward me: and Thou hast delivered my soul from the lowest hell.

O God, the proud are risen against me: and the assemblies of violent men have sought after my soul and have not set Thee before them.

But Thou, O Lord, art a God full of compassion and gracious: long-suffering and plenteous in mercy and truth.

Oh, turn unto me and have mercy upon me: give Thy strength unto Thy servant and save the son of Thine handmaid.

Show me a token for good that they which hate me may see it and be ashamed: because Thou, Lord, hast holpen me and comforted me.

Psalm 87. Fundamenta eius

His foundation: is in the holy mountains.

The Lord loveth the gates of Zion: more than all the dwellings of Jacob.

Glorious things are spoken of thee: O city of God.

I will make mention of Rahab and Babylon to them that know Me: Behold Philistia and Tyre with Ethiopia; this man was born there.

And of Zion it shall be said, This and that man was born in her: and the Highest Himself shall establish her.

The Lord shall count when He writeth up the people: that this man was born there.

As well the singers as the players on instruments shall be there: all my springs are in thee.

Psalm 88. Domine, Deus

O LORD God of my salvation: I have cried day and night before Thee.

Let my prayer come before Thee: incline Thine ear unto my cry.

For my soul is full of troubles: and my life draweth nigh unto the grave.

I am counted with them that go down into the pit: I am as a man that hath no strength;

Free among the dead, like the slain that lie in the grave, whom Thou rememberest no more: and they are cut off from Thy hand.

Thou hast laid me in the lowest pit: in darkness, in the deeps.

Thy wrath lieth hard upon me: and Thou hast afflicted me with all Thy waves.

Thou hast put away mine acquaintance far from me; Thou hast made me an abomination unto them: I am shut up, and I cannot come forth.

Mine eye mourneth by reason of affliction: LORD, I have called daily upon Thee, I have stretched out my hands unto Thee.

Wilt Thou show wonders to the dead?: Shall the dead arise and praise Thee?

Shall Thy loving-kindness be declared in the grave: or Thy faithfulness in destruction?

Shall Thy wonders be known in the dark: and Thy righteousness in the land of forgetfulness?

But unto Thee have I cried, O LORD: and in the morning shall my prayer prevent Thee.

LORD, why castest Thou off my soul?: Why hidest Thou Thy face from me?

I am afflicted and ready to die from my youth up: while I suffer Thy terrors, I am distracted.

Thy fierce wrath goeth over me: Thy terrors have cut me off.

They came round about me daily like water: they compassed me about together.

Lover and friend hast Thou put far from me: and mine acquaintance into darkness.

Psalm 89. Misericordias Domini

I will sing of the mercies of the LORD forever: with my mouth will I make known Thy faithfulness to all generations.

For I have said, Mercy shall be built up forever: Thy faithfulness shalt Thou establish in the very heavens.

I have made a covenant with My chosen: I have sworn unto David, My servant,

Thy Seed will I establish forever: and build up Thy throne to all generations.

And the heavens shall praise Thy wonders, O LORD: Thy faithfulness also in the congregation of the saints.

For who in the heaven can be compared unto the LORD?: Who among the sons of the mighty can be likened unto the LORD?

God is greatly to be feared in the assembly of the saints: and to be had in reverence of all them that are about Him.

O LORD God of hosts, who is a strong LORD like unto Thee: or to Thy faithfulness round about Thee?

Thou rulest the raging of the sea: when the waves thereof arise, Thou stillest them.

Thou hast broken Rahab in pieces, as one that is slain: Thou hast scattered Thine enemies with Thy strong arm.

The heavens are Thine, the earth also is Thine: as for the world and the fullness thereof, Thou hast founded them.

The north and the south, Thou hast created them: Tabor and Hermon shall rejoice in Thy name.

Thou hast a mighty arm: strong is Thy hand, and high is Thy right hand.

Justice and judgment are the habitation of Thy throne: mercy and truth shall go before Thy face.

Blessed is the people that know the joyful sound: they shall walk, O LORD, in the light of Thy countenance.

In Thy name shall they rejoice all the day: and in Thy righteousness shall they be exalted.

For Thou art the glory of their strength: and in Thy favor our horn shall be exalted.

For the Lord is our Defense: and the Holy One of Israel is our King.

Then Thou spakest in vision to Thy Holy One and saidst: I have laid help upon one that is mighty; I have exalted one chosen out of the people.

I have found David, My Servant: with My holy oil have I anointed Him,

With whom My hand shall be established: Mine arm also shall strengthen Him.

The enemy shall not exact upon Him: nor the son of wickedness afflict Him.

And I will beat down His foes before His face: and plague them that hate Him.

But My faithfulness and My mercy shall be with Him: and in My name shall His horn be exalted.

I will set His hand also in the sea: and His right hand in the rivers.

He shall cry unto Me, Thou art My Father: My God, and the Rock of My salvation.

Also I will make Him My First-born: higher than the kings of the earth.

My mercy will I keep for Him forevermore: and My covenant shall stand fast with Him.

His seed also will I make to endure forever: and His throne as the days of heaven.

If His children forsake My Law: and walk not in My judgments;

If they break My statutes and keep not My commandments: then will I visit their transgression with the rod and their iniquity with stripes.

Nevertheless My loving-kindness will I not utterly take from Him: nor suffer My faithfulness to fail.

My covenant will I not break nor alter the thing that is gone out of My lips: Once I have I sworn by My holiness that I will not lie unto David.

His seed shall endure forever: and His throne as the sun before Me.

It shall be established forever as the moon: and as a faithful witness in heaven.

But Thou hast cast off and abhorred: Thou hast been wroth with Thine Anointed.

Thou hast made void the covenant of Thy Servant: Thou hast profaned His crown by casting it to the ground.

Thou hast broken down all His hedges: Thou hast brought His strongholds to ruin.

All that pass by the way spoil Him: He is a reproach to His neighbors.

Thou hast set up the right hand of His adversaries: Thou hast made all His enemies to rejoice.

Thou hast also turned the edge of His sword: and hast not made Him to stand in the battle.

Thou hast made His glory to cease: and cast His throne down to the ground.

The days of His youth hast Thou shortened: Thou hast covered Him with shame.

How long, Lord? Wilt Thou hide Thyself forever?: Shall Thy wrath burn like fire?

Remember how short My time is: wherefore hast Thou made all men in vain?

What man is he that liveth and shall not see death?: Shall he deliver his soul from the hand of the grave?

Lord, where are Thy former loving-kindnesses: which Thou swarest unto David in Thy truth?

Remember, Lord, the reproach of Thy servants: how I do bear in My bosom the reproach of all the mighty people,

Wherewith Thine enemies have reproached, O Lord, wherewith they have reproached the footsteps of Thine Anointed: Blessed be the Lord forevermore. Amen, and Amen.

Psalm 90. Domine, refugium

Lord, Thou hast been our Dwelling Place: in all generations.

Before the mountains were brought forth or ever Thou hadst formed the earth and the world: even from everlasting to everlasting, Thou art God.

Thou turnest man to destruction: and sayest, Return, ye children of men.

For a thousand years in Thy sight are but as yesterday when it is past: and as a watch in the night.

Thou carriest them away as with a flood; they are as a sleep: in the morning they are like grass which groweth up.

In the morning it flourisheth and groweth up: in the evening it is cut down and withereth.

For we are consumed by Thine anger: and by Thy wrath are we troubled.

Thou hast set our iniquities before Thee: our secret sins in the light of Thy countenance.

For all our days are passed away in Thy wrath: we spend our years as a tale that is told.

The days of our years are threescore years and ten; and if by reason of strength they be fourscore years; yet is their strength labor and sorrow; for it is soon cut off, and we fly away.

Who knoweth the power of Thine anger?: Even according to Thy fear, so is Thy wrath.

So teach us to number our days: that we may apply our hearts unto wisdom.

Return, O Lord, how long?: And let it repent Thee concerning Thy servants.

Oh, satisfy us early with Thy mercy: that we may rejoice and be glad all our days.

Make us glad according to the days wherein Thou hast afflicted us: and the years wherein we have seen evil.

Let Thy work appear unto Thy servants: and Thy glory unto their children.

And let the beauty of the Lord, our God, be upon us: and establish Thou the work of our hands upon us; yea, the work of our hands, establish Thou it.

Psalm 91. Qui habitat

He that dwelleth in the secret place of the Most High: shall abide under the shadow of the Almighty.

I will say of the LORD, He is my Refuge and my Fortress: my God; in Him will I trust.

Surely He shall deliver thee from the snare of the fowler: and from the noisome pestilence.

He shall cover thee with His feathers, and under His wings shalt thou trust: His truth shall be thy shield and buckler.

Thou shalt not be afraid for the terror by night: nor for the arrow that flieth by day;

Nor for the pestilence that walketh in darkness: nor for the destruction that wasteth at noonday.

A thousand shall fall at thy side and ten thousand at thy right hand: but it shall not come nigh thee.

Only with thine eyes shalt thou behold: and see the reward of the wicked.

Because thou hast made the LORD, which is my Refuge: even the Most High, thy habitation,

There shall no evil befall thee: neither shall any plague come nigh thy dwelling.

For He shall give His angels charge over thee: to keep thee in all thy ways.

They shall bear thee up in their hands: lest thou dash thy foot against a stone.

Thou shalt tread upon the lion and adder: the young lion and the dragon shalt thou trample under feet.

Because he hath set his love upon Me, therefore will I deliver him: I will set him on high because he hath known My name.

He shall call upon Me, and I will answer him: I will be with him in trouble; I will deliver him and honor him.

With long life will I satisfy him: and show him My salvation.

Psalm 92. Bonum est confiteri

It is a good thing to give thanks unto the LORD: and to sing praises unto Thy name, O Most High;

To show forth Thy loving-kindness in the morning: and Thy faithfulness every night,

Upon an instrument of ten strings and upon the psaltery: upon the harp with a solemn sound.

For Thou, LORD, hast made me glad through Thy work: I will triumph in the works of Thy hands.

O LORD, how great are Thy works!: And Thy thoughts are very deep.

A brutish man knoweth not: neither doth a fool understand this.

When the wicked spring as the grass, and when all the workers of iniquity do flourish: it is that they shall be destroyed forever; but Thou, LORD, art most high forevermore.

For, lo, Thine enemies, O LORD, for, lo, Thine enemies shall perish: all the workers of iniquity shall be scattered.

But my horn shalt Thou exalt like the horn of a unicorn: I shall be anointed with fresh oil.

Mine eye also shall see my desire on mine enemies: and mine ears shall hear my desire of the wicked that rise up against me.

The righteous shall flourish like the palm tree: he shall grow like a cedar in Lebanon.

Those that be planted in the house of the LORD: shall flourish in the courts of our God.

They shall still bring forth fruit in old age: they shall be fat and flourishing;

To show that the LORD is upright; He is my Rock: and there is no unrighteousness in Him.

Psalm 93. Dominus regnavit

The LORD reigneth; He is clothed with majesty: the LORD is clothed with strength, wherewith He hath girded Himself.

The world also is established: that it cannot be moved.

Thy throne is established of old: Thou art from everlasting.

The floods have lifted up, O LORD, the floods have lifted up their voice: the floods lift up their waves.

The LORD on high is mightier than the noise of many waters: yea, than the mighty waves of the sea.

Thy testimonies are very sure: holiness becometh Thine house, O LORD, forever.

Psalm 95. Venite, exultemus

Oh, come, let us sing unto the LORD: let us make a joyful noise to the Rock of our salvation.

Let us come before His presence with thanksgiving: and make a joyful noise unto Him with psalms.

For the LORD is a great God: and a great King above all gods.

In His hand are the deep places of the earth: the strength of the hills is His also.

The sea is His, and He made it: and His hands formed the dry land.

Oh, come, let us worship and bow

down: let us kneel before the LORD, our Maker!

For He is our God: and we are the people of His pasture and the sheep of His hand.

Today, if ye will hear His voice, harden not your heart: as in the provocation and as in the day of temptation in the wilderness,

When your fathers tempted Me: proved Me, and saw My work.

Forty years long was I grieved with this generation and said: It is a people that do err in their heart, and they have not known My ways;

Unto whom I sware in My wrath: that they should not enter into My rest.

Psalm 96. Cantate Domino

Oh, sing unto the LORD a new song: sing unto the LORD, all the earth.

Sing unto the LORD, bless His name: show forth His salvation from day to day.

Declare His glory among the heathen: His wonders among all people.

For the LORD is great and greatly to be praised: He is to be feared above all gods.

For all the gods of the nations are idols: but the LORD made the heavens.

Honor and majesty are before Him: strength and beauty are in His Sanctuary.

Give unto the LORD, O ye kindreds of the people: give unto the LORD glory and strength.

Give unto the LORD the glory due unto His name: bring an offering and come into His courts.

Oh, worship the LORD in the beauty of holiness: fear before Him, all the earth.

Say among the heathen that the LORD reigneth; the world also shall be established that it shall not be moved: He shall judge the people righteously.

Let the heavens rejoice, and let the earth be glad: let the sea roar and the fullness thereof.

Let the field be joyful, and all that is therein: then shall all the trees of the wood rejoice

Before the LORD; for He cometh, for He cometh to judge the earth: He shall judge the world with righteousness and the people with His truth.

Psalm 97. Dominus regnavit

The LORD reigneth, let the earth rejoice: let the multitude of isles be glad thereof.

Clouds and darkness are round about Him: righteousness and judgment are the habitation of His throne.

A fire goeth before Him: and burneth up His enemies round about.

His lightnings enlightened the world: the earth saw and trembled.

The hills melted like wax at the presence of the LORD: at the presence of the Lord of the whole earth.

The heavens declare His righteousness: and all the people see His glory.

Confounded be all they that serve graven images, that boast themselves of idols: worship Him, all ye gods.

Zion heard and was glad: and the daughters of Judah rejoiced because of Thy judgments, O LORD.

For Thou, LORD, art high above all the earth: Thou art exalted far above all gods.

Ye that love the LORD, hate evil: He preserveth the souls of His saints; He delivereth them out of the hand of the wicked.

Light is sown for the righteous: and gladness for the upright in heart.

Rejoice in the LORD, ye righteous: and give thanks at the remembrance of His holiness.

Psalm 98. Cantate Domino

Oh, sing unto the LORD a new song: for He hath done marvelous things.

His right hand and His holy arm: hath gotten Him the victory.

The LORD hath made known His salvation: His righteousness hath He openly showed in the sight of the heathen.

He hath remembered His mercy and His truth toward the house of Israel: all the ends of the earth have seen the salvation of our God.

Make a joyful noise unto the LORD, all the earth: make a loud noise and rejoice and sing praise.

Sing unto the LORD with the harp: with the harp and the voice of a psalm.

With trumpets and sound of cornet: make a joyful noise before the LORD, the King.

Let the sea roar and the fullness thereof: the world and they that dwell therein.

Let the floods clap their hands, let the hills be joyful together before the LORD: for He cometh to judge the earth.

With righteousness shall He judge the world: and the people with equity.

Psalm 100. Iubilate Deo

Make a joyful noise unto the LORD, all ye lands: serve the LORD with gladness, come before His presence with singing.

Know ye that the LORD, He is God: it is He that hath made us, and not we ourselves; we are His people and the sheep of His pasture.

Enter into His gates with thanksgiving and into His courts with praise: be thankful unto Him and bless His name.

For the LORD is good; His mercy is everlasting: and His truth endureth to all generations.

Psalm 102
Domine, exaudi orationem meam

Hear my prayer, O LORD: and let my cry come unto Thee.

Hide not Thy face from me in the day when I am in trouble: incline Thine ear unto me; in the day when I call, answer me speedily.

For my days are consumed like smoke: and my bones are burned as an hearth.

My heart is smitten and withered like grass: so that I forget to eat my bread.

By reason of the voice of my groaning: my bones cleave to my skin.

I am like a pelican of the wilderness: I am like an owl of the desert.

I watch and am as a sparrow: alone upon the housetop.

Mine enemies reproach me all the day: and they that are mad against me are sworn against me.

For I have eaten ashes like bread: and mingled my drink with weeping

Because of Thine indignation and Thy wrath: for Thou hast lifted me up and cast me down.

My days are like a shadow that declineth: and I am withered like grass.

But Thou, O LORD, shalt endure forever: and Thy remembrance unto all generations.

Thou shalt arise and have mercy upon Zion: for the time to favor her, yea, the set time, is come.

For Thy servants take pleasure in her stones: and favor the dust thereof.

So the heathen shall fear the name of the LORD: and all the kings of the earth Thy glory.

When the LORD shall build up Zion: He shall appear in His glory.

He will regard the prayer of the destitute: and not despise their prayer.

This shall be written for the generation to come: and the people which shall be created shall praise the LORD.

For He hath looked down from the height of His Sanctuary: from heaven did the LORD behold the earth

To hear the groaning of the prisoner: to loose those that are appointed to death;

To declare the name of the LORD in Zion: and His praise in Jerusalem,

When the people are gathered together: and the kingdoms, to serve the LORD.

He weakened my strength in the way: He shortened my days.

I said, O my God, take me not away in the midst of my days: Thy years are throughout all generations.

Of old hast Thou laid the foundation of the earth: and the heavens are the work of Thy hands.

They shall perish, but Thou shalt endure: yea, all of them shall wax old like a garment; as a vesture shalt Thou change them, and they shall be changed;

But Thou art the same: and Thy years shall have no end.

The children of Thy servants shall continue: and their seed shall be established before Thee.

Psalm 103
Benedic, anima mea, Domino, et omnia

Bless the LORD, O my soul: and all that is within me, bless His holy name.

Bless the LORD, O my soul: and forget not all His benefits:

Who forgiveth all thine iniquities: who healeth all thy diseases;

Who redeemeth thy life from destruction: who crowneth thee with loving-kindness and tender mercies;

Who satisfieth thy mouth with good things: so that thy youth is renewed like the eagle's.

The LORD executeth righteousness and judgment: for all that are oppressed.

He made known His ways unto Moses: His acts unto the Children of Israel.

The LORD is merciful and gracious: slow to anger and plenteous in mercy.

He will not always chide: neither will He keep His anger forever.

He hath not dealt with us after our sins: nor rewarded us according to our iniquities.

For as the heaven is high above the earth: so great is His mercy toward them that fear Him.

As far as the east is from the west: so far hath He removed our transgressions from us.

Like as a father pitieth his childen: so the Lord pitieth them that fear Him.

For He knoweth our frame: He remembereth that we are dust.

As for man, his days are as grass: as a flower of the field, so he flourisheth.

For the wind passeth over it, and it is gone: and the place thereof shall know it no more.

But the mercy of the LORD is from everlasting to everlasting upon them that fear Him: and His righteousness unto children's children,

To such as keep His covenant: and to those that remember His commandments to do them.

The LORD hath prepared His throne in the heavens: and His kingdom ruleth over all.

Bless the LORD, ye His angels, that excel in strength: that do His commandments, hearkening unto the voice of His word.

Bless ye the LORD, all ye His hosts: ye ministers of His that do His pleasure.

Bless the LORD, all His works, in all places of His dominion: Bless the LORD, O my soul.

Psalm 104. Benedic, anima mea

Bless the LORD, O my soul: O LORD, my God, Thou art very great; Thou art clothed with honor and majesty;

Who coverest Thyself with light as with a garment: who stretchest out the heavens like a curtain:

Who layeth the beams of His chambers in the waters: who maketh the clouds His chariot; who walketh upon the wings of the wind;

Who maketh His angels spirits: His ministers a flaming fire;

Who laid the foundations of the earth: that it should not be removed forever.

Thou coveredst it with the deep as with a garment: the waters stood above the mountains.

At Thy rebuke they fled: at the voice of Thy thunder they hastened away.

They go up by the mountains: they go down by the valleys, unto the place which Thou hast founded for them.

Thou hast set a bound that they may not pass over: that they turn not again to cover the earth.

He sendeth the springs into the valleys: which run among the hills.

They give drink to every beast of the field: the wild asses quench their thirst.

By them shall the fowls of the heaven have their habitation: which sing among the branches.

He watereth the hills from His chambers: the earth is satisfied with the fruit of Thy works.

He causeth the grass to grow for the cattle: and herb for the service of man,

That he may bring forth food out of the earth and wine that maketh glad the heart of man: and oil to make his face to shine, and bread, which strengtheneth man's heart.

The trees of the LORD are full of sap: the cedars of Lebanon, which He hath planted;

Where the birds make their nests: as for the stork, the fir trees are her house.

The high hills are a refuge for the wild goats: and the rocks for the conies.

He appointed the moon for seasons: the sun knoweth his going down.

Thou makest darkness, and it is night: wherein all the beasts of the forests do creep forth.

The young lions roar after their prey: and seek their meat from God.

The sun ariseth, they gather themselves together: and lay them down in their dens.

Man goeth forth unto his work and to his labor: until the evening.

O LORD, how manifold are Thy works!: In wisdom hast Thou made them all; the earth is full of Thy riches.

So is this great and wide sea: wherein are things creeping innumerable, both small and great beasts.

There go the ships; there is that leviathan: whom Thou hast made to play therein.

These wait all upon Thee: that Thou mayest give them their meat in due season.

That Thou givest them they gather: Thou openest Thine hand, they are filled with good.

Thou hidest Thy face, they are troubled: Thou takest away their breath, they die and return to their dust.

Thou sendest forth Thy Spirit, they are created: and Thou renewest the face of the earth.

The glory of the LORD shall endure forever: the LORD shall rejoice in His works.

He looketh on the earth, and it trembleth: He toucheth the hills, and they smoke.

I will sing unto the LORD as long as I live: I will sing praise to my God while I have my being.

My meditation of Him shall be sweet: I will be glad in the LORD.

Let the sinners be consumed out of the earth, and let the wicked be no more: Bless thou the LORD, O my soul. Praise ye the LORD.

Psalm 110. Dixit Dominus

The LORD said unto my Lord: Sit Thou at My right hand until I make Thine enemies Thy footstool.

The LORD shall send the rod of Thy strength out of Zion: rule Thou in the midst of Thine enemies.

Thy people shall be willing in the day of Thy power, in the beauties o holiness from the womb of the morning: Thou hast the dew of Thy youth.

The LORD hath sworn and will not repent: Thou art a Priest forever after the order of Melchizedek.

The LORD at Thy right hand: shall strike through kings in the day of His wrath.

He shall judge among the heathen, He shall fill the places with the dead bodies: He shall wound the heads over many countries.

He shall drink of the brook in the way: therefore shall He lift up the head.

Psalm 111. Confitebor tibi

Praise ye the LORD. I will praise the LORD with my whole heart: in the assembly of the upright and in the congregation.

The works of the LORD are great: sought out of all them that have pleasure therein.

His work is honorable and glorious: and His righteousness endureth forever.

He hath made His wonderful works to be remembered: the LORD is gracious and full of compassion.

He hath given meat unto them that fear Him: He will ever be mindful of His covenant.

He hath showed His people the power of His works: that He may give them the heritage of the heathen.

The works of His hands are verity and judgment: all His commandments are sure.

They stand fast forever and ever: and are done in truth and uprightness.

He sent redemption unto His people: He hath commanded His covenant forever; holy and reverend is His name.

The fear of the LORD is the beginning of wisdom: a good understanding have all they that do His commandments; His praise endureth forever.

Psalm 113. Laudate, pueri

Praise ye the LORD. Praise, O ye servants of the LORD: praise the name of the LORD.

Blessed be the name of the LORD: from this time forth and forevermore.

From the rising of the sun unto the going down of the same: the LORD's name is to be praised.

The LORD is high above all nations: and His glory above the heavens.

Who is like unto the LORD, our God, who dwelleth on high: who humbleth himself to behold the things that are in heaven and in the earth?

He raiseth up the poor out of the dust: and lifteth the needy out of the dunghill

That He may set him with princes: even with the princes of His people.

He maketh the barren woman to keep house: and to be a joyful mother of children. Praise ye the LORD.

Psalm 114. In exitu Israel

When Israel went out of Egypt: the house of Jacob from a people of strange language,

Judah was His sanctuary: and Israel His dominion.

The sea saw it and fled: Jordan was driven back.

The mountains skipped like rams: and the little hills like lambs.

What ailed thee, O thou sea, that thou fleddest?: thou Jordan, that thou wast driven back?

Ye mountains, that ye skipped like rams: and ye little hills, like lambs?

Tremble, thou earth, at the presence of the Lord: at the presence of the God of Jacob;

Which turned the rock into a standing water: the flint into a fountain of waters.

Psalm 115. Non nobis, Domine

Not unto us, O LORD, not unto us, but unto Thy name give glory: for Thy mercy and for Thy truth's sake.

Wherefore should the heathen say: Where is now their God?

But our God is in the heavens: He hath done whatsoever He hath pleased.

Their idols are silver and gold: the work of men's hands.

They have mouths, but they speak not: eyes have they, but they see not;

They have ears, but they hear not: noses have they, but they smell not;

They have hands, but they handle not; feet have they, but they walk not: neither speak they through their throat.

They that make them are like unto them: so is everyone that trusteth in them.

O Israel, trust thou in the LORD: He is their Help and their Shield.

O house of Aaron, trust in the LORD: He is their Help and their Shield.

Ye that fear the LORD, trust in the LORD: He is their Help and their Shield.

The LORD hath been mindful of us; He will bless us: He will bless the house of Israel; He will bless the house of Aaron.

He will bless them that fear the LORD: both small and great.

The LORD shall increase you more and more: you and your children.

Ye are blessed of the Lord: which made heaven and earth.

The heaven, even the heavens, are the Lord's: but the earth hath He given to the children of men.

The dead praise not the Lord: neither any that go down into silence.

But we will bless the Lord: from this time forth and forevermore. Praise the Lord.

Psalm 116. Dilexi quoniam

I love the Lord: because He hath heard my voice and my supplications.

Because He hath inclined His ear unto me: therefore will I call upon Him as long as I live.

The sorrows of death compassed me, and the pains of hell gat hold upon me: I found trouble and sorrow.

Then called I upon the name of the Lord: O Lord, I beseech Thee, deliver my soul.

Gracious is the Lord and righteous: yea, our God is merciful.

The Lord preserveth the simple: I was brought low, and He helped me.

Return unto thy rest, O my soul: for the Lord hath dealt bountifully with thee.

For Thou hast delivered my soul from death: mine eyes from tears, and my feet from falling.

I will walk before the Lord: in the land of the living.

I believed, therefore have I spoken; I was greatly afflicted: I said in my haste, All men are liars.

What shall I render unto the Lord: for all His benefits toward me?

I will take the cup of salvation: and call upon the name of the Lord.

I will pay my vows unto the Lord now: in the presence of all His people.

Precious in the sight of the Lord: is the death of His saints.

O Lord, truly I am Thy servant: I am Thy servant and the son of Thine handmaid; Thou hast loosed my bonds.

I will offer to Thee the sacrifice of thanksgiving: and will call upon the name of the Lord.

I will pay my vows unto the Lord now, in the presence of all His people: in the courts of the Lord's house, in the midst of thee, O Jerusalem. Praise ye the Lord.

Psalm 117. Laudate Dominum

Oh, praise the Lord, all ye nations: praise Him, all ye people.

For His merciful kindness is great toward us: and the truth of the Lord endureth forever. Praise ye the Lord.

Psalm 118. Confitemini Domino

Oh, give thanks unto the Lord, for He is good: because His mercy endureth forever.

Let Israel now say: that His mercy endureth forever.

Let the house of Aaron now say: that His mercy endureth forever.

Let them now that fear the Lord say: that His mercy endureth forever.

I called upon the Lord in distress: the Lord answered me and set me in a large place.

The Lord is on my side; I will not fear: what can man do unto me?

The Lord taketh my part with them that help me: therefore shall I see my desire upon them that hate me.

It is better to trust in the Lord: than to put confidence in man.

It is better to trust in the Lord: than to put confidence in princes.

All nations compassed me about: but in the name of the Lord will I destroy them.

They compassed me about; yea, they compassed me about: but in the name of the Lord I will destroy them.

They compassed me about like bees; they are quenched as the fire of thorns: for in the name of the Lord I will destroy them.

Thou hast thrust sore at me that I might fall: but the Lord helped me.

The Lord is my Strength and Song: and is become my Salvation.

The voice of rejoicing and salvation is in the tabernacles of the righteous: the right hand of the Lord doeth valiantly.

The right hand of the Lord is exalted: the right hand of the Lord doeth valiantly.

I shall not die but live: and declare the works of the Lord.

The Lord hath chastened me sore: but He hath not given me over unto death.

Open to me the gates of righteousness: I will go into them, and I will praise the Lord,

This gate of the Lord: into which the righteous shall enter.

I will praise Thee, for Thou hast heard me: and art become my Salvation

The stone which the builders refused: is become the headstone of the corner.

This is the Lord's doing: it is marvelous in our eyes.

This is the day which the Lord hath made: we will rejoice and be glad in it

Save now, I beseech Thee, O Lord O Lord, I beseech Thee, send now prosperity.

Blessed be he that cometh in the name of the Lord: we have blessed you out of the house of the Lord.

God is the Lord which hath showed us light: bind the sacrifice with cords, even unto the horns of the altar.

Thou art my God, and I will praise Thee: Thou art my God, I will exalt Thee.

Oh, give thanks unto the Lord; for He is good: for His mercy endureth forever.

Psalm 119

I. Beati immaculati

Blessed are the undefiled in the way: who walk in the Law of the Lord.

Blessed are they that keep His testimonies: and that seek Him with the whole heart.

They also do no iniquity: they walk in His ways.

Thou hast commanded us: to keep Thy precepts diligently.

Oh, that my ways were directed: to keep Thy statutes!

Then shall I not be ashamed: when I have respect unto all Thy commandments.

I will praise Thee with uprightness of heart: when I shall have learned Thy righteous judgments.

I will keep Thy statutes: Oh, forsake me not utterly!

II. In quo corrigit?

Wherewithal shall a young man cleanse his way?: By taking heed thereto according to Thy Word.

With my whole heart have I sought Thee: Oh, let me not wander from Thy commandments!

Thy Word have I hid in mine heart: that I might not sin against Thee.

Blessed art Thou, O Lord: teach me Thy statutes.

With my lips have I declared: all the judgments of Thy mouth.

I have rejoiced in the way of Thy testimonies: as much as in all riches.

I will meditate in Thy precepts: and have respect unto Thy ways.

I will delight myself in Thy statutes: I will not forget Thy Word.

III. Retribue servo tuo

Deal bountifully with Thy servant: that I may live and keep Thy Word.

Open Thou mine eyes: that I may behold wondrous things out of Thy Law.

I am a stranger in the earth: hide not Thy commandments from me.

My soul breaketh for the longing: that it hath unto Thy judgments at all times.

Thou hast rebuked the proud that are cursed: which do err from Thy commandments.

Remove from me reproach and contempt: for I have kept Thy testimonies.

Princes also did sit and speak against me: but Thy servant did meditate in Thy statutes.

Thy testimonies also are my delight: and my counselors.

IV. Adhaesit pavimento

My soul cleaveth unto the dust: quicken Thou me according to Thy Word.

I have declared my ways, and Thou heardest me: teach me Thy statutes.

Make me to understand the way of Thy precepts: so shall I talk of Thy wondrous works.

My soul melteth for heaviness: strengthen Thou me according unto Thy Word.

Remove from me the way of lying: and grant me Thy Law graciously.

I have chosen the way of truth: Thy judgments have I laid before me.

I have stuck unto Thy testimonies: O Lord, put me not to shame.

I will run the way of Thy commandments: when Thou shalt enlarge my heart.

V. Legem pone

Teach me, O Lord, the way of Thy statutes: and I shall keep it unto the end.

Give me understanding, and I shall keep Thy Law: yea, I shall observe it with my whole heart.

Make me to go in the path of Thy commandments: for therein do I delight.

Incline my heart unto Thy testimonies: and not to covetousness.

Turn away mine eyes from beholding vanity: and quicken Thou me in Thy way.

Stablish Thy Word unto Thy servant: who is devoted to Thy fear.

Turn away my reproach which I fear: for Thy judgments are good.

Behold, I have longed after Thy precepts: quicken me in Thy righteousness.

VI. Et veniat super me

Let Thy mercies come also unto me, O Lord: even Thy salvation, according to Thy Word.

So shall I have wherewith to answer him that reproacheth me: for I trust in Thy Word.

And take not the Word of Truth utterly out of my mouth: for I have hoped in Thy judgments.

So shall I keep Thy Law continually: forever and ever.

And I will walk at liberty: for I seek Thy precepts.

I will speak of Thy testimonies also before kings: and will not be ashamed.

And I will delight myself in Thy commandments: which I have loved.

My hands also will I lift up unto Thy commandments, which I have loved: and I will meditate in Thy statutes.

VII. Memor esto verbi tui

Remember the word unto Thy servant: upon which Thou hast caused me to hope.

This is my comfort in my affliction: for Thy Word hath quickened me.

The proud have had me greatly in derision: yet have I not declined from Thy Law.

I remembered Thy judgments of old, O Lord: and have comforted myself.

Horror hath taken hold upon me: because of the wicked that forsake Thy Law.

Thy statutes have been my songs: in the house of my pilgrimage.

I have remembered Thy name, O Lord, in the night: and have kept Thy Law.

This I had: because I kept Thy precepts.

VIII. Portio mea, Domine

Thou art my Portion, O Lord: I have said that I would keep Thy words.

I entreated Thy favor with my whole heart: be merciful unto me according to Thy Word.

I thought on my ways: and turned my feet unto Thy testimonies.

I made haste and delayed not: to keep Thy commandments.

The bands of the wicked have robbed me: but I have not forgotten Thy Law.

At midnight I will rise to give thanks unto Thee: because of Thy righteous judgments.

I am a companion of all them that fear Thee: and of them that keep Thy precepts.

The earth, O Lord, is full of Thy mercy: teach me Thy statutes.

IX. Bonitatem fecisti

Thou hast dealt well with Thy servant: O Lord, according unto Thy Word.

Teach me good judgment and knowledge: for I have believed Thy commandments.

Before I was afflicted, I went astray: but now have I kept Thy Word.

Thou art good, and doest good: teach me Thy statutes.

The proud have forged a lie against me: but I will keep Thy precepts with my whole heart.

Their heart is as fat as grease: but I delight in Thy Law.

It is good for me that I have been afflicted: that I might learn Thy statutes.

The Law of Thy mouth is better unto me: than thousands of gold and silver.

X. Manus tuae fecerunt me

Thy hands have made me and fashioned me: give me understanding that I may learn Thy commandments.

They that fear Thee will be glad when they see me: because I have hoped in Thy Word.

I know, O Lord, that Thy judgments are right: and that Thou in faithfulness hast afflicted me.

Let, I pray Thee, Thy merciful kindness be for my comfort: according to Thy word unto Thy servant.

Let Thy tender mercies come unto me that I may live: for Thy Law is my delight.

Let the proud be ashamed, for they dealt perversely with me without a cause: but I will meditate in Thy precepts.

Let those that fear Thee turn unto me: and those that have known Thy testimonies.

Let my heart be sound in Thy statutes: that I be not ashamed.

XI. Deficit anima mea

My soul fainteth for Thy salvation: but I hope in Thy Word.

Mine eyes fail for Thy Word: saying, When wilt Thou comfort me?

For I am become like a bottle in the smoke: yet do I not forget Thy statutes.

How many are the days of Thy servant?: When wilt Thou execute judgment on them that persecute me?

The proud have digged pits for me: which are not after Thy Law.

All Thy commandments are faithful: they persecute me wrongfully; help Thou me.

They had almost consumed me upon earth: but I forsook not Thy precepts.

Quicken me after Thy loving-kindness: so shall I keep the testimony of Thy mouth.

XII. In aeternum, Domine

Forever, O Lord: Thy Word is settled in heaven.

Thy faithfulness is unto all generations: Thou hast established the earth and it abideth.

They continue this day according to Thine ordinances: for all are Thy servants.

Unless Thy Law had been my delight: I should then have perished in mine affliction.

I will never forget Thy precepts: for with them Thou hast quickened me.

I am Thine, save me: for I have sought Thy precepts.

The wicked have waited for me to destroy me: but I will consider Thy testimonies.

I have seen an end of all perfection: but Thy commandment is exceeding broad.

XIII. Quomodo dilexi

Oh, how love I Thy Law!: It is my meditation all the day.

Thou through Thy commandments hast made me wiser than mine enemies: for they are ever with me.

I have more understanding than all my teachers: for Thy testimonies are my meditation.

I understand more than the ancients: because I keep Thy precepts.

I have refrained my feet from every evil way: that I might keep Thy Word.

I have not departed from Thy judgments: for Thou hast taught me.

How sweet are Thy words unto my taste!: yea, sweeter than honey to my mouth.

Through Thy precepts I get understanding: therefore I hate every false way.

XIV. Lucerna pedibus meis

Thy Word is a lamp unto my feet: and a light unto my path.

I have sworn, and I will perform it: that I will keep Thy righteous judgments.

I am afflicted very much: quicken me, O Lord, according unto Thy Word.

Accept, I beseech Thee, the freewill offerings of my mouth, O Lord: and teach me Thy judgments.

My soul is continually in my hand: yet do I not forget Thy Law.

The wicked have laid a snare for me: yet I erred not from Thy precepts.

Thy testimonies have I taken as an heritage forever: for they are the rejoicing of my heart.

I have inclined mine heart to perform Thy statutes alway: even unto the end.

XV. Iniquos odio habui

I hate vain thoughts: but Thy Law do I love.

Thou art my Hiding Place and my shield: I hope in Thy Word.

Depart from me, ye evildoers: for I will keep the commandments of my God.

Uphold me according unto Thy Word that I may live: and let me not be ashamed of my hope.

Hold Thou me up, and I shall be safe: and I will have respect unto Thy statutes continually.

Thou hast trodden down all them that err from Thy statutes: for their deceit is falsehood.

Thou puttest away all the wicked of the earth like dross: therefore I love Thy testimonies.

My flesh trembleth for fear of Thee: and I am afraid of Thy judgments.

XVI. Feci iudicium

I have done judgment and justice: leave me not to mine oppressors.

Be surety for Thy servant for good: let not the proud oppress me.

Mine eyes fail for Thy salvation: and for the Word of Thy righteousness.

Deal with Thy servant according unto Thy mercy: and teach me Thy statutes.

I am Thy servant; give me understanding: that I may know Thy testimonies.

It is time for Thee, Lord, to work: for they have made void Thy Law.

Therefore I love Thy commandments above gold: yea, above fine gold.

Therefore I esteem all Thy precepts concerning all things to be right; and I hate every false way.

XVII. Mirabilia testimonia tua

Thy testimonies are wonderful: therefore doth my soul keep them.

The entrance of Thy words giveth light: it giveth understanding unto the simple.

I opened my mouth and panted: for I longed for Thy commandments.

Look Thou upon me and be merciful unto me: as Thou usest to do unto those that love Thy name.

Order my steps in Thy Word: and let not any iniquity have dominion over me.

Deliver me from the oppression of man: so will I keep Thy precepts.

Make Thy face to shine upon Thy servant: and teach me Thy statutes.

Rivers of waters run down mine eyes: because they keep not Thy Law.

XVIII. Iustus es, Domine

Righteous art Thou, O Lord: and upright are Thy judgments.

Thy testimonies that Thou hast commanded: are righteous and very faithful.

My zeal hath consumed me: because mine enemies have forgotten Thy words.

Thy Word is very pure: therefore Thy servant loveth it.

I am small and despised: yet do I not forget Thy precepts.

Thy righteousness is an everlasting righteousness: and Thy Law is the truth.

Trouble and anguish have taken hold on me: yet Thy commandments are my delights.

The righteousness of Thy testimonies is everlasting: give me understanding, and I shall live.

XIX. Clamavi in toto corde meo

I cried with my whole heart: hear me, O LORD; I will keep Thy statutes.

I cried unto Thee: save me, and I shall keep Thy testimonies.

I prevented the dawning of the morning and cried: I hoped in Thy Word.

Mine eyes prevent the night-watches: that I might meditate in Thy Word.

Hear my voice according unto Thy loving-kindness: O LORD, quicken me according to Thy judgment.

They draw nigh that follow after mischief: they are far from Thy Law.

Thou art near, O LORD: and all Thy commandments are truth.

Concerning Thy testimonies, I have known of old: that Thou hast founded them forever.

XX. Vide humilitatem

Consider mine affliction and deliver me: for I do not forget Thy Law.

Plead my cause and deliver me: quicken me according to Thy Word.

Salvation is far from the wicked: for they seek not Thy statutes.

Great are Thy tender mercies, O LORD: quicken me according to Thy judgments.

Many are my persecutors and mine enemies: yet do I not decline from Thy testimonies.

I beheld the transgressors and was grieved: because they kept not Thy Word.

Consider how I love Thy precepts: quicken me, O LORD, according to Thy loving-kindness.

Thy Word is true from the beginning: and every one of Thy righteous judgments endureth forever.

XXI. Principes persecuti sunt

Princes have persecuted me without a cause: but my heart standeth in awe of Thy Word.

I rejoice at Thy Word: as one that findeth great spoil.

I hate and abhor lying: but Thy Law do I love.

Seven times a day do I praise Thee: because of Thy righteous judgments.

Great peace have they which love Thy Law: and nothing shall offend them.

LORD, I have hoped for Thy salvation: and done Thy commandments.

My soul hath kept Thy testimonies: and I love them exceedingly.

I have kept Thy precepts and Thy testimonies: for all my ways are before Thee.

XXII. Appropinquet deprecatio

Let my cry come near before Thee, O LORD: give me understanding according to Thy Word.

Let my supplication come before Thee: deliver me according to Thy Word.

My lips shall utter praise: when Thou hast taught me Thy statutes.

My tongue shall speak of Thy Word: for all Thy commandments are right-eousness.

Let Thine hand help me: for I have chosen Thy precepts.

I have longed for Thy salvation, O LORD: and Thy Law is my delight.

Let my soul live, and it shall praise Thee: and let Thy judgments help me.

I have gone astray like a lost sheep: seek Thy servant: for I do not forget Thy commandments.

Psalm 121. Levavi oculos

I will lift up mine eyes unto the hills: from whence cometh my help.

My help cometh from the LORD: which made heaven and earth.

He will not suffer thy foot to be moved: He that keepeth thee will not slumber.

Behold, He that keepeth Israel: shall neither slumber nor sleep.

The LORD is thy Keeper: the LORD is thy Shade upon thy right hand.

The sun shall not smite thee by day: nor the moon by night.

The LORD shall preserve thee from all evil: He shall preserve thy soul.

The LORD shall preserve thy going out and thy coming in: from this time forth and even forevermore.

Psalm 122. Laetatus sum

I was glad when they said unto me: Let us go into the house of the LORD.

Our feet shall stand within thy gates, O Jerusalem.

Jerusalem is builded: as a city that is compact together,

Whither the tribes go up, the tribes of the LORD: unto the testimony of Israel, to give thanks unto the name of the LORD.

For there are set thrones of judgment: the thrones of the house of David.

Pray for the peace of Jerusalem: they shall prosper that love thee.

Peace be within thy walls: and prosperity within thy palaces.

For my brethren and companions' sakes: I will now say, Peace be within thee.

Because of the house of the LORD, our God: I will seek thy good.

Psalm 124. Nisi quia Dominus

If it had not been the LORD who was on our side: now may Israel say;

If it had not been the LORD who was on our side: when men rose up against us,

Then they had swallowed us up quick: when their wrath was kindled against us;

Then the waters had overwhelmed us: the stream had gone over our soul.

Then the proud waters: had gone over our soul.

Blessed be the LORD: who hath not given us as a prey to their teeth.

Our soul is escaped as a bird out of the snare of the fowlers: the snare is broken, and we are escaped.

Our help is in the name of the LORD: who made heaven and earth.

Psalm 125. Qui confidunt

They that trust in the LORD shall be as Mount Zion: which cannot be removed, but abideth forever.

As the mountains are round about Jerusalem: so the LORD is round about His people from henceforth even forever.

For the rod of the wicked shall not rest upon the lot of the righteous: lest the righteous put forth their hands unto iniquity.

Do good, O LORD, unto those that be good: and to them that are upright in their hearts.

As for such as turn aside unto their crooked ways: the LORD shall lead them forth with the workers of iniquity; but peace shall be upon Israel.

Psalm 126. In convertendo

When the LORD turned again the captivity of Zion: we were like them that dream.

Then was our mouth filled with laughter: and our tongue with singing.

Then said they among the heathen: the LORD hath done great things for them.

The LORD hath done great things for us: whereof we are glad.

Turn again our captivity, O LORD: as the streams in the south.

They that sow in tears: shall reap in joy.

He that goeth forth and weepeth, bearing precious seed: shall doubtless come again with rejoicing, bringing his sheaves with him.

Psalm 130. De profundis

Out of the depths: have I cried unto Thee, O LORD.

Lord, hear my voice: let Thine ears be attentive to the voice of my supplications.

If Thou, LORD, shouldest mark iniquities: O Lord, who shall stand?

But there is forgiveness with Thee: that Thou mayest be feared.

I wait for the LORD, my soul doth wait: and in His Word do I hope.

My soul waiteth for the Lord more than they that watch for the morning: I say, more than they that watch for the morning.

Let Israel hope in the LORD, for with the LORD there is mercy: and with Him is plenteous redemption.

And He shall redeem Israel: from all his iniquities.

Psalm 132. Memento, Domine

LORD, remember David: and all his afflictions;

How he sware unto the LORD: and vowed unto the mighty God of Jacob;

Surely I will not come into the tabernacle of my house: nor go up into my bed;

I will not give sleep to mine eyes: or slumber to mine eyelids,

Until I find out a place for the LORD: a habitation for the mighty God of Jacob.

Lo, we heard of it at Ephratah: we found it in the fields of the wood.

We will go into His Tabernacles: we will worship at His footstool.

Arise, O LORD, into Thy rest: Thou and the Ark of Thy strength.

Let Thy priests be clothed with righteousness: and let Thy saints shout for joy.

For Thy servant David's sake: turn not away the face of Thine anointed.

The LORD hath sworn in truth unto David: He will not turn from it;

Of the fruit of thy body: will I set upon thy throne.

If thy children will keep My covenant and My testimony that I shall teach them: their children shall also sit upon thy throne forevermore.

For the LORD hath chosen Zion: He hath desired it for His habitation.

This is My rest forever: here will I dwell; for I have desired it.

I will abundantly bless her provision: I will satisfy her poor with bread.

I will also clothe her priests with salvation: and her saints shall shout aloud for joy.

There will I make the horn of David to bud: I have ordained a lamp for Mine anointed.

His enemies will I clothe with shame: but upon himself shall his crown flourish.

Psalm 136. Confitemini

Oh, give thanks unto the LORD; for He is good: for His mercy endureth forever.

Oh, give thanks unto the God of gods: for His mercy endureth forever.

Oh, give thanks to the Lord of Lords: for His mercy endureth forever;

To Him who alone doeth great wonders: for His mercy endureth forever;

To Him that by wisdom made the heavens: for His mercy endureth forever;

To Him that stretched out the earth above the waters: for His mercy endureth forever;

To Him that made great lights: for His mercy endureth forever;

The sun to rule by day: for His mercy endureth forever;

The moon and stars to rule by night: for His mercy endureth forever;

To Him that smote Egypt in their first-born: for His mercy endureth forever;

And brought out Israel from among them: for His mercy endureth forever;

With a strong hand and with a stretched-out arm: for His mercy endureth forever;

To Him which divided the Red Sea into parts: for His mercy endureth forever;

And made Israel to pass through the midst of it: for His mercy endureth forever;

But overthrew Pharaoh and his host in the Red Sea: for His mercy endureth forever;

To Him which led His people through the wilderness: for His mercy endureth forever;

To Him which smote great kings: for His mercy endureth forever;

And slew famous kings: for His mercy endureth forever;

Sihon, king of the Amorites: for His mercy endureth forever;

And Og, the king of Bashan: for His mercy endureth forever;

And gave their land for an heritage: for His mercy endureth forever;

Even an heritage unto Israel, His servant: for His mercy endureth forever;

Who remembered us in our low estate: for His mercy endureth forever;

And hath redeemed us from our enemies: for His mercy endureth forever;

Who giveth food to all flesh: for His mercy endureth forever.

Oh, give thanks unto the God of heaven: for His mercy endureth forever.

Psalm 138. Confitebor tibi

I will praise Thee with my whole heart: before the gods will I sing praise unto Thee.

I will worship toward Thy holy Temple and praise Thy name for Thy loving-kindness and for Thy truth: for Thou hast magnified Thy Word above all Thy name.

In the day when I cried, Thou answeredst me: and strengthenedst me with strength in my soul.

All the kings of the earth shall praise Thee, O LORD: when they hear the words of Thy mouth.

Yea, they shall sing in the ways of the LORD: for great is the glory of the LORD.

Though the LORD be high, yet hath He respect unto the lowly: but the proud He knoweth afar off.

Though I walk in the midst of trouble, Thou wilt revive me: Thou shalt stretch forth Thine hand against the wrath of mine enemies, and Thy right hand shall save me.

The LORD will perfect that which concerneth me: Thy mercy, O LORD, endureth forever; forsake not the work of Thine own hands.

Psalm 139. Domine, probasti

O LORD, Thou hast searched me and known me: Thou knowest my down sitting and mine uprising; Thou understandest my thought afar off.

Thou compassest my path and my lying down: and art acquainted with all my ways.

For there is not a word in my tongue but, lo, O LORD, Thou knowest it altogether.

Thou hast beset me behind and before: and laid Thine hand upon me.

Such knowledge is too wonderful for me: it is high, I cannot attain unto it.

Whither shall I go from Thy Spirit or whither shall I flee from Thy presence

If I ascend up into heaven, Thou

art there: if I make my bed in hell, behold, Thou art there.

If I take the wings of the morning: and dwell in the uttermost parts of the sea,

Even there shall Thy hand lead me: and Thy right hand shall hold me.

If I say, Surely the darkness shall cover me: even the night shall be light about me.

Yea, the darkness hideth not from Thee; but the night shineth as the day: the darkness and the light are both alike to Thee.

For Thou hast possessed my reins: Thou hast covered me in my mother's womb.

I will praise Thee; for I am fearfully and wonderfully made: marvelous are Thy works; and that my soul knoweth right well.

My substance was not hid from Thee when I was made in secret: and curiously wrought in the lowest parts of the earth.

Thine eyes did see my substance yet being unperfect: and in Thy book all my members were written,

Which in continuance were fashioned: when as yet there was none of them.

How precious also are Thy thoughts unto me, O God!: How great is the sum of them!

If I should count them, they are more in number than the sand: when I awake, I am still with Thee.

Surely Thou wilt slay the wicked, O God: depart from me, therefore, ye bloody men.

For they speak against Thee wickedly: and Thine enemies take Thy name in vain.

Do not I hate them, O LORD, that hate Thee: and am not I grieved with those that rise up against Thee?

I hate them with perfect hatred: I count them mine enemies.

Search me, O God, and know my heart: try me and know my thoughts;

And see if there be any wicked way in me: and lead me in the way everlasting.

Psalm 143. Domine, exaudi

Hear my prayer, O LORD, give ear to my supplications: in Thy faithfulness answer me and in Thy righteousness.

And enter not into judgment with Thy servant: for in Thy sight shall no man living be justified.

For the enemy hath persecuted my soul; he hath smitten my life down to the ground: he hath made me to dwell in darkness, as those that have been long dead.

Therefore is my spirit overwhelmed within me: my heart within me is desolate.

I remember the days of old; I meditate on all Thy works: I muse on the work of Thy hands.

I stretch forth my hands unto Thee: my soul thirsteth after Thee as a thirsty land.

Hear me speedily, O LORD; my spirit faileth: hide not Thy face from me lest I be like unto them that go down into the pit.

Cause me to hear Thy loving-kindness in the morning; for in Thee do I trust: cause me to know the way wherein I should walk; for I lift up my soul unto Thee.

Deliver me, O LORD, from mine enemies: I flee unto Thee to hide me.

Teach me to do Thy will; for Thou art my God: Thy Spirit is good; lead me into the land of uprightness.

Quicken me, O LORD, for Thy name's sake: for Thy righteousness' sake bring my soul out of trouble.

And of Thy mercy cut off mine enemies: and destroy all them that afflict my soul; for I am Thy servant.

Psalm 145. Exaltabo te, Deus

I will extol Thee, my God, O King: and I will bless Thy name forever and ever.

Every day will I bless Thee: and I will praise Thy name forever and ever.

Great is the LORD and greatly to be praised: and His greatness is unsearchable.

One generation shall praise Thy works to another: and shall declare Thy mighty acts.

I will speak of the glorious honor of Thy majesty: and of Thy wondrous works.

And men shall speak of the might of Thy terrible acts: and I will declare Thy greatness.

They shall abundantly utter the memory of Thy great goodness: and shall sing of Thy righteousness.

The LORD is gracious and full of compassion: slow to anger and of great mercy.

The LORD is good to all: and His tender mercies are over all His works.

All Thy works shall praise Thee, O LORD: and Thy saints shall bless Thee.

They shall speak of the glory of Thy kingdom: and talk of Thy power,

To make known to the sons of men His mighty acts: and the glorious majesty of His kingdom.

Thy kingdom is an everlasting kingdom: and Thy dominion endureth throughout all generations.

The LORD upholdeth all that fall: and raiseth up all those that be bowed down.

The eyes of all wait upon Thee: and Thou givest them their meat in due season.

Thou openest Thine hand: and satisfiest the desire of every living thing.

The LORD is righteous in all His ways: and holy in all His works.

The LORD is nigh unto all them that call upon Him: to all that call upon Him in truth.

He will fulfill the desire of them that fear Him: He also will hear their cry and will save them.

The LORD preserveth all them that love Him: but all the wicked will He destroy.

My mouth shall speak the praise of the LORD: and let all flesh bless His holy name forever and ever.

Psalm 146. Lauda, anima mea

Praise ye the LORD: Praise the LORD, O my soul.

While I live, will I praise the LORD: I will sing praises unto my God while I have any being.

Put not your trust in princes: nor in the son of man, in whom there is no help.

His breath goeth forth, he returneth to his earth: in that very day his thoughts perish.

Happy is he that hath the God of Jacob for his help: whose hope is in the LORD, his God;

Which made heaven and earth, the sea, and all that therein is: which keepeth truth forever;

Which executeth judgment for the oppressed: which giveth food to the hungry.

The LORD looseth the prisoners: the LORD openeth the eyes of the blind.

The LORD raiseth them that are bowed down: the LORD loveth the righteous.

The LORD preserveth the strangers; He relieveth the fatherless and widow: but the way of the wicked He turneth upside down.

The LORD shall reign forever, even Thy God, O Zion, unto all generations: Praise ye the LORD.

Psalm 147. Laudate Dominum

Praise ye the LORD, for it is good to sing praises unto our God: for it is pleasant; and praise is comely.

The LORD doth build up Jerusalem:

He gathereth together the outcasts of Israel.

He healeth the broken in heart: and bindeth up their wounds.

He telleth the number of the stars: He calleth them all by their names.

Great is our Lord and of great power: His understanding is infinite.

The LORD lifteth up the meek: He casteth the wicked down to the ground.

Sing unto the LORD with thanksgiving: sing praise upon the harp unto our God;

Who covereth the heaven with clouds, who prepareth rain for the earth: who maketh grass to grow upon the mountains.

He giveth to the beast his food: and to the young ravens which cry.

He delighteth not in the strength of the horse: He taketh not pleasure in the legs of a man.

The LORD taketh pleasure in them that fear Him: in those that hope in His mercy.

Praise the LORD, O Jerusalem: praise thy God, O Zion.

For He hath strengthened the bars of thy gates: He hath blessed thy children within thee.

He maketh peace in thy borders: and filleth thee with the finest of the wheat.

He sendeth forth His commandment upon earth: His word runneth very swiftly.

He giveth snow like wool: He scattereth the hoarfrost like ashes.

He casteth forth His ice like morsels: who can stand before His cold?

He sendeth out His word and melteth them: He causeth His wind to blow, and the waters flow.

He showeth His Word unto Jacob: His statutes and His judgments unto Israel.

He hath not dealt so with any nation: and as for His judgments, they have not known them. Praise ye the LORD.

Psalm 148. Laudate Dominum de coelis

Praise ye the LORD. Praise ye the LORD from the heavens: praise Him in the heights.

Praise ye Him, all His angels: praise ye Him, all His hosts.

Praise ye Him, sun and moon: praise Him, all ye stars of light.

Praise Him, ye heavens of heavens: and ye waters that be above the heavens.

Let them praise the name of the LORD: for He commanded, and they were created.

He hath also stablished them forever

and ever: He hath made a decree which shall not pass.

Praise the LORD from the earth: ye dragons and all deeps;

Fire and hail; snow and vapors: stormy wind fulfilling His word;

Mountains and all hills: fruitful trees and all cedars;

Beasts and all cattle: creeping things and flying fowl;

Kings of the earth and all people: princes and all judges of the earth;

Both young men and maidens: old men and children;

Let them praise the name of the LORD: for His name alone is excellent; His glory is above the earth and heaven.

He also exalteth the horn of His people, the praise of all His saints: even of the children of Israel, a people near unto Him. Praise ye the LORD.

Psalm 150

Laudate Dominum in sanctis eius

Praise ye the LORD. Praise God in His Sanctuary: praise Him in the firmament of His power.

Praise Him for His mighty acts: praise Him according to His excellent greatness.

Praise Him with the sound of the trumpet: praise Him with the psaltery and harp.

Praise Him with the timbrel and dance: praise Him with stringed instruments and organs.

Praise Him upon the loud cymbals: praise Him upon the high-sounding cymbals.

Let everything that hath breath praise the LORD: Praise ye the LORD.

Miscellaneous

The Movable Feasts and Festivals of the Church Year

The Movable Feasts and Festivals all depend upon Easter, except Advent.

Advent Sunday is always the nearest Sunday to the thirtieth day of November, whether before or after. *Easter* is always the first Sunday after the Full Moon which happens upon or next after the twenty-first day of March; and if the Full Moon happens upon a Sunday, Easter is the Sunday after. The time of Easter being found, the other Feasts and Festivals occur as follows:

Septuagesima Sunday is nine weeks before Easter. *Ash Wednesday,* or the beginning of Lent, is forty-six days before Easter. *Palmarum,* or the beginning of Holy Week, is seven days before Easter. *Maundy Thursday* is the Thursday before Easter. *Good Friday* is the Friday before Easter. *Ascension Day* is forty days after Easter. *Whitsunday* is seven weeks after Easter. *Trinity Sunday* is eight weeks after Easter.

Table of the Days on which Easter will Fall from 1941—2000

1941	April 13	1956	April 1	1971	April 11	1986	March 30
1942	April 5	1957	April 21	1972	April 2	1987	April 19
1943	April 25	1958	April 6	1973	April 22	1988	April 3
1944	April 9	1959	March 29	1974	April 14	1989	March 26
1945	April 1	1960	April 17	1975	March 30	1990	April 15
1946	April 21	1961	April 2	1976	April 18	1991	March 31
1947	April 6	1962	April 22	1977	April 10	1992	April 19
1948	March 28	1963	April 14	1978	March 26	1993	April 11
1949	April 17	1964	March 29	1979	April 15	1994	April 3
1950	April 9	1965	April 18	1980	April 6	1995	April 16
1951	March 25	1966	April 10	1981	April 19	1996	April 7
1952	April 13	1967	March 26	1982	April 11	1997	March 30
1953	April 5	1968	April 14	1983	April 3	1998	April 12
1954	April 18	1969	April 6	1984	April 22	1999	April 4
1955	April 10	1970	March 29	1985	April 7	2000	April 23

A Table of the Movable Feasts and Festivals
According to the several days that Easter can possibly fall upon

Easter	Sundays after Epiphany *	Septuagesima Sunday	Ash Wednesday	Ascension Day	Whitsunday	Sundays after Trinity	First Advent Sunday
March 22	1	Jan. 18	Feb. 4	April 30	May 10	27	Nov. 29
" 23	1	" 19	" 5	May 1	" 11	27	" 30
" 24	1	" 20	" 6	" 2	" 12	27	Dec. 1
" 25	2	" 21	" 7	" 3	" 13	27	" 2
" 26	2	" 22	" 8	" 4	" 14	27	" 3
" 27	2	" 23	' 9	" 5	" 15	26	Nov. 27
" 28	2	" 24	" 10	" 6	" 16	26	" 28
" 29	2	" 25	" 11	" 7	" 17	26	" 29
" 30	2	" 26	" 12	" 8	" 18	26	" 30
" 31	2	" 27	" 13	" 9	" 19	26	Dec. 1
April 1	3	" 29	" 15	" 10	" 20	26	" 2
" 2	3	" 29	" 15	" 11	" 21	26	" 3
" 3	3	" 30	" 16	" 12	" 22	25	Nov. 27
" 4	3	" 31	" 17	" 13	" 23	25	" 28
" 5	3	Feb. 1	" 18	" 14	" 24	25	" 29
" 6	3	" 2	" 19	" 15	" 25	25	" 30
" 7	3	" 3	" 20	" 16	" 26	25	Dec. 1
" 8	4	" 4	" 21	" 17	" 27	25	" 2
" 9	4	" 5	" 22	" 18	" 28	25	" 3
" 10	4	" 6	" 23	" 19	" 29	24	Nov. 27
" 11	4	" 7	" 24	" 20	" 30	24	" 28
" 12	4	" 8	" 25	" 21	" 31	24	" 29
" 13	4	" 9	" 26	" 22	June 1	24	" 30
" 14	4	" 10	" 27	" 23	" 2	24	Dec. 1
" 15	5	" 11	" 28	" 24	" 3	24	" 2
" 16	5	" 12	March 1	" 25	" 4	24	" 3
" 17	5	" 13	" 2	" 26	" 5	23	Nov. 27
" 18	5	" 14	" 3	" 27	" 6	23	" 28
" 19	5	" 15	" 4	" 28	" 7	23	" 29
" 20	5	" 16	" 5	" 29	" 8	23	" 30
" 21	5	" 17	" 6	" 30	" 9	23	Dec. 1
" 22	6	" 18	" 7	" 31	" 10	23	" 2
" 23	6	" 19	" 8	June 1	" 11	23	" 3
" 24	6	" 20	" 9	" 2	" 12	22	Nov. 27
" 25	6	" 21	" 10	" 3	" 13	22	" 28

* In a Leap Year, the number of Sundays after Epiphany is the same as if Easter had fallen one day later than it really does; and Septuagesima Sunday and Ash Wednesday fall one day later than that given in the Table unless the Table gives some day in March for Ash Wednesday; for in that case the day in the Table is right.

A Table of Lessons for the Sundays, Feasts, and Chief Festivals of the Church Year

Sunday and Feasts	First Series		Old Testament	Second Series		Psalms	
	Epistles	Gospels		Epistles	Gospels	Matins	Vespers
1. S. in Advent	Rom. 13:11-14	Matt. 21:1-9	Jer. 33:14-18	Col. 1:12-23	Luke 1:1-25	Ps. 1	Ps. 143
2. S. in Advent	Rom. 15:4-13	Luke 21:25-36	Micah 4:1-7	Rom. 2:1-16	Luke 1:26-35	Ps 42	Ps. 91
3. S. in Advent	1 Cor. 4:1-5	Matt. 11:2-10	Mal. 3:1-6	Rom. 1:16-25	Luke 1:39-56	Ps. 4	Ps. 98
4. S. in Advent	Phil. 4:4-7	John 1:19-28	Is. 40:1-8	Heb. 12:15-29	Luke 1:67-80	Ps. 5	Ps. 145
Christmas Day	Titus 2:11-14; Is. 9:2-7	Luke 2:1-14	Is. 7:10-14	Heb. 1:1-12	John 1:1-14	Pss. 19, 45, 85	Pss. 89, 110, 132
Second Christmas Day	Titus 3:4-7	Luke 2:15-20	Micah 5:2-4	1 John 4:7-16	John 1:15-18	Ps. 121	Ps. 111
Sunday after Christmas	Gal. 4:1-7	Luke 2:33-40	Is. 11:1-5	Heb. 2:9-16	Luke 2:22-32		
New Year's Eve			Is. 63:7-18	1 Pet. 1:22-25	Luke 13:6-10		
Circumcision and Name of Jesus	Gal. 3:23-29	Luke 2:21	Is. 55:1-13	Jas. 4:13-17	Luke 4:16-21	Pss. 122, 72	Pss. 90, 115
Sunday after New Year	1 Pet. 4:12-19	Matt. 2:13-23	Is. 42:1-9	Rom. 3:19-22	Matt. 3:1-12		
Epiphany	Is. 60:1-6	Matt. 2:1-12	Is. 49:1-7	Rom. 3:23-31	Matt. 3:13-17	Ps. 96	Ps. 72
1. S. after Epiphany	Rom. 12:1-5	Luke 2:41-52	Is. 61:1-3	Eph. 6:1-4	Mark 10:13-16	Ps. 13	Ps. 86
2. S. after Epiphany	Rom. 12:6-16 a	John 2:1-11	Deut. 18:15-19	Eph. 5:21-33	Luke 19:1-10	Ps. 14	Ps. 16
3. S. after Epiphany	Rcm. 12:16-21 b	Matt. 8:1-13	Jer. 33:6-9	Heb. 11:1-16	Luke 17:5-10	Ps. 15	Ps. 33
4. S. after Epiphany	Rom. 13:8-10	Matt. 8:23-27	Is. 43:1-3	Rom. 4:16-25	Matt. 14:22-33	Ps. 2	Ps. 97
5. S. after Epiphany	Col. 3:12-17		Jer. 17:5-10	1 Cor. 4:3-23	Matt. 13:44-52	Ps. 20	Ps. 86
The Transfiguration °	2 Pet. 1:16-21	Matt. 17:1-9	Is. 61:10, 11	2 Cor. 4:5, 6	Matt. 11:25-27	Ps. 87	Ps. 8
Septuagesima Sunday	2 Cor. 9:24—10:5	Matt. 20:1-16	Jer. 1:4-10	Acts 17:22-34	Matt. 25:14-30	Ps. 23	Ps. 114
Sexagesima Sunday	2 Cor. 11:19—12:9	Luke 8:4-15	Is. 55:10-13	2 Tim. 3:10—4:5	Mark 4:26-32	Ps. 24	Ps. 25
Quinquagesima Sunday	1 Cor. 13:1-13	Luke 18:31-43	Is. 35:3-7	1 Pet. 3:18-22	John 12:23-36	Ps. 26	Ps. 27
Ash Wednesday	Joel 2:12-19	Matt. 6:16-21	Jonah 3:1-10; or Is. 59:12-21	1 John 1:5-10	Luke 6:20-49	Ps. 6	Ps. 51
Inv., 1. S. in Lent	2 Cor. 6:1-10	Matt. 4:1-11	Gen. 3:1-24	Jas. 1:2-15	Luke 22:24-32	Ps. 32	Ps. 16
Rem., 2. S. in Lent	1 Thess. 4:1-7	Matt. 15:21-28	Is. 45:20-25	Jas. 5:13-20	Mark 9:17-29	Ps. 130	Ps. 25
Oculi, 3. S. in Lent	Eph. 5:1-9	Luke 11:14-28	2 Sam. 22:1-7	Rev. 2:1-7	John 8:42-51	Ps. 43	Ps. 86
Laet., 4. S. in Lent	Gal. 4:21-31	John 6:1-15	Is. 49:8-13	2 Pet. 1:2-11	John 6:36-51	Ps. 46	Ps. 139
Jud., 5. S. in Lent	Heb. 9:11-15	Matt. 21:1-9	Gen. 12:1-3	1 Cor. 1:21-31	Matt. 10:32-42	Ps. 54	Ps. 27
Palm., 6. S. in Lent	Phil. 2:5-11	John 12:1-23	Zech. 9:9, 10	Heb. 12:1-11	Mark 14:3-9	Ps. 61	Ps. 67
Monday of Holy Week	Jer. 11:18-20	John 12:24-43					
Tuesday of Holy Week	Is. 62:11—63:7	Luke 22:1—23:42					
Wednesday of Holy Week	1 Cor. 11:23-32	John 13:1-15					
Maundy Thursday		John 18:1—19:42	Ex. 12:1-14	1 Cor. 10:16, 17	Luke 22:14-20	Ps. 116	Ps. 70
Good Friday	Is. 52:13—53:12	Matt. 27:57-66	Is. 50:6-9	Rev. 5:6-10	Matt. 27:33-54	Pss. 22, 40, 54	Pss. 88, 69
Holy Saturday	1 Pet. 3:17-22	Mark 16:1-8					
Easter Sunday	Acts 10:34-41	Luke 24:13-35	Is. 52:13-15	1 Pet. 1:3-12	Matt. 28:1-8	Pss. 2, 57, 111	Pss. 113, 114, 118
Easter Monday	Acts 13:26-33	Luke 24:36-48	Hos. 13:14	1 Cor. 15:12-20	John 20:1-18	Ps. 62	Ps. 30
Easter Tuesday							
Sundays after Easter:							
1. Quasimodogeniti	1 John 5:4-10	John 20:19-31	Job 19:25-27	1 Pet. 1:17—2:3	John 21:15-19	Ps. 111	Ps. 4
2. Misericordias Domini	1 Pet. 2:21-25	John 10:11-16	Ezek. 34:11-16	Heb. 13:20, 21	John 5:22-30	Ps. 70	Ps. 23

° Always the last Sunday after Epiphany

Sunday and Feasts	First Series		Old Testament	Second Series		Psalms	
	Epistles	Gospels		Epistles	Gospels	Matins	Vespers
3. Jubilate	1 Pet. 2:11-20	John 16:16-23 c	Lam. 3:18-26	Heb. 4:14-16	John 14:1-11	Ps. 75	Ps. 146
4. Cantate	Jas. 1:16-21	John 16:5-15	Is. 12:1-6	2 Cor. 5:14-21	John 8:21-36	Ps. 82	Ps. 126
5. Rogate	Jas. 1:22-27	John 16:23-30 d	Jer. 29:11-14	Rom. 8:24-28	John 17:1-19	Ps. 84	Ps. 124
Ascension Day	Acts 1:1-11	Mark 16:14-20	Is. 57:15	Eph. 1:3-14	Luke 24:46-53	Pss. 8, 15, 21, 47	Pss. 24, 68, 148
Sunday after Ascension	1 Pet. 4:7-11 e	John 15:26—16:4	Ezek. 36:25-27	Rom. 8:29-39	John 17:20-26	Ps. 93	Ps. 97
Whitsunday	Acts 2:1-13	John 14:23-31	Joel 2:28-32	Eph. 4:7-16	John 14:15-21	Pss. 48, 68, 45	Pss. 104, 145
Whit-Monday	Acts 10:42-48 f	John 3:16-21	Is. 32:14-20	Acts 2:42-47	John 4:5-26	Ps. 90	Ps. 19
Whit-Tuesday	Acts 8:14-17	John 10:1-10	Ezek. 18:30-32	2 Cor. 13:14			
Trinity Sunday	Rom. 11:33-36	John 3:1-15	Jer. 9:23, 24	1 Tim. 6:6-19	Matt. 28:18-20	Pss. 67, 8, 148	Pss. 115, 143
1. S. after Trinity	1 John 4:16-21 g	Luke 16:19-31	Is. 25:6-9	Rev. 3:14-22	Luke 12:13-21	Ps. 119, 1st part	Ps. 34
2. S. after Trinity	1 John 3:13-18	Luke 14:16-24	Micah 7:18-20	Acts 9:1-18	Luke 14:25-35	Ps. 119, 2d part	Ps. 28
3. S. after Trinity	1 Pet. 5:6-11	Luke 15:1-10	Is. 58:6-12	Rom. 14:7-17	Luke 15:11-32	Ps. 119, 3d part	Ps. 25
4. S. after Trinity	Rom. 8:18-23	Luke 6:36-42	Jer. 16:14-21	1 Pet. 2:4-10	Matt. 5:43-48	Ps. 119, 4th part	Ps. 92
5. S. after Trinity	1 Pet. 3:8-15 h	Luke 5:1-11	Ex. 20:1-17	Eph. 2:4-10	Matt. 16:13-26	Ps. 119, 5th part	Ps. 113
6. S. after Trinity	Rom. 6:3-11	Matt. 5:20-26	Jer. 31:23-25	Acts 14:8-23	Matt. 19:16-30	Ps. 119, 6th part	Ps. 114
7. S. after Trinity	Rom. 6:19-23	Mark 8:1-9	Jer. 15:19-21	Acts 20:17-38	Matt. 10:24-31	Ps. 119, 7th part	Ps. 125
8. S. after Trinity	Rom. 8:12-17	Matt. 7:15-23	1 Chron. 29:10-13	2 Tim. 1:1-14	Matt. 7:22-29	Ps. 119, 8th part	Ps. 126
9. S. after Trinity	1 Cor. 10:6-13	Luke 16:1-9	Jer. 7:1-7	Heb. 3:7-15	Luke 12:32-48	Ps. 119, 9th part	Ps. 139
10. S. after Trinity	1 Cor. 12:1-11	Luke 19:41-48	2 Sam. 22:21-29	Jas. 3:1-12	Matt. 11:16-24	Ps. 119, 10th part	Ps. 143
11. S. after Trinity	1 Cor. 15:1-10	Luke 18:9-14	Is. 29:18, 19	Rom. 10:4-18	Luke 7:36-50	Ps. 119, 11th part	Ps. 147
12. S. after Trinity	2 Cor. 3:4-11	Mark 7:31-37	Lev. 18:1-5	1 Tim. 1:5-17	Matt. 12:31-42	Ps. 119, 12th part	Ps. 104
13. S. after Trinity	Gal. 3:15-22	Luke 10:23-37	Jer. 17:13, 14	Acts 3:1-10	Matt. 20:20-28	Ps. 119, 13th part	Ps. 84
14. S. after Trinity	Gal. 5:16-24	Luke 17:11-19	Deut. 6:4-7	Acts 8:26-39	John 5:1-15	Ps. 119, 14th part	Ps. 66
15. S. after Trinity	Gal. 5:25-6:10	Matt. 6:24-34	Deut. 32:39, 40	1 Cor. 15:21-28	Luke 10:38-42	Ps. 119, 15th part	Ps. 34
16. S. after Trinity	Eph. 3:13-21	Luke 7:11-17	1 Sam. 2:1-10	Jude 20-25	John 11:19-45	Ps. 119, 16th part	Ps. 36
17. S. after Trinity	Eph. 4:1-6	Luke 14:1-11	Deut. 10:12-21	1 John 3:1-8	Mark 2:18-28	Ps. 119, 17th part	Ps. 56
18. S. after Trinity	1 Cor. 1:4-9	Matt. 22:34-46	Is. 44:21-23	1 Cor. 12:12-24	John 15:1-17	Ps. 119, 18th part	Ps. 54
19. S. after Trinity	Eph. 4:22-28	Matt. 9:1-8	Is. 65:1, 2	Rom. 11:25-32	John 1:35-51	Ps. 119, 19th part	Ps. 61
20. S. after Trinity	Eph. 5:15-21	Matt. 22:1-14	Hos. 13:14	Rev. 3:7-13	Matt. 21:28-44	Ps. 119, 20th part	Ps. 57
21. S. after Trinity	Eph. 6:10-17	John 4:46-54 i	Deut. 7:9-11	Eph. 4:30-32	John 4:31-42	Ps. 119, 21st part	Ps. 31, 1st part
22. S. after Trinity	Phil. 1:3-11	Matt. 18:23-35	Is. 32:1-8	Rom. 13:1-7	Matt. 18:1-7	Ps. 119, 22d part	Ps. 31, 2d part
23. S. after Trinity	Phil. 3:17-21	Matt. 22:15-22	Is. 51:9-16	2 Cor. 5:1-10	John 5:17-29	Ps. 124	Ps. 31, 3d part
24. S. after Trinity	Col. 1:9-14	Matt. 9:18-26	Is. 49:12-17	2 Pet. 3:3-15	Luke 17:20-33	Ps. 125	Ps. 18, 1st part
25. S. after Trinity	1 Thess. 4:13-18	Matt. 24:15-28	Is. 40:9-11	Heb. 4:9-13	Matt. 11:25-30	Ps. 116	Ps. 18, 2d part
26. S. after Trinity	2 Thess. 1:3-10 or 2 Thess. 3:3-14: or	Matt. 25:31-46				Ps. 111	Ps. 18, 3d part
27. S. after Trinity	1 Thess. 5:1-11	Matt. 25:1-13	Is. 65:17-19	Rev. 21:1-7	Matt. 5:13-16	Ps. 103	Pss. 27, 97
St. Michael's Day	Rev. 12:7-12	Matt. 18:1-11	Gen. 28:10-22	Rev. 5:11-14	Luke 10:16-20	Pss. 8, 19	Pss. 24, 34
Reformation	Rev. 14:6, 7	Matt. 11:12-15	2 Chron. 29:12-19	Acts 14:15, 16	John 2:13-17	Pss. 126, 48	Pss. 138, 87
Harvest	Deut. 26:1-11	Luke 12:13-21	Mal. 3:10-12	Gal. 6:7-10	Matt. 3:1-12	Pss. 65, 100	Ps. 67
Thanksgiving	1 Tim. 2:1-8	Luke 17:11-19	Lam. 3:22-25	Heb. 10:1-31		Pss. 136, 104	Ps. 92
Humiliation	Joel 2:12-19	Matt. 6:16-21	Dan. 9:3-19	2 Tim. 3:14-17		Ps. 6	Ps. 32
Dedication	Rev. 21:1-5	Luke 19:1-10				Ps. 84	Ps. 27

a End: "men of low estate"
b Begin: "Be not wise in your own conceits"
c End: "ye shall ask Me nothing"
d Begin: "Verily, verily, I say"
e Begin: "Be ye therefore sober"
f End: "In the name of the Lord"
g Begin: "God is love"
h End: "sanctify the Lord God in your hearts"
i Begin: "And there was a certain nobleman"

A Table of Lessons for the Minor Festivals

	Epistles	Gospels
The Presentation	Mal. 3:1-4	Luke 2:22-32
The Annunciation	Is. 7:10-16	Luke 1:26-38
The Visitation	Is. 11:1-5	Luke 1:39-56
St. Thomas the Apostle	Eph. 1:3-6	John 19:24-31
St. Stephen the Martyr	Acts 6:8-15; 7:54-60	Matt. 23:34-39
St. John the Apostle	1 John 1:1-10	John 21:19-24
The Holy Innocents	Rev. 14:1-5	Matt. 2:13-18
The Conversion of St. Paul	Acts 9:1-22	Matt. 19:27-30
St. Matthias the Apostle	Acts 1:15-26	Matt. 11:25-30
St. Mark the Evangelist	Eph. 4:7-16	Luke 10:1-9
SS. Philip and James the Apostles	Eph. 2:19-22	John 14:1-14
St. John the Baptist	Is. 40:1-5	Luke 1:57-80
SS. Peter and Paul the Apostles	Acts 12:1-11	Matt. 16:13-20
St. Mary Magdalene	Prov. 31:10-31	Luke 7:36-50
St. James the Elder the Apostle	Rom. 8:28-39	Matt. 20:20-28
St. Bartholomew the Apostle	2 Cor. 4:7-10	Luke 22:24-30
St. Matthew the Apostle	Eph. 4:7-14	Matt. 9:9-13
St. Luke the Evangelist	2 Tim. 4:5-15	Luke 10:1-9
SS. Simon and Jude the Apostles	1 Pet. 1:3-9	John 15:17-21
All Saints	Rev. 7:2-17	Matt. 5:1-12
St. Andrew the Apostle	Rom. 10:8-18	Matt. 4:18-22

Lessons for Morning and Evening Throughout the Year

These Lessons may be used at Matins and Vespers or at Morning and Evening Prayer of the household on the days of the week.

The Lessons appointed for days between the *Fourth Sunday in Advent* and the *First Sunday after Epiphany* are to be omitted when the days for which they are appointed do not occur.

When there are not six *Sundays after Epiphany,* the Lessons for the week after the *First Sunday* may be omitted one year and those which follow another *Sunday,* the second year, and so on, in order that in the course of several years all the Lessons provided may be read.

The Lessons appointed for the days from the *Twentieth Sunday after Trinity* to the end of the year are to be read in every year, and those appointed for the weeks before the *Twentieth Sunday after Trinity* are to be omitted so far as necessary to this end.

[In this Table the first Lesson is for the Morning and the second for the Evening of each day.]

First Sunday in Advent

Mon.	Matt. 11:25-30	Gen. 3:1-24
Tues.	Acts 3:22-26	Gen. 9:1-19
Wed.	Col. 1:15-29	Gen. 22:1-19
Th.	Heb. 1:1-4	Gen. 49:1-28
Fri.	Heb. 2:1-4	Num. 24:14-25
Sat.	Eph. 3:1-12	Deut. 18:15-19

Second Sunday in Advent

Mon.	Acts 17:16-34	1 Chron. 17:1-27
Tues.	1 John 4:9-16	2 Chron. 7:11-22
Wed.	Col. 1:1-8	Is. 11:1-10
Th.	Phil. 2:12-18	Jer. 23:2-8
Fri.	Phil. 3:12-16	Jer. 30:1-22
Sat.	Col. 3:1-11	Jer. 33:14-26

Third Sunday in Advent

Mon.	Heb. 10:35-39	Is. 2:1-5
Tues.	Luke 21:5-24	Is. 24:21—25:5
Wed.	Luke 12:35-59	Is. 25:6-10
Th.	Jas. 5:7-11	Is. 26:1-21
Fri.	Luke 1:1-25	Is. 51:1-16
Sat.	Luke 1:26-38	Is. 52:1-12

Fourth Sunday in Advent

Mon.	Matt. 1:18-25	Is. 40:1-11
Tues.	Luke 1:39-45	Mal. 3:1-7
Wed.	Luke 1:46-56	Mal. 4:1-6
Th.	Luke 1:57-66	Is. 28:14-19
Fri.	Luke 1:67-80	Is. 7:1-17
Sat.	Matt. 1:1-17	Micah 5:1-5

Christmas

Jan. 3.	Matt. 2:19-23	Micah 4:1-8
Dec. 27.	John 1:15-18	Is. 32:1-8
Dec. 28.	Luke 2:15-20	Is. 46:3-13
Dec. 29.	Luke 2:22-24	Is. 49:1-13
Dec. 30.	Luke 2:25-32	Is. 55:1-13
Dec. 31.	Matt. 2:13-15	Is. 42:1-9
Jan. 2.	Matt. 2:16-18	Is. 61:1-11
Jan. 4.	Matt. 3:1-12	Is. 56:1-8
Jan. 5.	Luke 3:1-9	Is. 12:1-6

Epiphany

Mon.	Luke 3:10-14	Gen. 1:1-31
Tues.	Luke 3:15-20	Gen. 2:1-25
Wed.	Mark 1:1-8	Gen. 4:1-26
Th.	Mark 1:9-11	Gen. 5:1-32
Fri.	Luke 3:21, 22	Gen. 6:9-22
Sat.	Luke 3:23-38	Gen. 7:1-24

First Sunday after Epiphany

Mon.	John 1:29-34	Gen. 8:1-22
Tues.	John 1:35-42	Gen. 11:1-9
Wed.	John 1:43-51	Gen. 12:1-20
Th.	Luke 4:1-13	Gen. 13:1-18
Fri.	Mark 1:12-15	Gen. 14:8-24
Sat.	Matt. 4:12-17	Gen. 15:1-21

Second Sunday after Epiphany

Mon.	Matt. 4:18-25	Gen. 17:1-22
Tues.	Matt. 5:1-9	Gen. 18:1-33
Wed.	Matt. 5:27-48	Gen. 19:1-29
Th.	Matt. 6:1-23	Gen. 21:1-8
Fri.	Matt. 7:1-14	Gen. 24:1-28
Sat.	Matt. 7:24-29	Gen. 24:29-67

Third Sunday after Epiphany

Mon.	Matt. 8:14-22	Gen. 25:19-34
Tues.	Matt. 8:28-34	Gen. 27:1-45
Wed.	Matt. 9:9-17	Gen. 27:46—28:22
Th.	Matt. 9:27-38	Gen. 29:1-20
Fri.	Matt. 10:1-16	Gen. 31:1-18
Sat.	Matt. 10:17—11:1	Gen. 32:3-32

Fourth Sunday after Epiphany

Mon.	Matt. 11:11-24	Gen. 33:1-20
Tues.	Matt. 12:1-21	Gen. 35:1-21
Wed.	Matt. 12:22-50	Gen. 37:1-36
Th.	Matt. 13:1-23	Gen. 39:1-23
Fri.	Matt. 14:1-36	Gen. 40:1-23
Sat.	Matt. 15:1-20	Gen. 41:1-37

Fifth Sunday after Epiphany

Mon.	Matt. 15:29-39	Gen. 41:38-57
Tues.	Matt. 16:1-12	Gen. 42:1-38
Wed.	Matt. 16:21-28	Gen. 43:1-34
Th.	Matt. 17:9-27	Gen. 44:1-34
Fri.	Matt. 19:1-15	Gen. 45:1-28
Sat.	Matt. 20:17-34	Gen. 46:1-34

Sixth Sunday after Epiphany

Mon.	Matt. 21:10-46	Gen. 47:1-31
Tues.	Matt. 23:1-39	Gen. 48:1-22
Wed.	Mark 1:16-45	Ex. 1:1-22
Th.	Mark 2:1-28	Ex. 2:1-25
Fri.	Mark 3:1-35	Ex. 3:1-22
Sat.	Mark 5:1-20	Ex. 4:1-31

Septuagesima Sunday

Mon.	Mark 5:21-43	Ex. 5:1-23
Tues.	Mark 6:1-29	Ex. 6:1-13
Wed.	Mark 6:30-56	Ex. 11:1-10
Th.	Mark 7:1-30	Ex. 12:1-28
Fri.	Mark 8:10—9:1	Ex. 12:29-42
Sat.	Mark 9:2-32	Ex. 13:1-22

Sexagesima Sunday

Mon.	Mark 10:1-31	Ex. 14:1-31
Tues.	Mark 10:32-52	Ex. 15:1-21
Wed.	Mark 11:1-33	Ex. 15:22—16:36
Th.	Mark 12:13-44	Ex. 17:1-16
Fri.	Luke 4:14-44	Ex. 19:1-25
Sat.	Luke 5:12-39	Ex. 20:1-23

Quinquagesima Sunday

Mon.	Luke 6:1-35	Ex. 24:1—25:9
Tues.	Luke 6:33-49	Ex. 31:18—32:35
Wed.	Luke 7:1-10	Ex. 33:1-23
Th.	Luke 7:18—8:3	Ex. 34:1-10
Fri.	Luke 8:16-56	Ex. 34:27-35
Sat.	Luke 9:1-27	Ex. 40:1-38

First Sunday in Lent

Mon.	Luke 9:28-62	Num. 3:5-13
Tues.	Luke 10:1-22	Num. 10:11-36
Wed.	Luke 10:38—11:13	Num. 11:1-35
Th.	Luke 11:29-36	Num. 12:1-15
Fri.	Luke 11:37-54	Num. 13:1-25
Sat.	Luke 12:1-34	Num. 13:26-33

Second Sunday in Lent

Mon.	Luke 13:1-17	Num. 14:1-45
Tues.	Luke 14:25-35	Num. 16:1-22
Wed.	Luke 15:11-32	Num. 16:23-50
Th.	Luke 16:10-18	Num. 17:1-13
Fri.	Luke 17:1-10	Num. 20:1-29
Sat.	Luke 18:1-8	Num. 21:1—22:1

Third Sunday in Lent

Mon.	Luke 18:15-30	Num. 22:2-41
Tues.	Luke 19:1-40	Num. 23:1-30
Wed.	Luke 20:1—21:4	Num. 24:1-13
Th.	Luke 21:37—22:38	Num. 27:12-23
Fri.	Luke 22:39-71	Deut. 5:1-33
Sat.	Luke 23:1-25	Deut. 8:1-20

Fourth Sunday in Lent

Mon.	Luke 23:26-56	Deut. 9:1-29
Tues.	Matt. 26:1-35	Deut. 10:1-22
Wed.	Matt. 26:36-75	Deut. 11:1-32
Th.	Matt. 27:1-38	Deut. 28:1-14
Fri.	Matt. 27:39-66	Deut. 28:15-68
Sat.	Mark 14:1-31	Deut. 34:1-12

Fifth Sunday in Lent

Mon.	Mark 14:32-72	Jer. 2:1-19
Tues.	Mark 15:1-19	Hos. 13:9-14
Wed.	Mark 15:20-47	Zeph. 3:1-8
Th.	John 12:1-19	Micah 3:9-12
Fri.	John 12:20-50	Is. 66:1-9
Sat.	John 13:16-38	Zech. 9:1-17

Palm Sunday

Mon.	John 18:1-18	Jer. 7:1-15
Tues.	John 18:19-40	Is. 50:4-11
Wed.	John 19:1-12	Jer. 11:18-23
Th.	John 19:13-24	Zech. 3:1-10
Fri.	John 19:25-37	Lam. 2:8-15
Sat.	John 19:38-42	Is. 52:13-15

Easter

EASTER MONDAY

Tues.	Matt. 28:1-15	Ezek. 21:25-27
Wed.	John 20:1-18	Hag. 2:20-23
Th.	Luke 24:1-12	Zech. 6:9-15
Fri.	Luke 24:36-49	Ezek. 17:22-24
Sat.	Mark 16:9-14	Is. 44:21-28

First Sunday after Easter

Mon.	John 21:1-25	Jonah 1:1-16
Tues.	John 2:12-25	Jonah 1:17—2:1
Wed.	John 3:22-36	Jonah 3:1-10
Th.	John 4:1-27	Jonah 4:1-11
Fri.	John 4:28-38	Is. 33:2-6
Sat.	John 4:39-45	Is. 42:10-17

Second Sunday after Easter

Mon.	John 5:1-17	Micah 2:12, 13
Tues.	John 5:18-30	Is. 30:19-26
Wed.	John 5:31-47	Jer. 3:11-19
Th.	John 6:16-29	Ezek. 34:1-11
Fri.	John 6:30-40	Ezek. 34:12-22
Sat.	John 6:41-59	Ezek. 34:23-31

Third Sunday after Easter

Mon.	John 6:60-71	Ezek. 36:1-15
Tues.	John 7:1-13	Ezek. 36:16-32
Wed.	John 7:14-24	Ezek. 36:33-38
Th.	John 7:25-36	Hag. 2:2-9
Fri.	John 7:37-53	Zech. 2:1-13
Sat.	John 8:1-11	Zech. 11:1-17

Fourth Sunday after Easter

Mon.	John 8:12-20	Zech. 12:1-14
Tues.	John 8:21-29	Is. 65:1-7
Wed.	John 8:30-45	Is. 65:8-16
Th.	John 9:1-13	Jer. 8:4-13
Fri.	John 9:14-34	Zech. 8:18-23
Sat.	John 9:35-41	Is. 49:22-26

Fifth Sunday after Easter

Mon.	John 10:1-5	Amos 9:8-15
Tues.	John 10:6-10	Is. 4:2-6
Wed.	Matt. 28:16-20	Is. 29:18-24
ASCENSION DAY		
Fri.	Luke 24:50-53	Micah 7:7-13
Sat.	Acts 1:12-26	Micah 7:14-20

Sunday after Ascension

Mon.	John 10:17-21	Zech. 13:7-9
Tues.	John 10:22-31	Zech. 14:1-21
Wed.	John 10:32-42	Is. 46:10-24
Th.	John 11:1-27	Jer. 46:27, 28
Fri.	John 11:28-44	Is. 32:9-20
Sat.	John 11:45-57	Is. 57:15-21

Whitsunday

MONDAY		
Tues.	Acts 2:14-36	Ezek. 47:1-12
Wed.	Acts 2:37-47	Is. 45:18-21
Th.	John 14:1-22	Is. 45:22-25
Fri.	John 15:1-25	Jer. 9:23-26
Sat.	John 16:31—17:26	Is. 44:6-8

Trinity Sunday

Mon.	Acts 3:1-21	Josh. 1:1-18
Tues.	Acts 4:1-37	Josh. 3:1-17
Wed.	Acts 5:1-42	Josh. 4:1-24
Th.	Acts 6:1-15	Josh. 6:1-27
Fri.	Acts 7:1-60	Josh. 8:1-35
Sat.	Acts 8:1-40	Josh. 9:1-27

First Sunday after Trinity

Mon.	Acts 9:1-43	Josh. 10:1-15
Tues.	Acts 10:1-33	Josh. 11:1-23
Wed.	Acts 11:1-30	Josh. 23:1-16
Th.	Acts 12:1-25	Josh. 24:1-31
Fri.	Acts 13:1-52	Judg. 2:1-23
Sat.	Acts 14:1-28	Judg. 6:1-40

Second Sunday after Trinity

Mon.	Acts 15:1-41	Judg. 7:1-25
Tues.	Acts 16:1-40	Judg. 13:1-25
Wed.	Acts 17:1-15	Judg. 14:1-20
Th.	Acts 18:1-28	Judg. 15:1-20
Fri.	Acts 19:1-41	Judg. 16:4-31
Sat.	Acts 20:1-38	1 Sam. 1:1-28

Third Sunday after Trinity

Mon.	Acts 21:1-39	1 Sam. 2:1-21
Tues.	Acts 21:40—22:29	1 Sam. 3:1-21
Wed.	Acts 22:30—23:35	1 Sam. 4:1-22
Th.	Acts 24:1-27	1 Sam. 5:1-12
Fri.	Acts 25:1-27	1 Sam. 7:1-17
Sat.	Acts 26:1-32	1 Sam. 8:1-22

Fourth Sunday after Trinity

Mon.	Acts 27:1-44	1 Sam. 9:1-27
Tues.	Acts 28:1-31	1 Sam. 10:1-27
Wed.	Rom. 1:1-15	1 Sam. 12:1-25
Th.	Rom. 1:16-32	1 Sam. 13:1-14
Fri.	Rom. 2:1-29	1 Sam. 15:1-35
Sat.	Rom. 3:1-31	1 Sam. 16:1-23

Fifth Sunday after Trinity

Mon.	Rom. 4:1-25	1 Sam. 17:1-58
Tues.	Rom. 5:1—6:2	1 Sam. 18:1-21
Wed.	Rom. 6:12-18	1 Sam. 19:1-24
Th.	Rom. 7:1-25	1 Sam. 20:1-42
Fri.	Rom. 2:1-29	1 Sam. 22:1-23
Sat.	Rom. 13:1-7	1 Sam. 24:1-22

Sixth Sunday after Trinity

Mon.	Rom. 14:1—15:3	1 Sam. 26:1-25
Tues.	Rom. 14:14-33	1 Sam. 28:3-25
Wed.	Rom. 16:1-27	1 Sam. 31:1-13
Th.	1 Cor. 1:10-31	2 Sam. 1:1-27
Fri.	1 Cor. 2:1-16	2 Sam. 5:1-25
Sat.	1 Cor. 4:6—5:5	2 Sam. 6:1-23

Seventh Sunday after Trinity

Mon.	1 Cor. 5:9—6:20	1 Chron. 16:1-43
Tues.	1 Cor. 7:1-40	2 Sam. 7:1-29
Wed.	1 Cor. 8:1-13	2 Sam. 12:1-23
Th.	1 Cor. 9:1-23	2 Sam. 15:1-15
Fri.	1 Cor. 10:14-33	2 Sam. 16:5-35
Sat.	1 Cor. 11:1-22	2 Sam. 18:1-13

Eighth Sunday after Trinity

Mon.	1 Cor. 12:12-31	2 Sam. 19:1-23
Tues.	1 Cor. 14:1-40	1 Chron. 21:1-30
Wed.	1 Cor. 15:58—16:24	1 Chron. 22:1-19
Th.	2 Cor. 1:1-24	1 Chron. 28:1-21
Fri.	2 Cor. 2:1—3:3	2 Chron. 29:1-23
Sat.	2 Cor. 6:11—7:16	2 Chron. 1:1-13

Ninth Sunday after Trinity

Mon.	2 Cor. 8:1-24	1 Kings 3:16-28
Tues.	2 Cor. 9:1-15	1 Kings 4:22-34
Wed.	2 Cor. 10:1-18	1 Kings 5:1-18
Th.	2 Cor. 11:1-18	2 Chron. 3:1-17
Fri.	2 Cor. 12:19—13:13	1 Kings 8:1-66
Sat.	Gal. 1:1-24	1 Kings 7:1-12

Tenth Sunday after Trinity

Mon.	Gal. 2:1-21	1 Kings 9:1-28
Tues.	Gal. 3:1-14	1 Kings 10:1-29
Wed.	Gal. 4:8-20	1 Kings 11:1-43
Th.	Gal. 5:1-15	1 Kings 12:1-33
Fri.	Gal. 6:11-18	1 Kings 13:1-34
Sat.	Eph. 6:1-9	1 Kings 14:1-31

Eleventh Sunday after Trinity

Mon.	Eph. 6:18-24	1 Kings 16:29—17:24
Tues.	Phil. 1:12—2:4	1 Kings 18:1-46
Wed.	Phil. 2:19-30	1 Kings 19:1-21
Th.	Phil. 3:1-11	1 Kings 21:1-29
Fri.	Phil. 4:1-3	1 Ks. 22:51, 2 Ks. 1:17
Sat.	Phil. 4:8-23	2 Kings 2:1-25

Twelfth Sunday after Trinity

Mon.	Col. 2:1-23	2 Kings 4:1-44
Tues.	Col. 3:18—4:18	2 Kings 5:1-27
Wed.	1 Thess. 1:1-10	2 Kings 6:1-23
Th.	1 Thess. 2:1-20	2 Kings 6:24—7:20
Fri.	1 Thess. 3:1-13	2 Kings 8:1-15
Sat.	1 Thess. 4:8-12	2 Kings 9:1-37

Thirteenth Sunday after Trinity

Mon.	1 Thess. 5:12-28	2 Kings 10:1-36
Tues.	1 Tim. 1:1-20	2 Chron. 22:1-12
Wed.	1 Tim. 2:1-15	2 Chron. 23:1-21
Th.	1 Tim. 3:1-16	2 Chron. 24:1-27
Fri.	1 Tim. 4:1-16	2 Kings 14:1-29
Sat.	1 Tim. 5:1-25	2 Kings 15:1-38

Fourteenth Sunday after Trinity

Mon.	1 Tim. 6:1-21	Is. 6:1-13
Tues.	2 Tim. 1:1-18	Amos 7:7-17
Wed.	2 Tim. 2:1-26	2 Kings 16:1-20
Th.	Titus 1:1-16	2 Kings 17:1-23
Fri.	Titus 2:1-10	2 Kings 18:1-37
Sat.	Titus 2:15—3:3	2 Kings 19:1-37

Fifteenth Sunday after Trinity

Mon.	Titus 3:8-15	2 Kings 20:1-21
Tues.	Philemon 1:25	2 Kings 21:1-26
Wed.	Heb. 1:1-14	2 Chron. 34:1-33
Th.	Heb. 2:5—3:6	2 Chron. 35:20—36:10
Fri.	Heb. 4:14—5:14	Jer. 22:1-30
Sat.	Heb. 6:1-20	Jer. 25:1-14

Sixteenth Sunday after Trinity

Mon.	Heb. 7:1-28	Jer. 37:1-21
Tues.	Heb. 8:1-13	Jer. 38:1-28
Wed.	Heb. 9:1-10	Jer. 32:1-44
Th.	Heb. 9:16-28	Jer. 39:1-18
Fri.	Heb. 10:1-34	Jer. 29:1-23
Sat.	Heb. 11:1-7	Dan. 1:1-21

Seventeenth Sunday after Trinity

Mon.	Heb. 11:17-40	Dan. 3:1-30
Tues.	Heb. 12:1-17	Dan. 4:1-37
Wed.	Heb. 13:1-25	Dan. 5:1-30
Th.	Jas. 1:1-15	Dan. 5:31—6:28
Fri.	Jas. 2:1-13	Ezra 1:1-11
Sat.	Jas. 2:14-26	Ezra 3:1-13

Eighteenth Sunday after Trinity

Mon.	Jas. 3:1-18	Ezra 4:1-24
Tues.	Jas. 4:1—5:6	Hag. 1:1-15
Wed.	Jas. 5:12-20	Ezra 5:1-17
Th.	1 Pet. 3:1-7	Ezra 6:1-22
Fri.	1 Pet. 3:15-22	Ezra 7:1-28
Sat.	1 Pet. 5:1-5	Ezra 8:31—9:15

Nineteenth Sunday after Trinity

Mon.	1 John 1:1-10	Neh. 1:1-11
Tues.	1 John 2:1-17	Neh. 2:1-20
Wed.	1 John 5:1-3	Neh. 4:1-23
Th.	1 John 5:10-21	Neh. 8:1-18
Fri.	2 John 1-13	Neh. 9:1-38
Sat.	3 John 1-14	Zech. 8:1-23

Twentieth Sunday after Trinity

Mon.	Mark 4:1-41	Is. 43:1-13
Tues.	Luke 13:18-35	Is. 41:1-20
Wed.	Matt. 13:31-58	Hab. 2:1-4
Th.	Matt. 16:13-20	Is. 63:7-19
Fri.	2 Cor. 3:10—4:18	Is. 64:1-12
Sat.	2 Cor. 5:1-21	Is. 5:1-7

Twenty-First Sunday after Trinity

Mon.	Eph. 1:1-23	Micah 6:1-9
Tues.	Eph. 2:1-22	Is. 58:1-14
Wed.	Eph. 4:7-21	Is. 59:1-21
Th.	Eph. 4:29-32	Jer. 31:1-22
Fri.	Eph. 5:10-14	Jer. 31:23-40
Sat.	Eph. 5:22, 23	Is. 48:1-22

Twenty-Second Sunday after Trinity

Mon.	Matt. 18:1-22	Micah 4:9—5:1
Tues.	Mark 9:33-50	Is. 49:14-21
Wed.	Luke 17:20-37	Is. 2:10-21
Th.	Rom. 8:24-39	Is. 63:1-6
Fri.	Mark 12:1-12	Joel 2:1-11
Sat.	Matt. 25:14-30	Joel 2:12-27

Twenty-Third Sunday after Trinity

Mon.	1 Cor. 3:1-23	Joel 3:1-13
Tues.	Matt. 19:16-30	Joel 3:14-21
Wed.	Luke 14:12-15	Obad. 1—21
Th.	Mark 13:1-37	Nah. 1:1-14
Fri.	Rom. 9:1-23	Nah. 1:15—3:19
Sat.	Rom. 10:1-21	Is. 10:5-27

Twenty-Fourth Sunday after Trinity

Mon.	Rom. 11:1-33	Is. 13:1-22
Tues.	2 Thess. 1:11—2:17	Is. 14:1-27
Wed.	2 Thess. 3:1-18	Is. 47:1-15
Th.	2 Tim. 3:1-17	Dan. 2:27-45
Fri.	2 Tim. 4:1-22	Dan. 7:1-28
Sat.	Matt. 24:1-14	Dan. 9:1-27

Twenty-Fifth Sunday after Trinity

Mon.	Matt. 24:29-51	Dan. 11:36—12:13
Tues.	Matt. 22:23-33	Ezek. 38:1-23
Wed.	1 Cor. 15:11-50	Ezek. 39:1-29
Th.	Heb. 3:7—4:13	Is. 43:14-25
Fri.	Heb. 11:8-16	Is. 33:17-24
Sat.	Heb. 12:18-29	Ezek. 37:1-14

Twenty-Sixth Sunday after Trinity

Mon.	1 Pet. 1:1-12	Zeph. 3:9-20
Tues.	1 Pet. 1:13—2:10	Is. 34:1-17
Wed.	1 Pet. 4:1-7	Is. 35:1-10
Th.	1 Pet. 4:12-19	Is. 54:1-17
Fri.	2 Pet. 1:1-15	Is. 60:7-22
Sat.	2 Pet. 2:1-22	Is. 62:1-12

Twenty-Seventh Sunday after Trinity

Mon.	2 Pet. 3:1-18	Is. 65:17-25
Tues.	Jude 1-25	Ezek. 37:15-28
Wed.	1 John 2:18-29	Hab. 3:1-19
Th.	1 John 3:1-12	Is. 40:27-31
Fri.	1 John 3:19-24	Jer. 14:7-9
Sat.	1 John 4:1-8	Mal. 3:7-18

Psalms for the Sundays, Feasts, and Festivals of the Church Year

1. Sunday in Advent — 25, 85, 145, 93, 24, 122, 110, 6

2. Sunday in Advent — 80, 50, 85, 1, 75, 96, 126, 38

3. Sunday in Advent — 85, 90, 111, 81, 4, 106, 9, 102

4. Sunday in Advent — 19, 145, 9, 27, 8, 5, 21, 143

Christmas, the Feast of the Nativity of Our Lord — 2, 8, 19, 45, 72, 85, 96, 98, 132, 145, 95, 80, 24, 93

St. Stephen — 119, III. XI. I; 12, 26, 52, 56, 59, 116

St. John, Apostle, Evangelist — 92, 11, 119, XII; 125, 145, 91, 56

The Holy Innocents — 9, 124, 113, 37, 72, 79, 94, 23

Sunday after Christmas — 93, 45, 91, 26, 110, 111, 84

The Circumcision — 98, 8, 40, 92, 85, 117, 67

2. Sunday after Christmas — 8, 106, 145, 138, 16, 72, 97

The Epiphany of Our Lord — 72, 19, 45, 47, 48, 67, 87, 96, 100

1. Sunday after Epiphany — 145, 100, 72, 50, 51, 119, I. II. V; 128, 27, 40, 122

2. Sunday after Epiphany — 66, 107, 15, 145, 36, 115, 127, 128, 23

3. Sunday after Epiphany — 97, 102, 118, 101, 144, 56, 103, 116, 117

4. Sunday after Epiphany — 7, 119, XII. XIII; 29, 65, 77, 20, 107

5. Sunday after Epiphany — 32, 92, 105, 28, 36, 78:1-24

6. Sunday after Epiphany — 77, 84, 112, 45, 110, 61, 97, 104, 16, 63

Septuagesima — 18, 9, 130, 92, 31, 86, 102, 42

Sexagesima — 44, 83, 60, 17, 43, 143, 25, 83

Quinquagesima — 31, 77, 100, 119, I. II. III; 15, 78, 146, 33

The Presentation of Christ and the Purification of Mary — 48, 134, 2, 26, 76, 36, 87

Ash Wednesday — 6, 32, 38, 51, 102, 130, 143, 69, 57, 79

Invocavit — 91, 31, 1, 42, 32, 34, 121, 55, 27, 73

Reminiscere — 25, 119, X; 5, 15, 38, 39, 141, 60

Oculi — 25, 9, 19, 84, 123, 12, 40, 6

Laetare — 122, 125, 135, 5, 37, 33, 105, 51

Judica — 43, 143, 129, 119, I. IV; 120, 69, 109

Palmarum — 22, 73, 69, 7, 57, 24, 92, 41, 35

Monday of Holy Week — 6, 7, 35, 63, 70, 79, 102

Tuesday of Holy Week — 12, 38, 39, 55, 59, 74, 83

Wednesday of Holy Week — 51, 88, 120, 130, 142, 143

Maundy Thursday — 86, 67, 23, 111, 114, 78:1-29, 105, 81, 116, 41, 55, 140

Good Friday — 22, 56, 57, 69, 40, 3, 43, 49, 119, XI. XVI; 142, 143

Easter, the Feast of the Resurrection of Our Lord — 139, 118, 76, 2, 8, 16, 34, 61, 81, 100, 105, 110, 114, 116, 124, 132, 135, 138, 1, 23, 30, 66, 113

The Annunciation — 45, 72, 85, 98, 110, 33, 76, 132, 149

Quasimodogeniti — 81, 91, 19, 9, 92, 134, 101, 145

Misericordias Domini — 33, 63, 23, 80, 21, 121, 146, 95, 100

Jubilate — 66, 146, 82, 101, 40, 30, 17, 124

Cantate — 99, 66, 136, 145, 148, 104, 83, 117

Rogate — 66, 54, 96, 1, 15, 26, 20, 64, 121

Ascension — 47, 68, 21, 24, 67, 110, 99, 93, 96, 97

Exaudi — 27, 47, 104, 146, 10, 119, XI. XII; 51

Whitsunday — The Feast of Pentecost — 68, 104, 33, 145, 48, 87, 84, 81, 18, 67, 46, 80, 117, 100, 78, 99, 76, 9, 50, 101, 75

The Feast of the Holy Trinity — 8, 33, 48, 75, 86, 115, 135, 67

1. Sunday after Trinity — 13, 41, 5, 9, 58, 39, 14, 119, I. II

2. Sunday after Trinity — 18, 120, 7, 6, 64, 26, 49, 119, III. IV

3. Sunday after Trinity — 25, 55, 9, 17, 107, 32, 103, 119, V. VI

St. John the Baptist — 92, 44, 105, 110, 136, 147, 116

4. Sunday after Trinity — 27, 79, 13, 15, 52, 107, 119, VII. VIII

The Visitation — 45, 2, 110, 132, 138, 145, 149

5. Sunday after Trinity — 27, 84, 71, 16, 112, 119, IX. X

6. Sunday after Trinity — 28, 90, 17, 36, 53, 129, 119, XI. XII

7. Sunday after Trinity — 47, 34, 65, 107, 145, 146, 119, XIII. XIV

8. Sunday after Trinity — 48, 31, 34, 70, 75, 1, 140, 119, XV. XVI

9. Sunday after Trinity — 54, 8, 81, 19, 62, 12, 119, XVII. XVIII

10. Sunday after Trinity — 55, 17, 88, 74, 81, 5, 58, 119, XIX. XX

11. Sunday after Trinity — 68, 27, 90, 30, 51, 32, 131, 119, XXI. XXII

12. Sunday after Trinity — 70, 34, 95, 104, 115, 143, 147

13. Sunday after Trinity — 74, 31, 15, 89, 149, 62, 112

14. Sunday after Trinity — 84, 92, 34, 38, 30, 36, 41, 39, 146

15. Sunday after Trinity — 86, 118, 108, 40, 28, 107, 133

16. Sunday after Trinity — 86, 102, 40, 71, 23, 84, 91, 39

St. Michael and All Angels — 103, 91, 34, 8, 68, 104, 33

17. Sunday after Trinity — 119, XVIII; 33, 76, 26, 48, 92, 37

18. Sunday after Trinity — 122, 96, 100, 81, 42, 110, 82, 149

19. Sunday after Trinity — 35, 48, 141, 119, IV. V; 138, 52, 71, 32

20. Sunday after Trinity — 48, 145, 130, 137, 43, 75, 111
21. Sunday after Trinity — 119, I; 90, 146, 27, 91, 136, 119, XIV; 42
22. Sunday after Trinity — 130, 133, 32, 36, 63, 82, 72
23. Sunday after Trinity — 85, 44, 147, 17, 140, 116, 99
24. Sunday after Trinity — 100, 116, 36, 71, 119, IX; 38, 14, 56
25. Sunday after Trinity — 31, 74, 46, 102, 29, 94, 10
26. Sunday after Trinity — 54, 50, 15, 20, 21, 126, 9, 96
27. Sunday after Trinity — 45, 73, 3, 17, 75, 110, 124, 87
St. Thomas — 9, 120, 101, 2, 139, 136, 11
St. Matthias — 68, 4, 140, 56, 87, 99, 32
St. Mark — 45, 64, 37, 89, 52, 67, 46
SS. Philip and James — 19, 43, 4, 1, 81, 16, 84
SS. Peter and Paul — 21, 45, 46, 48, 44, 113, 117
St. Mary Magdalene — 45, 112, 32, 51, 63, 92, 103
St. James the Elder — 139, 19, 1, 13, 26, 119, VIII. XXI
St. Bartholomew — 56, 9, 53, 54, 37, 129, 147
St. Matthew — 68, 62, 80, 132, 149, 137, 84
St. Luke — 45, 19, 34, 67, 84, 87, 117
SS. Simon and Jude — 1, 7, 20, 36, 80, 92, 138
The Festival of the Reformation — 46, 48, 62, 73, 78, 85, 97, 119, VI; 124, 125
St. Andrew — 139, 19, 44, 45, 26, 122, 3
Dedication — 93, 138, 84, 46, 111, 99, 122, 132, 2, 21
Thanksgiving — 150, 144, 103, 104, 100, 67, 65
Humiliation — 6, 38, 51, 102, 130, 143, 32, 25, 90

The Psalter Distributed over Thirty-One Days

(In months having thirty days the psalms for the thirty-first day are to be read on the thirtieth day; in the morning, Pss. 146, 147; in the evening, Pss. 148-150. On the twenty-eighth of February Pss. 140-144 are to be read in the morning, Pss. 145-150 in the evening.)

Morning	Evening	Morning	Evening	Morning	Evening
1. 1-4	5-8	12. 64, 65	66-68	23. 112-115	116-118
2. 9-11	12-17	13. 69	70-72	24. 119:1-40	119:41-88
3. 18	19-22	14. 73	74-76	25. 119:89-128	119:129ff.
4. 23-25	26-30	15. 77	78	26. 120-125	126-132
5. 31, 32	33, 34	16. 79, 80	81-83	27. 133-135	136-139
6. 35	36, 37	17. 84, 85	86-88	28. 140, 141	142, 143
7. 38	39-41	18. 89	90-92	29. 144	145
8. 42-44	45-48	19. 93-95	96-100	30. 146	147
9. 49	50, 51	20. 101, 102	103, 104	31. 148	149, 150
10. 52-54	55-57	21. 105	106		
11. 58, 59	60-63	22. 107	108-111		

The Psalms

With reference to their import

I. OF PRAYER

For the Church: 3, 5, 28, 59, 64, 71, 74, 77, 79, 80, 83, 94, 112 125
Against the Enemies of the Church: 7, 19, 26, 27, 42, 54, 56, 57, 62, 141
Against the Pope and the Papists: 10, 12, 36, 44, 55, 69, 70, 94, 109, 120
For Peace in the Church: 60, 86, 137, 140
For the Divine Word: 67, 69, 119
For Forgiveness of Sin and Spiritual Direction: 38, 59, 86, 90, 130, 141, 142
For the State: 20, 62
Against an Evil Conscience: 6, 38, 88

II. OF REPENTANCE

6, 32, 38, 51, 102, 130, 143

III. OF THANKSGIVING

For the Divine Word and Other Spiritual Gifts: 34, 42, 66, 103, 109, 122, 138, 145, 147
For Bodily Blessings: 33, 105, 107, 108, 114, 116, 139, 144, 146
For the Preservation of the Church: 76, 86, 108, 111, 116, 135, 136
For Deliverance from Tyranny and Other Distresses: 9, 18, 30, 66, 113

IV. OF DOCTRINE

Concerning the Forgiveness of Sin: 51, 139
Concerning Trust in God Alone: 4, 33, 91, 112, 115, 131, 146, 148
Concerning God's Word and the Fear of God: 1, 15, 41, 78, 81, 92, 95, 96, 100, 112, 149
Concerning the Prosperity of the Wicked and the Misfortunes of the Godly: 37, 39, 49, 52, 63, 73, 92, 129
For the Teachers of the Church: 134, 150
For Rulers and for the Household: 2, 82, 101, 125, 127, 128, 133, 144

V. OF CONSOLATION

God Preserves the Church and Destroys Her Enemies: 3, 11, 23, 33, 36, 46, 47, 76, 124, 125, 126

VI. OF PROPHECY

Concerning Christ's Person and Office: 2, 110, 118, 138
Concerning Christ's Sufferings and Exaltation: 2, 8, 16, 21, 22, 41, 68, 69, 109
Concerning the Spread of the Gospel: 19, 40, 45, 47, 50, 72, 78, 93, 97, 98

VII. OF PARTICULAR SEASONS

Morning: 63, 103, 130
Midday: 4, 7, 19, 104, 121
Evening: 3, 4, 8, 91, 104, 127, 134, 139

Glossary of Liturgical Terms

Agnus Dei: Lamb of God

Amen: So be it

Antiphon: A piece of devotional verse or prose responsively sung

Athanasian Creed: The third ecumenical creed, ascribed to Athanasius

Benedicamus: Bless we

Benedictus: The Song of Zacharias, Luke 1:68-79

Bidding Prayer: Prayer with petitions for specified objects or classes of persons

Cantate: Latin opening of Introit: Oh, sing

Collect: A short prayer of the Church with a fixed form or pattern

Creed: A statement of faith

Doxology: An exultant hymn or psalm of praise to God, especially to God
as *triune*

Eleison: Have mercy

Epiphany: Manifestation

Exultemus: Let us sing

Exaudi: Latin opening of Introit "Hear, O Lord"

Gloria in Excelsis: Glory in the highest; the Greater Doxology

Gloria Patri: Glory be to the Father; the Lesser Doxology

Gradual: Response of praise between Epistle and Gospel

Hallelujah or Alleluia: Praise the Lord

Hosanna: Save now, we pray. An exclamation of praise

Introit: Entrance, or opening psalm or sentences

Invitatory: Psalm sung at the beginning of Matins

Invocavit: Latin opening of Introit "He shall call upon Me"

Jubilate: Latin opening of Introit "Make a joyful noise"

Judica: Latin opening of Introit "Judge me"

Kyrie: O Lord

Laetare: Latin opening of Introit "Rejoice ye"

Lection: A lesson or selection of Holy Scripture

Litany: A form of liturgical prayer, related to the General Prayer

Magnificat: Song of Mary, Luke 1:46-55

Matins: Early morning service

Misericordias Domini: Latin opening of Introit "The goodness of God"

Nicene Creed: Creed adopted by the Council of Nicaea, A.D. 325

Nunc Dimittis: Simeon's song, Luke 2:29-32

Oculi: Latin opening of Introit "Mine eyes"

Offertory: Having received the Word, we offer ourselves to God

Palmarum: Sunday of palms

Pax Domini: The peace of the Lord

Preface: Introduction of Communion service

Quasimodogeniti: Latin opening of Introit "As newborn babes"

Quinquagesima: Fiftieth

Reminiscere: Latin opening of Introit "Remember, O Lord"

Responsory: Response sung after or during a lesson

Rogate: Latin, "Pray ye." Reference to the Gospel for the Day

Salutation: Greeting of pastor and congregation's response

Sanctus: Holy! Song of the angels, Is. 6:3

Septuagesima: Seventieth

Sexagesima: Sixtieth

Sequence: Hymn sung after Epistle and Gradual

Suffrage: A petition to God

Te Deum Laudamus: We praise Thee, O God

Tract: Tractus, the verses of Scripture sung in pre-Lent and Lent after the
Gradual instead of the Hallelujah

Venite: O come

Whitsunday: White Sunday; Pentecost (50th day after Easter)

Explanations of Terms and Abbreviations
Used in Hymn Section

Ab. — abridged, or abbreviated (when only one stanza of original hymn has been dropped)

Ad. — adapted

Alt. — altered

Anon. — anonymous

Arr. — arranged

Asc. — ascribed to

C. — circa, about

Cento — A hymn made up of separate stanzas of a longer original

C. M. — common meter (4 lines: 8, 6, 8, 6 syllables)

D. — double

H. M. — hallelujah meter (6 lines: 6, 6, 6, 6, 8, 8, or 8 lines: 6, 6, 6, 6, 4, 4, 4, 4 syllables)

L. M. — long meter (4 lines: 8, 8, 8, 8 syllables)

S. — syllables

S. M. — short meter (4 lines: 6, 6, 8, 6 syllables)

St. — stanza or stanzas

Tr. — translator or translation

LET the Word of Christ dwell in you richly in all wisdom, teaching and admonishing one another with psalms and hymns and spiritual songs, singing with grace in your hearts to the Lord. ——————————— Col. 3:16

O GOD, our Father, whose praise is in the Church, uplift our souls to the holiness of Thy presence that with pure hearts we may adore Thee and worship Thee with joyful lips; through Jesus Christ, Thy Son, our Lord, who liveth and reigneth with Thee and the Holy Ghost, ever one God, world without end. Amen.

The Hymns

Adoration

Open Now Thy Gates of Beauty

1

8. 7. 8. 7. 7. 7.

Ps. 100 : 4
Tut mir auf die schöne Pforte
Benjamin Schmolck, 1732, cento
Tr., Catherine Winkworth, 1863, alt.

Neander
Joachim Neander, 1680

1 O - pen now thy gates of beau-ty, Zi - on, let me en-ter there,
2 Lord, my God, I come be-fore Thee, Come Thou al - so un-to me;
3 Here Thy praise is glad-ly chant-ed, Here Thy seed is du-ly sown;

Where my soul in joy-ful du - ty Waits for Him who an-swers prayer.
Where we find Thee and a - dore Thee, There a heav'n on earth must be.
Let my soul, where it is plant-ed, Bring forth pre-cious sheaves a-lone,

Oh, how bless-ed is this place, Filled with sol-ace, light, and grace!
To my heart, oh, en - ter Thou, Let it be Thy tem-ple now!
So that all I hear may be Fruit-ful un - to life in me. A-men.

4 Thou my faith increase and quicken,
   Let me keep Thy gift divine,
Howsoe'er temptations thicken;
   May Thy Word still o'er me shine
As my guiding star through life,
   As my comfort in my strife.

5 Speak, O God, and I will hear Thee,
   Let Thy will be done indeed;
May I undisturbed draw near Thee
   While Thou dost Thy people feed.
Here of life the fountain flows,
Here is balm for all our woes.

2

To Thy Temple I Repair

7. 7. 7. 7.

Heb. 9: 14
James Montgomery, 1812

Gott sei Dank
"Neues geistreiches Gesangbuch"
Halle, 1704

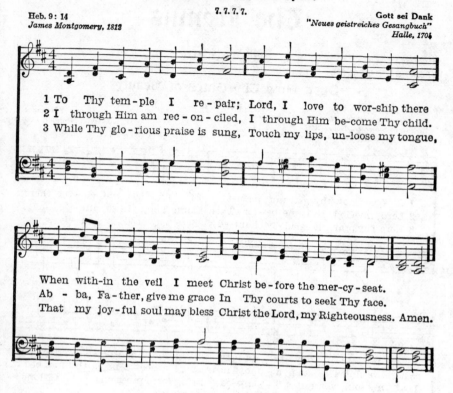

1 To Thy tem-ple I re-pair; Lord, I love to wor-ship there
2 I through Him am rec-on-ciled, I through Him be-come Thy child.
3 While Thy glo-rious praise is sung, Touch my lips, un-loose my tongue,

When with-in the veil I meet Christ be-fore the mer-cy-seat.
Ab - ba, Fa-ther, give me grace In Thy courts to seek Thy face.
That my joy-ful soul may bless Christ the Lord, my Righteousness. Amen.

4 While the prayers of saints ascend,
God of Love, to mine attend.
Hear me, for Thy Spirit pleads;
Hear, for Jesus intercedes.

5 While I hearken to Thy Law,
Fill my soul with humble awe
Till Thy Gospel bring to me
Life and immortality.

6 While Thy ministers proclaim
Peace and pardon in Thy name,
Through their voice, by faith, may I
Hear Thee speaking from the sky.

7 From Thy house when I return,
May my heart within me burn,
And at evening let me say,
"I have walked with God today."

Lord Jesus Christ, Be Present Now

L. M.

Ps. 95 : 2
Herr Jesu Christ, dich zu uns wend
Author unknown, 1651
Tr., Catherine Winkworth, 1863, alt.

Herr Jesu Christ, dich
"Cantionale Germanicum"
Dresden, 1628

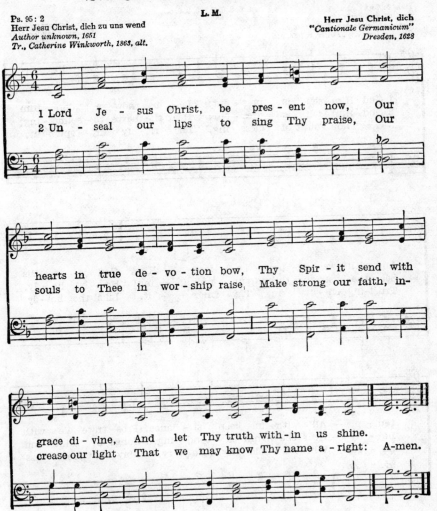

1 Lord Jesus Christ, be pres-ent now, Our
2 Un-seal our lips to sing Thy praise, Our

hearts in true de-vo-tion bow, Thy Spir-it send with
souls to Thee in wor-ship raise, Make strong our faith, in-

grace di-vine, And let Thy truth with-in us shine.
crease our light That we may know Thy name a-right: A-men.

3 Until we join the hosts that cry,
"Holy art Thou, O Lord, most high!"
And in the light of that blest place
Fore'er behold Thee face to face.

4 Glory to God the Father, Son,
And Holy Spirit, Three in One!
To Thee, O blessèd Trinity,
Be praise throughout eternity!

4

God Himself Is Present

Hab. 2:20
Gott ist gegenwärtig
Gerhard Tersteegen, 1729, cento
Tr., Frederick W. Foster, c. 1826, alt.

6. 6. 8. 6. 6. 8. 3. 3. 6. 6.

Wunderbarer König
Joachim Neander, 1680

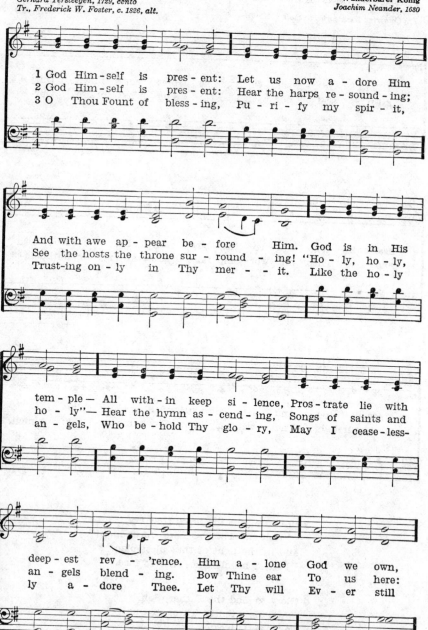

1 God Him-self is pres-ent: Let us now a-dore Him
2 God Him-self is pres-ent: Hear the harps re-sound-ing;
3 O Thou Fount of bless-ing, Pu-ri-fy my spir-it,

And with awe ap-pear be-fore Him. God is in His
See the hosts the throne sur-round-ing! "Ho-ly, ho-ly,
Trust-ing on-ly in Thy mer-it. Like the ho-ly

tem-ple— All with-in keep si-lence, Pros-trate lie with
ho-ly"— Hear the hymn as-cend-ing, Songs of saints and
an-gels, Who be-hold Thy glo-ry, May I cease-less-

deep-est rev-'rence. Him a-lone God we own,
an-gels blend-ing. Bow Thine ear To us here:
ly a-dore Thee. Let Thy will Ev-er still

God Himself Is Present

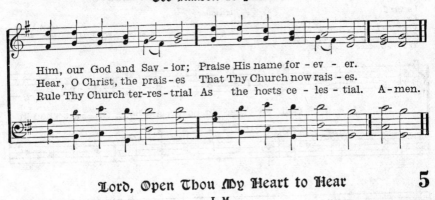

Him, our God and Sav - ior; Praise His name for - ev - er.
Hear, O Christ, the prais - es That Thy Church now rais - es.
Rule Thy Church ter - res - trial As the hosts ce - les - tial. A - men.

Lord, Open Thou My Heart to Hear 5

L. M.

Ps. 119: 140
Herr, öffne mir die Herzenstür
Johannes Olearius, 1671
Tr., Matthias Loy, 1880

Erhalt uns, Herr
"Geistliche Lieder"
Wittenberg, 1543

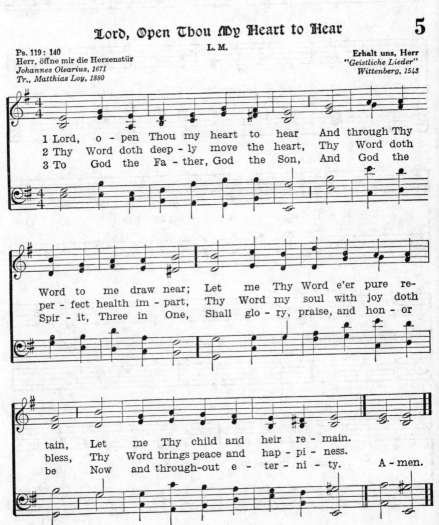

1 Lord, o - pen Thou my heart to hear, And through Thy
2 Thy Word doth deep - ly move the heart, Thy Word doth
3 To God the Fa - ther, God the Son, And God the

Word to me draw near; Let me Thy Word e'er pure re-
per - fect health im - part, Thy Word my soul with joy doth
Spir - it, Three in One, Shall glo - ry, praise, and hon - or

tain, Let me Thy child and heir re - main.
bless, Thy Word brings peace and hap - pi - ness.
be Now and through-out e - ter - ni - ty. A - men.

6 Kyrie, God Father in Heaven Above

Ps. 28 : 2

Kyrie, Gott Vater in Ewigkeit
From the Latin, c. 1100
German author unknown, c. 1541
Tr., W. Gustave Polack, 1939

Irregular

Kyrie, Gott Vater
Based on "Kyrie fons bonitatis," c. 800

Kyr - i - e, God Fa - ther in heav'n a - bove, Great art Thou in

grace and love, Of all things the Mak - er and Pre - serv - er.

E - le - i - son, e - le - i - son! Kyr - i - e, O

Christ, our King, Sal - va - tion for sin - ners Thou didst bring.

O Lord Je - sus, God's own Son, Our Me - di - a - tor at the

Kyrie, God Father in Heaven Above

heav'n-ly throne, Hear our cry and grant our sup-pli-ca - tion.

E - le - i - son, e - le - i - son! Kyr - i - e, O

God the Ho - ly Ghost, Guard our faith, the gift we need the most;

Do Thou our last hour bless; Let us leave this sin - ful world with

glad - ness. E - le - i - son, e - le - i - son! A - men.

7 As We Begin Another Week

Rev. 1: 10
Heut' fangen wir in Gottes Nam'n
Martin Wandersleben, 11668
Tr., W. Gustave Polack, 1940

L. M.

Herr Jesu Christ, mein's
"As Hymnodus Sacer"
Leipzig, 1625

1 As we be-gin an-oth-er week, In Je-sus'
2 Thy gen-tle bless-ings, Lord, out-pour On all our

name this boon we seek: God, grant that thro' these sev-en
la-bor ev-er-more; Our hearts with Thy good Spir-it

days No e-vil may be-fall our ways.
fill That we may glad-ly do Thy will. A-men.

3 In every season, every place
May we regard Thy Word of grace
Until, when life's brief day is past
We reach eternal joy at last

4 And keep with angels in Thy rest
The endless Sabbaths of the blest.
This grant to us through Christ, Thy Son,
Who reigns with Thee upon Thy throne.

Father, Who the Light This Day

7. 7. 7. 7. 7. 7.

Gen. 1: 3
Julia A. Elliot, 1855, cento, alt.

Fred til Bod
Ludvig M. Lindeman, 1871

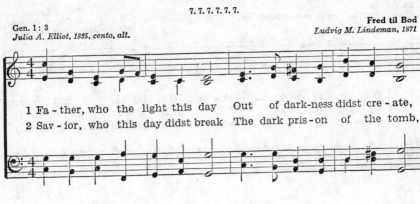

1 Fa - ther, who the light this day Out of dark-ness didst cre - ate,
2 Sav - ior, who this day didst break The dark pris - on of the tomb,

Shine up - on us now, we pray, While with - in Thy courts we wait.
Bid our slum-b'ring souls a - wake, Shine thro' all their sin and gloom;

Wean us from the works of night, Make us chil-dren of the light.
Let us, from our bonds set free, Rise from sin and live to Thee. A - men.

3 Blessed Spirit, Comforter,
    Sent this day from Christ on high,
Lord, on us Thy gifts confer,
    Cleanse, illumine, sanctify.
All Thy fulness shed abroad;
Lead us to the truth of God.

9 O Day of Rest and Gladness

Ps. 118 : 24
Christopher Wordsworth, 1862, cento, alt.

7. 6. 7. 6. D.

Ellacombe
"Gesangbuch d. Herzogl.
Württemberg. Hofkapelle," 1784

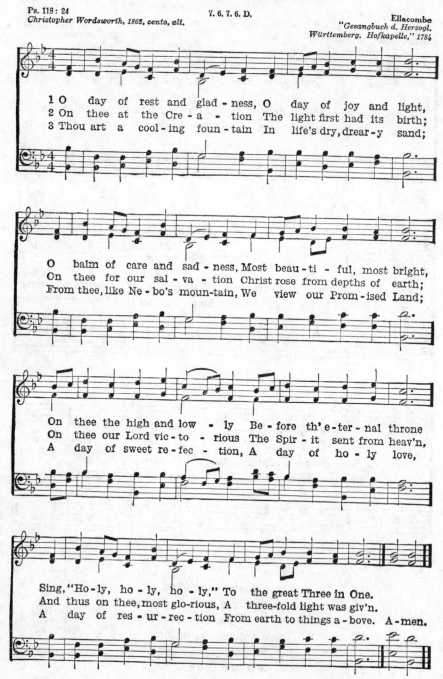

1 O day of rest and glad - ness, O day of joy and light,
2 On thee at the Cre - a - tion The light first had its birth;
3 Thou art a cool - ing foun - tain In life's dry, drear - y sand;

O balm of care and sad - ness, Most beau - ti - ful, most bright,
On thee for our sal - va - tion Christ rose from depths of earth;
From thee, like Ne - bo's moun-tain, We view our Prom - ised Land;

On thee the high and low - ly Be - fore th' e-ter - nal throne
On thee our Lord vic - to - rious The Spir - it sent from heav'n,
A day of sweet re - fec - tion, A day of ho - ly love,

Sing, "Ho - ly, ho - ly, ho - ly," To the great Three in One.
And thus on thee, most glo - rious, A three-fold light was giv'n.
A day of res - ur - rec - tion From earth to things a - bove. A - men.

O Day of Rest and Gladness

4 Today on weary nations
　The heavenly manna falls;
To holy convocations
　The silver trumpet calls,
Where Gospel-light is glowing
　With pure and radiant beams
And living water flowing
　With soul-refreshing streams.

5 New graces ever gaining
　From this our day of rest,
We reach the rest remaining
　To spirits of the blest.
To Holy Ghost be praises,
　To Father, and to Son;
The Church her voice upraises
　To Thee, blest Three in One.

This Is the Day the Lord Hath Made 　10

C. M.

Ps. 118: 24
Isaac Watts, 1719

Num danket all'
Johann Crüger, 1653

1 This is the day the Lord hath made; He calls the hours His own;
2 To - day He rose and left the dead, And Sa-tan's em - pire fell;
3 Ho - san-na to th' a-noint-ed King, To Da-vid's ho - ly Son!

Let heav'n re-joice, let earth be glad　And praise surround the throne.
To - day the saints His triumphs spread And all His won - ders tell.
Help us, O Lord; de-scend and bring Sal - va-tion from the throne. A-men.

4 Blest be the Lord, who comes to men
　With messages of grace;
Who comes in God His Father's name
　To save our sinful race.

5 Hosanna in the highest strains
　The Church on earth can raise.
The highest heavens, in which He reigns,
　Shall give Him nobler praise.

11 Safely through Another Week

Ps. 65: 4
John Newton, 1774, alt.

7. 7. 7. 7. 7. 7.

Voller Wunder
Johann G. Ebeling, 1666

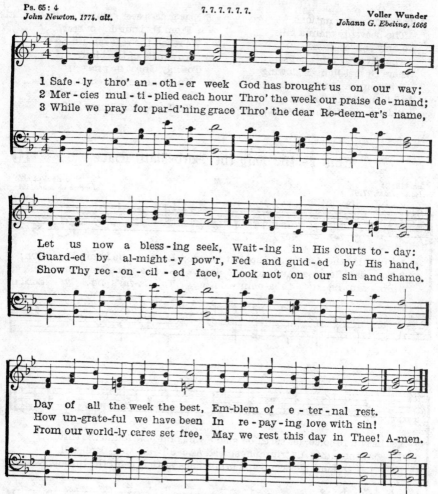

1 Safe - ly thro' an - oth - er week God has brought us on our way;
2 Mer - cies mul - ti - plied each hour Thro' the week our praise de - mand;
3 While we pray for par - d'ning grace Thro' the dear Re - deem - er's name,

Let us now a bless - ing seek, Wait - ing in His courts to - day:
Guard - ed by al - might - y pow'r, Fed and guid - ed by His hand,
Show Thy rec - on - cil - ed face, Look not on our sin and shame.

Day of all the week the best, Em - blem of e - ter - nal rest.
How un - grate - ful we have been In re - pay - ing love with sin!
From our world - ly cares set free, May we rest this day in Thee! A - men.

4 As we come Thy name to praise,
  May we feel Thy presence near;
May Thy glory meet our eyes
  While we in Thy house appear!
Here afford us, Lord, a taste
Of our everlasting feast.

5 May Thy Gospel's joyful sound
  Conquer sinners, comfort saints;
Make the fruits of grace abound,
  Bring relief for all complaints.
Thus may all our Sabbaths prove
Till we join the Church above.

This Day at Thy Creating Word

12

L. M.

Gen. 1: 5
William W. How, 1871

Winchester New
"Musikalisches Handbuch"
Hamburg, 1690

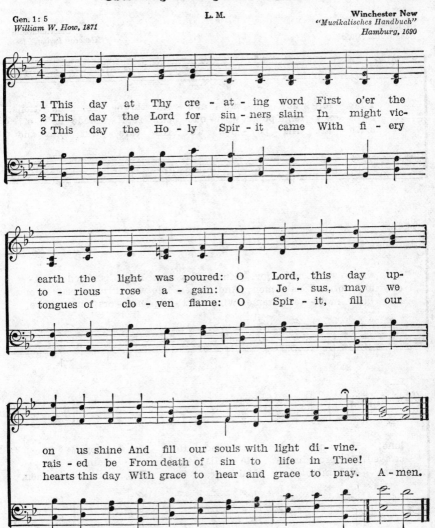

1 This day at Thy cre-at-ing word First o'er the
2 This day the Lord for sin-ners slain In might vic-
3 This day the Ho-ly Spir-it came With fi-ery

earth the light was poured: O Lord, this day up-
to-rious rose a-gain: O Je-sus, may we
tongues of clo-ven flame: O Spir-it, fill our

on us shine And fill our souls with light di-vine.
rais-ed be From death of sin to life in Thee!
hearts this day With grace to hear and grace to pray. A-men.

4 O day of light and life and grace,
From earthly toil sweet resting-place,
Thy hallowed hours, blest gift of love,
Give we again to God above.

5 All praise to God the Father be,
All praise, eternal Son, to Thee,
Whom, with the Spirit, we adore
Forever and forevermore.

13 Before Jehovah's Awe=full Throne

L. M.

Ps. 100
Isaac Watts, 1719, alt.

Old Hundredth
"Genevan Psalter," 1551

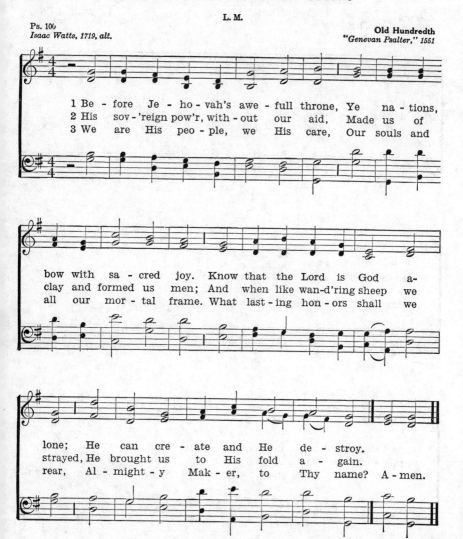

1 Be - fore Je - ho - vah's awe - full throne, Ye na - tions,
2 His sov - 'reign pow'r, with - out our aid, Made us of
3 We are His peo - ple, we His care, Our souls and

bow with sa - cred joy. Know that the Lord is God a -
clay and formed us men; And when like wan - d'ring sheep we
all our mor - tal frame. What last - ing hon - ors shall we

lone; He can cre - ate and He de - stroy.
strayed, He brought us to His fold a - gain.
rear, Al - might - y Mak - er, to Thy name? A - men.

4 We'll crowd Thy gates with thankful songs,
High as the heavens our voices raise;
And earth, with her ten thousand tongues,
Shall fill Thy courts with sounding praise.

5 Wide as the world is Thy command,
Vast as eternity Thy love;
Firm as a rock Thy truth must stand
When rolling years shall cease to move.

All People that on Earth do Dwell

14

L. M.

Ps. 100
William Kethe, 1561

Old Hundredth
"Genevan Psalter," 1551

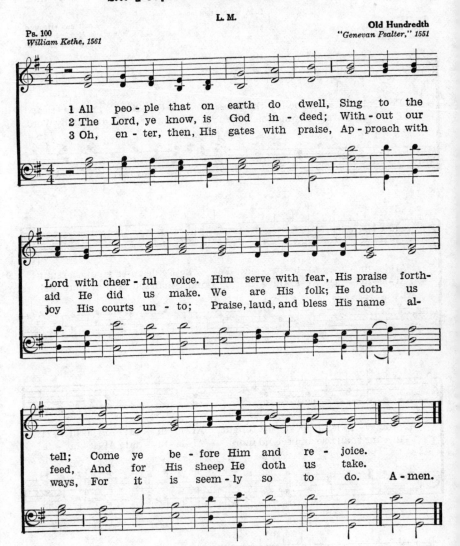

1 All peo-ple that on earth do dwell, Sing to the
2 The Lord, ye know, is God in-deed; With-out our
3 Oh, en-ter, then, His gates with praise, Ap-proach with

Lord with cheer-ful voice. Him serve with fear, His praise forth-
aid He did us make. We are His folk; He doth us
joy His courts un-to; Praise, laud, and bless His name al-

tell; Come ye be-fore Him and re-joice.
feed, And for His sheep He doth us take.
ways, For it is seem-ly so to do. A-men.

4 For why? The Lord, our God, is good;
His mercy is forever sure.
His truth at all times firmly stood
And shall from age to age endure.

5 To Father, Son, and Holy Ghost,
The God whom heaven and earth adore,
From men and from the angel host
Be praise and glory evermore.

15 From All that Dwell below the Skies

L. M. with Alleluias

Ps. 117
Isaac Watts, 1719

Lasst uns erfreuen
"Geistliche Kirchengesäng"
Cologne, 1623

1 From all that dwell be-low the skies   Let   the Cre - a-tor's praise a - rise;
2 E - ter-nal are Thy mer-cies, Lord;   E - ter-nal truth at-tends Thy Word:

Al - le-lu - ia!   Al - le-lu - ia!   Let   the Re-deem-er's name be sung
Al - le-lu - ia!   Al - le-lu - ia!   Thy praise shall sound from shore to shore.

Thro' ev - 'ry land, by ev - 'ry tongue.   Al - le-lu - ia! Al - le-lu - ia!
Till suns shall rise and set no more.   Al - le-lu - ia! Al - le-lu - ia!

Al - le - lu - ia! Al - le-lu - ia!   Al - le - lu - ia!
Al - le - lu - ia! Al - le-lu - ia!   Al - le - lu - ia!   A - men.

Blessed Jesus, at Thy Word

16

7. 8. 7. 8. 8. 8.

Luke 11 : 28
Liebster Jesu, wir sind hier
St. 1–3, Tobias Clausnitzer, 1667
St. 4, author unknown, 1707
Tr., Catherine Winkworth, 1858
Tr., st. 4, unknown

Liebster Jesu
Johann R. Ahle, 1664

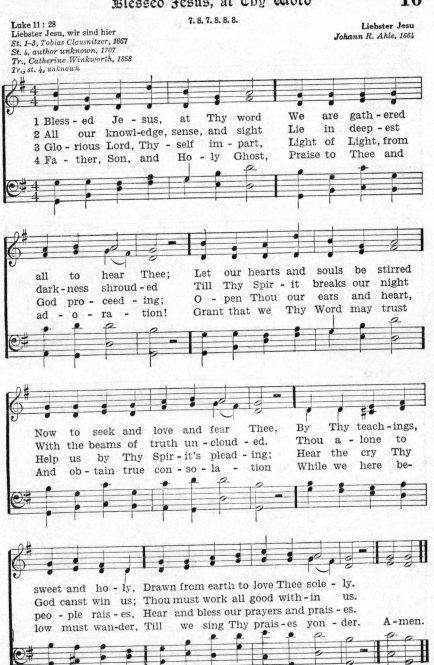

1 Bless - ed Je - sus, at Thy word We are gath - ered
2 All our knowl-edge, sense, and sight Lie in deep - est
3 Glo - rious Lord, Thy - self im - part, Light of Light, from
4 Fa - ther, Son, and Ho - ly Ghost, Praise to Thee and

all to hear Thee; Let our hearts and souls be stirred
dark - ness shroud - ed Till Thy Spir - it breaks our night
God pro - ceed - ing; O - pen Thou our ears and heart,
ad - o - ra - tion! Grant that we Thy Word may trust

Now to seek and love and fear Thee, By Thy teach - ings,
With the beams of truth un - cloud - ed. Thou a - lone to
Help us by Thy Spir - it's plead - ing; Hear the cry Thy
And ob - tain true con - so - la - tion While we here be -

sweet and ho - ly, Drawn from earth to love Thee sole - ly.
God canst win us; Thou must work all good with - in us.
peo - ple rais - es, Hear and bless our prayers and prais - es.
low must wan - der, Till we sing Thy prais - es yon - der. A - men.

17
Oh, Worship the King

5. 5. 5. 5. 6. 5. 6. 5.

Ps. 104
Robert Grant, 1833, alt.

Hanover
"New Version," Supplement, 1708

1 Oh, wor - ship the King All glo - rious a - bove;
2 Oh, tell of His might, Oh, sing of His grace,
3 This earth, with its store Of won - ders un - told,
4 Thy boun - ti - ful care What tongues can re - cite?

Oh, grate - ful - ly sing His pow'r and His love,
Whose robe is the light, Whose can - o - py space!
Al - might - y, Thy pow'r Hath found - ed of old,
It breathes in the air, It shines in the light,

Our Shield and De - fend - er, The An - cient of Days,
His char - iots of wrath The deep thun - der - clouds form,
Hath stab - lished it fast By a change - less de - cree,
It streams from the hills, It de - scends to the plain,

Pa - vil - ioned in splen - dor And gird - ed with praise!
And dark is His path On the wings of the storm.
And round it hath cast, Like a man - tle, the sea.
And sweet - ly dis - tils In the dew and the rain. A - men.

Oh, Worship the King

5 Frail children of dust
    And feeble as frail,
In Thee do we trust
    Nor find Thee to fail.
Thy mercies, how tender,
    How firm to the end,
Our Maker, Defender,
    Redeemer, and Friend!

6 O measureless Might,
    Ineffable Love,
While angels delight
    To hymn Thee above,
Thy humbler creation,
    Though feeble their lays,
With true adoration
    Shall sing to Thy praise.

Lord, We Come Before Thee Now 18

7. 7. 7. 7.

Ps. 27 : 8
William Hammond, 1745
Cento by Martin Madan, 1760

Vienna
Justin H. Knecht, 1797

1 Lord, we come be - fore Thee now, At Thy feet we hum - bly bow;
2 Lord, on Thee our souls de - pend; In com - pas-sion now de - scend,
3 In Thine own ap - point-ed way Now we seek Thee, here we stay.
4 Send some mes-sage from Thy Word That may joy and peace af - ford;

Oh, do not our suit dis-dain! Shall we seek Thee, Lord, in vain?
Fill our hearts with Thy rich grace, Tune our lips to sing Thy praise.
Lord, we know not how to go Till a bless-ing Thou be-stow.
Let Thy Spir-it now im-part Full sal-va - tion to each heart. A-men.

5 Comfort those who weep and mourn,
    Let the time of joy return;
    Those that are cast down lift up,
    Make them strong in faith and hope.

6 Grant that all may seek and find
    Thee a gracious God and kind.
    Heal the sick, the captive free;
    Let us all rejoice in Thee.

19 All Praise to God, Who Reigns Above

Deut. 32: 3
Sei Lob und Ehr' dem höchsten Gut
Johann J. Schütz, 1675, cento
Tr., composite

8. 7. 8. 7. 8. 8. 7.

Lobet den Herrn, ihr
Melchior Vulpius, 1609

1 All praise to God, who reigns a-bove, The God of all cro-
2 What God's al-might-y pow'r hath made His gra-cious mer-cy
3 I cried to Him in time of need: Lord God, oh, hear my
4 The Lord for-sak-eth not His flock, His cho-sen gen-er-

a-tion, The God of won-ders, pow'r, and love, The God of
keep-eth; By morn-ing dawn or eve-ning shade His watch-ful
call-ing! For death He gave me life in-deed And kept my
a-tion; He is their Ref-uge and their Rock, Their Peace and

our sal-va-tion! With heal-ing balm my soul He fills, The God who
eye ne'er sleep-eth; With-in the king-dom of His might, Lo, all is
feet from fall-ing. For this my thanks shall endless be; Oh, thank Him,
their Sal-va-tion. As with a moth-er's ten-der hand He leads His

ev-'ry sor-row stills,—To God all praise and glo-ry!
just and all is right,—To God all praise and glo-ry!
thank our God, with me,—To God all praise and glo-ry!
own, His cho-sen band,—To God all praise and glo-ry! A-men.

All Praise to God, Who Reigns Above

5 Ye who confess Christ's holy name,
    To God give praise and glory!
Ye who the Father's power proclaim,
    To God give praise and glory!
All idols under foot be trod,
The Lord is God! The Lord is God!
    To God all praise and glory!

6 Then come before His presence now
    And banish fear and sadness;
To your Redeemer pay your vow
    And sing with joy and gladness:
Though great distress my soul befell,
The Lord, my God, did all things well —
    To God all praise and glory!

God of Mercy, God of Grace

20

7. 7. 7. 7. 7. 7.

Ps. 67
Henry F. Lyte, 1834

Ratisbon
"Sächsisches Choralbuch"
Leipzig, 1815

1 God of mer-cy, God of grace, Show the bright-ness of Thy face;
2 Let the peo-ple praise Thee, Lord! Be by all that live a-dored;
3 Let the peo-ple praise Thee, Lord! Earth shall then her fruits af-ford,

Shine up-on us, Sav-ior, shine, Fill Thy Church with light di-vine,
Let the na-tions shout and sing Glo-ry to their Sav-ior King,
God to man His bless-ing give, Man to God de-vot-ed live;

And Thy sav-ing health ex-tend Un-to earth's re-mot-est end.
At Thy feet their trib-ute pay, And Thy ho-ly will o-bey.
All be-low and all a-bove One in joy and light and love. A-men.

21 Jehovah, Let Me Now Adore Thee

John 16: 23. Gal. 4: 6
9. 10. 9. 10. 10. 10.

Dir, dir, Jehova, will ich singen
Bartholomäus Crasselius, 1697, cento
Tr., Catherine Winkworth, 1863, alt.

Dir, dir, Jehova
"Geistreiches Gesangbuch"
Halle, 1704

1 Je - ho - vah, let me now a - dore Thee, For where is
2 O Fa - ther, draw me to my Sav - ior That Thy dear
3 Grant that Thy Spir - it prompt my prais - es, Then shall my
4 For He can plead for me with sigh - ings That are un-

there a God such, Lord, as Thou? With songs I fain would
Son may draw me un - to Thee; Thy Spir - it guide my
sing - ing sure - ly please Thine ear; Sweet are the sounds my
speak - a - ble to lips like mine; He bids me pray with

come be - fore Thee; Oh, let Thy Ho - ly Spir - it teach me
whole be - hav - ior And rule both sense and rea - son thus in
heart then rais - es, My prayer in truth and spir - it Thou wilt
ear - nest cry - ings, Bears wit - ness with my soul that I am

now To praise Thee in His name thro' whom a - lone
me That, Lord, Thy peace from me may ne'er de - part,
hear. Then shall Thy Spir - it raise my heart to Thee
Thine, Joint heir with Christ, and thus may dare to say:

Jehovah, Let Me Now Adore Thee

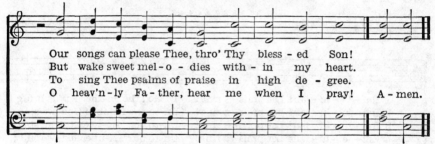

Our songs can please Thee, thro' Thy bless-ed Son!
But wake sweet mel-o-dies with-in my heart.
To sing Thee psalms of praise in high de-gree.
O heav'n-ly Fa-ther, hear me when I pray! A-men.

5 When thus my heart in prayer ascendeth,
  Through Thine own Holy Spirit, unto Thee,
Thy heart, O Father, kindly bendeth
  Its fervent love and favor unto me,
Rejoicing my petition to fulfil
Which I have made according to Thy will.

6 And what Thy Spirit thus hath taught me
  To seek from Thee must needs be such a prayer
As Thou wilt grant, through Him who bought me
  And raised me up to be Thy child and heir.
In Jesus' name I boldly seek Thy face
And take from Thee, my Father, grace for grace.

Lord, When We Bend Before Thy Throne 22

C. M.

Ps. 32: 1
Joseph D. Carlyle, 1802

St. Flavian
"Psalter"
John Day, 1562

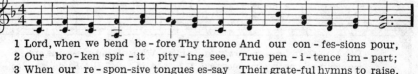

1 Lord, when we bend be-fore Thy throne And our con-fes-sions pour,
2 Our bro-ken spir-it pity-ing see, True pen-i-tence im-part;
3 When our re-spon-sive tongues es-say Their grate-ful hymns to raise,

Teach us to feel the sins we own And hate what we de-plore.
Then let a kindling glance from Thee Beam hope up-on the heart.
Grant that our souls may join the lay And mount to Thee in praise. A-men.

4 When we disclose our wants in prayer,
  May we our wills resign
And not a thought our bosom share·
  That is not wholly Thine.

5 May faith each meek petition fill
  And waft it to the skies;
And teach our hearts 'tis goodness still
  That grants it or denies.

23 Hallelujah! Let Praises Ring

8. 8. 7. 8. 8. 7. 4. 4. 4. 4. 8.

Rev. 19:1
Halleluja! Lob, Preis und Ehr'
Author unknown, 1698
Tr., composite

Wie schön leuchtet
Philipp Nicolai, 1599

1 Hal - le - lu - jah! Let prais-es ring! To God the Fa-ther let us bring
2 Hal - le - lu - jah! Let prais-es ring! Un-to the Lamb of God we sing,
3 Hal - le - lu - jah! Let prais-es ring! Un-to the Ho-ly Ghost we sing
4 Hal - le - lu - jah! Let prais-es ring! Un-to our Tri-une God we sing;

Our songs of ad-o-ra-tion. To Him thro' ev-er-last-ing days
In whom we are e-lect-ed. He bo't His Church with His own blood,
For our re-gen-er-a-tion. The sav-ing faith in us He wrought
Blest be His name for-ev-er! With an-gel hosts let us a-dore

Be wor-ship, hon-or, pow'r, and praise, Whose hand sus-tains cre-a-
He cleansed her in that bless-ed flood, And as His Bride se-lect-
And us un-to the Bridegroom bro't, Made us His cho-sen na-
And sing His prais-es more and more For all His grace and fa-

tion. Sing-ing, ring-ing: Ho-ly, ho-ly, God is ho-ly,—
ed. Ho-ly, ho-ly Is our un-ion And com-mun-ion.
tion. Glo-ry! Glo-ry! Joy e-ter-nal, Bliss su-per-nal;
vor! Sing-ing, ring-ing: Ho-ly, ho-ly, God is ho-ly,—

Hallelujah! Let Praises Ring

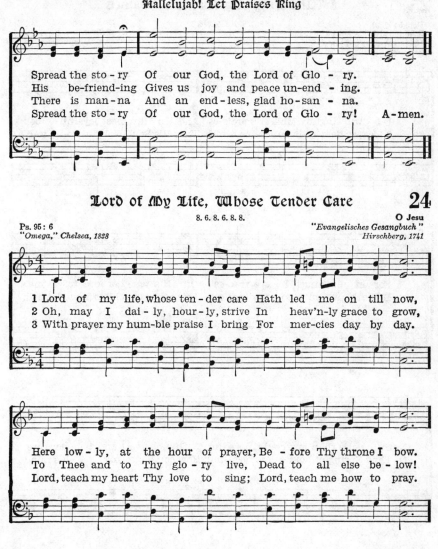

Spread the sto-ry Of our God, the Lord of Glo - ry.
His be-friend-ing Gives us joy and peace un-end - ing.
There is man-na And an end-less, glad ho-san - na.
Spread the sto-ry Of our God, the Lord of Glo - ry! A-men.

Lord of My Life, Whose Tender Care   24

8. 6. 8. 6. 8. 8.

O Jesu
"Evangelisches Gesangbuch"
Hirschberg, 1741

Ps. 95: 6
"Omega," Chelsea, 1838

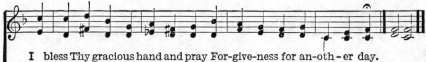

1 Lord of my life, whose ten-der care Hath led me on till now,
2 Oh, may I dai-ly, hour-ly, strive In heav'n-ly grace to grow,
3 With prayer my hum-ble praise I bring For mer-cies day by day.

Here low-ly, at the hour of prayer, Be - fore Thy throne I bow.
To Thee and to Thy glo-ry live, Dead to all else be - low!
Lord, teach my heart Thy love to sing; Lord, teach me how to pray.

I bless Thy gracious hand and pray For-give-ness for an-oth - er day.
Tread in the path my Sav-ior trod, Tho' thorn-y, yet the path of God.
All that I have and am, to Thee I of - fer thro' e - ter-ni - ty. A-men.

25 I Will Sing My Maker's Praises

Eph. 5 : 19, 20
Sollt' ich meinem Gott nicht singen
Paul Gerhardt, 1659, cento
Tr., composite

8. 7. 8. 7. 8. 7. 7. 8. 7. 7.

Sollt' ich meinem Gott
Johann Schop, 1641

1 I will sing my Mak-er's prais-es And in Him most joy-ful be,
2 Yea, so dear did He es-teem me That His Son He loved so well

For in all things I see trac-es Of His ten-der love to me.
He hath giv-en to re-deem me From the quenchless flames of hell.

Noth-ing else than love could move Him With such sweet and ten-der care
O Thou Spring of bound-less bless-ing, How could e'er my fee-ble mind

Ev-er-more to raise and bear All who try to serve and love Him.
Of Thy depth the bot-tom find Tho' my ef-forts were un-ceas-ing?

I Will Sing My Maker's Praises

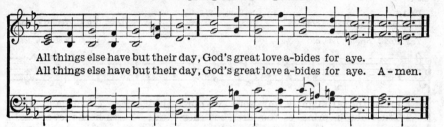

All things else have but their day, God's great love a-bides for aye.
All things else have but their day, God's great love a-bides for aye. A-men.

3 All that for my soul is needful
   He with loving care provides,
Nor of that is He unheedful
   Which my body needs besides.
When my strength cannot avail me,
   When my powers can do no more,
   Doth my God His strength outpour;
In my need He doth not fail me.
   All things else have but their day,
   God's great love abides for aye.

4 When I sleep, He still is near me,
   O'er me rests His guardian eye;
And new gifts and blessings cheer me
   When the morning streaks the sky.
Were it not for God's protection,
   Had His countenance not been
   Here my guide, I had not seen
E'er the end of my affliction.
   All things else have but their day,
   God's great love abides for aye.

5 As a father never turneth
   Wholly from a wayward child,
For the prodigal still yearneth,
   Longing to be reconciled,
So my many sins and errors
   Find a tender, pardoning God,
   Chastening frailty with His rod,
Not, in vengeance, with His terrors.
   All things else have but their day,
   God's great love abides for aye.

6 Since, then, neither change nor coldness,
   In my Father's love can be,
Lo! I lift my hands with boldness,
   As Thy child I come to Thee.
Grant me grace, O God, I pray Thee,
   That I may with all my might,
   All my lifetime, day and night,
Love and trust Thee and obey Thee
   And, when this brief life is o'er,
   Praise and love Thee evermore.

26 Praise the Almighty, My Soul, Adore Him

Ps. 146
Lobe den Herren, o meine Seele
Johann D. Herrnschmidt, 1714
Tr., Alfred Brauer, 1925, alt.

10. 8. 10. 8. 8. 8. 4. 4.

Lobe den Herren, o meine
"Seelenharfe"
Onolzbach, 1665

1 Praise the Al-might-y, my soul, a-dore Him! Yea, I will laud Him un-til death. With songs and an-thems I'll come be-fore Him As long as He doth give me breath. From Him my life and all things came; Bless, O my soul, His ho-ly name. Hal-le-lu-jah! Hal-le-lu-jah!

2 Trust not in princ-es, they are but mor-tal; Earth-born they are and soon de-cay. Naught are their coun-sels at life's last por-tal, When the dark grave doth claim its prey. Since, then, no man can help af-ford, Trust ye in Christ, our God and Lord. Hal-le-lu-jah! Hal-le-lu-jah!

3 Bless-ed, yea, bless-ed is he for-ev-er Whose help is in the Lord most high, Whom from the sav-ing faith naught can sev-er, And who in hope to Christ draws nigh. To all who trust in Him, our Lord, Coun-sel and aid He doth af-ford. Hal-le-lu-jah! Hal-le-lu-jah!

4 God the Al-might-y, the great Cre-a-tor, Rul-er of sky and land and sea, All things or-dain-ed, and soon-er or lat-er They come to pass un-fail-ing-ly. His rule is o-ver rich and poor, His prom-ise ev-er stand-eth sure. Hal-le-lu-jah! Hal-le-lu-jah! A-men.

Praise the Almighty, My Soul, Adore Him

5 Penitent sinners, for mercy crying,
  Pardon and peace from Him obtain;
Ever the wants of the poor supplying,
  Their faithful God He doth remain.
He helps His children in distress,
The widows and the fatherless.
  Hallelujah! Hallelujah!

6 Praise, O mankind, now the name so holy
  Of Him who doth such wondrous things!
All that hath being, to praise Him solely,
  With happy heart its "Amen" sings!
Children of God, with angel host
Praise Father, Son, and Holy Ghost!
  Hallelujah! Hallelujah!

Oh, Bless the Lord, My Soul   27

Ps. 103:1-7   S. M.   St. Thomas
Isaac Watts, 1719   *Aaron Williams, 1770*

1 Oh, bless the Lord, my soul! Let all with-in me join
2 Oh, bless the Lord, my soul, Nor let His mer-cies lie
3 'Tis He for-gives thy sins; 'Tis He re-lieves thy pain;
4 He crowns thy life with love When ran-somed from the grave;

And aid my tongue to bless His name Whose fa-vors are di-vine.
For-got-ten in un-thank-ful-ness And with-out prais-es die!
'Tis He that heals thy sick-ness-es And makes thee young a-gain.
He that re-deemed my soul from hell Hath sov-'reign pow'r to save. A-men.

5 He fills the poor with good;
  He gives the sufferers rest:
The Lord hath judgments for the proud
  And justice for th' opprest.

6 His wondrous works and ways
  He made by Moses known,
But sent the world His truth and grace
  By His belovèd Son.

28 Now Let All Loudly Sing Praise

1 Chron. 29 : 11, 12
Nun preiset alle Gottes Barmherzigkeit
Matthäus A. v. Löwenstern, 1644
Tr., Catherine Winkworth, 1863, alt.

5. 6. 5. 6. 9. 10.

Nun preiset alle
"Apellislieder"
Breslau, 1644

1 Now let all loud-ly Sing praise to God the Lord;
2 For the Lord reign-eth O - ver the u - ni -verse,
3 Come, hea-then rac - es, Cast off all grief and care,

Chris - ten-dom, proud-ly Laud Him with one ac - cord.
All He sus - tain-eth, All things His praise re - hearse,
For pleas-ant plac - es Your Sav - ior doth pre-pare,

Gen - tly He bids thee come be - fore Him;
The an - gel host His glo - ry tell - ing,
Where His blest Word a - broad is sound - ed,

Haste, then, O Is - ra - el, now a - dore Him;
Psal - ter and harp are the an - them swell - ing;
Par - don for sin - ners and grace un - bound - ed;

Haste, then, O Is - ra - el, now a - dore Him.
Psal - ter and harp are the an - them swell - ing.
Par - don for sin - ners and grace un-bound - ed. A - men.

Now Let All Loudly Sing Praise

4 Richly He feeds us
  Always and everywhere;
Gently He leads us
  With a true father's care;
The late and early rains He sends us,
Daily His blessing, His love, attends us.

5 Sing we His praises
  Who is thus merciful;
Christendom raises
  Songs to His glorious rule.
Rejoice! No foe shall now alarm us;
He will protect us, and who can harm us?

Through All the Changing Scenes of Life   29

Ps. 34   C. M.   Ich singe dir
Nicholas Brady and   "Harmonischer Liederschatz"
Nahum Tate, 1696, alt.   Frankfurt, 1738

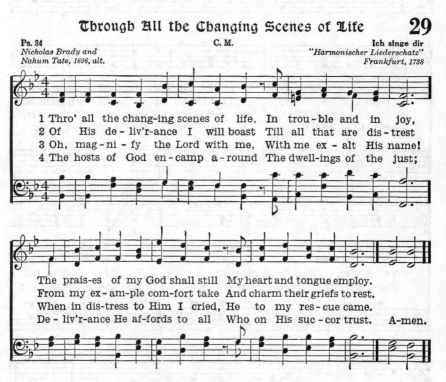

1 Thro' all the chang-ing scenes of life, In trou-ble and in joy,
2 Of His de-liv'r-ance I will boast Till all that are dis-trest
3 Oh, mag-ni-fy the Lord with me, With me ex-alt His name!
4 The hosts of God en-camp a-round The dwell-ings of the just;

The prais-es of my God shall still My heart and tongue employ.
From my ex-am-ple com-fort take And charm their griefs to rest.
When in dis-tress to Him I cried, He to my res-cue came.
De-liv'r-ance He af-fords to all Who on His suc-cor trust.   A-men.

5 Oh, make but trial of His love!
  Experience will decide
How blest are they, and only they,
  Who in His truth confide.

6 Fear Him, ye saints, and you will then
  Have nothing else to fear;
Make you His service your delight,
  He'll make your wants His care.

30 Oh, that I Had a Thousand Voices

9. 8. 9. 8. 8. 8.

Ps. 126 : 3
O dass ich tausend Zungen hätte
Johann Mentzer, 1704, cento
Tr., composite

O dass ich tausend
Johann B. König, 1738

Oh, that I Had a Thousand Voices

5 Lord, I will tell, while I am living,
    Thy goodness forth with every breath
  And greet each morning with thanksgiving
    Until my heart is still in death;
  Yea, when at last my lips grow cold,
  Thy praise shall in my sighs be told.

6 O Father, deign Thou, I beseech Thee,
    To listen to my earthly lays;
  A nobler strain in heaven shall reach Thee,
    When I with angels hymn Thy praise
  And learn amid their choirs to sing
  Loud hallelujahs to my King.

When All Thy Mercies, O My God   31

C. M.

Ps. 33 : 1
Joseph Addison, 1712

Winchester Old
"Psalter"
Thomas Este, 1592

1 When all Thy mer-cies, O my God, My ris-ing soul sur-veys,
2 Ten thou-sand thou-sand pre-cious gifts My dai-ly thanks em-ploy;
3 Thro' ev-'ry pe-riod of my life Thy good-ness I'll pur-sue

Trans-port-ed with the view, I'm lost In won-der, love, and praise.
Nor is the least a cheer-ful heart That tastes those gifts with joy.
And af-ter death, in dis-tant worlds, The glo-rious theme re-new. A-men.

4 When nature fails and day and night
  Divide Thy works no more,
  My ever grateful heart, O Lord,
  Thy mercies shall adore.

5 Through all eternity to Thee
  A joyful song I'll raise;
  But, oh! eternity's too short
  To utter all Thy praise.

32

Redeemed, Restored, Forgiven

7. 6. 7. 6. D.

Luke 15: 24
Henry W. Baker, 1876

Ich dank' dir, lieber Herre
"Musika Deutsch"
Nürnberg, 1532

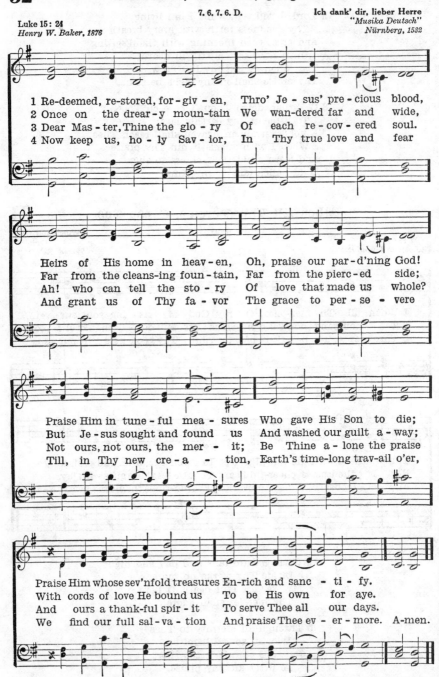

1 Re-deemed, re-stored, for-giv-en, Thro' Je-sus' pre-cious blood,
2 Once on the drear-y moun-tain We wan-dered far and wide,
3 Dear Mas-ter, Thine the glo-ry Of each re-cov-ered soul.
4 Now keep us, ho-ly Sav-ior, In Thy true love and fear

Heirs of His home in heav-en, Oh, praise our par-d'ning God!
Far from the cleans-ing foun-tain, Far from the pierc-ed side;
Ah! who can tell the sto-ry Of love that made us whole?
And grant us of Thy fa-vor The grace to per-se-vere

Praise Him in tune-ful mea-sures Who gave His Son to die;
But Je-sus sought and found us And washed our guilt a-way;
Not ours, not ours, the mer-it; Be Thine a-lone the praise
Till, in Thy new cre-a-tion, Earth's time-long trav-ail o'er,

Praise Him whose sev'nfold treasures En-rich and sanc-ti-fy.
With cords of love He bound us To be His own for aye.
And ours a thank-ful spir-it To serve Thee all our days.
We find our full sal-va-tion And praise Thee ev-er-more. A-men.

The Lord hath Helped Me Hitherto

33

1 Sam. 7: 12
Bis hieher hat mich Gott gebracht
Ämilie Juliane, 1699
Tr., August Crull, 1882

8. 7. 8. 7. 8. 8. 7.

Allein Gott in der Höh'
Nikolaus Decius, 1539, asc.

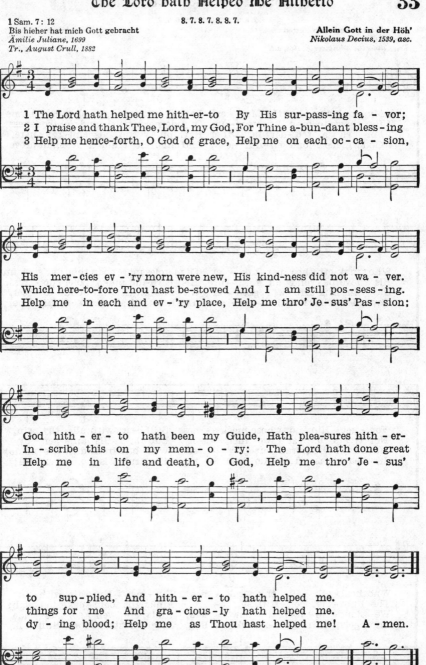

1 The Lord hath helped me hith-er-to   By His sur-pass-ing fa - vor;
2 I praise and thank Thee, Lord, my God, For Thine a-bun-dant bless - ing
3 Help me hence-forth, O God of grace, Help me on each oc-ca - sion,

His mer-cies ev - 'ry morn were new, His kind-ness did not wa - ver.
Which here-to-fore Thou hast be-stowed And I am still pos-sess-ing.
Help me in each and ev - 'ry place, Help me thro' Je-sus' Pas - sion;

God hith - er - to hath been my Guide, Hath plea-sures hith - er-
In - scribe this on my mem - o - ry: The Lord hath done great
Help me in life and death, O God, Help me thro' Je - sus'

to sup - plied, And hith - er - to hath helped me.
things for me And gra - cious - ly hath helped me.
dy - ing blood; Help me as Thou hast helped me! A - men.

34 My Soul, Now Bless Thy Maker

Ps. 103

7. 8. 7. 8. 7. 6. 7. 6. 7. 6. 7. 6.

Nun lob, mein' Seel', den Herren
Johann Gramann, 1525
Tr., Catherine Winkworth, 1863, alt.

Nun lob, mein' Seel'
"Concentus Novi"
Augsburg, 1540

1 My soul, now bless thy Mak - er! Let all with - in me bless His name
2 He shows to man His treas - ure Of judgment, truth, and righteousness,
3 For as a ten - der fa - ther Hath pit - y on his chil - dren here,
4 God's grace a - lone en - dur - eth, And children's children yet shall prove

Who mak - eth thee par - tak - er Of mercies more than thou dar'st claim.
His love be - yond all meas - ure, His yearn - ing pit - y o'er dis - tress,
He in His arms will gath - er All who are His in child - like fear.
How He with strength as - sur - eth The hearts of all that seek His love.

For - get Him not whose meek - ness Still bears with all thy sin,
Nor treats us as we mer - it, But lays His an - ger by.
He knows how frail our pow - ers Who but from dust are made;
In heav'n is fixed His dwell - ing, His rule is o - ver all;

Who heal - eth all thy weak - ness, Re - news thy life with - in;
The hum - ble, con - trite spir - it Finds His com - pas - sion nigh;
We flour - ish like the flow - ers, And e - ven so we fade;
An - gels, in might ex - cel - ling, Bright hosts, be - fore Him fall.

My Soul, Now Bless Thy Maker

Whose grace and care are end - less, And saved thee thro' the past;
And high as heav'n a - bove us, As break from close of day,
The wind but o'er them pass - es, And all their bloom is o'er,-
Praise Him who ev - er reign - eth, All ye who hear His Word,

Who leaves no suf - f'rer friend-less, But rights the wronged at last.
So far, since He doth love us, He puts our sins a - way.
We with - er like the grass - es, Our place knows us no more.
Nor our poor hymns dis-dain-eth — My soul, O bless the Lord! A-men.

Songs of Praise the Angels Sang

35

Job 38 : 7
James Montgomery, 1819, alt.

7. 7. 7. 7.

Innocents
French melody, 13th century

1 Songs of praise the an - gels sang, Heav'n with al - le - lu - ias rang,
2 Songs of praise a - woke the morn When the Prince of Peace was born;
3 Heav'n and earth must pass a - way; Songs of praise shall crown that day.
4 And shall man a - lone be dumb Till that glo-rious king-dom come?

When cre - a - tion was be - gun, When God spake and it was done.
Songs of praise a-rose when He Cap - tive led cap-tiv - i - ty.
God will make new heav'ns and earth; Songs of praise shall hail their birth.
No; the Church delights to raise Psalms and hymns and songs of praise. Amen.

5 Saints below, with heart and voice,
Still in songs of praise rejoice;
Learning here, by faith and love,
Songs of praise to sing above.

6 Borne upon their latest breath,
Songs of praise shall conquer death;
Then, amidst eternal joy,
Songs of praise their powers employ.

36 Now Thank We All Our God

Ecclus. 50 : 22–24
Nun danket alle Gott
Martin Rinckart, 1636
Tr., Catherine Winkworth, 1858

6. 7. 6. 7. 6. 6. 6. 6.

Nun danket alle Gott
Johann Crüger, 1648

1 Now thank we all our God With heart and hands and voic - es,
2 Oh, may this boun-teous God Thro' all our life be near us,
3 All praise and thanks to God The Fa-ther now be giv - en,

Who won-drous things hath done, In whom His world re - joic - es;
With ev - er joy - ful hearts And bless-ed peace to cheer us
The Son, and Him who reigns With them in high-est heav - en:

Who from our moth-er's arms Hath blessed us on our way
And keep us in His grace And guide us when per - plexed
The one e - ter - nal God, Whom earth and heav'n a - dore!

With count-less gifts of love And still is ours to - day.
And free us from all ills In this world and the next!
For thus it was, is now, And shall be ev - er - more. A - men.

Lord, 'Tis Not that I did Choose Thee

37

8. 7. 8. 7. D.

John 15: 16
Josiah Conder, 1843, alt.

O du Liebe
"Musikalischer Christenschatz"
Basel, 1745

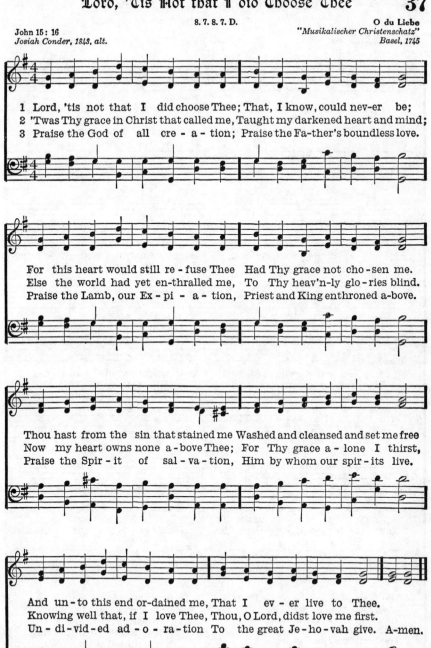

1 Lord, 'tis not that I did choose Thee; That, I know, could nev-er be;
2 'Twas Thy grace in Christ that called me, Taught my darkened heart and mind;
3 Praise the God of all cre-a-tion; Praise the Fa-ther's boundless love.

For this heart would still re-fuse Thee Had Thy grace not cho-sen me.
Else the world had yet en-thralled me, To Thy heav'n-ly glo-ries blind.
Praise the Lamb, our Ex-pi-a-tion, Priest and King enthroned a-bove.

Thou hast from the sin that stained me Washed and cleansed and set me free
Now my heart owns none a-bove Thee; For Thy grace a-lone I thirst,
Praise the Spir-it of sal-va-tion, Him by whom our spir-its live.

And un-to this end or-dained me, That I ev-er live to Thee.
Knowing well that, if I love Thee, Thou, O Lord, didst love me first.
Un-di-vid-ed ad-o-ra-tion To the great Je-ho-vah give. A-men.

38 The Lord, My God, be Praised

Deut. 32 : 3
Gelobet sei der Herr
Johann Olearius, 1671
Tr., August Crull, †1923, alt.

6. 7. 6. 7. 6. 6. 6. 6.

Nun danket alle Gott
Johann Crüger, 1648

1 The Lord, my God, be praised, My Light, my Life from heav-en;
2 The Lord, my God, be praised, My Trust, my Life from heav-en,
3 The Lord, my God, be praised, My Hope, my Life from heav-en,

My Mak-er, who to me Hath soul and bod-y giv-en;
The Fa-ther's own dear Son, Whose life for me was giv-en;
The Spir-it, whom the Son In love to me hath giv-en.

My Fa-ther, who doth shield And keep me day by day,
Who for my sin a-toned With His most pre-cious blood,
'Tis He re-vives my heart, 'Tis He that gives me pow'r,

Doth make each mo-ment yield New bless-ings on my way.
Who giv-eth me by faith The high-est heav'n-ly good.
Help, com-fort, and sup-port In sor-row's gloom-y hour. A-men.

4 The Lord, my God, be praised,
   My God, who ever liveth,
To whom the heavenly host
   All praise and honor giveth.
The Lord, my God, be praised,
   In whose great name I boast,
God Father, God the Son,
   And God the Holy Ghost.

5 To Him with joyful song
   Our praises we are bringing
And with the angel throng
   Thrice "Holy" we are singing.
With one united voice
   The Church doth Him adore.
The Lord, my God, be praised
   Now and forevermore.

Praise to the Lord, the Almighty

Neh. 9: 6

Lobe den Herren, den mächtigen
Joachim Neander, 1679
Tr., Catherine Winkworth, 1863, alt.

14. 14. 4. 7. 8.

Lobe den Herren, den
"Erneuertes Gesangbuch"
Stralsund, 1665

1 Praise to the Lord, the Al-might-y, the King of cre-a - - tion!
2 Praise to the Lord, who o'er all things so won-drous-ly reign - eth,
3 Praise to the Lord, who hath fear-ful-ly, won-drous-ly, made thee;
4 Praise to the Lord, who doth pros-per thy work and de-fend thee,

O my soul, praise Him, for He is thy Health and Sal-va - - tion!
Who, as on wings of an ea - gle, up-lift-eth, sus-tain - eth.
Health hath vouchsafed and, when heed-less-ly fall-ing, hath stayed thee.
Who from the heav-ens the streams of His mer-cy doth send thee.

Join the full throng; Wake, harp and psal-ter and song;
Hast thou not seen How thy de-sires all have been
What need or grief Ev - er hath failed of re - lief?—
Pon - der a - new What the Al-might-y can do,

Sound forth in glad ad-o - ra - - tion!
Grant-ed in what He or-dain - - eth?
Wings of His mer-cy did shade thee.
Who with His love doth be-friend thee. A - men.

5 Praise to the Lord! Oh, let all that is in me adore Him!
All that hath life and breath, come now with praises before Him!
Let the Amen
Sound from His people again;
Gladly for aye we adore Him.

40 The God of Abraham Praise

6. 6. 8. 4. D.

Ex. 3 : 6
Thomas Olivers, c. 1770, cento

Yigdal
Hebrew melody, 17th century

1 The God of A-br'ham praise; All prais-ed be His name
2 The God of A-br'ham praise, At whose su-preme com-mand
3 He by Him-self hath sworn,—I on His oath de-pend,—
4 The whole tri-um-phant host Give thanks to God on high;

Who was and is and is to be And still the same!
From earth I rise and seek the joys At His right hand.
I shall, on ea-gles' wings up-borne, To heav'n as-cend;
"Hail, Fa-ther, Son, and Ho-ly Ghost!" They ev-er cry.

The one e-ter-nal God, Ere aught that now ap-pears;
I all on earth for-sake, Its wis-dom, fame, and pow'r,
I shall be-hold His face, I shall His pow'r a-dore
Hail, A-br'ham's God and mine!— I join the heav'n-ly lays —

The First, the Last: be-yond all tho't His time-less years!
And Him my on-ly Por-tion make, My Shield and Tow'r.
And sing the won-ders of His grace For-ev-er-more.
All might and maj-es-ty are Thine And end-less praise. A-men.

Wondrous King, All=Glorious

41

Ps. 150: 6
Wunderbarer König
Joachim Neander, 1680
Tr., Wm. J. Schaefer, 1938

6. 6. 8. 6. 6. 8. 3. 3. 6. 6.

Wunderbarer König
Joachim Neander, 1680

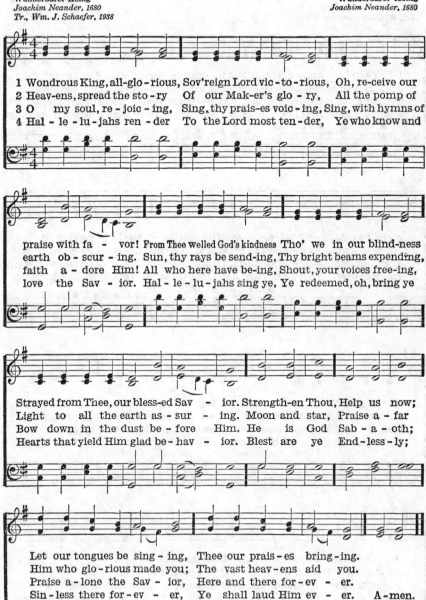

1 Wondrous King, all-glo-rious, Sov'reign Lord vic-to-rious, Oh, re-ceive our
2 Heav-ens, spread the sto-ry Of our Mak-er's glo-ry, All the pomp of
3 O my soul, re-joic-ing, Sing, thy prais-es voic-ing, Sing, with hymns of
4 Hal-le-lu-jahs ren-der To the Lord most ten-der, Ye who know and

praise with fa - vor! From Thee welled God's kindness Tho' we in our blind-ness
earth ob-scur-ing. Sun, thy rays be send-ing, Thy bright beams expending,
faith a-dore Him! All who here have be-ing, Shout, your voices free-ing,
love the Sav - ior. Hal-le-lu-jahs sing ye, Ye redeemed, oh, bring ye

Strayed from Thee, our bless-ed Sav - ior. Strength-en Thou, Help us now;
Light to all the earth as-sur - ing. Moon and star, Praise a-far
Bow down in the dust be-fore Him. He is God Sab-a-oth;
Hearts that yield Him glad be-hav - ior. Blest are ye End-less-ly;

Let our tongues be sing-ing, Thee our prais-es bring-ing.
Him who glo-rious made you; The vast heav-ens aid you.
Praise a-lone the Sav-ior, Here and there for-ev-er.
Sin-less there for-ev-er, Ye shall laud Him ev-er. A-men.

42 O Thou Love Unbounded

John 16 : 27
Unumschränkte Liebe
Johann J. Rambach, 1735
Tr., W. Gustave Polack, 1940

6. 6. 8. 6. 6. 8. 3. 3. 6. 6.

Wunderbarer König
Joachim Neander, 1680

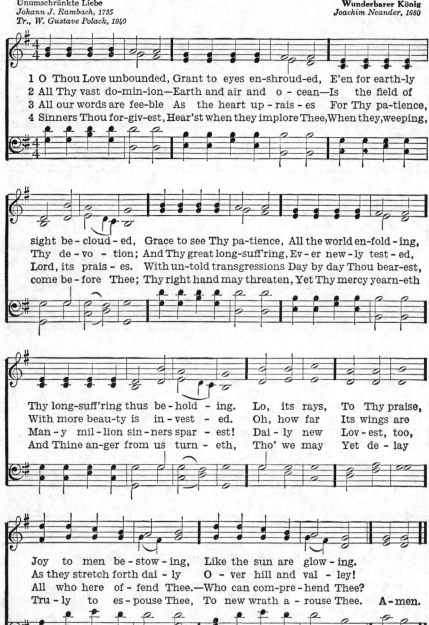

1 O Thou Love unbounded, Grant to eyes en-shroud-ed, E'en for earth-ly
sight be-cloud-ed, Grace to see Thy pa-tience, All the world en-fold-ing,
Thy long-suff'ring thus be-hold-ing. Lo, its rays, To Thy praise,
Joy to men be-stow-ing, Like the sun are glow-ing.

2 All Thy vast do-min-ion—Earth and air and o-cean—Is the field of
Thy de-vo-tion; And Thy great long-suff'ring, Ev-er new-ly test-ed,
With more beau-ty is in-vest-ed. Oh, how far Its wings are
As they stretch forth dai-ly O-ver hill and val-ley!

3 All our words are fee-ble As the heart up-rais-es For Thy pa-tience,
Lord, its prais-es. With un-told transgressions Day by day Thou bear-est,
Man-y mil-lion sin-ners spar-est! Dai-ly new Lov-est, too,
All who here of-fend Thee.—Who can com-pre-hend Thee?

4 Sinners Thou for-giv-est, Hear'st when they implore Thee, When they, weeping,
come be-fore Thee; Thy right hand may threaten, Yet Thy mercy yearn-eth
And Thine an-ger from us turn-eth, Tho' we may Yet de-lay
Tru-ly to es-pouse Thee, To new wrath a-rouse Thee. A-men.

O Thou Love Unbounded

5 Lord, no·one has ever,
   Who on Thee believèd,
   Justice here for grace receivèd.
All guilt Thou removest
   When we bow before Thee
   And in penitence implore Thee;
For our smart
Moves Thy heart;
   Thou wouldst mercy show us
   And with grace endow us.

6 O Most High, we praise Thee
   That Thou us regardest
   Nor our evil deeds rewardest!
Zion's Hope, continue
   Thy dominion o'er us,
   Wielding well Thy scepter for us
Lovingly.
Patient be,
   Lord, we now implore Thee:
   Thine shall be the glory!

We Sing the Almighty Power of God — 43

C. M.

Ps. 149
Isaac Watts, 1715

Ich singe dir
"Harmonischer Liederschatz"
Frankfurt, 1738

1 We sing th' al-might-y pow'r of God, Who bade the moun-tains rise,
2 We sing the wis-dom that or-dained The sun to rule the day;
3 We sing the good-ness of the Lord, Who fills the earth with food,
4 Lord, how Thy won-ders are dis-played Wher-e'er we turn our eyes,

Who spread the flow-ing seas a-broad And built the loft-y skies.
The moon shines, too, at His command, And all the stars o-bey.
Who formed His creatures by a word And then pronounced them good.
When-e'er we view the ground we tread Or gaze up-on the skies! A-men.

5 There's not a plant nor flower below
   But makes Thy glories known;
And clouds arise and tempests blow
   By order from Thy throne.

6 On Thee each moment we depend;
   If Thou withdraw, we die.
Oh, may we ne'er that God offend
   Who is forever nigh!

44 Ye Lands, to the Lord Make a Jubilant Noise

11. 5. 12. 9.

Ps. 100
Al Verden nu raabe for Herren med Fryd
Ulrik V. Koren, 1874
Tr., Harriet R. Spaeth, 1899, alt.

Guds Menighed, syng
Erik Hoff, c. 1860

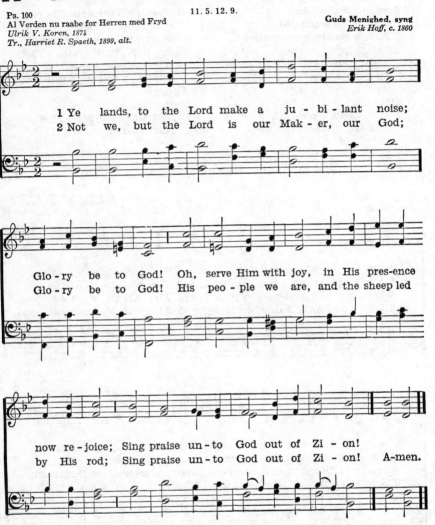

1 Ye lands, to the Lord make a ju-bi-lant noise;
2 Not we, but the Lord is our Mak-er, our God;

Glo-ry be to God! Oh, serve Him with joy, in His pres-ence
Glo-ry be to God! His peo-ple we are, and the sheep led

now re-joice; Sing praise un-to God out of Zi-on!
by His rod; Sing praise un-to God out of Zi-on! A-men.

3 Oh, enter His gates with thanksgiving and praise;
   Glory be to God!
   To bless Him and thank Him our voices we will raise;
   Sing praise unto God out of Zion!

4 For good is the Lord, and His mercy is sure;
   Glory be to God!
   To all generations His truth shall still endure;
   Sing praise unto God out of Zion!

Now, the Hour of Worship O'er

45

7. 8. 7. 8. 8. 8.

Ps. 121 : 8
Nun Gott Lob, es ist vollbracht
Hartman Schenck, 1680
Tr., st. 1-2, composite; st. 3, Oscar Kaiser, 1938

Liebster Jesu
Johann R. Ahle, 1664

1 Now, the hour of wor-ship o'er, Teach-ing, hear-ing,
2 Now the Bless-ing cheers our heart, By His grace to
3 Bless our go-ing out, we pray, Bless our en-trance

pray-ing, sing-ing, Let us glad-ly God a-dore,
us ex-tend-ed. Let us joy-ful-ly de-part;
in like mea-sure; Bless our bread, O Lord, each day,

For His Word our prais-es bring-ing; For the rich re-
Be our souls to God com-mend-ed. May His Spir-it
Bless our toil, our rest, our plea-sure; Bless us when we

past He gave us Bless the Lord, who deigned to save us.
ev-er guide us And with all good gifts pro-vide us!
reach death's por-tal, Bless us then with life im-mor-tal. A-men.

46 On What has Now been Sown

6. 6. 6. 6. 8. 8.

1 Cor. 3: 6
John Newton, 1779, cento, alt.

Darwall's 148th
John Darwall, 1770

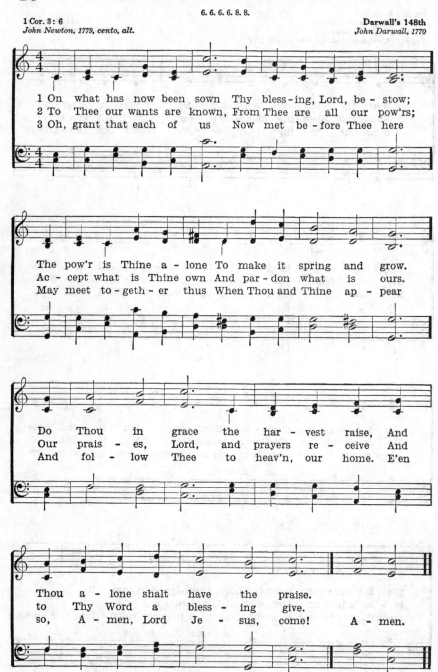

1 On what has now been sown Thy bless-ing, Lord, be-stow;
2 To Thee our wants are known, From Thee are all our pow'rs;
3 Oh, grant that each of us Now met be-fore Thee here

The pow'r is Thine a-lone To make it spring and grow.
Ac-cept what is Thine own And par-don what is ours.
May meet to-geth-er thus When Thou and Thine ap-pear

Do Thou in grace the har-vest raise, And
Our prais-es, Lord, and prayers re-ceive And
And fol-low Thee to heav'n, our home. E'en

Thou a-lone shalt have the praise.
to Thy Word a bless-ing give.
so, A-men, Lord Je-sus, come! A-men.

Savior, Again to Thy Dear Name We Raise   47

10. 10. 10. 10.

Ps. 110: 2
John Ellerton, 1866

Ellers
Edward J. Hopkins, 1869

1 Sav - ior, a - gain to Thy dear name we raise
2 Grant us Thy peace up - on our home-ward way;
3 Grant us Thy peace, Lord, through the com - ing night;

With one ac - cord our part - ing hymn of praise.
With Thee be - gan, with Thee shall end, the day.
Turn Thou for us its dark - ness in - to light.

Once more we bless Thee ere our wor - ship cease,
Guard Thou the lips from sin, the hearts from shame,
From harm and dan - ger keep Thy chil - dren free;

Then, low - ly bend - ing, wait Thy word of peace.
That in this house have called up - on Thy name.
For dark and light are both a - like to Thee. A - men.

4 Grant us Thy peace throughout our earthly life,
Our Balm in sorrow and our Stay in strife;
Then, when Thy voice shall bid our conflict cease,
Call us, O Lord, to Thine eternal peace.

48 How Blest Are They Who Hear God's Word

Is. 61: 3

8. 8. 7. 8. 8. 7. 7.

O salig den Guds Ord har hört
Johan N. Brun, 1786
Tr., Oluf H. Smeby, 1913

Min Själ og Aand
"Psalmebog," 1569

1 How blest are they who hear God's Word And keep and heed what
2 God's Word a trea-sure is to me, Thro' sor-row's night my
3 To-day I was my Sav-ior's guest, My soul was here so

they have heard! They wis-dom dai-ly gath-er; Their light shines
sun shall be, The shield of faith in bat-tle. The Fa-ther's
rich-ly blest, The Bread of Life re-ceiv-ing. Oh, may there-

bright-er day by day, And while they tread life's wea-ry way, They
hand hath writ-ten there My ti-tle as His child and heir, "The
by my faith pre-vail, So that its fruits shall nev-er fail Till

have the oil of glad-ness To soothe their pain and sad-ness.
king-dom's thine for-ev-er." That prom-ise fail-eth nev-er.
my ac-count is giv-en Be-fore the throne in heav-en! A-men.

Almighty God, Thy Word is Cast

C. M.

Mark 4: 3–9
John Cawood, 1819

Dundee
"Scottish Psalter," 1615

1 Al - might - y God, Thy Word is cast Like
2 Let not the foe of Christ and man This

seed in - to the ground; Now let the dew of
ho - ly seed re - move, But give it root in

heav'n de - scend And right - eous fruits a - bound.
ev - 'ry heart To bring forth fruits of love. A - men.

3 Let not the world's deceitful cares
   The rising plant destroy,
But let it yield a hundredfold
   The fruits of peace and joy.

4 Oft as the precious seed is sown,
   Thy quickening grace bestow
That all whose souls the truth receive
   Its saving power may know.

50 Lord, Dismiss Us with Thy Blessing

8. 7. 8. 7. 8. 7.

Num. 6: 24–26
John Fawcett, 1773

(*FIRST TUNE*)

Regent Square
Henry Smart, 1867

1 Lord, dis - miss us with Thy bless-ing, Fill our hearts with joy and peace. Let us each, Thy love pos-sess - ing, Tri - umph in re - deem-ing grace. Oh, re - fresh us, Oh, re-fresh us, Trav-'ling thro' this wil - der - ness! A-men.

2 Thanks we give and adoration
   For Thy Gospel's joyful sound.
   May the fruits of Thy salvation
   In our hearts and lives abound;
   Ever faithful, Ever faithful
   To the Truth may we be found!

Lord, Dismiss Us with Thy Blessing

3 So whene'er the signal's given
Us from earth to call away,
Borne on angels' wings to heaven,
Glad the summons to obey,
May we ever, May we ever,
Reign with Christ in endless day!

Lord, Dismiss Us with Thy Blessing

8. 7. 8. 7. 8. 7.

(*SECOND TUNE*)

Num. 6: 24–26
John Fawcett, 1773

New Ulm
Fritz Reuter, 1910

1 Lord, dis-miss us with Thy bless-ing, Fill our hearts with

joy and peace. Let us each, Thy love pos-sess-ing,

Tri-umph in re-deem-ing grace. Oh, re-fresh us,

Oh, re-fresh us, Trav-'ling thro' this wil-der-ness! A-men.

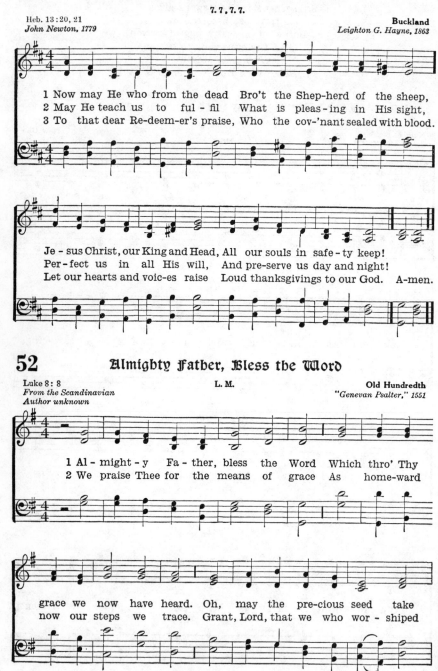

51 Now May He Who from the Dead

7.7.7.7.

Heb. 13:20, 21
John Newton, 1779

Buckland
Leighton G. Hayne, 1863

1 Now may He who from the dead Bro't the Shep-herd of the sheep,
2 May He teach us to ful - fil What is pleas-ing in His sight,
3 To that dear Re-deem-er's praise, Who the cov-'nant sealed with blood.

Je - sus Christ, our King and Head, All our souls in safe - ty keep!
Per - fect us in all His will, And pre-serve us day and night!
Let our hearts and voic-es raise Loud thanksgivings to our God. A-men.

52 Almighty Father, Bless the Word

Luke 8: 8
From the Scandinavian
Author unknown

L. M.

Old Hundredth
"Genevan Psalter," 1551

1 Al - might - y Fa - ther, bless the Word Which thro' Thy
2 We praise Thee for the means of grace As home-ward

grace we now have heard. Oh, may the pre-cious seed take
now our steps we trace. Grant, Lord, that we who wor - shiped

Almighty Father, Bless the Word

| root, | Spring | up, | and | bear | a - | bun - | dant | fruit! |
| here | May | all | at | last | in | heav'n ap - | pear. | A - men. |

Abide, O Dearest Jesus

53

Luke 24 : 29
Ach bleib mit deiner Gnade
Josua Stegmann, 1628
Tr., August Crull, †1923

7. 6. 7. 6.

Christus, der ist mein
Melchior Vulpius, 1609

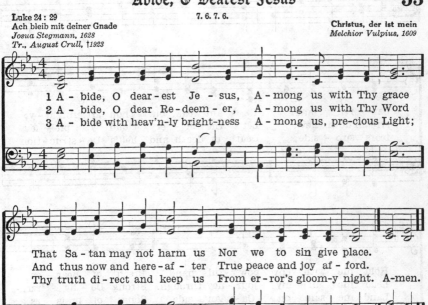

1 A - bide, O dear-est Je - sus, A - mong us with Thy grace
2 A - bide, O dear Re-deem - er, A - mong us with Thy Word
3 A - bide with heav'n-ly bright-ness A - mong us, pre-cious Light;

That Sa - tan may not harm us Nor we to sin give place.
And thus now and here - af - ter True peace and joy af - ford.
Thy truth di - rect and keep us From er - ror's gloom-y night. A-men.

4 Abide with richest blessings
  Among us, bounteous Lord;
  Let us in grace and wisdom
  Grow daily through Thy Word.

5 Abide with Thy protection
  Among us, Lord, our Strength,
  Lest world and Satan fell us
  And overcome at length.

6 Abide, O faithful Savior,
  Among us with Thy love;
  Grant steadfastness and help us
  To reach our home above.

54 Guide Me, O Thou Great Jehovah

Ex. 13: 21
Arglwydd arwain trwy'r Anialwch
William Williams, 1745
Tr., William and Peter Williams, 1771-2

8. 7. 8. 7. 4. 7.

Guide Me
George W. Warren, 1884

1 Guide me, O Thou great Je - ho - vah, Pil - grim through this
2 O - pen now the crys - tal foun - tain Whence the heal - ing
3 When I tread the verge of Jor - dan, Bid my anx - ious

bar - ren land. I am weak, but Thou art might - y;
stream doth flow; Let the fi - ery, cloud - y pil - lar
fears sub - side; Death of death and hell's De - struc - tion,

Hold me with Thy pow'r - ful hand. Bread of heav - en,
Lead me all my jour - ney through. Strong De - liv - 'rer,
Land me safe on Ca - naan's side. Songs of prais - es

Feed me till I want no more.
Be Thou still my Strength and Shield.
I will ev - er give to Thee. A - men.

ADVENT

Come, Thou Precious Ransom, Come

55

Matt. 21 : 5
Komm, du wertes Lösegeld
Johann G. Olearius, 1664
Tr., August Crull, †1923, alt.

7. 8. 7. 8. 7. 7.

Meinen Jesum lass' ich nicht
"Neuverfertigtes Gesangbuch"
Darmstadt, 1699

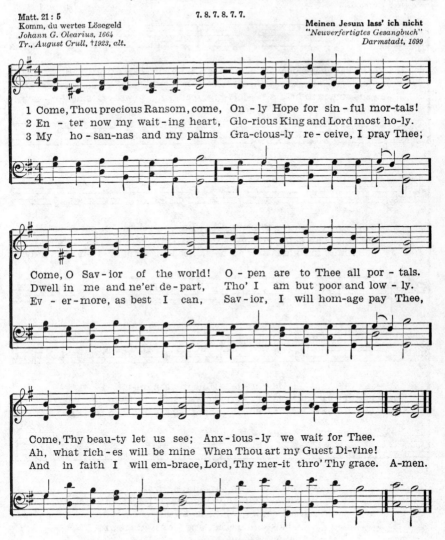

1 Come, Thou precious Ransom, come, On - ly Hope for sin - ful mor-tals!
2 En - ter now my wait-ing heart, Glo-rious King and Lord most ho-ly.
3 My ho - san-nas and my palms Gra-cious-ly re - ceive, I pray Thee;

Come, O Sav-ior of the world! O - pen are to Thee all por - tals.
Dwell in me and ne'er de-part, Tho' I am but poor and low - ly.
Ev - er-more, as best I can, Sav-ior, I will hom-age pay Thee,

Come, Thy beau-ty let us see; Anx-ious-ly we wait for Thee.
Ah, what rich - es will be mine When Thou art my Guest Di-vine!
And in faith I will em-brace, Lord, Thy mer-it thro' Thy grace. A-men.

4 Hail, hosanna, David's Son!
Help, Lord, hear our supplication!
Let Thy kingdom, scepter, crown,
Bring us blessing and salvation,
That forever we may sing:
Hail, hosanna! to our King.

56 Jesus Came, the Heavens Adoring

8. 7. 8. 7. 8. 7.

Zech. 9: 9
Godfrey Thring, 1864

Sieh, hier bin ich
"Geistreiches Gesangbuch"
Darmstadt, 1698

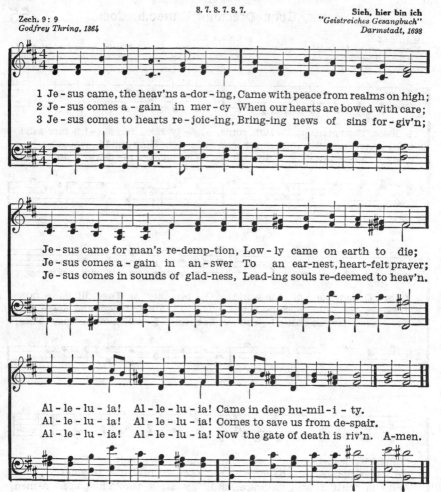

1 Je-sus came, the heav'ns a-dor-ing, Came with peace from realms on high;
2 Je-sus comes a-gain in mer-cy When our hearts are bowed with care;
3 Je-sus comes to hearts re-joic-ing, Bring-ing news of sins for-giv'n;

Je-sus came for man's re-demp-tion, Low-ly came on earth to die;
Je-sus comes a-gain in an-swer To an ear-nest, heart-felt prayer;
Je-sus comes in sounds of glad-ness, Lead-ing souls re-deemed to heav'n.

Al-le-lu-ia! Al-le-lu-ia! Came in deep hu-mil-i-ty.
Al-le-lu-ia! Al-le-lu-ia! Comes to save us from de-spair.
Al-le-lu-ia! Al-le-lu-ia! Now the gate of death is riv'n. A-men.

4 Jesus comes in joy and sorrow,
   Shares alike our hopes and fears;
Jesus comes, whate'er befalls us,
   Glads our hearts, and dries our tears;
Alleluia! Alleluia!
   Cheering e'en our failing years.

5 Jesus comes on clouds triumphant
   When the heavens shall pass away;
Jesus comes again in glory.
   Let us, then, our homage pay,
Alleluia! ever singing
   Till the dawn of endless day.

O Bride of Christ, Rejoice

57

6. 6. 7. 7. 7. 7.

Luke 19: 28-40
Fryd dig, du Kristi Brud
Danish author unknown, c. 1600
Tr., Victor O. Petersen, 1899

Wo soll ich fliehen hin
"Der bussfertige Sünder"
Nürnberg, 1679

1 O bride of Christ, re-joice; Ex-ul-tant raise thy voice
2 Let shouts of glad-ness rise Tri-um-phant to the skies.
3 He wears no king-ly crown, Yet as a King is known;

To hail the day of glo-ry Fore-told in sa-cred sto-ry.
Now comes the King most glo-rious To reign o'er all vic-to-rious.
Tho' not ar-rayed in splen-dor, He still makes death sur-ren-der.

Ho-san-na, praise, and glo-ry! Our King, we bow be-fore Thee.
Ho-san-na, praise, and glo-ry! Our King, we bow be-fore Thee.
Ho-san-na, praise, and glo-ry! Our King, we bow be-fore Thee. A-men.

4 The weak and timid find
How meek He is and kind;
To them He gives a treasure
Of bliss beyond all measure.
Hosanna, praise, and glory!
Our King, we bow before Thee.

5 Thy heart now open wide,
Bid Christ with thee abide.
He graciously will hear thee
And be forever near thee.
Hosanna, praise, and glory!
Our King, we bow before Thee.

6 Then go thy Lord to meet;
Strew palm-leaves at His feet;
Thy garments spread before Him
And honor and adore Him.
Hosanna, praise, and glory!
Our King, we bow before Thee.

7 E'en babes with one accord
With thee shall praise the Lord
And every Gentile nation
Respond with exultation:
Hosanna, praise, and glory!
Our King, we bow before Thee.

58 O Lord, How Shall I Meet Thee

Matt. 21 : 1–9
Wie soll ich dich empfangen
Paul Gerhardt, 1653, cento
Tr., composite

7. 6. 7. 6. D.

(FIRST TUNE)

Valet will ich dir geben
Melchior Teschner, 1613

1 O Lord, how shall I meet Thee, How wel-come Thee a-right?

Thy peo-ple long to greet Thee, My Hope, my heart's De-light!

Oh, kin-dle, Lord most ho-ly, Thy lamp with-in my breast

To do in spir-it low-ly All that may please Thee best. A-men.

2 Thy Zion strews before Thee
    Green boughs and fairest palms,
And I, too, will adore Thee
    With joyous songs and psalms.
My heart shall bloom forever
    For Thee with praises new
And from Thy name shall never
    Withhold the honor due.

3 I lay in fetters, groaning,
    Thou com'st to set me free;
I stood, my shame bemoaning,
    Thou com'st to honor me;
A glory Thou dost give me,
    A treasure safe on high,
That will not fail or leave me
    As earthly riches fly.

4 Love caused Thy incarnation,
    Love brought Thee down to me;
Thy thirst for my salvation
    Procured my liberty.
O love beyond all telling,
    That led Thee to embrace,
In love all love excelling,
    Our lost and fallen race!

5 Rejoice, then, ye sad-hearted,
    Who sit in deepest gloom,
Who mourn o'er joys departed
    And tremble at your doom.
Despair not, He is near you,
    Yea, standing at the door,
Who best can help and cheer you
    And bids you weep no more.

O Lord, How Shall I Meet Thee

6 Ye need not toil nor languish
Nor ponder day and night
How in the midst of anguish
Ye draw Him by your might.
He comes, He comes all willing,
Moved by His love alone,
Your woes and troubles stilling;
For all to Him are known.

7 Sin's debt, that fearful burden,
Let not your souls distress;
Your guilt the Lord will pardon
And cover by His grace.
He comes, for men procuring
The peace of sin forgiven,
For all God's sons securing
Their heritage in heaven.

8 What though the foes be raging,
Heed not their craft and spite;
Your Lord, the battle waging,
Will scatter all their might.
He comes, a King most glorious,
And all His earthly foes
In vain His course victorious
Endeavor to oppose.

9 He comes to judge the nations,
A terror to His foes,
A Light of consolations
And blessèd Hope to those
Who love the Lord's appearing.
O glorious Sun, now come,
Send forth Thy beams most cheering,
And guide us safely home.

O Lord, How Shall I Meet Thee

Matt. 21 : 1-9
Wie soll ich dich empfangen
Paul Gerhardt, 1653, cento
Tr. composite

7. 6. 7. 6. D.

(*SECOND TUNE*)

Wie soll ich dich
Johann Crüger, 1653

1 O Lord, how shall I meet Thee, How wel-come Thee a - right?

Thy peo - ple long to greet Thee, My Hope, my heart's De - light!

Oh, kin - dle, Lord, most ho - ly, Thy lamp with - in my breast

To do in spir - it low - ly All that may please Thee best. A - men.

59 Hail to the Lord's Annointed

7. 6. 7. 6. D.

Ps. 72
James Montgomery, 1821

Freut euch, ihr lieben
Leonhart Schröter, 1587

1 Hail to the Lord's A-noint-ed, Great Da-vid's great-er Son!
2 He comes with suc-cor speed-y To those who suf-fer wrong;
3 He shall come down like show-ers Up-on the fruit-ful earth,
4 A-ra-bia's des-ert ran-ger To Him shall bow the knee,

Hail, in the time ap-point-ed, His reign on earth be-gun!
To help the poor and need-y And bid the weak be strong;
And joy and hope, like flow-ers, Spring in His path to birth.
The E-thi-o-pian stran-ger His glo-ry come to see;

He comes to break op-pres-sion, To set the cap-tive free,
To give them songs for sigh-ing, Their dark-ness turn to light,
Be-fore Him on the moun-tains Shall peace, the her-ald, go
With of-f'rings of de-vo-tion Ships from the isles shall meet

To take a-way trans-gres-sion, And rule in eq - ui-ty.
Whose souls, condemned and dying, Were pre-cious in His sight.
And righteousness, in foun-tains, From hill to val - ley flow.
To pour the wealth of o-cean In trib-ute at His feet. A-men.

Hail to the Lord's Anointed

5 Kings shall bow down before Him
  And gold and incense bring;
All nations shall adore Him,
  His praise all peoples sing;
To Him shall prayer unceasing
  And daily vows ascend,
His kingdom still increasing,
  A kingdom without end.

6 O'er every foe victorious,
  He on His throne shall rest,
From age to age more glorious,
  All blessing and all-blest.
The tide of time shall never
  His covenant remove;
His name shall stand forever —
  That name to us is Love.

Hark, a Thrilling Voice is Sounding   60

Rom. 13 : 11
Vox clara ecce intonat
Latin, c. 900
Tr., Edward Caswall, 1849

8. 7. 8. 7.

O der alles
"Neues geistreiches Gesangbuch"
Halle, 1705

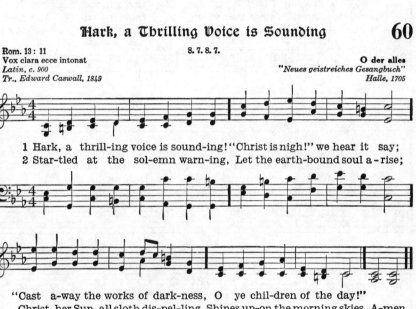

1 Hark, a thrill-ing voice is sound-ing! "Christ is nigh!" we hear it say;
2 Star-tled at the sol-emn warn-ing, Let the earth-bound soul a-rise;

"Cast a-way the works of dark-ness, O ye chil-dren of the day!"
Christ, her Sun, all sloth dis-pel-ling, Shines up-on the morning skies. A-men.

3 Lo, the Lamb, so long expected.
  Comes with pardon down from heaven.
Let us haste, with tears of sorrow,
  One and all, to be forgiven,

4 That, when next He comes with glory
  And the world is wrapped in fear
He may shield us with His mercy
  And with words of love draw near.

5 Honor, glory, might, dominion,
  To the Father and the Son.
With the everlasting Spirit,
  While eternal ages run!

61 Comfort, Comfort, Ye My People

Is. 40 : 1–8   8. 7. 8. 7. 7. 7. 8. 8.

Tröstet, tröstet meine Lieben
Johann Olearius, 1671
Tr., Catherine Winkworth, 1863, alt.

Freu dich sehr
"Genevan Psalter," 1551

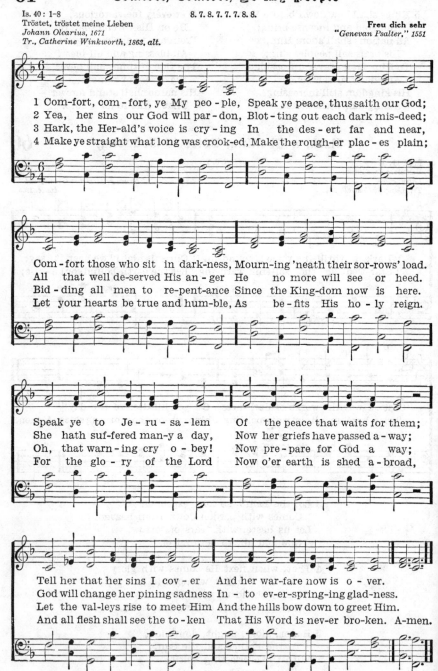

1 Com-fort, com-fort, ye My peo-ple, Speak ye peace, thus saith our God;
2 Yea, her sins our God will par-don, Blot-ting out each dark mis-deed;
3 Hark, the Her-ald's voice is cry-ing In the des-ert far and near,
4 Make ye straight what long was crook-ed, Make the rough-er plac-es plain;

Com-fort those who sit in dark-ness, Mourn-ing 'neath their sor-rows' load.
All that well de-served His an-ger He no more will see or heed.
Bid-ding all men to re-pent-ance Since the King-dom now is here.
Let your hearts be true and hum-ble, As be-fits His ho-ly reign.

Speak ye to Je-ru-sa-lem Of the peace that waits for them;
She hath suf-fered man-y a day, Now her griefs have passed a-way;
Oh, that warn-ing cry o-bey! Now pre-pare for God a way;
For the glo-ry of the Lord Now o'er earth is shed a-broad,

Tell her that her sins I cov-er And her war-fare now is o-ver.
God will change her pining sadness In-to ev-er-spring-ing glad-ness.
Let the val-leys rise to meet Him And the hills bow down to greet Him.
And all flesh shall see the to-ken That His Word is nev-er bro-ken. A-men.

Oh, Come, Oh, Come, Emmanuel

Is. 59 : 20

8. 8. 8. 8. 8. 8.

Veni, veni, Emmanuel
Latin author unknown, c. 1100
Tr., John M. Neale, 1851, 1859, ab.

Veni, Emmanuel
Plain-song melody, c. 1200

1 Oh, come, Oh, come, Em-man - u - el, And ran-som cap-tive
2 Oh, come, Thou Rod of Jes - - se, free Thine own from Sa - tan's
3 Oh, come, Thou Day-spring from on high, And cheer us by Thy
4 Oh, come, Thou Key of Da - - vid, come And o - pen wide our

Is - - ra - el That mourns in lone-ly ex - - ile here Un-
tyr - an-ny; From depths of hell Thy peo - - ple save And
draw - ing nigh; Dis - perse the gloom-y clouds of night And
heav'n - ly home; Make safe the way that leads on high And

til the Son of God ap - pear. Re - joice! Re - joice! Em-
give them vic - t'ry o'er the grave. Re - joice! Re - joice! Em-
death's dark shad-ows put to flight. Re - joice! Re - joice! Em-
close the path to mis - er - y. Re - joice! Re - joice! Em-

man - u - el Shall come to thee, O Is - - ra - el.
man - u - el Shall come to thee, O Is - - ra - el.
man - u - el Shall come to thee, O Is - - ra - el.
man - u - el Shall come to thee, O Is - - ra - el. A-men.

63 On Jordan's Bank the Baptist's Cry

Is. 40: 3; Matt. 3: 3   **L. M.**
Jordanis oras praevia
Charles Coffin, 1736, ab.
St. 1–3, tr., John Chandler, 1837
St. 4, 5, tr., unknown

                                  Puer nobis nascitur
                              "Musae Sioniae," VI, 1609

1 On   Jor - dan's bank   the   Bap - tist's cry   An - nounc - es
2 Then cleansed be   ev - 'ry   Chris - tian breast   And fur - nished
3 For Thou   art   our   Sal - va - tion, Lord,   Our Ref - uge,

that   the   Lord   is   nigh; Come, then, and heark - en, for   he
for   so   great   a   Guest. Yea,   let   us   each   our   hearts pre -
and   our   great   Re - ward. With - out Thy grace   our   souls must

brings Glad ti - dings from   the   King   of   kings.
pare   For Christ   to   come   and   en - ter   there.
fade   And with - er   like   a   flow'r de - cayed.   A - men.

4 Lay on the sick Thy healing hand
   And make the fallen strong to stand;
   Show us the glory of Thy face
   Till beauty springs in every place.

5 All praise, eternal Son, to Thee
   Whose advent sets Thy people free,
   Whom, with the Father, we adore
   And Holy Ghost forevermore.

Jesus, Thy Church with Longing Eyes

64

L. M.

Rev. 1: 7
William H. Bathurst, 1831, ab.

O Jesu Christ, mein's
"Nürnbergisches Gesangbuch," 1676

1 Je - sus, Thy Church with long - ing eyes For Thine ex -
2 E'en now, when tem - pests round us fall And win - try
3 Come, gra - cious Lord, our hearts re - new, Our foes re -

pect - ed com - ing waits. When will the prom - ised light a -
clouds o'er - cast the sky, Thy words with plea - sure we re -
pel, our wrongs re - dress, Man's root - ed en - mi - ty sub -

rise And glo - ry beam from Zi - on's gates?
call And deem that our re - demp - tion's nigh.
due, And crown Thy Gos - pel with suc - cess. A - men.

4 Oh, come and reign o'er every land;
Let Satan from his throne be hurled,
All nations bow to Thy command,
And grace revive a dying world.

5 Teach us in watchfulness and prayer
To wait for the appointed hour
And fit us by Thy grace to share
The triumphs of Thy conquering power.

65 When Sinners See Their Lost Condition

John 20: 19-26
Naar Synderen ret ser sin Vaade
Magnus B. Landstad, 1863
Tr., Oluf H. Smeby, 1909, alt.

9. 8. 9. 8. 8. 8.

Wer weiss, wie nahe
Christian Möck, 1818

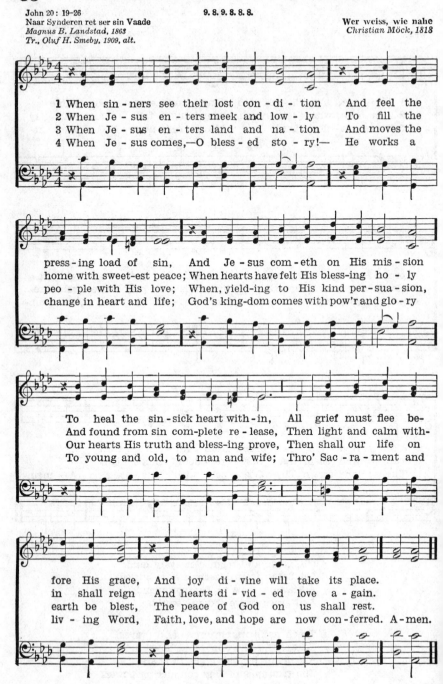

1 When sin - ners see their lost con - di - tion   And feel the
2 When Je - sus en - ters meek and low - ly   To fill the
3 When Je - sus en - ters land and na - tion   And moves the
4 When Je - sus comes,—O bless - ed sto - ry!—   He works a

press - ing load of sin,   And Je - sus com - eth on His mis - sion
home with sweet-est peace;   When hearts have felt His bless-ing ho - ly
peo - ple with His love;   When, yield-ing to His kind per - sua - sion,
change in heart and life;   God's king-dom comes with pow'r and glo - ry

To heal the sin - sick heart with - in,   All grief must flee be-
And found from sin com-plete re - lease,   Then light and calm with-
Our hearts His truth and bless-ing prove,   Then shall our life on
To young and old, to man and wife;   Thro' Sac - ra - ment and

fore His grace,   And joy di - vine will take its place.
in shall reign   And hearts di - vid - ed love a - gain.
earth be blest,   The peace of God on us shall rest.
liv - ing Word,   Faith, love, and hope are now con - ferred. A - men.

When Sinners See Their Lost Condition

5 Then stilled are cries and lamentation,
    Then loosed is Satan's every band;
In death is hope and consolation,
    The soul is safe in Jesus' hand.
When we shall walk through death's dark **vale,**
    His rod and staff shall never fail.

6 Oh, may He soon to every nation
    Find entrance where He is unknown,
With life and light and full salvation,
    That heathendom may be o'erthrown
And healing to the hearts may come
In heathen land and Christian home!

Hark the Glad Sound! The Savior Comes   66

C. M.

Is. 61 : 1, 2; Luke 4 : 18
Philip Doddridge, 1735, cento

Chesterfield
Thomas Haweis, 1792

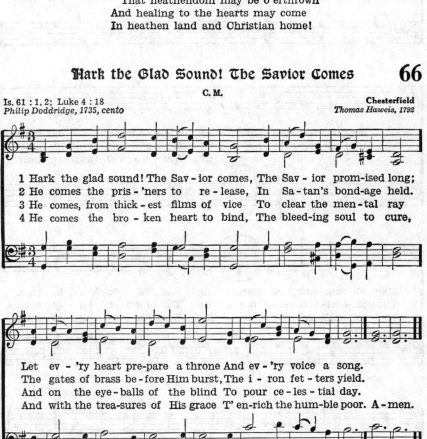

1 Hark the glad sound! The Sav - ior comes, The Sav - ior prom-ised long;
2 He comes the pris - 'ners to re - lease, In Sa-tan's bond-age held.
3 He comes, from thick - est films of vice To clear the men -tal ray
4 He comes the bro - ken heart to bind, The bleed-ing soul to cure,

Let ev - 'ry heart pre-pare a throne And ev-'ry voice a song.
The gates of brass be-fore Him burst, The i - ron fet - ters yield.
And on the eye-balls of the blind To pour ce - les - tial day.
And with the trea-sures of His grace T' en-rich the hum-ble poor. A - men.

5 Our glad hosannas, Prince of Peace,
    Thy welcome shall proclaim
And heaven's eternal arches ring
    With Thy belovèd name.

67 The Bridegroom Soon Will Call Us

Matt. 25: 6

Der Bräut'gam wird bald rufen
Johann Walther, 1552, cento
Tr., Matthias Loy, 1880

7. 6. 7. 6. D.

Ach Gott vom Himmelreiche
"Musae Sioniae," VII, 1609

1 The Bride-groom soon will call us: Come, all ye wed-ding-guests!
2 There shall we see de-light-ed Our dear Re-deem-er's face,
3 They will not blush to own us As broth-ers, sis-ters dear;

May not His voice ap-pal us While slum-ber binds our breasts!
Who leads our souls be-night-ed To glo-ry by His grace.
Love ev-er will be shown us When we with them ap-pear.

May all our lamps be burn-ing And oil be found in store
The pa-tri-archs shall meet us, The proph-ets' ho-ly band,
We all shall come be-fore Him Who for us man be-came,

That we, with Him re-turn-ing, May o-pen find the door!
A-pos-tles, mar-tyrs, greet us In that ce-les-tial land.
As Lord and God a-dore Him, And ev-er bless His name. A-men.

The Bridegroom Soon Will Call Us

4 Our Father, rich in blessing,
   Will give us crowns of gold
And, to His bosom pressing,
   Impart a bliss untold,
Will welcome with embraces
   Of never-ending love,
And deck us with His graces
   In blissful realms above.

5 In yonder home shall never
   Be silent music's voice;
With hearts and lips forever
   We shall in God rejoice.
The angels shall adore Him,
   All saints shall sing His praise
And bring with joy before Him
   Their sweetest heavenly lays.

6 In mansions fair and spacious
   Will God the feast prepare
And, ever kind and gracious,
   Bid us its riches share.
There bliss that knows no measure
   From springs of love shall flow,
And never-changing pleasure
   His bounty will bestow.

7 Thus God shall from all evil
   Forever make us free,
From sin, and from the devil,
   From all adversity,
From sickness, pain, and sadness,
   From troubles, cares, and fears,
And grant us heavenly gladness
   And wipe away our tears.

The Advent of Our King   68

S. M.

Zech. 9 : 9
Instantis adventum Dei
Charles Coffin, 1736
Tr., John Chandler, 1837, alt.

St. Thomas
Aaron Williams, 1770

1 The ad-vent of our King Our prayers must now em-ploy,
2 The ev-er-last-ing Son In-car-nate deigns to be;
3 O Zi-on's Daugh-ter, rise To meet thy low-ly King,
4 As Judge, on clouds of light, He soon will come a-gain

And we must hymns of wel-come sing In strains of ho-ly joy.
Him-self a serv-ant's form puts on To set His serv-ants free.
Nor let thy faith-less heart de-spise The peace He comes to bring.
And His true mem-bers all u-nite With Him in heav'n to reign. A-men.

5 Before the dawning day
   Let sin's dark deeds be gone,
The old man all be put away,
   The new man all put on.

6 All glory to the Son,
   Who comes to set us free,
With Father, Spirit, ever One,
   Through all eternity.

69 Arise, Sons of the Kingdom

Luke 19 : 38

Auf, auf, ihr Reichsgenossen
Johann Rist, 1651, cento
Tr. based on Catherine Winkworth, 1858

7. 6. 7. 6. 6. 7. 7. 6.

Aus meines Herzens Grunde
"Neu Catechismus-Gesangbüchlein"
Hamburg, 1598

1 A - rise, sons of the King - dom! The King is draw-ing nigh;
2 A - rise, ye droop-ing mourn-ers! The King is ver - y near;
3 A - rise, ye much af - flict - ed! The King is not a - far.
4 A - rise, ye poor and need - y! The King pro - vides for you;

A - rise and hail with glad - ness The Ru - ler from on high.
A - way with grief and sor - row! For, lo, your Help is here.
Re - joice, ye long de - ject - ed, Be - hold the Morn-ing Star!
He comes with suc - cor speed - y, With mer - cy ev - er new.

Ye Chris-tians, hast - en forth! Your praise and hom - age bring Him
Be - hold, in man - y a place— Oh, bless - ed con - so - la - tion!—
The Lord will give you joy; Tho' trou - bles now dis - tress you,
Re - ceive your gra-cious King, The Giv - er of all bless - ing,

And glad ho-san-nas sing Him; Naught else your love is worth.
You find Him, your Sal - va - tion, With - in His means of grace.
With com-fort He will bless you, E'en death will He de - stroy.
Hail Him, His name con-fess - ing, And glad ho - san-nas sing. A-men.

Arise, Sons of the Kingdom

5 Be righteous, ye His subjects,
  The King is just and true;
Prepare for Him a highway,
  Make all things straight and new.
For, lo, He means it well;
  Then willing bear the crosses
  That He Himself imposes,
Nor let your courage fail.

6 Oh, rich the gifts Thou bringest,
  Thyself made poor and weak!
O Love beyond expression,
  That thus can sinners seek!
For this, O Lord, will we
  Our joyous tribute bring Thee
  And glad hosannas sing Thee
And ever grateful be.

Hosanna to the Living Lord 70

Matt. 21: 9
Reginald Heber. 1811. 1827. ab.

L. M.

Vom Himmel hoch
"Geistliche Lieder"
Leipzig, 1539

1 Ho - san - na to the liv - ing Lord! Ho-
2 O Sav - ior, with pro - tect - ing care A-
3 But, chief - est, in our cleans - ed breast, E-
4 So in the last and dread - ful Day, When

san - na to th' In - car - nate Word! To Christ, Cre - a - tor,
bide in this Thy house of prayer, Where we Thy part - ing
ter - nal, bid Thy Spir - it rest And make our se - cret
earth and heav'n shall melt a - way, Thy flock, re - deemed from

Sav - ior, King, Let earth, let heav'n, ho - san - na sing.
prom - ise claim, As - sem - bled in Thy sa - cred name.
soul to be A tem - ple pure and wor - thy Thee.
sin - ful stain, Shall swell the sound of praise a - gain. A - men.

71 Watchman, Tell Us of the Night

7. 7. 7. 7. D.

Is. 21: 11
John Bowring, 1825

St. George
George J. Elvey, 1858

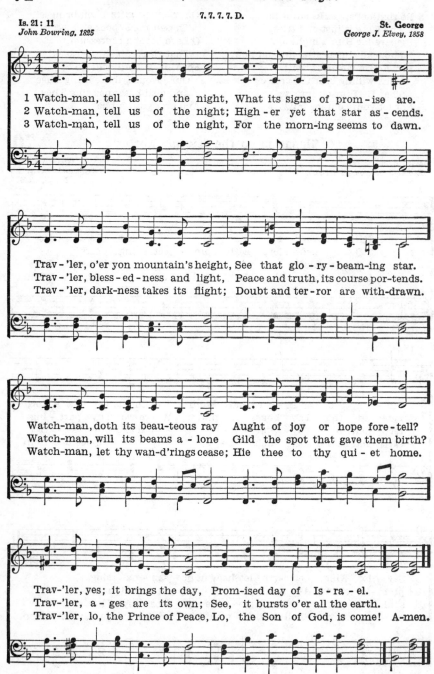

1 Watch-man, tell us of the night, What its signs of prom-ise are.
2 Watch-man, tell us of the night; High-er yet that star as-cends.
3 Watch-man, tell us of the night, For the morn-ing seems to dawn.

Trav-'ler, o'er yon mountain's height, See that glo-ry-beam-ing star.
Trav-'ler, bless-ed-ness and light, Peace and truth, its course por-tends.
Trav-'ler, dark-ness takes its flight; Doubt and ter-ror are with-drawn.

Watch-man, doth its beau-teous ray Aught of joy or hope fore-tell?
Watch-man, will its beams a-lone Gild the spot that gave them birth?
Watch-man, let thy wan-d'rings cease; Hie thee to thy qui-et home.

Trav-'ler, yes; it brings the day, Prom-ised day of Is-ra-el.
Trav-'ler, a-ges are its own; See, it bursts o'er all the earth.
Trav-'ler, lo, the Prince of Peace, Lo, the Son of God, is come! A-men.

Rejoice, Rejoice, Believers

7. 6. 7. 6. D.

Matt. 25: 6
Ermuntert euch, ihr Frommen
Laurentius Laurenti, 1700, cento
Tr., Sarah Findlater, 1854, alt.

Valet will ich dir geben
Melchior Teschner, 1613

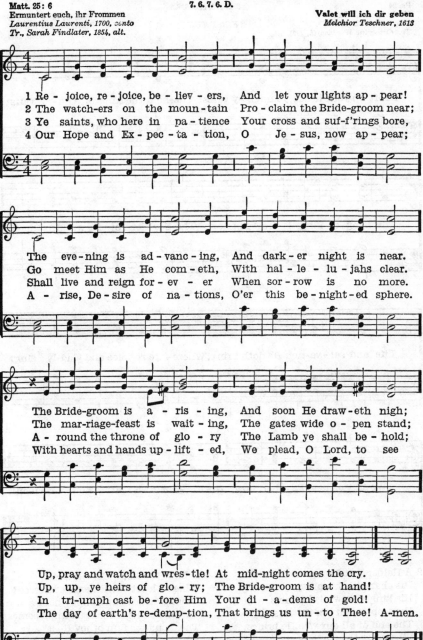

1 Re - joice, re - joice, be - liev - ers, And let your lights ap - pear!
2 The watch-ers on the moun-tain Pro - claim the Bride-groom near;
3 Ye saints, who here in pa - tience Your cross and suf-f'rings bore,
4 Our Hope and Ex - pec - ta - tion, O Je - sus, now ap - pear;

The eve-ning is ad - vanc - ing, And dark - er night is near.
Go meet Him as He com - eth, With hal - le - lu - jahs clear.
Shall live and reign for - ev - er When sor - row is no more.
A - rise, De - sire of na - tions, O'er this be - night-ed sphere.

The Bride-groom is a - ris - ing, And soon He draw-eth nigh;
The mar-riage-feast is wait - ing, The gates wide o - pen stand;
A - round the throne of glo - ry The Lamb ye shall be - hold;
With hearts and hands up - lift - ed, We plead, O Lord, to see

Up, pray and watch and wres - tle! At mid-night comes the cry.
Up, up, ye heirs of glo - ry; The Bride-groom is at hand!
In tri-umph cast be - fore Him Your di - a - dems of gold!
The day of earth's re-demp-tion, That brings us un - to Thee! A-men.

73 Lift Up Your Heads, Ye Mighty Gates

Ps. 24
Macht hoch die Tür
Georg Weissel, 1642
Tr., Catherine Winkworth, 1855, alt.

8. 8. 8. 8. 8. 8. 6. 6.

(FIRST TUNE)

Macht hoch die Tür
"Praxis Pietatis Melica"
Berlin, 1661

1 Lift up your heads, ye might-y gates! Be-hold, the King of Glo-ry waits;
The King of kings is draw-ing near, The Sav-ior of the world is here.
Life and sal-va-tion He doth bring, Where-fore re-joice and glad-ly sing:
We praise Thee, Fa-ther, now, Cre-a-tor, wise art Thou! A-men.

2 A Helper just He comes to thee,
His chariot is humility,
His kingly crown is holiness,
His scepter, pity in distress.
The end of all our woe He brings,
Wherefore the earth is glad and sings:
We praise Thee, Savior, now,
Mighty in deed art Thou!

3 O blest the land, the city blest,
Where Christ the Ruler is confessed!
O happy hearts and happy homes
To whom this King in triumph comes!
The cloudless Sun of joy He is,
Who bringeth pure delight and bliss.
We praise Thee, Spirit, now,
Our Comforter art Thou!

Lift Up Your Heads, Ye Mighty Gates

4 Fling wide the portals of your heart;
  Make it a temple set apart
  From earthly use for Heaven's employ,
  Adorned with prayer and love and joy.
  So shall your Sovereign enter in
  And new and nobler life begin.
    To Thee, O God, be praise
    For word and deed and grace!

5 Redeemer, come! I open wide
  My heart to Thee; here, Lord, abide!
  Let me Thine inner presence feel,
  Thy grace and love in me reveal;
  Thy Holy Spirit guide us on
  Until our glorious goal is won.
    Eternal praise and fame
    We offer to Thy name.

Lift Up Your Heads, Ye Mighty Gates

Ps. 24
Macht hoch die Tür
Georg Weissel, 1642
Tr., Catherine Winkworth, 1855, alt.

8. 8. 8. 8. 8. 8. 6. 6.
(*SECOND TUNE*)

Macht hoch die Tür
Johann A. Freylinghausen, 1704

1 Lift up your heads, ye might-y gates! Be-hold, the King of Glo-ry waits;

The King of kings is draw-ing near, The Sav-ior of the world is here.

Life and sal-va-tion He doth bring, Where-fore re-joice and glad-ly sing:

We praise Thee, Fa-ther, now, Cre-a-tor, wise art Thou! A-men.

Lift Up Your Heads, Ye Mighty Gates

Ps. 24
Macht hoch die Tür
Georg Weissel, 1642
Tr., Catherine Winkworth, 1855, alt

8. 8. 8. 8. 8. 8. 6. 6.

(*THIRD TUNE*)

Macht hoch die Tür
August Lemke, 1849

1 Lift up your heads, ye might-y gates! Be-hold, the King of Glo-ry waits;

The King of kings is draw-ing near, The Sav-ior of the world is here.

Life and sal-va-tion He doth bring, Where-fore re-joice and glad-ly sing:

We praise Thee, Fa-ther, now, Cre-a-tor, wise art Thou! A-men.

2 A Helper just He comes to thee,
His chariot is humility,
His kingly crown is holiness,
His scepter, pity in distress.
The end of all our woe He brings;
Wherefore the earth is glad and sings:
We praise Thee, Savior, now,
Mighty in deed art Thou!

3 O blest the land, the city blest,
Where Christ the Ruler is confessed!
O happy hearts and happy homes
To whom this King in triumph comes!
The cloudless Sun of joy He is,
Who bringeth pure delight and bliss.
We praise Thee, Spirit, now,
Our Comforter art Thou!

Lift Up Your Heads, Ye Mighty Gates

4 Fling wide the portals of your heart;
  Make it a temple set apart
  From earthly use for Heaven's employ,
  Adorned with prayer and love and joy.
  So shall your Sovereign enter in
  And new and nobler life begin.
    To Thee, O God, be praise
    For word and deed and grace!

5 Redeemer, come! I open wide
  My heart to Thee; here, Lord, abide!
  Let me Thine inner presence feel,
  Thy grace and love in me reveal;
  Thy Holy Spirit guide us on
  Until our glorious goal is won.
    Eternal praise and fame
    We offer to Thy name.

Once He Came in Blessing 74

6. 6. 6. 6. 6. 6.

Luke 4 : 18
Gottes Sohn ist kommen
Johann Roh, 1544, cento
Tr., Catherine Winkworth, 1863

Gottes Sohn ist kommen
Michael Weisse, 1531

1 Once He came in bless-ing,   All our ills re-dress-ing;
2 Still He comes with-in   us,   Still His voice would win   us,
3 Thus, if thou hast known Him,   Not a-shamed to own Him,
4 He who thus en-dur-eth   Bright re-ward se-cur-eth.

Came in like-ness low-ly,   Son of God most ho-ly;
From the sins that hurt   us;   Would to Truth con-vert   us;
But wilt trust Him bold-ly   Nor dost love Him cold-ly,
Come, then, O Lord Je-sus,   From our sins re-lease   us:

Bore the cross to save   us,   Hope and free-dom gave   us.
From our fool-ish er-rors   Ere He comes in ter-rors.
He will then re-ceive thee,   Heal thee, and for-give   thee.
Let us here con-fess Thee   Till in heav'n we bless   Thee. A-men.

75 Ye Sons of Men, Oh, Hearken

Luke 3 : 4, 5
Mit Ernst, o Menschenkinder
Valentin Thilo, Jr., 1659, alt.
Tr., based on Arthur T. Russell, 1851

7. 6. 7. 6. 6. 7. 7. 6.

Aus meines Herzens Grunde
"Neu Catechismus-Gesangbüchlein"
Hamburg, 1598

1 Ye sons of men, oh, heark - en: Your heart and mind pre - pare;
2 Pre - pare the way be - fore Him; Pre - pare for Him the best.
3 The hum - ble heart and low - ly God lift - eth up on high;
4 Pre - pare my heart, Lord Je - sus, Turn not from me a - side,

To hail th' Al-might-y Sav - ior, O sin - ners, be your care.
Cast out what-e'er of - fend - eth This great, this heav'n-ly Guest.
Be - neath His feet in an - guish The haugh-ty soul shall lie.
And grant that I re - ceive Thee This bless - ed Ad - vent-tide.

He who of grace a - lone Our Life and Light was giv - en,
Make straight, make plain, the way: The low - ly val - leys rais - ing,
The heart, sin - cere and right, That heeds God's in - vi - ta - tion
From stall and man - ger low Come Thou to dwell with - in me;

The prom-ised Lord from heav-en, Un - to our world is shown.
The heights of pride a - bas - ing, His path all e - ven lay.
And makes true prep-a-ra - tion, It is the Lord's de - light.
Loud prais-es will I sing Thee And forth Thy glo - ry show. A-men.

A Great and Mighty Wonder

1 Tim. 3: 16
Μέγα καὶ παράδοξον Θαῦμα
St. Germanus, †734
Tr., John M. Neale, 1862, ab.

7. 6. 7. 6. 6. 7. 6.

Es ist ein' Ros'
"Alte geistliche Kirchengesäng"
Cologne, 1599

1 A great and might-y won-der, A full and ho-ly cure: The Vir-gin bears the In-fant With vir-gin hon-or pure! Re-peat the hymn a-gain: "To God on high be glo-ry And peace on earth to men!"

2 The Word be-comes in-car-nate And yet re-mains on high, And cher-u-bim sing an-thems To shep-herds from the sky. Re-peat the hymn a-gain: "To God on high be glo-ry And peace on earth to men!"

3 While thus they sing your Mon-arch, Those bright an-gel-ic bands, Re-joice, ye vales and moun-tains, Ye o-ceans, clap your hands. Re-peat the hymn a-gain: "To God on high be glo-ry And peace on earth to men!" A-men.

4 Since all He comes to ransom,
By all be He adored,
The Infant born in Bethl'em,
The Savior and the Lord.
Repeat the hymn again:
"To God on high be glory
And peace on earth to men!"

5 And idol forms shall perish,
And error shall decay,
And Christ shall wield His scepter,
Our Lord and God for aye.
Repeat the hymn again:
"To God on high be glory
And peace on earth to men!"

77 All My Heart This Night Rejoices

Luke 2: 11
Fröhlich soll mein Herze springen
Paul Gerhardt, 1653
Tr., Catherine Winkworth, 1858, alt.

8. 8. 8. 6. 8. 8. 8. 6.

Fröhlich soll mein **Herze**
Johann Crüger, 1653

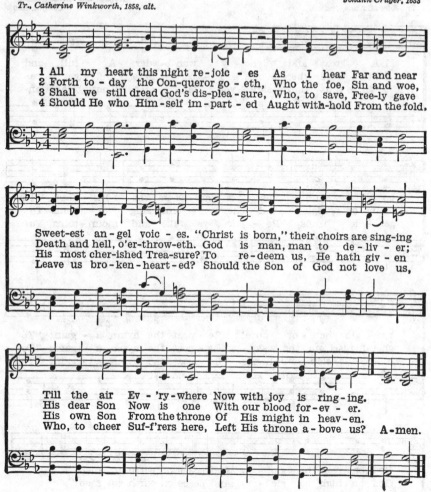

1 All my heart this night re - joic - es As I hear Far and near
2 Forth to - day the Con-queror go - eth, Who the foe, Sin and woe,
3 Shall we still dread God's dis-plea - sure, Who, to save, Free-ly gave
4 Should He who Him-self im-part - ed Aught with-hold From the fold.

Sweet-est an - gel voic - es. "Christ is born," their choirs are sing-ing
Death and hell, o'er-throw-eth. God is man, man to de - liv - er;
His most cher-ished Trea-sure? To re - deem us, He hath giv - en
Leave us bro-ken-heart-ed? Should the Son of God not love us,

Till the air Ev - 'ry-where Now with joy is ring-ing.
His dear Son Now is one With our blood for-ev - er.
His own Son From the throne Of His might in heav-en.
Who, to cheer Suf-f'rers here, Left His throne a - bove us? A-men.

5 If our blessed Lord and Maker
  Hated men, Would He then
Be of flesh partaker?
  If He in our woe delighted,
Would He bear All the care
  Of our race benighted?

6 He becomes the Lamb that taketh
  Sin away And for aye
Full atonement maketh.
  For our life His own He tenders
And our race, By His grace,
  Meet for glory renders.

All My Heart This Night Rejoices

7 Hark! a voice from yonder manger,
   Soft and sweet, Doth entreat:
"Flee from woe and danger.
   Brethren, from all ills that grieve you
You are freed; All you need
   I will surely give you."

8 Come, then, banish all your sadness,
   One and all, Great and small;
Come with songs of gladness.
   Love Him who with love is glowing;
Hail the Star Near and far
   Light and joy bestowing.

9 Ye whose anguish knew no measure,
   Weep no more; See the door
To celestial pleasure.
   Cling to Him, for He will guide you
Where no cross, Pain, or loss
   Can again betide you.

10 Hither come, ye heavy-hearted,
   Who for sin, Deep within,
Long and sore have smarted;
   For the poisoned wounds you're feeling
Help is near, One is here
   Mighty for their healing.

11 Hither come, ye poor and wretched;
   Know His will Is to fill
Every hand outstretchèd.
   Here are riches without measure;
Here forget All regret,
   Fill your hearts with treasure.

12 Let me in my arms receive Thee;
   On Thy breast Let me rest,
Savior, ne'er to leave Thee.
   Since Thou hast Thyself presented
Now to me, I shall be
   Evermore contented.

13 Guilt no longer can distress me;
   Son of God, Thou my load
Bearest to release me.
   Stain in me Thou findest never;
I am clean, All my sin
   Is removed forever.

14 I am pure, in Thee believing,
   From Thy store Evermore
Righteous robes receiving.
   In my heart I will enfold Thee,
Treasure rare, Let me there,
   Loving, ever hold Thee.

15 Dearest Lord, Thee will I cherish.
   Though my breath Fail in death,
Yet I shall not perish,
   But with Thee abide forever
There on high, In that joy
   Which can vanish never.

78 Hail the Day So Rich in Cheer

7. 6. 7. 6. 7. 7. 6. 7. 7. 6.

Is. 9: 6
Dies est laetitia
Author unknown, 15th century
Tr., W. Gustave Polack, 1940

Der Tag, der ist
German melody, 15th century

1 Hail the day so rich in cheer For each earth-born crea - ture!
2 Child of won-der, vir-gin-born, King of all cre - a - tion,

God's own Son from heav'n draws near, Takes our hu-man na - ture;
On this hap-py Christ-mas morn Come for our sal-va - tion!

Of a vir-gin born is He; Ma-ry, by the Lord's de-cree,
Were this Child for us not born, We should all be lost, for-lorn,

Is be-come a moth-er. See the mir-a-cle of love:
No true hope pos-sess-ing. Dear Lord Je-sus, thanks to Thee

God Him-self, from heav'n a-bove, Came to be our Broth-er!
Now and thro' e-ter-ni-ty For this grace and bless-ing! A-men.

Rejoice, Rejoice, This Happy Morn

8. 8. 7. 8. 8. 7. 4. 4. 4. 4. 8.

Luke 2 : 11
Os er idag en Frelser född
Birgitte Boye, 1778
Tr., Carl Döving, 1911

Wie schön leuchtet
Philipp Nicolai, 1599

Re-joice, re-joice, this hap-py morn, A Sav-ior un-to us is born,

The Christ, the Lord of Glo - ry. His low-ly birth in Beth-le-hem

The an-gels from on high proclaim And sing re-demp-tion's sto - ry.

My soul, ex - tol God's great fa-vor, Bless Him ev-er For sal-va-tion,

Give Him praise and ad - o - ra - tion. A - men.

80 All Praise to Thee, Eternal God

L. M., with Hallelujah

John 1 : 14
Gelobet seist du, Jesu Christ
Based on Latin sequence, 11th century
German, st. 1, 1370
Martin Luther, 1524, cento
Tr., unknown, 1858

Gelobet seist du, Jesu
Ancient melody, c. 1400

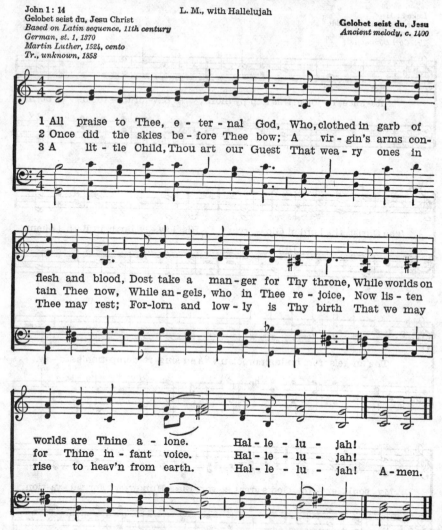

1 All praise to Thee, e - ter - nal God, Who, clothed in garb of flesh and blood, Dost take a man - ger for Thy throne, While worlds on worlds are Thine a - lone. Hal - le - lu - jah!

2 Once did the skies be - fore Thee bow; A vir - gin's arms con - tain Thee now, While an - gels, who in Thee re - joice, Now lis - ten for Thine in - fant voice. Hal - le - lu - jah!

3 A lit - tle Child, Thou art our Guest That wea - ry ones in Thee may rest; For-lorn and low - ly is Thy birth That we may rise to heav'n from earth. Hal - le - lu - jah! A - men.

4 Thou comest in the darksome night
To make us children of the light,
To make us in the realms divine,
Like Thine own angels, round Thee shine.
Hallelujah!

5 All this for us Thy love hath done;
By this to Thee our love is won;
For this our joyful songs we raise
And shout our thanks in ceaseless praise.
Hallelujah!

O Jesus Christ, Thy Manger Is

4. 4. 11. 4. 4. 11.

Luke 2: 7
O Jesu Christ, dein Kripplein ist
Paul Gerhardt, 1653, cento
Tr., composite

O Jesu Christ, dein Kripplein
Johann Crüger, 1653

1 O Je-sus Christ, Thy man-ger is My par-a-dise at which my
2 He whom the sea And wind o-bey Doth come to serve the sin-ner
3 Thy light and grace Our guilt ef-face, Thy heav'n-ly rich-es all our
4 Thou Christian heart, Who-e'er thou art, Be of good cheer and let no

soul re-clin-eth. For there, O Lord, Doth lie the Word
in great meek-ness. Thou, God's own Son, With us art one,
loss re-triev-ing. Im-man-u-el, Thy birth doth quell
sor-row move thee! For God's own Child, In mer-cy mild,

Made flesh for us; here-in Thy grace forth shin-eth.
Dost join us and our chil-dren in our weak-ness.
The pow'r of hell and Sa-tan's bold de-ceiv-ing.
Joins thee to Him; how great-ly God must love thee! A-men.

5 Remember thou
   What glory now
The Lord prepared thee for all earthly sadness.
   The angel host
   Can never boast
Of greater glory, greater bliss or gladness.

6 The world may hold
   Her wealth and gold;
But thou, my heart, keep Christ as thy true Treasure.
   To Him hold fast
   Until at last
A crown be thine and honor in full measure.

82 Come Rejoicing, Praises Voicing

Luke 2: 1–14
Čas radosti
Juraj Tranovský, †1637
Tr., composite

4. 4. 6. 4. 4. 6. 6. 6. 11.

Gladness
Bohemian melody, 12th century

1 Come re-joic-ing, Prais-es voic-ing, Christ-mas Day is break-ing;
2 Un - a - bat - ed For Him wait-ed Man - y gen-er-a - tions;
3 Ten - der Flow-er, Might-y Tow-er, Je - sus Christ, our Sav-ior;

Now th' E-ter - nal, Lord su - per - nal, Hu - man form is tak - ing.
Him now proud-ly An - gels loud - ly Praise the Hope of na - tions.
Heav'n-ly Trea-sure, With-out mea-sure Thee we love for - ev - er.

On the hay— lo, be-hold Vir-gin's Son, as fore-told—
Let us, then, glad - ly sing, Let our songs gai - ly ring,
Lord and King with - out end, Our poor hearts now be - friend,

Lies the pre - cious In - fant in the win - try cold,
As we to this ho - ly Child our prais - es bring,
All Thy gifts of grace and good - ness to us send,

Come Rejoicing, Praises Voicing

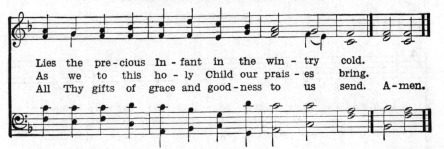

Lies the pre-cious In-fant in the win-try cold.
As we to this ho-ly Child our prais-es bring.
All Thy gifts of grace and good-ness to us send. A-men.

Hark! What Mean Those Holy Voices

83

8. 7. 8. 7.

Stuttgart
"Psalmodia Sacra"
Gotha, 1715

Luke 2: 14
John Cawood, 1819, alt.

1 Hark! what mean those ho-ly voic-es Sweet-ly sound-ing thro' the skies?
2 Lis-ten to the won-drous sto-ry Which they chant in hymns of joy,
3 Peace on earth, good will from heav-en, Reach-ing far as man is found;
4 Christ is born, the great A-noint-ed; Heav'n and earth, His prais-es sing!

Lo, th' an-gel-ic host re-joic-es, Heav'n-ly hal-le-lu-jahs rise.
Glo-ry in the high-est, glo-ry! Glo-ry be to God most high!
Souls re-deemed and sins for-giv-en! Loud our gold-en harps shall sound.
Oh, re-ceive whom God ap-point-ed For your Prophet, Priest, and King! Amen.

5 Hasten, mortals, to adore Him,
    Learn His name and taste His joy,
Till in heaven ye sing before Him,
    "Glory be to God most high!"

6 Let us learn the wondrous story
    Of our great Redeemer's birth;
Spread the brightness of His glory
    Till it cover all the earth.

84 Christians, Awake, Salute the Happy Morn

10. 10. 10. 10. 10. 10.

Luke 2 : 1–18
John Byrom, 1749, cento, alt.

Yorkshire
John Wainwright, 1750

1 Chris - tians, a - wake, sa - lute the hap - py morn
2 Then to the watch - ful shep - herds it was told,
3 He spake; and straight - way the ce - les - tial choir

Where - on the Sav - ior of the world was born.
Who heard th' an - gel - ic her - ald's voice, "Be - hold,
In hymns of joy, un - known be - fore, con - spire;

Rise to a - dore the mys - ter - y of love
I bring good ti - dings of a Sav - ior's birth
The prais - es of re - deem - ing love they sang,

Which hosts of an - gels chant - ed from a - bove,
To you and all the na - tions up - on earth;
And heav'n's whole orb with al - le - lu - ias rang.

Christians, Awake, Salute the Happy Morn

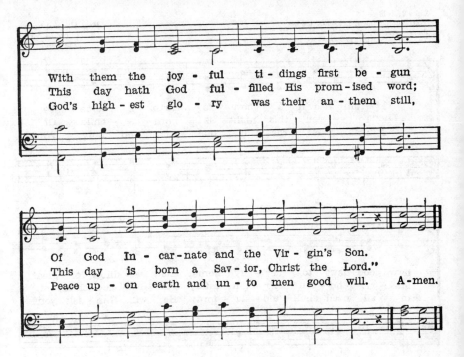

With them the joy - ful ti - dings first be - gun
This day hath God ful - filled His prom - ised word;
God's high - est glo - ry was their an - them still,

Of God In - car - nate and the Vir - gin's Son.
This day is born a Sav - ior, Christ the Lord."
Peace up - on earth and un - to men good will. A - men.

4 To Bethlehem straight th' enlightened shepherds ran
To see the wonder God had wrought for man
And found, with Joseph and the blessed maid,
Her Son, the Savior, in a manger laid;
Then to their flocks, still praising God, return,
And their glad hearts with holy rapture burn.

5 Oh, may we keep and ponder in our mind
God's wondrous love in saving lost mankind!
Trace we the Babe, who hath retrieved our loss,
From His poor manger to His bitter cross,
Tread in His steps, assisted by His grace,
Till man's first heavenly state again takes place.

6 Then may we hope, th' angelic hosts among,
To sing, redeemed, a glad triumphal song.
He that was born upon this joyful day
Around us all His glory shall display.
Saved by His love, incessant we shall sing
Eternal praise to heaven's almighty King.

85 From Heaven Above to Earth I Come

Luke 2: 1-18
Vom Himmel hoch, da komm' ich her
Martin Luther, 1535
Tr., Catherine Winkworth, 1855, alt.

L. M.

Vom Himmel hoch
"Geistliche Lieder"
Leipzig, 1539

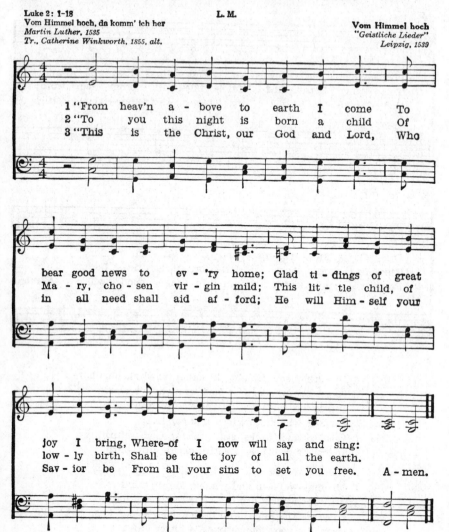

1 "From heav'n a - bove to earth I come To
2 "To you this night is born a child Of
3 "This is the Christ, our God and Lord, Who

bear good news to ev - 'ry home; Glad ti - dings of great
Ma - ry, cho - sen vir - gin mild; This lit - tle child, of
in all need shall aid af - ford; He will Him - self your

joy I bring, Where-of I now will say and sing:
low - ly birth, Shall be the joy of all the earth.
Sav - ior be From all your sins to set you free. A - men.

4 "He will on you the gifts bestow
Prepared by God for all below,
That in His kingdom, bright and fair,
You may with us His glory share.

5 "These are the tokens ye shall mark:
The swaddling-clothes and manger dark;
There ye shall find the Infant laid
By whom the heavens and earth were made."

From Heaven Above to Earth I Come

6 Now let us all with gladsome cheer
   Go with the shepherds and draw near
   To see the precious Gift of God,
   Who hath His own dear Son bestowed.

7 Give heed, my heart, lift up thine eyes!
   What is it in yon manger lies?
   Who is this child, so young and fair?
   The blessed Christ-child lieth there.

8 Welcome to earth, Thou noble Guest,
   Through whom the sinful world is blest!
   Thou com'st to share my misery;
   What thanks shall I return to Thee?

9 Ah, Lord, who hast created all,
   How weak art Thou, how poor and small,
   That Thou dost choose Thine infant bed
   Where humble cattle lately fed!

10 Were earth a thousand times as fair,
   Beset with gold and jewels rare,
   It yet were far too poor to be
   A narrow cradle, Lord, for Thee.

11 For velvets soft and silken stuff
   Thou hast but hay and straw so rough,
   Whereon Thou, King, so rich and great,
   As 'twere Thy heaven, art throned in state.

12 And thus, dear Lord, it pleaseth Thee
   To make this truth quite plain to me,
   That all the world's wealth, honor, might,
   Are naught and worthless in Thy sight.

13 Ah, dearest Jesus, holy Child,
   Make Thee a bed, soft, undefiled,
   Within my heart, that it may be
   A quiet chamber kept for Thee.

14 My heart for very joy doth leap,
   My lips no more can silence keep;
   I, too, must sing with joyful tongue
   That sweetest ancient cradle-song:

15 Glory to God in highest heaven,
   Who unto us His Son hath given!
   While angels sing with pious mirth
   A glad new year to all the earth.

86 Christ the Lord to Us is Born

Luke 2: 11
Narodil se Kristus Pán
Bohemian author unknown, c. 1400
Tr., st. 1–4, Vincent Pisek, †1929
Tr., st. 5–6, John Bajus, 1939

7. 4. 7. 4. 6. 6. 6.

Salvator natus
Bohemian melody, c. 1400

1 Christ the Lord to us is born, Hal-le-lu – jah! On this joy-ous
2 Proph-e-sied in days of old, Hal-le-lu – jah! God has sent Him
3 Our poor hu-man form He took, Hal-le-lu – jah! Realms of heav-en
4 Pros-trate lies the E-vil One, Hal-le-lu – jah! God has saved us

Christ-mas morn, Hal-le-lu – jah! Of a vir-gin low-ly,
as fore-told, Hal-le-lu – jah! Of a vir-gin low-ly,
He for-sook, Hal-le-lu – jah! Of a vir-gin low-ly,
through His Son, Hal-le-lu – jah! Of a vir-gin low-ly,

He, the King most ho – ly, Born this day to save us.
He, the King most ho – ly, Born this day to save us.
He, the King most ho – ly, Born this day to save us.
He, the King most ho – ly, Born this day to save us. A-men.

5 Grace divine, be with us still, Hallelujah!
Keep us from all harm and ill, Hallelujah!
For the sake of Jesus,
Who from sin now saves us,
Grant to us Thy mercy.

6 Grant us, Lord, a blessed end, Hallelujah!
To our souls Thy comfort send, Hallelujah!
Come to us, dear Jesus,
Born this day to save us,
Bless us all forever.

Joy to the World, the Lord is Come

C. M.

Luke 2: 10; Ps. 98
Isaac Watts, 1719

Antioch
Georg F. Händel, 1742, arr.

Congregation and Choir

1 Joy to the world, the Lord is come! Let earth re-
2 Joy to the earth, the Sav - ior reigns! Let men their
3 No more let sins and sor - rows grow Nor thorns in-
4 He rules the world with truth and grace And makes the

Choir only

ceive her King; Let ev - 'ry heart pre - pare Him
songs em - ploy, While fields and floods, rocks, hills, and
fest the ground; He comes to make His bless - ings
na - tions prove The glo - ries of His right - eous-

room And heav'n and na - ture sing, And heav'n and na - ture
plains Re - peat the sound-ing joy, Re - peat the sound-ing
flow Far as the curse is found, Far as the curse is
ness And won-ders of His love, And won-ders of His

Congregation and Choir

sing, And heav'n, and heav'n and na - ture sing.
joy, Re - peat, re - peat the sound-ing joy.
found, Far as, far as the curse is found.
love, And won - ders, won - ders of His love. A - men.

88 This Night a Wondrous Revelation

Luke 1: 78, 79

Dies ist die Nacht, da mir erschienen
Caspar F. Nachtenhöfer, c. 1683, ab.
Tr., Anna Hoppe, 1922

9. 8. 9. 8. 8. 8.

O dass ich tausend
Johann B. König, 1738

1 This night a won-drous rev - e - la - tion Makes known to
2 The Sun of Grace for thee is beam - ing; Re - joice, my
3 This light, which all thy gloom can ban - ish, The bliss of

me God's love and grace; The Child that mer-its ad - o - ra - tion
soul, in Je - sus' birth! The light from yon-der man-ger stream-ing
heav - en glo - ri - fies; When sun and moon and stars shall van - ish,

Brings light to our be-night-ed race; And though a thou-sand
Sends forth its rays o'er all the earth. It drives the night of
Its rays shall still il-lume the skies. This light thro' all e-

suns did shine, Still bright-er were that Light di - vine.
sin a - way And turns our dark-ness in - to day.
ter - ni - ty Thy heav'n and all to thee shall be. A-men.

4 O Jesus, precious Sun of gladness,
  Fill Thou my soul with light, I pray.
Dispel the gloomy night of sadness
  And teach Thou me this Christmas Day
How I a child of light may be,
Aglow with light that comes from Thee.

To Thee My Heart I Offer

Luke 2: 7
Mein Herz will ich dir schenken
Author unknown, 1653
Tr., composite

7. 6. 7. 6. 8. 8. 8. 6.

Cordis donum
"Clausener Gesangbuch," 1653

1 To Thee my heart I of-fer, O Christ-child sweet and dear,
2 My heart with-in is glow-ing, O Christ-child sweet and dear;
3 What bro't Thee to the man-ger, O Christ-child sweet and dear?

Up-on Thy love re-ly-ing; Oh, be Thou ev-er near!
I love Thee, Lord and Sav-ior, Oh, be Thou ev-er near!
Thy love for me, a stran-ger— Oh, be Thou ev-er near!

Take Thou my heart and give me Thine And let it be for-ev-er mine,
I see Thee in a man-ger laid, Near cat-tle rest-ing un-a-fraid;
O Lord, how great is this Thy love That reaches down from heav'n a-bove,

O Je-sus, ho-ly, un-de-filed, My Sav-ior meek and mild.
I see Thy deep hu-mil-i-ty And low-ly bow to Thee.
Thy love for us, by sin de-filed, That made Thee, God, a child! A-men.

4 With all my heart and being,
   O Christ-child sweet and dear,
 I love Thee, and Thee only;
   Oh, be Thou ever near!
 My heart I in Thy manger lay;
 Let it remain there and for aye
 Draw it to Thee that it may be
 Secure eternally.

5 Let me be Thine forever,
   O Christ-child sweet and dear;
 Uphold me with Thy mercy,
   And be Thou ever near.
 From Thee I gladly all receive,
 And what is mine to Thee I give,
 My heart, my soul, and all I own.
 Let these be Thine alone.

90 Come, Your Hearts and Voices Raising

Luke 2: 15
Kommt und lasst uns Christum ehren
Paul Gerhardt, 1667
Tr., composite

8. 8. 8. 7.

Quem pastores
14th-century melody

1 Come, your hearts and voic-es rais-ing, Christ the
2 Sin and death may well be groan-ing, Sa-tan
3 See how God, for us pro-vid-ing, Gave His

Lord with glad-ness prais-ing; Loud-ly sing His love a-
now may well be moan-ing; We, our full sal-va-tion
Son and life a-bid-ing; He our wea-ry steps is

maz-ing, Wor-thy folk of Chris-ten-dom.
own-ing, Cast our ev-'ry care a-way.
guid-ing From earth's woe to heav'n-ly joy.

A - men.

4 Christ, from heaven to us descending
And in love our race befriending,
In our need His help extending,
Saved us from the wily Foe.

5 Jacob's Star in all its splendor
Beams with comfort sweet and tender,
Forcing Satan to surrender,
Breaking all the powers of hell.

6 From the bondage that oppressed us,
From sin's fetters that possessed us,
From the grief that sore distressed us,
We, the captives, now are free.

Come, Your Hearts and Voices Raising

7 Oh, the joy beyond expressing
  When by faith we grasp this blessing
  And to Thee we come confessing
    That our freedom Thou hast wrought!

8 Gracious Child, we pray Thee, hear us,
  From Thy lowly manger cheer us,
  Gently lead us and be near us
    Till we join th' angelic choir.

Let the Earth Now Praise the Lord   91

7. 7. 7. 7.

Luke 24 : 27
Gott sei Dank durch alle Welt
Heinrich Held, 1659
Tr., Catherine Winkworth, 1863
Tr., st. 7, unknown

Nun komm, der Heiden Heiland
"Geistliches Gesangbüchlein"
Wittenberg, 1524, ad.

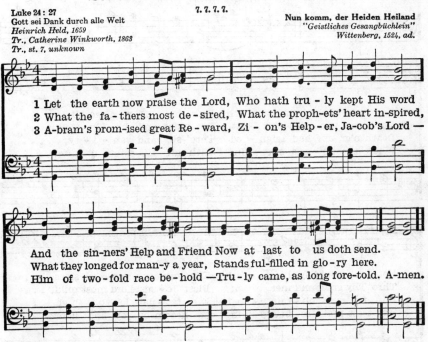

1 Let the earth now praise the Lord, Who hath tru-ly kept His word
2 What the fa-thers most de-sired, What the proph-ets' heart in-spired,
3 A-bram's prom-ised great Re-ward, Zi-on's Help-er, Ja-cob's Lord —

And the sin-ners' Help and Friend Now at last to us doth send.
What they longed for man-y a year, Stands ful-filled in glo-ry here.
Him of two-fold race be-hold —Tru-ly came, as long fore-told. A-men.

4 Welcome, O my Savior, now!
  Hail! My Portion, Lord, art Thou.
  Here, too, in my heart, I pray,
  Oh, prepare Thyself a way!

5 King of Glory, enter in;
  Cleanse it from the filth of sin,
  As Thou hast so often done;
  It belongs to Thee alone.

6 As Thy coming was in peace,
  Quiet, full of gentleness,
  Let the same mind dwell in me
  That was ever found in Thee.

7 Comfort my desponding heart;
  Thou my Strength and Refuge art.
  I am weak, and cunningly
  Satan lays his snares for me.

8 Bruise for me the Serpent's head
  That, set free from doubt and dread,
  I may cleave to Thee in faith,
  Safely kept through life and death,

9 And when Thou dost come again
  As a glorious King to reign,
  I with joy may see Thy face,
  Freely ransomed by Thy grace.

92
Now Sing We, Now Rejoice

Luke 2: 1–14
In dulci iubilo
Author unknown, c. 1300
Tr., Arthur T. Russell, 1851, alt.

6. 6. 6. 6. 6. 6. 5. 5.

In dulci iubilo
German melody, 14th century

1 Now sing we, now re-joice, Now raise to heav'n our voice;
2 Come from on high to me; I can-not rise to Thee.
3 Now thro' His Son doth shine The Fa-ther's grace di-vine.
4 Oh, where shall joy be found? Where but on heav'n-ly ground?

He from whom joy stream-eth Poor in a man-ger lies; ....
Cheer my wea-ried spir-it, O pure and ho-ly Child; ...
Death o'er us had reign-ed Thro' sin and van-i-ty; ...
Where the an-gels sing-ing With all His saints u-nite, ...

Not so bright-ly beam-eth The sun in yon-der skies. ...
Thro' Thy grace and mer-it, Blest Je-sus, Lord most mild, ...
He for us ob-tain-ed E-ter-nal joy on high. ...
Sweet-est prais-es bring-ing In heav'n-ly joy and light. ...

Thou my Sav-ior art! .... Thou my Sav-ior art!
Draw me un-to Thee! ... Draw me un-to Thee!
May we praise Him there! ... May we praise Him there!
Oh, that we were there! ... Oh, that we were there! A-men.

O Lord, We Welcome Thee

93

6. 7. 6. 7. 6. 6. 6. 6.

Is. 9: 6
Ich freue mich in dir
Caspar Ziegler, 1648
Tr., composite

Nun danket alle Gott
Johann Crüger, 1648

1 O Lord, we wel-come Thee, Our hearts for joy are leap-ing.
2 The might-y Son of God, His maj-es-ty con-ceal-ing,
3 Ah, sweet and gen-tle name! Its ech-oes far are sound-ing,
4 To Thee a-lone we cling, For Thee all else for-sak-ing;

Thou, Je-sus, dear-est Child, Thy pre-cious prom-ise keep-ing,
Dwells with our fall-en race To give us balm and heal-ing.
It pierc-es hearts of stone And tells of love a-bound-ing.
On Thee a-lone we build Tho' heav'n and earth be quak-ing.

Art come from heav'n to earth To be our Broth-er dear;
The ev-er-last-ing God De-scends from realms a-bove,
O Je-sus, dear-est Child, On Thee will we re-ly,
To Thee a-lone we live, In Thee a-lone we die;

Thou, gra-cious Son of God, Wilt ban-ish all our fear.
Be-comes a win-some Child, Re-veals His Fa-ther's love.
And, call-ing on Thy name, We die not when we die.
O Je-sus, dear-est Lord, With Thee we reign on high. A-men.

94 Hark! The Herald Angels Sing

7. 7. 7. 7. D., with Refrain

Luke 2: 14
Charles Wesley, 1739, et al.

Mendelssohn
Felix Mendelssohn, 1840, ad.

1 Hark! the her-ald an-gels sing, "Glo-ry to the new-born King;
2 Christ, by high-est heav'n a-dored, Christ, the ev-er-last-ing Lord,
3 Hail, the heav'n-ly Prince of Peace! Hail, the Sun of Right-eous-ness!
4 Come, De-sire of na-tions, come, Fix in us Thy hum-ble home;

Peace on earth and mer-cy mild, God and sin-ners rec-on-ciled!"
Late in time be-hold Him come, Off-spring of a vir-gin's womb.
Light and life to all He brings, Ris'n with heal-ing in His wings.
Oh, to all Thy-self im-part, Formed in each be-liev-ing heart!

Joy-ful, all ye na-tions, rise, Join the tri-umph of the skies;
Veiled in flesh the God-head see, Hail th' in-car-nate De-i-ty!
Mild He leaves His throne on high, Born that man no more may die;
Hark! the her-ald an-gels sing, "Glo-ry to the new-born King;

With th' an-gel-ic host pro-claim, "Christ is born in Beth-le-hem!"
Pleased as Man with man to dwell; Je-sus, our Im-man-u-el!
Born to raise the sons of earth; Born to give them sec-ond birth.
Peace on earth and mer-cy mild, God and sin-ners rec-on-ciled!"

Hark! the Herald Angels Sing

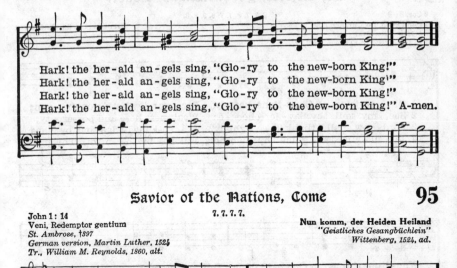

Hark! the her-ald an-gels sing, "Glo-ry to the new-born King!"
Hark! the her-ald an-gels sing, "Glo-ry to the new-born King!"
Hark! the her-ald an-gels sing, "Glo-ry to the new-born King!"
Hark! the her-ald an-gels sing, "Glo-ry to the new-born King!" A-men.

Savior of the Nations, Come 95

7. 7. 7. 7.

John 1: 14
Veni, Redemptor gentium
St. Ambrose, †397
German version, Martin Luther, 1524
Tr., William M. Reynolds, 1860, alt.

Nun komm, der Heiden Heiland
"Geistliches Gesangbüchlein"
Wittenberg, 1524, ad.

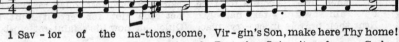

1 Sav - ior of the na-tions, come, Vir-gin's Son, make here Thy home!
2 Not by hu-man flesh and blood, By the Spir-it of our God,
3 Won-drous birth! O won-drous Child Of the Vir-gin un-de-filed!

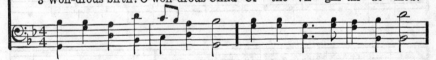

Mar-vel now, O heav'n and earth, That the Lord chose such a birth.
Was the Word of God made flesh—Woman's Offspring, pure and fresh.
Tho' by all the world dis-owned, Still to be in heav'n enthroned. A-men.

4 From the Father forth He came
And returneth to the same,
Captive leading death and hell—
High the song of triumph swell!

5 Thou, the Father's only Son,
Hast o'er sin the victory won.
Boundless shall Thy kingdom be;
When shall we its glories see?

6 Brightly doth Thy manger shine,
Glorious is its light divine.
Let not sin o'ercloud this light;
Ever be our faith thus bright.

7 Praise to God the Father sing,
Praise to God the Son, our King,
Praise to God the Spirit be
Ever and eternally.

96 Oh, Rejoice, Ye Christians, Loudly

2 Cor. 8: 9
8. 7. 7. 8. 7. 7. 8. 8. 8. 8.

Freuet euch, ihr Christen alle
Christian Keimann, 1646
Tr., Catherine Winkworth, 1863, alt.

Freuet euch, ihr Christen
Andreas Hammerschmidt, 1646

1 Oh, re-joice, ye Chris-tians, loud-ly, For our joy hath now be-gun;
2 See, my soul, thy Sav-ior choos-es Weak-ness here and pov-er-ty;
3 Lord, how shall I thank Thee right-ly? I ac-knowl-edge that by Thee
4 Je-sus, guard and guide Thy mem-bers, Fill Thy breth-ren with Thy grace,

Won-drous things our God hath done. Tell a-broad His good-ness proud-ly
In such love He comes to thee Nor the hard-est couch re-fus-es;
I am saved e-ter-nal-ly. Let me not for-get it light-ly,
Hear their prayers in ev-'ry place. Quick-en now life's faint-est em-bers;

Who our race hath hon-ored thus That He deigns to
All He suf-fers for thy good, To re-deem thee
But to Thee at all times cleave And my heart true
Grant all Chris-tians, far and near, Ho-ly peace, a

dwell with us. Joy, O joy, be-yond all glad-ness.
by His blood. Joy, O joy, be-yond all glad-ness,
peace re-ceive. Joy, O joy, be-yond all glad-ness,
glad New Year! Joy, O joy, be-yond all glad-ness,

Ob, Rejoice, Ye Christians, Loudly

Christ hath done a - way with sad - ness! Hence, all sor - row
Christ hath done a - way with sad - ness! Hence, all sor - row
Christ hath done a - way with sad - ness! Hence, all sor - row
Christ hath done a - way with sad - ness! Hence, all sor - row

and re - pin - ing, For the Sun of Grace is shin-ing!
and re - pin - ing, For the Sun of Grace is shin-ing!
and re - pin - ing, For the Sun of Grace is shin-ing!
and re - pin - ing, For the Sun of Grace is shin-ing! A - men.

Let Us All with Gladsome Voice   97

2 Cor. 8: 9   7. 6. 7. 6. Trochaic   Lasst uns alle
Lasst uns alle fröhlich sein   "Gesangbuch, Ander Teil"
Author unknown, 1632   Dresden, 1632
Tr., Catherine Winkworth, 1863, alt.

1 Let us all with glad-some voice Praise the God of heav - en,
2 To this vale of tears He comes, Here to serve in sad - ness,
3 We are rich, for He was poor; Is not this a won - der?
4 O Lord Christ, our Sav - ior dear, Be Thou ev - er near us.

Who, to bid our hearts re - joice, His own Son hath giv - en.
That with Him in heav'n's fair homes We may reign in glad - ness.
There-fore praise God ev - er - more Here on earth and yon - der.
Grant us now a glad new year. A - men, Je - sus, hear us! A-men.

98 Of the Father's Love Begotten

1 Tim. 3 : 16
Corde natus ex Parentis
Aurelius C. Prudentius, †413, cento
Tr., John M. Neale, 1854, and
Henry W. Baker, 1861

8. 7. 8. 7. 8. 7. 7.

Divinum mysterium
Plain-song tune, 12th century

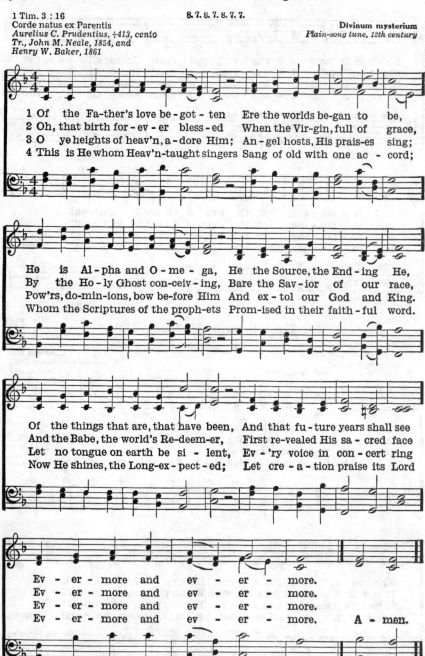

1 Of the Fa-ther's love be-got-ten Ere the worlds be-gan to be,
2 Oh, that birth for-ev-er bless-ed When the Vir-gin, full of grace,
3 O ye heights of heav'n, a-dore Him; An-gel hosts, His prais-es sing;
4 This is He whom Heav'n-taught singers Sang of old with one ac-cord;

He is Al-pha and O-me-ga, He the Source, the End-ing He,
By the Ho-ly Ghost con-ceiv-ing, Bare the Sav-ior of our race,
Pow'rs, do-min-ions, bow be-fore Him And ex-tol our God and King.
Whom the Scriptures of the proph-ets Prom-ised in their faith-ful word.

Of the things that are, that have been, And that fu-ture years shall see
And the Babe, the world's Re-deem-er, First re-vealed His sa-cred face
Let no tongue on earth be si-lent, Ev-'ry voice in con-cert ring
Now He shines, the Long-ex-pect-ed; Let cre-a-tion praise its Lord

Ev-er-more and ev-er-more.
Ev-er-more and ev-er-more.
Ev-er-more and ev-er-more.
Ev-er-more and ev-er-more. A-men.

Of the Father's Love Begotten

5 Christ, to Thee, with God the Father,
  And, O Holy Ghost, to Thee
Hymn and chant and high thanksgiving
  And unending praises be,
Honor, glory, and dominion,
  And eternal victory
    Evermore and evermore.

Now Are the Days Fulfilled 99

Gal. 4: 4
Nun ist die Zeit erfüllt
Author unknown, 1746
Tr., Frederick W. Herzberger, †1930, alt.

6. 7. 6. 7. 6. 6. 6. 6.

Was frag' ich nach der Welt
Ahasverus Fritsch, 1679

1 Now are the days ful-filled, God's Son is man-i-fest-ed.
2 Now are the days ful-filled, Lo, Ja-cob's Star is shin-ing;
3 Now are the days ful-filled, The child of God re-joic-es;

Now His great maj-es-ty In hu-man flesh is vest-ed.
The gloom-y night has fled Where-in the world lay pin-ing.
No bond-age of the Law, No curs-es that it voic-es,

Be-hold the might-y God, By whom all wrath is stilled,
Now, Is-rael, look on Him Who long thy heart hath thrilled;
Can fill our hearts with fear; On Christ our hope we build.

The wom-an's prom-ised Seed— Now are the days ful-filled.
Hear Zi-on's watch-men cry: Now are the days ful-filled.
Be-hold the Prince of Peace— Now are the days ful-filled. A-men.

100 Christians, Sing Out with Exultation

1 John 4 : 2
Faisons éclater notre joie
Benedict Pictet, 1705, ab.
Tr., Henry L. Jenner, 1886

9. 8. 9. 8. D.

Navarre
Louis Bourgeois, 1544

1 Chris-tians, sing out with ex-ul-ta-tion And praise your Ben-e-fac-tor's name! To-day the Au-thor of sal-va-tion, The Fa-ther's Well-be-lov-ed, came. Of un-de-fil-ed vir-gin moth-er An In-fant all di-vine was born, And God Him-self be-

2 In Him e-ter-nal might and pow-er To hu-man weak-ness hath in-clined; And this poor Child brings rich-est dow-er Of gifts and grac-es to man-kind. While here, His maj-es-ty dis-guis-ing, A serv-ant's form the Mas-ter wears, Be-hold the beams of

3 A sta-ble serves Him for a dwell-ing And for a bed a man-ger mean; Yet o'er His head, His ad-vent tell-ing, A new and won-drous star is seen. An-gels re-hearse to men the sto-ry, The joy-ful sto-ry of His birth; To Him they raise the

4 For thro' this ho-ly in-car-na-tion The pri-mal curse is done a-way; And bless-ed peace o'er all cre-a-tion Hath shed its pure and gen-tle ray. Then, in that heav'n-ly con-cert join-ing, O Chris-tian men, with one ac-cord, Your voic-es tune-ful-

Christians, Sing Out with Exultation

came your Broth - er   Up - on this hap - py Christ-mas morn.
glo - ry ris - ing   E'en from His pov - er - ty and tears.
an - them—"Glo - ry   To   God on high and peace on earth!"
ly com-bin - ing,   Sa - lute the birth-day of your Lord. A-men.

O Gladsome Light, O Grace   101

6. 6. 7. 6. 6. 7.

John 1: 9
Φῶς ἱλαρὸν ἁγίας δόξης
Author unknown, c. 200
Tr., Robert Bridges, 1895

Nunc dimittis
"Genevan Psalter," 1549

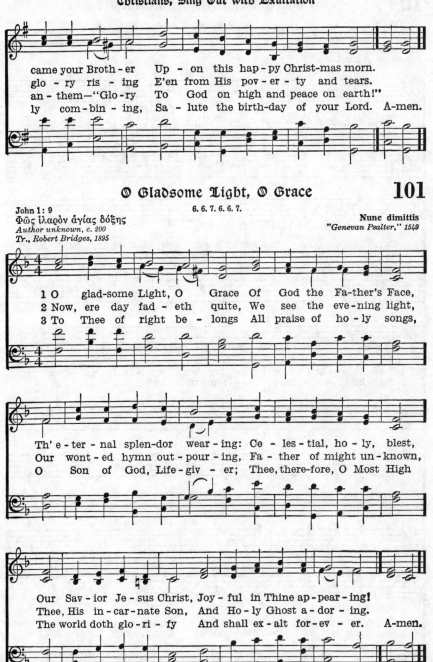

1 O   glad-some Light, O   Grace Of   God the Fa-ther's Face,
2 Now, ere day fad - eth   quite, We   see the eve-ning light,
3 To   Thee of right be - longs All praise of ho - ly songs,

Th' e - ter - nal splen-dor wear - ing: Ce - les - tial, ho - ly, blest,
Our wont-ed hymn out - pour - ing, Fa - ther of might un - known,
O   Son of God, Life - giv - er; Thee, there-fore, O Most High

Our Sav - ior Je - sus Christ, Joy - ful in Thine ap - pear - ing!
Thee, His in - car-nate Son, And Ho - ly Ghost a - dor - ing.
The world doth glo - ri - fy   And shall ex - alt for - ev - er.   A-men.

102

Oh, Come, All Ye Faithful

Luke 2 : 15
Adeste fideles
Author unknown, 18th century
Tr., Edward Caswall and
Philip Schaff, 1849, 1870

Irregular

Adeste fideles
"Cantus Diversi," 1751

1 Oh, come, all ye faith - ful, tri - um - phant - ly sing;
2 True Son of the Fa - ther, He comes from the skies;

Come, see in the man - ger our Sav - ior and King!
To be born of a vir - gin He doth not de - spise.

To Beth - le - hem has - ten with joy - ful ac - cord;
To Beth - le - hem has - ten with joy - ful ac - cord;

Oh, come, let us a - dore Him, Oh, come, let us a - dore Him,
Oh, come, let us a - dore Him, Oh, come, let us a - dore Him,

Oh, come, let us a - dore Him, Christ the Lord!
Oh, come, let us a - dore Him, Christ the Lord! A - men.

Oh, Come, All Ye Faithful

3 Hark, hark, to the angels all singing in heaven,
"To God in the highest all glory be given!"
To Bethlehem hasten with joyful accord;
Oh, come, let us adore Him, Christ the Lord!

4 To Thee, then, O Jesus, this day of Thy birth
Be glory and honor through heaven and earth,
True Godhead incarnate, omnipotent Word!
Oh, come, let us adore Him, Christ the Lord!

To Shepherds as They Watched by Night 103

Luke 2: 10, 11
Vom Himmel kam der Engel Schar
Martin Luther, 1543
Tr., Richard Massie, 1854, alt.

L. M.

Puer nobis nascitur
"Musae Sioniae," VI, 1609

1 To shep-herds as they watched by night Ap-peared a host of an-gels bright; Be-hold the ten-der Babe, they said, In yon-der low-ly man-ger laid,

2 At Beth-le-hem, in Da-vid's town, As Mi-cah did of old make known; 'Tis Je-sus Christ, your Lord and King, Who doth to all sal-va-tion bring.

3 Oh, then re-joice that thro' His Son God is with sin-ners now at one; Made like your-selves of flesh and blood, Your broth-er is th' e-ter-nal God.

4 What harm can sin and death then do? The true God now a-bides with you. Let hell and Sa-tan rage and chafe, Christ is your Broth-er— ye are safe. A-men.

5 Not one He will or can forsake
Who Him his confidence doth make.
Let all his wiles the Tempter try,
You may his utmost powers defy.

6 Ye shall and must at last prevail;
God's own ye are, ye cannot fail.
To God forever sing your praise
With joy and patience all your days.

104 Now Praise We Christ, the Holy One

Phil. 2: 6, 7

L. M.

A solis ortus cardine
Coelius Sedulius, c. 450
German version, Martin Luther. 1524, ab.
Tr., Richard Massie, 1854, alt.

Christum wir sollen loben schon
"Enchiridion"
Erfurt, 1524

1 Now praise we Christ, the Ho- ly One, The bless- ed vir- gin
2 He who Him- self all things did make A ser-vant's form vouch-
3 The grace and pow'r of God the Lord Up- on the moth- er
4 The no- ble moth-er bore a Son — For so did Ga- briel's

Ma- ry's Son, Far as the glo- rious sun doth shine
safed to take That He as man man-kind might win
was out-poured; A vir- gin pure and un- de- filed
prom- ise run,— Whom John con- fessed and leaped with joy

Ending for st. 1–6:   *Ending for last stanza:*

E'en to the world's re- mote con- fine.
And save His crea-tures from their sin.
In won-drous wise con-ceived a child.
Ere yet the moth-er knew her Boy. 7 time be lost. A-men.

5 Upon a manger filled with hay
   In poverty content He lay;
   With milk was fed the Lord of all,
   Who feeds the ravens when they call.

6 The heavenly choirs rejoice and raise
   Their voice to God in songs of praise.
   To humble shepherds is proclaimed
   The Shepherd who the world hath framed.

7 All honor unto Christ be paid,
   Pure Offspring of the favored maid,
   With Father and with Holy Ghost,
   Till time in endless time be lost.

Praise God the Lord, Ye Sons of Men

105

C. M.

Luke 2 : 1–14
Lobt Gott, ihr Christen allzugleich
Nikolaus Herman, 1560
Tr., August Crull, †1923, alt.

Lobt Gott, ihr Christen
Nikolaus Herman, 1554

1 Praise God the Lord, ye sons of men, Be - fore His
2 He leaves His heav'n - ly Fa - ther's throne, Is born an
3 He veils in flesh His pow'r di - vine A ser - vant's
4 He nes - tles at His moth - er's breast, Re - ceives her

high - est throne; To - day He o - pens heav'n a - gain And
In - fant small, And in a man - ger, poor and lone, Lies
form to take; In want and low - li - ness must pine Who
ten - der care, Whom an - gels hail with joy most blest, King

gives us His own Son, And gives us His own Son.
in a hum - ble stall, Lies in a hum - ble stall.
heav'n and earth did make, Who heav'n and earth did make.
Da - vid's roy - al Heir, King Da - vid's roy - al Heir. A - men.

5 'Tis He who in these latter days
    From Judah's tribe should come,
By whom the Father would upraise
    The Church, His Christendom.

6 A wondrous change which He does make!
    He takes our flesh and blood,
And He conceals for sinners' sake
    His majesty of God.

7 He serves that I a lord may be;
    A great exchange indeed!
Could Jesus' love do more for me
    To help me in my need?

8 He opens us again the door
    Of Paradise today;
The angel guards the gate no more.
    To God our thanks we pay.

106 The People That in Darkness Sat

C. M.

Is. 9 : 2; Matt. 4 : 16
John Morison, 1770, alt.

Lobt Gott, ihr Christen
Nikolaus Herman, 1554

1 The peo-ple that in dark-ness sat A glo-rious
2 To hail Thee, Sun of Right-eous-ness, The gath-'ring
3 For Thou their bur-den dost re-move And break the

light have seen; The light has shined on them who long In
na-tions come; They joy as when the reap-ers bear Their
ty-rant's rod As in the day when Mid-ian fell Be-

shades of death have been, In shades of death have been.
har-vest trea-sures home, Their har-vest trea-sures home.
fore the sword of God, Be-fore the sword of God. A-men.

4 To us a Child of hope is born,
   To us a Son is given,
And on His shoulder ever rests
   All power in earth and heaven.

5 His name shall be the Prince of Peace,
   The Everlasting Lord,
The Wonderful, the Counselor,
   The God by all adored.

6 His righteous government and power
   Shall over all extend;
On judgment and on justice based,
   His reign shall have no end.

7 Lord Jesus, reign in us, we pray,
   And make us Thine alone,
Who with the Father ever art
   And Holy Spirit, one.

We Christians May Rejoice Today

Luke 2 : 20
Wir Christenleut' hab'n jetzund Freud'
Caspar Füger, 1592
Tr., Catherine Winkworth, 1863

4. 4. 11. 4. 4. 11.

O Jesu Christ, dein Kripplein
Johann Crüger, 1653

1 We Christians may Re - joice to - day, When Christ was born to com - fort
2 Oh, won-drous joy That God most high Should take our flesh and thus our
3 Sin bro't us grief, But Christ re - lief, When down to earth He came for

and to save us. Who thus be - lieves No long - er grieves,
race should hon - or! A vir - gin mild Hath borne this Child;
our sal - va - tion. Since God with us Is dwell - ing thus,

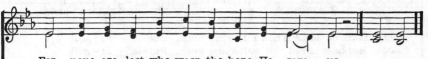

For none are lost who grasp the hope He gave us.
Such grace and glo - ry God hath put up - on her.
Who dares to speak the Chris-tian's con-dem-na - tion? A - men.

4 Then hither throng With happy song
   To Him whose birth and death are our assurance;
Through whom are we At last set free
   From sins and burdens that surpassed endurance.

5 Yea, let us praise Our God and raise
   Loud hallelujahs to the skies above us.
The bliss bestowed Today by God
   To ceaseless thankfulness and joy should move us.

108 We Sing, Immanuel, Thy Praise

Matt. 1: 23

Wir singen dir, Immanuel
Paul Gerhardt, 1653, cento
Tr., composite

L. M., with Hallelujah

Erschienen ift
Nikolaus Herman, 1560

1 We sing, Im-man-u-el, Thy praise, Thou Prince of
Life and Fount of grace, Thou Flow'r of heav'n and Star of morn,
Thou Lord of lords, Thou Vir-gin-born. Hal-le-lu-jah!

2 For Thee, since first the world was made, So man-y
hearts have watched and prayed; The pa-tri-archs' and proph-ets' throng
For Thee have hoped and wait-ed long. Hal-le-lu-jah!

3 Now art Thou here, Thou Ev-er-blest! In low-ly
man-ger dost Thou rest. Thou, mak-ing all things great, art small;
So poor art Thou, yet cloth-est all. Hal-le-lu-jah!

4 From Thee a-bove all glad-ness flows, Yet Thou must
bear such bit-ter woes; The Gen-tiles' Light and Hope Thou art,
Yet find-est none to soothe Thine heart. Hal-le-lu-jah! A-men.

5 But I, Thy servant, Lord, today
Confess my love and freely say,
I love Thee truly, but I would
That I might love Thee as I should.
Hallelujah!

6 I have the will, the power is weak;
Yet, Lord, my humble offering take
And graciously the love receive
Which my poor heart to Thee can give.
Hallelujah!

7 Had I no load of sin to bear,
Thy grace, O Lord, I could not share;
In vain hadst Thou been born for me
If from God's wrath I had been free.
Hallelujah!

8 Thus will I sing Thy praises here
With joyful spirit year by year;
And when we reckon years no more,
May I in heaven Thy name adore!
Hallelujah!

While Shepherds Watched Their Flocks by Night 109

C. M. D.

Luke 2: 11
Nahum Tate, 1700

Bethlehem
Gottfried W. Fink, 1842

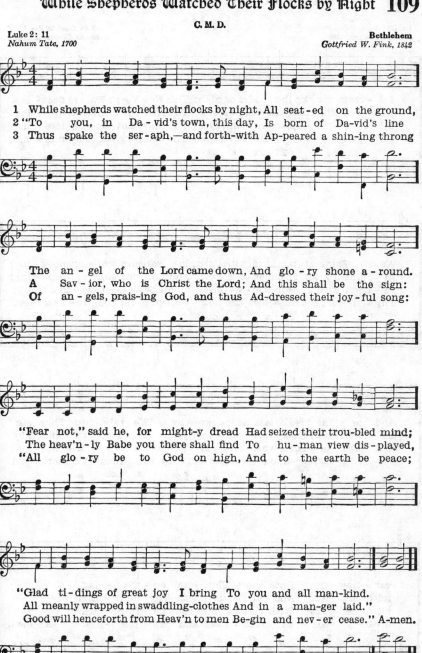

1 While shepherds watched their flocks by night, All seat-ed on the ground,
2 "To you, in Da-vid's town, this day, Is born of Da-vid's line
3 Thus spake the ser-aph,—and forth-with Ap-peared a shin-ing throng

The an-gel of the Lord came down, And glo-ry shone a-round.
A Sav-ior, who is Christ the Lord; And this shall be the sign:
Of an-gels, prais-ing God, and thus Ad-dressed their joy-ful song:

"Fear not," said he, for might-y dread Had seized their trou-bled mind;
The heav'n-ly Babe you there shall find To hu-man view dis-played,
"All glo-ry be to God on high, And to the earth be peace;

"Glad ti-dings of great joy I bring To you and all man-kind.
All meanly wrapped in swaddling-clothes And in a man-ger laid."
Good will henceforth from Heav'n to men Be-gin and nev-er cease." A-men.

110 Across the Sky the Shades of Night

8. 7. 8. 7. 8. 8. 7.

Ps. 121 : 1
James Hamilton, 1888

Allein Gott in der Höh'
Nikolaus Decius, 1539, asc.

1 A - cross the sky the shades of night This New Year's Eve are fleet - ing.
2 Be - fore the cross sub-dued we bow, To Thee our prayers ad-dress-ing,
3 And while we pray, we lift our eyes To dear ones gone be - fore us,
4 We gath - er up in this brief hour The mem-'ry of Thy mer - cies:

We deck Thine al - tar, Lord, with light, In sol-emn wor-ship meet - ing;
Re - count-ing all Thy mer-cies now, And all our sins con - fess - ing;
Safe home with Thee in Par - a - dise, Whose peace de-scend-eth o'er us;
Thy won-drous goodness, love, and pow'r Our grate-ful song re - hears - es;

And as the year's last hours go by, We raise to Thee our
Be - seech-ing Thee this com - ing year To keep us in Thy
And beg of Thee, when life is past, To re - u - nite us
For Thou hast been our Strength and Stay In man - y a dark and

ear - nest cry, Once more Thy love en - treat - ing.
faith and fear And crown us with Thy bless - ing.
all at last With those who've gone be - fore us.
drear - y day Of sor - row and re - vers - es. A - men.

Across the Sky the Shades of Night

5 In many an hour when fear and dread,
　Like evil spells, have bound us
And clouds were gathering overhead,
　Thy providence hath found us.
In many a night when seas ran high,
Thy gracious presence, drawing nigh,
　Hath made all calm around us.

6 Then, O great God, in years to come,
　Whatever may betide us,
Right onward through our journey home
　Be Thou at hand to guide us;
Nor leave us till at close of life,
Safe from all perils, toil, and strife,
　Heaven shall enfold and hide us.

Thou Who Roll'st the Year Around   111

Ps. 90: 12
Ray Palmer, 1832

7. 7. 7. 7.

Aus der Tiefe
"Nürnbergisches Gesangbuch," 1676

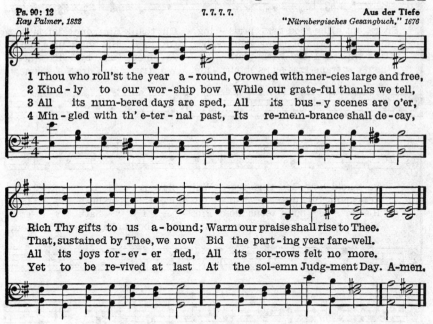

1 Thou who roll'st the year a-round, Crowned with mer-cies large and free,
2 Kind-ly to our wor-ship bow While our grate-ful thanks we tell,
3 All its num-bered days are sped, All its bus-y scenes are o'er,
4 Min-gled with th' e-ter-nal past, Its re-mem-brance shall de-cay,

Rich Thy gifts to us a-bound; Warm our praise shall rise to Thee.
That, sustained by Thee, we now Bid the part-ing year fare-well.
All its joys for-ev-er fled, All its sor-rows felt no more.
Yet to be re-vived at last At the sol-emn Judg-ment Day. A-men.

5 All our follies, Lord, forgive;
　Cleanse us from each guilty stain.
Let Thy grace within us live
　That we spend not years in vain.

6 Then, when life's last eve shall come,
　Happy spirits, may we fly
To our everlasting home,
　To our Father's house on high!

112 To God the Anthem Raising

Ps. 101 : 1
Helft mir Gott's Güte preisen
Paul Eber, 1571
Tr., Carl Döving, 1907

7. 6. 7. 6. 6. 7. 7. 6.

Helft mir Gott's Güte
Wolfgang Figulus, 1575

1 To God the an-them rais-ing, Sing, Christians, great and small;
2 Let us con-sid-er right-ly His mer-cies man-i-fold,
3 To Church and State He grant-ed His peace in ev-'ry place,
4 His Fa-ther heart is yearn-ing To take us for His own

Sing out, His good-ness prais-ing, Oh, thank Him, one and all!
And let us not think light-ly Of all His gifts un-told.
His vine-yard He hath plant-ed A-mong us by His grace.
When, our trans-gres-sions mourn-ing, We trust in Christ a-lone;

Be-hold how God this year, Which now is safe-ly end-ed,
Let thank-ful-ness re-call How God this year hath led us,
His ev-er boun-teous hand Pros-per-i-ty hath giv-en
When in His name we pray And hum-bly make con-fes-sion,

Hath in His love be-friend-ed His chil-dren far and near.
How He hath clothed and fed us, The great ones and the small.
And want and fam-ine driv-en From this our na-tive land.
He par-dons our trans-gres-sion And is our faith-ful Stay. A-men.

To God the Anthem Raising

5 Our God hath well defended,
  Hath kept us through His grace;
But if He had contended
  With us our sins to trace
And given us our meed,
  We all would then be lying
  In sin and sorrow, dying,
Each one for his misdeed.

6 O Father dear in heaven,
  For all Thy gifts of love
Which Thou to us hast given
  We lift our thanks above.
In Jesus' name we here,
  To Thee our prayers addressing,
  Still ask Thee for Thy blessing:
Grant us a joyful year.

While with Ceaseless Course the Sun 113

7. 7. 7. 7. D.

Ps. 90 : 12
John Newton, 1774

Christe, wahres Seelenlicht
"Neues geistreiches Gesangbuch"
Halle, 1704

1 While with cease-less course the sun Hast-ed thro' the for-mer year,
2 As the wing-ed ar-row flies Speed-i-ly the mark to find;
3 Thanks for mer-cies past re-ceive, Par-don of our sins re-new;

Man-y souls their race have run, Nev-er-more to meet us here;
As the light-ning from the skies Darts and leaves no trace be-hind,
Teach us hence-forth how to live With e-ter-ni-ty in view.

Fixed in an e-ter-nal state, They have done with all be-low.
Swift-ly thus our fleet-ing days Bear us down life's rap-id stream.
Bless Thy Word to young and old, Fill us with a Sav-ior's love;

We a lit-tle lon-ger wait, But how lit-tle, none can know.
Up-ward, Lord, our spir-its raise; All be-low is but a dream.
And when life's short tale is told, May we dwell with Thee a-bove. A-men.

114 Jesus! Name of Wondrous Love

7.7.7.7.

Luke 1 : 31
William W. How, 1854. alt.

Gott sei Dank
"Neues geistreiches Gesangbuch"
Halle, 1704

1 Je - sus! Name of won-drous love, Name all oth - er
2 Je - sus! Name de - creed of old, To the maid - en
3 Je - sus! Name of price - less worth To the fall - en

names a - bove, Un - to which must ev - 'ry knee
moth - er told— Kneel - ing in her low - ly cell—
sons of earth For the prom - ise that it gave,

Bow in deep hu - mil - i - ty.
By the an - gel Ga - bri - el.
"Je - sus shall His peo - ple save." A - men.

4 Jesus! Name of mercy mild,
Given to the holy Child
When the cup of human woe
First He tasted here below.

5 Jesus! Only name that's given
Under all the mighty heaven
Whereby man, to sin enslaved,
Bursts his fetters and is saved.

6 Jesus! Name of wondrous love,
Human name of God above;
Pleading only this, we flee,
Helpless, O our God, to Thee.

O Blessed Day When First was Poured

Gal. 4 : 4–5
Felix dies, quam proprio
Sebastian Besnault, 1726
Tr., John Chandler, 1837, alt.

L. M.

Angelus
"Heilige Seelenlust"
Breslau, 1657, ad.

1 O bless-ed day when first was poured The blood of
2 While from His moth-er's bos-om fed, His pre-cious
3 Scarce come to earth, His Fa-ther's will With prompt o-

our re-deem-ing Lord! O bless-ed day when Christ be-gan
blood He wills to shed; A fore-taste of His death He feels,
be-dience to ful-fil, A vic-tim e-ven now He lies

His sav-ing work for sin-ful man!
An ear-nest of His love re-veals.
Be-fore the day of sac-ri-fice. A-men.

4 In love our guilt He undertakes;
   Sinless, for sin atonement makes.
   The great Lawgiver for our aid
   Obedient to the Law is made.

5 Lord, circumcise our heart, we pray,
   And take what is not Thine away.
   Write Thine own name upon our hearts,
   Thy Law within our inward parts.

6 O Lord, the Virgin-born, to Thee
   Eternal praise and glory be,
   Whom with the Father we adore
   And Holy Ghost forevermore.

116 To the Name of Our Salvation

Acts 4: 12
Gloriosi Salvatoris
Author unknown, 1496
Tr., John M. Neale, 1851, alt.

8. 7. 8. 7. 8. 7.

Sieh, hier bin ich
"Geistreiches Gesangbuch"
Darmstadt, 1698

1 To the name of our sal-va-tion Laud and hon-or let us pay,
2 Je-sus is the name we trea-sure, Name be-yond what words can tell;
3 'Tis the name for ad - o - ra-tion; 'Tis the name of vic-to - ry;

Which for man-y a gen - er - a - tion Hid in God's fore-knowl-edge lay;
Name of glad-ness, name of plea-sure, Ear and heart de-light-ing well;
'Tis the name for med-i - ta - tion In this vale of mis-er - y;

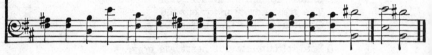

But with ho - ly ex - ul - ta-tion We may sing a-loud to - day.
Name of sweetness, passing measure, Sav-ing us from sin and hell.
'Tis the name for ven - er - a - tion By the cit - i - zens on high. A-men.

4 'Tis the name that whoso preacheth
Speaks like music to the ear;
Who in prayer this name beseecheth
Sweetest comfort findeth near;
Who its perfect wisdom reacheth
Heavenly joy possesseth here.

To the Name of Our Salvation

5 Jesus is the name prevailing
  Over every name by right;
At this name, in terror quailing,
  Powers of hell are put to flight;
God, in mercy never failing,
  Saves us by this name of might.

6 Therefore we in love adoring
  This most blessed name revere.
Holy Jesus, Thee imploring
  So to write it in us here
That hereafter, heavenward soaring,
  We may sing with angels there.

The Ancient Law Departs   117

Luke 2: 21
Debilis cessant elementa legis
Sebastian Besnault, 1736
Tr., composite, 1861, alt.

S. M.

Potsdam
"Church Psalter," 1854
Johann S. Bach, †1750, ad.

1 The an-cient Law de - parts, And all its fears re - move,
2 The Light of Light Di - vine, True bright-ness un - de - filed,
3 His in-fant bod-y now Be - gins the cross to feel;

For Je-sus makes with faithful hearts A cov-e-nant of love.
He bears for us the pain of sin, A ho-ly, spot-less Child.
Those precious drops of blood that flow For death the Vic-tim seal.   A-men.

4 Today the name is Thine
At which we bend the knee.
They call Thee Jesus, Child Divine;
Our Jesus deign to be.

5 All praise, eternal Son,
For Thy redeeming love,
With Father, Spirit, ever One
In glorious might above.

118

Father, Let Me Dedicate

7. 5. 7. 5. D.

1 Pet. 2: 9
Lawrence Tuttiett, 1864

Glorification
Gossner's "Choralbuch"
Leipzig, 1832, ad.

1 Fa - ther, let me ded - i - cate   All   this year to   Thee,
2 Can a child pre-sume to choose Where or how to   live?
3 If   in mer - cy Thou wilt spare Joys that yet are mine;
4 If   Thou call - est to the cross And its shad-ow come,

In   what - ev - er earth - ly state Thou wilt have me   be.
Can a   fa - ther's love re - fuse All the best to   give?
If   on   life, se - rene and fair, Bright-er rays may shine,
Turn-ing all my gain to loss, Shroud-ing heart and home,

Not   from sor - row, pain, or care Free-dom dare I   claim;
More Thou giv - est ev - 'ry day Than the best can claim
Let   my glad heart while it sings Thee in all pro - claim
Let   me think how Thy dear Son To   His glo - ry came

This a - lone shall be my prayer: Glo - ri - fy Thy name.
Nor with-hold-est aught that may Glo - ri - fy Thy name.
And, what-e'er the fu - ture brings, Glo - ri - fy Thy name.
And in deep-est woe pray on: "Glo - ri - fy Thy name." A - men.

Great God, We Sing That Mighty Hand

L. M.

Ps. 92: 1
Philip Doddridge, 1755, alt.

Mendon
German melody
Arr. by Samuel Dyer, 1828

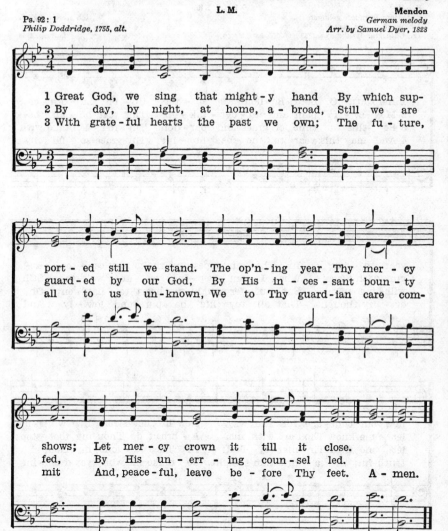

1 Great God, we sing that might-y hand By which sup-
2 By day, by night, at home, a-broad, Still we are
3 With grate-ful hearts the past we own; The fu-ture,

port-ed still we stand. The op'n-ing year Thy mer-cy
guard-ed by our God, By His in-ces-sant boun-ty
all to us un-known, We to Thy guard-ian care com-

shows; Let mer-cy crown it till it close.
fed, By His un-err-ing coun-sel led.
mit And, peace-ful, leave be-fore Thy feet. A-men.

4 In scenes exalted or depressed
Be Thou our Joy and Thou our Rest.
Thy goodness all our hopes shall raise,
Adored through all our changing days.

5 When death shall interrupt our songs
And seal in silence mortal tongues,
Our Helper, God, in whom we trust,
In better worlds our soul shall boast.

120 Help Us, O Lord! Behold, We Enter

Heb. 13 : 8
Hilf, Herr Jesu, lass gelingen
Johann Rist, 1642, cento
Tr., Catherine Winkworth, 1863

9. 8. 9. 8. 8. 8.

Ich sterbe täglich
Ms., Municipal Library
Leipzig, 1756

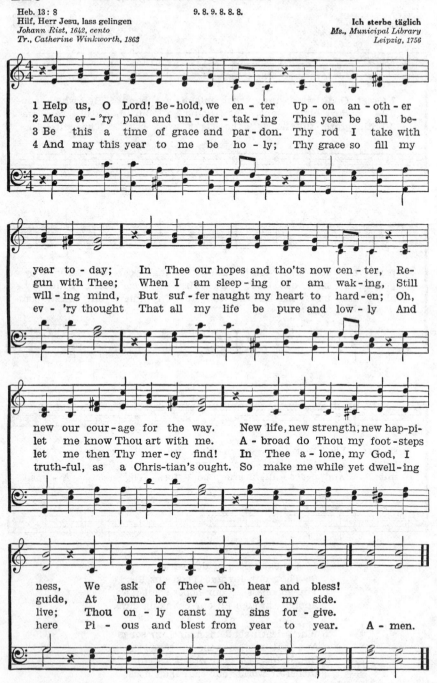

1 Help us, O Lord! Be-hold, we en-ter Up-on an-oth-er
2 May ev-'ry plan and un-der-tak-ing This year be all be-
3 Be this a time of grace and par-don. Thy rod I take with
4 And may this year to me be ho-ly; Thy grace so fill my

year to-day; In Thee our hopes and tho'ts now cen-ter, Re-
gun with Thee; When I am sleep-ing or am wak-ing, Still
will-ing mind, But suf-fer naught my heart to hard-en; Oh,
ev-'ry thought That all my life be pure and low-ly And

new our cour-age for the way. New life, new strength, new hap-pi-
let me know Thou art with me. A-broad do Thou my foot-steps
let me then Thy mer-cy find! In Thee a-lone, my God, I
truth-ful, as a Chris-tian's ought. So make me while yet dwell-ing

ness, We ask of Thee—oh, hear and bless!
guide, At home be ev-er at my side.
live; Thou on-ly canst my sins for-give.
here Pi-ous and blest from year to year. A-men.

Help Us, O Lord! Behold, We Enter

5 Jesus, be with me and direct me;
  Jesus, my plans and hopes inspire;
Jesus, from tempting thoughts protect me;
  Jesus, be all my heart's Desire;
Jesus, be in my thoughts all day
Nor suffer me to fall away.

6 And grant, Lord, when the year is over,
  That it for me in peace may close;
In all things care for me and cover
  My head in time of fear and woes.
So may I when my years are gone
Appear with joy before Thy throne.

For Thy Mercy and Thy Grace

121

7. 7. 7. 7.

Ps. 59: 16
Henry Downton, 1841, ab. and alt.

Culbach
"Heilige Seelenlust"
Breslau, 1657, ad.

1 For Thy mer - cy and Thy grace, Faith-ful thro' an - oth - er year,
2 Lo, our sins on Thee we cast, Thee, our per - fect Sac - ri - fice,
3 Dark the fu - ture; let Thy light Guide us, bright and Morn-ing Star.
4 In our weak-ness and dis - tress, Rock of strength, be Thou our Stay;

Hear our song of thank-ful-ness; Sav - ior and Re-deem - er, hear!
And, for - get-ting all the past, Press un - to our glo-rious prize.
Fierce our foes and hard the fight; Arm us, Sav-ior, for the war.
In the path-less wil-der - ness Be our true and liv-ing Way. A-men.

5 Who of us death's awful road
  In the coming year shall tread,
With Thy rod and staff, O God,
  Comfort Thou his dying bed.

6 Keep us faithful, keep us pure,
  Keep us evermore Thine own.
Help, oh, help us to endure;
  Fit us for the promised crown.

122 Now Let Us Come Before Him

Ps. 91 : 1
Nun lasst uns gehn und treten
Paul Gerhardt, 1653, cento
Tr., John Kelly, 1867, alt.

7. 7. 7. 7. Iambic

Nun lasst uns Gott, dem Herren
"Christliche Psalmen"
Leipzig, 1587

1 Now let us come be-fore Him, With song and prayer a - dore Him,
2 The stream of years is flow-ing, And we are on-ward go - ing,
3 In woe we of - ten lan-guish And pass thro' times of an-guish
4 As moth-ers watch are keep-ing O'er chil-dren who are sleep-ing,

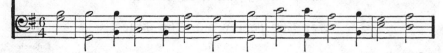

Who to our life hath giv - en All need-ed strength from heaven.
From old to new sur-viv-ing And by His mer-cy thriv-ing.
Of wars and trep-i-da - tion A-larm-ing ev-'ry na-tion.
Their fear and grief as-suag-ing When an-gry storms are rag-ing, A-men.

5 So God His own is shielding
And help to them is yielding.
When need and woe distress them,
His loving arms caress them.

6 O Thou who dost not slumber,
Remove what would encumber
Our work, which prospers never
Unless Thou bless it ever.

7 O God of Mercy, hear us;
Our Father, be Thou near us;
Mid crosses and in sadness
Be Thou our Fount of gladness.

8 To all who bow before Thee
And for Thy grace implore Thee,
Oh, grant Thy benediction
And patience in affliction.

9 Be Thou a Helper speedy
To all the poor and needy,
To all forlorn a Father;
Thine erring children gather.

10 Be with the sick and ailing,
Their Comforter unfailing;
Dispelling grief and sadness,
Oh, give them joy and gladness!

11 Above all else, Lord, send us
Thy Spirit to attend us,
Within our hearts abiding,
To heaven our footsteps guiding.

12 All this Thy hand bestoweth,
Thou Life, whence our life floweth.
To all Thy name confessing
Grant, Lord, Thy New Year's blessing!

Our God, Our Help in Ages Past

C. M.

Ps. 90
Isaac Watts, 1719, ab.

St. Anne
William Croft, 1708

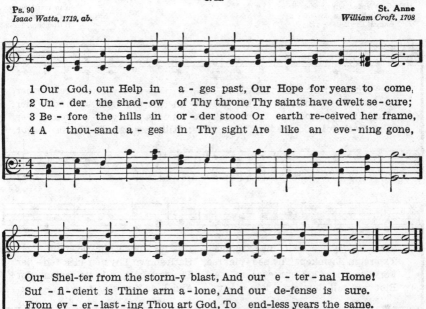

1 Our God, our Help in   a - ges past, Our Hope for years to   come,
2 Un - der   the shad - ow   of Thy throne Thy saints have dwelt se - cure;
3 Be - fore   the hills in   or - der stood Or   earth re-ceived her frame,
4 A   thou-sand a - ges   in Thy sight Are   like an   eve - ning gone,

Our Shel-ter from the storm-y blast, And our   e - ter - nal Home!
Suf - fi - cient is Thine arm a - lone, And our de-fense is   sure.
From ev - er - last - ing Thou art God, To   end-less years the same.
Short as the watch that ends the night Be - fore the ris - ing sun.   A-men.

5 Thy word commands our flesh to dust:
   "Return, ye sons of men!"
 All nations rose from earth at first
   And turn to earth again.

6 Time, like an ever-rolling stream,
   Bears all its sons away;
 They fly forgotten as a dream
   Dies at the opening day.

7 Like flowery fields the nations stand,
   Pleased with the morning light;
 The flowers beneath the mower's hand
   Lie withering ere 'tis night.

8 Our God, our Help in ages past,
   Our Hope for years to come,
 Be Thou our Guard while troubles last
   And our eternal Home!

124 O Lord, Our Father, Thanks to Thee

Ps. 107: 1
Herr Gott Vater, wir preisen dich
Cyriacus Schneegass, 1597
Tr., August Crull, 1880, alt.

8. 7. 8. 7. 8. 8. 7.

Nun freut euch
"Etlich' christliche Lieder"
Wittenberg, 1524

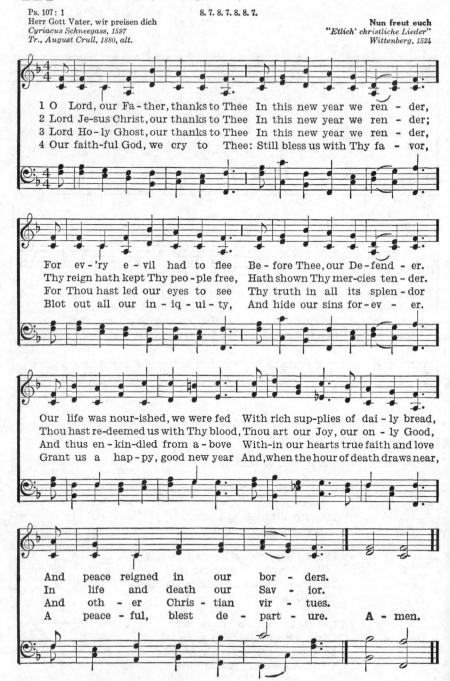

1 O Lord, our Fa - ther, thanks to Thee In this new year we ren - der,
2 Lord Je - sus Christ, our thanks to Thee In this new year we ren - der;
3 Lord Ho - ly Ghost, our thanks to Thee In this new year we ren - der,
4 Our faith-ful God, we cry to Thee: Still bless us with Thy fa - vor,

For ev - 'ry e - vil had to flee Be - fore Thee, our De - fend - er.
Thy reign hath kept Thy peo - ple free, Hath shown Thy mer-cies ten - der.
For Thou hast led our eyes to see Thy truth in all its splen - dor
Blot out all our in - iq - ui - ty, And hide our sins for - ev - er.

Our life was nour-ished, we were fed With rich sup-plies of dai - ly bread,
Thou hast re-deemed us with Thy blood, Thou art our Joy, our on - ly Good,
And thus en - kin-dled from a - bove With-in our hearts true faith and love
Grant us a hap-py, good new year And, when the hour of death draws near,

And peace reigned in our bor - ders.
In life and death our Sav - ior.
And oth - er Chris - tian vir - tues.
A peace - ful, blest de - part - ure. A - men.

The Old Year Now hath Passed Away

125

L. M.

John 15: 4
Das alte Jahr vergangen ist
Johann Steuerlein, 1588, asc.
Tr., Catherine Winkworth, 1863

Herr Jesu Christ, dich
"Cantionale Germanicum"
Dresden, 1628

1 The old year now hath passed a-way; We thank Thee, O our
2 We pray Thee, O e - ter-nal Son, Who with the Fa - ther
3 Take not Thy sav - ing Word a-way, Our souls' true com - fort,

God, to - day That Thou hast kept us through the year
reign'st as One, To guard and rule Thy Chris - ten - dom
staff, and stay. A - bide with us and keep us free

When dan - ger and dis - tress were near.
Through all the a - ges yet to come.
From er - rors, fol - l'wing on - ly Thee. A - men.

4 Oh, help us to forsake all sin,
A new and holier course begin!
Mark not what once was done amiss;
A happier, better year be this,

5 Wherein as Christians we may live
Or die in peace that Thou canst give,
To rise again when Thou shalt come
And enter Thine eternal home.

6 There shall we thank Thee and adore
With all the angels evermore.
Lord Jesus Christ, increase our faith
To praise Thy name through life and death.

126 Arise and Shine in Splendor

Is. 60 : 1–6
Brich auf und werde lichte
Martin Opitz, 1628, ab.
Tr., Gerhard Gieschen, 1937

7. 7. 6. 7. 7. 8.

O Welt, ich muss dich lassen
Heinrich Isaak, c. 1490

1 A - rise and shine in splen-dor, Let night to day sur-ren-der;
2 See earth in dark-ness ly - ing, The hea-then na-tions dy - ing
3 The world's re-mot-est rac - es, Up - on whose wea-ry fac - es

Thy Light is draw-ing near. A - bove thee day is beam-ing,
In hope-less gloom and night. To thee the Lord of heav-en—
The sun looks from the sky, Shall run with zeal un - tir - ing,

In matchless beau-ty gleaming; The glo-ry of the Lord is here.
Thy Life, thy Hope—hath giv-en Great glo-ry, hon - or, and de-light.
With joy thy Light de-sir - ing That breaks upon them from on high. A-men.

4 Lift up thine eyes in wonder;
    See, nations gather yonder,
        They all come unto thee.
    The world has heard thy story,
    Thy sons come to thy glory,
        And daughters haste thy Light to see.

5 Thy heart will leap for gladness
    When from the realms of sadness
        They come o'er land and sea.
    Thine eyes will wake from slumber
    When people without number
        Come thronging from afar to thee.

As with Gladness Men of Old

7. 7. 7. 7. 7. 7.

Matt. 2: 1-11
William C. Dix, 1860

Dix
Konrad Kocher, 1838

1 As with glad-ness men of old Did the guid-ing star be-hold;
2 As with joy-ful steps they sped, Sav-ior, to Thy low-ly bed,
3 As they of-fered gifts most rare At Thy cra-dle, rude and bare,

As with joy they hailed its light, Lead-ing on-ward, beam-ing bright,
There to bend the knee be-fore Thee whom heav'n and earth a-dore,
So may we with ho-ly joy, Pure and free from sin's al-loy,

So, most gracious Lord, may we Ev-er-more be led by Thee!
So may we with will-ing feet Ev-er seek Thy mer-cy-seat!
All our cost-liest treasures bring, Christ, to Thee, our heav'nly King! A-men.

4 Holy Jesus, every day
Keep us in the narrow way;
And, when earthly things are past,
Bring our ransomed souls at last
Where they need no star to guide,
Where no clouds Thy glory hide.

5 In the heavenly country bright
Need they no created light;
Thou its Light, its Joy, its Crown,
Thou its Sun which goes not down.
There forever may we sing
Alleluias to our King!

128 Brightest and Best of the Sons of the Morning

11. 10. 11. 10.

Matt. 2 : 11
Reginald Heber, 1811

Morning Star
John P. Harding, 1892

1 Bright-est and best of the sons of the morn-ing,
Dawn on our dark-ness and lend us thine aid;
Star of the East, the ho-ri-zon a-dorn-ing,
Guide where our in-fant Re-deem-er is laid.

2 Cold on His cra-dle the dew-drops are shin-ing;
Low lies His head with the beasts of the stall.
An-gels a-dore Him in slum-ber re-clin-ing,
Mak-er and Mon-arch and Sav-ior of all.

3 Shall we not yield Him, in cost-ly de-vo-tion,
O-dors of E-dom and of-f'rings di-vine,
Gems of the moun-tain and pearls of the o-cean,
Myrrh from the for-est and gold from the mine? A-men.

4 Vainly we offer each ample oblation,
  Vainly with gifts would His favor secure.
Richer by far is the heart's adoration;
  Dearer to God are the prayers of the poor.

Brightest and Best of the Sons of the Morning

5 Brightest and best of the sons of the morning,
   Dawn on our darkness and lend us thine aid;
   Star of the East, the horizon adorning,
   Guide where our infant Redeemer is laid.

Hail, Thou Source of Every Blessing 129

8. 7. 8. 7. D.

O Durchbrecher
"Neues geistreiches Gesangbuch"
Halle, 1704

Matt. 2: 11
Basil Woodd, c. 1810

1 Hail, Thou Source of ev-'ry bless-ing, Sov-'reign Fa-ther of man-kind!
2 Once far off, but now in-vit-ed, We ap-proach Thy sa-cred throne;
3 Hail, Thou all-in-vit-ing Sav-ior! Gen-tiles now their of-f'rings bring;

Gen-tiles now, Thy grace pos-sess-ing, In Thy courts ad-mis-sion find.
In Thy cov-e-nant u-nit-ed, Rec-on-ciled, re-deemed, made one.
In Thy tem-ples seek Thy fa-vor, Je-sus Christ, our Lord and King.

Grate-ful now we fall be-fore Thee, In Thy Church ob-tain a place,
Now re-vealed to East-ern sa-ges, See the Star of Mer-cy shine;
May we, bod-y, soul, and spir-it, Live de-vot-ed to Thy praise,

Now by faith be-hold Thy glo-ry, Praise Thy truth, adore Thy grace.
Mys-t'ry hid in for-mer a-ges, Mys-t'ry great of love di-vine.
Glo-rious realms of bliss in-her-it, Grate-ful an-thems ev-er raise! A-men.

130 O Jesus, King of Glory

Matt. 2: 1–12

7. 6. 7. 6. D.

O König aller Ehren
Martin Behm, 1606
Tr., *Catherine Winkworth, 1863, alt.*

Valet will ich dir geben
Melchior Teschner, 1613

1 O Je-sus, King of Glo-ry, Both Da-vid's Lord and Son!
2 The East-ern sa-ges, bring-ing Their trib-ute gifts to Thee,
3 Thou art a might-y Mon-arch, As by Thy Word is told,
4 Yet art Thou decked with beau-ty, With rays of glo-rious light;

Thy realm en-dures for-ev-er, In heav'n is fixed Thy throne.
Bear wit-ness to Thy king-dom And hum-bly bow the knee.
Yet car-est Thou but lit-tle For earth-ly goods or gold;
Thy works pro-claim Thy good-ness, And all Thy ways are right.

Help that in earth's do-min-ions, Thro'-out from pole to pole,
To Thee the star is point-ing, And the pro-phet-ic Word;
On no proud steed Thou rid-est, Thou wear'st no jew-eled crown
Vouch-safe to shield Thy peo-ple With Thine al-might-y arm

Thy reign may spread sal-va-tion To each be-night-ed soul.
Hence joy-ous-ly we hail Thee: Our Sav-ior and our Lord!
Nor dwell'st in lord-ly cas-tle, But bear-est scoff and frown.
That they may dwell in safe-ty From those who mean them harm. Amen.

O Jesus, King of Glory

5 Ah, look on me with pity
  Though I am weak and poor;
Admit me to Thy kingdom
  To dwell there, blest and sure.
I pray Thee, guide and keep me
  Safe from my bitter foes,
From sin and death and Satan;
  Free me from all my woes.

6 And bid Thy Word within me
  Shine as the fairest star;
Keep sin and all false doctrine
  Forever from me far.
Help me confess Thee truly
  And with Thy Christendom
Here own Thee King and Savior
  And in the world to come.

The Star Proclaims the King Is Here 131

Matt. 2: 9
Hostis Herodes impie
Coelius Sedulius, c. 450
Tr., John M. Neale, 1852, alt.

L. M.

Wo Gott zum Haus
"Geistliche Lieder"
Wittenberg, 1535

1 The star pro-claims the King is here; But, Her - od, why this sense-less fear? He takes no realms of earth a - way Who gives the realms of heav'n-ly day.

2 The wis - er Ma - gi see from far And fol - low on His guid-ing star; And led by light, to light they press And by their gifts their God con - fess.

3 With - in the Jor-dan's crys - tal flood In meek-ness stands the Lamb of God And, sin - less, sanc - ti - fies the wave, Man-kind from sin to cleanse and save.

A - men.

4 At Cana first His power is shown;
  His might the blushing waters own
And, changing as He speaks the word,
  Flow wine, obedient to their Lord.

5 All glory, Jesus, be to Thee
  For this Thy glad epiphany;
Whom with the Father we adore
  And Holy Ghost forevermore.

132 O God of God, O Light of Light

L. M. D.

Ps. 43: 3
John Julian, 1883

O grosser Gott
"Gesang- und Notenbuch"
Stuttgart, 1744

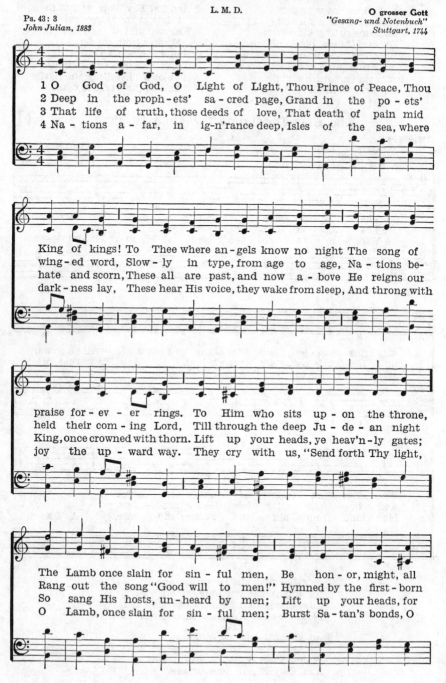

1 O God of God, O Light of Light, Thou Prince of Peace, Thou King of kings! To Thee where an-gels know no night The song of praise for-ev-er rings. To Him who sits up-on the throne, The Lamb once slain for sin-ful men, Be hon-or, might, all

2 Deep in the proph-ets' sa-cred page, Grand in the po-ets' wing-ed word, Slow-ly in type, from age to age, Na-tions be-held their com-ing Lord, Till through the deep Ju-de-an night Rang out the song "Good will to men!" Hymned by the first-born

3 That life of truth, those deeds of love, That death of pain mid hate and scorn, These all are past, and now a-bove He reigns our King, once crowned with thorn. Lift up your heads, ye heav'n-ly gates; So sang His hosts, un-heard by men; Lift up your heads, for

4 Na-tions a-far, in ig-n'rance deep, Isles of the sea, where dark-ness lay, These hear His voice, they wake from sleep, And throng with joy the up-ward way. They cry with us, "Send forth Thy light, O Lamb, once slain for sin-ful men; Burst Sa-tan's bonds, O

O God of God, O Light of Light

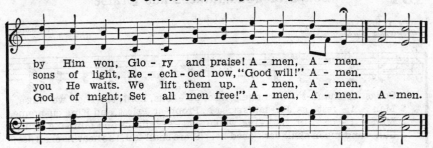

by Him won, Glo-ry and praise! A-men, A-men.
sons of light, Re-ech-oed now, "Good will!" A-men.
you He waits. We lift them up. A-men, A-men.
God of might; Set all men free!" A-men, A-men. A-men.

5 Sing to the Lord a glorious song,
  Sing to His name, His love forthtell;
Sing on, heaven's host, His praise prolong;
Sing, ye who now on earth do dwell:
  Worthy the Lamb for sinners slain;
    From angels praise and thanks from men;
  Worthy the Lamb, enthroned to reign,
    Glory and power! Amen, Amen.

Within the Father's House

133

S. M.

Franconia
"Harmonischer Liederschatz"
Frankfurt, 1738

Luke 2: 41-52
James R. Woodford, 1863

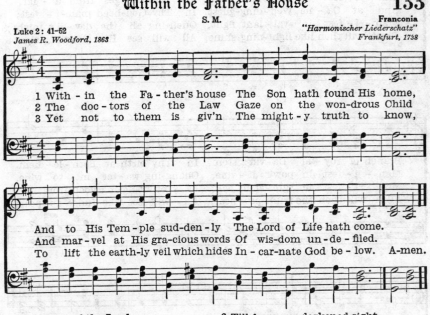

1 With-in the Fa-ther's house The Son hath found His home,
2 The doc-tors of the Law Gaze on the won-drous Child
3 Yet not to them is giv'n The might-y truth to know,

And to His Tem-ple sud-den-ly The Lord of Life hath come.
And mar-vel at His gra-cious words Of wis-dom un-de-filed.
To lift the earth-ly veil which hides In-car-nate God be-low. A-men.

4 The secret of the Lord
  Escapes each human eye,
And faithful pondering hearts await
  The full epiphany.

5 Lord, visit Thou our souls
  And teach us by Thy grace
Each dim revealing of Thyself
  With loving awe to trace,

6 Till from our darkened sight
  The cloud shall pass away
And on the cleansed soul shall burst
  The everlasting day,

7 Till we behold Thy face
  And know as we are known
Thee, Father, Son, and Holy Ghost,
  Coequal Three in One.

134 Songs of Thankfulness and Praise

7. 7. 7. 7. D.

1 Pet. 1: 20
Christopher Wordsworth, 1862

St. George
George J. Elvey, 1858

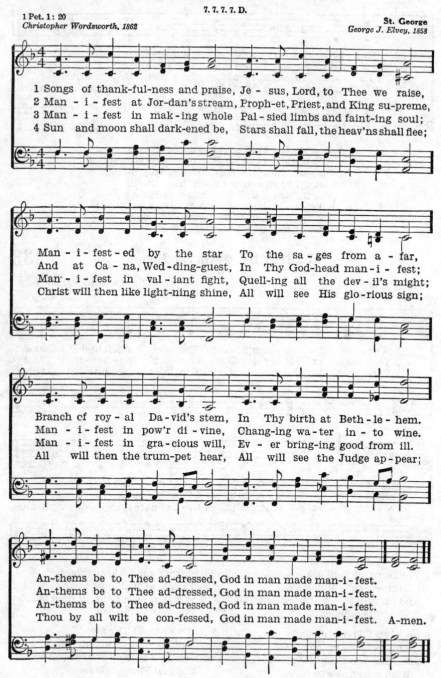

1 Songs of thank-ful-ness and praise, Je - sus, Lord, to Thee we raise,
2 Man - i - fest at Jor-dan's stream, Proph-et, Priest, and King su-preme,
3 Man - i - fest in mak-ing whole Pal - sied limbs and faint-ing soul;
4 Sun and moon shall dark-ened be, Stars shall fall, the heav'ns shall flee;

Man - i - fest-ed by the star To the sa - ges from a - far,
And at Ca - na, Wed-ding-guest, In Thy God-head man-i - fest;
Man - i - fest in val-iant fight, Quell-ing all the dev-il's might;
Christ will then like light-ning shine, All will see His glo-rious sign;

Branch of roy - al Da-vid's stem, In Thy birth at Beth - le - hem.
Man - i - fest in pow'r di - vine, Chang-ing wa - ter in - to wine.
Man - i - fest in gra-cious will, Ev - er bring-ing good from ill.
All will then the trum-pet hear, All will see the Judge ap-pear;

An-thems be to Thee ad-dressed, God in man made man-i - fest.
An-thems be to Thee ad-dressed, God in man made man-i - fest.
An-thems be to Thee ad-dressed, God in man made man-i - fest.
Thou by all wilt be con-fessed, God in man made man-i - fest. A-men.

Songs of Thankfulness and Praise

5 Grant us grace to see Thee, Lord,
  Mirrored in Thy holy Word;
  May we imitate Thee now
  And be pure as pure art Thou
  That we like to Thee may be
  At Thy great Epiphany
  And may praise Thee, ever blest,
  God in man made manifest.

TRANSFIGURATION

'Tis Good, Lord, to Be Here

135

S. M.

Potsdam
"Church Psalter," 1854
Johann S. Bach, †1750, ad.

Matt. 17: 4
Joseph A. Robinson, 1888

1 'Tis good, Lord, to be here, Thy glo-ry fills the night;
2 'Tis good, Lord, to be here, Thy beau-ty to be-hold
3 Ful-fill-er of the past, Prom-ise of things to be,

Thy face and garments, like the sun, Shine with unborrowed light.
Where Mo-ses and E-li-jah stand, Thy mes-sen-gers of old.
We hail Thy bod-y glo-ri-fied And our re-demp-tion see. A-men.

4 Before we taste of death,
  We see Thy kingdom come;
  We fain would hold the vision bright
  And make this hill our home.

5 'Tis good, Lord, to be here.
  Yet we may not remain;
  But since Thou bidst us leave the mount,
  Come with us to the plain.

136 Angels from the Realms of Glory

8. 7. 8. 7. 4. 4. 7.

Matt. 2: 2
James Montgomery, 1816, 1825, ab.

Regent Square
Henry Smart, 1867

1 An - gels from the realms of glo - ry, Wing your flight o'er
2 Shep-herds in the fields a - bid - ing, Watch-ing o'er your
3 Sa - ges, leave your con - tem - pla-tions, Bright-er vi - sions
4 Saints be - fore the al - tar bend-ing, Watch-ing long in

all the earth; Ye who sang cre - a - tion's sto - ry,
flocks by night, God with man is now re - sid - ing,
beam a - far; Seek the great De - sire of na - tions,
hope and fear, Sud - den - ly the Lord, de - scend-ing,

Now pro - claim Mes - si - ah's birth: Come and wor-ship,
Yon - der shines the In - fant Light: Come and wor-ship,
Ye have seen His na - tal star: Come and wor-ship,
In His Tem - ple shall ap - pear: Come and wor-ship,

Come and wor-ship; Wor-ship Christ, the new-born King.
Come and wor-ship; Wor-ship Christ, the new-born King.
Come and wor-ship; Wor-ship Christ, the new-born King.
Come and wor-ship; Wor-ship Christ, the new-born King. A - men.

In Peace and Joy I Now Depart

8. 5. 8. 4. 7. 7.

Luke 2 : 29–32
Mit Fried' und Freud' ich fahr' dahin
Martin Luther, 1524
Tr., Leonard W. Bacon, 1884, alt.

Mit Fried' und Freud'
"Geistliches Gesangbüchlein"
Wittenberg, 1524

1 In peace and joy I now de-part At God's dis-pos - ing;
2 'Tis Christ that wrought this work for me, My faith-ful Sav - ior,

For full of com-fort is my heart, Soft re-pos - ing.
Whom Thou hast made mine eyes to see By Thy fa - vor.

So the Lord hath promised me, And death is but a slum - ber.
Now I know He is my Life, My Help in need and dy - ing. A-men.

3 Him Thou hast unto all set forth
   Their great Salvation
And to His kingdom called the earth,
   Every nation,
By Thy dear and wholesome Word,
   In every place resounding.

4 He is the Hope and saving Light
   Of lands benighted;
By Him are they who dwelt in night
   Fed and lighted.
He is Israel's Praise and Bliss,
   Their Joy, Reward, and Glory.

138 Thou Light of Gentile Nations

Luke 2 : 32
Herr Jesu, Licht der Heiden
Johann Franck, 1674
Tr., Catherine Winkworth, 1863, alt.

7. 6. 7. 6. D.

Valet will ich dir geben
Melchior Teschner, 1613

1 Thou Light of Gen-tile na-tions, Thou Sav-ior from a-bove,
2 Yea, Lord, Thy ser-vants meet Thee In ev-'ry ho-ly place
3 Be Thou our Joy and Bright-ness, Our Cheer in pain and loss,
4 Let us, O Lord, be faith-ful Like Sim-eon to the end,

Drawn by Thy Spir-it's lead-ing, We come with joy and love
Where Thy true Word has prom-ised That we should see Thy face.
Our Sun in dark-est ter-ror, The Glo-ry round our cross,
So that his prayer ex-ul-tant May from our hearts as-cend:

In-to Thy ho-ly tem-ple And wait with ear-nest mind
To-day Thou still dost grant us Who gath-er round Thee here
A Star for sink-ing spir-its, A Bea-con in dis-tress,
"O Lord, now let Thy ser-vant De-part in peace, I pray,

As Sim-eon once had wait-ed His God and Lord to find.
In arms of faith to bear Thee As did that a-ged seer.
Phy-si-cian, Friend, in sick-ness, In death our Hap-pi-ness.
Since I have seen my Sav-ior And here be-held His day." A-men.

Thou Light of Gentile Nations

5 My Savior, I behold Thee
  With faith's enlightened eye;
Of Thee no foe can rob me,
  His threats I can defy.
Within Thy heart abiding,
  As Thou, O Lord, in me,
Death can no longer frighten
  Nor part my soul from Thee.

6 Lord, here on earth Thou seemest
  At times to frown on me,
And through my tears I often
  Can scarce distinguish Thee;
But in the heavenly mansions
  Shall nothing dim my sight;
There shall I see Thy glory
  In never-changing light.

In His Temple Now Behold Him   139

Luke 2: 22
St. 1–3, Henry J. Pye, 1851
St. 4, William Cooke, 1853

8. 7. 8. 7. 8. 7.

Sieh, hier bin ich
"Geistreiches Gesangbuch"
Darmstadt, 1698

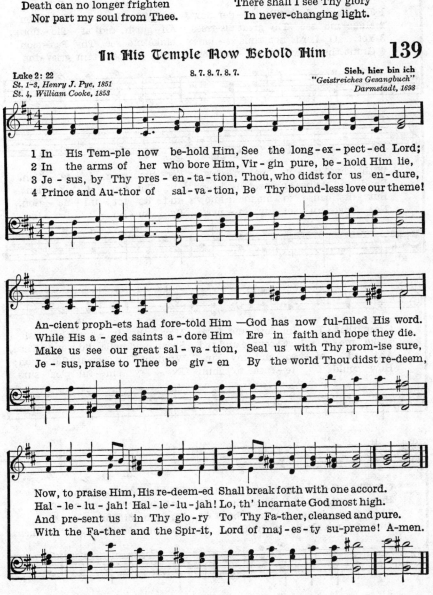

1 In His Tem-ple now be-hold Him, See the long-ex-pect-ed Lord;
2 In the arms of her who bore Him, Vir - gin pure, be-hold Him lie,
3 Je - sus, by Thy pres - en - ta - tion, Thou, who didst for us en - dure,
4 Prince and Au-thor of sal - va-tion, Be Thy bound-less love our theme!

An-cient proph-ets had fore-told Him —God has now ful-filled His word.
While His a - ged saints a - dore Him Ere in faith and hope they die.
Make us see our great sal - va - tion, Seal us with Thy prom-ise sure,
Je - sus, praise to Thee be giv - en By the world Thou didst re-deem,

Now, to praise Him, His re-deem-ed Shall break forth with one accord.
Hal - le - lu - jah! Hal - le - lu - jah! Lo, th' incarnate God most high.
And pre-sent us in Thy glo - ry To Thy Fa-ther, cleansed and pure.
With the Fa-ther and the Spir - it, Lord of maj - es - ty su-preme! A-men.

140 Jesus, I Will Ponder Now

7. 6. 7. 6. D. Trochaic

Luke 18: 31–34
Jesu, deine Passion
Sigismund v. Birken, 1653
Tr., August Crull, †1923, alt.

Jesu Kreuz, Leiden und Pein
Melchior Vulpius, 1609

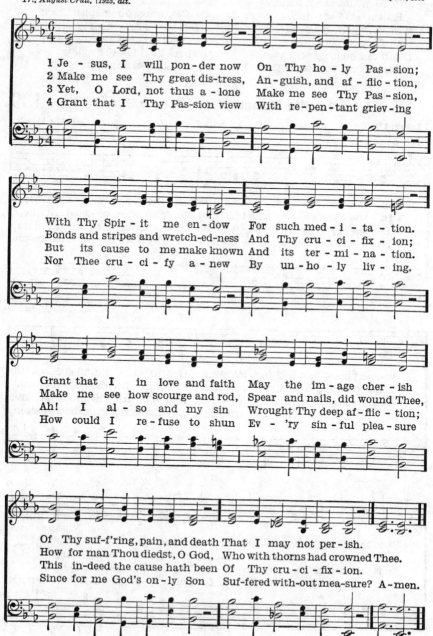

1 Je - sus, I will pon-der now On Thy ho - ly Pas-sion;
2 Make me see Thy great dis-tress, An-guish, and af - flic-tion,
3 Yet, O Lord, not thus a - lone Make me see Thy Pas-sion,
4 Grant that I Thy Pas-sion view With re-pen-tant griev-ing

With Thy Spir - it me en-dow For such med - i - ta - tion.
Bonds and stripes and wretch-ed-ness And Thy cru - ci - fix - ion;
But its cause to me make known And its ter - mi - na - tion.
Nor Thee cru - ci - fy a - new By un - ho - ly liv - ing.

Grant that I in love and faith May the im - age cher - ish
Make me see how scourge and rod, Spear and nails, did wound Thee,
Ah! I al - so and my sin Wrought Thy deep af - flic - tion;
How could I re - fuse to shun Ev - 'ry sin - ful plea - sure

Of Thy suf-f'ring, pain, and death That I may not per - ish.
How for man Thou diedst, O God, Who with thorns had crowned Thee.
This in-deed the cause hath been Of Thy cru - ci - fix - ion.
Since for me God's on - ly Son Suf-fered with-out mea-sure? A - men.

Jesus, I Will Ponder Now

5 If my sins give me alarm
  And my conscience grieve me,
Let Thy cross my fear disarm,
  Peace of conscience give me.
Grant that I may trust in Thee
  And Thy holy Passion.
If His Son so loveth me,
  God must have compassion.

6 Grant that I may willingly
  Bear with Thee my crosses,
Learning humbleness of Thee,
  Peace mid pain and losses.
May I give Thee love for love!
  Hear me, O my Savior,
That I may in heaven above
  Sing Thy praise forever.

Enslaved by Sin and Bound in Chains   141

L. M.

1 Pet. 1: 18, 19
Anne Steele, 1760

Wenn wir in höchsten Nöten
"Genevan Psalter," 1547

1 En-slaved by sin and bound   in   chains,   Be-neath its dread-ful
2 Nor gold nor gems could buy   our   peace,   Nor all the world's col-
3 Je - sus, the Lord, the might - y   God,   An all - suf - fi - cient
4 Je - sus the Sac - ri - fice   be - came   To res - cue guilt-y

ty - rant sway,   And doomed to ev - er - last - ing pains,
lect - ed store   Suf - fice to pur - chase our re - lease;
ran - som paid.   O match-less price! His pre - cious blood
souls from hell;   The spot - less, bleed-ing, dy - ing Lamb

We wretch - ed, guilt - y cap - tives lay.
A thou - sand worlds were all too poor.
For vile, re - bel - lious trai - tors shed.
Be - neath a - veng - ing Jus - tice fell.   A - men.

5 Amazing goodness! Love divine!
  Oh, may our grateful hearts adore
The matchless grace nor yield to sin
  Nor wear its cruel fetters more!

142 A Lamb Goes Uncomplaining Forth

Is. 53: 7
Ein Lämmlein geht
Paul Gerhardt, 1648, cento
Tr., composite

8. 7. 8. 7. 8. 8. 7. 8. 7.

An Wasserflüssen Babylon
"Deutsch Kirchenamt"
Strassburg, 1525

1 A Lamb goes un-com-plain-ing forth, The guilt of all men bear-ing;
2 This Lamb is Christ, the soul's great Friend, The Lamb of God, our Sav-ior;
3 "Yea, Fa-ther, yea, most will-ing-ly I'll bear what Thou commandest;
4 From morn till eve my theme shall be Thy mercy's wondrous mea-sure;

And la-den with the sins of earth, None else the bur-den
Him God the Fa-ther chose to send To gain for us His
My will con-forms to Thy de-cree, I do what Thou de-
To sac-ri-fice my-self for Thee Shall be my aim and

shar-ing! Goes pa-tient on, grows weak and faint, To slaugh-ter
fa-vor. "Go forth, My Son," the Fa-ther saith, "And free men
mand-est." O won-drous Love, what hast Thou done! The Fa-ther
plea-sure. My stream of life shall ev-er be A cur-rent

led with-out com-plaint, That spot-less life to of-fer;
from the fear of death, From guilt and con-dem-na-tion.
of-fers up His Son! The Son, con-tent, de-scend-eth!
flow-ing cease-less-ly, Thy con-stant praise out-pour-ing.

A Lamb Goes Uncomplaining Forth

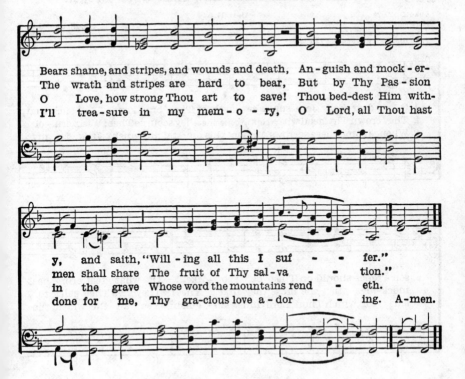

Bears shame, and stripes, and wounds and death, An-guish and mock-er-
The wrath and stripes are hard to bear, But by Thy Pas-sion
O Love, how strong Thou art to save! Thou bed-dest Him with-
I'll trea-sure in my mem-o-ry, O Lord, all Thou hast

y, and saith, "Will-ing all this I suf - - fer."
men shall share The fruit of Thy sal-va - - tion."
in the grave Whose word the mountains rend - eth.
done for me, Thy gra-cious love a-dor - - ing. A-men.

5 Of death I am no more afraid,
   New life from Thee is flowing;
Thy cross affords me cooling shade
   When noonday's sun is glowing.
When by my grief I am opprest,
On Thee my weary soul shall rest
   Serenely as on pillows.
Thou art my Anchor when by woe
My bark is driven to and fro
   On trouble's surging billows.

6 And when Thy glory I shall see
   And taste Thy kingdom's pleasure,
Thy blood my royal robe shall be,
   My joy beyond all measure;
When I appear before Thy throne,
Thy righteousness shall be my crown,—
   With these I need not hide me.
And there, in garments richly wrought
As Thine own bride, I shall be brought
   To stand in joy beside Thee.

143 O Dearest Jesus, What Law Hast Thou Broken

Luke 23: 20–24
Herzliebster Jesu
Johann Heermann, 1630
Tr., Catherine Winkworth, 1863, alt.

11. 11. 11. 5.

Herzliebster Jesu
Johann Crüger, 1640

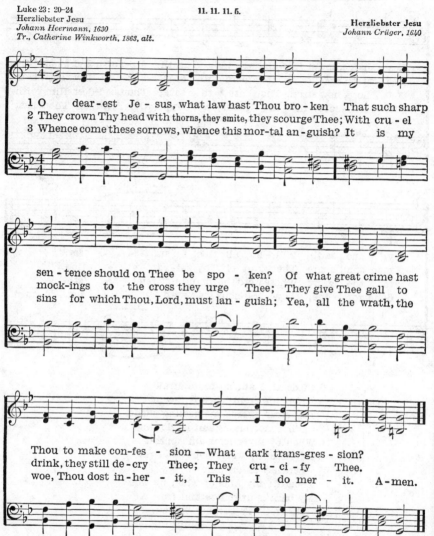

1 O   dear-est Je - sus, what law hast Thou bro-ken   That such sharp
2 They crown Thy head with thorns, they smite, they scourge Thee; With cru - el
3 Whence come these sorrows, whence this mor-tal an-guish? It   is my

sen - tence should on Thee be spo - ken? Of what great crime hast
mock-ings to   the cross they urge   Thee; They give Thee gall to
sins   for which Thou, Lord, must lan - guish; Yea, all the wrath, the

Thou to make con-fes - sion — What   dark trans-gres - sion?
drink, they still de - cry   Thee; They   cru - ci - fy   Thee.
woe, Thou dost in - her - it, This   I do mer - it. A - men.

4 What punishment so strange is suffered yonder!
  The Shepherd dies for sheep that loved to wander;
  The Master pays the debt His servants owe Him,
  Who would not know Him.

5 The sinless Son of God must die in sadness;
  The sinful child of man may live in gladness;
  Man forfeited his life and is acquitted —
  God is committed.

O Dearest Jesus, What Law Hast Thou Broken

6 There was no spot in me by sin untainted;
Sick with sin's poison, all my heart had fainted;
My heavy guilt to hell had well-nigh brought me,
Such woe it wrought me.

7 O wondrous love, whose depth no heart hath sounded,
That brought Thee here, by foes and thieves surrounded!
All worldly pleasures, heedless, I was trying
While Thou wert dying.

8 O mighty King, no time can dim Thy glory!
How shall I spread abroad Thy wondrous story?
How shall I find some worthy gifts to proffer?
What dare I offer?

9 For vainly doth our human wisdom ponder —
Thy woes, Thy mercy, still transcend our wonder.
Oh, how should I do aught that could delight Thee!
Can I requite Thee?

10 Yet unrequited, Lord, I would not leave Thee;
I will renounce whate'er doth vex or grieve Thee
And quench with thoughts of Thee and prayers most lowly
All fires unholy.

11 But since my strength will nevermore suffice me
To crucify desires that still entice me,
To all good deeds, oh, let Thy Spirit win me
And reign within me!

12 I'll think upon Thy mercy without ceasing,
That earth's vain joys to me no more be pleasing;
To do Thy will shall be my sole endeavor
Henceforth forever.

13 Whate'er of earthly good this life may grant me,
I'll risk for Thee; no shame, no cross, shall daunt me.
I shall not fear what man can do to harm me
Nor death alarm me.

14 But worthless is my sacrifice, I own it;
Yet, Lord, for love's sake Thou wilt not disown it;
Thou wilt accept my gift in Thy great meekness
Nor shame my weakness.

15 And when, dear Lord, before Thy throne in heaven
To me the crown of joy at last is given,
Where sweetest hymns Thy saints forever raise Thee,
I, too, shall praise Thee.

144 Jesus, Grant that Balm and Healing

8. 7. 8. 7. 7. 7. 8. 8.

1 Pet. 2 : 24
Jesu, deine tiefen Wunden
Johann Heermann, 1644, ab.
Tr., composite

Der am Kreuz
Johann B. König, 1738

1 Je - sus, grant that balm and heal-ing In Thy ho - ly wounds I find,
2 Should some lust or sharp temp-ta-tion Prove too strong for flesh and blood,
3 If the world my heart en - tic - es On the broad and eas - y road
4 Ev - 'ry wound that pains or grieves me, By Thy stripes, Lord, is made whole;

Ev - 'ry hour that I am feel-ing Pains of bod - y and of mind.
Let me think up - on Thy Pas-sion, And the breach is soon made good.
With its mirth and lur - ing vi - ces, Let me think up - on the load
When I'm faint, Thy Cross re - vives me, Grant-ing new life to my soul.

Should some e - vil tho't with-in Tempt my treach'rous heart to sin,
Or should Sa - tan press me hard, Let me then be on my guard,
Thou didst car - ry and en - dure That I flee all tho'ts im - pure,
Yea, Thy com-fort ren - ders sweet Ev - 'ry bit - ter cup I meet;

Show the per-il, and from sinning Keep me ere its first be - gin - ning.
Saying, "Christ for me was wounded," That the Tempter flee confounded.
Ban - ish-ing each wild e-mo-tion, Calm and blest in my de - vo - tion.
For Thy all - a - ton-ing Pas-sion Has procured my soul's sal - va - tion. A-men.

Jesus, Grant that Balm and Healing

5 O my God, my Rock and Tower,
   Grant that in Thy death I trust,
Knowing Death has lost his power
   Since Thou trodd'st him in the dust.
Savior, let Thine agony
Ever help and comfort me;
When I die, be my Protection,
Light and Life and Resurrection.

Jesus, Refuge of the Weary   145

8. 7. 8. 7. D.

Mark 15: 29, 30
Giesù sommo conforto
Girolamo Savonarola, 1563
Tr., Jane F. Wilde, 1853

O du Liebe
"Musikalischer Christenschatz"
Basel, 1745

1 Je - sus, Ref-uge of the wea-ry, Blest Re-deem-er, whom we love,
2 Do we pass that cross un-heed-ing, Breath-ing no re-pen-tant vow,
3 Je - sus, may our hearts be burn-ing With more fer-vent love for Thee!

Foun-tain in life's des-ert drear-y, Sav-ior from the world a-bove,
Tho' we see Thee wound-ed, bleed-ing, See Thy thorn-en-cir-cled brow?
May our eyes be ev-er turn-ing To Thy cross of ag-o-ny

Oh, how oft Thine eyes, of-fend-ed, Gaze up-on the sin-ner's fall!
Yet Thy sin-less death hath bro't us Life e-ter-nal, peace, and rest;
Till in glo-ry, part-ed nev-er From the bless-ed Sav-ior's side,

Yet, up-on the cross ex-tend-ed, Thou didst bear the pain of all.
On-ly what Thy grace hath taught us Calms the sinner's stormy breast.
Grav-en in our hearts for-ev-er, Dwell the cross, the Cru-ci-fied! A-men.

146

Lamb of God, Pure and Holy

John 1: 29
O Lamm Gottes, unschuldig
Nikolaus Decius, 1531
Tr., composite

7. 7. 7. 7. 7. 7. 5. 6.

O Lamm Gottes, unschuldig
"Christl. Kirchenordnung"
Erfurt, 1542

1 Lamb of God, pure and ho - - ly, Who on the cross didst suf-fer,
2 Lamb of God, pure and ho - - ly, Who on the cross didst suf-fer,
3 Lamb of God, pure and ho - - ly, Who on the cross didst suf-fer,

Ev - er pa-tient and low - - ly, Thy-self to scorn didst of - fer.
Ev - er pa-tient and low - - ly, Thy-self to scorn didst of - fer.
Ev - er pa-tient and low - - ly, Thy-self to scorn didst of - fer.

All sins Thou bor-est for us, Else had de-spair reigned o'er us:
All sins Thou bor-est for us, Else had de-spair reigned o'er us:
All sins Thou bor-est for us, Else had de-spair reigned o'er us:

Have mer-cy on us, O Je - sus! O Je - sus!
Have mer-cy on us, O Je - sus! O Je - sus!
Thy peace be with us, O Je - sus! O Je - sus! A-men.

O Christ, Thou Lamb of God

Irregular

John 1: 29
Christe, du Lamm Gottes
From the German, 1528
Tr., unknown

Christe, du Lamm Gottes
Johann Bugenhagen's "Kirchenordnung"
Braunschweig, 1528

O Christ, Thou Lamb of God, that tak-est a-way the sin of the world,

have mer-cy up-on us! O Christ, Thou Lamb of God, that

tak-est a-way the sin of the world, have mer-cy up-on us!

O Christ, Thou Lamb of God, that tak-est a-way the sin of the world,

grant us Thy peace! . . . A - - - - - men.

148 Lord Jesus Christ, My Life, My Light

Luke 23: 33
O Jesu Christ, mein's Lebens Licht
Martin Behm, 1610, cento
Tr., Catherine Winkworth, 1858, 1863, alt.

L. M.

O Jesu Christ, mein's
"*Nürnbergisches Gesangbuch,*" 1676

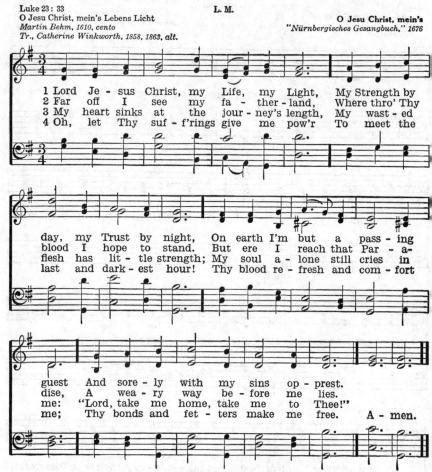

1 Lord Jesus Christ, my Life, my Light, My Strength by day, my Trust by night, On earth I'm but a passing guest And sorely with my sins opprest.

2 Far off I see my fatherland, Where thro' Thy blood I hope to stand. But ere I reach that Paradise, A weary way before me lies.

3 My heart sinks at the journey's length, My wasted flesh has little strength; My soul alone still cries in me: "Lord, take me home, take me to Thee!"

4 Oh, let Thy suff'rings give me pow'r To meet the last and darkest hour! Thy blood refresh and comfort me; Thy bonds and fetters make me free. A-men.

5 Oh, let Thy holy wounds for me
Clefts in the rock forever be
Where as a dove my soul can hide
And safe from Satan's rage abide.

6 And when my spirit flies away,
Thy dying words shall be my stay.
Thy cross shall be my staff in life,
Thy holy grave my rest from strife.

7 Lord, in Thy nail-prints let me read
That Thou to save me hast decreed
And grant that in Thine opened side
My troubled soul may ever hide.

8 Since Thou hast died, the Pure, the Just,
I take my homeward way in trust.
The gates of heaven, Lord, open wide
When here I may no more abide.

Lord Jesus Christ, My Life, My Light

9 And when the last Great Day shall come
And Thou, our Judge, shalt speak the **doom,**
Let me with joy behold the light
And set me then upon Thy right.

10 Renew this wasted flesh of mine
That like the sun it there may shine
Among the angels pure and bright,
Yea, like Thyself in glorious light.

11 Ah, then I'll have my heart's desire,
When, singing with the angels' choir,
Among the ransomed of Thy grace,
Forever I'll behold Thy face!

Come to Calvary's Holy Mountain   149

8. 7. 8. 7. 7. 7.

Matt. 11: 28
James Montgomery, 1819

Consolation
Ludvig M. Lindeman, 1871

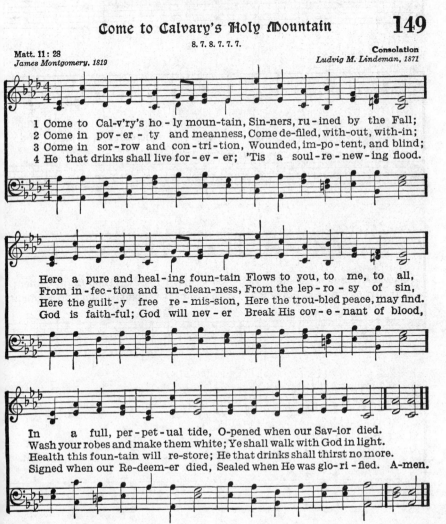

1 Come to Cal-v'ry's ho - ly moun-tain, Sin-ners, ru - ined by the Fall;
2 Come in pov - er - ty and meanness, Come de-filed, with-out, with-in;
3 Come in sor-row and con-tri-tion, Wounded, im-po-tent, and blind;
4 He that drinks shall live for - ev - er; 'Tis a soul-re - new-ing flood.

Here a pure and heal-ing foun-tain Flows to you, to me, to all,
From in-fec-tion and un-clean-ness, From the lep-ro-sy of sin,
Here the guilt-y free re-mis-sion, Here the trou-bled peace, may find.
God is faith-ful; God will nev - er Break His cov-e-nant of blood,

In a full, per-pet-ual tide, O-pened when our Sav-ior died.
Wash your robes and make them white; Ye shall walk with God in light.
Health this foun-tain will re-store; He that drinks shall thirst no more.
Signed when our Re-deem-er died, Sealed when He was glo-ri-fied. A-men.

150 Lord Jesus, Thou art Going Forth

John 19: 16–17
So gehst du nun, mein Jesu, hin
St. 1–3, 5, Kaspar F. Nachtenhöfer, 1651
St. 4, Magnus D. Omeis, 1699
Tr., W. Gustave Polack, 1940

8. 7. 8. 7. 4. 4. 7. 4. 4. 7.

So gehst du nun
"Geistreiches Gesangbuch"
Darmstadt, 1698

1 (*The Soul:*) Lord Je-sus, Thou art go-ing forth For me Thy
2 (*Jesus:*) O Soul, at-tend thou and be-hold The fruit of

life to of-fer; For me, a sin-ner from my birth, Who
thy trans-gres-sion! My por-tion is the curse of old And

caused all Thou must suf-fer. So be it, then, Thou Hope of men;
for man's sin My Pas-sion. Now comes the night Of sin's dread might,

Thee I shall fol-low weep-ing, Tears flow-ing free
Man's guilt I here am bear-ing. Oh, weigh it, Soul;

Lord Jesus, Thou art Going Forth

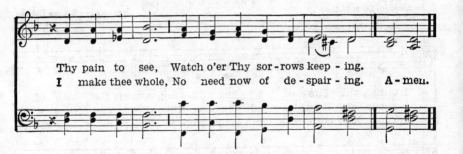

Thy pain to see, Watch o'er Thy sor-rows keep-ing.
I make thee whole, No need now of de-spair-ing. A-men.

3 (*The Soul:*) 'Tis I, Lord Jesus, I confess,
　　　　Who should have borne sin's wages
And lost the peace of heavenly bliss
　　　　Through everlasting ages.
　　　　　Instead 'tis Thou
　　　　　Who goest now
My punishment to carry.
　　　　Thy death and blood
　　　　Lead me to God;
By grace I there may tarry.

4 (*Jesus:*)　　O Soul, I take upon Me now
　　　　The pain thou shouldst have suffered.
Behold, with grace I thee endow,
　　　　Grace freely to thee offered.
　　　　　The curse I choose
　　　　　That thou mightst lose
Sin's curse and guilt forever.
　　　　My gift of love
　　　　From heaven above
Will give thee blessing ever.

5 (*The Soul:*) What can I for such love divine
　　　　To Thee, Lord Jesus, render?
No merit has this heart of mine;
　　　　Yet while I live, I'll tender
　　　　　Myself alone,
　　　　　And all I own,
In love to serve before Thee;
　　　　Then when time's past,
　　　　Take me at last
To Thy blest home in glory.

151 Christ, the Life of All the Living

Matt. 26: 64-67
Jesu, meines Lebens Leben
Ernst C. Homburg, 1659, ab.
Tr., Catherine Winkworth, 1863, alt.

8. 7. 8. 7. 8. 8. 7. 7.

Jesu, meines Lebens Leben
"Kirchengesangbuch"
Darmstadt, 1687

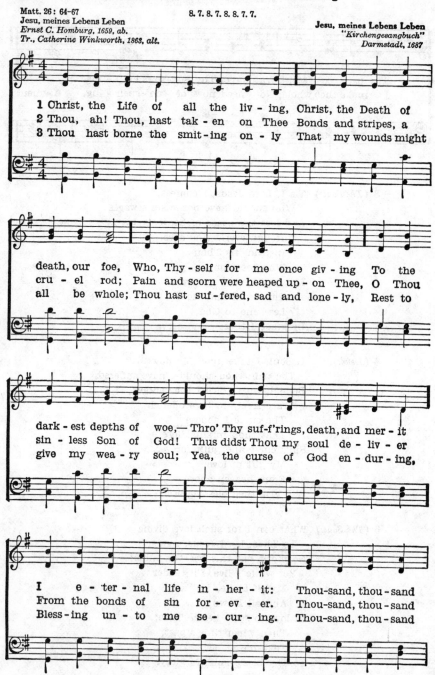

1 Christ, the Life of all the liv-ing, Christ, the Death of
2 Thou, ah! Thou, hast tak-en on Thee Bonds and stripes, a
3 Thou hast borne the smit-ing on-ly That my wounds might

death, our foe, Who, Thy-self for me once giv-ing To the
cru-el rod; Pain and scorn were heaped up-on Thee, O Thou
all be whole; Thou hast suf-fered, sad and lone-ly, Rest to

dark-est depths of woe,— Thro' Thy suf-f'rings, death, and mer-it
sin-less Son of God! Thus didst Thou my soul de-liv-er
give my wea-ry soul; Yea, the curse of God en-dur-ing,

I e-ter-nal life in-her-it: Thou-sand, thou-sand
From the bonds of sin for-ev-er. Thou-sand, thou-sand
Bless-ing un-to me se-cur-ing. Thou-sand, thou-sand

Christ, the Life of All the Living

thanks shall be, Dear-est Je-sus, un-to Thee.
thanks shall be, Dear-est Je-sus, un-to Thee.
thanks shall be, Dear-est Je-sus, un-to Thee. A-men.

4 Heartless scoffers did surround Thee,
    Treating Thee with shameful scorn
And with piercing thorns they crowned Thee.
    All disgrace Thou, Lord, hast borne
That as Thine Thou mightest own me
And with heavenly glory crown me.
    Thousand, thousand thanks shall be,
    Dearest Jesus, unto Thee.

5 Thou hast suffered men to bruise Thee
    That from pain I might be free;
Falsely did Thy foes accuse Thee,—
    Thence I gain security;
Comfortless Thy soul did languish
Me to comfort in my anguish.
    Thousand, thousand thanks shall be,
    Dearest Jesus, unto Thee.

6 Thou hast suffered great affliction
    And hast borne it patiently,
Even death by crucifixion,
    Fully to atone for me;
Thou didst choose to be tormented
That my doom should be prevented.
    Thousand, thousand thanks shall be,
    Dearest Jesus, unto Thee.

7 Then, for all that wrought my pardon,
    For Thy sorrows deep and sore,
For Thine anguish in the Garden,
    I will thank Thee evermore,
Thank Thee for Thy groaning, sighing,
For Thy bleeding and Thy dying,
    For that last triumphant cry,
    And shall praise Thee, Lord, on high.

152 When o'er My Sins I Sorrow

Heb. 10: 14

Wenn meine Sünd' mich kränken

7. 6. 7. 6. 8. 7. 6.

Justus Gesenius, 1646, cento
Tr., st. 1, Catherine Winkworth, 1863
Tr., st. 2–4, composite

Wenn meine Sünd'
Michael Prätorius, 1609

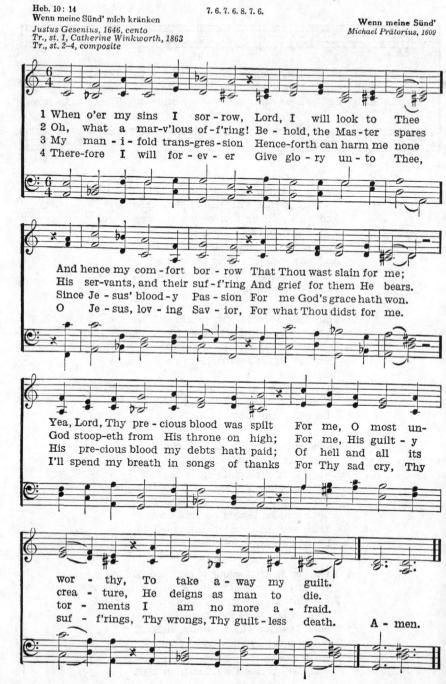

1 When o'er my sins I sor-row, Lord, I will look to Thee
2 Oh, what a mar-v'lous of-f'ring! Be-hold, the Mas-ter spares
3 My man-i-fold trans-gres-sion Hence-forth can harm me none
4 There-fore I will for-ev-er Give glo-ry un-to Thee,

And hence my com-fort bor-row That Thou wast slain for me;
His ser-vants, and their suf-f'ring And grief for them He bears.
Since Je-sus' blood-y Pas-sion For me God's grace hath won.
O Je-sus, lov-ing Sav-ior, For what Thou didst for me.

Yea, Lord, Thy pre-cious blood was spilt For me, O most un-
God stoop-eth from His throne on high; For me, His guilt-y
His pre-cious blood my debts hath paid; Of hell and all its
I'll spend my breath in songs of thanks For Thy sad cry, Thy

wor-thy, To take a-way my guilt.
crea-ture, He deigns as man to die.
tor-ments I am no more a-fraid.
suf-f'rings, Thy wrongs, Thy guilt-less death. A-men.

Stricken, Smitten, and Afflicted

153

8. 7. 8. 7. D.

Is. 53 : 3–5
Thomas Kelly, 1804

O mein Jesu, ich muss sterben
"Geistliche Volkslieder"
Paderborn, 1850

1 Strick-en, smit-ten, and af-flict-ed, See Him dy-ing on the tree!
2 Tell me, ye who hear Him groan-ing, Was there ev-er grief like His?
3 Ye who think of sin but light-ly Nor sup-pose the e-vil great
4 Here we have a firm foun-da-tion, Here the ref-uge of the lost;

'Tis the Christ by man re-ject-ed; Yes, my soul, 'tis He, 'tis He!
Friends thro' fear His cause dis-own-ing, Foes in-sult-ing His dis-tress;
Here may view its na-ture right-ly, Here its guilt may es-ti-mate.
Christ's the Rock of our sal-va-tion, His the name of which we boast.

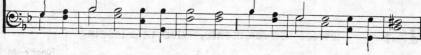

'Tis the long-ex-pect-ed Proph-et, Da-vid's Son, yet Da-vid's Lord;
Man-y hands were raised to wound Him, None would in-ter-pose to save;
Mark the Sac-ri-fice ap-point-ed, See who bears the aw-ful load;
Lamb of God, for sin-ners wound-ed, Sac-ri-fice to can-cel guilt!

Proofs I see suf-fi-cient of it: 'Tis the true and faith-ful Word.
But the deepest stroke that pierced Him Was the stroke that Justice gave.
'Tis the WORD, the LORD'S ANOINTED, Son of Man and Son of God.
None shall ev-er be con-found-ed Who on Him their hope have built. A-men.

154 Alas! and Did My Savior Bleed

C. M.

Luke 23 : 44–46
Isaac Watts, 1707

Martyrdom
Hugh Wilson, †1824

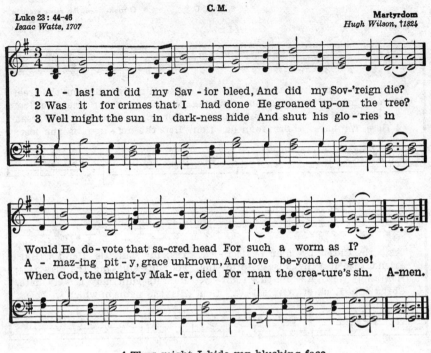

1 A - las! and did my Sav - ior bleed, And did my Sov-'reign die?
2 Was it for crimes that I had done He groaned up-on the tree?
3 Well might the sun in dark-ness hide And shut his glo - ries in

Would He de-vote that sa-cred head For such a worm as I?
A - maz-ing pit - y, grace unknown, And love be-yond de-gree!
When God, the might-y Mak-er, died For man the crea-ture's sin. A-men.

4 Thus might I hide my blushing face
   While His dear cross appears,
   Dissolve my heart in thankfulness,
   And melt mine eyes to tears.

5 But drops of grief can ne'er repay
   The debt of love I owe;
   Here, Lord, I give myself away,
   'Tis all that I can do.

155 Sweet the Moments, Rich in Blessing

8. 7. 8. 7.

1 John 1: 7
Walter Shirley, 1770, ad., alt.

Ringe recht
"Musikalischer Christenschatz"
Basel, 1745

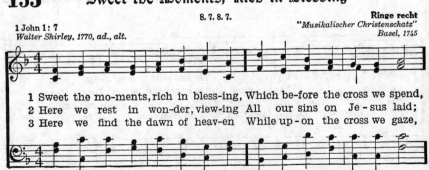

1 Sweet the mo-ments, rich in bless-ing, Which be-fore the cross we spend,
2 Here we rest in won-der, view-ing All our sins on Je - sus laid;
3 Here we find the dawn of heav-en While up - on the cross we gaze,

Sweet the Moments, Rich in Blessing

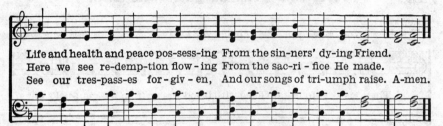

Life and health and peace pos-sess-ing From the sin-ners' dy-ing Friend.
Here we see re-demp-tion flow-ing From the sac-ri-fice He made.
See our tres-pass-es for-giv-en, And our songs of tri-umph raise. A-men.

4 Oh, that, near the cross abiding,
   We may to the Savior cleave,
Naught with Him our hearts dividing,
   All for Him content to leave!

5 Lord, in loving contemplation
   Fix our hearts and eyes on Thee
Till we taste Thy full salvation
   And Thine unveiled glory see.

Not All the Blood of Beasts   156

S. M.

Heb. 10: 4
Isaac Watts, 1709

Southwell
"Psalter"
William Daman, 1579

1 Not all the blood of beasts On Jew-ish al-tars slain
2 But Christ, the heav'n-ly Lamb, Takes all our sins a-way;
3 My faith would lay her hand On that dear head of Thine

Could give the guilt-y con-science peace Or wash a-way the stain.
A sac-ri-fice of no-bler name And rich-er blood than they.
While like a pen-i-tent I stand And there con-fess my sin. A-men.

4 My soul looks back to see
   The burden Thou didst bear
When hanging on the cursed tree
   And knows her guilt was there.

5 Believing, we rejoice
   To see the curse remove;
We bless the Lamb with cheerful voice
   And sing His bleeding love.

157 There Is a Fountain Filled with Blood

C. M.

Zech. 13: 1
William Cowper, 1771, cento

(FIRST TUNE)

Horsley
William Horsley, 1844

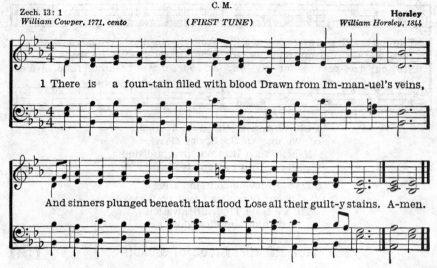

1 There is a foun-tain filled with blood Drawn from Im-man-uel's veins,

And sinners plunged beneath that flood Lose all their guilt-y stains. A-men.

2 The dying thief rejoiced to see
   That fountain in his day;
   And there have I, as vile as he,
   Washed all my sins away.

3 Dear dying Lamb, Thy precious blood
   Shall never lose its power
   Till all the ransomed Church of God
   Be saved to sin no more.

4 E'er since by faith I saw the stream
   Thy flowing wounds supply,
   Redeeming love has been my theme
   And shall be till I die.

5 When this poor lisping, stammering tongue
   Lies silent in the grave,
   Then in a nobler, sweeter song
   I'll sing Thy power to save.

There Is a Fountain Filled with Blood

C. M.

Zech. 13: 1
William Cowper, 1771, cento

(SECOND TUNE)

Cowper
Lowell Mason, 1830

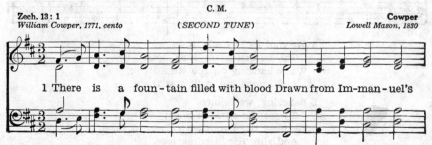

1 There is a foun-tain filled with blood Drawn from Im-man-uel's

There Is a Fountain Filled with Blood

veins, And sin-ners plunged be-neath that flood Lose all their guilt-y stains, Lose all their guilt-y stains. A-men.

Glory Be to Jesus

158

6. 5. 6. 5.

1 Pet. 1: 19
Viva! viva! Gesù
Italian, 18th century, cento
Tr., Edward Caswall, 1857

Wem in Leidenstagen
Friedrich Filitz, 1847

1 Glo-ry be to Je-sus, Who in bit-ter pains
2 Grace and life e-ter-nal In that blood I find;
3 Blest through end-less a-ges Be the pre-cious stream
4 A-bel's blood for ven-geance Plead-ed to the skies;

Poured for me the life-blood From His sa-cred veins!
Blest be His com-pas-sion, In-fi-nite-ly kind!
Which from end-less tor-ments Did the world re-deem!
But the blood of Je-sus For our par-don cries. A-men.

5 Oft as earth exulting
　Wafts its praise on high,
Angel hosts rejoicing
　Make their glad reply.

6 Lift we, then, our voices,
　Swell the mighty flood,
Louder still and louder
　Praise the precious blood!

159 Go to Dark Gethsemane

7. 7. 7. 7. 7. 7.

Lam. 3 : 19
James Montgomery, 1820, 1825

Gethsemane
Richard Redhead, 1853

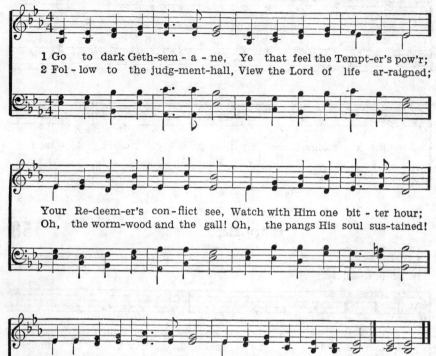

1 Go to dark Geth-sem-a-ne, Ye that feel the Tempt-er's pow'r;
2 Fol-low to the judg-ment-hall, View the Lord of life ar-raigned;

Your Re-deem-er's con-flict see, Watch with Him one bit-ter hour;
Oh, the worm-wood and the gall! Oh, the pangs His soul sus-tained!

Turn not from His griefs a-way, Learn of Je-sus Christ to pray.
Shun not suff'ring, shame, or loss; Learn of Him to bear the cross. A-men.

3 Calvary's mournful mountain climb;
    There, adoring at His feet,
Mark that miracle of time,
    God's own sacrifice complete.
"It is finished!" hear Him cry;
Learn of Jesus Christ to die.

4 Early hasten to the tomb
    Where they laid His breathless clay;
All is solitude and gloom,—
    Who hath taken Him away?
Christ is risen! He meets our eyes.
Savior, teach us so to rise.

All Glory, Laud, and Honor 160

Matt. 21 : 16
Gloria, laus et honor
St. Theodulph of Orleans, c. 820
Tr., *John M. Neale, 1854, alt.*

7. 6. 7. 6. D.

Valet will ich dir geben
Melchior Teschner, 1613

1 All glo - ry, laud, and hon - or To Thee, Re-deem - er, King,
2 All glo - ry, laud, and hon - or To Thee, Re-deem - er, King,
3 All glo - ry, laud, and hon - or To Thee, Re-deem - er, King,

To whom the lips of chil - dren Made sweet ho - san - nas ring.
To whom the lips of chil - dren Made sweet ho - san - nas ring.
To whom the lips of chil - dren Made sweet ho - san - nas ring.

Thou art the King of Is - rael, Thou Da - vid's roy - al Son,
The com - pa - ny of an - gels Are prais-ing Thee on high,
The peo - ple of the He - brews With palms be - fore Thee went;

Who in the Lord's name com-est, The King and Bless - ed One.
And mor - tal men and all things Cre - at - ed make re - ply.
Our praise and prayer and an-thems Be - fore Thee we pre-sent. A - men.

4 All glory, laud, and honor
  To Thee, Redeemer, King,
To whom the lips of children
  Made sweet hosannas ring.
To Thee, before Thy Passion,
  They sang their hymns of praise;
To Thee, now high exalted,
  Our melody we raise.

5 All glory, laud, and honor
  To Thee, Redeemer, King,
To whom the lips of children
  Made sweet hosannas ring.
Thou didst accept their praises;
  Accept the prayers we bring,
Who in all good delightest,
  Thou good and gracious King.

161

Hosanna, Loud Hosanna

7. 6. 7. 6. D.

Matt. 21: 15
Jeannette Threlfall, 1873

Ellacombe
*"Gesangbuch d. Herzogl.
Württemberg. Hofkapelle," 1784*

1 Ho - san - na, loud ho - san - na, The lit - tle chil-dren sang;
2 From Ol - i - vet they fol - lowed Mid an ex - ul-tant crowd;
3 "Ho - san - na in the high - est!" That an-cient song we sing,

Thro' pil - lared court and Tem - ple The love - ly an -them rang.
The vic - tor palm branch wav - ing And chant-ing clear and loud.
For Christ is our Re - deem - er, The Lord of heav'n our King.

To Je - sus, who had blessed them, Close fold-ed to His breast,
The Lord of men and an - gels Rode on in low - ly state
Oh, may we ev - er praise Him With heart and life and voice

The chil-dren sang their prais - es, The sim-plest and the best.
Nor scorned that lit-tle chil - dren Should on His bid-ding wait.
And in His bliss-ful pres - ence E - ter-nal-ly re-joice! A-men.

Ride On, Ride On, in Majesty

162

L. M.

Matt. 21: 9
Henry H. Milman, 1827, alt.

Winchester New
"Musikalisches Handbuch"
Hamburg, 1690

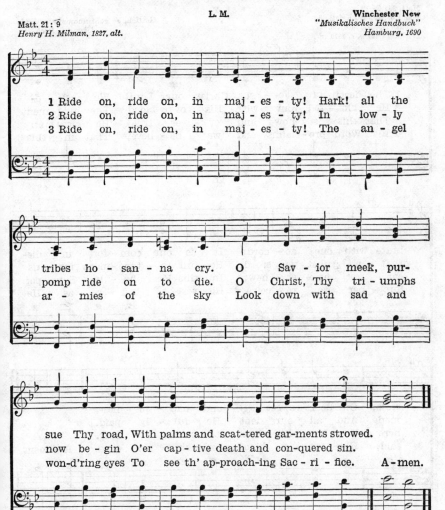

1 Ride on, ride on, in maj-es-ty! Hark! all the
2 Ride on, ride on, in maj-es-ty! In low-ly
3 Ride on, ride on, in maj-es-ty! The an-gel

tribes ho-san-na cry. O Sav-ior meek, pur-
pomp ride on to die. O Christ, Thy tri-umphs
ar-mies of the sky Look down with sad and

sue Thy road, With palms and scat-tered gar-ments strowed.
now be-gin O'er cap-tive death and con-quered sin.
won-d'ring eyes To see th' ap-proach-ing Sac-ri-fice. A-men.

4 Ride on, ride on, in majesty!
Thy last and fiercest strife is nigh;
The Father on His sapphire throne
Expects His own anointed Son.

5 Ride on, ride on, in majesty!
In lowly pomp ride on to die.
Bow Thy meek head to mortal pain,
Then take, O Christ, Thy power and reign.

163 The Death of Jesus Christ, Our Lord

Matt. 26: 26-29

Wår Herres Jesu Kristi död
Haquin Spegel, 1686, ab.
Tr., Olof Olsson, c. 1910, alt.

L. M.

Gottlob, es geht nunmehr zu Ende
Johann S. Bach, 1736

1 The death of Je - sus Christ, our Lord, We cel - e -
2 He blot - ted out with His own blood The judg - ment
3 That this is now and ev - er true He gives an
4 His Word pro - claims, and we be - lieve, That in this

brate with one ac - cord; It is our com - fort in dis -
that a - gainst us stood; He full a - tone - ment for us
ear - nest ev - er new: In this His ho - ly Sup - per
Sup - per we re - ceive His ver - y bod - y, as He

tress, Our heart's sweet joy and hap - pi - ness.
made, And all our debt He ful - ly paid.
here We taste His love so sweet, so near.
said, His ver - y blood for sin - ners shed. A - men.

5 A precious food is this indeed,—
It never fails us in our need,—
A heavenly manna for our soul,
Until we safely reach our goal.

6 Oh, blest is each believing guest
Who in this promise finds his rest;
For Jesus will in love abide
With those who do in Him confide.

7 The guest that comes with true intent
To turn to God and to repent,
To live for Christ, to die to sin,
Will thus a holy life begin.

The Death of Jesus Christ, Our Lord

8 They who His Word do not believe
This food unworthily receive,
Salvation here will never find,—
May we this warning keep in mind!

9 Help us sincerely to believe
That we may worthily receive
Thy Supper and in Thee find rest.
Amen, he who believes is blest.

'Twas on That Dark, That Doleful Night   **164**

1 Cor. 11: 23ff.
Isaac Watts, 1709, ab.

L. M.

St. Cross
John B. Dykes, 1861

1 'Twas on that dark, that dole-ful night When pow'rs of
2 Be - fore the mourn-ful scene be - gan, He took the
3 "This is My bod - y, broke for sin; Re - ceive and
4 "Do this," He said, "till time shall end, In mem-'ry

earth and hell a - rose A - gainst the Son of God's de-
bread and blessed and brake. What love thro' all His ac - tions
eat the liv - ing food"; Then took the cup and blessed the
of your dy - ing Friend. Meet at My ta - ble and re-

light And friends be - trayed Him to His foes.
ran! What won-drous words of grace He spake!
wine: "'Tis the new cov - 'nant in My blood."
cord The love of your de - part - ed Lord." A - men.

5 Jesus, Thy feast we celebrate;
We show Thy death, we sing Thy name,
Till Thou return and we shall eat
The marriage supper of the Lamb.

165

Behold the Lamb of God!

6. 6. 6. 4. 8. 8. 4.

John 1: 29
Matthew Bridges, 1848, ab., alt.

Ecce Agnus
"Neues Gesangbuch"
Dresden, 1593, ad.

1 Be - hold the Lamb of God! O Thou for sin - ners slain,
2 Be - hold the Lamb of God! In - to the sa - cred flood
3 Be - hold the Lamb of God! All hail, in - car - nate Word!
4 Be - hold the Lamb of God! Wor - thy is He a - lone

Let it not be in vain That Thou hast died!
Of Thy most pre - cious blood My soul I cast.
Thou ev - er - last - ing Lord, Purge out our leav'n;
To sit up - on the throne Of God a - bove,

Thee for my Sav - ior let me take, My on - ly ref - uge
Wash me and make me pure and clean, Up - hold me thro' life's
Clothe us with god - li - ness and good, Feed us with Thy ce -
One with the An - cient of all days, One with the Par - a -

let me make Thy pierc - ed side.
change - ful scene, Till all be past.
les - tial food, Man - na from heav'n.
clete in praise, All Light, all Love! A - men.

Savior, When in Dust to Thee

166

7. 7. 7. 7. D.

Luke 18: 13
Robert Grant, 1815, ab.

Spanish Chant
Spanish melody, c. 1600

1 Sav - ior, when in dust to Thee Low we bow th' a-dor-ing knee,
2 By Thy help-less in-fant years, By Thy life of want and tears,
3 By Thine hour of dire de-spair, By Thine ag - o - ny of prayer,
4 By Thy deep ex - pir-ing groan, By the sad se - pul-chral stone,

When, re - pen-tant, to the skies Scarce we lift our weep-ing eyes,
By Thy days of sore dis-tress In the sav - age wil - der - ness,
By the cross, the nail, the thorn, Pierc-ing spear, and torturing scorn,
By the vault whose dark a - bode Held in vain the ris - ing God,

Oh, by all Thy pains and woe Suf-fered once for man be - low,
By the dread, mys-te - rious hour Of th' in-sult-ing Tempt-er's pow'r,
By the gloom that veiled the skies O'er the dread-ful sac - ri - fice,
Oh, from earth to heav'n re-stored, Might-y, re - as-cend-ed Lord,

Bend-ing from Thy throne on high, Hear our sol-emn lit - a - ny!
Turn, O turn, a fa-v'ring eye, Hear our sol-emn lit - a - ny!
Lis - ten to our hum-ble cry, Hear our sol-emn lit - a - ny!
Lis - ten, lis - ten, to the cry, Hear our sol-emn lit - a - ny! A-men.

167 O Darkest Woe

Acts 3 : 15
O Traurigkeit, o Herzeleid
St. 1, "Würzburger Gesangbuch," 1628
St. 2–7, Johann Rist, 1641, ab.
Tr., Catherine Winkworth, 1863, alt.

4. 4. 7. 7. 6.

O Traurigkeit
"Würzburger Gesangbuch," 1628

1 O dark - est woe! Ye tears, forth flow! Has
2 O sor - row dread! God's Son is dead! But
3 O sin - ful man! It was the ban Of
4 Lo, stained with blood, The Lamb of God, The

earth so sad a won - der? God the Fa - ther's
by His ex - pi - a - tion Of our guilt up -
death on thee that brought Him Down to suf - fer
Bride - groom, lies be - fore thee, Pour - ing out His

on - ly Son Now is bur - ied yon - der.
on the cross Gained for us sal - va - tion.
for thy sins And such woe hath wrought Him.
life that He May to life re - store thee. A - men.

5 O Ground of faith,
Laid low in death,
Sweet lips, now silent sleeping!
Surely all that live must mourn
Here with bitter weeping.

6 O blest shall be
Eternally
Who oft in faith will ponder
Why the glorious Prince of Life
Should be buried yonder.

7 O Jesus blest,
My Help and Rest,
With tears I now entreat Thee:
Make me love Thee to the last,
Till in heaven I greet Thee.

The Royal Banners Forward Go

168

Ps. 96: 10
Vexilla Regis prodeunt
Venantius Fortunatus, 569, cento
Tr., John M. Neale, 1851, alt.

L. M.

Vexilla Regis
John Hampton, 1875, ad.

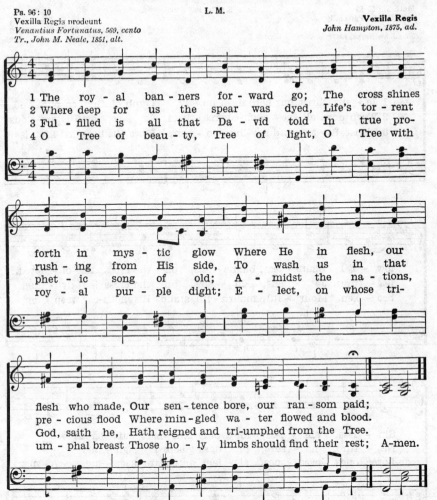

1 The roy - al ban - ners for - ward go; The cross shines
2 Where deep for us the spear was dyed, Life's tor - rent
3 Ful - filled is all that Da - vid told In true pro -
4 O Tree of beau - ty, Tree of light, O Tree with

forth in mys - tic glow Where He in flesh, our
rush - ing from His side, To wash us in that
phet - ic song of old; A - midst the na - tions,
roy - al pur - ple dight; E - lect, on whose tri -

flesh who made, Our sen - tence bore, our ran - som paid;
pre - cious flood Where min - gled wa - ter flowed and blood.
God, saith he, Hath reigned and tri - umphed from the Tree.
um - phal breast Those ho - ly limbs should find their rest; A-men.

5 On whose dear arms, so widely flung,
The weight of this world's ransom hung
The price of humankind to pay
And spoil the spoiler of his prey.

6 O Cross, our one reliance, hail!
So may thy power with us avail
To give new virtue to the saint
And pardon to the penitent.

7 To Thee, eternal Three in One,
Let homage meet by all be done
Whom by the cross Thou dost restore,
Preserve, and govern evermore.

169 Jesus Christ, Our Lord Most Holy

Matt. 27: 50–53
Jezu Kriste, Pane milý
Michal Grodzki, c. 1550
Tr., John Bajus, 1939

8. 8. 10. 10.

Teshiniens
Polish melody, c. 1500

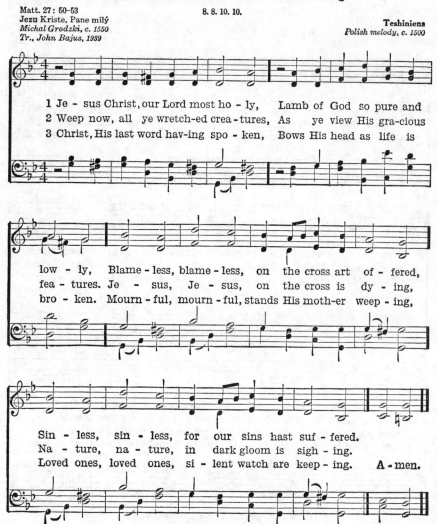

1 Je - sus Christ, our Lord most ho - ly, Lamb of God so pure and
2 Weep now, all ye wretch-ed crea - tures, As ye view His gra-cious
3 Christ, His last word hav-ing spo - ken, Bows His head as life is

low - ly, Blame - less, blame - less, on the cross art of - fered,
fea - tures. Je - sus, Je - sus, on the cross is dy - ing,
bro - ken. Mourn - ful, mourn - ful, stands His moth-er weep - ing,

Sin - less, sin - less, for our sins hast suf - fered.
Na - ture, na - ture, in dark gloom is sigh - ing.
Loved ones, loved ones, si - lent watch are keep - ing.   A - men.

4 The great veil was torn asunder,
   Earth did quake mid roars of thunder,
   Boulders, boulders, into bits were breaking;
   Sainted, sainted dead from death were waking.

5 As His side with spear was riven,
   Blood and water forth were given.
   Jesus, Jesus, sinners' only Savior,
   Mercy, mercy, grant to us forever.

O Perfect Life of Love!

170

S. M.

John 19: 30
Henry W. Baker. 1875

Southwell
"Psalter"
William Daman, 1579

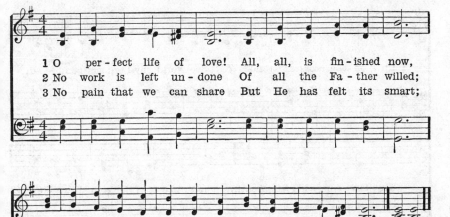

1 O per-fect life of love! All, all, is fin-ished now,
2 No work is left un-done Of all the Fa-ther willed;
3 No pain that we can share But He has felt its smart;

All that He left His throne a-bove To do for us be-low.
His toil, His sor-rows, one by one, The Scriptures have ful-filled.
All forms of hu-man grief and care Have pierced that tender heart. A-men.

4 And on His thorn-crowned head
   And on His sinless soul
Our sins in all their guilt were laid
   That He might make us whole.

5 In perfect love He dies;
   For me He dies, for me.
O all-atoning Sacrifice,
   I cling by faith to Thee.

6 In every time of need,
   Before the judgment-throne,
Thy works, O Lamb of God, I'll plead,
   Thy merits, not mine own.

7 Yet work, O Lord, in me
   As Thou for me hast wrought;
And let my love the answer be
   To grace Thy love has brought.

171 Upon the Cross Extended

Heb. 9 : 28
O Welt, sieh hier dein Leben
Paul Gerhardt, 1648, cento
Tr., John Kelly, 1867, alt.

7. 7. 6. 7. 7. 8.

(*FIRST TUNE*)

O Welt, sieh hier
Heinrich Friese, 1703

1 Up - on the cross ex - tend - ed, See, world, thy Lord sus - pend - ed.

Thy Sav - ior yields His breath. The Prince of Life from heav - en

Him - self hath free - ly giv - en To shame and blows and bitter death. Amen.

2 Come hither now and ponder,
'Twill fill thy soul with wonder,
Blood streams from every pore.
Through grief whose depth none
knoweth,
From His great heart there floweth
Sigh after sigh of anguish o'er.

3 Who is it that hath bruised Thee?
Who hath so sore abused Thee
And caused Thee all Thy woe?
While we must make confession
Of sin and dire transgression,
Thou deeds of evil dost not know.

4 I caused Thy grief and sighing
By evils multiplying
As countless as the sands.
I caused the woes unnumbered
With which Thy soul is cumbered,
Thy sorrows raised by wicked hands.

5 'Tis I who should be smitten,
My doom should here be written:
Bound hand and foot in hell.
The fetters and the scourging,
The floods around Thee surging,
'Tis I who have deserved them well.

6 The load Thou takest on Thee,
That pressed so sorely on me,
It crushed me to the ground.
The cross for me enduring,
The crown for me securing,
My healing in Thy wounds is found.

7 A crown of thorns Thou wearest,
My shame and scorn Thou bearest,
That I might ransomed be.
My Bondsman, ever willing,
My place with patience filling,
From sin and guilt hast made me
free.

Upon the Cross Extended

8 Thy cords of love, my Savior,
  Bind me to Thee forever,
    I am no longer mine.
  To Thee I gladly tender
  All that my life can render
    And all I have to Thee resign.

9 Thy cross I'll place before me,
  Its saving power be o'er me,
    Wherever I may be;
  Thine innocence revealing,
  Thy love and mercy sealing,
    The pledge of truth and constancy.

10 How God at our transgression
   To anger gives expression,
     How loud His thunders roll,
   How fearfully He smiteth,
   How sorely He requiteth,—
     All this Thy sufferings teach my soul.

11 When evil men revile me,
   With wicked tongues defile me,
     I'll curb my vengeful heart.
   The unjust wrong I'll suffer,
   Unto my neighbor offer
     Forgiveness for each bitter smart.

12 Thy groaning and Thy sighing,
   Thy bitter tears and dying,
     With which Thou wast opprest,—
   They shall, when life is ending,
   Be guiding and attending
     My way to Thine eternal rest.

Upon the Cross Extended

Heb. 9: 23
O Welt, sieh hier dein Leben
Paul Gerhardt, 1648, cento
Tr., John Kelly, 1867, alt.

7. 7. 6. 7. 7. 8.
(*SECOND TUNE*)

O Welt, ich muss dich lassen
Heinrich Isaak, c. 1490

1 Up - on the cross ex - tend - ed, See, world, thy Lord sus - pend - ed,

Thy Sav - ior yields His breath. The Prince of Life from heav - en

Him - self hath free - ly giv - en To shame and blows and bitter death. A - men.

172 O Sacred Head, Now Wounded

7. 6. 7. 6. D.

Is. 50: 6
O Haupt voll Blut und Wunden
Based on the Latin
Bernard of Clairvaux, †1153, asc.
Paul Gerhardt, 1656
Tr., composite

Herzlich tut mich
Hans L. Hassler, 1601

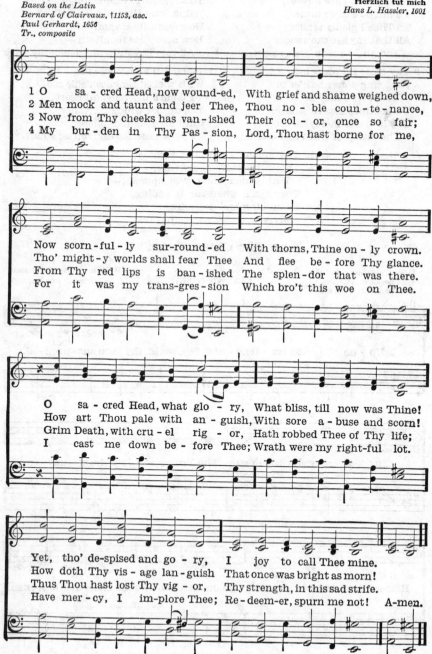

1 O   sa - cred Head, now wound-ed,   With grief and shame weighed down,
2 Men mock and taunt and jeer Thee,   Thou no - ble coun - te - nance,
3 Now from Thy cheeks has van - ished   Their col - or, once so fair;
4 My   bur - den in   Thy Pas - sion,   Lord, Thou hast borne for me,

Now scorn - ful - ly   sur - round - ed   With thorns, Thine on - ly crown.
Tho' might - y worlds shall fear Thee   And flee be - fore Thy glance.
From Thy red lips   is ban - ished   The splen - dor that was there.
For   it   was my trans - gres - sion   Which bro't this woe on Thee.

O   sa - cred Head, what glo - ry,   What bliss, till now was Thine!
How art Thou pale with an - guish,   With sore a - buse and scorn!
Grim Death, with cru - el   rig - or,   Hath robbed Thee of Thy life;
I   cast me down be - fore Thee;   Wrath were my right-ful lot.

Yet, tho' de-spised and go - ry,   I   joy to call Thee mine.
How doth Thy vis - age lan - guish   That once was bright as morn!
Thus Thou hast lost Thy vig - or,   Thy strength, in this sad strife.
Have mer - cy, I   im-plore Thee;   Re - deem-er, spurn me not!   A-men.

O Sacred Head, Now Wounded

5 My Shepherd, now receive me;
   My Guardian, own me Thine.
Great blessings Thou didst give me,
   O Source of gifts divine.
Thy lips have often fed me
   With words of truth and love;
Thy Spirit oft hath led me
   To heavenly joys above.

6 Here I will stand beside Thee,
   From Thee I will not part;
O Savior, do not chide me!
   When breaks Thy loving heart,
When soul and body languish
   In death's cold, cruel grasp,
Then, in Thy deepest anguish,
   Thee in mine arms I'll clasp.

7 The joy can ne'er be spoken,
   Above all joys beside,
When in Thy body broken
   I thus with safety hide.
O Lord of Life, desiring
   Thy glory now to see,
Beside Thy cross expiring,
   I'd breathe my soul to Thee.

8 What language shall I borrow
   To thank Thee, dearest Friend,
For this Thy dying sorrow,
   Thy pity without end?
Oh, make me Thine forever!
   And should I fainting be,
Lord, let me never, never,
   Outlive my love for Thee.

9 My Savior, be Thou near me
   When death is at my door;
Then let Thy presence cheer me,
   Forsake me nevermore!
When soul and body languish,
   Oh, leave me not alone,
But take away mine anguish
   By virtue of Thine own!

10 Be Thou my Consolation,
   My Shield, when I must die;
Remind me of Thy Passion
   When my last hour draws nigh.
Mine eyes shall then behold Thee,
   Upon Thy cross shall dwell,
My heart by faith enfold Thee.
   Who dieth thus dies well.

173 Lord Jesus, We Give Thanks to Thee

Heb. 13 : 15
Wir danken dir, Herr Jesu Christ
Christoph Fischer, 1597
Tr., August Crull, †1923

L. M.

Wir danken dir
"Bergkreyen"
Wittenberg, 1562

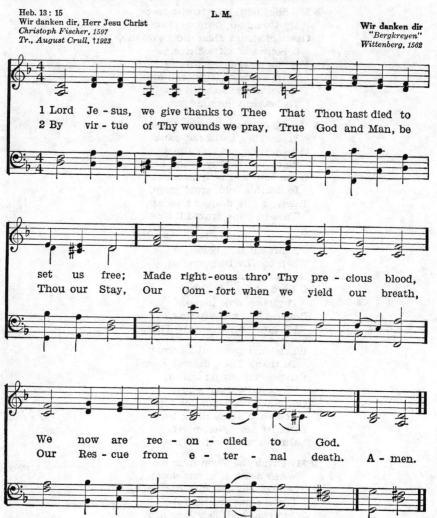

1 Lord Je - sus, we give thanks to Thee That Thou hast died to
2 By vir - tue of Thy wounds we pray, True God and Man, be

set us free; Made right-eous thro' Thy pre - cious blood,
Thou our Stay, Our Com - fort when we yield our breath,

We now are rec - on - ciled to God.
Our Res - cue from e - ter - nal death. A - men.

3 Defend us, Lord, from sin and shame;
Help us by Thine almighty name
To bear our crosses patiently,
Consoled by Thy great agony,

4 And thus the full assurance gain
That Thou to us wilt true remain
And not forsake us in our strife
Until we enter into life.

Throned upon the Awe=full Tree

7. 7. 7. 7. 7. 7.

174

Mark 15: 34
John Ellerton, 1875

Gethsemane
Richard Redhead, 1853

1 Throned up-on the awe-full tree, King of grief, I watch with Thee.
2 Si - lent thro' those three dread hours, Wres-tling with the e - vil pow'rs,

Dark-ness veils Thine anguished face; None its lines of woe can trace,
Left a - lone with hu-man sin, Gloom a-round Thee and with-in,

None can tell what pangs unknown Hold Thee si-lent and a - lone.
Till th' ap-point-ed time is nigh, Till the Lamb of God may die. A-men.

3 Hark the cry that peals aloud
Upward through the whelming cloud!
Thou, the Father's only Son,
Thou, His own Anointed One,
Thou dost ask Him, Can it be?
"Why hast Thou forsaken Me?"

4 Lord, should fear and anguish roll
Darkly o'er my sinful soul,
Thou, who once wast thus bereft
That Thine own might ne'er be left,
Teach me by that bitter cry
In the gloom to know Thee nigh.

175 When I Survey the Wondrous Cross

L. M.

(FIRST TUNE)

Gal. 6:14
Isaac Watts, 1707, ab. and alt.

Hamburg
*Based on First Gregorian Chant
Arr. by Lowell Mason, 1824*

1 When I sur-vey the won-drous cross On which the
Prince of Glo-ry died, My rich-est gain I count but
loss And pour con-tempt on all my pride. A-men.

2 Forbid it, Lord, that I should boast
   Save in the death of Christ, my God;
  All the vain things that charm me most,
   I sacrifice them to His blood.

3 See, from His head, His hands, His feet,
   Sorrow and love flow mingled down.
  Did e'er such love and sorrow meet
   Or thorns compose so rich a crown?

4 Were the whole realm of nature mine,
   That were a tribute far too small;
  Love so amazing, so divine,
   Demands my soul, my life, my all.

When I Survey the Wondrous Cross

L. M.

(SECOND TUNE)

Gal. 6:14
Isaac Watts, 1707, ab. and alt.

Rockingham Old
Edward Miller, 1790

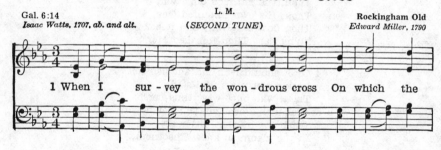

1 When I sur-vey the won-drous cross On which the

When I Survey the Wondrous Cross

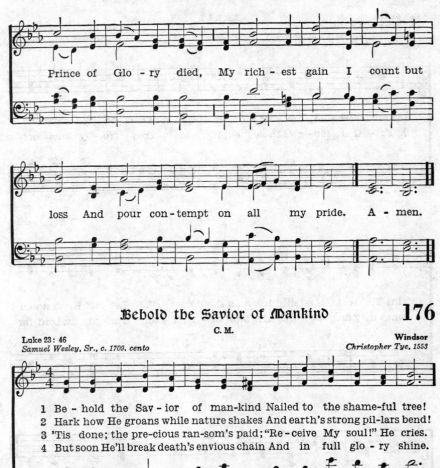

Prince of Glo-ry died, My rich-est gain I count but loss And pour con-tempt on all my pride. A - men.

Behold the Savior of Mankind

176

C. M.

Luke 23: 46
Samuel Wesley, Sr., c. 1709, cento

Windsor
Christopher Tye, 1553

1 Be - hold the Sav - ior of man-kind Nailed to the shame-ful tree!
2 Hark how He groans while nature shakes And earth's strong pil-lars bend!
3 'Tis done; the pre-cious ran-som's paid; "Re - ceive My soul!" He cries.
4 But soon He'll break death's envious chain And in full glo - ry shine.

How vast the love that Him in-clined To bleed and die for thee!
The Tem-ple's veil in sun-der breaks, The sol - id mar-bles rend.
See where He bows His sa-cred head; He bows His head and dies.
O Lamb of God, was ev - er pain, Was ev - er love, like Thine? A-men.

177 Our Blessed Savior Seven Times Spoke

Heb. 5: 7
Da Jesus an des Kreuzes Stamm
Johann Böschenstain, c. 1515, alt.
Tr., Frances E. Cox, 1841, alt.

8. 8. 7. 8. 7.

Da Jesus an des Kreuzes
German melody, c. 1400

1 Our bless - ed Sav - ior sev'n times spoke When on the cross our
2 "Fa - ther, for - give these men; for, lo, They tru - ly know not

sins He took And died lest man should per - ish. Let us His last and
what they do." So far His love ex - tend - ed. For - give us, Lord, for

dy - ing words In our re-mem-brance cher - ish.
we, too, have Thro' ig - no-rance of - fend - ed. A - men.

3 Now to the contrite thief He cries:
"Thou, verily, in Paradise
Shalt meet Me ere tomorrow."
Lord, take us to Thy kingdom soon
Who linger here in sorrow.

Our Blessed Savior Seven Times Spoke

4 To weeping Mary, standing by,
  "Behold thy son," now hear Him cry;
    To John, "Behold thy mother."
  Provide, O Lord, for those we leave;
    Let each befriend the other.

5 The Savior's fourth word was "I thirst."
  O mighty Prince of Life, Thy thirst
    For us and our salvation
  Is truly great; do help us, then,
    That we escape damnation.

6 The fifth, "My God, My God, O why
  Forsake Me?" Hark, the awe-full cry!
    Lord, Thou wast here forsaken
  That we might be received on high;
    Let this hope not be shaken.

7 The sixth, when victory was won,
  "'Tis finished!" for Thy work was done.
    Grant, Lord, that, onward pressing,
  We may the work Thou dost impose
    Fulfil with Thine own blessing.

8 The last, as woe and sufferings end,
  "O God, My Father, I commend
    Into Thy hands My spirit."
  Be this, dear Lord, my dying wish;
    O heavenly Father, hear it.

9 Whoe'er, by sense of sin opprest,
  Upon these words his thoughts will rest,
    He joy and hope obtaineth
  And through God's love and boundless grace
    A peaceful conscience gaineth.

10 O Jesus Christ, Thou Crucified,
  Who hast for our offenses died,
    Grant that we e'er may ponder
  Thy wounds, Thy cross, Thy bitter death,
    Both here below and yonder.

178 We Sing the Praise of Him Who Died

L. M.

Gal. 6: 14
Thomas Kelly, 1815

O Jesu Christ, mein's
"Nürnbergisches Gesangbuch," 1676

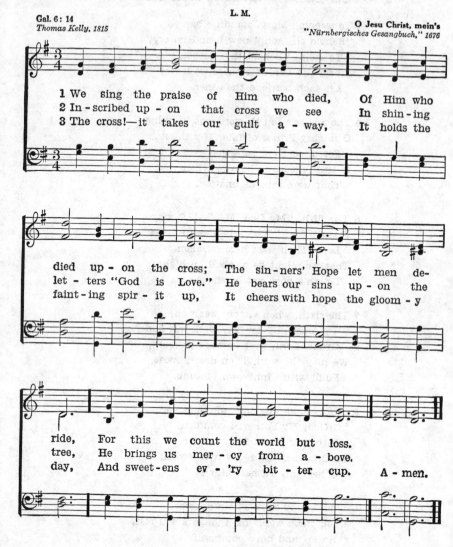

1 We sing the praise of Him who died, Of Him who
2 In-scribed up-on that cross we see In shin-ing
3 The cross!—it takes our guilt a-way, It holds the

died up-on the cross; The sin-ners' Hope let men de-
let-ters "God is Love." He bears our sins up-on the
faint-ing spir-it up, It cheers with hope the gloom-y

ride, For this we count the world but loss.
tree, He brings us mer-cy from a-bove.
day, And sweet-ens ev-'ry bit-ter cup. A-men.

4 It makes the coward spirit brave
And nerves the feeble arm for fight;
It takes all terror from the grave
And gilds the bed of death with light.

5 The balm of life, the cure of woe,
The measure and the pledge of love,
The sinners' refuge here below,
The angels' theme in heaven above.

On My Heart Imprint Thine Image

179

8. 7. 8. 7. 7. 8. 8.

Luke 23 : 38
Skriv dig, Jesu, paa mit Hjerte
Thomas Kingo, 1689
Tr., Peer O. Strömme, 1898, alt.

Der am Kreuz
Johann B. König, 1738

On my heart im-print Thine im-age, Bless-ed Je-sus, King of Grace,

That life's rich-es, cares, and plea-sures Have no pow'r Thee to ef-face.

This the su-per-scrip-tion be: Je-sus, cru-ci-

fied for me, Is my Life, my hope's Foun-da-tion,

And my Glo-ry and Sal-va-tion. A-men.

180 The Seven Words on the Cross

I

Jesus, in Thy Dying Woes

Luke 23 : 34
Thomas B. Pollock, 1870

7. 7. 7. 6.

Septem Verba
Bernhard Schumacher, 1939

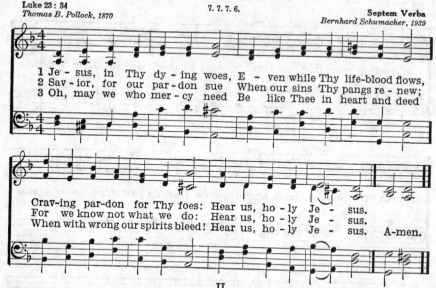

1 Je - sus, in Thy dy - ing woes, E - ven while Thy life-blood flows,
2 Sav - ior, for our par - don sue When our sins Thy pangs re - new;
3 Oh, may we who mer - cy need Be like Thee in heart and deed

Crav-ing par-don for Thy foes: Hear us, ho - ly Je - sus.
For we know not what we do: Hear us, ho - ly Je - sus.
When with wrong our spirits bleed! Hear us, ho - ly Je - sus. A-men.

II

181 Jesus, Pitying the Sighs

Luke 23 : 43

1 Jesus, pitying the sighs
Of the thief who near Thee dies,
Promising him Paradise:
Hear us, holy Jesus.

2 May we in our guilt and shame
Still Thy love and mercy claim,
Calling humbly on Thy name:
Hear us, holy Jesus.

3 May our hearts to Thee incline,
Looking from our cross to Thine;
Cheer our souls with hope divine:
Hear us, holy Jesus.

III

182 Jesus, Loving to the End

John 19 : 26, 27

1 Jesus, loving to the end
Her whose heart Thy sorrows rend,
And Thy dearest human friend:
Hear us, holy Jesus.

2 May we in Thy sorrows share,
For Thy sake all peril dare,
And enjoy Thy tender care:
Hear us, holy Jesus.

3 May we all Thy loved ones be,
All one holy family,
Loving for the love of Thee:
Hear us, holy Jesus.

IV

Jesus, Whelmed in Fears Unknown

Matt. 27 : 46

183

1 Jesus, whelmed in fears unknown,
  With our evil left alone,
  While no light from heaven is shown:
      Hear us, holy Jesus.

2 When we vainly seem to pray
  And our hope seems far away,
  In the darkness be our Stay:
      Hear us, holy Jesus.

3 Though no Father seem to hear,
  Though no light our spirits cheer,
  May we know that God is near:
      Hear us, holy Jesus.

V

Jesus, in Thy Thirst and Pain

John 19 : 28

184

1 Jesus, in Thy thirst and pain,
  While Thy wounds Thy life-blood drain,
  Thirsting more our love to gain:
      Hear us, holy Jesus.

2 Thirst for us in mercy still,
  All Thy holy work fulfil,
  Satisfy Thy loving will:
      Hear us, holy Jesus.

3 May we thirst Thy love to know;
  Lead us in our sin and woe
  Where the healing waters flow:
      Hear us, holy Jesus.

VI

Jesus, All Our Ransom Paid

John 19 : 30

185

1 Jesus, all our ransom paid,
  All Thy Father's will obeyed,
  By Thy sufferings perfect made:
      Hear us, holy Jesus.

2 Save us in our soul's distress,
  Be our Help to cheer and bless
  While we grow in holiness:
      Hear us, holy Jesus.

3 Brighten all our heavenward way
  With an ever holier ray
  Till we pass to perfect day:
      Hear us, holy Jesus.

VII

Jesus, All Thy Labor Vast

Luke 23 : 46

186

1 Jesus, all Thy labor vast,
  All Thy woe and conflict past,
  Yielding up Thy soul at last:
      Hear us, holy Jesus.

2 When the death shades round us lower,
  Guard us from the Tempter's power,
  Keep us in that trial hour:
      Hear us, holy Jesus.

3 May Thy life and death supply
  Grace to live and grace to die,
  Grace to reach the home on high:
      Hear us, holy Jesus.

187 Christ is Arisen

1 Cor. 15: 20
Christ ist erstanden
Author unknown, c. 1100
Tr., W. Gustave Polack, 1939

Irregular

Christ ist erstanden
Latin melody, c. 1100

Christ is a - ris - en From the grave's dark pris - on.

We now re-joice with glad - ness; Christ will end all sad - ness.

Lord, have mer - cy. All our hopes were end - ed

Had Je - sus not as - cend - ed From the grave tri-um-phant-ly.

Christ is Arisen

For this, Lord Christ, we wor-ship Thee. Lord, have mer - cy.

Hal - le - lu - jah! Hal - le - lu - jah!

Hal - le - lu - jah! We now re-joice with glad - ness;

Christ will end all sad - ness. Lord, have mer - cy. A - men.

188 Hallelujah! Jesus Lives!

7. 7. 7. 7. 7. 7.

John 20: 15
Halleluja, Christus lebt
Carl B. Garve, 1825, cento
Tr., Jane Borthwick, 1862

Fred til Bod
Ludvig M. Lindeman, 1871

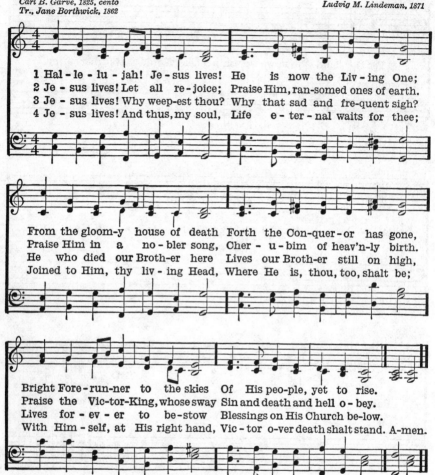

1 Hal - le - lu - jah! Je - sus lives! He is now the Liv - ing One;
2 Je - sus lives! Let all re - joice; Praise Him, ran-somed ones of earth.
3 Je - sus lives! Why weep-est thou? Why that sad and fre-quent sigh?
4 Je - sus lives! And thus, my soul, Life e - ter - nal waits for thee;

From the gloom-y house of death Forth the Con-quer-or has gone,
Praise Him in a no - bler song, Cher - u - bim of heav'n-ly birth.
He who died our Broth-er here Lives our Broth-er still on high,
Joined to Him, thy liv - ing Head, Where He is, thou, too, shalt be;

Bright Fore - run - ner to the skies Of His peo-ple, yet to rise.
Praise the Vic-tor-King, whose sway Sin and death and hell o - bey.
Lives for - ev - er to be-stow Blessings on His Church be-low.
With Him - self, at His right hand, Vic - tor o-ver death shalt stand. A-men.

5 Jesus lives! To Him my heart
   Draws with ever new delight.
Earthly vanities, depart,
   Hinder not my heavenward flight.
Let this spirit ever rise
To its Magnet in the skies.

6 Hallelujah, angels, sing!
   Join us in our hymn of praise;
Let your chorus swell the strain
   Which our feebler voices raise:
Glory to our God above
And on earth His peace and love!

He is Arisen! Glorious Word!

189

8. 8. 7. 8. 8. 7. 4. 4. 4. 4. 8.

Rom. 4 : 25
Han er opstanden! Store Bud!
Birgitte K. Boye, 1778
Tr., George T. Rygh, 1909

Wie schön leuchtet
Philipp Nicolai, 1599

He is a - ris-en! Glorious Word! Now rec-on-ciled is God, my Lord;

The gates of heav'n are o - pen. My Je - sus did tri-um-phant die,

And Sa-tan's ar-rows bro-ken lie, De-stroyed hell's dir-est weap-on.

Oh, hear What cheer! Christ vic-to-rious Riseth glo-rious, Life He giv-eth—

He was dead, but see, He liv - eth! A - men.

190 Christ the Lord is Risen Again

Mark 16: 6
Christus ist erstanden
Michael Weisse, 1531
Tr., Catherine Winkworth, 1863

7. 7. 7. 7., with Hallelujah

Christus ist erstanden
Based on "Christ ist erstanden"
Latin melody, c. 1100

1 Christ the Lord is ris'n a-gain; Christ has bro-ken
2 He who gave for us His life, Who for us en-
3 He who bore all pain and loss Com-fort-less up-
4 He whose path no rec-ords tell Hath de-scend-ed

death's strong chain. Hark, the an-gels shout for joy,
dured the strife, Is our Pas-chal Lamb to-day.
on the cross Lives in glo-ry now on high,
in-to hell; He the strong man armed hath bound

Sing-ing ev-er-more on high: Hal-le-lu-jah!
We, too, sing for joy and say: Hal-le-lu-jah!
Pleads for us and hears our cry: Hal-le-lu-jah!
And in high-est heav'n is crowned. Hal-le-lu-jah! A-men.

5 He who slumbered in the grave
Is exalted now to save;
Now through Christendom it rings
That the Lamb is King of kings. Hallelujah!

6 Now He bids us tell abroad
How the lost may be restored,
How the penitent forgiven,
How we, too, may enter heaven. Hallelujah!

7 Thou our Paschal Lamb indeed,
Christ, today Thy people feed;
Take our sins and guilt away
That we all may sing for aye: Hallelujah!

Christ the Lord is Risen Today; Alleluia!

7. 7. 7. 7., with Alleluias

Mark 16: 6
Victimae Paschali, c. 1100
Author unknown
Tr., Jane E. Leeson, 1851

Llanfair
Robert Williams, 1817

1 Christ the Lord is ris'n to-day; Al - le-lu - ia!
2 For the sheep the Lamb hath bled, Al - le-lu - ia!
3 Christ, the Vic-tim un-de-filed, Al - le-lu - ia!
4 Chris-tians, on this hap-py day Al - le-lu - ia!

Chris-tians, haste your vows to pay; Al - le-lu - ia!
Sin-less in the sin-ners' stead. Al - le-lu - ia!
God and man hath rec-on-ciled Al - le-lu - ia!
Haste with joy your vows to pay. Al - le-lu - ia!

Of - fer ye your prais-es meet Al - le-lu - ia!
"Christ is ris'n," to-day we cry; Al - le-lu - ia!
While in strange and awe-full strife Al - le-lu - ia!
"Christ is ris'n," to-day we cry; Al - le-lu - ia!

At the Pas-chal Vic-tim's feet. Al - le-lu - ia!
Now He lives no more to die. Al - le-lu - ia!
Met to-geth-er Death and Life. Al - le-lu - ia!
Now He lives no more to die. Al - le-lu - ia! A-men.

5 Christ, who once for sinners bled,
Now the First-born from the dead,
Throned in endless might and power,
Lives and reigns forevermore.

6 Hail, eternal Hope on high!
Hail, Thou King of victory!
Hail, Thou Prince of Life adored!
Help and save us, gracious Lord.

192 Awake, My Heart, with Gladness

Col. 2: 15
Auf, auf, mein Herz, mit Freuden
Paul Gerhardt, 1648, ab.
Tr., John Kelly, 1867, alt.

7. 6. 7. 6. 6. 6. 6. 6.

Auf, auf, mein Herz
Johann Crüger, 1648

1 A - wake, my heart, with glad - ness, See what to - day is done;
2 The Foe in tri - umph shout - ed When Christ lay in the tomb;
3 This is a sight that glad - dens; What peace it doth im - part!
4 Now hell, its prince, the dev - il, Of all their pow'r are shorn;

Now, af - ter gloom and sad - ness, Comes forth the glo - rious Sun.
But, lo, he now is rout - ed, His boast is turned to gloom.
Now noth - ing ev - er sad - dens The joy with - in my heart.
Now I am safe from e - vil, And sin I laugh to scorn.

My Sav - ior there was laid Where our bed must be made
For Christ a - gain is free; In glo - rious vic - to - ry
No gloom shall ev - er shake, No foe shall ev - er take,
Grim Death with all his might Can - not my soul af - fright;

When to the realms of light Our spir - it wings its flight.
He who is strong to save Has tri - umphed o'er the grave.
The hope which God's own Son In love for me hath won.
He is a pow'r-less form, How-e'er he rave and storm. A - men.

Awake, My Heart, with Gladness

5 The world against me rageth,
　Its fury I disdain;
Though bitter war it wageth,
　Its work is all in vain.
My heart from care is free,
No trouble troubles me.
Misfortune now is play,
And night is bright as day.

6 Now I will cling forever
　To Christ, my Savior true;
My Lord will leave me never,
　Whate'er He passeth through.
He rends Death's iron chain,
He breaks through sin and pain,
He shatters hell's dark thrall,—
I follow Him through all.

7 To halls of heavenly splendor
　With Him I penetrate;
And trouble ne'er may hinder
　Nor make me hesitate.
Let tempests rage at will,
My Savior shields me still;
He grants abiding peace
And bids all tumult cease.

8 He brings me to the portal
　That leads to bliss untold,
Whereon this rime immortal
　Is found in script of gold:
"Who there My cross hath shared
Finds here a crown prepared;
Who there with Me hath died
Shall here be glorified."

Christ the Lord is Risen Today　193

7. 7. 7. 7.

1 Cor. 15 : 57
Charles Wesley, 1739, cento

Orientis partibus
French melody, c. 1200, ad.

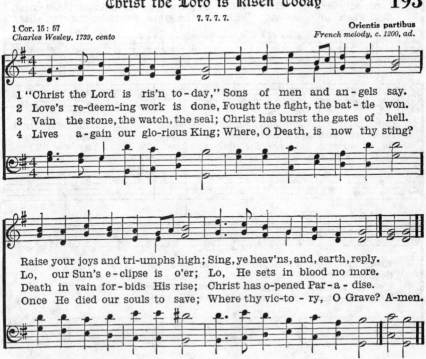

1 "Christ the Lord is ris'n to-day," Sons of men and an-gels say.
2 Love's re-deem-ing work is done, Fought the fight, the bat-tle won.
3 Vain the stone, the watch, the seal; Christ has burst the gates of hell.
4 Lives a-gain our glo-rious King; Where, O Death, is now thy sting?

Raise your joys and tri-umphs high; Sing, ye heav'ns, and, earth, reply.
Lo, our Sun's e-clipse is o'er; Lo, He sets in blood no more.
Death in vain for-bids His rise; Christ has o-pened Par-a-dise.
Once He died our souls to save; Where thy vic-to-ry, O Grave? A-men.

5 Soar we now where Christ has led,
　Following our exalted Head.
Made like Him, like Him we rise;
Ours the cross, the grave, the skies.

6 Hail the Lord of earth and heaven!
　Praise to Thee by both be given!
Thee we greet triumphant now:
Hail, the Resurrection Thou!

194 Abide with Us, the Day is Waning

Luke 24: 13-35
Bliv hos os, Mester, Dagen helder
Caspar J. Boye, 1834
Tr., Oluf H. Smeby, 1909

9. 8. 9. 8. 8. 8.

Wer nur den lieben Gott
Georg Neumark, 1640

1 "A - bide with us, the day is wan-ing," Thus prayed the
2 At e - ven - tide, Thy Spir - it send-ing, Help us, O
3 A - bide with us; with heav'n-ly glad-ness Il - lu - mine,
4 A - bide with us, O Sav - ior ten - der, That bit - ter

two while on the way; We read that Thou, O Lord, re-main-ing,
Lord, our watch to keep, In prayer de - vout be - fore Thee bend-ing
Lord, our dark-est day; And when we weep in pain and sad-ness,
day when life shall end, When to the grave we must sur-ren-der,

Didst all their doubts and fears al - lay. In - cline Thine ear, Thou
Ere we our eye - lids close in sleep, Con-fess - ing sin in
Be Thou our Sol - ace, Strength, and Stay. Tell of Thy woe, Thy
And fear and pain our hearts shall rend. The shield of faith do

King of Grace, When, pray-ing thus, we seek Thy face.
deed and word With hope of mer - cy from the Lord.
vic - t'ry won, When Thou didst pray: "Thy will be done."
Thou be - stow When trem-bling we must meet the foe. A - men.

5 When earthly help no more availeth,
  To sup with us Thou wilt be nigh;
Thou givest strength that never faileth,
  In Thee we grave and death defy.
While earth is fading from our sight,
Our eyes behold the realms of light.

Christ Jesus Lay in Death's Strong Bands

195

8. 7. 8. 7. 7. 8. 7. 4.

Acts 2:24
Christ lag in Todesbanden
Martin Luther, 1524, cento
Tr., Richard Massie, 1854, alt.

Christ lag in Todesbanden
Based on "Christ ist erstanden"
Latin melody, c. 1100

1 Christ Je - sus lay in death's strong bands, For our of - fens - es giv - en;
2 It was a strange and dread-ful strife When Life and Death con-tend-ed;
3 Here the true Pas-chal Lamb we see, Whom God so free-ly gave us;
4 So let us keep the fes - ti - val Where-to the Lord in-vites us;

But now at God's right hand He stands And brings us life from heav-en;
The vic - to - ry re-mained with Life, The reign of Death was end-ed;
He died on the ac - curs - ed tree— So strong His love!—to save us.
Christ is Him-self the Joy of all, The Sun that warms and lights us.

There-fore let us joy - ful be And sing to God right thank-ful - ly
Ho - ly Scrip-ture plain-ly saith That Death is swal-lowed up by Death,
See, His blood doth mark our door; Faith points to it, Death pass-es o'er,
By His grace He doth im-part E - ter - nal sun-shine to the heart;

Loud songs of hal - le - lu - jah. Hal - le - lu - jah!
His sting is lost for - ev - er. Hal - le - lu - jah!
And Sa - tan can - not harm us. Hal - le - lu - jah!
The night of sin is end - ed. Hal - le - lu - jah! A-men

5 Then let us feast this Easter Day
    On Christ, the Bread of heaven;
The Word of Grace hath purged away
    The old and evil leaven.
Christ alone our souls will feed,
He is our meat and drink indeed;
    Faith lives upon no other. Hallelujah!

196 I Am Content! My Jesus Liveth Still

John 11: 25
Ich habe g'nug
Johann J. Möller, 1704
Tr., August Crull, †1923, alt.

10. 6. 10. 6. 9. 9. 4. 4.

Es ist genug
"Geistliche Arien"
Mühlhausen, 1672

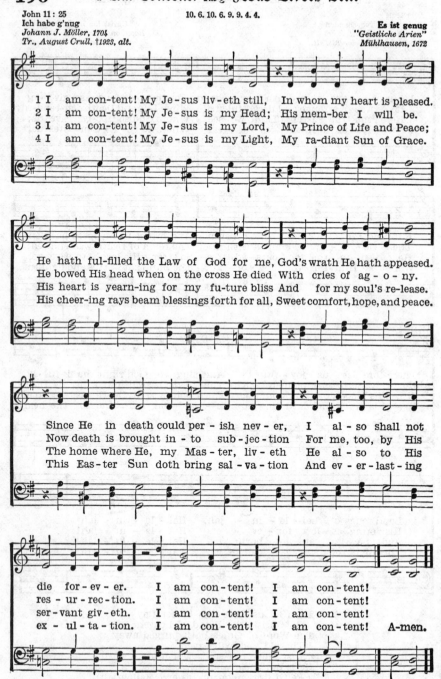

1 I am con-tent! My Je-sus liv-eth still, In whom my heart is pleased.
2 I am con-tent! My Je-sus is my Head; His mem-ber I will be.
3 I am con-tent! My Je-sus is my Lord, My Prince of Life and Peace;
4 I am con-tent! My Je-sus is my Light, My ra-diant Sun of Grace.

He hath ful-filled the Law of God for me, God's wrath He hath appeased.
He bowed His head when on the cross He died With cries of ag-o-ny.
His heart is yearn-ing for my fu-ture bliss And for my soul's re-lease.
His cheer-ing rays beam blessings forth for all, Sweet comfort, hope, and peace.

Since He in death could per-ish nev-er, I al-so shall not
Now death is brought in-to sub-jec-tion For me, too, by His
The home where He, my Mas-ter, liv-eth He al-so to His
This Eas-ter Sun doth bring sal-va-tion And ev-er-last-ing

die for-ev-er. I am con-tent! I am con-tent!
res-ur-rec-tion. I am con-tent! I am con-tent!
ser-vant giv-eth. I am con-tent! I am con-tent!
ex-ul-ta-tion. I am con-tent! I am con-tent! A-men.

I Am Content! My Jesus Liveth Still

5 I am content! Lord, draw me unto Thee
And wake me from the dead
That I may rise forevermore to be
With Thee, my living Head.
The fetters of my body sever,
Then shall my soul rejoice forever.
I am content! I am content!

Where Wilt Thou Go Since Night Draws Near 197

Luke 24 : 29   L. M.
Wo willst du hin, weil's Abend ist   **Ach bleib bei uns**
Author unknown, 1674   *"Geistliche Lieder"*
Tr., August Crull, †1923, alt.   *Leipzig, 1589*

1 Where wilt Thou go since night draws near, O Je - sus
2 Grant my re - quest, O dear - est Friend, For tru - ly
3 The day is now far spent and gone, The shades of

Christ, Thou Pil - grim dear? Lord, make me hap - py, be my Guest,
I the best in - tend; Thou know-est that Thou ev - er art
night come quick - ly on; A - bide with me, Thou heav'n-ly Light,

And in my heart, oh, deign to rest.
A wel - come Guest un - to my heart.
And do not leave me in this night. A - men.

4 Enlighten me that from the way
That leads to heaven I may not stray,
That I may never be misled
Though night of sin is round me spread.

5 And when I on my death-bed lie,
Help me that I in peace may die.
Abide! I will not let Thee go.
Thou wilt not leave me, Lord, I know.

198 He's Risen, He's Risen, Christ Jesus, the Lord

1 Cor. 15: 55
Erstanden! Erstanden!
C. Ferdinand W. Walther, 1860, cento
Tr., Anna M. Meyer, 1937

11. 11. 11. 11.

Walther
C. Ferdinand W. Walther, 1860

1 He's ris - en, He's ris - en, Christ Je - sus, the Lord;
2 The Foe was tri - um - phant when on Cal - va - ry
3 But short was their tri - umph, the Sav - ior a - rose,
4 Oh, where is thy sting, Death? We fear thee no more;

He o - pened Death's pris - on, the In - car - nate Word.
The Lord of cre - a - tion was nailed to the tree.
And Death, hell, and Sa - tan He van-quished, His foes;
Christ rose, and now o - pen is fair E - den's door.

Break forth, hosts of heav - en, in ju - bi - lant song,
In Sa - tan's do - main did the hosts shout and jeer,
The con - quer - ing Lord lifts His ban - ner on high.
For all our trans - gres - sions His blood does a - tone;

And, earth, sea, and moun-tain, the pae - an pro - long.
For Je - sus was slain, whom the e - vil ones fear.
He lives, yea, He lives, and will nev - er-more die.
Re - deemed and for - giv - en, we now are His own.

A - men.

5 Then sing your hosannas and raise your glad voice;
Proclaim the blest tidings that all may rejoice.
Laud, honor, and praise to the Lamb that was slain,
Who sitteth in glory and ever shall reign.

Jesus Christ is Risen Today, Alleluia!

199

7. 7. 7. 7., with Alleluias

Rev. 1: 18
Surrexit Christus hodie
Author unknown, c. 1372
Tr., unknown, 1708–1882

Easter Hymn
"Lyra Davidica," 1708, alt.

1 Je - sus Christ is ris'n to - day, Al - - le - lu - ia!
2 Hymns of praise, then, let us sing, Al - - le - lu - ia!
3 But the pains which He en - dured, Al - - le - lu - ia!
4 Sing we to our God a - bove, Al - - le - lu - ia!

Our tri - um-phant ho - ly day, Al - - le - lu - ia!
Un - to Christ, our heav'n-ly King, Al - - le - lu - ia!
Our sal - va - tion have pro - cured. Al - - le - lu - ia!
Praise e - ter - nal as His love: Al - - le - lu - ia!

Who did once up - on the cross, Al - - le - lu - ia!
Who en - dured the cross and grave, Al - - le - lu - ia!
Now a - bove the sky He's King, Al - - le - lu - ia!
Praise Him, all ye heav'n - ly host, Al - - le - lu - ia!

Suf - fer to re - deem our loss. Al - - le - lu - ia!
Sin - ners to re - deem and save. Al - - le - lu - ia!
Where the an - gels ev - er sing. Al - - le - lu - ia!
Fa - ther, Son, and Ho - ly Ghost. Al - - le - lu - ia! A-men.

200 I Know that My Redeemer Lives

L. M.

Job 19: 25–27
Samuel Medley. 1775, ab.

Duke Street
John Hatton, 1793

1 I know that my Re-deem-er lives; What com-fort this sweet sen-tence gives! He lives, He lives, who once was dead; He lives, my ev-er-liv-ing Head.

2 He lives tri-um-phant from the grave, He lives e-ter-nal-ly to save, He lives all-glo-rious in the sky, He lives ex-alt-ed there on high.

3 He lives to bless me with His love, He lives to plead for me a-bove, He lives my hun-gry soul to feed, He lives to help in time of need.

4 He lives to grant me rich sup-ply, He lives to guide me with His eye, He lives to com-fort me when faint, He lives to hear my soul's com-plaint. A-men.

5 He lives to silence all my fears,
He lives to wipe away my tears,
He lives to calm my troubled heart,
He lives all blessings to impart.

6 He lives, my kind, wise, heavenly Friend,
He lives and loves me to the end;
He lives, and while He lives, I'll sing;
He lives, my Prophet, Priest, and King.

7 He lives and grants me daily breath;
He lives, and I shall conquer death;
He lives my mansion to prepare;
He lives to bring me safely there.

8 He lives, all glory to His name!
He lives, my Jesus, still the same.
Oh, the sweet joy this sentence gives,
"I know that my Redeemer lives!"

Jesus Lives! The Victory's Won

201

Rom. 8: 11
Jesus lebt, mit ihm auch ich
Christian F. Gellert, 1757, ab.
Tr., Frances E. Cox, 1841, alt.

7. 8. 7. 8. 7. 7.

Jesus, meine Zuversicht
Johann Crüger, 1656

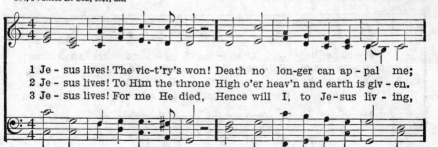

1 Je - sus lives! The vic-t'ry's won! Death no lon-ger can ap - pal me;
2 Je - sus lives! To Him the throne High o'er heav'n and earth is giv - en.
3 Je - sus lives! For me He died, Hence will I, to Je-sus liv - ing,

Je - sus lives! Death's reign is done! From the grave Christ will re - call me.
I shall go where He is gone, Live and reign with Him in heav-en.
Pure in heart and act a - bide, Praise to Him and glo - ry giv - ing.

Bright-er scenes will then commence; This shall be my con - fi-dence.
God is faith-ful. Doubtings, hence! This shall be my con - fi-dence.
Free - ly God doth aid dis - pense; This shall be my con - fi-dence. A-men.

4 Jesus lives! I know full well
   Naught from me His love shall sever;
Life nor death nor powers of hell
   Part me now from Christ forever.
God will be a sure Defense;
This shall be my confidence.

5 Jesus lives! and now is death
   But the gate of life immortal;
This shall calm my trembling breath
   When I pass its gloomy portal.
Faith shall cry, as fails each sense,
Jesus is my confidence!

202 Welcome, Happy Morning!

Acts 10: 40
Salve, festa dies
Venantius Fortunatus, c. 590, cento
Tr., John Ellerton, 1868, alt.

6. 5. 6. 5. D., with Refrain

Sei du mir gegrüsset
"Enchiridion"
Lübeck, 1545

1 "Wel-come, hap-py morn-ing!" Age to age shall say;
2 Mak-er and Re-deem-er, Life and Health of all,
3 Thou, of life the Au-thor, Death didst un-der-go,
4 Loose the souls long pris-oned, Bound with Sa-tan's chain;

"Hell to-day is van-quished, Heav'n is won to-day!"
Thou from heav'n be-hold-ing Hu-man na-ture's fall,
Tread the path of dark-ness, Sav-ing strength to show.
All that now is fall-en Raise to life a-gain.

Lo, the Dead is liv-ing, God for-ev-er-more!
Of the Fa-ther's God-head, True and on-ly Son,
Come, then, True and Faith-ful, Now ful-fil Thy word;
Show Thy face in bright-ness, Bid the na-tions see;

Him, their true Cre-a-tor, All His works a-dore.
Man-hood to de-liv-er Man-hood didst put on.
'Tis Thine own third morn-ing— Rise, O bur-ied Lord
Bring a-gain our day-light; Day re-turns with Thee.

Welcome, Happy Morning!

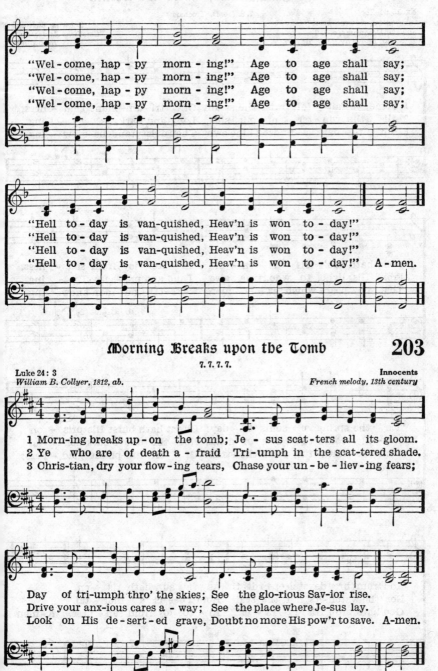

"Wel - come, hap - py morn - ing!" Age to age shall say;
"Wel - come, hap - py morn - ing!" Age to age shall say;
"Wel - come, hap - py morn - ing!" Age to age shall say;
"Wel - come, hap - py morn - ing!" Age to age shall say;

"Hell to - day is van-quished, Heav'n is won to - day!"
"Hell to - day is van-quished, Heav'n is won to - day!"
"Hell to - day is van-quished, Heav'n is won to - day!"
"Hell to - day is van-quished, Heav'n is won to - day!" A - men.

Morning Breaks upon the Tomb   203
7. 7. 7. 7.

Luke 24 : 3
William B. Collyer, 1812, ab.

Innocents
French melody, 13th century

1 Morn-ing breaks up-on the tomb; Je - sus scat-ters all its gloom.
2 Ye who are of death a - fraid Tri - umph in the scat-tered shade.
3 Chris-tian, dry your flow-ing tears, Chase your un - be - liev-ing fears;

Day of tri-umph thro' the skies; See the glo-rious Sav-ior rise.
Drive your anx-ious cares a - way; See the place where Je-sus lay.
Look on His de - sert-ed grave, Doubt no more His pow'r to save. A - men.

204 Come, Ye Faithful, Raise the Strain

Ex. 15 : 1–21
Αἴσωμεν, πάντες λαοί
John of Damascus, c. 750
Tr., *John M. Neale, 1859, alt., ab.*

7. 6. 7. 6. D. Trochaic

Schwing dich auf
"Geistliche Andachten"
Berlin, 1666

1 Come, ye faith-ful, raise the strain Of tri-um-phant glad - ness;
2 All the win-ter of our sins, Long and dark, is fly - ing
3 But to - day a - midst Thine own Thou didst stand, be-stow - ing

God hath bro't His Is - ra - el In - to joy from sad - ness.
From His light, to whom we give Laud and praise un - dy - ing.
That Thy peace which ev - er - more Pass-eth hu - man know - ing.

'Tis the spring of souls to - day: Christ hath burst His pris - on
Nei - ther could the gates of death Nor the tomb's dark por - tal
Come, ye faith - ful, raise the strain Of tri-um-phant glad - ness;

And from three days' sleep in death As a sun hath ris - en.
Nor the watch-ers nor the seal Hold Thee as a mor - tal.
God hath bro't His Is - ra - el In - to joy from sad - ness. A-men.

The Day of Resurrection

205

Ps. 118: 15
Ἀναστάσεως ἡμέρα
John of Damascus, c. 750
Tr., John M. Neale, 1863, alt.

7. 6. 7. 6. D.

Lancashire
Henry Smart, 1836

1 The day of res - ur - rec - tion, Earth, tell it out a - broad,
2 Our hearts be pure from e - vil That we may see a - right
3 Now let the heav'ns be joy - ful, Let earth her song be - gin,

The Pass - o - ver of glad - ness, The Pass - o - ver of God.
The Lord in rays e - ter - nal Of res - ur - rec - tion light
Let all the world keep tri - umph And all that is there - in.

From death to life e - ter - nal, From this world to the sky,
And, lis - t'ning to His ac - cents, May hear, so calm and plain,
Let all things, seen and un - seen, Their notes of glad - ness blend;

Our Christ hath bro't us o - ver With hymns of vic - to - ry.
His own "All hail!" and, hear - ing, May raise the vic - tor strain.
For Christ the Lord hath ris - en,—Our joy that hath no end. A - men.

206 Jesus Christ, My Sure Defense

1 Cor. 15: 35ff.
Jesus, meine Zuversicht
Author unknown, 1653
Tr., based on Catherine Winkworth, 1863

7. 8. 7. 8. 7. 7.

Jesus, meine Zuversicht
Johann Crüger, 1653

1 Je-sus Christ, my sure De-fense And my Sav-ior, ev-er liv-eth;
2 Je-sus, my Re-deem-er, lives; I, too, un-to life shall wak-en.

Know-ing this, my con-fi-dence Rests up-on the hope it giv-eth
End-less joy my Sav-ior gives; Shall my cour-age, then, be shak-en?

Though the night of death be fraught Still with man-y an anx-ious tho't.
Shall I fear, or could the Head Rise and leave His members dead? A-men.

3 Nay, too closely am I bound
    Unto Him by hope forever;
Faith's strong hand the Rock hath found,
    Grasped it, and will leave it never;
Even death now cannot part
From its Lord the trusting heart.

4 I am flesh and must return
    Unto dust, whence I am taken;
But by faith I now discern
    That from death I shall awaken
With my Savior to abide
In His glory, at His side.

Jesus Christ, My Sure Defense

5 Glorified, I shall anew
  With this flesh then be enshrouded;
 In this body I shall view
  God, my Lord, with eyes unclouded;
 In this flesh I then shall see
 Jesus Christ eternally.

6 Then these eyes my Lord shall know,
  My Redeemer and my Brother;
 In His love my soul shall glow —
  I myself, and not another!
 Then the weakness I feel here
 Shall forever disappear.

7 They who sorrow here and moan
  There in gladness shall be reigning;
 Earthly here the seed is sown,
  There immortal life attaining.
 Here our sinful bodies die,
 Glorified to dwell on high.

8 Then take comfort and rejoice,
  For His members Christ will cherish.
 Fear not, they will hear His voice;
  Dying, they shall never perish;
 For the very grave is stirred
 When the trumpet's blast is heard.

9 Laugh to scorn the gloomy grave
  And at death no longer tremble;
 He, the Lord, who came to save
  Will at last His own assemble.
 They will go their Lord to meet,
 Treading death beneath their feet.

10 Oh, then, draw away your hearts
  Now from pleasures base and hollow.
 There to share what He imparts,
  Here His footsteps ye must follow.
 Fix your hearts beyond the skies,
 Whither ye yourselves would rise.

207 Like the Golden Sun Ascending

Acts 2: 32
Som den gyldne Sol frembryder
Thomas Kingo, 1689, cento
Tr., George T. Rygh, 1908

8. 7. 8. 7. 7. 7. 8. 8.

Werde munter
Johann Schop, 1642

1 Like the gold-en sun as-cend-ing, Break-ing thro' the gloom of night, On the earth his glo-ry spend-ing So that dark-ness takes to flight, Thus my Je-sus from the grave And Death's dis-mal, dread-ful cave Rose tri-um-phant Eas-ter

2 Thanks to Thee, O Christ vic-to-rious! Thanks to Thee, O Lord of Life! Death hath now no pow-er o'er us, Thou hast con-quered in the strife. Thanks be-cause Thou didst a-rise And hast o-pened Par-a-dise! None can ful-ly sing the

Like the Golden Sun Ascending

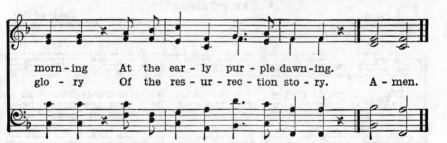

morn-ing At the ear-ly pur-ple dawn-ing.
glo-ry Of the res-ur-rec-tion sto-ry. A-men.

3 Though I be by sin o'ertaken,
   Though I lie in helplessness,
  Though I be by friends forsaken
   And must suffer sore distress,
  Though I be despised, contemned,
  And by all the world condemned,
  Though the dark grave yawn before me,
  Yet the light of hope shines o'er me.

4 Thou hast died for my transgression,
   All my sins on Thee were laid;
  Thou hast won for me salvation,
   On the cross my debt was paid.
  From the grave I shall arise
  And shall meet Thee in the skies.
  Death itself is transitory;
  I shall lift my head in glory.

5 Grant me grace, O blessed Savior,
   And Thy Holy Spirit send
  That my walk and my behavior
   May be pleasing to the end;
  That I may not fall again
  Into Death's grim pit and pain,
  Whence by grace Thou hast retrieved me
  And from which Thou hast relieved me.

6 For the joy Thine advent gave me,
   For Thy holy, precious Word;
  For Thy Baptism, which doth save me,
   For Thy blest Communion board;
  For Thy death, the bitter scorn,
  For Thy resurrection morn,
  Lord, I thank Thee and extol Thee,
  And in heaven I shall behold Thee.

208 Ye Sons and Daughters of the King

John 20
O filii et filiae
Author unknown, c. 1600
Tr., John M. Neale, 1851

8. 8. 8., with Alleluias

Gelobt sei Gott
Melchior Vulpius, 1609

1 Ye sons and daugh-ters of the King, Whom heav'n-ly hosts in
2 On that first morn-ing of the week, Be-fore the day be-
3 An an-gel bade their sor-row flee, For thus he spake un-

glo-ry sing, To-day the grave hath lost its sting:
gan to break, The Ma-rys went their Lord to seek:
to the three: "Your Lord doth go to Gal-i-lee":

Al-le-lu-ia!... Al-le-lu-ia!... Al-le-lu-ia!
Al-le-lu-ia!... Al-le-lu-ia!... Al-le-lu-ia!
Al-le-lu-ia!... Al-le-lu-ia!... Al-le-lu-ia! A-men.

4 That night the Apostles met in fear,
   Amidst them came their Lord most dear
   And said: "Peace be unto you here":
       Alleluia!

5 When Thomas afterwards had heard
   That Jesus had fulfilled His word,
   He doubted if it were the Lord:
       Alleluia!

6 "Thomas, behold My side," saith He,
   "My hands, My feet, My body, see;
   And doubt not, but believe in Me":
       Alleluia!

7 No longer Thomas then denied;
   He saw the feet, the hands, the side;
   "Thou art my Lord and God," he cried:
       Alleluia!

Ye Sons and Daughters of the King

8 Blessèd are they that have not seen
And yet whose faith hath constant been,
In life eternal they shall reign:
Alleluia!

9 On this most holy day of days
To God your hearts and voices raise
In laud and jubilee and praise:
Alleluia!

10 And we with holy Church unite,
As evermore is just and right,
In glory to the King of light:
Alleluia!

Who Is This that Comes from Edom   209

8. 7. 8. 7. 7. 7.

2 Tim. 1 : 10
Thomas Kelly, 1809, alt.

Neander
Joachim Neander, 1680

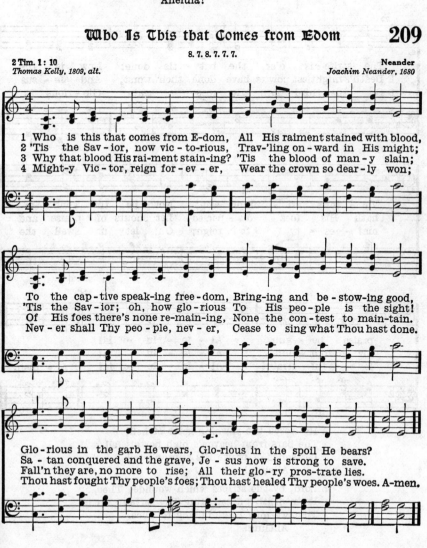

1 Who is this that comes from E-dom, All His raiment stained with blood,
2 'Tis the Sav-ior, now vic-to-rious, Trav-'ling on-ward in His might;
3 Why that blood His rai-ment stain-ing? 'Tis the blood of man-y slain;
4 Might-y Vic-tor, reign for-ev-er, Wear the crown so dear-ly won;

To the cap-tive speak-ing free-dom, Bring-ing and be-stow-ing good,
'Tis the Sav-ior; oh, how glo-rious To His peo-ple is the sight!
Of His foes there's none re-main-ing, None the con-test to main-tain.
Nev-er shall Thy peo-ple, nev-er, Cease to sing what Thou hast done.

Glo-rious in the garb He wears, Glo-rious in the spoil He bears?
Sa-tan conquered and the grave, Je-sus now is strong to save.
Fall'n they are, no more to rise; All their glo-ry pros-trate lies.
Thou hast fought Thy people's foes; Thou hast healed Thy people's woes. A-men.

210 The Strife Is O'er, the Battle Done

Ps. 98: 1
Finita iam sunt praelia
Author unknown, 1695
Tr., Francis Pott, c. 1859, alt.

8. 8. 8. 4., with Alleluias

Palestrina
Giovanni P. da Palestrina, 1591, ad.

1 Al - le - lu - ia! Al - le - lu - ia! Al - le - lu - ia!

The strife is o'er, the bat - tle done; Now is the
2 Death's mightiest pow'rs have done their worst, And Je - sus
3 On the third morn He rose a - gain Glo - rious in

Vic - tor's tri - umph won; Now be the song of
hath His foes dis - persed; Let shouts of praise and
maj - es - ty to reign; Oh, let us swell the

praise be - gun. Al - le - lu - ia!
joy out - burst. Al - le - lu - ia!
joy - ful strain! Al - le - lu - ia! A - men.

4 He closed the yawning gates of hell;
The bars from heaven's high portals fell.
Let songs of praise His triumph tell.
Alleluia!

5 Lord, by the stripes which wounded Thee,
From death's dread sting Thy servants free
That we may live and sing to Thee.
Alleluia!

Lo, Judah's Lion Wins the Strife

211

Rev. 5: 5
Aj, ten silný lev udatný
From the Bohemian, c. 1650
Tr., John Bajus, 1940

8. 8. 4. 7.

Judah's Lion
Bohemian melody, c. 1600

1 Lo, Judah's Lion wins the strife And reigns o'er death to give us life. Hallelujah! Oh, let us sing His praises!

2 'Tis He whom David did portray When he did strong Goliath slay. Hallelujah! Oh, sing with gladsome voices!

3 Like Samson, Christ great strength employed And conquered hell, its gates destroyed. Hallelujah! Oh, let us sing His praises! A-men.

4 The power of death He brake in twain
When He to life arose again.
Hallelujah!
To Him all praise be given!

5 He led to freedom all oppressed
And pardon won for sin-distressed.
Hallelujah!
Oh, praise Him for His mercy!

6 In festal spirit, song, and word,
To Jesus, our victorious Lord,
Hallelujah!
All praise and thanks be rendered.

7 All honor, glory, praise be given
Our Triune God, who reigns in heaven.
Hallelujah!
Now gladly sing we: Amen.

212 A Hymn of Glory Let Us Sing

Acts 1: 11

Hymnum canamus gloriae
The Venerable Bede, †735
Tr., Benjamin Webb, 1854, alt.

L. M., with Alleluias

Lasst uns erfreuen
"Geistliche Kirchengesäng"
Cologne, 1623

1 A hymn of glo - ry let us sing; New songs thro'-out the
2 The ho - ly ap - os - tol - ic band Up - on the Mount of
3 To whom the an - gels, draw-ing nigh, "Why stand and gaze up -
4 "A - gain shall ye be - hold Him so As ye to - day have

world shall ring: Al - le - lu - ia! Al - le - lu - ia! Christ,
Ol - ives stand; Al - le - lu - ia! Al - le - lu - ia! And
on the sky? Al - le - lu - ia! Al - le - lu - ia! This
seen Him go, Al - le - lu - ia! Al - le - lu - ia! In

by a road be - fore un - trod, As - cend-eth to the
with His fol - low - ers they see Je - sus' re - splen-dent
is the Sav - ior," thus they say; "This is His no - ble
glo - rious pomp as - cend-ing high, Up to the por - tals

throne of God. Al - le - lu - ia! Al - le - lu - ia!
maj - es - ty. Al - le - lu - ia! Al - le - lu - ia!
tri - umph - day. Al - le - lu - ia! Al - le - lu - ia!
of the sky." Al - le - lu - ia! Al - le - lu - ia!

A Hymn of Glory Let Us Sing

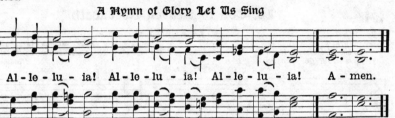

Al - le - lu - ia! Al - le - lu - ia! Al - le - lu - ia! A - men.

5 Oh, grant us thitherward to tend
   And with unwearied hearts ascend—Alleluia!
   Unto Thy kingdom's throne, where Thou,
   As is our faith, art seated now.—Alleluia!

6 Be Thou our Joy and strong Defense,
   Who art our future Recompense:—Alleluia!
   So shall the light that springs from Thee
   Be ours through all eternity.—Alleluia!

7 O risen Christ, ascended Lord,
   All praise to Thee let earth accord,—Alleluia!
   Who art, while endless ages run,
   With Father and with Spirit One.—Alleluia!

Hail the Day that Sees Him Rise 213

Acts 1: 9
Charles Wesley, 1739, cento, alt.

7. 7. 7. 7.

Orientis partibus
French melody, c. 1200, ad.

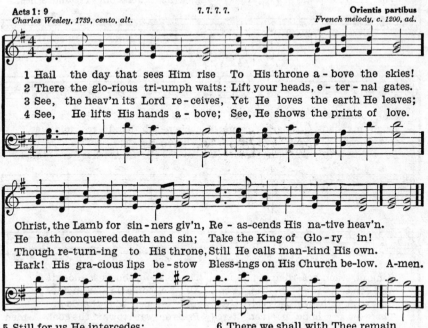

1 Hail the day that sees Him rise To His throne a-bove the skies!
2 There the glo-rious tri-umph waits: Lift your heads, e-ter-nal gates.
3 See, the heav'n its Lord re-ceives, Yet He loves the earth He leaves;
4 See, He lifts His hands a-bove; See, He shows the prints of love.

Christ, the Lamb for sin-ners giv'n, Re-as-cends His na-tive heav'n.
He hath conquered death and sin; Take the King of Glo-ry in!
Though re-turn-ing to His throne, Still He calls man-kind His own.
Hark! His gra-cious lips be-stow Bless-ings on His Church be-low. A-men.

5 Still for us He intercedes;
   His prevailing death He pleads,
   Near Himself prepares our place,
   Harbinger of human race.

6 There we shall with Thee remain
   Partners of Thy endless reign,
   There Thy face unclouded see,
   Find our heaven of heavens in Thee.

214 Lo, God to Heaven Ascendeth

Ps. 47: 5-7
Gott fähret auf gen Himmel
Gottfried W. Sacer, 1661, cento
Tr., Frances E. Cox, 1841, alt.

7. 6. 7. 6. 6. 7. 7. 6.

Aus meines Herzens Grunde
"Neu Catechismus-Gesangbüchlein"
Hamburg, 1598

1 Lo, God to heav'n as-cend-eth! Thro'-out its re-gions vast
2 With joy is heav'n re-sound-ing Christ's glad re-turn to see;
3 From cross to throne as-cend-ing, We fol-low Christ on high
4 Our place He is pre-par-ing; To heav'n we, too, shall rise,

With shouts tri-um-phant blend-eth The trum-pet's thrill-ing blast:
Be-hold the saints sur-round-ing The Lord who set them free.
And know the path-way wend-ing To man-sions in the sky.
With Him His glo-ry shar-ing, Be where our Trea-sure lies.

Sing praise to Christ the Lord; Sing praise with ex-ul-ta-tion,
Bright myr-iads, throng-ing, come; The cher-ub band re-joic-es,
Our Lord is gone be-fore; Yet here He will not leave us,
Be-stir thy-self, my soul! Where Je-sus Christ has en-tered,

King of each hea-then na-tion, The God of hosts a-dored!
And loud se-raph-ic voic-es All wel-come Je-sus home.
But soon in heav'n re-ceive us And o-pen wide the door.
There let thy hope be cen-tered; Press on-ward toward the goal. A-men.

Lo, God to Heaven Ascendeth

5 Let all our thoughts be winging
    To where Thou didst ascend,
And let our hearts be singing:
    "We seek Thee, Christ, our Friend,
Thee, God's exalted Son,
    Our Life, and Way to heaven,
    To whom all power is given,
Our Joy and Hope and Crown."

Draw Us to Thee 215

Solomon's Song 1: 4
Zeuch uns nach dir
Friedrich Funcke, 1686
Tr., August Crull, †1923

4. 4. 7. 4. 4. 7.

Ach Gott und Herr
C. Peter, "Andachts-Zymbeln"
Freyberg, 1655

1 Draw us to Thee, For then shall we Walk in Thy
2 Draw us to Thee, Lord, lov-ing-ly; Let us de-
3 Draw us to Thee; Oh, grant that we May walk the

steps for-ev-er And hast-en on Where Thou art
part with glad-ness That we may be For-ev-er
road to heav-en! Di-rect our way Lest we should

gone To be with Thee, dear Sav-ior.
free From sor-row, grief, and sad-ness.
stray And from Thy paths be driv-en. A-men.

4 Draw us to Thee
    That also we
Thy heavenly bliss inherit
    And ever dwell
    Where sin and hell
No more can vex our spirit.

5 Draw us to Thee
    Unceasingly,
Into Thy kingdom take us;
    Let us fore'er
    Thy glory share,
Thy saints and joint heirs make us.

216 On Christ's Ascension I Now Build

John 14: 3
Auf Christi Himmelfahrt allein
Josua Wegelin, 1636
Tr., William M. Czamanske, 1938

8. 7. 8. 7. 8. 8. 7.

Nun freut euch
"Etlich' christliche Lieder"
Wittenberg, 1524

1 On Christ's as-cen-sion I now build The hope of mine as-cen-sion;
2 Since He re-turned to claim His throne, Great gifts for men ob-tain-ing,
3 Oh, grant, dear Lord, this grace to me, Re-call-ing Thine as-cen-sion,

This hope a-lone has ev-er stilled All doubt and ap-pre-hen-sion;
My heart shall rest in Him a-lone, No oth-er rest re-main-ing;
That I may ev-er walk with Thee, A-dorn-ing Thy re-demp-tion;

For where the Head is, there full well I know His mem-bers are to dwell
For where my Trea-sure went be-fore, There all my tho'ts shall ev-er soar
And then, when all my days shall cease, Let me de-part in joy and peace

When Christ shall come and call them.
To still their deep-est yearn-ing.
In an-swer to my plead-ing. A-men.

Oh, Sing with Exultation

217

7. 6. 7. 6. 6. 7. 7. 6.

Ps. 118: 15, 16
Om Salighed og Gläde
Anders C. Arrebo, 1623, cento
Tr., Carl Döving, 1907

Aus meines Herzens Grunde
"Neu Catechismus-Gesangbüchlein"
Hamburg, 1598

1 Oh, sing with ex - ul - ta - tion, Sing to the Lord, re - joice,
2 Since Christ, our Lord, is liv - ing, We nev - er - more shall die;
3 Christ is the sure Foun - da - tion The build - ers did re - ject,
4 To Thee, O Christ, be glo - ry, Who cam - est in His name!

And in His con - gre - ga - tion Shout with tri - um - phant voice.
To God the glo - ry giv - ing, We rise to Him on high.
But He for our sal - va - tion Is pre - cious and e - lect
Thy peo - ple sing the sto - ry Thy prais - es to pro - claim.

For, lo, at God's right hand Is Christ in glo - ry seat - ed;
Tho' chas-tened we may be And to our graves be tak - en,
And made the Cor - ner-stone On which the Church is found - ed;
We thank Thee and a - dore, O Christ, our Lord and Sav - ior;

With death and hell de - feat - ed, As Vic - tor doth com-mand.
We un - to life shall wak - en And live e - ter - nal - ly.
This mar - vel now is sound-ed, The work of God a - lone.
Thy grace and bound-less fa - vor Stand fast for - ev - er-more. A-men.

218 See, the Conqueror Mounts in Triumph

8. 7. 8. 7. D.

Ps. 68 : 18
Christopher Wordsworth, 1862, cento

Rex Gloriae
Henry Smart, 1868

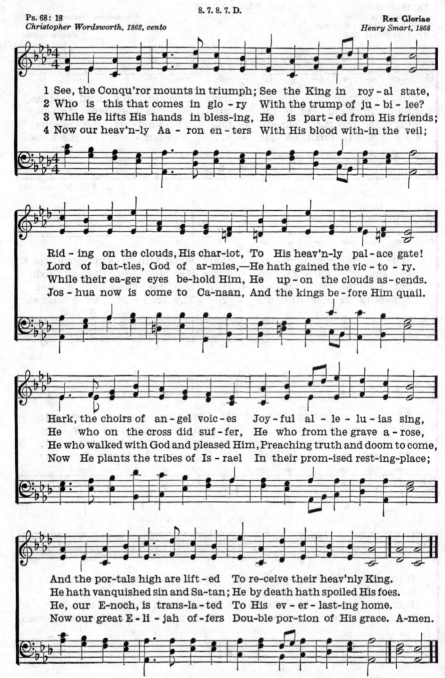

1 See, the Conqu'ror mounts in triumph; See the King in roy-al state,
2 Who is this that comes in glo-ry With the trump of ju-bi-lee?
3 While He lifts His hands in bless-ing, He is part-ed from His friends;
4 Now our heav'n-ly Aa-ron en-ters With His blood with-in the veil;

Rid-ing on the clouds, His char-iot, To His heav'n-ly pal-ace gate!
Lord of bat-tles, God of ar-mies,—He hath gained the vic-to-ry.
While their ea-ger eyes be-hold Him, He up-on the clouds as-cends.
Jos-hua now is come to Ca-naan, And the kings be-fore Him quail.

Hark, the choirs of an-gel voic-es Joy-ful al-le-lu-ias sing,
He who on the cross did suf-fer, He who from the grave a-rose,
He who walked with God and pleased Him, Preaching truth and doom to come,
Now He plants the tribes of Is-rael In their prom-ised rest-ing-place;

And the por-tals high are lift-ed To re-ceive their heav'nly King.
He hath vanquished sin and Sa-tan; He by death hath spoiled His foes.
He, our E-noch, is trans-la-ted To His ev-er-last-ing home.
Now our great E-li-jah of-fers Dou-ble por-tion of His grace. A-men.

See, the Conqueror Mounts in Triumph

5 Thou hast raised our human nature
   On the clouds to God's right hand;
There we sit in heavenly places,
   There with Thee in glory stand.
Jesus reigns, adored by angels;
   Man with God is on the throne.
Mighty Lord, in Thine ascension
   We by faith behold our own.

6 Glory be to God the Father;
   Glory be to God the Son,
Dying, risen, ascending for us,
   Who the heavenly realm hath won;
Glory to the Holy Spirit!
   To One God in Persons Three
Glory both in earth and heaven,
   Glory, endless glory, be.

The Head that Once was Crowned with Thorns 219

C. M.

Heb. 2: 10
Thomas Kelly, 1820

St. Magnus
Jeremiah Clarke, 1709

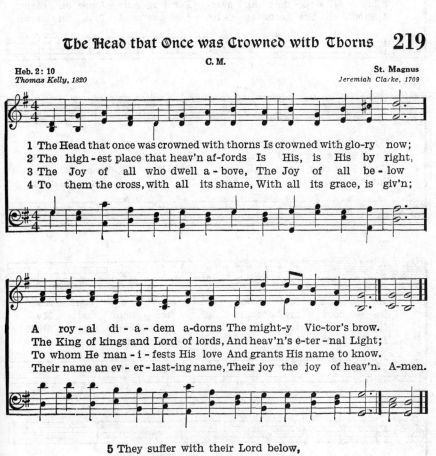

1 The Head that once was crowned with thorns Is crowned with glo-ry now;
2 The high-est place that heav'n af-fords Is His, is His by right,
3 The Joy of all who dwell a-bove, The Joy of all be-low
4 To them the cross, with all its shame, With all its grace, is giv'n;

A roy-al di-a-dem a-dorns The might-y Vic-tor's brow.
The King of kings and Lord of lords, And heav'n's e-ter-nal Light;
To whom He man-i-fests His love And grants His name to know.
Their name an ev-er-last-ing name, Their joy the joy of heav'n. A-men.

5 They suffer with their Lord below,
   They reign with Him above,
Their profit and their joy to know
   The mystery of His love.

6 The cross He bore is life and health,
   Though shame and death to Him:
His people's hope, His people's wealth,
   Their everlasting theme.

220 Jesus, My Great High Priest

Heb. 9: 11, 12
Join All the Glorious Names
Isaac Watts, 1709, cento

6. 6. 6. 6. 8. 8.

Bevan
John Goss, 1853

1 Je - sus, my great High Priest, Of - fered His blood and died;
2 To this dear Sure - ty's hand Will I com - mit my cause;
3 My Ad - vo - cate ap - pears For my de - fense on high;
4 Should all the hosts of death And pow'rs of hell un - known

My guilt - y con - science seeks No sac - ri - fice be - side.
He an - swers and ful - fils His Fa - ther's bro - ken laws.
The Fa - ther bows His ears And lays His thun - der by.
Put their most dread - ful forms Of rage and mis - chief on,

His pow'r - ful blood did once a - tone, And
Be - hold my soul at free - dom set; My
Not all that hell or sin can say Shall
I shall be safe, for Christ dis - plays Su -

now it pleads be - fore the Throne.
Sure - ty paid the dread - ful debt.
turn His heart, His love, a - way.
pe - rior pow'r and guard - ian grace. A - men.

Hark! Ten Thousand Harps and Voices

8. 7. 8. 7. 7. 7.

Heb. 1: 6
Thomas Kelly, 1806, ab.

Neander
Joachim Neander, 1680

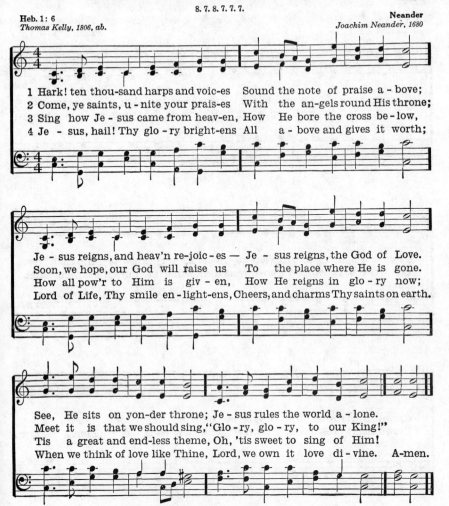

1 Hark! ten thou-sand harps and voic-es Sound the note of praise a - bove;
2 Come, ye saints, u - nite your prais-es With the an-gels round His throne;
3 Sing how Je - sus came from heav-en, How He bore the cross be - low,
4 Je - sus, hail! Thy glo - ry bright-ens All a - bove and gives it worth;

Je - sus reigns, and heav'n re-joic-es — Je - sus reigns, the God of Love.
Soon, we hope, our God will raise us To the place where He is gone.
How all pow'r to Him is giv - en, How He reigns in glo - ry now;
Lord of Life, Thy smile en - light-ens, Cheers, and charms Thy saints on earth.

See, He sits on yon-der throne; Je - sus rules the world a - lone.
Meet it is that we should sing, "Glo - ry, glo - ry, to our King!"
Tis a great and end-less theme, Oh, 'tis sweet to sing of Him!
When we think of love like Thine, Lord, we own it love di - vine. A-men.

5 King of Glory, reign forever;
   Thine an everlasting crown.
Nothing from Thy love shall sever
   Those whom Thou hast made Thine own,
Happy objects of Thy grace,
Destined to behold Thy face.

6 Savior, hasten Thine appearing;
   Bring, oh, bring, the glorious day
When, the awe-full summons hearing,
   Heaven and earth shall pass away;
Then with golden harps we'll sing,
"Glory, glory, to our King!"

222 Look, Ye Saints, the Sight Is Glorious

8. 7. 8. 7. 4. 7.

Phil. 2: 9–11
Thomas Kelly, 1809

Coronae
William H. Monk, 1871

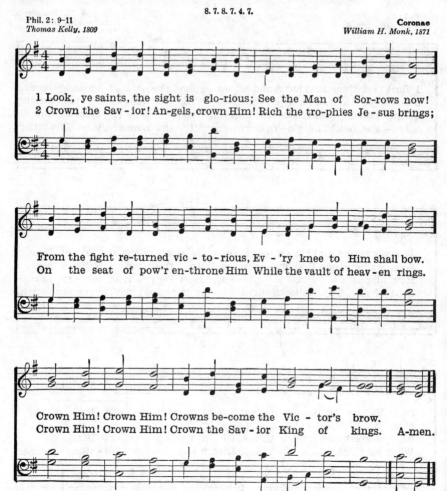

1 Look, ye saints, the sight is glo-rious; See the Man of Sor-rows now!
2 Crown the Sav-ior! An-gels, crown Him! Rich the tro-phies Je-sus brings;

From the fight re-turned vic-to-rious, Ev-'ry knee to Him shall bow.
On the seat of pow'r en-throne Him While the vault of heav-en rings.

Crown Him! Crown Him! Crowns be-come the Vic-tor's brow.
Crown Him! Crown Him! Crown the Sav-ior King of kings. A-men.

3 Sinners in derision crowned Him,
    Mocking thus the Savior's claim;
Saints and angels crowd around Him,
    Own His title, praise His name.
Crown Him! Crown Him!
    Spread abroad the Victor's fame.

4 Hark, those bursts of acclamation!
    Hark, those loud triumphant chords!
Jesus takes the highest station;
    Oh, what joy the sight affords!
Crown Him! Crown Him!
    King of kings and Lord of lords!

We Thank Thee, Jesus, Dearest Friend

223

L. M., with Hallelujah

Eph. 4: 8
Wir danken dir, Herr Jesu Christ
Author unknown, 1607, cento.
Tr., Matthias Loy, 1880, alt.

Erschienen ist
Nikolaus Herman, 1560

1 We thank Thee, Je - sus, dear - est Friend, That Thou didst
2 As - cend - ed to His throne on high, Hid from our
3 The man who trusts in Him is blest And finds in

in - to heav'n as - cend. O bless - ed Sav - ior, bid us live
sight, yet al - ways nigh, He rules and reigns at God's right hand
Him e - ter - nal rest; This world's al-lure-ments we de - spise

And strength to soul and bod - y give. Hal - le - lu - jah!
And has all pow'r at His com-mand. Hal - le - lu - jah!
And fix on Christ a - lone our eyes. Hal - le - lu - jah! A - men.

4 We therefore heartily rejoice
And sing His praise with cheerful voice;
He captive led captivity,
From bitter death He set us free.
Hallelujah!

5 Through Him we heirs of heaven are made;
O Brother, Christ, extend Thine aid
That we may firmly trust in Thee
And through Thee live eternally.
Hallelujah!

224 Come, Holy Ghost, God and Lord!

Acts 2: 4
Komm, Heiliger Geist, Herre Gott
Martin Luther, 1524
Tr., composite

7. 8. 8. 8. 8. 8. 8. 8. 10. 8.

Komm, Heiliger Geist, Herre Gott
15th-century melody

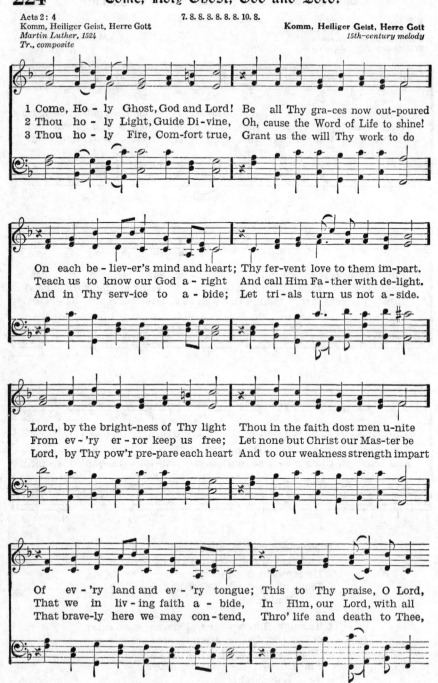

1 Come, Ho - ly Ghost, God and Lord! Be all Thy gra - ces now out-poured
2 Thou ho - ly Light, Guide Di - vine, Oh, cause the Word of Life to shine!
3 Thou ho - ly Fire, Com-fort true, Grant us the will Thy work to do

On each be - liev-er's mind and heart; Thy fer-vent love to them im-part.
Teach us to know our God a - right And call Him Fa - ther with de-light.
And in Thy serv-ice to a - bide; Let tri - als turn us not a - side.

Lord, by the bright-ness of Thy light Thou in the faith dost men u-nite
From ev - 'ry er - ror keep us free; Let none but Christ our Mas-ter be
Lord, by Thy pow'r pre-pare each heart And to our weakness strength impart

Of ev - 'ry land and ev - 'ry tongue; This to Thy praise, O Lord,
That we in liv - ing faith a - bide, In Him, our Lord, with all
That brave-ly here we may con-tend, Thro' life and death to Thee,

Come, Holy Ghost, God and Lord!

our God, be sung. Hal - le - lu - jah! Hal - le - lu - jah!
our might con - fide. Hal - le - lu - jah! Hal - le - lu - jah!
our Lord, as - cend. Hal - le - lu - jah! Hal - le - lu - jah! A - men.

Come, Holy Spirit, Come

225

Ps. 51 : 10–12
Joseph Hart, 1759, cento

S. M.

Boylston
Lowell Mason, 1832

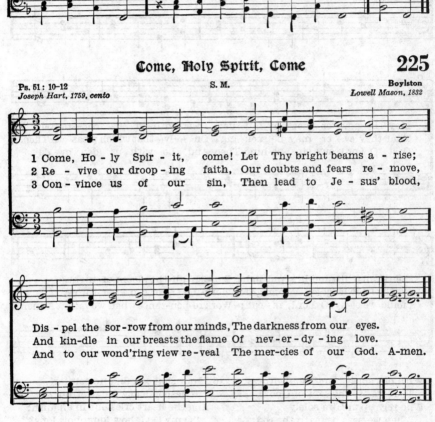

1 Come, Ho - ly Spir - it, come! Let Thy bright beams a - rise;
2 Re - vive our droop - ing faith, Our doubts and fears re - move,
3 Con - vince us of our sin, Then lead to Je - sus' blood,

Dis - pel the sor - row from our minds, The darkness from our eyes.
And kin - dle in our breasts the flame Of nev - er - dy - ing love.
And to our wond'ring view re - veal The mer - cies of our God. A - men.

4 'Tis Thine to cleanse the heart,
To sanctify the soul,
To pour fresh life into each part,
And new-create the whole.

5 Dwell therefore in our hearts;
Our minds from bondage free;
Then shall we know and praise and love
The Father, Son, and Thee.

226 Come, Oh, Come, Thou Quickening Spirit

Rom. 8: 15
8. 7. 8. 7. 7. 7.

Komm, o komm, du Geist des Lebens
Heinrich Held, c. 1664
Tr., Charles W. Schaeffer, 1866, alt.

Komm, o komm, du Geist
J. Christoph Bach, 1680

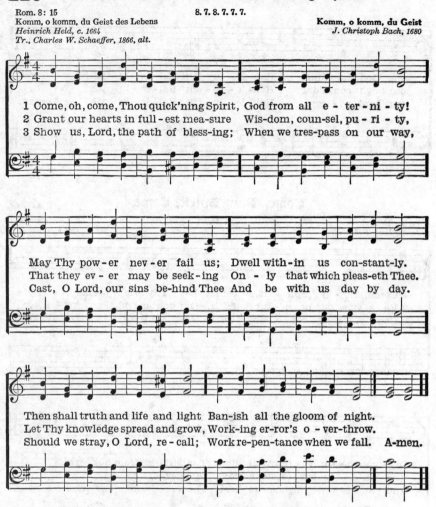

1 Come, oh, come, Thou quick'ning Spirit, God from all e - ter - ni - ty!
2 Grant our hearts in full - est mea - sure Wis-dom, coun-sel, pu - ri - ty,
3 Show us, Lord, the path of bless-ing; When we tres-pass on our way,

May Thy pow-er nev-er fail us; Dwell with-in us con-stant-ly.
That they ev - er may be seek-ing On - ly that which pleas-eth Thee.
Cast, O Lord, our sins be-hind Thee And be with us day by day.

Then shall truth and life and light Ban-ish all the gloom of night.
Let Thy knowledge spread and grow, Work-ing er-ror's o - ver-throw.
Should we stray, O Lord, re - call; Work re-pen-tance when we fall. A-men.

4 With our spirit bear Thou witness
　　That we are the sons of God
Who rely upon Him solely
　　When we pass beneath the rod;
For we know, as children should,
That the cross is for our good.

5 Prompt us, Lord, to come before Him
　　With a childlike heart to pray;
Sigh in us, O Holy Spirit,
　　When we know not what to say.
Then our prayer is not in vain,
And our faith new strength shall gain.

6 If our soul can find no comfort,
　　If despondency grows strong,
And the heart cries out in anguish:
　　"O my God, how long, how long?"
Comfort then our aching breast,
Grant it courage, patience, rest.

7 Holy Spirit, strong and mighty,
　　Thou who makest all things new,
Make Thy work within us perfect
　　And the evil Foe subdue.
Grant us weapons for the strife
And with victory crown our life.

Come, Oh, Come, Thou Quickening Spirit

8 Guard, O God, our faith forever;
  Let not Satan, death, or shame
Ever part us from our Savior;
  Lord our Refuge is Thy name.
Though our flesh cry ever: Nay!
Be Thy Word to us still Yea!

9 And when life's frail thread is breaking,
  Then assure us more and more,
As the heirs of life unending,
  Of the glory there in store,
Glory never yet expressed,
Glory of the saints at rest.

Come, Holy Ghost, in Love   227

6. 6. 4. 6. 6. 6. 4.

Ezek. 36: 26
Veni, Sancte Spiritus
Latin author unknown, c. 1200
Tr., Ray Palmer, 1858

Italian Hymn
Felice de Giardini, 1769

1 Come, Ho - ly Ghost, in love Shed on us from a - bove
2 Come, ten-d'rest Friend and best, Our most de - light - ful Guest,
3 Come, Light se - rene and still, Our in-most bos - oms fill,

Thine own bright ray. Di - vine - ly good Thou art; Thy sa - cred
With sooth-ing pow'r. Rest which the wea - ry know, Shade mid the
Dwell in each breast. We know no dawn but Thine; Send forth Thy

gifts im-part To glad-den each sad heart. Oh, come to - day!
noon-tide glow, Peace when deep griefs o'erflow, Cheer us this hour.
beams di-vine On our dark souls to shine And make us blest. A - men.

4 Exalt our low desires,
  Extinguish passion's fires,
    Heal every wound.
  Our stubborn spirits bend,
  Our icy coldness end,
  Our devious steps attend
    While heavenward bound.

5 Come, all the faithful bless;
  Let all who Christ confess
    His praise employ.
  Give virtue's rich reward,
  Victorious death accord
  And, with our glorious Lord,
    Eternal joy.

228   Oh, Enter, Lord, Thy Temple

Acts 2: 17   7. 6. 7. 6. 6. 7. 7. 6.

Zeuch ein zu deinen Toren
Paul Gerhardt, 1653, cento
Tr., Catherine Winkworth, 1863, alt.

Zeuch ein
Johann Crüger, 1653

1 Oh, en-ter, Lord, Thy tem-ple, Be Thou my spir-it's Guest,
2 Oh, en-ter, let me know Thee And feel Thy pow'r with-in,
3 Thou art, O Ho-ly Spir-it, The true a-noint-ing Oil

Who gav-est me, the earth-born, A sec-ond birth more blest!
The pow'r that breaks our fet-ters And res-cues us from sin!
Thro' which are con-se-cra-ted Soul, bod-y, rest, and toil

Thou in the God-head, Lord, Tho' here to dwell Thou deign-est,
Oh, wash and cleanse Thou me That I may serve Thee tru-ly
To Christ, whose guardian wings, Wher-e'er their lot ap-point-ed,

For-ev-er e-qual reign-est, Art e-qual-ly a-dored.
And ren-der hon-or du-ly With per-fect heart to Thee!
Pro-tect His own a-noint-ed, His prophets, priests, and kings. A-men.

4 Thou, Holy Spirit, teachest
     The soul to pray aright;
Thy songs have sweetest music,
     Thy prayers have wondrous might.
Unheard they cannot fall,
     They pierce the highest heaven
     Till He His help hath given
Who surely helpeth all.

5 Thy gift is joy, O Spirit,
     Thou wouldst not have us pine;
In darkest hours Thy comfort
     Doth ever brightly shine.
And, oh, how oft Thy voice
     Hath shed its sweetness o'er me
     And opened heaven before me
And bid my heart rejoice!

Oh, Enter, Lord, Thy Temple

6 All love is Thine, O Spirit;
Thou hatest enmity;
Thou lovest peace and friendship,
All strife wouldst have us flee.
Where wrath and discord reign,
Thy whisper kindly pleadeth
And to the heart that heedeth
Brings love and light again.

7 Our path in all things order
According to Thy mind,
And when this life is over
And all must be resigned,
Oh, grant us then to die
With calm and fearless spirit
And after death inherit
Eternal life on high!

Holy Spirit, Hear Us 229

1 Cor. 12: 7–9
From the German by
Joseph Mohr, 1816
Tr., Claudia F. Hernaman, †1898

6. 5. 6. 5.

Wem in Leidenstagen
Friedrich Filitz, 1847

1 Ho - ly Spir - it, hear us On this sa - cred day;
2 Come as once Thou cam - est To the faith - ful few
3 Up to heav'n as - cend - ing, Our dear Lord has gone;

Come to us with bless - ing, Come with us to stay.
Pa - tient - ly a - wait - ing Je - sus' prom - ise true.
Yet His lit - tle chil - dren Leaves He not a - lone. A - men.

4 To His blessed promise
Now in faith we cling.
Comforter most holy,
Spread o'er us Thy wing.

5 Lighten Thou our darkness,
Be Thyself our Light;
Strengthen Thou our weakness,
Spirit of all might.

6 Spirit of Adoption,
Make us overflow
With Thy sevenfold blessing
And in grace to grow.

7 Into Christ baptized,
Grant that we may be
Day and night, dear Spirit,
Perfected by Thee.

230 Holy Spirit, God of Love

John 15: 26

7. 6. 7. 6. 7. 7. 6. 7. 6.

O Lue fra Guds Kjaerlighed
Birgitte K. Boye, 1778
Tr., George T. Rygh, 1908, alt.

Der Tag, der ist
German melody, 15th century

Ho-ly Spir-it, God of Love, Who our night dost bright-en,

Poured on us from heav'n a-bove, Now our faith en-light-en.

In Thy light we gath-er here; Show us that Christ's prom-ise clear

Is A-men for-ev-er. Je-sus, our as-cend-ed Lord,

Oh, ful-fil Thy gra-cious Word: Bless us with Thy fa-vor! A-men.

We Now Implore God the Holy Ghost

231

John 16: 13
Nun bitten wir den Heiligen Geist
St. 1, author unknown, c. 1250
St. 2-4, Martin Luther, 1524
Tr., composite

9. 9. 11. 10. 4.

Nun bitten wir
Sacred melody, c. 1100

1 We now im-plore God the Ho-ly Ghost
2 Shine in our hearts, O most pre-cious Light,
3 Thou sa-cred Love, grace on us be-stow,
4 Thou high-est Com-fort in ev-'ry need,

For the true faith, which we need the most,
That we Je-sus Christ may know a-right,
Set our hearts with heav'n-ly fire a-glow
Grant that nei-ther shame nor death we heed,

That in our last mo-ments He may be-friend us
Cling-ing to our Sav-ior, whose blood hath bought us,
That with hearts u-nit-ed we love each oth-er,
That e'en then our cour-age may nev-er fail us

And, as home-ward we jour-ney, at-tend us. Lord, have mer-cy!
Who a-gain to our home-land hath bro't us. Lord, have mer-cy!
Of one mind, in peace with ev-'ry broth-er. Lord, have mer-cy!
When the Foe shall ac-cuse and as-sail us. Lord, have mer-cy! A-men.

232
Let Songs of Praises Fill the Sky

Rom. 5: 5
Thomas Cotterill, 1819

8. 6. 8. 6. 8. 8.

Erfurt
Herman Ilse, 1910

1 Let songs of prais-es fill the sky: Christ, our as-cend-ed Lord,
2 The Spir-it by His heav'nly breath Cre-ates new life with-in;
3 The things of Christ the Spir-it takes And shows them un-to men;
4 Come, Ho-ly Spir-it, from a-bove With Thy ce-les-tial fire;

Sends down His Spir-it from on high Ac-cord-ing to His word.
He quick-ens sin-ners from the death Of tres-pass-es and sin.
The fall-en soul His tem-ple makes, God's im-age stamps a-gain.
Come and with flames of zeal and love Our hearts and tongues in-spire.

All hail the day of Pen-te-cost, The com-ing of the Ho-ly Ghost!
All hail the day of Pen-te-cost, The com-ing of the Ho-ly Ghost!
All hail the day of Pen-te-cost, The com-ing of the Ho-ly Ghost!
Be this our day of Pen-te-cost, The com-ing of the Ho-ly Ghost! **A-men.**

233
Come, Holy Ghost, Creator Blest

John 14: 26
Veni, Creator Spiritus, Mentes
Rhabanus Maurus, 1856, asc.
Tr., Edward Caswall, 1849, alt.

L. M.

Komm, Gott Schöpfer
Based on "Veni, Creator Spiritus," c. 600

1 Come, Ho-ly Ghost, Cre-a-tor blest, Vouchsafe within our souls to rest;
2 To Thee, the Com-fort-er, we cry, To Thee, the Gift of God Most High,
3 The sev'n-fold gifts of grace are Thine, O Fin-ger of the Hand Di-vine;

Come, Holy Ghost, Creator Blest

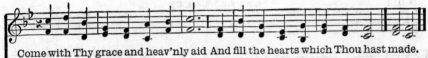

Come with Thy grace and heav'nly aid And fill the hearts which Thou hast made.
The Fount of life, the Fire of love, The soul's Anointing from a-bove.
True Promise of the Father Thou, Who dost the tongue with speech endow. Amen.

4 Thy light to every thought impart
And shed Thy love in every heart;
The weakness of our mortal state
With deathless might invigorate.

5 Drive far away our wily Foe
And Thine abiding peace bestow;
If Thou be our protecting Guide,
No evil can our steps betide.

6 Make Thou to us the Father known,
Teach us the eternal Son to own
And Thee, whose name we ever bless,
Of both the Spirit, to confess.

7 Praise we the Father and the Son
And Holy Spirit, with them One;
And may the Son on us bestow
The gifts that from the Spirit flow!

Holy Ghost, with Light Divine 234

1 Thess. 5 : 23
Andrew Reed, 1817

7. 7. 7. 7.

Light Divine
Orlando Gibbons, 1623

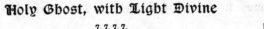

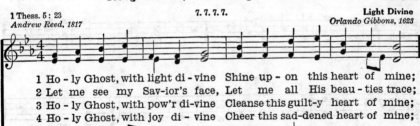

1 Ho-ly Ghost, with light di-vine Shine up-on this heart of mine;
2 Let me see my Sav-ior's face, Let me all His beau-ties trace;
3 Ho-ly Ghost, with pow'r di-vine Cleanse this guilt-y heart of mine;
4 Ho-ly Ghost, with joy di-vine Cheer this sad-dened heart of mine;

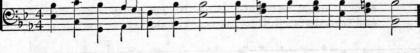

Chase the shades of night a-way, Turn the dark-ness in-to day.
Show those glo-rious truths to me Which are on-ly known to Thee.
In Thy mer-cy pit-y me, From sin's bondage set me free.
Yield a sa-cred, set-tled peace, Let it grow and still in-crease. A-men.

5 Holy Spirit, all divine,
Dwell within this heart of mine;
Cast down every idol throne,
Reign supreme, and reign alone.

6 See, to Thee I yield my heart,
Shed Thy life through every part;
A pure temple I would be,
Wholly dedicate to Thee.

235 O Holy Spirit, Enter In

Is. 11 : 2

O Heil'ger Geist, kehr bei uns ein
Michael Schirmer, 1640, alt.
Tr., Catherine Winkworth, 1863, alt.

8. 8. 7. 8. 8. 7. 4. 4. 4. 4. 8.

Wie schön leuchtet
Philipp Nicolai, 1599

1 O Ho-ly Spir-it, en-ter in And in our hearts Thy work be-gin,
2 Give to Thy Word impressive pow'r That in our hearts, from this good hour,

Thy tem-ple deign to make us; Sun of the soul, Thou Light Divine,
As fire it may be glow-ing; That we con-fess the Fa-ther, Son,

A-round and in us bright-ly shine, To joy and glad-ness wake us
And Thee, the Spirit, Three in One, Thy glo-ry ev-er show-ing.

That we, In Thee Tru-ly liv-ing, To Thee giv-ing Prayer un-ceas-ing,
Stay Thou, Guide now Our souls ev-er That they nev-er May for-sake Thee,

O Holy Spirit, Enter In

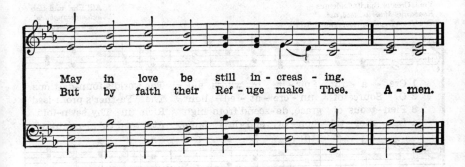

May in love be still in-creas-ing.
But by faith their Ref-uge make Thee. A-men.

3 Thou Fountain whence all wisdom flows
Which God on pious hearts bestows,
  Grant us Thy consolation
That in our pure faith's unity
We faithful witnesses may be
  Of grace that brings salvation.
Hear us, Cheer us
By Thy teaching; Let our preaching
And our labor
Praise Thee, Lord, and serve our neighbor.

4 Left to ourselves, we shall but stray;
Oh, lead us on the narrow way,
  With wisest counsel guide us,
And give us steadfastness that we
May ever faithful prove to Thee
  Whatever woes betide us.
Come, Friend, And mend
Hearts now broken, Give a token
Thou art near us,
Whom we trust to light and cheer us.

5 Thy heavenly strength sustain our heart
That we may act the valiant part,
  With Thee as our Reliance;
Be Thou our Refuge and our Shield
That we may never quit the field,
  But bid all foes defiance.
Descend, Defend
From all errors And earth's terrors.
Thy salvation
Be our constant consolation.

6 O mighty Rock, O Source of Life,
Let Thy dear Word, mid doubt and strife,
  Be strong within us burning
That we be faithful unto death,
In Thy pure love and holy faith,
  From Thee true wisdom learning.
Thy grace And peace
On us shower; By Thy power
Christ confessing,
Let us win our Savior's blessing.

7 O gentle Dew, from heaven now fall
With power upon the hearts of all,
  Thy tender love instilling,
That heart to heart more closely bound,
In kindly deeds be fruitful found,
  The law of love fulfilling.
Dwell thus In us;
Envy banish; Strife will vanish
Where Thou livest.
Peace and love and joy Thou givest.

8 Grant that our days, while life shall last,
In purest holiness be passed,
  Be Thou our Strength and Tower,
From sinful lust and vanity
And from dead works set Thou us free
  In every evil hour.
Keep Thou Pure now
From offenses Heart and senses.
Blessed Spirit,
Let us heavenly life inherit.

236 Creator Spirit, by Whose Aid

Rom. 8: 9

Veni, Creator Spiritus, Mentes
Rhabanus Maurus, 1856, asc.
Tr., *John Dryden, 1693, cento, alt.*

8. 8. 8. 8. 8. 8.

All' Ehr' und Lob
"Kirchengesangbuch"
Strassburg, 1541

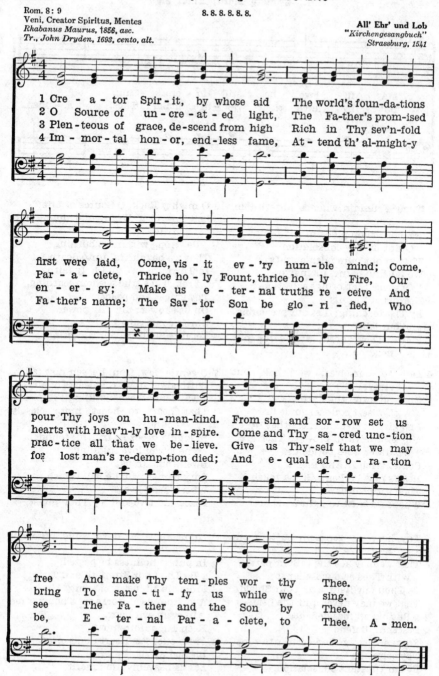

1 Cre - a - tor Spir - it, by whose aid The world's foun-da-tions
2 O Source of un - cre - at - ed light, The Fa-ther's prom-ised
3 Plen -teous of grace, de-scend from high Rich in Thy sev'n-fold
4 Im - mor - tal hon-or, end-less fame, At - tend th' al-might-y

first were laid, Come, vis - it ev - 'ry hum - ble mind; Come,
Par - a - clete, Thrice ho - ly Fount, thrice ho - ly Fire, Our
en - er - gy; Make us e - ter - nal truths re - ceive And
Fa -ther's name; The Sav - ior Son be glo - ri - fied, Who

pour Thy joys on hu - man-kind. From sin and sor - row set us
hearts with heav'n-ly love in - spire. Come and Thy sa - cred unc - tion
prac - tice all that we be - lieve. Give us Thy-self that we may
for lost man's re - demp-tion died; And e - qual ad - o - ra - tion

free And make Thy tem - ples wor - thy Thee.
bring To sanc - ti - fy us while we sing.
see The Fa - ther and the Son by Thee.
be, E - ter - nal Par - a - clete, to Thee. A - men.

All Glory Be to God on High

8. 7. 8. 7. 8. 8. 7.

Luke 2 : 14
Allein Gott in der Höh' sei Ehr'
Nikolaus Decius, 1525
Tr., Catherine Winkworth, 1863, alt.

Allein Gott in der Höh'
Nikolaus Decius, 1539, asc.

1 All glo-ry be to God on high, Who hath our race be-friend-ed!
2 We praise, we wor-ship Thee, we trust, And give Thee thanks for-ev-er,
3 O Je-sus Christ, Thou on-ly Son Of God, Thy heav'n-ly Fa-ther,
4 O Ho-ly Ghost, Thou precious Gift, Thou Com-fort-er un-fail-ing,

To us no harm shall now come nigh, The strife at last is end-ed.
O Fa-ther, that Thy rule is just And wise and chang-es nev-er.
Who didst for all our sins a-tone And Thy lost sheep dost gath-er:
O'er Sa-tan's snares our souls up-lift And let Thy pow'r a-vail-ing

God show-eth His good will to men, And peace shall reign on
Thy bound-less pow'r o'er all things reigns, Done is what-e'er Thy
Thou Lamb of God, to Thee on high From out our depths we
A-vert our woes and calm our dread. For us the Sav-ior's

earth a-gain; Oh, thank Him for His good-ness!
will or-dains: Well for us that Thou rul-est.
sin-ners cry, Have mer-cy on us, Je-sus!
blood was shed; We trust in Thee to save us. A-men.

238 All Glory Be to God Alone

Luke 2: 14
All' Ehr' und Lob soll Gottes sein
Author unknown, 1543
Tr., W. Gustave Polack, 1940

8. 8. 8. 8. 8. 8.

All' Ehr' und Lob
"*Kirchengesangbuch*"
Strassburg, 1541

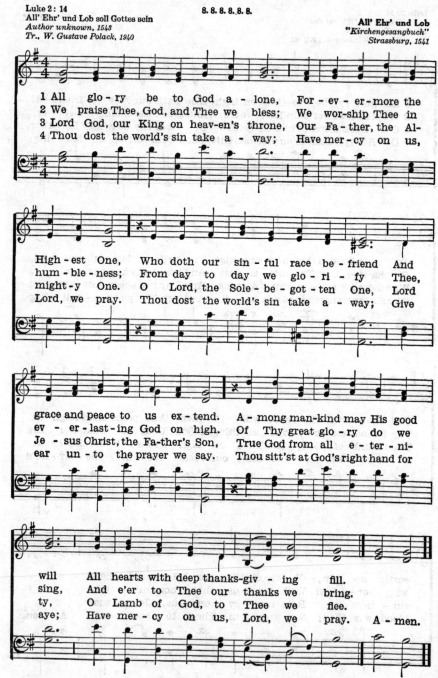

1 All glo-ry be to God a-lone, For-ev-er-more the
2 We praise Thee, God, and Thee we bless; We wor-ship Thee in
3 Lord God, our King on heav-en's throne, Our Fa-ther, the Al-
4 Thou dost the world's sin take a-way; Have mer-cy on us,

High-est One, Who doth our sin-ful race be-friend And
hum-ble-ness; From day to day we glo-ri-fy Thee,
might-y One. O Lord, the Sole-be-got-ten One, Lord
Lord, we pray. Thou dost the world's sin take a-way; Give

grace and peace to us ex-tend. A-mong man-kind may His good
ev-er-last-ing God on high. Of Thy great glo-ry do we
Je-sus Christ, the Fa-ther's Son, True God from all e-ter-ni-
ear un-to the prayer we say. Thou sitt'st at God's right hand for

will All hearts with deep thanks-giv-ing fill.
sing, And e'er to Thee our thanks we bring.
ty, O Lamb of God, to Thee we flee.
aye; Have mer-cy on us, Lord, we pray. A-men.

All Glory Be to God Alone

5 Thou only art the Holy One;
Thou art o'er all things Lord alone.
O Jesus Christ, we glorify
Thee only as the Lord Most High;
Thou art, the Holy Ghost with Thee,
One in the Father's majesty.

6 Amen, this ever true shall be,
As angels sing adoringly.
By all creation, far and wide,
Thou, Lord, art ever glorified;
And Thee all Christendom doth praise
Now and through everlasting days.

Come, Thou Almighty King 239

6. 6. 4. 6. 6. 6. 4.

Rev. 4: 8
Author unknown, c. 1757, ab.

Italian Hymn
Felice de Giardini, 1769

1 Come, Thou al - might - y King, Help us Thy name to sing, Help us to praise. Fa - ther all - glo - ri - ous, O'er all vic - to - ri-ous, Come and reign o - ver us, An-cient of Days.

2 Come, Thou In - car - nate Word, Gird on Thy might - y sword, Our prayer at - tend. Come and Thy peo - ple bless And give Thy Word success; Stab-lish Thy right-eous-ness, Sav-ior and Friend!

3 Come, ho - ly Com - fort - er, Thy sa - cred wit - ness bear In this glad hour. Thou, who al - might - y art, Now rule in ev - 'ry heart And ne'er from us de-part, Spir-it of Pow'r!

4 To the great One in Three E - ter - nal prais - es be Hence ev - er - more! His sov - 'reign maj - es - ty May we in glo - ry see And to e - ter - ni - ty Love and a - dore! A - men.

240 Father Most Holy, Merciful, and Tender

2 Cor. 13: 14
O Pater Sancte, c. 900
Tr., Percy Dearmer, 1906

11. 11. 11. 5.

Herzliebster Jesu
Johann Crüger, 1640

1 Fa - ther most ho - ly, mer - ci - ful, and ten - der; Je - sus, our
2 Trin - i - ty sa - cred, U - ni - ty un - shak - en; De - i - ty
3 Mak - er of all things, all Thy crea - tures praise Thee; Lo, all things
4 To the all - rul - ing Tri - une God be glo - ry! High - est and

Sav - ior, with the Fa - ther reign - ing; Spir - it all - kind - ly,
per - fect, giv - ing and for - giv - ing, Light of the an - gels,
serve Thee thro' Thy whole cre - a - tion. Hear us, Al - might - y,
Great - est, help Thou our en - deav - or; We, too, would praise Thee,

Ad - vo - cate, De - fend - er, Light nev - er wan - ing.
Life of the for - sak - en, Hope of all liv - ing.
hear us as we raise Thee Our ad - o - ra - tion.
giv - ing hon - or wor - thy Now and for - ev - er. A - men.

241 Father, in Whom We Live

Acts 17: 28
Charles Wesley, 1747, cento

S. M.

Dover
Aaron Williams, 1770

1 Fa - ther, in whom we live, In whom we are and move,
2 O Thou In - car - nate Word, Let all Thy ran - somed race
3 Spir - it of Ho - li - ness, Let all Thy saints a - dore
4 E - ter - nal Tri - une Lord, Let all the hosts a - bove,

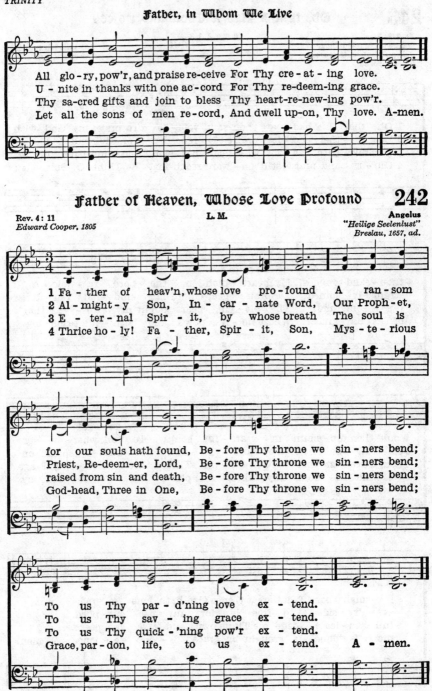

Father, in Whom We Live

All glo-ry, pow'r, and praise re-ceive For Thy cre-at-ing love.
U - nite in thanks with one ac-cord For Thy re-deem-ing grace.
Thy sa-cred gifts and join to bless Thy heart-re-new-ing pow'r.
Let all the sons of men re-cord, And dwell up-on, Thy love. A-men.

Father of Heaven, Whose Love Profound 242

Rev. 4: 11
Edward Cooper, 1805

L. M.

Angelus
"Heilige Seelenlust"
Breslau, 1657, ad.

1 Fa - ther of heav'n, whose love pro - found   A ran - som
2 Al - might - y Son, In - car - nate Word,   Our Proph-et,
3 E - ter - nal Spir - it, by whose breath   The soul is
4 Thrice ho - ly! Fa - ther, Spir - it, Son,   Mys - te - rious

for our souls hath found, Be - fore Thy throne we sin - ners bend;
Priest, Re-deem-er, Lord, Be - fore Thy throne we sin - ners bend;
raised from sin and death, Be - fore Thy throne we sin - ners bend;
God-head, Three in One, Be - fore Thy throne we sin - ners bend;

To us Thy par - d'ning love ex - tend.
To us Thy sav - ing grace ex - tend.
To us Thy quick - 'ning pow'r ex - tend.
Grace, par - don, life, to us ex - tend.   A - men.

243 Oh, that I Had a Thousand Voices

Ps. 148: 1
O dass ich tausend Zungen hätte
Johann Mentzer, 1704, cento
Tr., composite

9. 8. 9. 8. 8. 8.

O dass ich tausend
Kornelius Dretzel, 1731

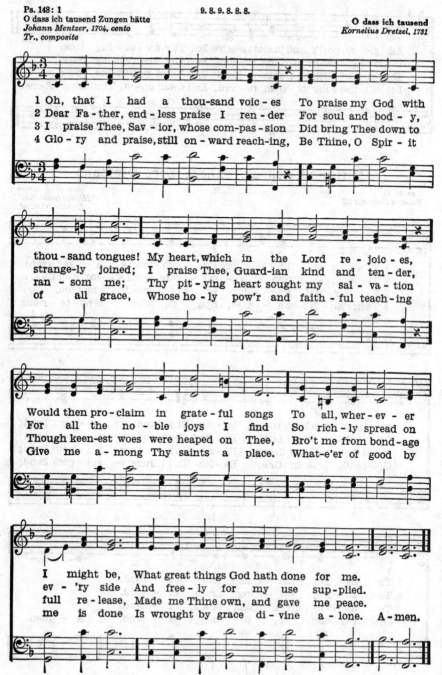

1 Oh, that I had a thou-sand voic-es To praise my God with
2 Dear Fa-ther, end-less praise I ren-der For soul and bod-y,
3 I praise Thee, Sav-ior, whose com-pas-sion Did bring Thee down to
4 Glo-ry and praise, still on-ward reach-ing, Be Thine, O Spir-it

thou-sand tongues! My heart, which in the Lord re-joic-es,
strange-ly joined; I praise Thee, Guard-ian kind and ten-der,
ran-som me; Thy pit-ying heart sought my sal-va-tion
of all grace, Whose ho-ly pow'r and faith-ful teach-ing

Would then pro-claim in grate-ful songs To all, wher-ev-er
For all the no-ble joys I find So rich-ly spread on
Though keen-est woes were heaped on Thee, Bro't me from bond-age
Give me a-mong Thy saints a place. What-e'er of good by

I might be, What great things God hath done for me.
ev-'ry side And free-ly for my use sup-plied.
full re-lease, Made me Thine own, and gave me peace.
me is done Is wrought by grace di-vine a-lone. A-men.

Ob, that I Had a Thousand Voices

5 Shall I not, then, be filled with gladness?
Shall I not praise Thee evermore
And triumph over fear and sadness,
E'en when my cup of woe runs o'er?
Though heaven and earth shall pass away,
Thy loving-kindness stands for aye.

Glory Be to God the Father — 244

8. 7. 8. 7. 4. 7.

Rev. 19 : 1
Horatius Bonar, 1866

Worcester
Walter G. Whinfield, †1919

1 Glo - ry be to God the Fa - ther, Glo - ry be to God the Son,
2 Glo - ry be to Him who loved us, Washed us from each spot and stain;
3 Glo - ry to the King of an - gels, Glo - ry to the Church's King,
4 Glo - ry, bless-ing, praise e - ter - nal! Thus the choir of an - gels sings;

Glo - ry be to God the Spir - it: Great Je - ho - vah, Three in One!
Glo - ry be to Him who bo't us, Made us kings with Him to reign!
Glo - ry to the King of na - tions; Heav'n and earth, your prais-es bring!
Hon - or, rich - es, pow'r, do - min - ion! Thus its praise cre - a - tion brings.

Glo - ry, glo - ry, While e - ter - nal a - ges run!
Glo - ry, glo - ry, To the Lamb that once was slain!
Glo - ry, glo - ry, To the King of Glo - ry sing!
Glo - ry, glo - ry, Glo - ry to the King of kings! A - men.

245 God Loved the World So that He Gave

John 3 : 16
Also hat Gott die Welt geliebt
Author unknown, 1791, cento
Tr., August Crull, †1923, alt.

L. M.

St. Crispin
George J. Elvey, 1862

1 God loved the world so that He gave His on-ly
2 Christ Je-sus is the Ground of faith, Who was made
3 God would not have the sin-ner die, His Son with
4 Be of good cheer, for God's own Son For-gives all

Son the lost to save That all who would in Him be-lieve
flesh and suf-fered death; All that con-fide in Him a-lone
sav-ing grace is nigh, His Spir-it in the Word doth teach
sins which thou hast done, And, jus-ti-fied by Je-sus' blood,

Should ev-er-last-ing life re-ceive.
Are built on this chief Cor-ner-stone.
How man the bless-ed goal may reach.
Thy Bap-tism grants the high-est good. A-men.

5 If thou be sick, if death draw near,
   This truth thy troubled heart can cheer:
   Christ Jesus saves my soul from death;
   That is the firmest ground of faith.

6 Glory to God the Father, Son,
   And Holy Spirit, Three in One!
   To Thee, O blessed Trinity,
   Be praise now and eternally!

Holy, Holy, Holy, Lord God Almighty

246

Rev. 4: 8
Reginald Heber, 1827

11. 12. 12. 10.

Nicæa
John B. Dykes, 1861

1 Ho - ly, ho - ly, ho - ly! Lord God Al - might - y!
2 Ho - ly, ho - ly, ho - ly! All the saints a - dore Thee,
3 Ho - ly, ho - ly, ho - ly! Tho' the dark - ness hide Thee,
4 Ho - ly, ho - ly, ho - ly! Lord God Al - might - y!

Ear - ly in the morn - ing our song shall rise to Thee;
Cast - ing down their gold - en crowns a - round the glass - y sea;
Tho' the eye of sin - ful man Thy glo - ry may not see,
All Thy works shall praise Thy name in earth and sky and sea.

Ho - ly, ho - ly, ho - ly, mer - ci - ful and might - y!
Cher - u - bim and ser - a - phim fall - ing down be - fore Thee,
On - ly Thou art ho - ly; there is none be - side Thee,
Ho - ly, ho - ly, ho - ly, mer - ci - ful and might - y!

God in Three Per - sons, bless - ed Trin - i - ty!
Which wert and art and ev - er - more shalt be.
Per - fect in pow'r, in love, and pu - ri - ty.
God in Three Per - sons, bless - ed Trin - i - ty! A - men.

247 God the Father, Be Our Stay

Ps. 18 : 18
Gott der Vater wohn' uns bei
Author unknown, c. 1400
Tr., Richard Massie, 1854, alt.

7s. 14 lines

Gott der Vater wohn'
14th-century melody

1 God the Fa-ther, be our Stay;
2 Je - sus Christ, be Thou our Stay; } Oh, let us per-ish nev - er!
3 Ho - ly Ghost, be Thou our Stay;

Cleanse us from our sins, we pray, And grant us life for-ev - er.

Keep us from the E - vil One; Up-hold our faith most ho - ly,

Grant us to trust Thee sole - ly With hum-ble hearts and low - ly.

Let us put God's ar-mor on, With all true Chris-tians run - ning

God the Father, Be Our Stay

Our heav'n-ly race and shun-ning The dev-il's wiles and cun-ning.

A-men, A-men, this be done; So sing we, Hal-le-lu - jah! A-men.

Father of Glory, to Thy Name   248

C. M.

Ps. 135: 1
Isaac Watts, c. 1721

Nun danket all'
Johann Crüger, 1653

1 Fa - ther of glo - ry, to Thy name Im-mor-tal praise we give,
2 Im-mor-tal hon - or to the Son, Who makes Thine an-ger cease;
3 To Thine al-might-y Spir-it be Im-mor-tal glo - ry giv'n,

Who dost an act of grace pro-claim And bid us reb-els live.
Our lives He ran-somed with His own And died to make our peace.
Whose teachings bring us near to Thee And train us up for heav'n. A-men.

4 Let men with their united voice
   Adore the eternal God
And spread His honors and their joys
   Through nations far abroad.

5 Let faith and love and duty join
   One grateful song to raise;
Let saints in earth and heaven combine
   In harmony and praise.

249 Isaiah, Mighty Seer, in Days of Old

Is. 6: 1–4   10s. 16 lines

Jesaia, dem Propheten, das geschah
Martin Luther, 1526
Tr., composite

Jesaia, dem Propheten
Martin Luther, 1526

I - sa - iah, might-y seer, in days of old The Lord of

all in spir - it did be - hold High on a loft - y throne, in

splen - dor bright, With flow - ing train that filled the Tem - ple quite.

A - bove the throne were state - ly ser - a - phim; Six wings had

they, these mes - sen - gers of Him. With twain they veiled their fac - es,

as was meet, With twain in rev-'rent awe they hid their feet,

Isaiah, Mighty Seer, in Days of Old

And with the oth-er twain a-loft they soared, One to the oth-er called and praised the Lord: "Ho-ly is God, the Lord of Sab-a-oth! Ho-ly is God, the Lord of Sab-a-oth! Ho-ly is God, the Lord of Sab-a-oth! Be-hold, His glo-ry fill-eth all the earth!" The beams and lin-tels trem-bled at the cry, And clouds of smoke enwrapped the throne on high. A-men.

250 Holy God, We Praise Thy Name

Luke 2: 14
Grosser Gott, wir loben dich
Author unknown; based on the Te Deum
Tr., Clarence A. Walworth, 1853, alt.

7. 8. 7. 8. 7. 7.

Grosser Gott
"Allgemeines Gesangbuch"
Vienna, 1775

1 Ho - ly God, we praise Thy name; Lord of all, we
2 Hark! the glad ce - les - tial hymn An - gel choirs a -
3 Lo, th' a - pos - tles' ho - ly train Join Thy sa - cred
4 Ho - ly Fa - ther, ho - ly Son, Ho - ly Spir - it,

bow be - fore Thee. All on earth Thy scep - ter claim,
bove are rais - ing; Cher - u - bim and ser - a - phim,
name to hal - low; Proph-ets swell the glad re - frain,
three we name Thee; Though in es - sence on - ly one,

All in heav'n a - bove a - dore Thee. In - fi - nite Thy
In un - ceas - ing cho - rus prais-ing, Fill the heav'ns with
And the white-robed mar - tyrs fol - low, And from morn to
Un - di - vid - ed God we claim Thee And, a - dor - ing,

vast do - main, Ev - er - last - ing is Thy reign.
sweet ac - cord: Ho - ly, ho - ly, ho - ly, Lord!
set of sun Thro' the Church the song goes on.
bend the knee While we own the mys - ter - y. A - men.

We All Believe in One True God

The Nicene Creed
Wir glauben all' an *einen* **Gott**
Martin Luther, 1525
Tr., *composite*

8s. 10 lines

(*FIRST TUNE*)

Wir glauben all' an einen Gott
"Manuskript Gesangbuch"
Langenöls, 1742

1 We all be-lieve in one true God, Who cre-at-ed earth and heav-en,
2 We all be-lieve in Je-sus Christ, His own Son, our Lord, pos-sess-ing
3 We all con-fess the Ho-ly Ghost, Who sweet grace and comfort giv-eth

The Fa-ther, who to us in love Hath the right of chil-dren giv-en.
An e-qual Godhead, throne, and might, Source of ev-'ry grace and bless-ing.
And with the Fa-ther and the Son In e-ter-nal glo-ry liv-eth;

He both soul and bod-y feed-eth, All we need He doth pro-vide us;
Born of Ma-ry, vir-gin moth-er, By the pow-er of the Spir-it,
Who the Church, His own cre-a-tion, Keeps in u-ni-ty of spir-it.

He thro' snares and per-ils lead-eth, Watch-ing that no harm be-tide us.
Made true man, our eld-er Broth-er, That the lost might life in-her-it;
Here for-give-ness and sal-va-tion Dai-ly come thro' Je-sus' mer-it.

He car-eth for us day and night, All things are governed by His might.
Was cru-ci-fied for sin-ful men And raised by God to life a-gain
All flesh shall rise, and we shall be In bliss with God e-ter-nal-ly. A-men.

TRINITY

251 We All Believe in One True God

The Nicene Creed
Wir glauben all' an *einen* Gott
Martin Luther, 1525
Tr., composite

8s. 10 lines

(*SECOND TUNE*)

Wir glauben all' an einen Gott
Latin Credo, c. 1300

1 We all be-lieve in one true God, Who cre-at-ed earth and heav-en,
2 We all be-lieve in Je-sus Christ, His own Son, our Lord, pos-sess-ing
3 We all con-fess the Ho-ly Ghost, Who sweet grace and comfort giveth

The Fa-ther, who to us in love Hath the right of chil-dren giv-en.
An e-qual Godhead, throne, and might, Source of ev-'ry grace and bless-ing.
And with the Fa-ther and the Son In e-ter-nal glo-ry liv-eth;

He both soul and bod-y feed-eth, All we need He doth pro-vide us;
Born of Ma-ry, vir-gin moth-er, By the pow-er of the Spir-it,
Who the Church, His own cre-a-tion, Keeps in u-ni-ty of spir-it.

He thro' snares and per-ils lead-eth, Watch-ing that no harm be-tide us,
Made true man, our eld-er Broth-er, That the lost might life in-her-it;
Here for-give-ness and sal-va-tion Dai-ly come thro' Je-sus' mer-it.

He car-eth for us day and night, ...
Was cru-ci-fied for sin-ful men . . . .
All flesh shall rise, and we shall be . . . .

We All Believe in One True God

All things are gov-erned by His might.
And raised by God to life a-gain.
In bliss with God e-ter-nal-ly. A-men.

We All Believe in One True God · 252

8. 7. 7. 7. 7. 7.

The Apostles' Creed
Wir glauben all' an *einen* Gott
Tobias Clausnitzer, 1668
Tr., Catherine Winkworth, 1863, alt.

Wir glauben all' an einen Gott
"Kirchengesangbuch"
Darmstadt, 1699

1 We all be-lieve in one true God, Fa-ther, Son, and Ho-ly Ghost,
2 We all be-lieve in Je-sus Christ, Son of God and Ma-ry's Son,
3 We all con-fess the Ho-ly Ghost, Who from both for-e'er pro-ceeds;

Ev-er-pres-ent Help in need, Praised by all the heav'n-ly host,
Who de-scend-ed from His throne And for us sal-va-tion won;
Who up-holds and com-forts us In all tri-als, fears, and needs.

By whose mighty pow'r a-lone All is made and wrought and done.
By whose cross and death are we Rescued from all mis-er-y.
Blest and Ho-ly Trin-i-ty, Praise for-ev-er be to Thee! A-men.

253   In One True God We All Believe

The Apostles' Creed
Věříme v všemohoucího
Juraj Tranovský, †1637
Tr., composite

8. 8. 8. 7.

Resurgenti Nazareno
Bohemian melody, 1505

1 In   one true God we all be-lieve   And to His name all glo-ry give.
2 We   all be-lieve in God's own Son,   Our Lord, the Sole-be-got-ten One;
3 By   Pon-tius Pi-late cru-ci-fied,   He suf-fered on the Tree and died;
4 The same Lord Christ of Naz-a-reth   Who for all sin-ners tast-ed death

Cre-a-tor of all things is He   In the heav'n, the earth, the sea.
And by the Ho-ly Ghost the same Of   a vir-gin man be-came.
To show of Sa-tan's reign the end, He did in-to hell de-scend.
The third day af-ter He had died   Rose with bod-y glo-ri-fied.   A-men.

5 In full accord with God's own Word
  This holy body of our Lord,
  Although in death's grim grasp it be,
  Never would corruption see.

6 He then ascended into heaven,
  Where endless power to Him was given;
  And there for us in all our needs
  Graciously He intercedes.

7 From thence He'll come, as once He said
  To judge the living and the dead.
  O righteous Judge, our Savior, come,
  Take us to our heavenly home!

8 We all confess the Holy Ghost,
  Who guides the Church, a chosen host,
  And binds the saints in purest love
  Here on earth and there above.

9 And to this truth we also cleave,
  That we forgiveness do receive,
  True peace and joy and comfort sweet,
  Daily from the Paraclete.

10 From death our bodies shall arise
   To endless life beyond the skies;
   By grace through Jesus we shall rest
   There in heaven, forever blest.

Lord God, We All to Thee Give Praise

254

L. M.

Heb. 1: 14
Dicimus grates tibi, summe rerum
Philipp Melanchthon, 1543, cento
Tr., Paul Eber, 1554
English tr., Emanuel Cronenwett, 1880, alt.

Old Hundredth
"Genevan Psalter," 1551

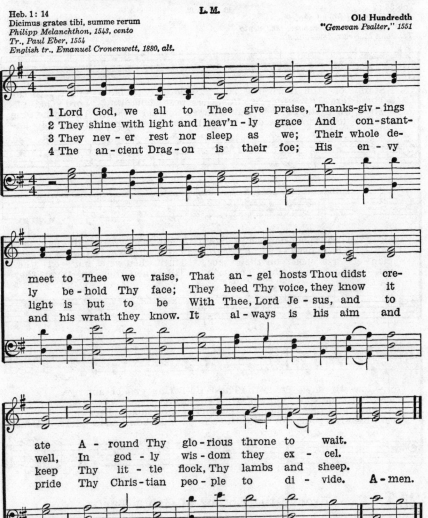

1 Lord God, we all to Thee give praise, Thanks-giv-ings meet to Thee we raise, That an-gel hosts Thou didst cre-ate A-round Thy glo-rious throne to wait.

2 They shine with light and heav'n-ly grace And con-stant-ly be-hold Thy face; They heed Thy voice, they know it well, In god-ly wis-dom they ex-cel.

3 They nev-er rest nor sleep as we; Their whole de-light is but to be With Thee, Lord Je-sus, and to keep Thy lit-tle flock, Thy lambs and sheep.

4 The an-cient Drag-on is their foe; His en-vy and his wrath they know. It al-ways is his aim and pride Thy Chris-tian peo-ple to di-vide. A-men.

5 As he of old deceived the world
And into sin and death has hurled,
So now he subtly lies in wait
To ruin school and Church and State.

6 A roaring lion, round he goes,
No halt nor rest he ever knows;
He seeks the Christians to devour
And slay them by his dreadful power.

7 But watchful is the angel band
That follows Christ on every hand
To guard His people where they go
And break the counsel of the Foe.

8 For this, now and in days to be,
Our praise shall rise, O Lord, to Thee,
Whom all the angel hosts adore
With grateful songs forevermore.

255 Stars of the Morning, So Gloriously Bright

Job 38 : 7   10. 10. 10. 10.

Φωστῆρες τῆς ἀΰλου οὐσίας   **O quanta qualia**
St. Joseph the Hymnographer, †883, cento   *Plain-song melody, c. 1650*
Tr., John M. Neale, 1862, ab., alt.

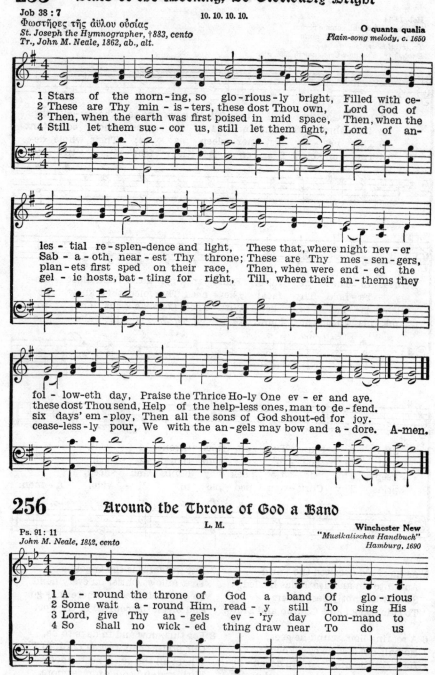

1 Stars of the morn-ing, so glo-rious-ly bright, Filled with ce-
2 These are Thy min - is - ters, these dost Thou own, Lord God of
3 Then, when the earth was first poised in mid space, Then, when the
4 Still let them suc - cor us, still let them fight, Lord of an-

les - tial re - splen-dence and light, These that, where night nev - er
Sab - a - oth, near-est Thy throne; These are Thy mes - sen - gers,
plan - ets first sped on their race, Then, when were end - ed the
gel - ic hosts, bat - tling for right, Till, where their an - thems they

fol - low-eth day, Praise the Thrice Ho-ly One ev - er and aye.
these dost Thou send, Help of the help-less ones, man to de - fend.
six days' em - ploy, Then all the sons of God shout-ed for joy.
cease-less - ly pour, We with the an - gels may bow and a - dore. A-men.

256 Around the Throne of God a Band

                                    L. M.
Ps. 91 : 11   **Winchester New**
John M. Neale, 1842, cento   *"Musikalisches Handbuch"*
                                    Hamburg, 1690

1 A - round the throne of God a band Of glo - rious
2 Some wait a - round Him, read - y still To sing His
3 Lord, give Thy an - gels ev - 'ry day Com-mand to
4 So shall no wick - ed thing draw near To do us

Around the Throne of God a Band

an - gels ev - er stand; Bright things they see, sweet
praise and do His will; And some, when He com -
guide us on our way And bid them ev - 'ry
harm or cause us fear; And we shall dwell, when

harps they hold, And on their heads are crowns of gold.
mands them, go To guard His ser - vants here be - low.
eve - ning keep Their watch a - round us while we sleep.
life is past, With an - gels round Thy throne at last. A - men.

Jesus, Brightness of the Father 257

8. 7. 8. 7. 7. 7.

Ps. 91 : 11
Tibi, Christe, splendor Patris
Rhabanus Maurus, †856, asc.
Tr., *Edward Caswall, 1849, alt.*

Neander
Joachim Neander, 1680

1 Je - sus, Brightness of the Fa - ther, Life and Strength of all who live,
2 Bless-ed Lord, by their pro - tec - tion Shel - ter us from harm this day,
3 Glo - ry to th' al - might - y Fa - ther Sing we with the heav'n - ly host;

For cre - at - ing guard-ian an - gels, Glo - ry to Thy name we give
Keep us pure in flesh and spir - it, Save us from the Foe, we pray,
Glo - ry to the great Re - deem - er, Glo - ry to the Ho - ly Ghost;

And Thy wondrous praise rehearse, Sing-ing in har - mo-nious verse.
And vouch-safe us by Thy grace In Thy Par - a - dise a place.
Three in One and One in Three, Thro'-out all e - ter - ni - ty! A - men.

258 Lord of Our Life and God of Our Salvation

Ps. 79: 9
Christe, du Beistand
Matthäus A. von Löwenstern, 1644
Tr., Philip Pusey, 1840, alt.

11. 11. 11. 5.

Herzliebster Jesu
Johann Crüger, 1640

1 Lord of our life and God of our sal - va - tion, Star of our
2 See round Thine ark the hun-gry bil-lows curl-ing; See how Thy
3 Lord, Thou canst help when earth-ly ar-mor fail - eth; Lord, Thou canst

night and Hope of ev - 'ry na - tion, Hear and re-ceive Thy
foes their ban-ners are un-furl - ing. Lord, while their darts en-
save when dead-ly sin as-sail - eth; Lord, o'er Thy Church nor

Church's sup - pli - ca - tion, Lord God Al-might - y.
ven-omed they are hurl - ing, Thou canst pre-serve us.
death nor hell pre - vail - eth; Grant us Thy peace, Lord: A-men.

4 Peace in our hearts, our evil thoughts assuaging;
    Peace in Thy Church where brothers are engaging;
    Peace when the world its busy war is waging.
    Calm Thy foes' raging.

5 Grant us Thy help till backward they are driven;
    Grant them Thy truth that they may be forgiven;
    Grant peace on earth or, after we have striven,
    Peace in Thy heaven.

Flung to the Heedless Winds

6. 6. 6. 6. D.

Acts 7: 59
Ein neues Lied wir heben an
Martin Luther, 1523, st. 9
Tr., John A. Messenger, 1843

Denby
Charles J. Dale, 1904

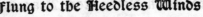

1 Flung to the heed-less winds Or on the wa-ters cast,
The mar-tyrs' ash-es, watched, Shall gath-ered be at last.
And from that scat-tered dust, A-round us and a-broad,
Shall spring a plen-teous seed Of wit-ness-es for God.

2 The Fa-ther hath re-ceived Their lat-est liv-ing breath,
And vain is Sa-tan's boast Of vic-t'ry in their death.
Still, still, tho' dead, they speak, And, trum-pet-tongued, pro-claim
To man-y a wak-'ning land The one a-vail-ing Name. A-men.

260 O Lord, Look Down from Heaven, Behold

Ps. 12

Ach Gott vom Himmel, sieh darein

Martin Luther, 1523
Tr., composite

8. 7. 8. 7. 8. 8. 7.

Ach Gott vom Himmel
"Enchiridion"
Erfurt, 1524

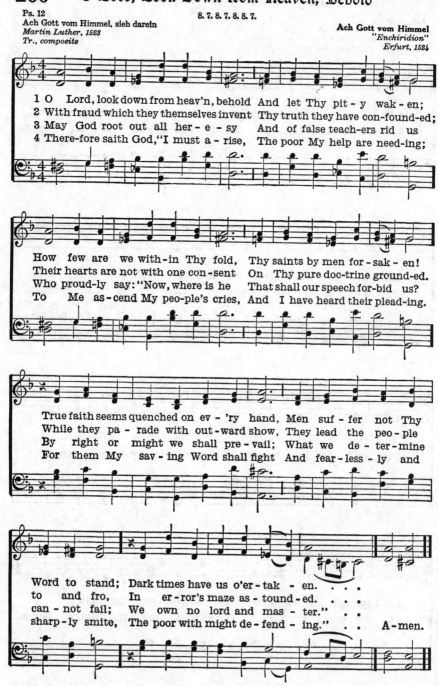

1 O Lord, look down from heav'n, behold And let Thy pit-y wak-en;
2 With fraud which they themselves invent Thy truth they have con-found-ed;
3 May God root out all her-e-sy And of false teach-ers rid us
4 There-fore saith God, "I must a-rise, The poor My help are need-ing;

How few are we with-in Thy fold, Thy saints by men for-sak-en!
Their hearts are not with one con-sent On Thy pure doc-trine ground-ed.
Who proud-ly say: "Now, where is he That shall our speech for-bid us?
To Me as-cend My peo-ple's cries, And I have heard their plead-ing.

True faith seems quenched on ev-'ry hand, Men suf-fer not Thy
While they pa-rade with out-ward show, They lead the peo-ple
By right or might we shall pre-vail; What we de-ter-mine
For them My sav-ing Word shall fight And fear-less-ly and

Word to stand; Dark times have us o'er-tak-en. . . .
to and fro, In er-ror's maze as-tound-ed. . . .
can-not fail; We own no lord and mas-ter." . . .
sharp-ly smite, The poor with might de-fend-ing." . . . A-men.

O Lord, Look Down from Heaven, Behold

5 As silver tried by fire is pure
  From all adulteration,
 So thro' God's Word shall men endure
  Each trial and temptation.
 Its light beams brighter thro' the cross,
 And, purified from human dross,
  It shines through every nation.

6 Defend Thy truth, O God, and stay
  This evil generation;
 And from the error of its way
  Keep Thine own congregation.
 The wicked everywhere abound
 And would Thy little flock confound;
  But Thou art our Salvation.

Lord, Keep Us Steadfast in Thy Word 261

L. M.

John 8: 31
Erhalt uns, Herr, bei deinem Wort
Martin Luther, 1541
Tr., Catherine Winkworth, 1863

Erhalt uns, Herr
"Geistliche Lieder"
Wittenberg, 1543

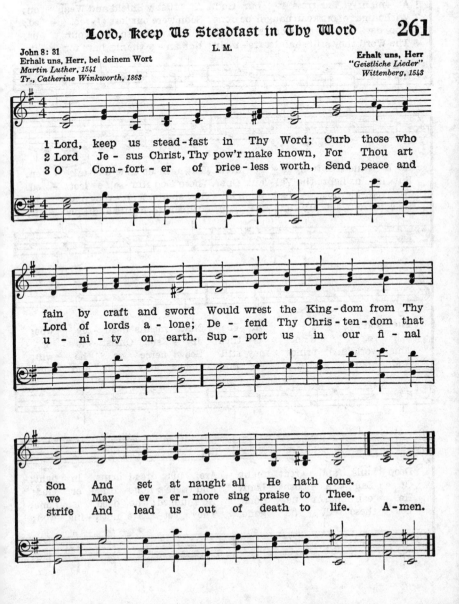

1 Lord, keep us stead-fast in Thy Word; Curb those who
2 Lord Je-sus Christ, Thy pow'r make known, For Thou art
3 O Com-fort-er of price-less worth, Send peace and

fain by craft and sword Would wrest the King-dom from Thy
Lord of lords a-lone; De-fend Thy Chris-ten-dom that
u-ni-ty on earth. Sup-port us in our fi-nal

Son And set at naught all He hath done.
we May ev-er-more sing praise to Thee.
strife And lead us out of death to life. A-men.

262 A Mighty Fortress Is Our God

Ps. 46
Ein' feste Burg ist unser Gott
Martin Luther, 1529
Tr., composite

8. 7. 8. 7. 5. 5. 5. 6. 7.

Ein' feste Burg
Martin Luther, 1529

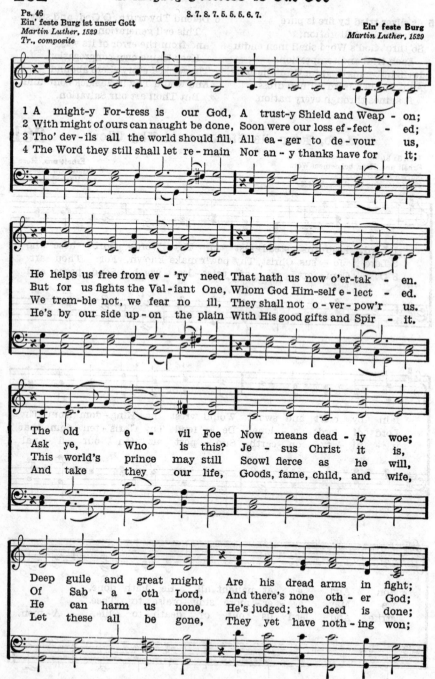

1 A might-y For-tress is our God, A trust-y Shield and Weap - on;
2 With might of ours can naught be done, Soon were our loss ef-fect - ed;
3 Tho' dev-ils all the world should fill, All ea-ger to de-vour us;
4 The Word they still shall let re-main Nor an-y thanks have for it;

He helps us free from ev-'ry need That hath us now o'er-tak - en.
But for us fights the Val-iant One, Whom God Him-self e-lect - ed.
We trem-ble not, we fear no ill, They shall not o-ver-pow'r us.
He's by our side up-on the plain With His good gifts and Spir - it.

The old e - vil Foe Now means dead-ly woe;
Ask ye, Who is this? Je - sus Christ it is,
This world's prince may still Scowl fierce as he will,
And take they our life, Goods, fame, child, and wife,

Deep guile and great might Are his dread arms in fight;
Of Sab-a-oth Lord, And there's none oth-er God;
He can harm us none, He's judged; the deed is done;
Let these all be gone, They yet have noth-ing won;

A Mighty Fortress Is Our God

On earth is not his e - - - qual.
He holds the field for - ev - - - er.
One lit - tle word can fell . . . . . him.
The King - dom ours re - main - - eth.   A - men.

O Little Flock, Fear Not the Foe   263

8. 8. 6. 8. 8. 6.

Luke 12 : 32
Verzage nicht, du Häuflein klein
Johann M. Altenburg, 1632, asc., ab.
Tr., Catherine Winkworth, 1855, alt.

Kommt her zu mir
German melody, c. 1400

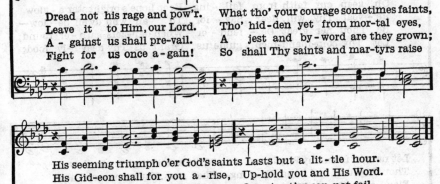

1 O   lit - tle flock, fear not the Foe   Who mad-ly seeks your o - ver-throw;
2 Be of good cheer; your cause belongs To Him who can avenge your wrongs;
3 As true as God's own Word is true, Not earth nor hell with all their crew
4 A - men, Lord Jesus, grant our prayer; Great Captain, now Thine arm make bare,

Dread not his rage and pow'r.   What tho' your courage sometimes faints,
Leave it   to Him, our Lord.   Tho' hid-den yet from mor-tal eyes,
A - gainst us shall pre-vail.   A   jest and by-word are they grown;
Fight for us once a-gain!   So   shall Thy saints and mar-tyrs raise

His seeming triumph o'er God's saints Lasts but a lit-tle hour.
His Gid-eon shall for you a - rise, Up-hold you and His Word.
God is with us, we are His own; Our vic - t'ry can-not fail.
A might-y cho-rus to Thy praise, World without end. A-men.   A-men.

264 Preserve Thy Word, O Savior

Jude 20, 21
Erhalt uns deine Lehre
Andreas Gryphius, 1676, ab.
Tr., William J. Schaefer, 1933

7. 6. 7. 6. D.

Herzlich tut mich
Hans L. Hassler, 1601

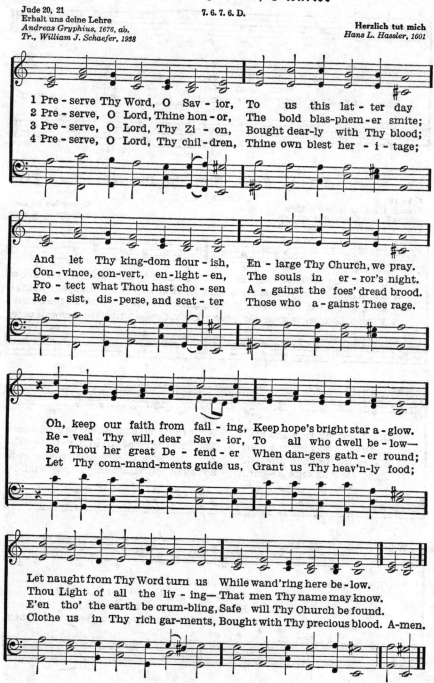

1 Pre - serve Thy Word, O Sav - ior, To us this lat - ter day
2 Pre - serve, O Lord, Thine hon - or, The bold blas-phem-er smite;
3 Pre - serve, O Lord, Thy Zi - on, Bought dear-ly with Thy blood;
4 Pre - serve, O Lord, Thy chil - dren, Thine own blest her - i - tage;

And let Thy king-dom flour - ish, En - large Thy Church, we pray.
Con - vince, con-vert, en-light - en, The souls in er - ror's night.
Pro - tect what Thou hast cho - sen A - gainst the foes' dread brood.
Re - sist, dis - perse, and scat - ter Those who a - gainst Thee rage.

Oh, keep our faith from fail - ing, Keep hope's bright star a - glow.
Re - veal Thy will, dear Sav - ior, To all who dwell be - low—
Be Thou her great De - fend - er When dan-gers gath - er round;
Let Thy com-mand-ments guide us, Grant us Thy heav'n-ly food;

Let naught from Thy Word turn us While wand'ring here be - low.
Thou Light of all the liv - ing— That men Thy name may know.
E'en tho' the earth be crum-bling, Safe will Thy Church be found.
Clothe us in Thy rich gar-ments, Bought with Thy precious blood. A-men.

Preserve Thy Word, O Savior

5 Preserve Thy Word and preaching,
The truth that makes us whole,
The mirror of Thy glory,
The power that saves the soul.
Oh, may this living water,
This dew of heavenly grace,
Sustain us while here living
Until we see Thy face!

6 Preserve in wave and tempest
Thy storm-tossed little flock;
Assailed by wind and weather,
May it endure each shock.
Take Thou the helm, O Pilot,
And set the course aright;
Thus we shall reach the harbor
In Thine eternal light.

Thine Honor Save, O Christ, Our Lord   265

L. M.

Ps. 118: 25
Rett, o Herr Jesu, rett dein' Ehr'
Johann Heermann, 1630
Tr., Matthias Loy, 1880, alt.

Erhalt uns, Herr
"Geistliche Lieder"
Wittenberg, 1543

1 Thine hon-or save, O Christ, our Lord! Hear Zi-on's
2 Their craft and pomp in-deed are great, And of their
3 For-give, O Lord, our sins for-give; Grant us Thy

cries and help af-ford; De-stroy the wiles of might-y
pow'r they boast and prate; Our hope they scorn-ful-ly de-
grace and let us live. Con-vince Thy foes through-out the

foes Who now Thy Word and truth op-pose.
ride And deem us noth-ing in their pride.
land That god-less coun-sels shall not stand. A-men.

4 That Thou art with us, Lord, proclaim
And put our enemies to shame;
Confound them in their haughtiness
And help Thine own in their distress.

5 Preserve Thy little flock in peace,
Nor let Thy boundless mercy cease;
To all the world let it appear
That Thy true Church indeed is here.

266
O God, Our Lord, Thy Holy Word

Rev. 14: 6, 7

O Herre Gott, dein göttlich Wort
Author unknown, 1527, cento
Tr., W. Gustave Polack, 1939, ad.

4. 4. 7. 4. 4. 7. D.

O Herre Gott
"Enchiridion"
Erfurt, 1527

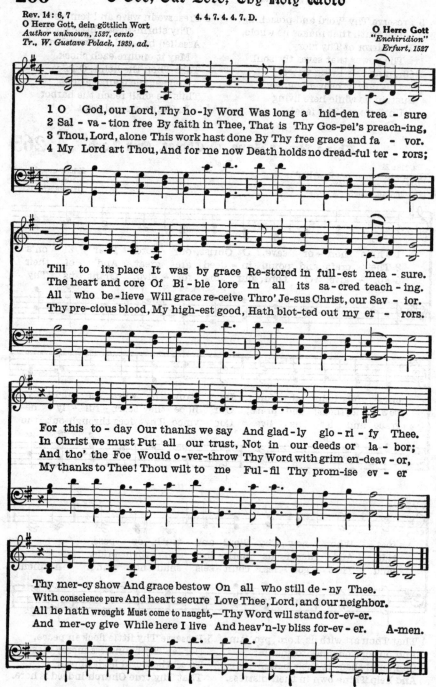

1 O God, our Lord, Thy ho-ly Word Was long a hid-den trea - sure
2 Sal - va - tion free By faith in Thee, That is Thy Gos-pel's preach-ing,
3 Thou, Lord, alone This work hast done By Thy free grace and fa - vor.
4 My Lord art Thou, And for me now Death holds no dread-ful ter - rors;

Till to its place It was by grace Re-stored in full-est mea - sure.
The heart and core Of Bi - ble lore In all its sa-cred teach - ing.
All who be-lieve Will grace re-ceive Thro' Je-sus Christ, our Sav - ior.
Thy pre-cious blood, My high-est good, Hath blot-ted out my er - rors.

For this to - day Our thanks we say And glad-ly glo - ri - fy Thee.
In Christ we must Put all our trust, Not in our deeds or la - bor;
And tho' the Foe Would o - ver-throw Thy Word with grim en-deav - or,
My thanks to Thee! Thou wilt to me Ful - fil Thy prom-ise ev - er

Thy mer-cy show And grace bestow On all who still de - ny Thee.
With conscience pure And heart secure Love Thee, Lord, and our neighbor.
All he hath wrought Must come to naught,—Thy Word will stand for-ev-er.
And mer-cy give While here I live And heav'n-ly bliss for-ev - er. A-men.

If God Had Not Been on Our Side 267

8. 7. 8. 7. 8. 8. 7.

Ps. 124
Wär' Gott nicht mit uns diese Zeit
Martin Luther, 1524
Tr., composite

Wär' Gott nicht mit uns
"Gesangbuch"
Wittenberg, 1537

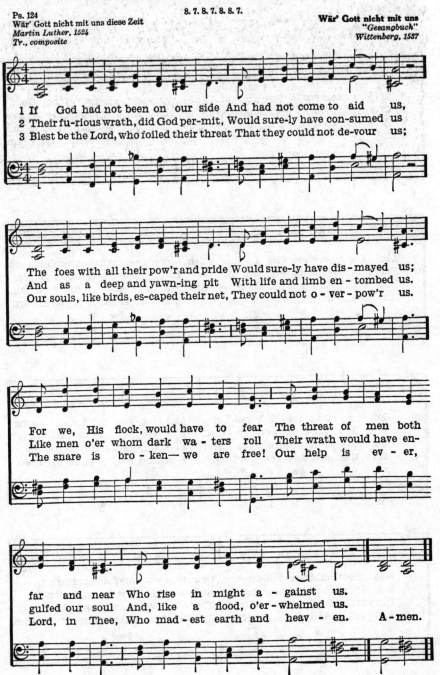

1 If God had not been on our side And had not come to aid us,
2 Their fu-rious wrath, did God per-mit, Would sure-ly have con-sumed us
3 Blest be the Lord, who foiled their threat That they could not de-vour us;

The foes with all their pow'r and pride Would sure-ly have dis-mayed us;
And as a deep and yawn-ing pit With life and limb en - tombed us.
Our souls, like birds, es-caped their net, They could not o - ver-pow'r us.

For we, His flock, would have to fear The threat of men both
Like men o'er whom dark wa - ters roll Their wrath would have en-
The snare is bro - ken— we are free! Our help is ev - er,

far and near Who rise in might a - gainst us.
gulfed our soul And, like a flood, o'er-whelmed us.
Lord, in Thee, Who mad - est earth and heav - en. A - men.

268 Zion Mourns in Fear and Anguish

Is. 49: 14–17
Zion klagt mit Angst und Schmerzen
Johann Heermann, 1636, ab.
Tr., Catherine Winkworth, 1869, alt.

8. 7. 8. 7. 7. 7. 8. 8.

Zion klagt
J. Hermann Schein, 1623

1 Zi - on mourns in fear and an - guish, Zi - on, cit - y of our God.
2 "Once," she mourns, "He promised plain-ly That His help should e'er be near;
3 "Zi - on, sure - ly I do love thee," Thus to her the Sav-ior saith,
4 "Let not Sa - tan make thee cra - ven; He can threat-en but not harm.

"Ah," she says, "how sore I lan - guish, Bowed be-neath the chast'ning rod!
Yet I now must seek Him vain - ly In my days of woe and fear.
"Tho' with man - y woes I prove thee And thy soul is sad to death.
On My hands thy name is grav - en, And thy shield is My strong arm.

For my God for-sook me quite And for-got my sor - ry plight
Will His an - ger nev - er cease? Will He not re - new His peace?
For My troth is pledged to thee; Zi - on, thou art dear to Me.
How, then, could it ev - er be I should not re-mem-ber thee,

Mid these troubles now distressing, Countless woes my soul oppressing.
Will He not show forth compassion And a-gain forgive transgression?"
Deep within My heart I've set thee, That I nev-er can for-get thee.
Fail to build thy walls, My cit-y, And look down on thee with pity? A-men.

Zion Mourns in Fear and Anguish

5 "Ever shall Mine eyes behold thee;
   On My bosom thou art laid.
Ever shall My love enfold thee;
   Never shalt thou lack Mine aid.
Neither Satan, war, nor stress
Then shall mar thy happiness:
With this blessèd consolation
Be thou firm in tribulation."

O Lord, Our Father, shall We be Confounded 269

Ps. 22: 5

11. 11. 11. 5.

Herr, unser Gott, lass nicht zuschanden werden
Johann Heermann, 1630
Tr., Catherine Winkworth, 1869, alt.

Herzliebster Jesu
Johann Crüger, 1640

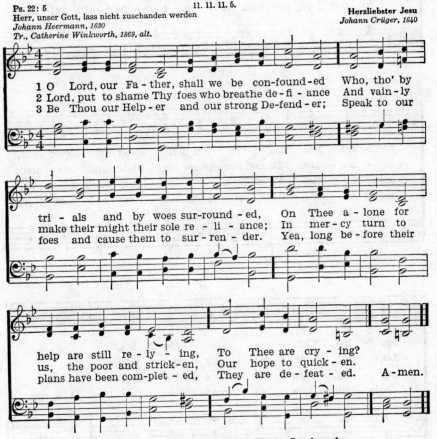

1 O Lord, our Fa-ther, shall we be con-found-ed Who, tho' by
2 Lord, put to shame Thy foes who breathe de-fi-ance And vain-ly
3 Be Thou our Help-er and our strong De-fend-er; Speak to our

tri-als and by woes sur-round-ed, On Thee a-lone for
make their might their sole re-li-ance; In mer-cy turn to
foes and cause them to sur-ren-der. Yea, long be-fore their

help are still re-ly-ing, To Thee are cry-ing?
us, the poor and strick-en, Our hope to quick-en.
plans have been com-plet-ed, They are de-feat-ed. A-men.

4 'Tis vain to trust in man; for Thou, Lord, only
   Art the Defense and Comfort of the lonely.
With Thee to lead, the battle shall be glorious
   And we victorious.

5 Thou art our Hero, all our foes subduing;
   Save Thou Thy little flock they are pursuing.
We seek Thy help; for Jesus' sake be near us.
   Great Helper, hear us!

270 Jesus Calls Us; o'er the Tumult

8. 7. 8. 7.

John 1 : 40
Cecil F. Alexander, 1852

Stuttgart
"*Psalmodia Sacra*"
Gotha, 1715

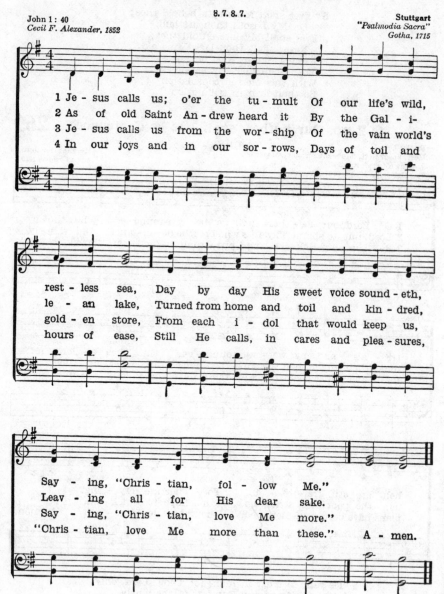

1 Je - sus calls us; o'er the tu - mult Of our life's wild,
2 As of old Saint An - drew heard it By the Gal - i-
3 Je - sus calls us from the wor - ship Of the vain world's
4 In our joys and in our sor - rows, Days of toil and

rest - less sea, Day by day His sweet voice sound - eth,
le - an lake, Turned from home and toil and kin - dred,
gold - en store, From each i - dol that would keep us,
hours of ease, Still He calls, in cares and plea - sures,

Say - ing, "Chris - tian, fol - low Me."
Leav - ing all for His dear sake.
Say - ing, "Chris - tian, love Me more."
"Chris - tian, love Me more than these." A - men.

5 Jesus calls us; by Thy mercies,
Savior, make us hear Thy call;
Give our hearts to Thine obedience,
Serve and love Thee best of all.

Word Supreme, Before Creation

271

8. 7. 8. 7. 8. 7.

John 21 : 20
John Keble, 1856, cento

Sieh, hier bin ich
"Geistreiches Gesangbuch"
Darmstadt, 1698

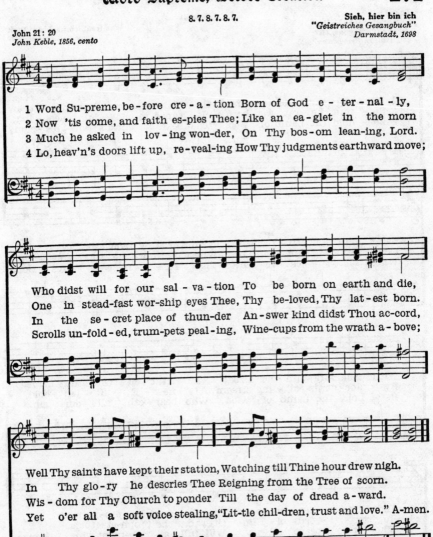

1 Word Su-preme, be-fore cre-a-tion Born of God e-ter-nal-ly,
2 Now 'tis come, and faith es-pies Thee; Like an ea-glet in the morn
3 Much he asked in lov-ing won-der, On Thy bos-om lean-ing, Lord.
4 Lo, heav'n's doors lift up, re-veal-ing How Thy judgments earthward move;

Who didst will for our sal-va-tion To be born on earth and die,
One in stead-fast wor-ship eyes Thee, Thy be-loved, Thy lat-est born.
In the se-cret place of thun-der An-swer kind didst Thou ac-cord,
Scrolls un-fold-ed, trum-pets peal-ing, Wine-cups from the wrath a-bove;

Well Thy saints have kept their station, Watching till Thine hour drew nigh.
In Thy glo-ry he descries Thee Reigning from the Tree of scorn.
Wis-dom for Thy Church to ponder Till the day of dread a-ward.
Yet o'er all a soft voice stealing, "Lit-tle chil-dren, trust and love." A-men.

5 Thee, th' almighty King eternal,
    Father of th' eternal Word,
  Thee, the Father's Word supernal,
    Thee, of both the Breath adored,
  Heaven and earth and realms infernal
    Own one glorious God and Lord.

272 When All the World was Cursed

Luke 1: 41
Es war die ganze Welt
Johann G. Olearius, 1697
Tr., Paul E. Kretzmann, 1940

6. 7. 6. 7. 6. 6. 6. 6.

Was frag' ich nach der Welt
Ahasverus Fritsch, 1679

1 When all the world was cursed By Mo-ses' con-dem-na-tion,
2 Be-fore he yet was born, He leaped in joy-ful meet-ing,
3 Be-hold the Lamb of God That bears the world's trans-gres-sion,

Saint John the Bap-tist came With words of con-so-la-tion.
Con-fess-ing Him as Lord Whose moth-er he was greet-ing.
Whose sac-ri-fice re-moves The En-e-my's op-pres-sion.

With true fore-run-ner's zeal The Great-er One he named,
By Jor-dan's roll-ing stream, A new E-li-jah bold,
Be-hold the Lamb of God, Who bear-eth all our sin,

And Him, as yet un-known, As Sav-ior he pro-claimed.
He tes-ti-fied of Him Of whom the proph-ets told:
Who for our peace and joy Will full a-tone-ment win. A-men.

4 Thrice blessèd every one
  Who heeds the proclamation
Which John the Baptist brought,
  Accepting Christ's salvation.
He who believes this truth
  And comes with love unfeigned
Has righteousness and peace
  In fullest measure gained.

5 Oh, grant, Thou Lord of Love,
  That we receive, rejoicing,
The word proclaimed by John,
  Our true repentance voicing;
That gladly we may walk
  Upon our Savior's way
Until we live with Him
  In His eternal day.

Sweet Flowerets of the Martyr Band

273

L. M.

Rev. 14 : 4
Salvete, flores martyrum
Aurelius C. Prudentius, †413, cento
Tr., Henry W. Baker, 1875, alt.

Das walt' Gott Vater
Daniel Vetter, 1713

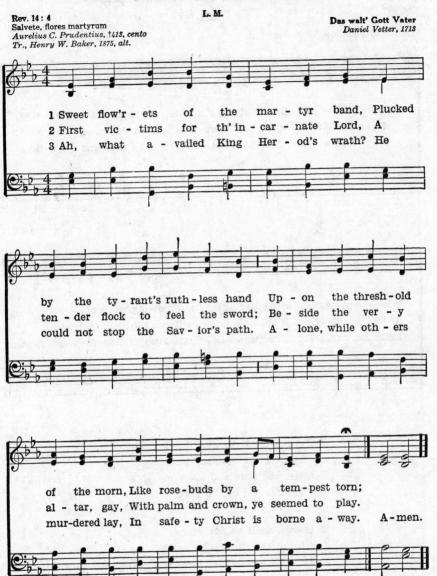

1 Sweet flow'r-ets of the mar-tyr band, Plucked by the ty-rant's ruth-less hand Up-on the thresh-old of the morn, Like rose-buds by a tem-pest torn;

2 First vic-tims for th' in-car-nate Lord, A ten-der flock to feel the sword; Be-side the ver-y al-tar, gay, With palm and crown, ye seemed to play.

3 Ah, what a-vailed King Her-od's wrath? He could not stop the Sav-ior's path. A-lone, while oth-ers mur-dered lay, In safe-ty Christ is borne a-way. A-men.

4 O Lord, the Virgin-born, to Thee
Eternal praise and glory be,
Whom with the Father we adore
And Holy Ghost forevermore.

274 Praise We the Lord This Day

S. M.

Matt. 1: 23
Author unknown, 1846

Swabia
Johann M. Spiess, 1745

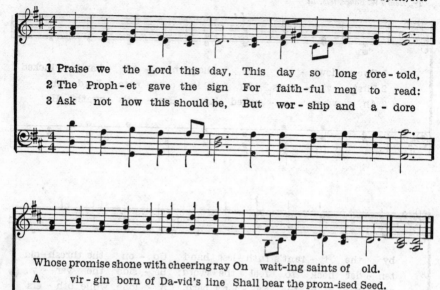

1 Praise we the Lord this day, This day so long fore-told,
2 The Proph-et gave the sign For faith-ful men to read:
3 Ask not how this should be, But wor-ship and a-dore

Whose promise shone with cheering ray On wait-ing saints of old.
A vir-gin born of Da-vid's line Shall bear the prom-ised Seed.
Like her whom God's own maj-es-ty Came down to shad-ow o'er. A-men.

4 She meekly bowed her head
    To hear the gracious word,
  Mary, the pure and lowly maid,
    The favored of the Lord.

5 Blessèd shall be her name
    In all the Church on earth
  Through whom that wondrous mercy came,
    Th' incarnate Savior's birth.

6 Jesus, the Virgin's Son,
    We praise Thee and adore,
  Who art with God the Father One
    And Spirit evermore.

My Soul doth Magnify the Lord

L. M.

Luke 1: 47-55
Mein' Seel', o Gott, muss loben dich
Author unknown, 1535, cento.
Tr., J. Theodore Mueller, 1940

Wo Gott zum Haus
"Geistliche Lieder"
Wittenberg, 1535

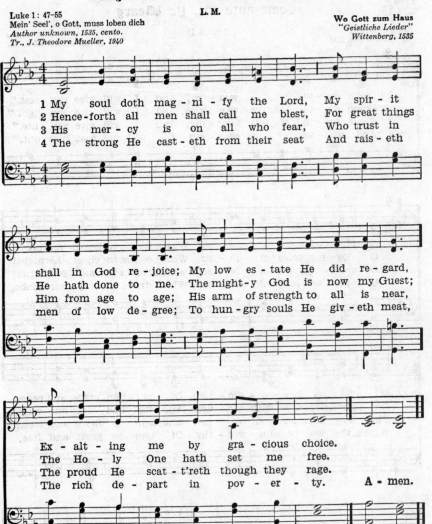

1 My soul doth mag-ni-fy the Lord, My spir-it
2 Hence-forth all men shall call me blest, For great things
3 His mer-cy is on all who fear, Who trust in
4 The strong He cast-eth from their seat And rais-eth

shall in God re-joice; My low es-tate He did re-gard,
He hath done to me. The might-y God is now my Guest;
Him from age to age; His arm of strength to all is near,
men of low de-gree; To hun-gry souls He giv-eth meat,

Ex-alt-ing me by gra-cious choice.
The Ho-ly One hath set me free.
The proud He scat-t'reth though they rage.
The rich de-part in pov-er-ty. A-men.

5 He helped His servant Israel;
  Remembering His eternal grace,
    As from of old He did foretell
      To Abraham and all his race.

6 So praise with me the Holy One,
  Who cometh in humility.
  Divine Redeemer, God's own Son,
    Eternal glory be to Thee!

Invitation

276   Come unto Me, Ye Weary

John 6: 37
William C. Dix, 1867

7. 6. 7. 6. D.

Anthes
Friedrich K. Anthes, 1847

1 "Come un-to Me, ye wea-ry, And I will give you rest."
2 "Come un-to Me, ye wan-d'rers, And I will give you light."
3 "Come un-to Me, ye faint-ing, And I will give you life."
4 "And who-so-ev-er com-eth, I will not cast him out."

O bless-ed voice of Je-sus, Which comes to hearts op-prest!
O lov-ing voice of Je-sus, Which comes to cheer the night!
O cheer-ing voice of Je-sus, Which comes to aid our strife!
O pa-tient love of Je-sus, Which drives a-way our doubt,

It tells of ben-e-dic-tion, Of par-don, grace, and peace,
Our hearts were filled with sad-ness, And we had lost our way;
The Foe is stern and ea-ger, The fight is fierce and long;
Which, tho' we be un-wor-thy Of love so great and free,

Of joy that hath no end-ing, Of love which can-not cease.
But Thou hast bro't us glad-ness And songs at break of day.
But Thou hast made us might-y And strong-er than the strong.
In-vites us ver-y sin-ners To come, dear Lord, to Thee! A-men.

I Heard the Voice of Jesus Say

C. M. D.

John 6: 35
Horatius Bonar, 1846

Vox dilecti
John B. Dykes, 1868

1 I heard the voice of Je - sus say, "Come un-to Me and rest;
2 I heard the voice of Je - sus say, "Be - hold, I free - ly give
3 I heard the voice of Je - sus say, "I am this dark world's Light.

Lay down, thou wea - ry one, lay down Thy head up - on My breast."
The liv - ing wa - ter; thirst - y one, Stoop down and drink and live."
Look un - to Me; thy morn shall rise And all thy day be bright."

I came to Je - sus as I was, Wea - ry and worn and sad;
I came to Je - sus, and I drank Of that life - giv - ing stream.
I looked to Je - sus, and I found In Him my Star, my Sun;

I found in Him a rest-ing place, And He has made me glad.
My thirst was quenched, my soul revived, And now I live in Him.
And in that Light of Life I'll walk Till trav-'ling days are done. A-men.

278 Delay Not, Delay Not, O Sinner, Draw Near

Acts 24 : 25
Thomas Hastings, 1831

11. 11. 11. 11.

Maldwyn
Welsh melody, c. 1600

1 De - lay not, de - lay not, O sin - ner, draw near,
2 De - lay not, de - lay not, O sin - ner, to come,
3 De - lay not, de - lay not! The Spir - it of Grace,
4 De - lay not, de - lay not! The hour is at hand;

The wa - ters of life are now flow - ing for thee.
For mer - cy still lin - gers and calls thee to - day.
Long grieved and re - sist - ed, may take His sad flight
The earth shall dis - solve, and the heav - ens shall fade.

No price is de - mand - ed; the Sav - ior is here;
Her voice is not heard in the vale of the tomb;
And leave thee in dark - ness to fin - ish thy race,
The dead, small and great, in the Judg - ment shall stand;

Re - demp - tion is pur - chased, sal - va - tion is free.
Her mes - sage, un - heed - ed, will soon pass a - way.
To sink in the gloom of e - ter - ni - ty's night.
What pow'r, then, O sin - ner, shall lend thee its aid? A - men.

5 Delay not, delay not! Why longer abuse
  The love and compassion of Jesus, thy God?
A fountain is opened; how canst thou refuse
  To wash and be cleansed in His pardoning blood?

Today Thy Mercy Calls Us

7. 6. 7. 6. D.

Rev. 3: 8
Oswald Allen, 1861

Anthes
Friedrich K. Anthes, 1847

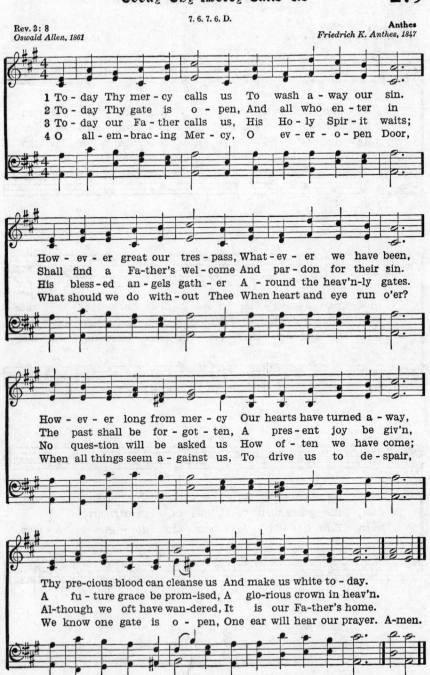

1 To - day Thy mer - cy calls us To wash a - way our sin.
2 To - day Thy gate is o - pen, And all who en - ter in
3 To - day our Fa - ther calls us, His Ho - ly Spir - it waits;
4 O all - em - brac - ing Mer - cy, O ev - er - o - pen Door,

How - ev - er great our tres - pass, What - ev - er we have been,
Shall find a Fa-ther's wel - come And par - don for their sin.
His bless - ed an - gels gath - er A - round the heav'n-ly gates.
What should we do with - out Thee When heart and eye run o'er?

How - ev - er long from mer - cy Our hearts have turned a - way,
The past shall be for - got - ten, A pres - ent joy be giv'n,
No ques-tion will be asked us How of - ten we have come;
When all things seem a - gainst us, To drive us to de - spair,

Thy pre-cious blood can cleanse us And make us white to - day.
A fu - ture grace be prom-ised, A glo-rious crown in heav'n.
Al-though we oft have wan-dered, It is our Fa-ther's home.
We know one gate is o - pen, One ear will hear our prayer. A-men.

280 Return, O Wanderer, Return

L. M.

Luke 15: 18
William B. Collyer, 1806, cento, alt.

Abends
Herbert S. Oakeley, 1874

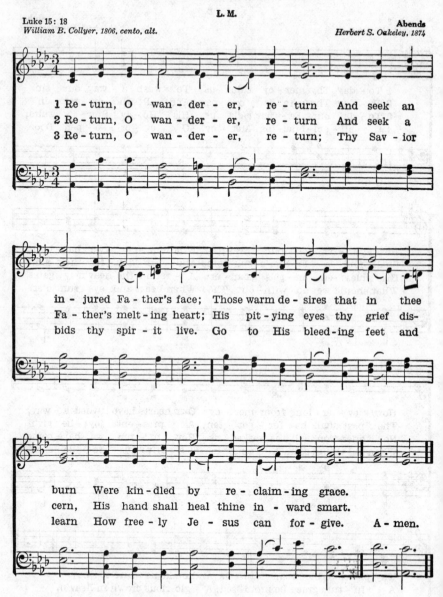

1 Re - turn, O wan - der - er, re - turn And seek an in - jured Fa - ther's face; Those warm de - sires that in thee burn Were kin - dled by re - claim - ing grace.

2 Re - turn, O wan - der - er, re - turn And seek a Fa - ther's melt - ing heart; His pit - ying eyes thy grief dis - cern, His hand shall heal thine in - ward smart.

3 Re - turn, O wan - der - er, re - turn; Thy Sav - ior bids thy spir - it live. Go to His bleed - ing feet and learn How free - ly Je - sus can for - give. A - men.

4 Return, O wanderer, return
   And wipe away the falling tear;
   'Tis God who says, "No longer mourn";
   'Tis Mercy's voice invites thee near.

The Savior Calls; Let Every Ear

C. M.

Matt. 11: 28
Anne Steele, 1760

Azmon
Carl G. Gläser, †1829

1 The Sav - ior calls; let ev - 'ry ear At-
2 For ev - 'ry thirst - y, long - ing heart Here
3 Here springs of sa - cred plea - sures rise To
4 Ye sin - ners, come, 'tis Mer - cy's voice; The

tend the heav'n - ly sound. Ye doubt-ing souls, dis-
streams of boun - ty flow And life and health and
ease your ev - 'ry pain; Im - mor - tal foun - tain,
gra - cious call o - bey; Mer - cy in - vites to

miss your fear; Hope smiles re - viv - ing round.
bliss im - part To ban-ish mor - tal woe.
full sup - plies! Nor shall you thirst in vain.
heav'n - ly joys, And can you yet de - lay? A - men.

5 Dear Savior, draw reluctant hearts;
To Thee let sinners fly
And take the bliss Thy love imparts
And drink and never die.

The Word

282   Christians, Come, in Sweetest Measures

Gen. 2 : 10
Iucundare, plebs fidelis
Adam of St. Victor, c. 1150, cento
Tr., Robert Campbell, 1850, alt.

8. 8. 7. 8. 8. 7.

Alles ist an Gottes Segen
Johann B. König, 1738

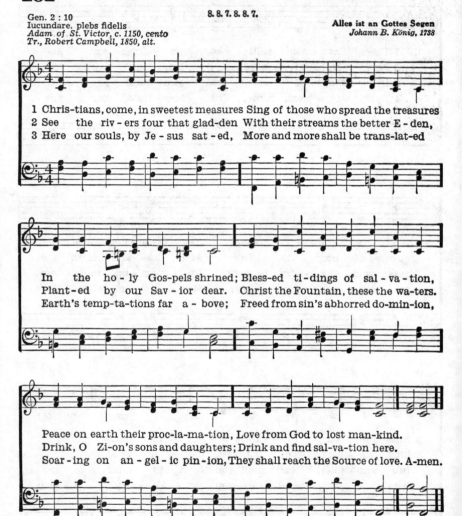

1 Chris-tians, come, in sweetest measures Sing of those who spread the treasures
2 See the riv-ers four that glad-den With their streams the better E - den,
3 Here our souls, by Je-sus sat - ed, More and more shall be trans-lat-ed

In the ho - ly Gos-pels shrined; Bless-ed ti-dings of sal - va - tion,
Plant-ed by our Sav - ior dear. Christ the Fountain, these the wa-ters.
Earth's temp-ta-tions far a - bove; Freed from sin's abhorred do-min-ion,

Peace on earth their proc-la-ma-tion, Love from God to lost man-kind.
Drink, O Zi-on's sons and daughters; Drink and find sal-va-tion here.
Soar-ing on an - gel - ic pin - ion, They shall reach the Source of love. A-men.

4 Then shall thanks and praise ascending
For Thy mercies without ending
Rise to Thee, O Savior blest.
With Thy gracious aid defend us,
Let Thy guiding light attend us,
Bring us to Thy place of rest.

God's Word Is Our Great Heritage 283

Ps. 16: 6
Guds Ord det er vort Arvegods
Nikolai F. S. Grundtvig, 1817
Tr., Ole G. Belsheim, 1909

8. 7. 8. 7. 6. 6. 6. 6. 7.

Reuter
Fritz Reuter, 1916

God's Word is our great her-i-tage And shall be ours for-ev-er;

To spread its light from age to age Shall be our chief en-deav-or.

Through life it guides our way, In death it is our stay.

Lord, grant, while worlds en-dure, We keep its teach-ings pure

Through-out all gen-er-a - tions. A-men.

284 Father of Mercies, in Thy Word

C. M.

Ps. 119: 127
Anne Steele, 1760, cento

Bedford
William Wheall, 1729

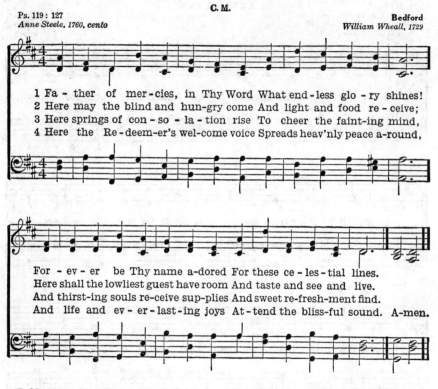

1 Fa - ther of mer - cies, in Thy Word What end - less glo - ry shines!
2 Here may the blind and hun-gry come And light and food re - ceive;
3 Here springs of con - so - la - tion rise To cheer the faint-ing mind,
4 Here the Re - deem-er's wel-come voice Spreads heav'nly peace a-round,

For - ev - er be Thy name a-dored For these ce - les - tial lines.
Here shall the lowliest guest have room And taste and see and live.
And thirst-ing souls re-ceive sup-plies And sweet re-fresh-ment find.
And life and ev - er - last-ing joys At - tend the bliss-ful sound. A-men.

5 Oh, may these heavenly pages be
    My ever dear delight;
  And still new beauties may I see
    And still increasing light!

6 Divine Instructor, gracious Lord,
    Be Thou forever near;
  Teach me to love Thy sacred Word
    And view my Savior here.

285 How Precious Is the Book Divine

C. M.

Ps. 119: 105
John Fawcett, 1782

Walder
Johann J. Walder, 1788

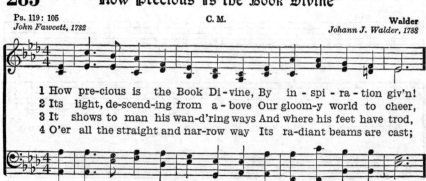

1 How pre-cious is the Book Di - vine, By in - spi - ra - tion giv'n!
2 Its light, de-scend-ing from a - bove Our gloom-y world to cheer,
3 It shows to man his wan-d'ring ways And where his feet have trod,
4 O'er all the straight and nar-row way Its ra-diant beams are cast;

How Precious Is the Book Divine

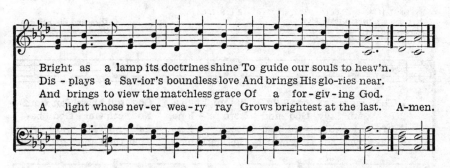

Bright as a lamp its doctrines shine To guide our souls to heav'n.
Dis - plays a Sav-ior's boundless love And brings His glo-ries near.
And brings to view the matchless grace Of a for-giv-ing God.
A light whose nev-er wea-ry ray Grows brightest at the last. A-men.

5 It sweetly cheers our drooping hearts
   In this dark vale of tears.
Life, light, and joy it still imparts
   And quells our rising fears.

6 This lamp through all the tedious night
   Of life shall guide our way
Till we behold the clearer light
   Of an eternal day.

How Shall the Young Secure Their Hearts   286

C. M.

Ps. 119: 9   St. Peter
Isaac Watts, 1719, cento   *Alexander R. Reinagle, 1836*

1 How shall the young se-cure their hearts And guard their lives from sin?
2 'Tis, like the sun, a heav'n-ly light That guides us all the day,
3 The star-ry heav'ns Thy rule o - bey, The earth maintains her place;

Thy Word the choic-est rules im-parts To keep the conscience clean.
And thro' the dan-gers of the night A lamp to lead our way.
And these Thy servants, night and day, Thy skill and pow'r ex-press. A-men.

4 But still Thy Law and Gospel, Lord,
   Have lessons more divine;
Not earth stands firmer than Thy Word,
   Nor stars so nobly shine.

5 Thy Word is everlasting truth;
   How pure is every page!
That holy Book shall guide our youth
   And well support our age.

287 That Man a Godly Life Might Live

Ex. 20: 1–17
Dies sind die heil'gen zehn Gebot'
Martin Luther, 1524
Tr., Richard Massie, 1854, alt.

8. 8. 8. 7. 4.

Dies sind die heil'gen
German melody, c. 1200

1 That man a god-ly life might live, God did these Ten Com-
2 I am thy God and Lord a-lone, No oth-er God be-
3 By i-dle word and speech pro-fane Take not My ho-ly
4 Hal-low the day which God hath blest That thou and all thy

mand-ments give By His true ser-vant Mo-ses, high
side Me own; Put thy whole con-fi-dence in Me
name in vain And praise but that as good and true
house may rest; Keep hand and heart from la-bor free

Up-on the Mount Si-na-i. Have mer-cy, Lord!
And love Me e'er cor-dial-ly. Have mer-cy, Lord!
Which I My-self say and do. Have mer-cy, Lord!
That God may so work in thee. Have mer-cy, Lord! A-men.

5 Give to thy parents honor due,
Be dutiful, and loving, too,
And help them when their strength
decays;
So shalt thou have length of days.
Have mercy, Lord!

6 In sinful wrath thou shalt not kill
Nor hate nor render ill for ill;
Be patient and of gentle mood,
And to thy foe do thou good.
Have mercy, Lord!

7 Be faithful to thy marriage vows,
Thy heart give only to thy spouse;
Thy life keep pure, and lest thou sin,
Use temperance and discipline.
Have mercy, Lord!

8 Steal not; all usury abhor
Nor wring their life-blood from the
poor,
But open wide thy loving hand
To all the poor in the land.
Have mercy, Lord!

That Man a Godly Life Might Live

9 Bear not false witness nor belie
Thy neighbor by foul calumny.
Defend his innocence from blame;
With charity hide his shame.
Have mercy, Lord!

10 Thy neighbor's house desire thou
not,
His wife, nor aught that he hath got,
But wish that his such good may be
As thy heart doth wish for thee.
Have mercy, Lord!

11 God these commandments gave
therein
To show thee, child of man, thy sin
And make thee also well perceive
How man unto God should live.
Have mercy, Lord!

12 Help us, Lord Jesus Christ, for we
A Mediator have in Thee.
Our works cannot salvation gain;
They merit but endless pain.
Have mercy, Lord!

Lord, Help Us Ever to Retain 288

Ex. 20: 1-17   L. M.
Herr Gott, erhalt uns für und für
Ludwig Helmbold, 1594
Tr., Matthias Loy, 1880, alt.

Herr Jesu Christ, mein's
"As Hymnodus Sacer"
Leipzig, 1625

1 Lord, help us ev-er to re-tain The Cat-e-chism's doc-trine plain As Lu-ther taught the Word of Truth In sim-ple style to ten-der youth.

2 Help us Thy ho-ly Law to learn, To mourn our sin, and from it turn In faith to Thee and to Thy Son, And Ho-ly Spir-it, Three in One.

3 Hear us, dear Fa-ther, when we pray For need-ed help from day to day That as Thy chil-dren we may live, Whom Thou in Bap-tism didst re-ceive.

4 Lord, when we fall and sin doth stain, Ab-solve and lift us up a-gain; And thro' the Sac-ra-ment in-crease Our faith till we de-part in peace. A-men.

289 The Law Commands and Makes Us Know

Ps. 19: 9
Isaac Watts, 1709

L. M.

Old Hundredth
"Genevan Psalter," 1551

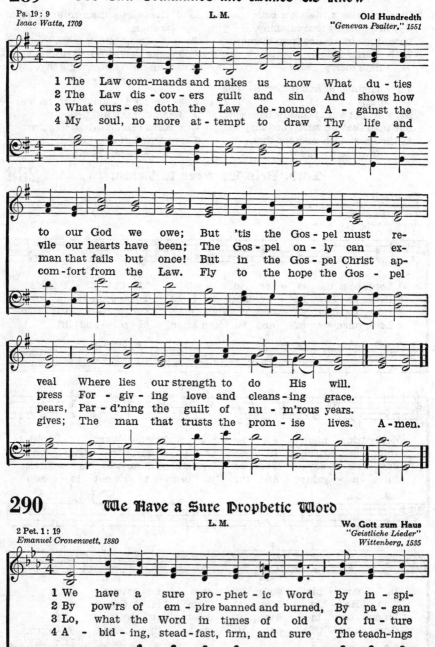

1 The Law com-mands and makes us know What du - ties
to our God we owe; But 'tis the Gos - pel must reveal Where lies our strength to do His will.

2 The Law dis - cov - ers guilt and sin And shows how
vile our hearts have been; The Gos - pel on - ly can ex-
press For - giv - ing love and cleans-ing grace.

3 What curs - es doth the Law de - nounce A - gainst the
man that fails but once! But in the Gos - pel Christ ap-
pears, Par - d'ning the guilt of nu - m'rous years.

4 My soul, no more at - tempt to draw Thy life and
com - fort from the Law. Fly to the hope the Gos - pel
gives; The man that trusts the prom - ise lives. A - men.

290 We Have a Sure Prophetic Word

L. M.

2 Pet. 1: 19
Emanuel Cronenwett, 1880

Wo Gott zum Haus
"Geistliche Lieder"
Wittenberg, 1535

1 We have a sure pro - phet - ic Word By in - spi-
2 By pow'rs of em - pire banned and burned, By pa - gan
3 Lo, what the Word in times of old Of fu - ture
4 A - bid - ing, stead-fast, firm, and sure The teach-ings

We Have a Sure Prophetic Word

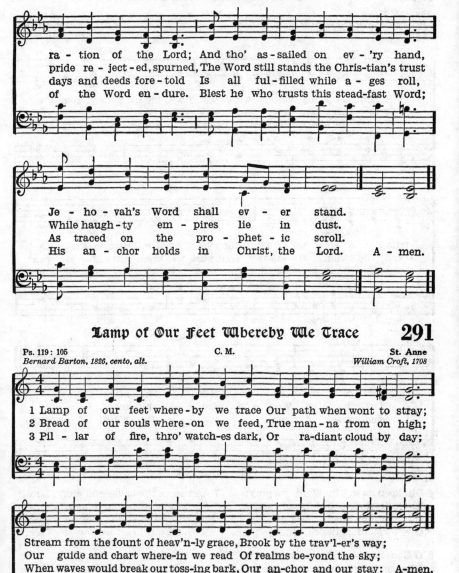

ra - tion of the Lord; And tho' as - sailed on ev - 'ry hand,
pride re - ject - ed, spurned, The Word still stands the Chris - tian's trust
days and deeds fore - told Is all ful - filled while a - ges roll,
of the Word en - dure. Blest he who trusts this stead - fast Word;

Je - ho - vah's Word shall ev - er stand.
While haugh - ty em - pires lie in dust.
As traced on the pro - phet - ic scroll.
His an - chor holds in Christ, the Lord. A - men.

Lamp of Our Feet Whereby We Trace 291

Ps. 119 : 105   C. M.   St. Anne
Bernard Barton, 1826, cento, alt.   *William Croft, 1708*

1 Lamp of our feet where - by we trace Our path when wont to stray;
2 Bread of our souls where - on we feed, True man - na from on high;
3 Pil - lar of fire, thro' watch - es dark, Or ra - diant cloud by day;

Stream from the fount of heav'n - ly grace, Brook by the trav'l - er's way;
Our guide and chart where - in we read Of realms be - yond the sky;
When waves would break our toss - ing bark, Our an - chor and our stay: A - men.

4 Word of the ever-living God,
    Will of His glorious Son;
Without thee, how could earth be trod
    Or heaven itself be won?

5 Lord, grant us all aright to learn
    The wisdom it imparts
And to its heavenly teaching turn
    With simple, childlike hearts.

292 Lord Jesus Christ, with Us Abide

Luke 24 : 29
L. M.

Ach bleib bei uns, Herr Jesu Christ
Nikolaus Selnecker et al., 1611
Tr., composite

Ach bleib bei uns
"Geistliche Lieder"
Leipzig, 1589

1 Lord Jesus Christ, with us abide, For round us
2 In these last days of sore distress Grant us, dear
3 Lord Jesus, help, Thy Church uphold, For we are

falls the eventide; Nor let Thy Word, that heav'nly light,
Lord, true steadfastness That pure we keep, till life is spent,
sluggish, thoughtless, cold. Oh, prosper well Thy Word of grace

For us be ever veiled in night.
Thy holy Word and Sacrament.
And spread its truth in ev'ry place! A-men.

4 Oh, keep us in Thy Word, we pray;
The guile and rage of Satan stay!
Oh, may Thy mercy never cease!
Give concord, patience, courage, peace.

5 O God, how sin's dread works abound!
Throughout the earth no rest is found,
And falsehood's spirit wide has spread,
And error boldly rears its head.

6 The haughty spirits, Lord, restrain
Who o'er Thy Church with might
  would reign
And always set forth something new,
Devised to change Thy doctrine true.

7 And since the cause and glory, Lord,
Are Thine, not ours, to us afford
Thy help and strength and constancy.
With all our heart we trust in Thee.

8 A trusty weapon is Thy Word,
Thy Church's buckler, shield, and
  sword.
Oh, let us in its power confide
That we may seek no other guide!

9 Oh, grant that in Thy holy Word
We here may live and die, dear Lord;
And when our journey endeth here,
Receive us into glory there.

O Holy Spirit, Grant Us Grace

293

8. 7. 8. 7. 8. 8. 7.

Ps. 19: 7
Gott Heil'ger Geist, hilf uns mit Grund
Bartholomäus Ringwaldt, 1581
Tr., Oluf H. Smeby, 1909

Es ist gewisslich
"Geistliche Lieder"
Wittenberg, 1535

1 O Ho-ly Spir-it, grant us grace That we our Lord and Sav-ior
2 Help us that we Thy sav-ing Word In faith-ful hearts may trea-sure;
3 And when our earth-ly race is run, Death's bit-ter hour im-pend-ing,

In faith and fer-vent love em-brace And tru-ly serve Him ev - er,
Let e'er that Bread of Life af-ford New grace in rich-est mea-sure.
Then may Thy work in us be-gun Con - tin-ue till life's end-ing,

So that when death is draw-ing nigh, We to His o-pen
Yea, let us die to ev-'ry sin, For heav'n cre-ate us
Un - til we glad-ly may com-mend Our souls in-to our

wounds may fly And find in them sal - va - tion.
new with - in That fruits of faith may flour - ish.
Sav - ior's hand To rest in peace e - ter - nal. A-men.

294

O Word of God Incarnate

7 6. 7. 6. D.

Ps. 119 : 105
William W. How, 1867

Munich
"Neuvermehrtes Gesangbuch"
Meiningen, 1693

1 O Word of God In-car-nate, O Wis-dom from on high,
2 The Church from her dear Mas-ter Re-ceived the gift di-vine,
3 It float-eth like a ban-ner Be-fore God's host un-furled;
4 Oh, make Thy Church, dear Sav-ior, A lamp of bur-nished gold

O Truth un-changed, un-chang-ing, O Light of our dark sky —
And still that light she lift-eth O'er all the earth to shine.
It shin-eth like a bea-con A-bove the dark-ling world;
To bear be-fore the na-tions Thy true light as of old!

We praise Thee for the ra-diance That from the hal-lowed page,
It is the gold-en cas-ket Where gems of truth are stored;
It is the chart and com-pass That o'er life's surg-ing sea,
Oh, teach Thy wan-d'ring pil-grims By this their path to trace

A lan-tern to our foot-steps, Shines on from age to age.
It is the heav'n-drawn pic-ture Of Christ, the liv-ing Word.
Mid mists and rocks and quicksands, Still guides, O Christ, to Thee.
Till, clouds and dark-ness end-ed, They see Thee face to face! A-men.

The Law of God Is Good and Wise

L. M.

Ps. 19: 8
Matthias Loy, 1863

295

Erhalt uns, Herr
"Geistliche Lieder"
Wittenberg, 1543

1 The Law of God is good and wise And sets His
2 Its light of ho - li - ness im - parts The knowl - edge
3 To those who help in Christ have found And would in
4 When men the of - fered help dis - dain And wil - ful -

will be - fore our eyes, Shows us the way of right - eous -
of our sin - ful hearts That we may see our lost es -
works of love a - bound It shows what deeds are His de -
ly in sin re - main, Its ter - ror in their ear re -

ness, And dooms to death when we trans - gress.
tate And seek de - liv - 'rance ere too late.
light And should be done as good and right.
sounds And keeps their wick - ed - ness in bounds. A - men.

5 The Law is good; but since the Fall
Its holiness condemns us all;
It dooms us for our sin to die
And has no power to justify.

6 To Jesus we for refuge flee,
Who from the curse has set us free,
And humbly worship at His throne,
Saved by His grace through faith alone.

296 Speak, O Lord, Thy Servant Heareth

1 Sam. 3: 10
Rede, liebster Jesus, rede
Anna Sophia of Hesse–Darmstadt, 1658, ab.
Tr., George T. Rygh, 1909

8. 7. 8. 7. 7. 7. 8. 8.

Werde munter
Johann Schop, 1642

1 Speak, O Lord, Thy ser-vant hear-eth, To Thy Word I
2 Oh, what bless-ing to be near Thee And to heark-en
3 Lord, Thy words are wa-ters liv-ing Where I quench my
4 Pre-cious Je-sus, I be-seech Thee, May Thy words take

now give heed; Life and spir-it Thy Word bear-eth, All Thy
to Thy voice! May I ev-er love and fear Thee That Thy
thirst-y need; Lord, Thy words are bread life-giv-ing, On Thy
root in me; May this gift from heav'n en-rich me So that

Word is true in-deed. Death's dread pow'r in me is rife;
Word may be my choice! Oft were har-dened sin-ners, Lord,
words my soul doth feed. Lord, Thy words shall be my light
I bear fruit for Thee! Take them nev-er from my heart

Je-sus, may Thy Word of Life Fill my soul with love's strong
Struck with ter-ror by Thy Word; But to him who for sin
Thro' death's vale and drear-y night; Yea, they are my sword pre-
Till I see Thee as Thou art, When in heav'n-ly bliss and

Speak, O Lord, Thy Servant Heareth

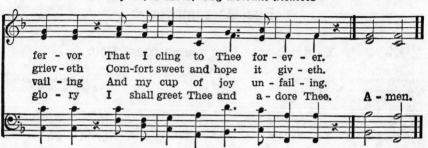

fer - vor   That I cling to Thee for - ev - er.
griev - eth   Com-fort sweet and hope it giv - eth.
vail - ing   And my cup of joy un - fail - ing.
glo - ry   I shall greet Thee and a - dore Thee.   A - men.

The Gospel Shows the Father's Grace   297

L. M.

John 3: 16
Matthias Loy, 1863

Herr Jesu Christ, dich
"Cantionale Germanicum"
Dresden, 1628

1 The Gos - pel shows the Fa-ther's grace, Who sent His Son to
2 It sets the Lamb be - fore our eyes, Who made th' a-ton - ing
3 It brings the Sav - ior's right-eous-ness Our souls to robe in
4 It is the pow'r of God to save From sin and Sa - tan

save our race, Pro - claims how Je - sus lived and died
sac - ri - fice, And calls the souls with guilt op - prest
roy - al dress; From all our guilt it brings re - lease
and the grave; It works the faith, which firm - ly clings

That man might thus be jus - ti - fied.
To come and find e - ter - nal rest.
And gives the trou - bled con-science peace.
To all the trea - sures which it brings.   A - men.

5 It bears to all the tidings glad
  And bids their hearts no more be sad;
  The heavy-laden souls it cheers
  And banishes their guilty fears.

6 May we in faith its tidings learn
  Nor thanklessly its blessings spurn;
  May we in faith its truth confess
  And praise the Lord our Righteousness!

298   Baptized into Thy Name Most Holy

Matt. 28: 19   9. 8. 9. 8. 8. 8.

Ich bin getauft auf deinen Namen   **O dass ich tausend**
Johann J. Rambach, 1734, ab.   *Kornelius Dretzel, 1731*
Tr., Catherine Winkworth, 1863, alt.

1 Bap-tized in-to Thy name most ho-ly, O Fa-ther, Son, and Ho-ly Ghost, I claim a place, though weak and low-ly, A-mong Thy seed, Thy cho-sen host. Bur-ied with Christ and dead to sin, Thy Spir-it now shall live with-in.

2 My lov-ing Fa-ther, Thou dost take me To be hence-forth Thy child and heir; My faith-ful Sav-ior, Thou dost make me The fruit of all Thy sor-rows share; Thou, Ho-ly Ghost, wilt com-fort me When dark-est clouds a-round I see.

3 And I have vowed to fear and love Thee And to o-bey Thee, Lord, a-lone; Be-cause the Ho-ly Ghost did move me, I dared to pledge my-self Thine own, Re-nounc-ing sin to keep the faith And war with e-vil un-to death.

4 My faith-ful God, Thou fail-est nev-er, Thy cov-'nant sure-ly will a-bide; Oh, cast me not a-way for-ev-er Should I trans-gress it on my side! Tho' I have oft my soul de-filed, Do Thou for-give, re-store, Thy child. A-men.

Baptized into Thy Name Most Holy

5 Yea, all I am and love most dearly
   I offer now, O Lord, to Thee.
Oh, let me make my vows sincerely
   And help me Thine own child to be!
Let naught within me, naught I own,
Serve any will but Thine alone.

6 And never let my purpose falter,
   O Father, Son, and Holy Ghost,
But keep me faithful to Thine altar
   Till Thou shalt call me from my post.
So unto Thee I live and die
And praise Thee evermore on high.

Dear Father, Who hast Made Us All   299

Gal. 3: 27   L. M.
O Vaterherz, das Erd' und Himmel schuf
Albert Knapp, 1841
Tr., William Czamanske, 1939

Herr Jesu Christ, dich
"Cantionale Germanicum"
Dresden, 1628

1 Dear Father, who hast made us all, To Thee Thy children humbly pray: Look on this babe who at Thy call Now enters on life's narrow way.

2 Dear Savior, for Thy love untold We bring this little child to Thee. Receive it, Shepherd, to Thy fold And keep it Thine eternally.

3 Dear Spirit, rest upon this child As Thou didst brood upon the sea, And make it pure and undefiled, A holy temple unto Thee.

4 O Triune God, we humbly pray That all Thy blessings be conferred Upon this child here cleansed today By means of water and the Word. A-men.

300 Dearest Jesus, We Are Here

7. 8. 7. 8. 8. 8.

Mark 10 : 13–16
Liebster Jesu, wir sind hier
Benjamin Schmolck, 1704, cento
Tr., Catherine Winkworth, 1863, alt.

Liebster Jesu
Johann R. Ahle, 1664

1 Dear-est Je-sus, we are here, Glad-ly Thy com-mand o-bey-ing; With this child we now draw near In ac-cord with Thine own say-ing That to Thee it shall be giv-en As a child and heir of heav-en.

2 Yea, Thy word is clear and plain, And we would o-bey it du-ly: "He who is not born a-gain, Heart and life re-new-ing tru-ly, Born of wa-ter and the Spir-it, Can My king-dom not in-her-it."

3 There-fore hast-en we to Thee, In our arms this in-fant bear-ing; Let us here Thy glo-ry see, Let this child, Thy mer-cy shar-ing In Thine arms be shield-ed ev-er, Thine on earth and Thine for-ev-er.

4 Gra-cious Head, Thy mem-ber own; Shep-herd, take Thy lamb and feed it; Prince of Peace, make here Thy throne; Way of Life, to heav-en lead it; Pre-cious Vine, let noth-ing sev-er From Thy side this branch for-ev-er. A-men.

Dearest Jesus, We Are Here

5 Now into Thy heart we pour
 Prayers that from our hearts proceeded.
Our petitions heavenward soar;
 May our warm desires be heeded!
Write the name we now have given,
Write it in the book of heaven.

He that Believes and is Baptized 301

Mark 16: 16   8. 7. 8. 7. 8. 8. 7.

Enhver som tror og bliver döbt
Thomas Kingo, 1689
Tr., George T. Rygh, 1909

Es ist das Heil
German melody, c. 1400

1 He that be-lieves and is bap-tized Shall see the Lord's sal-va-tion;
2 With one ac-cord, O God, we pray: Grant us Thy Ho-ly Spir-it;

Bap-tized in-to the death of Christ, He is a new cre-a-tion.
Look Thou on our in-firm-i-ty Thro' Je-sus' blood and mer-it.

Thro' Christ's re-demp-tion he shall stand A-mong the glo-rious
Grant us to grow in grace each day That by this Sac-ra-

heav'n-ly band Of ev-'ry tribe and na-tion.
ment we may E-ter-nal life in-her-it. A-men.

302

The Savior Kindly Calls

Mark 10: 14
S. M.
Franconia

Philip Doddridge, 1755, cento
"Harmonischer Liederschatz"

Henry U. Onderdonk, 1826, ad.
Frankfurt, 1738

1 The Sav - ior kind - ly calls Our chil - dren to His breast;
2 "Let them ap - proach," He cries, "Nor scorn their hum - ble claim;
3 With joy we bring them, Lord, De - vot - ing them to Thee,

He folds them in His gra - cious arms, Him - self de - clares them blest.
The heirs of heav'n are such as these, For such as these I came."
Im - plor - ing that, as we are Thine, Thine may our offspring be. A - men.

303

This Child We Dedicate to Thee

Luke 18: 17
L. M.
Uxbridge

From the German
Lowell Mason, 1830

Author unknown

Tr., Samuel Gilman, 1823

1 This child we ded - i - cate to Thee, O God of grace and pu - ri - ty;
2 Oh, may Thy Spir - it gen - tly draw Its will - ing soul to keep Thy Law!
3 We, too, be - fore Thy gra - cious sight Once shared the blest baptismal rite
4 Grant that with true and faithful heart We still may act the Christian's part,

Shield it from sin and threat'ning wrong, And let Thy love its life pro - long.
May vir - tue, pi - e - ty, and truth Dawn e - ven with its dawning youth!
And would re - new its sol - emn vow With love and thanks and praises now.
Cheered by each promise Thou hast giv'n And lab'ring for the prize in heav'n. Amen.

An Awe=full Mystery Is Here

L. M.

1 Cor. 11: 23–25
Matthias Loy, 1880

St. Crispin
George J. Elvey, 1862

304

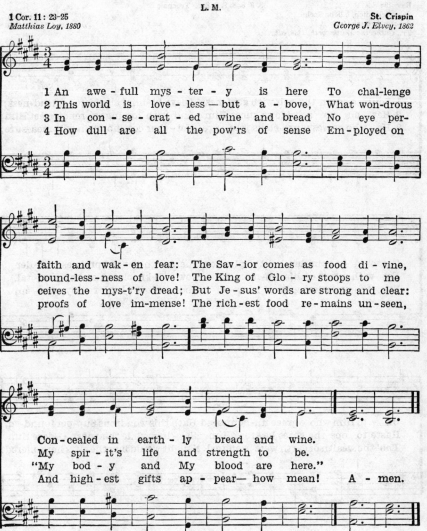

1 An awe-full mys-ter-y is here To chal-lenge faith and wak-en fear: The Sav-ior comes as food di-vine, Con-cealed in earth-ly bread and wine.

2 This world is love-less — but a-bove, What won-drous bound-less-ness of love! The King of Glo-ry stoops to me My spir-it's life and strength to be.

3 In con-se-crat-ed wine and bread No eye per-ceives the mys-t'ry dread; But Je-sus' words are strong and clear: "My bod-y and My blood are here."

4 How dull are all the pow'rs of sense Em-ployed on proofs of love im-mense! The rich-est food re-mains un-seen, And high-est gifts ap-pear— how mean! A - men.

5 But here we have no boon on earth,
And faith alone discerns its worth.
The Word, not sense, must be our guide,
And faith assure since sight's denied.

6 Lord, show us still that Thou art good
And grant us evermore this food.
Give faith to every wavering soul
And make each wounded spirit whole.

305 Soul, Adorn Thyself with Gladness

Rev. 19: 8
Schmücke dich, o liebe Seele
Johann Franck, 1649
Tr., Catherine Winkworth, 1858, alt.

8. 8. 8. 8. 8. 8. 8. 8. Trochaic

Schmücke dich
Johann Crüger, 1649

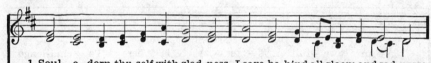

1 Soul, a-dorn thy-self with glad-ness, Leave be-hind all gloom and sad-ness;
2 Hast-en as a bride to meet Him And with lov-ing rev'rence greet Him;
3 He who craves a pre-cious trea-sure Nei-ther cost nor pain will mea-sure;

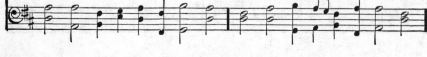

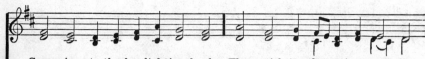

Come in-to the day-light's splendor, There with joy thy prais-es ren-der
For with words of life im-mor-tal Now He knock-eth at thy por-tal.
But the price-less gifts of heav-en God to us hath free-ly giv-en.

Un-to Him whose grace un-bound-ed Hath this wondrous Sup-per found-ed.
Haste to ope the gates be-fore Him, Say-ing, while thou dost a-dore Him,
Tho' the wealth of earth were proffered, Naught would buy the gifts here offered:

High o'er all the heav'ns He reigneth, Yet to dwell with thee He deigneth.
Suf-fer, Lord, that I re-ceive Thee, And I nev-er-more will leave Thee.
Christ's true bod-y, for thee riv-en, And His blood, for thee once given. Amen.

Soul, Adorn Thyself with Gladness

4 Ah, how hungers all my spirit
  For the love I do not merit!
  Oft have I, with sighs fast thronging,
  Thought upon this food with longing,
  In the battle well-nigh worsted,
  For this cup of life have thirsted,
  For the Friend who here invites us
  And to God Himself unites us.

5 In my heart I find ascending
  Holy awe, with rapture blending,
  As this mystery I ponder,
  Filling all my soul with wonder,
  Bearing witness at this hour
  Of the greatness of God's power;
  Far beyond all human telling
  Is the power within Him dwelling.

6 Human reason, though it ponder,
  Cannot fathom this great wonder
  That Christ's body e'er remaineth
  Though it countless souls sustaineth
  And that He His blood is giving
  With the wine we are receiving.
  These great mysteries unsounded
  Are by God alone expounded.

7 Jesus, Sun of Life, my Splendor,
  Jesus, Thou my Friend most tender,
  Jesus, Joy of my desiring,
  Fount of life, my soul inspiring —
  At Thy feet I cry, my Maker,
  Let me be a fit partaker
  Of this blessed food from heaven,
  For our good, Thy glory, given.

8 Lord, by love and mercy driven
  Thou hast left Thy throne in heaven
  On the cross for me to languish
  And to die in bitter anguish,
  To forego all joy and gladness
  And to shed Thy blood in sadness.
  By this blood redeemed and living,
  Lord, I praise Thee with thanksgiving.

9 Jesus, Bread of Life, I pray Thee,
  Let me gladly here obey Thee.
  By Thy love I am invited,
  Be Thy love with love requited;
  From this Supper let me measure,
  Lord, how vast and deep love's treasure.
  Through the gifts Thou here dost give me
  As Thy guest in heaven receive me.

306 Lord Jesus Christ, Thou hast Prepared

1 Cor. 11: 26   8. 7. 8. 7. 8. 8. 7.

Herr Jesu Christ, du hast bereit't
Samuel Kinner, 1638
Tr., Emanuel Cronenwett, 1880, ad.

Herr Jesu Christ, du hast bereit't
Peter Sohren, 1668

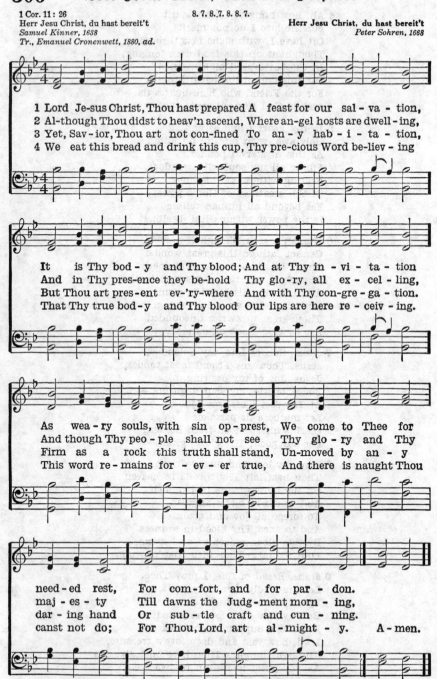

1 Lord Je-sus Christ, Thou hast prepared A feast for our sal - va - tion,
2 Al-though Thou didst to heav'n ascend, Where an-gel hosts are dwell-ing,
3 Yet, Sav - ior, Thou art not con-fined To an - y hab - i - ta - tion,
4 We eat this bread and drink this cup, Thy pre-cious Word be-liev - ing

It is Thy bod - y and Thy blood; And at Thy in - vi - ta - tion
And in Thy pres-ence they be-hold Thy glo-ry, all ex - cel - ling,
But Thou art pres-ent ev-'ry-where And with Thy con-gre - ga - tion.
That Thy true bod-y and Thy blood Our lips are here re - ceiv - ing.

As wea - ry souls, with sin op - prest, We come to Thee for
And though Thy peo - ple shall not see Thy glo - ry and Thy
Firm as a rock this truth shall stand, Un-moved by an - y
This word re - mains for - ev - er true, And there is naught Thou

need - ed rest, For com - fort, and for par - don.
maj - es - ty Till dawns the Judg-ment morn - ing,
dar - ing hand Or sub - tle craft and cun - ning.
canst not do; For Thou, Lord, art al-might - y. A - men.

Lord Jesus Christ, Thou hast Prepared

5 Though reason cannot understand
   Yet faith this truth embraces;
Thy body, Lord, is everywhere
   At once in many places.
How this can be I leave to Thee,
Thy word alone sufficeth me,
   I trust its truth unfailing.

6 Lord, I believe what Thou hast said,
   Help me when doubts assail me;
Remember that I am but dust
   And let my faith not fail me.
Thy Supper in this vale of tears
Refreshes me and stills my fears
   And is my priceless treasure.

7 Grant that we worthily receive
   Thy Supper, Lord, our Savior,
And, truly grieving o'er our sins,
   May prove by our behavior
That we are thankful for Thy grace
And day by day may run our race,
   In holiness increasing.

8 For Thy consoling Supper, Lord,
   Be praised throughout all ages!
Preserve it, for in every place
   The world against it rages.
Grant that this Sacrament may be
A blessed comfort unto me
   When living and when dying.

Draw Nigh and Take the Body of the Lord 307

Ps. 34: 8
Sancti, venite, corpus Christi sumite
Latin author unknown, c. 680
Tr., John M. Neale, 1851, cento, alt.

10. 10. 10. 10.

Old 124th
"Genevan Psalter," 1551

1 Draw nigh and take the bod-y of the Lord And drink the ho-ly blood for you out-poured. Of-fered was He for great-est and for least, Him-self the Vic-tim and Him-self the Priest.

2 He that His saints in this world rules and shields To all be-liev-ers life e-ter-nal yields, With heav'nly bread makes them that hunger whole, Gives liv-ing wa-ters to the thirst-ing soul.

3 Ap-proach ye, then, with faith-ful hearts sin-cere And take the pledg-es of sal-va-tion here. O Judge of all, our on-ly Sav-ior Thou, In this Thy feast of love be with us now. A-men.

308
Invited, Lord, by Boundless Grace

1 Cor. 11 : 26

L. M.

Das walt' Gott Vater

Emanuel Cronenwett, 1880

Daniel Vetter, 1713

1 In - vit - ed, Lord, by bound - less grace, I
2 How ho - ly is this Sac - ra - ment Where
3 Now let - test Thou Thy guest de - part With
4 When Thou shalt in Thy glo - ry come To

stand a guest be - fore Thy face; As Host Thou spreadst no
par - don, peace, and life are spent! This bread and cup my
full as - sur - ance in his heart. For such com - mun - ion,
gath - er all Thy peo - ple home, Then let me, as Thy

com - mon food: Here is Thy bod - y and Thy blood.
lips have pressed; Thou bless - edst, and my soul is blessed.
Lord, with Thee A new life may my of - f'ring be.
heav'n - ly guest, In an - thems praise Thee with the blest. A - men.

309
O Jesus, Blessed Lord, to Thee

2 Cor. 9 : 15

L. M.

Old Hundredth

O Jesu, söde Jesu, dig

"Genevan Psalter," 1551

Thomas Kingo, 1689

Tr., Arthur J. Mason, 1889

1 O Je - sus, bless - ed Lord, to Thee My heart - felt
2 Break forth, my soul, for joy and say: What wealth is

O Jesus, Blessed Lord, to Thee

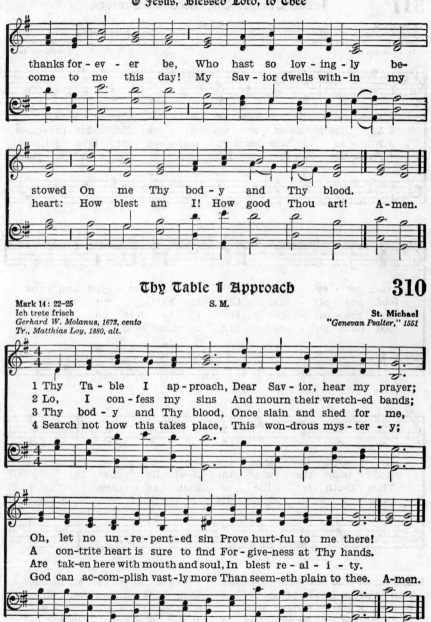

thanks for-ev-er be, Who hast so lov-ing-ly become to me this day! My Sav-ior dwells with-in my

stowed On me Thy bod-y and Thy blood.
heart: How blest am I! How good Thou art! A-men.

Thy Table I Approach

310

Mark 14: 22–25
Ich trete frisch
Gerhard W. Molanus, 1673, cento
Tr., Matthias Loy, 1880, alt.

S. M.

St. Michael
"Genevan Psalter," 1551

1 Thy Ta - ble I ap-proach, Dear Sav - ior, hear my prayer;
2 Lo, I con-fess my sins And mourn their wretch-ed bands;
3 Thy bod - y and Thy blood, Once slain and shed for me,
4 Search not how this takes place, This won-drous mys - ter - y;

Oh, let no un - re - pent-ed sin Prove hurt-ful to me there!
A con-trite heart is sure to find For - give-ness at Thy hands.
Are tak-en here with mouth and soul, In blest re - al - i - ty.
God can ac-com-plish vast-ly more Than seem-eth plain to thee. A-men.

5 Vouchsafe, O blessed Lord,
    That earth and hell combined
May ne'er about this Sacrament
    Raise doubt within my mind.

6 Oh, may I never fail
    To thank Thee day and night
For Thy true body and true blood,
    O God, my Peace and Light!

311
Jesus Christ, Our Blessed Savior

Heb. 10: 12
Iesus Christus, nostra salus
John Huss, 1415, cento, asc.
Tr. unknown

8. 8. 7. 8.

Jesus Christus, unser Heiland
"Geistliche Lieder"
Wittenberg, 1535

1 Je - sus Christ, our bless - ed Sav - ior, Turned a - way God's
2 As His pledge of love un - dy - ing He, this pre - cious
3 Who - so to this Board re - pair - eth May take heed how
4 Praise the Fa - ther, who from heav - en Un - to us such

wrath for - ev - er; By His bit - ter grief and woe
food sup - ply - ing, Gives His bod - y with the bread
he pre - par - eth; For if he does not be - lieve,
food hath giv - en And, to mend what we have done,

He saved us from the e - vil Foe.
And with the wine the blood He shed.
Then death for life he shall re - ceive.
Gave in - to death His on - ly Son. A - men.

5 Thou shalt hold with faith unshaken
That this food is to be taken
By the sick who are distrest,
By hearts that long for peace and rest.

6 Christ says: "Come, all ye that labor,
And receive My grace and favor;
They who feel no want nor ill
Need no physician's help nor skill.

7 "Useless were for thee My Passion
If thy works thy weal could fashion.
This feast is not spread for thee
If thine own savior thou wilt be."

8 If thy heart this truth professes
And thy mouth thy sin confesses,
His dear guest thou here shalt be,
And Christ Himself shall banquet thee.

Lord Jesus Christ, Thou Living Bread

312

John 6: 48
Du Lebensbrot, Herr Jesu Christ
Johann Rist, 1654, cento
Tr., Arthur T. Russell, 1851, alt.

8. 7. 8. 7. 8. 8. 7.

Herr, wie du willst
"Deutsch Kirchenamt"
Strassburg, 1525

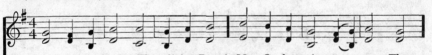

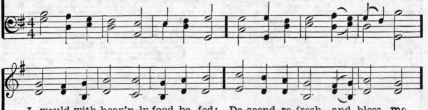

1 Lord Je-sus Christ, Thou living Bread, May I for mine pos-sess Thee.
2 Thou me to pas-tures green dost guide, To qui-et wa-ters lead me;
3 O Bread of Heav'n, my soul's De-light, For full and free re-mis-sion
4 I mer-it not Thy fa-vor, Lord, Sin now up-on me li-eth;

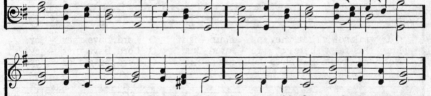

I would with heav'n-ly food be fed; De-scend, re-fresh, and bless me.
Thy Ta-ble Thou dost well pro-vide And from Thy hand dost feed me.
With prayer I come be-fore Thy sight, In sor-row and con-tri-tion.
Be-neath my bur-den, self-ab-horred, To Thee my spir-it cri-eth.

Now make me meet for Thee, O Lord; Now, hum-bly by my heart im-plored,
Sin, weakness, and in-fir-mi-ty Am I; O Sav-ior, give to me
With faith a-dorn my soul that I May to Thy Ta-ble now draw nigh
In all my grief this com-forts me, That Thou on sin-ners gra-cious-ly,

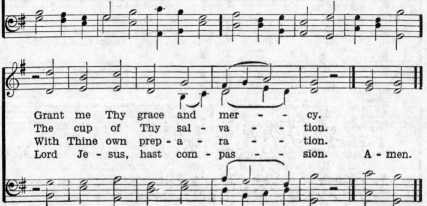

Grant me Thy grace and mer - - cy.
The cup of Thy sal-va - - tion.
With Thine own prep-a-ra - - tion.
Lord Je-sus, hast com-pas - - sion. A-men.

313 O Lord, We Praise Thee

Ps. 118: 1
Gott sei gelobet und gebenedeiet
St. 1, author unknown, c. 1400
St. 2, 3, Martin Luther, 1524
Tr., composite

11. 8. 11. 8. 5. 9. 9. 6. 7. 5.

Gott sei gelobet
German melody, c. 1400

1 O Lord, we praise Thee, bless Thee, and a-dore Thee, In thanks-giv-ing
2 Thy ho-ly bod-y in-to death was giv-en, Life to win for
3 May God be-stow on us His grace and fa-vor To please Him with

bow be-fore Thee. Thou with Thy bod-y and Thy blood didst nourish
us in heav-en. No great-er love than this to Thee could bind us;
our be-hav-ior And live as breth-ren here in love and u-nion

Our weak souls that they may flour-ish: O Lord, have mer-cy!
May this feast there-of re-mind us! O Lord, have mer-cy!
Nor re-pent this blest Com-mu-nion! O Lord, have mer-cy!

May Thy bod-y, Lord, born of Ma-ry, That our sins and
Lord, Thy kind-ness did so con-strain Thee That Thy blood should
Let not Thy good Spir-it for-sake us; Grant that heav'n-ly-

sor-rows did car-ry, And Thy blood for us plead
bless and sus-tain me. All our debt Thou hast paid;
mind-ed He make us; Give Thy Church, Lord, to see

O Lord, We Praise Thee

In all tri - al, fear, and need: O Lord, have mer - cy!
Peace with God once more is made: O Lord, have mer - cy!
Days of peace and u - ni - ty: O Lord, have mer - cy! A-men.

Lord Jesus Christ, We Humbly Pray 314

L. M.

1 Cor. 10: 17
Henry E. Jacobs, 1910

Herr Jesu Christ, dich
"Cantionale Germanicum"
Dresden, 1628

1 Lord Je - sus Christ, we hum-bly pray That we may feed on
2 The chas-tened peace of sin for-giv'n, The fil - ial joy of
3 Our trem-bling hearts cleave to Thy Word; All Thou hast said Thou

Thee to - day; Be - neath these forms of bread and wine
heirs of heav'n, Grant as we share this won-drous food,
dost af - ford, All that Thou art we here re - ceive,

En - rich us with Thy grace di - vine.
Thy bod - y bro - ken and Thy blood.
And all we are to Thee we give. A - men.

4 One bread, one cup, one body, we,
United by our life in Thee,
Thy love proclaim till Thou shalt come
To bring Thy scattered loved ones
home.

5 Lord Jesus Christ, we humbly pray
To keep us steadfast to that day
That each may be Thy welcomed guest
When Thou shalt spread Thy heavenly
feast.

315 I Come, O Savior, to Thy Table

1 Cor. 11 : 28
Ich komm' zu deinem Abendmahle
Friedrich C. Heyder, 1710, *cento*
Tr., composite

9. 8. 9. 8. 8. 8.

Ich sterbe täglich
Ms., Municipal Library
Leipzig, 1756

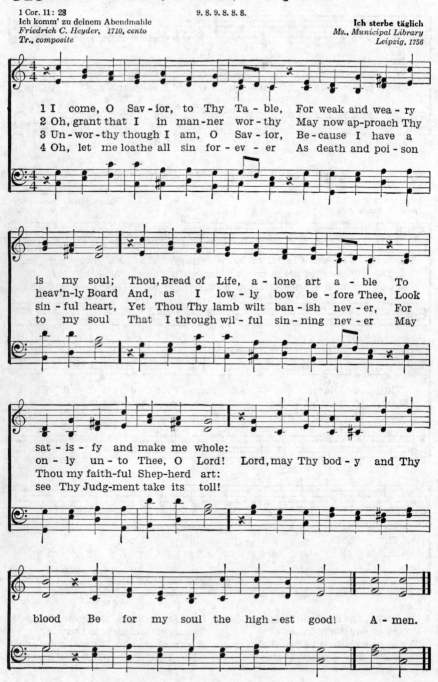

1 I come, O Sav-ior, to Thy Ta-ble, For weak and wea-ry
2 Oh, grant that I in man-ner wor-thy May now ap-proach Thy
3 Un-wor-thy though I am, O Sav-ior, Be-cause I have a
4 Oh, let me loathe all sin for-ev-er As death and poi-son

is my soul; Thou, Bread of Life, a-lone art a-ble To
heav'n-ly Board And, as I low-ly bow be-fore Thee, Look
sin-ful heart, Yet Thou Thy lamb wilt ban-ish nev-er, For
to my soul That I through wil-ful sin-ning nev-er May

sat-is-fy and make me whole:
on-ly un-to Thee, O Lord! Lord, may Thy bod-y and Thy
Thou my faith-ful Shep-herd art:
see Thy Judg-ment take its toll!

blood Be for my soul the high-est good! A-men.

¶ Come, O Savior, to Thy Table

5 Thy heart is filled with fervent yearning
    That sinners may salvation see
Who, Lord, to Thee in faith are turning;
    So I, a sinner, come to Thee.

6 Weary am I and heavy laden,
    With sin my soul is sore opprest;
Receive me graciously and gladden
    My heart, for I am now Thy guest.

7 Thou here wilt find a heart most lowly
    That humbly falls before Thy feet,
That duly weeps o'er sin, yet solely
    Thy merit pleads, as it is meet.

8 By faith I call Thy holy Table
    The testament of Thy deep love;
For, lo, thereby I now am able
    To see how love Thy heart doth move.

9 What higher gift can we inherit?
    It is faith's bond and solid base;
It is the strength of heart and spirit,
    The covenant of hope and grace.

10 This feast is manna, wealth abounding
    Unto the poor, to weak ones power,
To angels joy, to hell confounding,
    And life for me in death's dark hour.

11 Thy body, given for me, O Savior,
    Thy blood which Thou for me didst shed,
These are my life and strength forever,
    By them my hungry soul is fed.

12 With Thee, Lord, I am now united;
    I live in Thee and Thou in me.
No sorrow fills my soul, delighted
    It finds its only joy in Thee.

13 Who can condemn me now? For surely
    The Lord is nigh, who justifies.
No hell I fear, and thus securely
    With Jesus I to heaven rise.

14 Though death may threaten with disaster,
    It cannot rob me of my cheer;
For He who is of death the Master
    With aid and comfort e'er is near.

15 My heart has now become Thy dwelling,
    O blessed, holy Trinity.
With angels I, Thy praises telling,
    Shall live in joy eternally.

316
O Living Bread from Heaven

Matt. 26 : 26-29
Wie wohl hast du gelabet
Johann Rist, 1651, cento
Tr., Catherine Winkworth, 1858, alt.

7. 8. 7. 8. 7. 6. 7. 6. 7. 6. 7. 6.

Nun lob, mein' Seel'
"Concentus Novi"
Augsburg, 1540

1 O liv-ing Bread from heav - en, How rich-ly hast Thou fed Thy guest!
2 My God, Thou here hast led me With-in Thy tem-ple's ho-liest place
3 A heart that hath re-pent-ed And mourns for sin with bit-ter sighs,—

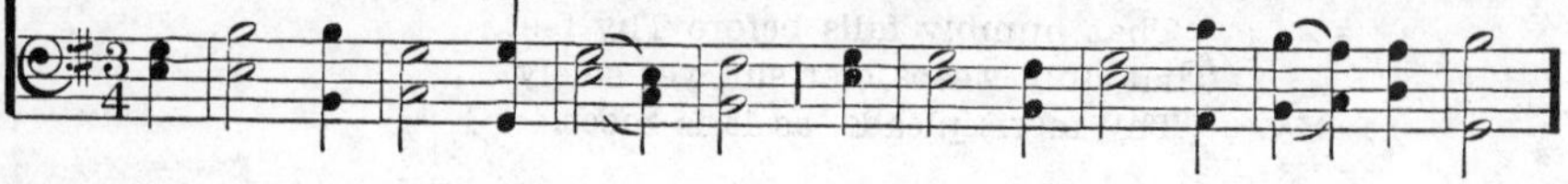

The gifts Thou now hast giv - en Have filled my heart with joy and rest.
And there Thy-self hast fed me With all the trea-sures of Thy grace.
Thou, Lord, art well con-tent-ed With this my on-ly sac-ri-fice.

O won-drous food of bless-ing, O cup that heals our woes!
Oh, bound-less is Thy kind-ness, And right-eous is Thy pow'r,
I know that in my weak-ness Thou wilt de-spise me not,

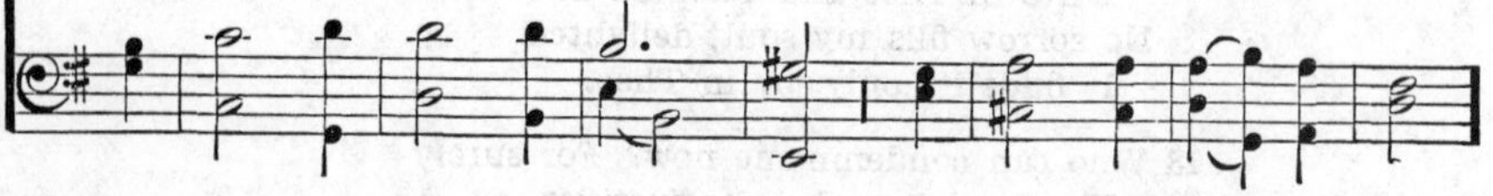

My heart, this gift pro-fess-ing, In thank-ful songs o'er-flows!
While I in sin-ful blind-ness Am err-ing hour by hour;
But grant me in Thy meek-ness The bless-ing I have sought;

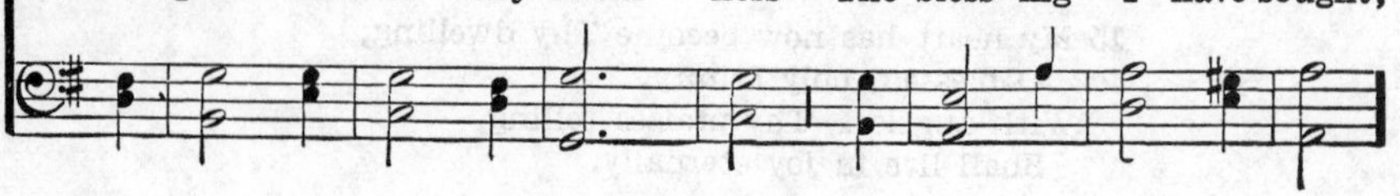

O Living Bread from Heaven

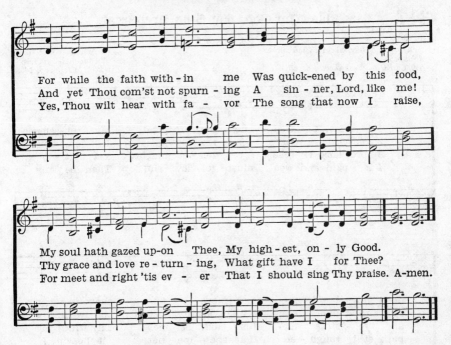

For while the faith with-in me Was quick-ened by this food,
And yet Thou com'st not spurn-ing A sin-ner, Lord, like me!
Yes, Thou wilt hear with fa-vor The song that now I raise,

My soul hath gazed up-on Thee, My high-est, on-ly Good.
Thy grace and love re-turn-ing, What gift have I for Thee?
For meet and right 'tis ev-er That I should sing Thy praise. A-men.

4 Grant what I have partaken
   May through Thy grace so work in me
That sin be all forsaken
   And I may cleave alone to Thee
And all my soul be heedful
   How I Thy love may know;
For this alone is needful
   Thy love should in me glow.
Then let no beauty ever,
   No joy, allure my heart,
But what is Thine, my Savior,
   What Thou dost here impart.

5 Oh, well for me that, strengthened
   With heavenly food and comfort here,
Howe'er my course be lengthened,
   I now may serve Thee free from fear!
Away, then, earthly pleasure!
   All earthly gifts are vain;
I seek a heavenly treasure,
   My home I long to gain,
My God, where I shall praise Thee,
   Where none my peace destroy,
And where my soul shall raise Thee
   Glad songs in endless joy.

317   Alas, My God, My Sins Are Great

Ps. 38 : 4   4. 4. 7. 4. 4. 7.

Ach Gott und Herr, wie gross und schwer
Johann Major, 1613
Tr., *Catherine Winkworth, 1863, alt.*

Ach Gott und Herr
"Andachts-Zymbeln"
Freyberg, 1655

1 A - las, my God,   my sins are great,   My con-science
2 And fled I hence   in my de-spair   In some lone
3 Lord, Thee I seek.   I mer-it naught;   Yet pit-y
4 If pain and woe   must fol-low sin,   Then be my

doth up-braid me;   And now I find   that in my
spot to hide me,   My griefs would still   be with me
and re-store me.   Just God, be not   Thy wrath my
path still rough-er.   Here spare me not;   if heav'n I

strait   No man hath pow'r to aid me.
there   And peace still be de-nied me.
lot;   Thy Son hath suf-fered for me.
win,   On earth I glad-ly suf-fer.   A - men.

5 But curb my heart, forgive my guilt,
   Make Thou my patience firmer;
For they must miss the good Thou wilt
Who at Thy chastenings murmur.

6 Then deal with me as seems Thee best —
   Thy grace will help me bear it
If but at last I see Thy rest
And with my Savior share it.

Before Thee, God, Who Knowest All

318

Ezra 9: 15
Jeg staar for Gud, som alting ved
Magnus B. Landstad, 1861
Tr., Carl Döving, 1909

8. 8. 8. 8. 8. 8.

Vater unser
"Geistliche Lieder"
Leipzig, 1539

1 Be - fore Thee, God, who know-est all, With grief and shame I
2 O Lord, my God, to Thee I pray: Oh, cast me not in
3 O Je - sus, let Thy pre-cious blood Be to my soul a

pros - trate fall. I see my sins a-gainst Thee, Lord, The
wrath a - way! Let Thy good Spir-it ne'er de-part, But
cleans-ing flood. Turn not, O Lord, Thy guest a - way, But

sins of thought, of deed, and word. They press me sore; I cry to
let Him draw to Thee my heart That tru-ly pen - i - tent I
grant that jus - ti - fied I may Go to my house at peace with

Thee: O God, be mer - ci - ful to me!
be: O God, be mer - ci - ful to me!
Thee: O God, be mer - ci - ful to me! A - men.

319

In Thee Alone, O Christ, My Lord

Rom. 3:25
Allein zu dir, Herr Jesu Christ
Johannes Schneesing, 1542, ab., asc.
Tr., Arthur T. Russell, 1851, alt.

8. 7. 8. 7. 8. 8. 8. 4. 8.

Allein zu dir
Separate Print, Nürnberg, 1541
Harm., Johann S. Bach, †1750

1 In Thee a-lone, O Christ, my Lord, My hope on earth re-main - - eth; I know Thou wilt Thine aid af-ford, Naught else my soul sus-tain - - eth. No strength of man, no earth-ly stay, Can help me in the e-vil day;

2 My sins, O Lord, a-gainst me rise, I mourn them with con-tri - - tion; Grant, thro' Thy death and sac - ri-fice, To me a full re-mis - - sion. Lord, show be-fore the Fa-ther's throne That Thou didst for my sins a-tone;

3 O Lord, in mer-cy stay my heart On faith's most sure foun-da - - tion And to my in-most soul im-part Thy per-fect con-so-la - - tion. Fill all my life with love to Thee, Toward all men grant me char-i-ty;

In Thee Alone, O Christ, My Lord

Thou, on - ly Thou, canst aid sup - ply. To Thee I cry;
So shall I from my load be freed. Thy Word I plead;
And at the last, when comes my end, Thy suc - cor send.

On Thee I bid my heart re - ly.
Keep me, O Lord, each hour of need.
From Sa - tan's wiles my soul de - fend. A - men.

Lord Jesus, Think on Me   320

Ps. 119: 133
Μνώεο Χριστέ
Synesius of Cyrene, †430
Tr., Allen W. Chatfield, 1876, cento

S. M.

Southwell
"Psalter"
William Daman, 1579

1 Lord Je - sus, think on me And purge a - way my sin;
2 Lord Je - sus, think on me, With man - y a care op - prest;
3 Lord Je - sus, think on me A - mid the bat - tle's strife;

From earth-born passions set me free And make me pure with - in.
Let me Thy lov - ing ser - vant be And taste Thy prom - ised rest.
In all my pain and mis - er - y Be Thou my Health and Life. A - men.

4 Lord Jesus, think on me
  Nor let me go astray;
Through darkness and perplexity
Point Thou the heavenly way.

5 Lord Jesus, think on me
  When floods the tempest high;
When on doth rush the enemy,
  O Savior, be Thou nigh!

6 Lord Jesus, think on me
  That, when the flood is past,
I may th' eternal brightness see
And share Thy joy at last.

7 Lord Jesus, think on me
  That I may sing above
To Father, Spirit, and to Thee
The strains of praise and love.

321 O Faithful God, Thanks Be to Thee

Ps. 6: 1   L. M.

Wir danken dir, o treuer Gott
Nikolaus Selnecker, 1572
Tr., composite

Wenn wir in höchsten Nöten
"Genevan Psalter," 1547

1 O faith-ful God, thanks be to Thee Who dost for-give in-
2 Thy ser-vant now de - clares to me: "Thy sins are all for-
3 O Lord, we bless Thy gra - cious heart, For Thou Thy-self dost
4 Give us Thy Spir - it, peace af - ford Now and for - ev - er,

iq - ui - ty. Thou grant-est help in sin's dis - tress,
giv - en thee. De - part in peace, but sin no more
heal our smart Thro' Christ our Sav - ior's pre - cious blood,
gra - cious Lord. Pre - serve to us till life is spent

And soul and bod - y dost Thou bless.
And e'er My par - d'ning grace a - dore."
Which for the sake of sin - ners flowed.
Thy ho - ly Word and Sac - ra - ment. A - men.

322 And Wilt Thou Pardon, Lord

Ps. 143: 4   S. M.

Τῶν ἁμαρτιῶν μου τὴν πληθῦν
Joseph the Hymnographer, c. 860, cento
Tr., John M. Neale, 1862

St. Bride
Samuel Howard, 1762

1 And wilt Thou par - don, Lord, A sin - ner such as I,
2 So deep are they en - graved, So ter - ri - ble their fear.
3 O Thou Phy - si - cian blest, Make clean my guilt - y soul
4 I know not how to praise Thy mer - cy and Thy love;

And Wilt Thou Pardon, Lord

Al-though Thy book his crimes re-cord Of such a crim-son dye?
The right-eous scarce-ly shall be saved, And where shall I ap-pear?
And me, by man-y a sin op-prest, Re-store and keep me whole.
But deign my soul from earth to raise And learn from Thee a-bove. A-men.

With Broken Heart and Contrite Sigh 323

Luke 18: 13
Cornelius Elven, 1852
L. M.
St. Luke
Jeremiah Clarke, †1707

1 With bro-ken heart and con-trite sigh, A trem-bling sin-ner,
2 I smite up-on my trou-bled breast, With deep and con-scious
3 Far off I stand with tear-ful eyes Nor dare up-lift them

Lord, I cry. Thy par-d'ning grace is rich and free —
guilt op-prest; Christ and His Cross my on-ly plea —
to the skies; But Thou dost all my an-guish see —

O God, be mer-ci-ful to me!
O God, be mer-ci-ful to me!
O God, be mer-ci-ful to me! A-men.

4 Nor alms nor deeds that I have done
Can for a single sin atone.
To Calvary alone I flee —
O God, be merciful to me!

5 And when, redeemed from sin and hell,
With all the ransomed throng I dwell,
My raptured song shall ever be,
God has been merciful to me.

324

Jesus Sinners Doth Receive

Luke 15: 2
Jesus nimmt die Sünder an
Erdmann Neumeister, 1718
Tr., composite

7. 8. 7. 8. 7. 7.

Meinen Jesum lass' ich nicht
"Neuverfertigtes Gesangbuch"
Darmstadt, 1699

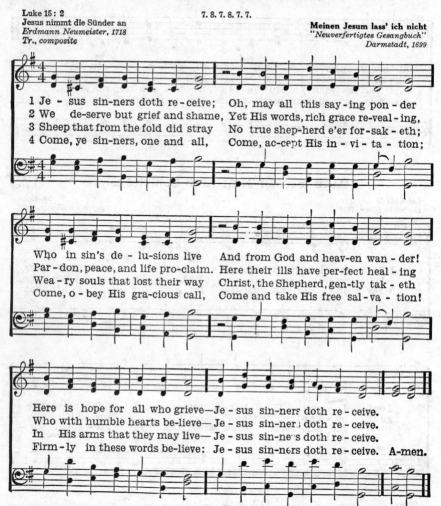

1 Je - sus sin-ners doth re-ceive; Oh, may all this say-ing pon - der
2 We de-serve but grief and shame, Yet His words, rich grace re-veal-ing,
3 Sheep that from the fold did stray No true shep-herd e'er for-sak - eth;
4 Come, ye sin-ners, one and all, Come, ac-cept His in - vi - ta - tion;

Who in sin's de - lu-sions live And from God and heav-en wan - der!
Par - don, peace, and life pro-claim. Here their ills have per-fect heal - ing
Wea - ry souls that lost their way Christ, the Shepherd, gen-tly tak - eth
Come, o - bey His gra-cious call, Come and take His free sal - va - tion!

Here is hope for all who grieve—Je - sus sin-ners doth re - ceive.
Who with humble hearts be-lieve—Je - sus sin-ners doth re - ceive.
In His arms that they may live—Je - sus sin-ners doth re - ceive.
Firm-ly in these words be-lieve: Je - sus sin-ners doth re - ceive. A-men.

5 I, a sinner, come to Thee
   With a penitent confession;
Savior, mercy show to me
   Grant for all my sins remission.
Let these words my soul relieve:
Jesus sinners doth receive.

6 Oh, how blest it is to know:
   Were as scarlet my transgression,
It shall be as white as snow
   By Thy blood and bitter Passion;
For these words I now believe:
Jesus sinners doth receive.

7 Now my conscience is at peace,
   From the Law I stand acquitted;
Christ hath purchased my release
   And my every sin remitted.
Naught remains my soul to grieve—
Jesus sinners doth receive.

8 Jesus sinners doth receive.
   Also I have been forgiven;
And when I this earth must leave,
   I shall find an open heaven.
Dying, still to Him I cleave—
Jesus sinners doth receive.

O Thou that Hear'st when Sinners Cry

L. M.

Ps. 51
Isaac Watts, 1719, cento, alt.

Hamburg
Based on First Gregorian Chant
Arr. by Lowell Mason, 1824

1 O Thou that hear'st when sin - ners cry Tho' all my
2 Cre - ate my na - ture pure with - in And form my
3 I can - not live with - out Thy light, Cast out and
4 Tho' I have grieved Thy Spir - it, Lord, His help and

crimes be - fore Thee lie, Be - hold them not with an - gry
soul a - verse to sin; Let Thy good Spir - it ne'er de -
ban - ished from Thy sight; Thy ho - ly joys, my God, re -
com - fort still af - ford And let me now come near Thy

look, But blot their mem - 'ry from Thy book.
part Nor hide Thy pres - ence from my heart.
store And guard me that I fall no more.
throne To plead the mer - its of Thy Son. A - men.

5 A broken heart, my God, my King,
Is all the sacrifice I bring.
Look down, O Lord, with pitying eye
And save the soul condemned to die.

6 Oh, may Thy love inspire my tongue!
Salvation shall be all my song;
And all my powers shall join to bless
The Lord, my Strength and Righteousness.

326

Lord, to Thee I Make Confession

Ps. 139: 7–10
Herr, ich habe missgehandelt
Johann Franck, 1649, cento
Tr., Catherine Winkworth, 1863, alt.

8. 7. 8. 7. 8. 8.

Herr, ich habe missgehandelt
Johann Crüger, 1649

1 Lord, to Thee I make con-fes - sion; I have sinned and
2 Yet, though con-science' voice ap-pal me, Fa - ther, I will
3 For Thy Son did suf-fer for me, Gave Him-self to
4 Then on Him I cast my bur-den, Sink it in the

gone a - stray, I have mul - ti - plied trans-gres - sion,
seek Thy face; Tho' Thy child I dare not call me,
res - cue me, Died to heal me and re - store me,
depths be - low. Let me know Thy gra - cious par - don,

Cho - sen for my-self my way. Led by Thee to see my
Yet re - ceive me to Thy grace. Do not for my sins for-
Rec - on - ciled me un - to Thee. 'Tis a - lone His cross can
Wash me, make me white as snow. Let Thy Spir - it leave me

er - rors, Lord, I trem-ble at Thy ter - rors.
sake me; Do not let Thy wrath o'er-take me.
van - quish These dark fears and soothe this an - guish.
nev - er; Make me on - ly Thine for - ev - er. A - men.

Out of the Deep I Call

327

S. M.

Southwell
"Psalter"

Ps. 130
Henry W. Baker, 1868

William Daman, 1579

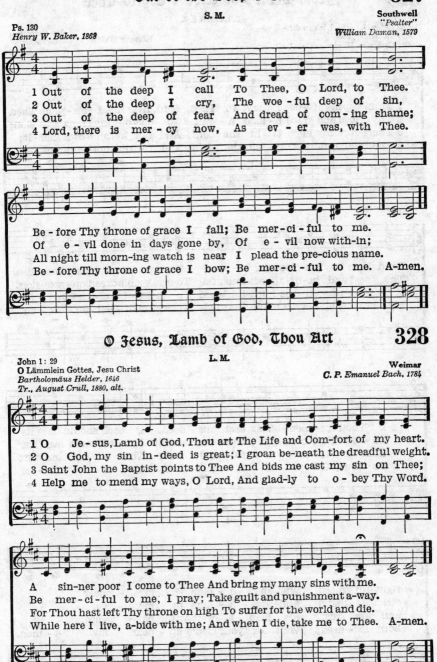

1 Out of the deep I call, To Thee, O Lord, to Thee.
2 Out of the deep I cry, The woe-ful deep of sin,
3 Out of the deep of fear And dread of com-ing shame;
4 Lord, there is mer-cy now, As ev-er was, with Thee.

Be - fore Thy throne of grace I fall; Be mer-ci-ful to me.
Of e - vil done in days gone by, Of e - vil now with-in;
All night till morn-ing watch is near I plead the pre-cious name.
Be - fore Thy throne of grace I bow; Be mer-ci-ful to me. A-men.

O Jesus, Lamb of God, Thou Art

328

L. M.

John 1: 29
O Lämmlein Gottes, Jesu Christ
Bartholomäus Helder, 1646
Tr., August Crull, 1880, alt.

Weimar
C. P. Emanuel Bach, 1784

1 O Je - sus, Lamb of God, Thou art The Life and Com-fort of my heart.
2 O God, my sin in-deed is great; I groan be-neath the dreadful weight.
3 Saint John the Baptist points to Thee And bids me cast my sin on Thee;
4 Help me to mend my ways, O Lord, And glad-ly to o-bey Thy Word.

A sin-ner poor I come to Thee And bring my many sins with me.
Be mer-ci-ful to me, I pray; Take guilt and punishment a-way.
For Thou hast left Thy throne on high To suffer for the world and die.
While here I live, a-bide with me; And when I die, take me to Thee. A-men.

329 From Depths of Woe I Cry to Thee

Ps. 130
Aus tiefer Not schrei' ich zu dir
8. 7. 8. 7. 8. 8. 7.

Martin Luther, 1523
Tr., Catherine Winkworth, 1863, alt.

Aus tiefer Not
Johann Walther's "Gesangbüchlein"
Wittenberg, 1524

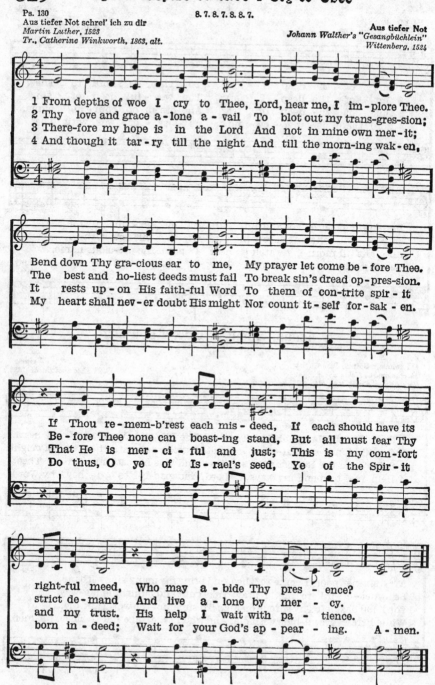

1 From depths of woe I cry to Thee, Lord, hear me, I im-plore Thee.
2 Thy love and grace a-lone a-vail To blot out my trans-gres-sion;
3 There-fore my hope is in the Lord And not in mine own mer-it;
4 And though it tar-ry till the night And till the morn-ing wak-en,

Bend down Thy gra-cious ear to me, My prayer let come be-fore Thee.
The best and ho-liest deeds must fail To break sin's dread op-pres-sion.
It rests up-on His faith-ful Word To them of con-trite spir-it
My heart shall nev-er doubt His might Nor count it-self for-sak-en.

If Thou re-mem-b'rest each mis-deed, If each should have its
Be-fore Thee none can boast-ing stand, But all must fear Thy
That He is mer-ci-ful and just; This is my com-fort
Do thus, O ye of Is-rael's seed, Ye of the Spir-it

right-ful meed, Who may a-bide Thy pres-ence?
strict de-mand And live a-lone by mer-cy.
and my trust. His help I wait with pa-tience.
born in-deed; Wait for your God's ap-pear-ing. A-men.

From Depths of Woe I Cry to Thee

5 Though great our sins and sore our woes,
   His grace much more aboundeth;
   His helping love no limit knows,
   Our utmost need it soundeth.
   Our Shepherd good and true is He,
   Who will at last His Israel free
   From all their sin and sorrow.

I Come to Thee, O Blessed Lord 330

John 6: 37   L. M.
Jeg kommer her, o söde Gud
Magnus B. Landstad, 1863
Tr., Carl Döving, 1910

Wenn wir in höchsten Nöten
"Genevan Psalter," 1547

1 I come to Thee, O bless - ed Lord, In - vit - ed by Thy
2 I come to Thee with sin and grief, For Thou a-lone canst
3 Shouldst Thou a strict ac - count de - mand, Who could, O Lord, be-

gra - cious Word To this Thy feast, to sup with Thee;
give re - lief. Thy death for me, dear Lord, I plead:
fore Thee stand? Purge all my se - cret sins a - way:

Grant that a wor - thy guest I be.
O Je - sus, help me in my need!
Be Thou, O Christ, the sin - ner's Stay! A - men.

4 O Jesus, Lamb of God, alone
  Thou didst for all our sins atone;
  Though I have sinned and gone astray,
  Turn not, O Lord, Thy guest away.

5 O Jesus, Lamb of God, alone
  Thou didst for all our sins atone;
  Be merciful, I Thee implore,
  Be merciful forevermore.

331

Yea, as I Live, Jehovah Saith

Ezek. 33 : 11

L. M.

So wahr ich leb', spricht Gott der Herr
Nikolaus Herman, 1560, cento
Tr., Matthias Loy, 1880, alt.

St. Luke
Jeremiah Clarke, †1707

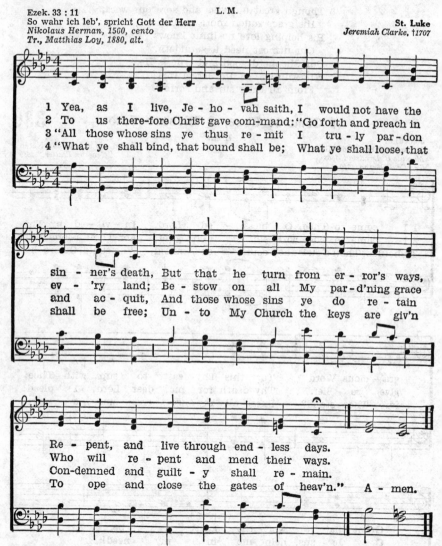

1 Yea, as I live, Je-ho-vah saith, I would not have the
sin-ner's death, But that he turn from er-ror's ways,
Re-pent, and live through end-less days.

2 To us there-fore Christ gave com-mand: "Go forth and preach in
ev-'ry land; Be-stow on all My par-d'ning grace
Who will re-pent and mend their ways.

3 "All those whose sins ye thus re-mit I tru-ly par-don
and ac-quit, And those whose sins ye do re-tain
Con-demned and guilt-y shall re-main.

4 "What ye shall bind, that bound shall be; What ye shall loose, that
shall be free; Un-to My Church the keys are giv'n
To ope and close the gates of heav'n." A-men.

5 The words which absolution give
Are His who died that we might live;
The minister whom Christ has sent
Is but His humble instrument.

6 When ministers lay on their hands,
Absolved by Christ the sinner stands;
He who by grace the Word believes
The purchase of His blood receives.

7 All praise, eternal Son, to Thee
For absolution full and free,
In which Thou showest forth Thy grace;
From false indulgence guard our race.

8 Praise God the Father and the Son
And Holy Spirit, Three in One,
As 'twas, is now, and so shall be
World without end, eternally!

Confirmation

Arm These Thy Soldiers, Mighty Lord

332

L. M.

Eph. 6: 13
Christopher Wordsworth, 1862, alt.

Erhalt uns, Herr
"Geistliche Lieder"
Wittenberg, 1543

1 Arm these Thy sol-diers, might-y Lord, With shield of
2 With ban-ner of the Cross un-furled, They o-ver-
3 Come, ev-er-bless-ed Spir-it, come And make Thy
4 En-rich that tem-ple's ho-ly shrine With sev'n-fold

faith and Spir-it's sword. Forth to the bat-tle may they
come the e-vil world And so at last re-ceive from
ser-vants' hearts Thy home. May each a liv-ing tem-ple
gifts of grace di-vine; With wis-dom, light, and knowl-edge

go And bold-ly fight a-gainst the Foe.
Thee The palm and crown of vic-to-ry.
be Hal-lowed for-ev-er, Lord, to Thee.
bless, With coun-sel, strength, fear, god-li-ness. A-men.

5 O Trinity in Unity,
   One only God and Persons Three,
   In whom, through whom, by whom, we live,
   To Thee we praise and glory give.

6 Oh, grant us so to use Thy grace
   That we may see Thy glorious face
   And ever with the heavenly host
   Praise Father, Son, and Holy Ghost!

333 Blessed Savior, Who hast Taught Me

8. 7. 8. 7. D.

Ezek. 16 : 60
John M. Neale, 1842, cento

O du Liebe
"Musikalischer Christenschatz"
Basel, 1745

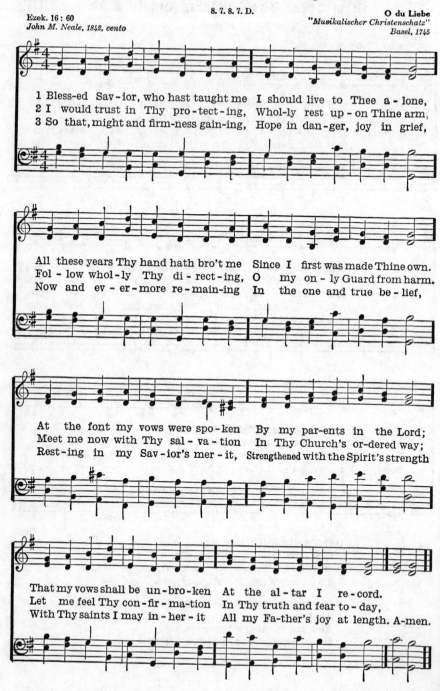

1 Bless-ed Sav-ior, who hast taught me I should live to Thee a - lone,
2 I would trust in Thy pro-tect-ing, Whol-ly rest up - on Thine arm,
3 So that, might and firm-ness gain-ing, Hope in dan-ger, joy in grief,

All these years Thy hand hath bro't me Since I first was made Thine own.
Fol - low whol-ly Thy di - rect-ing, O my on - ly Guard from harm.
Now and ev - er-more re - main-ing In the one and true be - lief,

At the font my vows were spo-ken By my par-ents in the Lord;
Meet me now with Thy sal - va - tion In Thy Church's or-dered way;
Rest-ing in my Sav-ior's mer - it, Strengthened with the Spirit's strength

That my vows shall be un-bro-ken At the al - tar I re-cord.
Let me feel Thy con - fir - ma-tion In Thy truth and fear to - day,
With Thy saints I may in - her - it All my Fa-ther's joy at length. A-men.

Let Me Be Thine Forever

334

7. 6. 7. 6. D.

Rom. 6: 16
Lass mich dein sein und bleiben
St. 1, Nikolaus Selnecker, 1572
St. 2, 3, author unknown, 1688
Tr., Matthias Loy, 1880, alt.

Ich dank' dir, lieber Herre
"Musika Deutsch"
Nürnberg, 1532

1 Let me be Thine for-ev - er, Thou faith-ful God and Lord;
2 Lord Je - sus, my Sal-va - tion, My Light, my Life di - vine,
3 And Thou, O Ho - ly Spir-it, My Com-fort-er and Guide,

Let me for-sake Thee nev - er Nor wan-der from Thy Word.
My on - ly Con - so - la - tion, Oh, make me whol-ly Thine!
Grant that in Je - sus' mer-it I al - ways may con - fide,

Lord, do not let me wa - ver, But give me stead-fast-ness,
For Thou hast dear - ly bought me With blood and bit - ter pain.
Him to the end con-fess - ing Whom I have known by faith.

And for such grace for-ev - er Thy ho - ly name I'll bless.
Let me, since Thou hast sought me, E - ter - nal life ob - tain.
Give me Thy con-stant bless-ing And grant a Chris - tian death. A-men.

335 **My Maker, Be Thou Nigh**

Ps. 119 : 8
Mein Schöpfer, steh mir bei
Johann J. Rambach, †1735
Tr., E. Taylor, 1925, alt.

6. 6. 6. 6. 7. 7. 7. 7. 8. 6.

Mein Schöpfer, steh mir bei
Franz H. Meyer, 1740

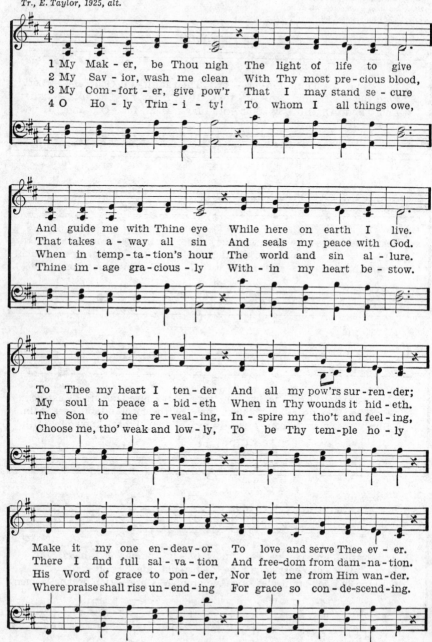

1 My Mak - er, be Thou nigh The light of life to give
2 My Sav - ior, wash me clean With Thy most pre - cious blood,
3 My Com - fort - er, give pow'r That I may stand se - cure
4 O Ho - ly Trin - i - ty! To whom I all things owe,

And guide me with Thine eye While here on earth I live.
That takes a - way all sin And seals my peace with God.
When in temp - ta - tion's hour The world and sin a - lure.
Thine im - age gra - cious - ly With - in my heart be - stow.

To Thee my heart I ten - der And all my pow'rs sur - ren - der;
My soul in peace a - bid - eth When in Thy wounds it hid - eth.
The Son to me re - veal - ing, In - spire my tho't and feel - ing,
Choose me, tho' weak and low - ly, To be Thy tem - ple ho - ly

Make it my one en - deav - or To love and serve Thee ev - er.
There I find full sal - va - tion And free - dom from dam - na - tion.
His Word of grace to pon - der, Nor let me from Him wan - der.
Where praise shall rise un - end - ing For grace so con - de - scend - ing.

My Maker, Be Thou Nigh

Up - on Thy prom-ise I re - ly; My Mak - er, be Thou nigh.
With-out Thee lost, de-filed by sin, My Sav - ior, wash me clean.
On me Thy gifts and grac-es show'r: My Com-fort-er, give pow'r!
O heav'n-ly bliss, Thine own to be, O Ho - ly Trin - i - ty! A-men.

My God, Accept My Heart This Day 336

C. M.

Ps. 119 : 10
Matthew Bridges, 1848

Winchester Old
"Psalter"
Thomas Este, 1592

1 My God, ac-cept my heart this day And make it al-ways Thine
2 Be - fore the cross of Him who died, Be - hold, I pros-trate fall;
3 A - noint me with Thy Spir-it's grace And seal me for Thine own

That I from Thee no more may stray, No more from Thee de-cline.
Let ev - 'ry sin be cru-ci-fied And Christ be all in all.
That I may see Thy glo-rious face And wor-ship near Thy throne. A-men.

4 May the dear blood once shed for me
    My blest atonement prove
That I from first to last may be
    The purchase of Thy love!

5 Let every thought and work and word
    To Thee be ever given;
Then life shall be Thy service, Lord,
    And death the gate of heaven.

337 Our Lord and God, Oh, Bless This Day

Is. 54 : 10
Lad denne Dag, o Herre Gud
Johan N. Brun, 1786
Tr., st. 1, 4, George T. Rygh, 1909
St. 2, 3, Carl Döving, 1909

8. 7. 8. 7. 6. 6. 6. 6. 7.

Reuter
Fritz Reuter, 1916

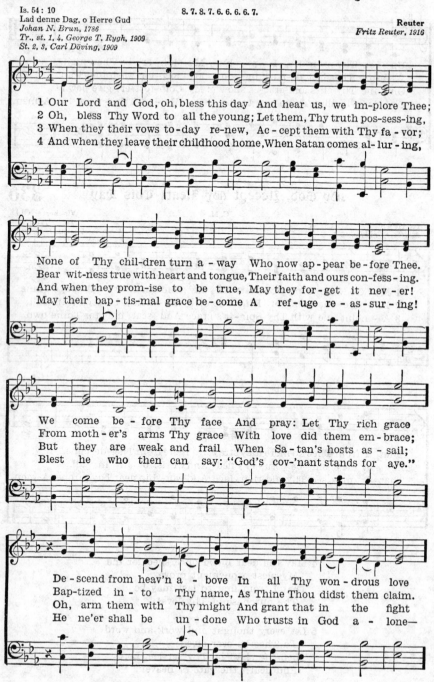

1 Our Lord and God, oh, bless this day And hear us, we im-plore Thee;
2 Oh, bless Thy Word to all the young; Let them, Thy truth pos-sess-ing,
3 When they their vows to-day re-new, Ac-cept them with Thy fa-vor;
4 And when they leave their childhood home, When Satan comes al-lur-ing,

None of Thy chil-dren turn a-way Who now ap-pear be-fore Thee.
Bear wit-ness true with heart and tongue, Their faith and ours con-fess-ing.
And when they prom-ise to be true, May they for-get it nev-er!
May their bap-tis-mal grace be-come A ref-uge re-as-sur-ing!

We come be-fore Thy face And pray: Let Thy rich grace
From moth-er's arms Thy grace With love did them em-brace;
But they are weak and frail When Sa-tan's hosts as-sail;
Blest he who then can say: "God's cov-'nant stands for aye."

De-scend from heav'n a-bove In all Thy won-drous love
Bap-tized in-to Thy name, As Thine Thou didst them claim.
Oh, arm them with Thy might And grant that in the fight
He ne'er shall be un-done Who trusts in God a-lone—

Our Lord and God, Oh, Bless This Day

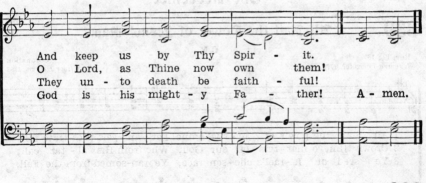

And keep us by Thy Spir - it.
O Lord, as Thine now own them!
They un - to death be faith - ful!
God is his might - y Fa - ther! A - men.

Thine Forever, God of Love

338

7. 7. 7. 7.

Mal. 3: 17
Mary F. Maude, 1847, cento

Vienna
Justin H. Knecht, 1797

1 Thine for - ev - er, God of Love! Hear us from Thy throne a - bove;
2 Thine for - ev - er! Oh, how blest They who find in Thee their rest!
3 Thine for - ev - er, Lord of Life! Shield us thro' our earth - ly strife.

Thine for - ev - er may we be Here and in e - ter - ni - ty!
Sav - ior, Guardian, heav'nly Friend, Oh, de - fend us to the end!
Thou, the Life, the Truth, the Way, Guide us to the realms of day. A - men.

4 Thine forever! Shepherd, keep
These Thy frail and trembling sheep.
Safe alone beneath Thy care,
Let us all Thy goodness share.

5 Thine forever! Thou our Guide,
All our wants by Thee supplied,
All our sins by Thee forgiven;
Lead us, Lord, from earth to heaven.

The Redeemer

339   All Hail the Power of Jesus' Name

C. M.

Rev. 19 : 16
Edward Perronet, 1779, ab., alt.

Coronation
Oliver Holden, 1793

1 All hail the pow'r of Je-sus' name! Let an-gels pros-trate fall;
2 Crown Him, ye mar-tyrs of our God, Who from His al-tar call;
3 Ye seed of Is-rael's cho-sen race, Ye ran-somed from the Fall,

Bring forth the roy-al di-a-dem And crown Him Lord of all.
Ex-tol the Stem of Jes-se's rod And crown Him Lord of all.
Hail Him who saves you by His grace And crown Him Lord of all.

Bring forth the roy-al di-a-dem And crown Him Lord of all.
Ex-tol the Stem of Jes-se's rod And crown Him Lord of all.
Hail Him who saves you by His grace And crown Him Lord of all. A-men.

4 Hail Him, ye heirs of David's line,
    Whom David Lord did call,
The God incarnate, Man divine,
    And crown Him Lord of all.

5 Sinners, whose love can ne'er forget
    The wormwood and the gall,
Go, spread your trophies at His feet
    And crown Him Lord of all.

6 Let every kindred, every tribe,
    On this terrestrial ball
To Him all majesty ascribe
    And crown Him Lord of all.

7 Oh, that with yonder sacred throng
    We at His feet may fall!
We'll join the everlasting song
    And crown Him Lord of all.

Awake, My Soul, to Joyful Lays

340

L. M.

Ps. 36 : 7
Samuel Medley, 1782, alt.

O heilige Dreifaltigkeit
Nikolaus Herman, 1560

1 A - wake, my soul, to joy - ful lays And sing thy
2 He saw me ru - ined in the Fall, Yet loved me
3 When I was Sa - tan's eas - y prey And deep in

great Re-deem-er's praise. He just - ly claims a song from me —
not - with-stand-ing all. He saved me from my lost es - tate —
debt and bond-age lay, He paid His life for my dis-charge —

His lov - ing - kind - ness, oh, how free!
His lov - ing - kind - ness, oh, how great!
His lov - ing - kind - ness, oh, how large! A - men.

4 Through mighty hosts of cruel foes,
Where earth and hell my way oppose,
He safely leads my soul along —
His loving-kindness, oh, how strong!

5 When trouble, like a gloomy cloud,
Has gathered thick and thundered
loud,
He near my soul has always stood —
His loving-kindness, oh, how good!

6 When earthly friends forsake me quite
And I have neither skill nor might,
He's sure my Helper to appear —
His loving-kindness, oh, how near!

7 Too oft I feel my sinful heart
Prone from my Jesus to depart;
But though I have Him oft forgot,
His loving-kindness changes not.

8 When I shall pass death's gloomy
vale
And all my mortal power must fail,
Oh, may my last, expiring breath
His loving-kindness sing in death!

9 Then shall I mount and soar away
To the bright world of endless day
And sing with rapture and surprise
His loving-kindness in the skies.

341 Crown Him with Many Crowns

S. M. D.

Rev. 19: 12
Matthew Bridges, 1851, cento, alt.

Diademata
George J. Elvey, 1868

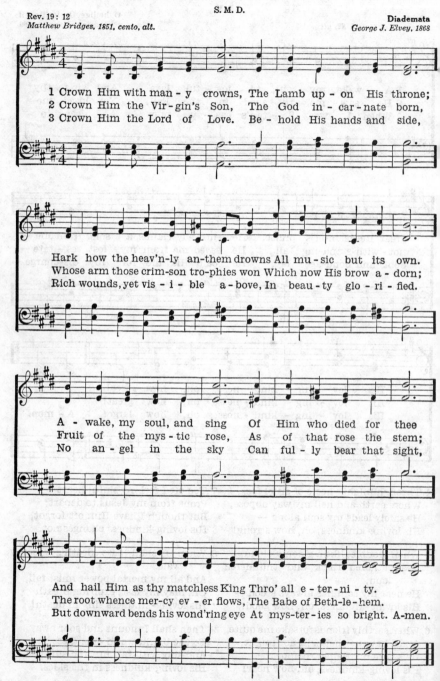

1 Crown Him with man - y crowns, The Lamb up - on His throne;
2 Crown Him the Vir - gin's Son, The God in - car - nate born,
3 Crown Him the Lord of Love. Be - hold His hands and side,

Hark how the heav'n-ly an-them drowns All mu - sic but its own.
Whose arm those crim-son tro-phies won Which now His brow a - dorn;
Rich wounds, yet vis - i - ble a - bove, In beau - ty glo - ri - fied.

A - wake, my soul, and sing Of Him who died for thee
Fruit of the mys - tic rose, As of that rose the stem;
No an - gel in the sky Can ful - ly bear that sight,

And hail Him as thy matchless King Thro' all e - ter - ni - ty.
The root whence mer - cy ev - er flows, The Babe of Beth-le-hem.
But downward bends his wond'ring eye At mys-ter - ies so bright. A-men.

Crown Him with Many Crowns

4 Crown Him the Lord of Life
  Who triumphed o'er the grave
And rose victorious in the strife
  For those He came to save.
His glories now we sing
  Who died and rose on high,
Who died eternal life to bring
  And lives that death may die.

5 Crown Him the Lord of Heaven,
  Enthroned in worlds above,
Crown Him the King to whom is given
  The wondrous name of Love.
Crown Him with many crowns
  As thrones before Him fall;
Crown Him, ye kings, with many crowns,
  For He is King of all.

Chief of Sinners Though I Be   342

7. 7. 7. 7. 7. 7.

Rom. 5: 8
William McComb, 1864

Gethsemane
Richard Redhead, 1853

1 Chief of sin-ners though I be, Je - sus shed His blood for me;
2 Oh, the height of Je - sus' love! High-er than the heav'ns a - bove,
3 Je - sus on - ly can im-part Balm to heal the smit-ten heart;

Died that I might live on high, Lived that I might nev - er die.
Deep - er than the depths of sea, Last - ing as e - ter - ni - ty.
Peace that flows from sin for-giv'n, Joy that lifts the soul to heav'n;

As the branch is to the vine, I am His, and He is mine.
Love that found me -wondrous tho't!-Found me when I sought Him not.
Faith and hope to walk with God In the way that E-noch trod. A-men.

4 Chief of sinners though I be,
  Christ is All in all to me;
All my wants to Him are known,
  All my sorrows are His own.
Safe with Him from earthly strife,
  He sustains the hidden life.

5 O my Savior, help afford
  By Thy Spirit and Thy Word!
When my wayward heart would stray,
  Keep me in the narrow way;
Grace in time of need supply
  While I live and when I die.

343 How Lovely Shines the Morning Star

Rev. 22: 16
Wie schön leuchtet der Morgenstern
Philipp Nicolai, 1597
Tr., composite

8. 8. 7. 8. 8. 7. 4. 4. 4. 4. 8.

Wie schön leuchtet
Philipp Nicolai, 1599

1 How love-ly shines the Morning Star! The na-tions see and hail a - far
2 O high-est joy by mor-tals won, True Son of God and Ma-ry's Son,
3 Now rich-ly to my wait-ing heart, O Thou, my God, deign to im-part

The light in Ju-dah shin-ing. Thou Da-vid's Son of Ja-cob's race,
Thou high-born King of a - ges! Thou art my heart's most beauteous Flow'r,
The grace of love un-dy-ing. In Thy blest bod-y let me be,

My Bridegroom and my King of Grace, For Thee my heart is pin - ing.
And Thy blest Gospel's sav-ing pow'r My rap-tured soul en - gag - es.
E'en as the branch is in the tree, Thy life my life sup-ply - ing.

Low - ly, Ho - ly, Great and glorious, Thou victorious Prince of grac-es,
Thou mine, I Thine; Sing ho-san-na! Heav'nly manna Tasting, eat-ing,
Sigh-ing, Cry-ing, For the sa-vor Of Thy fa-vor; Rest-ing nev-er

Fill - ing all the heav'n-ly plac - es.
Whilst Thy love in songs re - peat - ing.
Till I rest in Thee for-ev - er. A - men.

How Lovely Shines the Morning Star

4 A pledge of peace from God I see
  When Thy pure eyes are turned to me
    To show me Thy good pleasure.
  Jesus, Thy Spirit and Thy Word,
  Thy body and Thy blood, afford
    My soul its dearest treasure.
        Keep me Kindly
  In Thy favor, O my Savior!
  Thou wilt cheer me;
  Thy Word calls me to draw near Thee.

5 Thou, mighty Father, in Thy Son
  Didst love me ere Thou hadst begun
    This ancient world's foundation.
  Thy Son hath made a friend of me,
  And when in spirit Him I see,
    I joy in tribulation.
        What bliss Is this!
  He that liveth To me giveth
  Life forever;
  Nothing me from Him can sever.

6 Lift up the voice and strike the string,
  Let all glad sounds of music ring
    In God's high praises blended.
  Christ will be with me all the way,
  Today, tomorrow, every day,
    Till traveling days be ended.
        Sing out, Ring out
  Triumph glorious, O victorious,
  Chosen nation;
  Praise the God of your salvation.

7 Oh, joy to know that Thou, my Friend,
  Art Lord, Beginning without end,
    The First and Last, Eternal!
  And Thou at length—O glorious grace!—
  Wilt take me to that holy place,
    The home of joys supernal.
        Amen, Amen!
  Come and meet me! Quickly greet me!
  With deep yearning,
  Lord, I look for Thy returning.

Come, Let Us Join Our Cheerful Songs 344

Rev. 5: 12
Isaac Watts, 1707, ab.

C. M.

Nun danket all'
Johann Crüger, 1653

1 Come, let us join our cheer-ful songs With an-gels round the throne.
2 "Wor - thy the Lamb that died," they cry, "To be ex - alt - ed thus."
3 Je - sus is wor - thy to re - ceive Hon - or and pow'r di - vine;
4 Let all cre - a - tion join in one To bless the sa - cred name

Ten thousand thousand are their tongues, But all their joys are one.
"Wor-thy the Lamb," our lips re - ply, For He was slain for us.
And blessings more than we can give Be, Lord, for-ev - er Thine.
Of Him that sits up - on the throne And to a - dore the Lamb. A-men.

345 Jesus, Lover of My Soul

7. 7. 7. 7. D.

Is. 32: 2
Charles Wesley, 1740

Martyn
Simeon B. Marsh, 1834

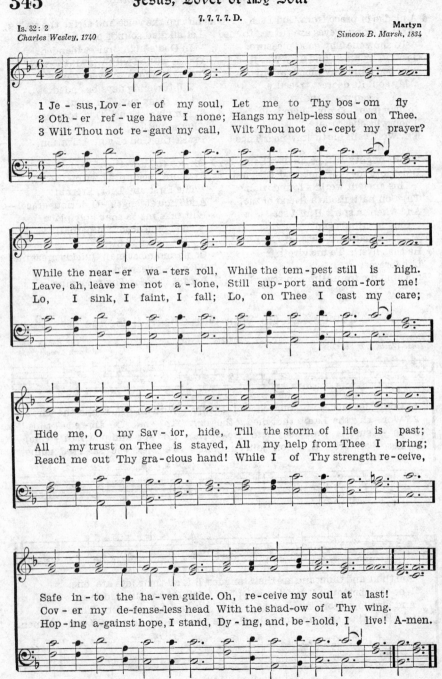

1 Je - sus, Lov - er of my soul, Let me to Thy bos - om fly
2 Oth - er ref - uge have I none; Hangs my help - less soul on Thee.
3 Wilt Thou not re - gard my call, Wilt Thou not ac - cept my prayer?

While the near - er wa - ters roll, While the tem - pest still is high.
Leave, ah, leave me not a - lone, Still sup - port and com - fort me!
Lo, I sink, I faint, I fall; Lo, on Thee I cast my care;

Hide me, O my Sav - ior, hide, Till the storm of life is past;
All my trust on Thee is stayed, All my help from Thee I bring;
Reach me out Thy gra - cious hand! While I of Thy strength re - ceive,

Safe in - to the ha - ven guide. Oh, re - ceive my soul at last!
Cov - er my de - fense - less head With the shad - ow of Thy wing.
Hop - ing a - gainst hope, I stand, Dy - ing, and, be - hold, I live! A - men.

Jesus, Lover of My Soul

4 Thou, O Christ, art all I want;
　More than all in Thee I find.
Raise the fallen, cheer the faint,
　Heal the sick, and lead the blind.
Just and holy is Thy name;
　I am all unrighteousness,
False and full of sin I am;
　Thou art full of truth and grace.

5 Plenteous grace with Thee is found,
　Grace to cover all my sin.
Let the healing streams abound;
　Make and keep me pure within.
Thou of life the Fountain art,
　Freely let me take of Thee;
Spring Thou up within my heart,
　Rise to all eternity.

Jesus! and Shall It Ever Be　　346

Mark 8: 38
Joseph Grigg, 1765
Alt., Benjamin Francis, 1787

L. M.

Federal Street
Henry K. Oliver, 1832

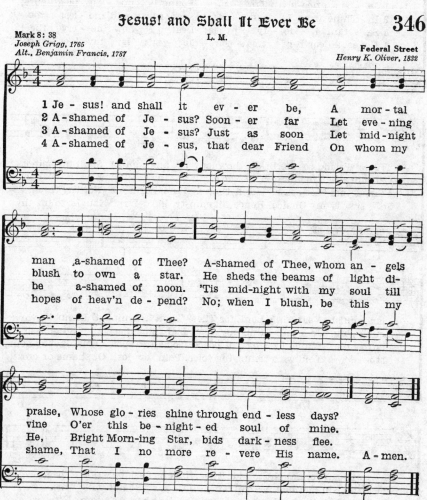

1 Je - sus! and shall it ev - er be, A mor - tal
2 A - shamed of Je - sus? Soon - er far Let eve - ning
3 A - shamed of Je - sus? Just as soon Let mid - night
4 A - shamed of Je - sus, that dear Friend On whom my

man a - shamed of Thee? A - shamed of Thee, whom an - gels
blush to own a star. He sheds the beams of light di-
be a - shamed of noon. 'Tis mid - night with my soul till
hopes of heav'n de - pend? No; when I blush, be this my

praise, Whose glo - ries shine through end - less days?
vine O'er this be - night - ed soul of mine.
He, Bright Morn - ing Star, bids dark - ness flee.
shame, That I no more re - vere His name. A - men.

5 Ashamed of Jesus? Yes, I may
When I've no guilt to wash away,
No tear to wipe, no good to crave,
No fear to quell, no soul to save.

6 Till then—nor is my boasting vain—
Till then I boast a Savior slain;
And oh, may this my glory be,
That Christ is not ashamed of me!

347 Jesus, Priceless Treasure

Matt. 13: 46

6. 6. 5. 6. 6. 5. 3. 4. 8. 6.

Jesu, meine Freude
Johann Franck, 1655
Tr., composite

Jesu, meine Freude
Johann Crüger, 1649

1 Je - sus, price-less Trea - sure, Fount of pur - est plea - sure,
2 In Thine arms I rest me; Foes who would mo - lest me
3 Sa - tan, I de - fy thee; Death, I now de - cry thee;
4 Hence, all earth-ly trea - sure! Je - sus is my Plea - sure,

Tru-est Friend to me. Ah, how long in an - guish Shall my spir-it
Can-not reach me here. Tho' the earth be shak - ing, Ev - 'ry heart be
Fear, I bid thee cease. World, thou shalt not harm me Nor thy threats a-
Je - sus is my Choice. Hence, all emp-ty glo - ry! Naught to me thy

lan - guish, Yearn-ing, Lord, for Thee? Thou art mine, O Lamb di - vine!
quak - ing, Je - sus calms my fear. Lightnings flash And thunders crash;
larm me While I sing of peace. God's great pow'r Guards ev'ry hour;
sto - ry Told with tempt-ing voice. Pain or loss, Or shame or cross,

I will suf-fer naught to hide Thee, Naught I ask be - side Thee.
Yet, tho' sin and hell as - sail me, Je - sus will not fail me.
Earth and all its depths a-dore Him, Si - lent bow be - fore Him.
Shall not from my Sav-ior move me Since He deigns to love me. A-men.

Jesus, Priceless Treasure

5 Evil world, I leave thee;
  Thou canst not deceive me,
    Thine appeal is vain.
  Sin that once did blind me,
  Get thee far behind me,
    Come not forth again.
  Past thy hour, O pride and power;
  Sinful life, thy bonds I sever,
  Leave thee now forever.

6 Hence, all fear and sadness!
  For the Lord of gladness,
    Jesus, enters in.
  Those who love the Father,
  Though the storms may gather,
    Still have peace within.
  Yea, whate'er I here must bear,
  Thou art still my purest Pleasure,
  Jesus, priceless Treasure!

Jesus, Jesus, Only Jesus   348

Eph. 3 : 19
Jesus, Jesus, nichts als Jesus
Ludämilia Elisabeth, 1687
Tr., August Crull, 1880, alt.

8. 7. 8. 7. 7. 7.

Jesus, Jesus, nichts als Jesus
"Vollkommenes Choralbuch," Hamburg, 1715

1 Je-sus, Je-sus, on-ly Je-sus, Can my heart-felt long-ing still.
2 One there is for whom I'm liv-ing, Whom I love most ten-der-ly;
3 What to me may seem a trea-sure But dis-pleas-ing is to Thee,

Lo, I pledge my-self to Je-sus What He wills a-lone to will.
Un-to Je-sus I am giv-ing What in love He gave to me.
Oh, re-move such harm-ful plea-sure; Give in-stead what prof-its me.

For my heart, which He hath filled, Ev-er cries, Lord, as Thou wilt.
Je-sus' blood hides all my guilt; Lord, oh, lead me as Thou wilt.
Let my heart by Thee be stilled; Make me Thine, Lord, as Thou wilt. Amen.

4 Let me earnestly endeavor
    Thy good pleasure to fulfil;
  In me, through me, with me, ever,
    Lord, accomplish Thou Thy will.
  In Thy holy image built,
  Let me die, Lord, as Thou wilt.

5 Jesus, constant be my praises,
    For Thou unto me didst bring
  Thine own self and all Thy graces
    That I joyfully may sing:
  Be it unto me, my Shield,
  As Thou wilt, Lord, as Thou wilt.

349 Jesus, Thy Boundless Love to Me

John 14: 15
8. 8. 8. 8. 8. 8.

O Jesu Christ, mein schönstes Licht
Paul Gerhardt, 1653, cento
Tr., John Wesley, 1739, alt.

Vater unser
"Geistliche Lieder"
Leipzig, 1539

1 Je - sus, Thy bound-less love to me No thought can reach, no tongue de - clare; U - nite my thank-ful heart with Thee And reign with-out a ri - val there. To Thee a - lone, dear Lord, I live; My - self to Thee, dear Lord, I give.

2 Oh, grant that noth-ing in my soul May dwell but Thy pure love a - lone! Oh, may Thy love pos - sess me whole, My Joy, my Trea-sure, and my Crown! All cold-ness from my heart re - move; My ev - 'ry act, word, thought, be love.

3 O Love, how cheer-ing is Thy ray! All pain be - fore Thy pres - ence flies; Care, an - guish, sor - row, melt a - way Wher - e'er Thy heal - ing beams a - rise. O Je - sus, noth-ing may I see, Noth - ing de - sire or seek, but Thee!

4 This love un - wea - ried I pur - sue And daunt-less - ly to Thee as - pire. Oh, may Thy love my hope re - new, Burn in my soul like heav'n-ly fire! And day and night be all my care To guard this sa - cred trea - sure there. A - men.

Jesus, Thy Boundless Love to Me

5 Oh, draw me, Savior, e'er to Thee;
  So shall I run and never tire.
  With gracious words still comfort me;
  Be Thou my Hope, my sole Desire.
  Free me from every guilt and fear;
  No sin can harm if Thou art near.

6 Still let Thy love point out my way;
  What wondrous things Thy love hath wrought!
  Still lead me lest I go astray;
  Direct my work, inspire my thought;
  And if I fall, soon may I hear
  Thy voice and know that love is near!

7 In suffering be Thy love my peace,
  In weakness be Thy love my power;
  And when the storms of life shall cease,
  O Jesus, in that final hour,
  Be Thou my Rod and Staff and Guide
  And draw me safely to Thy side!

Jesus, the Very Thought of Thee 350

Song of Solomon 1: 3
Iesu dulcis memoria
Author unknown, 12th century, cento
Tr., Edward Caswall, 1849, alt.

C. M.

Clairvaux
Herman A. Polack, 1910

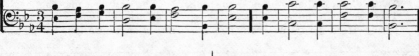

1 Je - sus, the ver - y tho't of Thee With sweet-ness fills the breast;
2 Nor voice can sing, nor heart can frame, Nor can the mem-'ry find
3 O Hope of ev - 'ry con-trite heart, O Joy of all the meek!

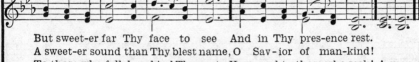

But sweet-er far Thy face to see And in Thy pres-ence rest.
A sweet-er sound than Thy blest name, O Sav-ior of man-kind!
To those who fall, how kind Thou art, How good to those who seek! A-men.

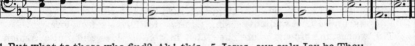

4 But what to those who find? Ah! this
  Nor tongue nor pen can show;
  The love of Jesus, what it is,
  None but His loved ones know.

5 Jesus, our only Joy be Thou
  As Thou our Prize wilt be!
  Jesus, be Thou our Glory now
  And through eternity.

O Savior, Precious Savior

352

1 Pet. 1: 8
Frances R. Havergal, 1870

7. 6. 7. 6. D.

Angel's Story
Arthur H. Mann, 1881

1 O   Sav-ior, pre-cious Sav-ior,   Whom, yet un-seen, we love;
2 O   Bring-er of   sal-va-tion,   Who won-drous-ly hast wrought
3 In Thee all ful-ness dwell-eth, All   grace and pow'r di-vine;
4 Oh, grant the con-sum-ma-tion Of   this our song a-bove

O Name of might and   fa-vor,   All   oth-er names a-bove,
Thy-self the rev-e-la-tion Of   love be-yond our thought,
The glo-ry that ex-cel-leth, O   Son of God, is Thine.
In end-less ad-o-ra-tion And   ev-er-last-ing love!

We wor-ship Thee, we   bless Thee, To   Thee, O Christ, we   sing;
We wor-ship Thee, we   bless Thee, To   Thee, O Christ, we   sing;
We wor-ship Thee, we   bless Thee, To   Thee, O Christ, we   sing;
Then shall we praise and   bless Thee Where per-fect prais-es   ring

We praise Thee and con-fess Thee, Our   ho-ly Lord and King.
We praise Thee and con-fess Thee, Our   gra-cious Lord and King.
We praise Thee and con-fess Thee, Our   glo-rious Lord and King.
And   ev-er-more con-fess Thee Our   Sav-ior and our King.   A-men.

353 Lord Jesus Christ, My Savior Blest

Ps. 119 : 170
4. 4. 7. 4. 4. 4. 7.

Herre Jesu Krist! Min Frelser du est
Hans C. Sthen, c. 1578
Tr., Harriet R. Spaeth, 1898

Herre Jesu Krist
Ludvig M. Lindeman, 1871

1 Lord Je - sus Christ, My Sav - ior blest, My Hope and my Sal-
2 As Thou dost will, Lead Thou me still That I may tru - ly
3 Most heart - i - ly I trust in Thee; Thy mer - cy fails me

va - tion! I trust in Thee; De - liv - er me From
serve Thee, My God, I pray, Teach me Thy way, To
nev - er. Dear Lord, a - bide; My Help - er tried, Thou

mis - er - y; Thy Word's my con - so - la - tion.
my last day In Thy true faith pre - serve me.
Cru - ci - fied, From e - vil keep me ev - er. A - men.

4 Now henceforth must
I put my trust
    In Thee, O dearest Savior.
Thy comfort choice,
Thy Word and voice,
My heart rejoice
    Despite my ill behavior.

5 When sorrows rise,
My refuge lies
    In Thy compassion tender.
Within Thine arm
Can naught alarm;
Keep me from harm,
    Be Thou my strong Defender.

6 I have Thy Word,
Christ Jesus, Lord;
    Thou never wilt forsake me.
This will I plead
In time of need.
Oh, help with speed
    When troubles overtake me!

7 Grant, Lord, I pray,
Thy grace each day
    That I, Thy Law revering,
May live with Thee
And happy be
Eternally,
    Before Thy throne appearing.

In the Cross of Christ I Glory

354

Gal. 6: 14
John Bowring, 1825

8. 7. 8. 7.

Rathbun
Ithamar Conkey, 1849

1 In the Cross of Christ I glo - ry, Tow'r-ing o'er the wrecks of time.
2 When the woes of life o'er-take me, Hopes de-ceive, and fears an - noy,
3 When the sun of bliss is beam-ing Light and love up - on my way,
4 Bane and bless-ing, pain and plea-sure, By the Cross are sanc - ti - fied;

All the light of sa - cred sto - ry Gathers round its head sub-lime.
Nev - er shall the Cross for-sake me; Lo, it glows with peace and joy.
From the Cross the radiance streaming Adds more lus-ter to the day.
Peace is there that knows no measure, Joys that thro' all time a - bide. A-men.

Thou Art the Way; to Thee Alone

355

John 14: 6
George W. Doane, 1824

C. M.

Dundee
"Scottish Psalter," 1615

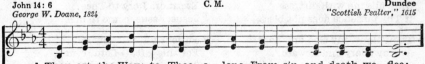

1 Thou art the Way; to Thee a - lone From sin and death we flee;
2 Thou art the Truth; Thy Word a - lone True wis-dom can im - part;
3 Thou art the Life; the rend - ing tomb Pro-claims Thy conqu'ring arm;
4 Thou art the Way, the Truth, the Life; Grant us that Way to know,

And he who would the Fa-ther seek Must seek Him, Lord, by Thee.
Thou on - ly canst in-form the mind And pu - ri - fy the heart.
And those who put their trust in Thee Nor death nor hell shall harm.
That Truth to keep, that Life to win, Whose joys e - ter - nal flow. A-men.

356 Jesus, Savior, Come to Me

Is. 26: 9
Jesu, komm doch selbst zu mir
Johann Scheffler, 1657, cento
Tr., Matthias Loy, 1861, alt.

7. 7. 7. 7.

Gott sei Dank
"Neues geistreiches Gesangbuch"
Halle, 1704

1 Je - sus, Sav-ior, come to me; Let me ev - er be with Thee.
2 Lord, for Thee I ev - er sigh, Noth-ing else can sat - is - fy.
3 Earth-ly joys can give no peace, Can-not bid my long-ing cease;

Come and nev-er-more de - part, Thou who reign-est in my heart.
Ev - er do I cry to Thee: Je - sus, Je - sus, come to me!
Still to have my Je - sus near, This is all my plea-sure here. A-men.

4 All that makes the angels glad,
In their garb of glory clad,
Only fills me with distress
If Thy presence does not bless.

5 Thou alone, my God and Lord,
Art my Glory and Reward.
Thou hast bled for me and died;
In Thy wounds I safely hide.

6 Come, then, Lamb for sinners slain,
Come and ease me of my pain.
Evermore I cry to Thee:
Jesus, Jesus, come to me!

7 Patiently I wait Thy Day;
For this gift, O Lord, I pray,
That, when death shall come to me,
My dear Jesus Thou wilt be.

357 Jesus, Thou Art Mine Forever

8. 7. 8. 7.

Stuttgart
"Psalmodia Sacra"
Gotha, 1715

Ps. 73: 24
Matthias Loy, 1863

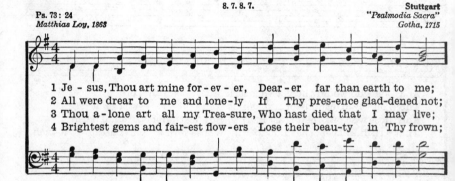

1 Je - sus, Thou art mine for - ev - er, Dear - er far than earth to me;
2 All were drear to me and lone - ly If Thy pres-ence glad-dened not;
3 Thou a - lone art all my Trea-sure, Who hast died that I may live;
4 Brightest gems and fair-est flow-ers Lose their beau-ty in Thy frown;

Jesus, Thou Art Mine Forever

Nei-ther life nor death shall sev-er Those sweet ties which bind to Thee.
While I sing to Thee, Thee on-ly, Mine's an ev - er bliss-ful lot.
Thou con-fer-rest noblest pleasure, Who dost all my sins for-give.
Joy and peace, like balmy showers, In Thy smile come gen-tly down. A-men.

5 Jesus, Thou art mine forever;
　　Never suffer me to stray.
　Let me in my weakness never
　　Cast my priceless pearl away.

6 Lamb of God, I do implore Thee,
　　Guard, support me, lest I fall.
　Let me evermore adore Thee;
　　Be my everlasting All.

Lamb of God, We Fall before Thee　　358

8. 7. 8. 7.

Heb. 12: 2
Joseph Hart, 1759, cento, alt.

Ringe recht
"Musikalischer Christenschatz"
Basel, 1745

1 Lamb of God, we　fall be-fore Thee, Hum-bly trust-ing　in Thy Cross.
2 Thee we own a　per-fect Sav-ior, On - ly Source of all that's good.
3 Je - sus gives us　true re-pen-tance By His Spir - it sent from heav'n;
4 Faith He grants us　to be-lieve it, Grate-ful hearts His love to prize;

That a-lone be　all our glo - ry; All things else are on - ly dross.
Ev - 'ry grace and ev-'ry fa-vor Comes to us thro' Je-sus' blood.
Whispers this transporting sentence, "Son, thy sins are all for-giv'n."
Want we wis-dom? He must give it, Hear-ing ears and see-ing eyes. A-men.

5 Jesus gives us pure affections,
　　Wills to do what He requires,
　Makes us follow His directions,
　　And what He commands, inspires.

6 All our prayers and all our praises,
　　Rightly offered in His name —
　He that dictates them is Jesus;
　　He that answers is the same.

359

Christ, Whose Glory Fills the Skies

7. 7. 7. 7. 7. 7.

Luke 1: 78
Charles Wesley, 1740

Ratisbon
"Sächsisches Choralbuch"
Leipzig, 1815

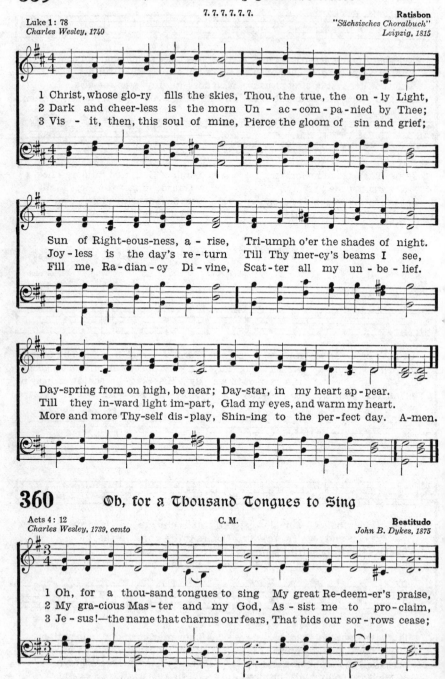

1 Christ, whose glo-ry fills the skies, Thou, the true, the on-ly Light,
2 Dark and cheer-less is the morn Un-ac-com-pa-nied by Thee;
3 Vis-it, then, this soul of mine, Pierce the gloom of sin and grief;

Sun of Right-eous-ness, a-rise, Tri-umph o'er the shades of night.
Joy-less is the day's re-turn Till Thy mer-cy's beams I see,
Fill me, Ra-dian-cy Di-vine, Scat-ter all my un-be-lief.

Day-spring from on high, be near; Day-star, in my heart ap-pear.
Till they in-ward light im-part, Glad my eyes, and warm my heart.
More and more Thy-self dis-play, Shin-ing to the per-fect day. A-men.

360

Oh, for a Thousand Tongues to Sing

Acts 4: 12
Charles Wesley, 1739, cento

C. M.

Beatitudo
John B. Dykes, 1875

1 Oh, for a thou-sand tongues to sing My great Re-deem-er's praise,
2 My gra-cious Mas-ter and my God, As-sist me to pro-claim,
3 Je-sus!—the name that charms our fears, That bids our sor-rows cease;

Oh, for a Thousand Tongues to Sing

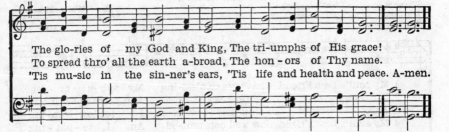

The glo-ries of my God and King, The tri-umphs of His grace!
To spread thro' all the earth a-broad, The hon-ors of Thy name.
'Tis mu-sic in the sin-ner's ears, 'Tis life and health and peace. A-men.

4 He breaks the power of canceled sin,
　He sets the prisoner free;
　His blood can make the foulest clean;
　His blood avails for me.

5 Look unto Him, ye nations; own
　Your God, ye fallen race.
　Look and be saved through faith alone,
　Be justified by grace.

6 See all your sins on Jesus laid;
　The Lamb of God was slain;
　His soul was once an offering made
　For every soul of man.

7 Glory to God and praise and love
　Be ever, ever given
　By saints below and saints above,
　The Church in earth and heaven.

O Jesus, King Most Wonderful　　361

1 Pet. 2: 7
Iesu, Rex admirabilis
Author unknown, 12th century, cento
Tr., Edward Caswall, 1848

C. M.

St. Agnes
John B. Dykes, 1866

1 O　Je-sus, King most won-der-ful, Thou Con-quer-or re-nowned,
2 When once Thou vis-it-est the heart, Then truth be-gins to shine,
3 O　Je-sus, Light of all be-low, Thou Fount of life and fire,

Thou Sweetness most in-ef-fa-ble, In whom all joys are found!
Then earth-ly van-i-ties de-part, Then kin-dles love di-vine.
Sur-pass-ing all the joys we know, All that we can de-sire — A-men.

4 May every heart confess Thy name
　And ever Thee adore
　And, seeking Thee, itself inflame
　To seek Thee more and more!

5 Thee may our tongues forever bless,
　Thee may we love alone,
　And ever in our lives express
　The image of Thine own!

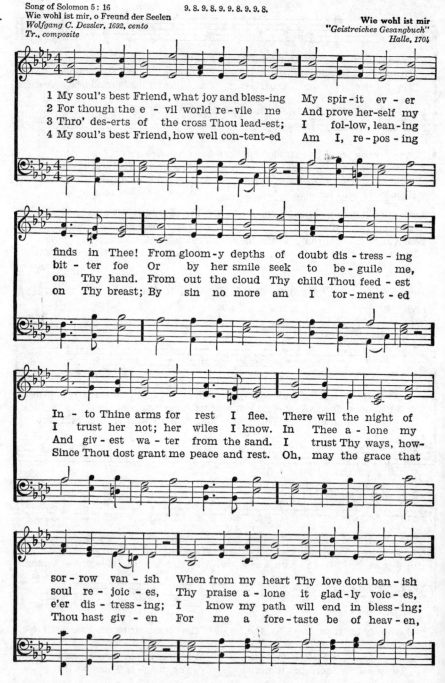

362 My Soul's Best Friend, What Joy and Blessing

Song of Solomon 5 : 16
Wie wohl ist mir, o Freund der Seelen
Wolfgang C. Dessler, 1692, cento
Tr., composite

9. 8. 9. 8. 9. 9. 8. 9. 9. 8.

Wie wohl ist mir
"Geistreiches Gesangbuch"
Halle, 1704

1 My soul's best Friend, what joy and bless-ing
2 For though the e - vil world re-vile me
3 Thro' des-erts of the cross Thou lead-est;
4 My soul's best Friend, how well con-tent-ed

My spir-it ev - er
And prove her-self my
I fol-low, lean-ing
Am I, re - pos-ing

finds in Thee! From gloom-y depths of doubt dis-tress-ing
bit - ter foe Or by her smile seek to be-guile me,
on Thy hand. From out the cloud Thy child Thou feed-est
on Thy breast; By sin no more am I tor-ment-ed

In - to Thine arms for rest I flee. There will the night of
I trust her not; her wiles I know. In Thee a - lone my
And giv-est wa - ter from the sand. I trust Thy ways, how-
Since Thou dost grant me peace and rest. Oh, may the grace that

sor - row van - ish When from my heart Thy love doth ban - ish
soul re - joic - es, Thy praise a - lone it glad-ly voic - es,
e'er dis - tress-ing; I know my path will end in bless-ing;
Thou hast giv - en For me a fore-taste be of heav - en,

My Soul's Best Friend, What Joy and Blessing

All an-guish and all pain and fear. Yea, here on earth be-
For Thou art true when friend-ships flee. The world may hate but
E - nough that Thou wilt be my Stay. For whom to hon - or
Where I shall bask in joys di - vine! A - way, vain world, with

gins my heav - en; Who would not joy - ful be when giv-
can - not fell me; Would might-y waves of tri - al quell
Thou in - tend - est Oft in - to sor - row's vale Thou send-
fleet - ing plea - sures; In Christ I have a - bid - ing trea-

en A lov - ing Sav - ior al - ways near!
me, I an - chor in Thy loy - al - ty.
est; The night must e'er pre - cede the day.
sures. Oh, com - fort sweet, my Friend is mine! A - men.

✱ Variant

en A lov - ing Sav - ior al - ways near!
me, I an - chor in . . . . Thy loy - al - ty.
est; The night must e'er . . . pre - cede the day.
sures. Oh, com - fort sweet, . . . my Friend is mine! A - men.

363
To Our Redeemer's Glorious Name

Ps. 135: 1
Anne Steele, 1760

C. M.

Bedford
William Wheall, 1729

1 To our Re-deem-er's glo-rious name A - wake the sa - cred song.
2 His love, what hu-man tho't can reach, What mor-tal tongue por-tray?
3 He left His ra-diant throne on high, Left realms of heav'n-ly bliss,

Oh, may His love, im-mor - tal flame, Tune ev - 'ry heart and tongue!
Im - ag - i - na-tion's utmost stretch In won-der dies a - way.
And came to earth to bleed and die —Was ev - er love like this? A-men.

4 Dear Lord, while we adoring pay
   Our humble thanks to Thee,
May every heart with rapture say,
   "The Savior died for me!"

5 Oh, may the sweet, the blissful theme
   Fill every heart and tongue
Till strangers love the charming name
   And join the sacred song!

364
How Sweet the Name of Jesus Sounds

Song of Solomon 1: 3
John Newton, 1779

C. M.

St. Peter
Alexander R. Reinagle, 1836

1 How sweet the name of Je - sus sounds In a be - liev - er's ear!
2 It makes the wound-ed spir - it whole And calms the trou-bled breast;
3 Dear name! The Rock on which I build, My Shield and Hid - ing-place;

It soothes his sorrows, heals his wounds, And drives a-way his fear.
'Tis man-na to the hun-gry soul And to the wea - ry, rest.
My nev - er - fail-ing Treasury, filled With boundless stores of grace. A-men.

How Sweet the Name of Jesus Sounds

4 By Thee my prayers acceptance gain
   Although with sin defiled.
Satan accuses me in vain,
   And I am owned a child.

5 Jesus, my Shepherd, Guardian, Friend,
   My Prophet, Priest, and King,
My Lord, my Life, my Way, my End,
   Accept the praise I bring.

6 Weak is the effort of my heart
   And cold my warmest thought;
But when I see Thee as Thou art,
   I'll praise Thee as I ought.

7 Till then I would Thy love proclaim
   With every fleeting breath;
And may the music of Thy name
   Refresh my soul in death!

Jesus I Will Never Leave   365

Luke 9: 57

7. 8. 7. 8. 7. 7.

Meinen Jesum lass' ich nicht
Christian Keimann, 1658, ab.
Tr., composite

Meinen Jesum lass' ich nicht
"Neuverfertigtes Gesangbuch"
Darmstadt, 1699

1 Je-sus I will nev-er leave, Who for me Him-self hath giv-en;
2 Je-sus I will nev-er leave While on earth I am a-bid-ing;
3 Tho' my sight shall pass a-way, Hear-ing, taste, and feel-ing fail me;

Firm-ly un-to Him I'll cleave Nor from Him be ev-er driv-en.
What I have to Him I give, In all cares in Him con-fid-ing.
Tho' my life's last light of day Shall o'er-take and sore as-sail me;

Life from Him doth light re-ceive,— Je-sus I will nev-er leave.
Naught shall me of Him be-reave,— Je-sus I will nev-er leave.
When His sum-mons I re-ceive, Je-sus I will nev-er leave. A-men.

4 Nor will I my Jesus leave
   When at last I shall come thither
Where His saints He will receive,
   Where in bliss they live together.
Endless joy to me He'll give,—
Jesus I will never leave.

5 Not for earth's vain joys I crave
   Nor, without Him, heaven's pleasure;
Jesus, who my soul did save,
   Evermore shall be my Treasure.
He redemption did achieve,—
Jesus I will never leave.

366 One Thing's Needful; Lord, This Treasure

Luke 10: 42

Eins ist not: ach, Herr, dies eine
Johann H. Schröder, 1697, cento
Tr., Frances E. Cox, 1841, alt.

8. 7. 8. 7. 12. 12. 11. 11.

Eins ist not
Friedrich Layriz, 1849

1 One thing's need-ful; Lord, this trea-sure   Teach me high-ly   to   re-gard;
2 Wilt thou find this one thing need-ful,   Turn from all cre-at-ed things
3 How were Ma-ry's tho'ts de-vot-ed   Her   e-ter-nal joy to find
4 Thus my long-ings, heav'nward tend-ing,   Je-sus, rest a-lone on Thee.

All   else, though it first give plea-sure,   Is   a yoke that press-es hard.
Un-to   Je-sus and be heed-ful   Of   the bless-ed joy He brings.
As   in-tent each word she not-ed,   At   her Sav-ior's feet re-clined!
Help me, thus on Thee de-pend-ing;   Sav-ior, come and dwell in   me.

Be-neath   it   the heart   is   still fret-ting and striv-ing,
For where God   and Man both   in   one   are u-nit-ed,
How kin-dled   her heart, how de-vout   was its   feel-ing,
Al-though all   the world should for-sake   and for-get Thee,

No   true, last-ing   hap-pi-ness ev-er   de-riv-ing.
With God's per-fect   ful-ness the heart   is   de-light-ed;
While hear-ing the   les-sons that Christ was   re-veal-ing!
In   love I   will   fol-low Thee, ne'er will   I   quit Thee.

One Thing's Needful; Lord, This Treasure

The gain of this one thing all loss can re - quite
There, there, is the wor - thi - est lot and the best,
For Je - sus all earth - ly con - cerns she for - got,
Lord Je - sus, both spir - it and life is Thy Word;

And teach me in all things to find true de - light.
My One and my All and my Joy and my Rest.
And all was re - paid in that one hap - py lot.
And is there a joy which Thou dost not af - ford? A - men.

5 Wisdom's highest, noblest treasure,
   Jesus, lies concealed in Thee;
Grant that this may still the measure
   Of my will and actions be,
Humility there and simplicity reigning,
In paths of true wisdom my steps ever training.
Oh, if I of Christ have this knowledge divine,
The fulness of heavenly wisdom is mine.

6 Naught have I, O Christ, to offer
   Naught but Thee, my highest Good.
Naught have I, O Lord, to proffer
   But Thy crimson-colored blood.
Thy death on the cross hath Death wholly defeated
And thereby my righteousness fully completed;
Salvation's white raiments I there did obtain,
And in them in glory with Thee I shall reign.

7 Therefore Thou alone, my Savior,
   Shalt be All in all to me;
Search my heart and my behavior,
   Root out all hypocrisy.
Restrain me from wand'ring on pathways unholy
And through all life's pilgrimage keep my heart lowly.
This one thing is needful, all others are vain;
I count all but loss that I Christ may obtain.

367 Hail, Thou Once Despised Jesus

8. 7. 8. 7. D.

Rev. 4 : 11
Author unknown, c. 1757

O Durchbrecher
"Neues geistreiches Gesangbuch"
Halle, 1704

1 Hail, Thou once de-spis-ed Je-sus! Hail, Thou Gal-i-le-an King!
2 Pas-chal Lamb, by God ap-point-ed, All our sins on Thee were laid;
3 Je-sus, hail, en-throned in glo-ry, There for-ev-er to a-bide!
4 Wor-ship, hon-or, pow'r, and bless-ing Thou art wor-thy to re-ceive;

Thou didst suf-fer to re-lease us; Thou didst free sal-va-tion bring.
By al-might-y love a-noint-ed, Thou hast full a-tone-ment made.
All the heav'n-ly host a-dore Thee, Seat-ed at Thy Fa-ther's side.
Loud-est prais-es, with-out ceas-ing, Meet it is for us to give.

Hail, Thou u-ni-ver-sal Sav-ior, Who hast borne our sin and shame,
Ev-'ry sin may be for-giv-en Thro' the vir-tue of Thy blood;
There for sin-ners Thou art plead-ing, There Thou dost our place pre-pare,
Help, ye bright an-gel-ic spir-its, Bring your sweet-est, no-blest lays;

By whose mer-its we find fa-vor! Life is giv-en thro' Thy name.
O-pen is the gate of heav-en, Peace is made 'twixt man and God.
Ev-er for us in-ter-ced-ing Till in glo-ry we ap-pear.
Help to sing our Sav-ior's mer-its, Help to chant Immanuel's praise. A-men.

The Lord My Pasture Shall Prepare

368

Ps. 23
Joseph Addison, 1712

8. 8. 8. 8. 8. 8.

Surrey
Henry Carey, 1723, alt.

1 The Lord my pas-ture shall pre-pare And feed me with a
2 When in the sul-try glebe I faint Or on the thirst-y
3 Tho' in the paths of death I tread, With gloom-y hor-rors
4 Tho' in a bare and rug-ged way, Thro' de-vious lone-ly

shep-herd's care; His pres-ence shall my wants sup-ply
moun-tain pant, To fer-tile vales and dew-y meads
o-ver-spread, My stead-fast heart shall fear no ill,
wilds, I stray, Thy boun-ty shall my pains be-guile;

And guard me with a watch-ful eye; My noon-day walks He
My wea-ry, wan-d'ring steps He leads, Where peace-ful riv-ers,
For Thou, O Lord, art with me still; Thy friend-ly crook shall
The bar-ren wil-der-ness shall smile, With sud-den greens and

shall at-tend And all my mid-night hours de-fend.
soft and slow, A-mid the ver-dant land-scape flow.
give me aid And guide me thro' the dread-ful shade.
herb-age crowned, And streams shall murmur all a-round. A-men.

Faith and Justification

369   All Mankind Fell in Adam's Fall

Rom. 3: 12   L. M.

Durch Adams Fall ist ganz verderbt
Lazarus Spengler, 1524, cento
Tr., Matthias Loy, 1880, alt.

Wenn wir in höchsten Nöten
"Genevan Psalter," 1547

1 All man-kind fell in Ad - - am's fall, One com-mon sin in-
2 Thro' all man's pow'rs cor-rup - - tion creeps And him in dread-ful
3 From hearts de-praved, to e - - vil prone, Flow tho'ts and deeds of
4 But Christ, the sec-ond Ad - - am, came To bear our sin and

fects us all; From sire to son the bane de-scends.
bond-age keeps; In guilt he draws his in-fant breath
sin a-lone; God's im-age lost, the dark-ened soul
woe and shame, To be our Life, our Light, our Way,

And o-ver all the curse im-pends.
And reaps its fruits of woe and death.
Nor seeks nor finds its heav'n-ly goal.
Our on-ly Hope, our on-ly Stay. A-men.

5 As by one man all mankind fell
And, born in sin, was doomed to hell,
So by one Man, who took our place,
We all received the gift of grace.

6 We thank Thee, Christ; new life is ours,
New light, new hope, new strength, new powers:
This grace our every way attend
Until we reach our journey's end!

My Hope is Built on Nothing Less

370

1 Tim. 1: 1
Edward Mote, c. 1834, cento

8. 8. 8. 8. 8. 8.

Magdalen
John Stainer, 1873, arr.

1 My hope is built on noth-ing less Than Je - sus' blood and
2 When dark-ness veils His love - ly face, I rest on His un-
3 His oath, His cov - e - nant, and blood Sup - port me in the
4 When He shall come with trum-pet sound, Oh, may I then in

right - eous - ness; I dare not trust the sweet - est frame, But
chang - ing grace; In ev - 'ry high and storm - y gale My
whelm - ing flood; When ev - 'ry earth - ly prop gives way, He
Him be found, Clothed in His right - eous - ness a - lone, Fault-

whol - ly lean on Je - sus' name. On Christ, the sol - id
an - chor holds with - in the veil. On Christ, the sol - id
then is all my Hope and Stay. On Christ, the sol - id
less to stand be - fore the throne. On Christ, the sol - id

Rock, I stand; All oth - er ground is sink - ing sand.
Rock, I stand; All oth - er ground is sink - ing sand.
Rock, I stand; All oth - er ground is sink - ing sand.
Rock, I stand; All oth - er ground is sink - ing sand. A - men.

371 Jesus, Thy Blood and Righteousness

1 John 1: 7
Christi Blut und Gerechtigkeit
Ludwig von Zinzendorf, 1739, cento
Tr., John Wesley, 1740

L. M.

St. Crispin
George J. Elvey, 1862

1 Je - sus, Thy blood and right - eous - ness, My beau - ty
2 Bold shall I stand in that great Day, For who aught
3 The ho - ly, meek, un - spot - ted Lamb, Who from the
4 Lord, I be - lieve Thy pre - cious blood, Which at the

are, my glo - rious dress; Midst flam-ing worlds, in these ar - rayed,
to my charge shall lay? Ful - ly thro' these ab - solved I am
Fa - ther's bos - om came, Who died for me, e'en me t'a - tone,
mer - cy seat of God For - ev - er doth for sin - ners plead,

With joy shall I lift up my head.
From sin and fear, from guilt and shame.
Now for my Lord and God I own.
For me— e'en for my soul— was shed. A - men.

5 Lord, I believe were sinners more
Than sands upon the ocean shore,
Thou hast for all a ransom paid,
For all a full atonement made.

6 When from the dust of death I rise
To claim my mansion in the skies,
E'en then this shall be all my plea:
Jesus hath lived and died for me.

7 Jesus, be endless praise to Thee,
Whose boundless mercy hath for me,
For me, and all Thy hands have made,
An everlasting ransom paid.

Through Jesus' Blood and Merit

372

7. 6. 7. 6. D.

Rom. 8: 35–39
Ich bin bei Gott in Gnaden
Simon Dach, 1651, cento
Tr., composite

Ich dank' dir, lieber Herre
"Musika Deutsch"
Nürnberg, 1532

1 Thro' Je - sus' blood and mer - it   I   am   at peace with   God;
2 There's naught that me can sev - er   From the great love   of   God;
3 Yea,   nei - ther life's temp-ta - tion   Nor death's so try - ing   hour,
4 Nor   an - y crea-ture ev - er   Shall from the love   of   God

What, then, can daunt my spir - it,   How - ev - er dark my   road?
No   want, no pain what-ev - er,   No   fam - ine, per - il,   flood.
Nor   an - gels of high sta - tion,   Nor an - y oth - er   pow'r,
This wretch - ed sin - ner sev - er;   For   in   my Sav - ior's   blood

My cour-age shall not fail   me,   For God   is   on my side;
Tho' thou-sand foes sur - round   me,   For slaugh-ter mark Thy sheep,
Nor things that now are pres - ent,   Nor things that are to come,
This love its foun-tain tak - eth;   He hears my faith-ful prayer

Tho' hell it-self as-sail me,   Its rage I   may   de - ride.
They nev-er shall con-found me,   The vic-t'ry I   shall reap.
Nor height, how-ev-er pleas-ant,   Nor depth of deep - est gloom,
And nev-er-more for-sak - eth   His own dear child   and heir. A-men.

373 By Grace I'm Saved, Grace Free and Boundless

Eph. 2 : 8, 9
Aus Gnaden soll ich selig werden
Christian L. Scheidt, 1742, cento
Tr., composite

9. 8. 9. 8. 8. 8.

O dass ich tausend
Kornelius H. Dretzel, 1731

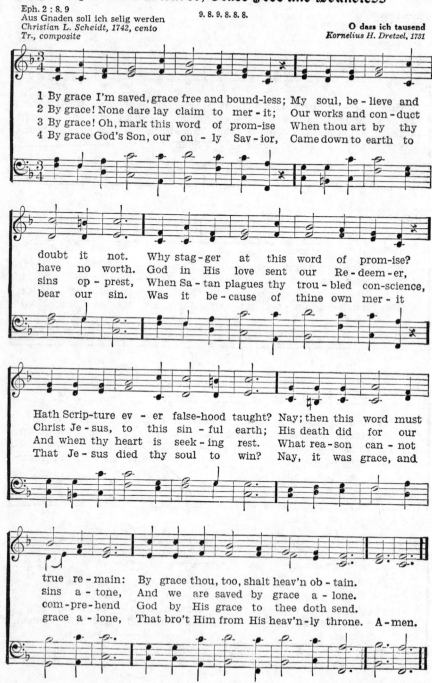

1 By grace I'm saved, grace free and bound-less; My soul, be - lieve and
2 By grace! None dare lay claim to mer - it; Our works and con - duct
3 By grace! Oh, mark this word of prom-ise When thou art by thy
4 By grace God's Son, our on - ly Sav-ior, Came down to earth to

doubt it not. Why stag-ger at this word of prom-ise?
have no worth. God in His love sent our Re - deem - er,
sins op - prest, When Sa - tan plagues thy trou - bled con-science,
bear our sin. Was it be - cause of thine own mer - it

Hath Scrip-ture ev - er false-hood taught? Nay; then this word must
Christ Je - sus, to this sin - ful earth; His death did for our
And when thy heart is seek - ing rest. What rea-son can - not
That Je - sus died thy soul to win? Nay, it was grace, and

true re - main: By grace thou, too, shalt heav'n ob - tain.
sins a - tone, And we are saved by grace a - lone.
com-pre-hend God by His grace to thee doth send.
grace a - lone, That bro't Him from His heav'n-ly throne. A - men.

By Grace I'm Saved, Grace Free and Boundless

5 By grace! This ground of faith is certain;
  So long as God is true, it stands.
What saints have penned by inspiration,
  What in His Word our God commands,
What our whole faith must rest upon,
  Is grace alone, grace in His Son.

6 By grace to timid hearts that tremble,
  In tribulation's furnace tried —
By grace, despite all fear and trouble,
  The Father's heart is open wide.
Where could I help and strength secure
If grace were not my anchor sure?

7 By grace! On this I'll rest when dying;
  In Jesus' promise I rejoice;
For though I know my heart's condition,
  I also know my Savior's voice.
My heart is glad, all grief has flown,
Since I am saved by grace alone.

Grace! 'Tis a Charming Sound 374

Eph. 2: 5   **S. M.**

St. 1, 2, 4, 6, *Philip Doddridge, 1755*
St. 3, 5, *Augustus M. Toplady, 1776, alt.*

Energy
William H. Monk, 1861

1 Grace! 'Tis a charm-ing sound, Har-mo-nious to the ear;
2 Grace first con-trived the way To save re-bel-lious man,
3 Grace first in-scribed my name In God's e-ter-nal book;
4 Grace led my wan-d'ring feet To tread the heav'n-ly road;

Heav'n with the ech-o shall re-sound, And all the earth shall hear.
And all the steps that grace dis-play Which drew the wondrous plan.
'Twas grace that gave me to the Lamb, Who all my sor-rows took.
And new sup-plies each hour I meet While press-ing on to God. A-men.

5 Grace taught my soul to pray
  And made mine eyes o'erflow;
'Twas grace that kept me to this day
  And will not let me go.

6 Grace all the work shall crown
  Through everlasting days;
It lays in heaven the topmost stone
  And well deserves the praise.

375 If Thy Beloved Son, O God

Gal. 2: 16   8. 7. 8. 7. 8. 8. 7.

Wenn dein herzliebster Sohn, o Gott
St. 1–4, Johann Heermann, 1630
St. 5, author unknown, 1661
Tr., composite

Nun freut euch
"Etlich' christliche Lieder"
Wittenberg, 1524

1 If   Thy be - lov - ed Son, O God, Had not to earth de - scend - ed
2 But now I find sweet peace and rest, De - spair no more reigns o'er me;
3 I   trust in Him with all my heart; Now all my sor - row ceas - es;
4 All right-eous-ness by works is vain, The Law brings con-dem-na - tion;

And   in our mor-tal flesh and blood Had not sin's pow - er end - ed,
No more am I   by sin op-prest, For Christ has borne sin for   me.
His words a - bid - ing peace im-part, His blood from guilt re - leas - es.
True right-eous-ness by faith I gain, Christ's work is my sal - va - tion.

Then this poor, wretch-ed soul of mine In hell e - ter - nal-
Up - on   the cross for   me He died That, rec - on - ciled, I
Free grace thro' Him   I   now ob - tain; He wash - es me from
His death, that per - fect sac - ri - fice, Has paid the all - suf-

ly would pine Be - cause of   its trans - gres - sion.
might a - bide With Thee, my God, for - ev - er.
ev - 'ry stain, And pure I   stand be - fore Him.
fi - cient price; In Him my hope is   an - chored. A - men.

If Thy Beloved Son, O God

5 My guilt, O Father, Thou hast laid
   On Christ, Thy Son, my Savior.
Lord Jesus, Thou my debt hast paid
   And gained for me God's favor.
O Holy Ghost, Thou Fount of grace,
The good in me to Thee I trace;
   In faith do Thou preserve me.

Rock of Ages, Cleft for Me 376
7. 7. 7. 7. 7. 7.

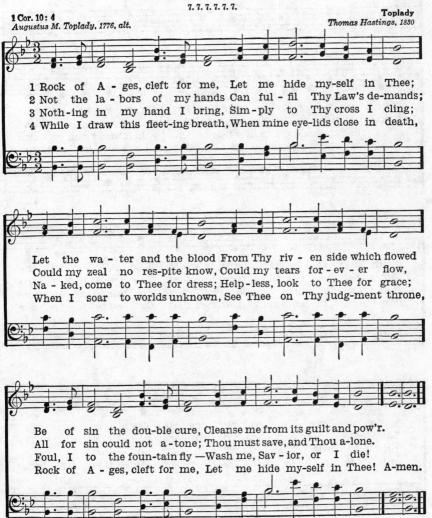

1 Cor. 10: 4
Augustus M. Toplady, 1776, alt.

Toplady
Thomas Hastings, 1830

1 Rock of A - ges, cleft for me, Let me hide my-self in Thee;
2 Not the la - bors of my hands Can ful - fil Thy Law's de-mands;
3 Noth-ing in my hand I bring, Sim - ply to Thy cross I cling;
4 While I draw this fleet-ing breath, When mine eye-lids close in death,

Let the wa - ter and the blood From Thy riv - en side which flowed
Could my zeal no res-pite know, Could my tears for - ev - er flow,
Na - ked, come to Thee for dress; Help-less, look to Thee for grace;
When I soar to worlds unknown, See Thee on Thy judg-ment throne,

Be of sin the dou-ble cure, Cleanse me from its guilt and pow'r.
All for sin could not a - tone; Thou must save, and Thou a-lone.
Foul, I to the foun-tain fly —Wash me, Sav - ior, or I die!
Rock of A - ges, cleft for me, Let me hide my-self in Thee! A-men.

377

Salvation unto Us has Come

8. 7. 8. 7. 8. 8. 7.

Rom. 3—5
Es ist das Heil uns kommen her
Paul Speratus, 1523, cento
Tr., composite

Es ist das Heil
German melody, c. 1400

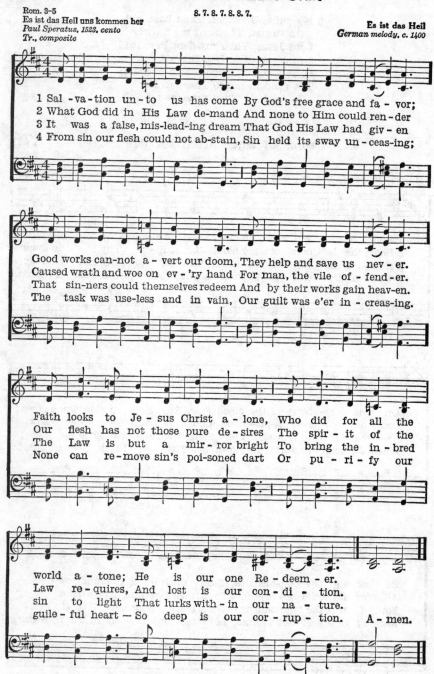

1 Sal - va - tion un - to us has come By God's free grace and fa - vor;
2 What God did in His Law de-mand And none to Him could ren - der
3 It was a false, mis-lead-ing dream That God His Law had giv - en
4 From sin our flesh could not ab-stain, Sin held its sway un - ceas-ing;

Good works can-not a - vert our doom, They help and save us nev - er.
Caused wrath and woe on ev - 'ry hand For man, the vile of - fend - er.
That sin-ners could themselves redeem And by their works gain heav-en.
The task was use-less and in vain, Our guilt was e'er in - creas-ing.

Faith looks to Je - sus Christ a - lone, Who did for all the
Our flesh has not those pure de - sires The spir - it of the
The Law is but a mir - ror bright To bring the in - bred
None can re-move sin's poi-soned dart Or pu - ri - fy our

world a - tone; He is our one Re - deem - er.
Law re - quires, And lost is our con - di - tion.
sin to light That lurks with - in our na - ture.
guile - ful heart — So deep is our cor - rup - tion. A - men.

Salvation unto Us has Come

5 Yet as the Law must be fulfilled
   Or we must die despairing,
 Christ came and hath God's anger
   stilled,
   Our human nature sharing.
 He hath for us the Law obeyed
 And thus the Father's vengeance stayed
   Which over us impended.

6 Since Christ hath full atonement made
   And brought to us salvation,
 Each Christian therefore may be glad
   And build on this foundation.
 Thy grace alone, dear Lord, I plead,
 Thy death is now my life indeed,
   For Thou hast paid my ransom.

7 Let me not doubt, but trust in Thee,
   Thy Word cannot be broken;
 Thy call rings out, "Come unto Me!"
   No falsehood hast Thou spoken.
 Baptized into Thy precious name,
 My faith cannot be put to shame,
   And I shall never perish.

8 The Law reveals the guilt of sin
   And makes men conscience-stricken;
 The Gospel then doth enter in
   The sinful soul to quicken.
 Come to the cross, trust Christ, and
   live;
 The Law no peace can ever give,
   No comfort and no blessing.

9 Faith clings to Jesus' cross alone
   And rests in Him unceasing;
 And by its fruits true faith is known,
   With love and hope increasing.
 Yet faith alone doth justify,
 Works serve thy neighbor and supply
   The proof that faith is living.

10 All blessing, honor, thanks, and praise
   To Father, Son, and Spirit,
 The God that saved us by His grace —
   All glory to His merit!
 O Triune God in heaven above,
 Who hast revealed Thy saving love,
   Thy blessed name be hallowed.

All that I Was, My Sin, My Guilt 378

C. M.

1 Cor. 15: 10
Horatius Bonar, 1845, alt.

St. Bernard
"Tochter Zion"
Cologne, 1741

1 All that I was, my sin, my guilt, My death, was all mine own;
2 The e-vil of my for-mer state Was mine, and on-ly mine;
3 The dark-ness of my for-mer state, The bond-age, all was mine;

All that I am I owe to Thee, My gra-cious God, a-lone.
The good in which I now re-joice Is Thine, and on-ly Thine.
The light of life in which I walk, The lib-er-ty, is Thine. A-men.

4 Thy Word first made me feel my sin,
   It taught me to believe;
 Then, in believing, peace I found,
   And now I live, I live!

5 All that I am, e'en here on earth,
   All that I hope to be,
 When Jesus comes and glory dawns,
   I owe it, Lord, to Thee.

379 I do Not Come Because My Soul

8. 8. 6. 8. 8. 6.

Rom. 7: 19–25
Frank B. St. John, 1878

Kommt her zu mir
German melody, c. 1400

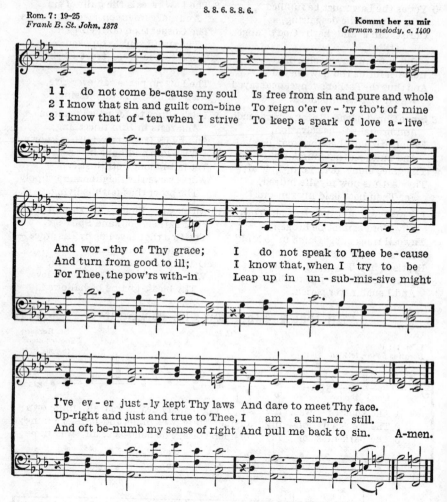

1 I   do not come be-cause my soul   Is free from sin and pure and whole
2 I know that sin and guilt com-bine   To reign o'er ev - 'ry tho't of mine
3 I know that of - ten when I strive   To keep a spark of love a - live

And wor - thy of Thy grace;   I   do not speak to Thee be - cause
And turn from good to ill;   I   know that, when I try to be
For Thee, the pow'rs with-in   Leap up in un - sub-mis-sive might

I've ev - er just - ly kept Thy laws   And dare to meet Thy face.
Up-right and just and true to Thee, I   am   a sin-ner still.
And oft be-numb my sense of right   And pull me back to sin.   A-men.

4 I know that, though in doing good
I spend my life, I never could
    Atone for all I've done;
But though my sins are black as night,
I dare to come before Thy sight
    Because I trust Thy Son.

5 In Him alone my trust I place,
Come boldly to Thy throne of grace,
    And there commune with Thee.
Salvation sure, O Lord, is mine,
And, all unworthy, I am Thine,
    For Jesus died for me.

Thy Works, Not Mine, O Christ

380

6. 6. 6. 6. 8. 8.

Phil. 3: 9
Horatius Bonar, 1857

St. John
"The Parish Choir," 1851

1 Thy works, not mine, O Christ, Speak glad-ness to this heart;
2 Thy wounds, not mine, O Christ, Can heal my bruis-ed soul;
3 Thy cross, not mine, O Christ, Has borne the awe-full load

They tell me all is done, They bid my fear de-part. To whom save
Thy stripes, not mine, con-tain The balm that makes me whole. To whom save
Of sins that none could bear But the in-car-nate God. To whom save

Thee, who canst a-lone For sin a-tone, Lord, shall I flee?
Thee, who canst a-lone For sin a-tone, Lord, shall I flee?
Thee, who canst a-lone For sin a-tone, Lord, shall I flee? A-men.

4 Thy death, not mine, O Christ,
  Has paid the ransom due;
Ten thousand deaths like mine
  Would have been all too few.
To whom save Thee, who canst alone
For sin atone, Lord, shall I flee?

5 Thy righteousness, O Christ,
  Alone can cover me;
No righteousness avails
  Save that which is of Thee.
To whom save Thee, who canst alone
For sin atone, Lord, shall I flee?

381

I Know My Faith is Founded

2 Tim. 1: 12

7. 8. 7. 8. 7. 6. 7. 6. 7. 6. 7. 6.

Ich weiss, an wen ich gläube
Erdmann Neumeister, 1718
Tr., composite

Nun lob, mein' Seel'
"Concentus Novi"
Augsburg, 1540

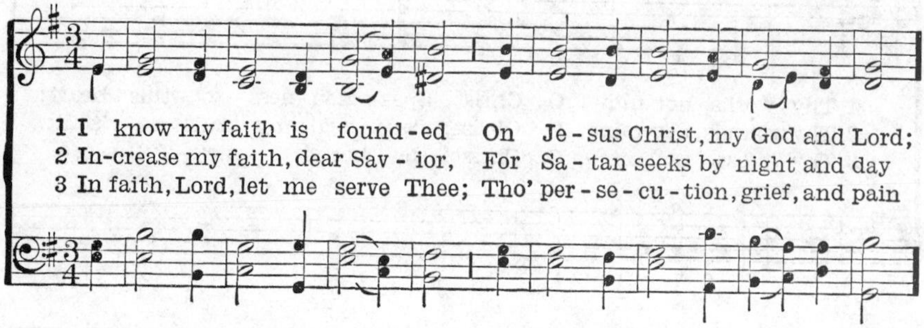

1 I know my faith is found-ed On Je-sus Christ, my God and Lord;
2 In-crease my faith, dear Sav-ior, For Sa-tan seeks by night and day
3 In faith, Lord, let me serve Thee; Tho' per-se-cu-tion, grief, and pain

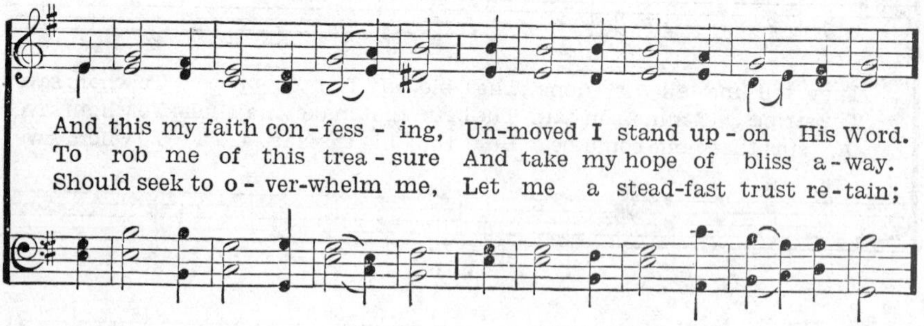

And this my faith con-fess-ing, Un-moved I stand up-on His Word.
To rob me of this trea-sure And take my hope of bliss a-way.
Should seek to o-ver-whelm me, Let me a stead-fast trust re-tain;

Man's rea-son can-not fath-om The truth of God pro-found;
But, Lord, with Thee be-side me, I shall be un-dis-mayed;
And then at my de-par-ture Take Thou me home to Thee

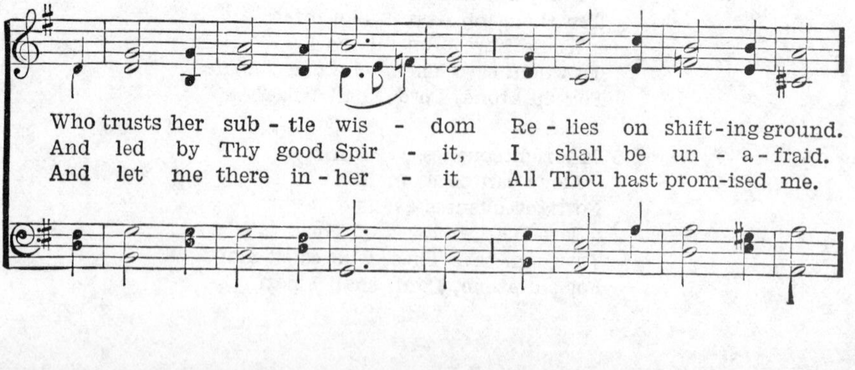

Who trusts her sub-tle wis-dom Re-lies on shift-ing ground.
And led by Thy good Spir-it, I shall be un-a-fraid.
And let me there in-her-it All Thou hast prom-ised me.

I Know My Faith is Founded

God's Word is all - suf - fi - cient, It makes di - vine - ly sure,
A - bide with me, O Sav - ior, A firm - er faith be - stow;
In life and death, Lord, keep me Un - til Thy heav'n I gain,

And trust-ing in its wis - dom, My faith shall rest se-cure.
Then I shall bid de - fi - ance To ev - 'ry e - vil foe.
Where I by Thy great mer - cy The end of faith at-tain. A - men.

Lord, We Confess Our Numerous Faults **382**

C. M.

Titus 3: 3, 7
Isaac Watts, 1709, alt.

St. Flavian
"Psalter"
John Day, 1562

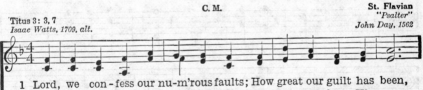

1 Lord, we con-fess our nu-m'rous faults; How great our guilt has been,
2 But, O my soul, for - ev - er praise, For - ev - er love, His name
3 'Tis not by works of right-eous-ness Which our own hands have done,
4 'Tis from the mer - cy of our God That all our hopes be - gin;

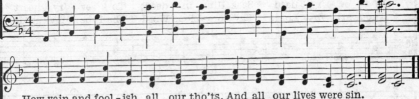

How vain and fool - ish all our tho'ts, And all our lives were sin.
Who turns thy feet from dang'rous ways Of fol - ly, sin, and shame.
But we are saved by God's free grace A-bound-ing thro' His Son.
'Tis by the Wa - ter and the Blood Our souls are washed from sin. A-men.

5 'Tis through the purchase of His death
  Who hung upon the tree
The Spirit is sent down to breathe
  On such dry bones as we.

6 Raised from the dead, we live anew;
  And justified by grace,
We shall appear in glory, too,
  And see our Father's face.

383 Seek Where Ye May to Find a Way

Acts 4: 12
Such', wer da will, ein ander Ziel
Georg Weissel, 1623
Tr., Arthur Voss, 1938

4. 4. 7. 4. 4. 7. 4. 4. 4. 4. 7.

Such', wer da will
Johann Stobäus, 1613, ad.

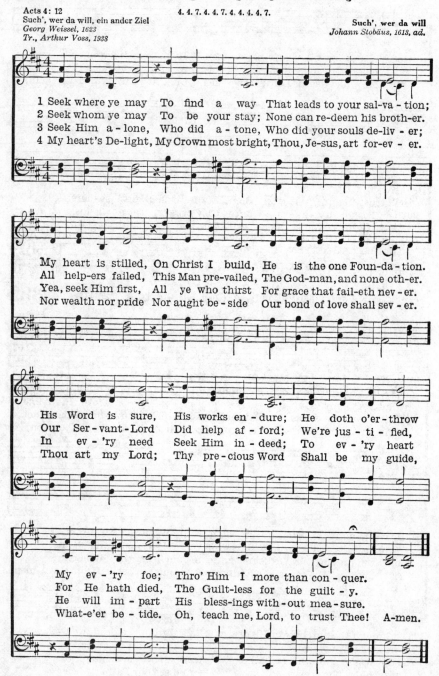

1 Seek where ye may   To find a way   That leads to your sal-va-tion;
2 Seek whom ye may   To be your stay; None can re-deem his broth-er.
3 Seek Him a-lone,   Who did a-tone, Who did your souls de-liv-er;
4 My heart's De-light, My Crown most bright, Thou, Je-sus, art for-ev-er.

My heart is stilled, On Christ I build, He is the one Foun-da-tion.
All help-ers failed, This Man pre-vailed, The God-man, and none oth-er.
Yea, seek Him first, All ye who thirst For grace that fail-eth nev-er.
Nor wealth nor pride Nor aught be-side Our bond of love shall sev-er.

His Word is sure, His works en-dure; He doth o'er-throw
Our Ser-vant-Lord Did help af-ford; We're jus-ti-fied,
In ev-'ry need Seek Him in-deed; To ev-'ry heart
Thou art my Lord; Thy pre-cious Word Shall be my guide,

My ev-'ry foe; Thro' Him I more than con-quer.
For He hath died, The Guilt-less for the guilt-y.
He will im-part His bless-ings with-out mea-sure.
What-e'er be-tide. Oh, teach me, Lord, to trust Thee! A-men.

Seek Where Ye May to Find a Way

5 Hide not from me, I ask of Thee,
Thy gracious face and favor.
Though floods of woe Should o'er me **flow,**
My faith shall never waver.
From pain and grief Grant sweet relief;
For tears I weep, Lord, let me reap
Thy heavenly joy and glory.

Oh, How Great Is Thy Compassion 384

2 Cor. 9: 15
Ach, wie gross ist deine Gnade
Johann Olearius, 1671
Tr., August Crull, †1923, alt.

8. 7. 7. 8. 7. 7.

Ach, was soll ich Sünder machen
"Hirtenlieder"
Altdorf, 1653

1 Oh, how great is Thy com-pas-sion, Faith-ful Fa - ther, God of grace,
2 Thy great love for this hath striv-en That we may from sin be free
3 And for this our soul's sal-va-tion Vouch-eth Thy good Spir-it, Lord,

That with all our fall-en race And in our deep deg-ra-tion
And for-ev-er live with Thee; Yea, Thy Son Him-self hath giv-en
In Thy Sac-ra-ments and Word. He im-part-eth con-so-la-tion,

Thou wast mer-ci-ful that we Might be saved e-ter-nal-ly!
In His grace an ear-nest call To His Sup-per un-to all.
Grant-eth us the gift of faith That we fear nor hell nor death. A-men.

4 Lord, Thy mercy will not leave me —
Truth doth evermore abide —
Then in Thee I will confide.
Since Thy Word cannot deceive me,
My salvation is to me
Well assured eternally.

5 I will praise Thy great compassion,
Faithful Father, God of grace,
That with all our fallen race
And in our deep degradation
Thou wast merciful that we
Might bring endless praise to Thee.

385 Now I have Found the Firm Foundation

1 Cor. 3: 11
Ich habe nun den Grund gefunden
Johann A. Rothe, 1727
Tr., composite

9. 8. 9. 8. 8. 8.

O dass ich tausend
Johann B. König, 1738

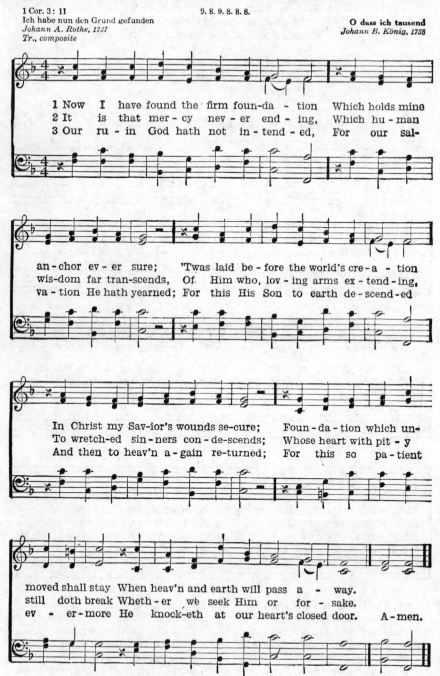

1 Now I have found the firm foun-da - tion Which holds mine
2 It is that mer - cy nev - er end - ing, Which hu - man
3 Our ru - in God hath not in - tend - ed, For our sal-

an - chor ev - er sure; 'Twas laid be - fore the world's cre - a - tion
wis-dom far tran-scends, Of Him who, lov - ing arms ex - tend-ing,
va - tion He hath yearned; For this His Son to earth de - scend - ed

In Christ my Sav-ior's wounds se-cure; Foun - da - tion which un-
To wretch-ed sin - ners con - de-scends; Whose heart with pit - y
And then to heav'n a - gain re-turned; For this so pa - tient

moved shall stay When heav'n and earth will pass a - way.
still doth break Wheth - er we seek Him or for - sake.
ev - er-more He knock-eth at our heart's closed door. A - men.

How I have Found the Firm Foundation

4 O depth of love, to me revealing
   The sea where my sins disappear!
In Christ my wounds find perfect healing,
   There is no condemnation here;
For Jesus' blood through earth and skies
Forever "Mercy! Mercy!" cries.

5 I never will forget this crying;
   In faith I'll trust it all my days,
And when o'er all my sins I'm sighing,
   Into the Father's heart I'll gaze;
For there is always to be found
Free mercy without end and bound.

6 Though I be robbed of every pleasure
   That makes my soul and body glad
And be deprived of earthly treasure
   And be forsaken, lone, and sad,
Though my desire for help seem vain,
His mercy shall with me remain.

7 Though earthly trials should oppress me
   And cares from day to day increase;
Though earth's vain things should sore distress me
   And rob me of my Savior's peace;
Though I be brought down to the dust,
Still in His mercy I will trust.

8 When all my deeds I am reviewing,
   The deeds that I admire the most,
I find in all my thought and doing
   That there is naught whereof to boast.
Yet this sweet comfort shall abide—
In mercy I can still confide.

9 Let mercy cause me to be willing
   To bear my lot and not to fret.
While He my restless heart is stilling,
   May I His mercy not forget!
Come weal, come woe, my heart to test,
His mercy is my only rest.

10 I'll stand upon this firm foundation
   As long as I on earth remain;
This shall engage my meditation
   While I the breath of life retain;
And then, when face to face with Thee,
I'll sing of mercy, great and free.

386

My Savior Sinners Doth Receive

Luke 15 : 2
Mein Heiland nimmt die Sünder an
Leopold F. Lehr, c. 1731, cento
Tr., composite

8. 9. 8. 9. 8. 8. 9. 9. 8. 8.

Mein Heiland
"Musikalischer Christenschatz"
Basel, 1745

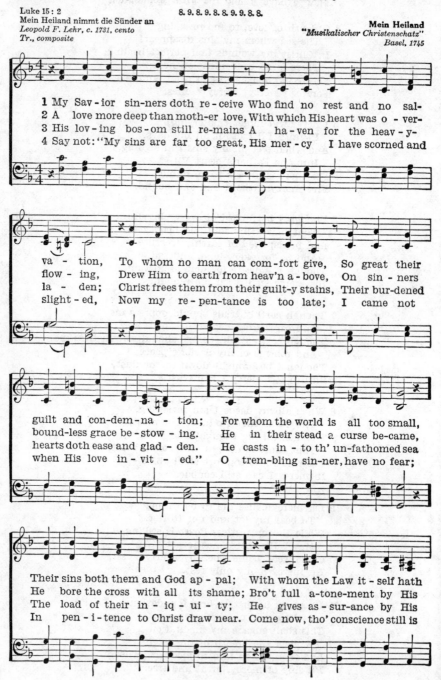

1 My Sav-ior sin-ners doth re-ceive Who find no rest and no sal-
2 A love more deep than moth-er love, With which His heart was o-ver-
3 His lov-ing bos-om still re-mains A ha-ven for the heav-y-
4 Say not: "My sins are far too great, His mer-cy I have scorned and

va - tion, To whom no man can com-fort give, So great their
flow - ing, Drew Him to earth from heav'n a-bove, On sin-ners
la - den; Christ frees them from their guilt-y stains, Their bur-dened
slight - ed, Now my re-pen-tance is too late; I came not

guilt and con-dem-na - tion; For whom the world is all too small,
bound-less grace be-stow - ing. He in their stead a curse be-came,
hearts doth ease and glad - den. He casts in-to th' un-fathomed sea
when His love in-vit - ed." O trem-bling sin-ner, have no fear;

Their sins both them and God ap - pal; With whom the Law it-self hath
He bore the cross with all its shame; Bro't full a-tone-ment by His
The load of their in-iq-ui-ty; He gives as-sur-ance by His
In pen-i-tence to Christ draw near. Come now, tho' conscience still is

My Savior Sinners Doth Receive

bro - ken, On whom its judg-ment hath been spo - ken,—
suf - f'ring, Gave up His life for them an of - f'ring.
Spir - it That they are saved through His own mer - it.
chid - ing; Ac - cept His mer - cy, e'er a - bid - ing.

To them the Gos - pel hope doth give: My Sav - ior sin - ners
This com-fort doth the Gos - pel give: My Sav - ior sin - ners
Yea, they shall live who this be - lieve: My Sav - ior sin - ners
Come; blest are they who this be - lieve: My Sav - ior sin - ners

doth re-ceive. My Sav - ior sin - ners doth re - ceive.
doth re-ceive. My Sav - ior sin - ners doth re - ceive.
doth re-ceive. My Sav - ior sin - ners doth re - ceive.
doth re-ceive. My Sav - ior sin - ners doth re - ceive. A - men.

5 Oh, draw us ever unto Thee,
   Thou Friend of sinners, gracious Savior;
Help us that we may fervently
   Desire Thy pardon, peace, and favor.
When guilty conscience doth reprove,
Reveal to us Thy heart of love.
May we, our wretchedness beholding,
See then Thy pardoning grace unfolding
And say: "To God all glory be:
My Savior, Christ, receiveth me."

387 Dear Christians, One and All, Rejoice

Rom. 3: 28
Nun freut euch, liebe Christen g'mein
Martin Luther, 1523
Tr., Richard Massie, 1854, alt.

8. 7. 8. 7. 8. 8. 7.

Nun freut euch
"Etlich' christliche Lieder"
Wittenberg, 1524

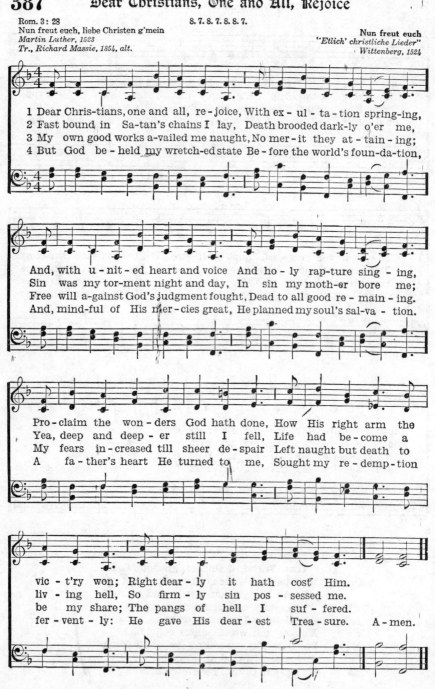

1 Dear Christians, one and all, re-joice, With ex-ul-ta-tion spring-ing,
2 Fast bound in Sa-tan's chains I lay, Death brooded dark-ly o'er me,
3 My own good works a-vailed me naught, No mer-it they at-tain-ing;
4 But God be-held my wretch-ed state Be-fore the world's foun-da-tion,

And, with u-nit-ed heart and voice And ho-ly rap-ture sing-ing,
Sin was my tor-ment night and day, In sin my moth-er bore me;
Free will a-gainst God's judgment fought, Dead to all good re-main-ing.
And, mind-ful of His mer-cies great, He planned my soul's sal-va-tion.

Pro-claim the won-ders God hath done, How His right arm the
Yea, deep and deep-er still I fell, Life had be-come a
My fears in-creased till sheer de-spair Left naught but death to
A fa-ther's heart He turned to me, Sought my re-demp-tion

vic-t'ry won; Right dear-ly it hath cost Him.
liv-ing hell, So firm-ly sin pos-sessed me.
be my share; The pangs of hell I suf-fered.
fer-vent-ly: He gave His dear-est Trea-sure. A-men.

Dear Christians, One and All, Rejoice

5 He spoke to His beloved Son:
　　'Tis time to have compassion.
Then go, bright Jewel of My crown,
　　And bring to man salvation;
From sin and sorrow set him free,
Slay bitter death for him that he
　　May live with Thee forever.

6 The Son obeyed His Father's will,
　　Was born of virgin mother,
And God's good pleasure to fulfill,
　　He came to be my Brother.
No garb of pomp or power He wore,
A servant's form, like mine, He bore,
　　To lead the devil captive.

7 To me He spake: Hold fast to Me,
　　I am thy Rock and Castle;
Thy Ransom I Myself will be,
　　For thee I strive and wrestle;
For I am with thee, I am thine,
And evermore thou shalt be Mine:
　　The Foe shall not divide us.

8 The Foe shall shed My precious blood,
　　Me of My life bereaving.
All this I suffer for thy good;
　　Be steadfast and believing.
Life shall from death the victory win,
My innocence shall bear thy sin;
　　So art thou blest forever.

9 Now to My Father I depart,
　　The Holy Spirit sending
And, heavenly wisdom to impart,
　　My help to thee extending.
He shall in trouble comfort thee,
Teach thee to know and follow Me,
　　And in all truth shall guide thee.

10 What I have done and taught, teach thou,
　　My ways forsake thou never;
So shall My kingdom flourish now
　　And God be praised forever.
Take heed lest men with base alloy
The heavenly treasure should destroy;
　　This counsel I bequeath thee.

388

Just as I Am, without One Plea

John 6: 37
Charlotte Elliott, 1836

L. M.
(*FIRST TUNE*)

St. Crispin
George J. Elvey, 1862

1 Just as I am, with-out one plea But that Thy blood was shed for me And that Thou bidd'st me come to Thee, O Lamb of God, I come, I come. A - men.

2 Just as I am and waiting not
To rid my soul of one dark blot,
To Thee, whose blood can cleanse each spot,
    O Lamb of God, I come, I come.

3 Just as I am, though tossed about
With many a conflict, many a doubt,
Fightings and fears within, without,
    O Lamb of God, I come, I come.

4 Just as I am, poor, wretched, blind;
Sight, riches, healing of the mind,
Yea, all I need, in Thee to find,
    O Lamb of God, I come, I come.

5 Just as I am, Thou wilt receive,
Wilt welcome, pardon, cleanse, relieve;
Because Thy promise I believe,
    O Lamb of God, I come, I come.

6 Just as I am; Thy love unknown
Has broken every barrier down.
Now to be Thine, yea, Thine alone,
    O Lamb of God, I come, I come.

Just as I Am, without One Plea

John 6: 37
Charlotte Elliott, 1836

L. M.
(*SECOND TUNE*)

Woodworth
William B. Bradbury, 1849

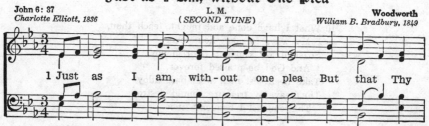

1 Just as I am, with-out one plea But that Thy

Just as I Am, without One Plea

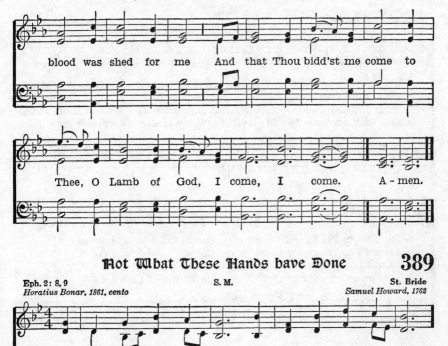

blood was shed for me And that Thou bidd'st me come to

Thee, O Lamb of God, I come, I come. A-men.

Not What These Hands have Done

389

Eph. 2: 8, 9
Horatius Bonar, 1861, cento

S. M.

St. Bride
Samuel Howard, 1762

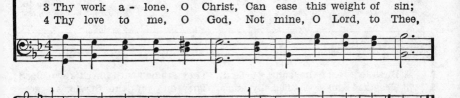

1 Not what these hands have done Can save this guilt-y soul;
2 Not what I feel or do Can give me peace with God;
3 Thy work a-lone, O Christ, Can ease this weight of sin;
4 Thy love to me, O God, Not mine, O Lord, to Thee,

Not what this toil-ing flesh has borne Can make my spir-it whole.
Not all my prayers and sighs and tears Can bear my awe-full load.
Thy blood a-lone, O Lamb of God, Can give me peace with-in.
Can rid me of this dark un-rest And set my spir-it free. A-men.

5 Thy grace alone, O God,
   To me can pardon speak;
Thy power alone, O Son of God,
   Can this sore bondage break.

6 I bless the Christ of God,
   I rest on love divine,
And with unfaltering lip and heart
   I call this Savior mine.

390 Drawn to the Cross, which Thou hast Blest

John 12: 32
Genevieve M. Irons, 1880

8. 8. 8. 6.

Dunstan
Joseph Barnby, 1883

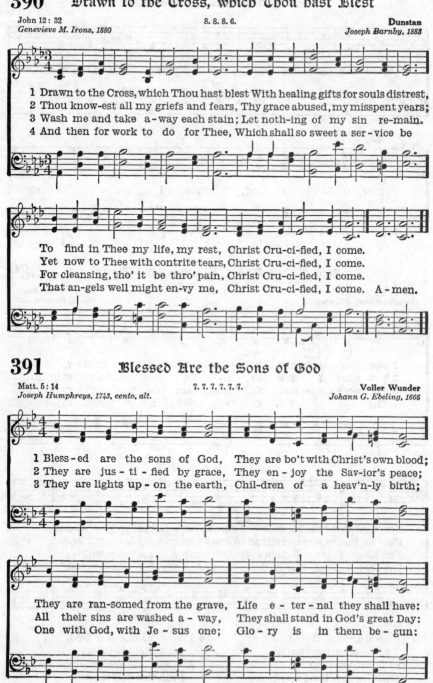

1 Drawn to the Cross, which Thou hast blest With healing gifts for souls distrest,
2 Thou know-est all my griefs and fears, Thy grace abused, my misspent years;
3 Wash me and take a-way each stain; Let noth-ing of my sin re-main.
4 And then for work to do for Thee, Which shall so sweet a ser-vice be

To find in Thee my life, my rest, Christ Cru-ci-fied, I come.
Yet now to Thee with contrite tears, Christ Cru-ci-fied, I come.
For cleansing, tho' it be thro' pain, Christ Cru-ci-fied, I come.
That an-gels well might en-vy me, Christ Cru-ci-fied, I come. A-men.

391 Blessed Are the Sons of God

Matt. 5: 14
Joseph Humphreys, 1743, cento, alt.

7. 7. 7. 7. 7. 7.

Voller Wunder
Johann G. Ebeling, 1666

1 Bless-ed are the sons of God, They are bo't with Christ's own blood;
2 They are jus-ti-fied by grace, They en-joy the Sav-ior's peace;
3 They are lights up-on the earth, Chil-dren of a heav'n-ly birth;

They are ran-somed from the grave, Life e-ter-nal they shall have:
All their sins are washed a-way, They shall stand in God's great Day:
One with God, with Je-sus one; Glo-ry is in them be-gun:

Blessed Are the Sons of God

With them numbered may we be Here and in e - ter - ni - ty!
With them numbered may we be Here and in e - ter - ni - ty!
With them numbered may we be Here and in e - ter - ni - ty! A-men.

Blest Is the Man, Forever Blest   392

Ps. 32
Isaac Watts, 1719

L. M.

O Jesu Christ, mein's
"*Nürnbergisches Gesangbuch,*" 1676

1 Blest is the man, for - ev - er blest, Whose guilt is
2 Blest is the man to whom the Lord Im - putes not
3 From guile his heart and lips are free; His hum - ble
4 How glo - rious is that right - eous - ness That hides and

par - doned by his God, Whose sins with sor - row are con -
his in - iq - ui - ties; He pleads no mer - it of re -
joy, his ho - ly fear, With deep re - pen - tance well a -
can - cels all his sins, While bright the ev - i - dence of

fessed And cov - ered with his Sav - ior's blood.
ward And not on works but grace re - lies.
gree And join to prove his faith sin - cere.
grace Thro' all his life ap - pears and shines! A - men.

393   From God Shall Naught Divide Me

Josh. 24 : 16
Von Gott will ich nicht lassen
Ludwig Helmbold, 1563, cento
Tr., Catherine Winkworth, 1863, alt.

7. 6. 7. 6. 6. 7. 7. 6.

Von Gott will ich nicht lassen
"Christliche Tischgesänge"
Erfurt, 1572

1 From God shall naught di - vide me, For He is true for aye
2 When man's help and af - fec - tion Shall un - a - vail - ing prove,
3 God shall be my Re - li - ance In sor-row's dark-est night;

And on my path will guide me, Who else should of - ten stray.
God grants me His pro - tec - tion And shows His pow'r and love.
Its dread I bid de - fi - ance When He is at my right.

His right hand hold - eth me; For me He tru - ly car - eth,
He helps in ev - 'ry need, From sin and shame re - deems me,
I un - to Him com - mend My bod - y, soul, and spir - it —

My bur - dens ev - er bear - eth Wher - ev - er I may be.
From chains and bonds re-claims me, Yea, e'en from death I'm freed.
They are His own by mer - it — All's well then at the end. A-men.

From God Shall Naught Divide Me

4 Oh, praise Him, for He never
  Forgets our daily need;
Oh, blest the hour whenever
  To Him our thoughts can speed;
Yea, all the time we spend
  Without Him is but wasted,
  Till we His joy have tasted,
The joy that hath no end.

5 Yea, when the world shall perish
  With all its pride and power,
Whatever worldlings cherish
  Shall vanish in that hour.

But though in death they make
  The deepest grave our cover,
  When there our sleep is over,
Our God will us awake.

6 What though I here must suffer
  Distress and trials sore,
I merit ways still rougher;
  And yet there is in store
For me eternal bliss,
  Yea, pleasures without measure,
  Since Christ is now my Treasure
And shall be evermore.

My Faith Looks Up to Thee   394

Eph. 3: 12
Ray Palmer, 1830

6. 6. 4. 6. 6. 6. 4.

Olivet
Lowell Mason, 1831

1 My faith looks up to Thee, Thou Lamb of Cal-va-ry,
2 May Thy rich grace im-part Strength to my faint-ing heart,
3 While life's dark maze I tread And griefs a-round me spread,
4 When ends life's tran-sient dream, When death's cold, sul-len stream

Sav-ior di-vine. Now hear me while I pray; Take all my
My zeal in-spire! As Thou hast died for me, Oh, may my
Be Thou my Guide. Bid dark-ness turn to day, Wipe sor-row's
Shall o'er me roll, Blest Sav-ior, then, in love, Fear and dis-

guilt a-way; Oh, let me from this day Be whol-ly Thine!
love to Thee Pure, warm, and changeless be, A liv-ing fire!
tears a-way, Nor let me ev-er stray From Thee a-side.
trust re-move; Oh, bear me safe a-bove, A ran-somed soul! A-men.

395

O God, Thou Faithful God

1 Kings 3: 5
O Gott, du frommer Gott
Johann Heermann, 1630
Tr., Catherine Winkworth, 1858, alt.

6. 7. 6. 7. 6. 6. 6. 6.

O Gott, du frommer Gott
"Neuvermehrtes Gesangbuch"
Meiningen, 1693

1 O God, Thou faith-ful God, Thou Foun-tain ev - er flow - ing,
2 Grant Thou me strength to do With read - y heart and will - ing
3 Oh, let me nev - er speak What bounds of truth ex - ceed - eth;
4 If dan - gers gath - er round, Still keep me calm and fear - less;

Who good and per - fect gifts In mer - cy art be - stow - ing,
What-e'er Thou shalt com-mand, My call - ing here ful - fill - ing;
Grant that no i - dle word From out my mouth pro - ceed - eth;
Help me to bear the cross When life is dark and cheer - less;

Give me a health - y frame, And may I have with - in
To do it when I ought, With all my might, and bless
And then, when in my place I must and ought to speak,
And let me win my foe With words and ac - tions kind.

A con-science free from blame, A soul un - hurt by sin!
The work I thus have wrought, For Thou must give suc - cess.
My words grant pow'r and grace Lest I of - fend the weak.
When coun-sel I would know, Good coun-sel let me find. A-men.

O God, Thou Faithful God

5 And let me with all men,
   As far as in me lieth,
In peace and friendship live.
   And if Thy gift supplieth
Great wealth and honor fair,
   Then this refuse me not,
That naught be mingled there
   Of goods unjustly got.

6 If Thou a longer life
   Hast here on earth decreed me;
If Thou through many ills
   To age at length wilt lead me,
Thy patience on me shed.
   Avert all sin and shame
And crown my hoary head
   With honor free from blame.

7 Let me depart this life
   Confiding in my Savior;
Do Thou my soul receive
   That it may live forever;
And let my body have
   A quiet resting-place
Within a Christian grave;
   And let it sleep in peace.

8 And on that solemn Day
   When all the dead are waking,
Stretch o'er my grave Thy hand,
   Thyself my slumbers breaking.
Then let me hear Thy voice,
   Change Thou this earthly frame,
And bid me aye rejoice
   With those who love Thy name.

Oh, for a Faith That Will Not Shrink   396

Luke 17: 5   C. M.   St. Peter
William H. Bathurst, 1831, alt.   Alexander R. Reinagle, 1836

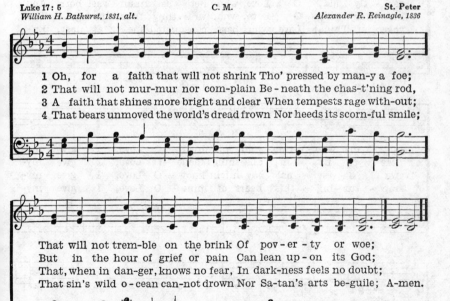

1 Oh, for a faith that will not shrink Tho' pressed by man-y a foe;
2 That will not mur-mur nor com-plain Be-neath the chas-t'ning rod,
3 A faith that shines more bright and clear When tempests rage with-out;
4 That bears unmoved the world's dread frown Nor heeds its scorn-ful smile;

That will not trem-ble on the brink Of pov-er-ty or woe;
But in the hour of grief or pain Can lean up-on its God;
That, when in dan-ger, knows no fear, In dark-ness feels no doubt;
That sin's wild o-cean can-not drown Nor Sa-tan's arts be-guile; A-men.

5 A faith that keeps the narrow way
   Till life's last spark is fled
And with a pure and heavenly ray
   Lights up the dying bed.

6 Lord, give us such a faith as this;
   And then, whate'er may come,
We'll taste e'en now the hallowed bliss
   Of an eternal home.

397 **O Love, Who Madest Me to Wear**

1 John 4 : 16
Liebe, die du mich zum Bilde
Johann Scheffler, 1657
Tr., Catherine Winkworth, 1858

8. 8. 8. 8. 8. 8.

Heut' triumphieret Gottes Sohn
"Deutsche geistliche Lieder"
Frankfurt a. O., 1601

1 O Love, who mad-est me to wear The im-age of Thy
2 O Love, who ere life's ear-liest dawn On me Thy choice hast
3 O Love, who once in time wast slain, Pierced thro' and thro' with
4 O Love, who thus hast bound me fast Be-neath that eas-y

God-head here; Who sought-est me with ten-der care Thro'
gen-tly laid; O Love, who here as man wast born And
bit-ter woe; O Love, who, wres-tling thus, didst gain That
yoke of Thine; Love, who hast con-quered me at last, En-

all my wan-d'rings wild and drear — O Love, I give my-
like to us in all things made — O Love, I give my-
we e-ter-nal joy might know — O Love, I give my-
rap-tur-ing this heart of mine — O Love, I give my-

self to Thee, Thine ev-er, on-ly Thine, to be.
self to Thee, Thine ev-er, on-ly Thine, to be.
self to Thee, Thine ev-er, on-ly Thine, to be.
self to Thee, Thine ev-er, on-ly Thine, to be. A-men.

O Love, Who Madest Me to Wear

5 O Love, who lovest me for aye,
    Who for my soul dost ever plead;
O Love, who didst my ransom pay,
    Whose power sufficeth in my stead —
O Love, I give myself to Thee,
Thine ever, only Thine, to be.

6 O Love, who once shalt bid me rise
    From out this dying life of ours;
O Love, who once above yon skies
    Shalt set me in the fadeless bowers —
O Love, I give myself to Thee,
Thine ever, only Thine, to be.

Renew Me, O Eternal Light   398

2 Cor. 3 : 18   **L. M.**

Erneure mich, o ew'ges Licht
Johann F. Ruopp, 1714, cento
Tr., August Crull, †1923

Herr Jesu Christ, mein's
"As Hymnodus Sacer"
Leipzig, 1625

1 Re-new me, O e-ter-nal Light, And let my heart and soul be bright, Il-lu-mined with the light of grace That is-sues from Thy ho-ly face.

2 De-stroy in me the lust of sin, From all im-pure-ness make me clean. Oh, grant me pow'r and strength, my God, To strive a-gainst my flesh and blood!

3 Cre-ate in me a new heart, Lord, That glad-ly I o-bey Thy Word And naught but what Thou wilt, de-sire; With such new life my soul in-spire.

4 Grant that I on-ly Thee may love And seek those things which are a-bove Till I be-hold Thee face to face, O Light e-ter-nal, through Thy grace. A-men.

399 Thee Will I Love, My Strength, My Tower

John 14: 23
Ich will dich lieben, meine Stärke
Johann Scheffler, 1657, cento
Tr., Catherine Winkworth, 1863, alt.

9. 8. 9. 8. 8. 6.

Ich will dich lieben
"Harmonischer Liederschatz"
Frankfurt, 1738

1 Thee will I love, my Strength, my Tow-er; Thee will I love, my
2 Thee will I love, my Life, my Sav-ior, Who art my best and
3 I thank Thee, Je-sus, Sun from heav-en, Whose radiance hath bro't
4 Oh, keep me watch-ful, then, and hum-ble And suf-fer me no

Hope, my Joy; Thee will I love with all my pow-er,
tru - est Friend; Thee will I love and praise for - ev - er,
light to me; I thank Thee, who hast rich - ly giv - en
more to stray; Up - hold me when my feet would stum - ble,

With ar - dor time shall ne'er de - stroy. Thee will I
For nev - er shall Thy kind-ness end; Thee will I
All that could make me glad and free; I thank Thee
Nor let me loi - ter by the way. Fill all my

love, O Light Di-vine, So long as life is mine.
love with all my heart, Thou my Re - deem - er art.
that my soul is healed By what Thy lips re - vealed.
na - ture with Thy light, O Ra-diance strong and bright! A - men.

Thee Will I Love, My Strength, My Tower

5 Oh, teach me, Lord, to love Thee truly
  With soul and body, head and heart,
  And grant me grace that I may duly
  Practice fore'er love's sacred art.
  Grant that my every thought may be
  Directed e'er to Thee.

6 Thee will I love, my Crown of gladness;
  Thee will I love, my God and Lord,
  Amid the darkest depths of sadness,
  Nor for the hope of high reward —
  For Thine own sake, O Light Divine,
  So long as life is mine.

Take My Life and Let It Be   400

Eph. 6: 24   7. 7. 7. 7.   Patmos
Frances R. Havergal, 1874   *William H. Havergal, 1869*

1 Take my life and let it be   Con - se - crat - ed, Lord, to Thee;
2 Take my hands and let them move   At the im-pulse of Thy love;
3 Take my voice and let me sing   Al - ways, on - ly, for my King;
4 Take my sil - ver and my gold,   Not a mite would I with-hold;

Take my moments and my days,   Let them flow in cease-less praise.
Take my feet and let them be   Swift and beau-ti-ful for Thee.
Take my lips and let them be   Filled with mes-sag-es from Thee.
Take my in - tel-lect and use   Ev - 'ry pow'r as Thou shalt choose. A-men.

5 Take my will and make it Thine,
  It shall be no longer mine;
  Take my heart, it is Thine own,
  It shall be Thy royal throne.

6 Take my love, my Lord, I pour
  At Thy feet its treasure store;
  Take myself, and I will be
  Ever, only, all, for Thee.

401 Praise to Thee and Adoration

Ps. 106: 1
Lov og Tak og evig Aere
Thomas Kingo, 1689
Tr., Kristen Kvamme et al., 1904

8. 7. 8. 7. 7. 7. 8. 8.

Freu dich sehr
"Genevan Psalter," 1551

1 Praise to Thee and ad - o - ra - tion, Bless-ed Je - sus, Son of God,
2 Let me nev - er, Lord, for-sake Thee, E'en tho' bit - ter pain and strife

Who, to serve Thine own cre - a - tion, Didst par-take of flesh and blood.
On my way shall o - ver-take me; But may I thro' all my life

Teach me that I nev - er may From Thy fold or pas-tures stray,
Walk in fer - vent love to Thee, In all woes for com-fort flee

But with zeal and joy ex-ceed-ing Fol-low where Thy steps are leading.
To Thy birth, Thy death, and Passion Till I see Thy full sal-va-tion. A-men.

O God, Forsake Me Not

402

Ps. 38: 22
Ach Gott, verlass mich nicht
Salomo Franck, 1714
Tr., August Crull, †1923, alt.

6. 7. 6. 7. 6. 6. 6. 6.

O Gott, du frommer Gott
"Neuvermehrtes Gesangbuch"
Meiningen, 1693

1 O God, for-sake me not! Thy gra-cious pres-ence lend me;
2 O God, for-sake me not! Take not Thy Spir-it from me
3 O God, for-sake me not! Lord, hear my sup-pli-ca-tion!

Lead Thou Thy help-less child; Thy Ho-ly Spir-it send me
And suf-fer not the might Of sin to o-ver-come me.
In ev-'ry e-vil hour Help me o'er-come temp-ta-tion;

That I my course may run. Be Thou my Light, my Lot,
In-crease my fee-ble faith, Which Thou Thy-self hast wrought.
And when the Prince of hell My con-science seeks to blot,

My Staff, my Rock, my Shield — O God, for-sake me not!
Be Thou my Strength and Pow'r —O God, for-sake me not!
Be Thou not far from me — O God, for-sake me not! A-men.

4 O God, forsake me not!
   Thy mercy I'm addressing;
O Father, God of Love,
   Grant me Thy heavenly blessing
To do when duty calls
   Whate'er Thou didst allot,
To do what pleaseth Thee —
   O God, forsake me not!

5 O God, forsake me not!
   Lord, I am Thine forever.
Grant me true faith in Thee;
   Grant that I leave Thee never.
Grant me a blessed end
   When my good fight is fought;
Help me in life and death —
   O God, forsake me not!

403 Savior, Thy Dying Love

Acts 9: 6
Sylvanus D. Phelps, 1862

6. 4. 6. 4. 6. 6. 6. 4.

Winterton
Joseph Barnby, 1892

1 Sav - ior, Thy dy - ing love Thou gav - est me;
2 O'er the blest mer - cy seat, Plead - ing for me,
3 Give me a faith - ful heart, Like - ness to Thee,
4 All that I am and have, Thy gifts so free,

Nor should I aught with-hold, Dear Lord, from Thee.
My fee - ble faith looks up, Je - sus, to Thee.
That each de - part - ing day Hence-forth may see
In joy, in grief, through life, Dear Lord, for Thee!

In love my soul would bow, My heart ful - fil its vow,
Help me the cross to bear, Thy won-drous love de - clare,
Some work of love be - gun, Some deed of kind - ness done,
And when Thy face I see, My ran-somed soul shall be

Some of - f'ring bring Thee now, Some-thing for Thee.
Some song to raise or prayer, Some-thing for Thee.
Some wan - d'rer sought and won, Some-thing for Thee.
Thro' all e - ter - ni - ty Some-thing for Thee. A - men.

Soul, What Return Has God, Thy Savior

404

9. 8. 9. 8. 8. 8.

Mark 12 : 17
Was gibst du denn, o meine Seele
Karl F. Lochner, 1673, ab.
Tr., composite

O dass ich tausend
Kornelius H. Dretzel, 1731

1 Soul, what re - turn has God, thy Sav-ior, For all He gives thee
2 Give un - to God thy heart's af - fec - tion, Who else can claim thee
3 Ac - cept the gift which Thou re - quir-est, My heart and soul, O
4 Whom should I give my heart's af - fec - tion But Thee, who giv - est

day by day? Oh, hast thou in thy gift a fa - vor
as His own? Should Sa-tan hold thee in sub - jec - tion?
gra - cious God, The first fruits Thou so much de - sir - est,
Thine to faith? Thy fer - vent love is my pro - tec - tion;

That can de - light and please Him?—Say! The best of of - f'rings
With him but pangs of hell are known. To Thee a - lone, O
For which Thy Son paid with His blood. To Thee I will - ing-
Lord, Thou hast loved me un - to death. My heart with Thine shall

He re - quires: Thy heart it is that He de - sires.
Lord di - vine, My heart and all I now re - sign.
ly as - sign My heart, dear Lord, for it is Thine.
ev - er be One heart through-out e - ter - ni - ty. A - men.

405 I Gave My Life for Thee

6. 6. 6. 6. 6. 6.

Phil. 1: 27
Frances R. Havergal, 1858

Old 120th
"Psalter"
Thomas Este, 1592

1 I gave My life for thee, My pre-cious blood I shed,
2 I spent long years for thee In wea-ri-ness and woe
3 My Fa-ther's home of light, My rain-bow-cir-cled throne,
4 I suf-fered much for thee, More than My tongue may tell,

That thou might'st ran-somed be And quick-ened from the dead.
That an e-ter-ni-ty Of joy thou might-est know.
I left for earth-ly night, For wan-d'rings sad and lone.
Of bit-t'rest ag-o-ny, To res-cue thee from hell.

I gave My life for thee; What hast thou giv'n for Me?
I spent long years for thee; Hast thou spent one for Me?
I left it all for thee; Hast thou left aught for Me?
I suf-fered much for thee; What canst thou bear for Me? A-men.

5 And I have brought to thee
    Down from My home above
Salvation full and free,
    My pardon and My love.
Great gifts I brought to thee;
What hast thou brought to Me?

6 Oh, let thy life be given,
    Thy years for Me be spent,
World's fetters all be riven,
    And joy with suffering blent!
I gave Myself for thee:
Give thou thyself to Me.

Lord, as Thou Wilt, Deal Thou with Me 406

8. 7. 8. 7. 8. 8. 7.

Ps. 40: 8
Herr, wie du willst, so schick's mit mir
Kaspar Bienemann, 1574
Tr., Emanuel Cronenwett, 1880, alt.

Herr, wie du willst
"Deutsch Kirchenamt"
Strassburg, 1525

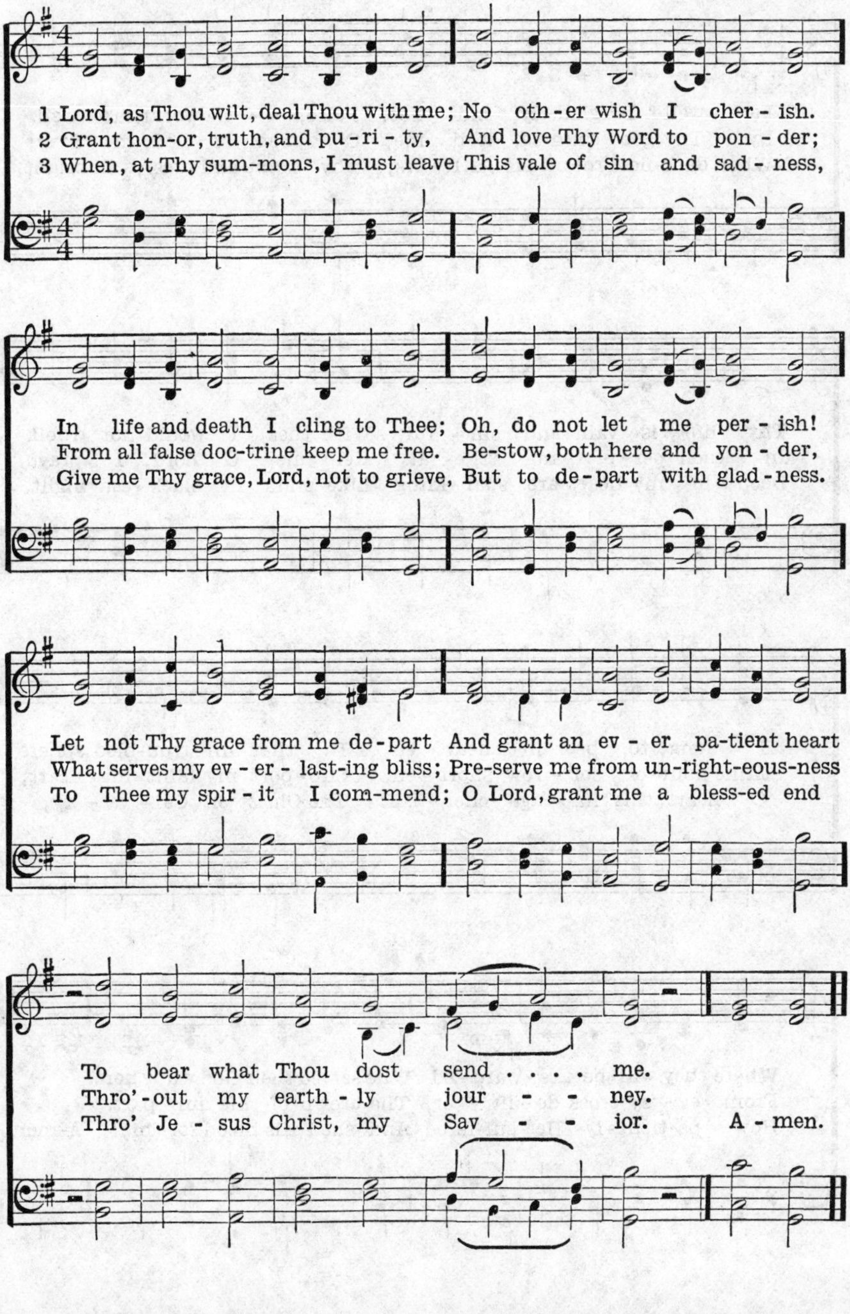

1 Lord, as Thou wilt, deal Thou with me; No oth-er wish I cher-ish.
2 Grant hon-or, truth, and pu-ri-ty, And love Thy Word to pon-der;
3 When, at Thy sum-mons, I must leave This vale of sin and sad-ness,

In life and death I cling to Thee; Oh, do not let me per-ish!
From all false doc-trine keep me free. Be-stow, both here and yon-der,
Give me Thy grace, Lord, not to grieve, But to de-part with glad-ness.

Let not Thy grace from me de-part And grant an ev-er pa-tient heart
What serves my ev-er-last-ing bliss; Pre-serve me from un-right-eous-ness
To Thee my spir-it I com-mend; O Lord, grant me a bless-ed end

To bear what Thou dost send . . . . me.
Thro'-out my earth-ly jour--ney.
Thro' Je-sus Christ, my Sav--ior. A-men.

407 Farewell I Gladly Bid Thee

Rev. 3: 5
7. 6. 7. 6. D.

Valet will ich dir geben
Valerius Herberger, 1613
Tr., Catherine Winkworth, 1863, alt.

Valet will ich dir geben
Melchior Teschner, 1613

1 Fare - well I glad - ly bid thee, False, e - vil world, fare - well.
2 By Thy good coun - sel lead me, O Son of God, my Stay;
3 When dark - ness round me gath - ers, Thy name and cross, still bright,

Thy life is vain and sin - ful, With thee I would not dwell.
In each per - plex - ing tri - al Help me, O Lord, I pray.
Deep in my heart are spar - kling Like stars in black - est night.

I long to be in heav - en, In that un - trou - bled sphere
Mine hour of sor - row short - en, Sup - port my faint - ing heart,
O heart, this im - age cher - ish: The Christ on Cal - va - ry,

Where they will be re - ward - ed Who served their God while here.
From ev - 'ry cross de - liv - er, The crown of life im - part.
How pa - tient - ly He suf - fered And shed His blood for me! A - men.

Farewell I Gladly Bid Thee

4 Lord, hide my soul securely
   Deep in Thy wounded side;
  From every danger shield me
   And to Thy glory guide.
  He has been truly blessèd
   Who reaches heaven above;
  He has found perfect healing
   Who rests upon Thy love.

5 Lord, write my name, I pray Thee,
   Now in the Book of Life
  And with all true believers
   Take me where joys are rife.
  There let me bloom and flourish,
   Thy perfect freedom prove,
  And tell, as I adore Thee,
   How faithful was Thy love.

Jesus Christ, My Pride and Glory   408

Luke 2: 41—52
Jesus selbst, mein Licht, mein Leben
Johann Olearius, 1671, cento
Tr., Paul E. Kretzmann, 1939

8. 7. 7. 8. 7. 7.

Ach, was soll ich Sünder machen
"Hirtenlieder"
Altdorf, 1653

1 Je - sus Christ, my Pride and Glo-ry, He, the true and liv-ing Light,
2 Let me live to praise Thee ev - er, Je - sus, Thou my heart's De-light,
3 Grant me, Lord, Thy Ho-ly Spir - it That in all I fol - low Him
4 From all pain and im - per - fec-tion, Gra-cious Lord, de - liv - er me,

Strengthens me with glo-rious might. Christ, re-vealed in sa - cred sto - ry,
Thou who lead-est me a - right. Let me cling to Thee for - ev - er,
Lest the light of faith grow dim. Let me ev - er trust Thy mer - it,
Heav - en's glo - ry let me see. Keep me un - der Thy di - rec - tion

Whom I now as Lord con - fess, Teach-es me true ho - li - ness.
All the flesh-ly lusts de - ny, And the dev - il's hosts de - fy.
Let Thy bless-ing me at - tend, From all e - vil me de - fend.
That the grace Thou gav-est me I may praise e - ter - nal - ly. A-men.

409 Let Us Ever Walk with Jesus

John 11: 16
Lasset uns mit Jesu ziehen
Sigismund von Birken, 1653
Tr., J. Adam Rimbach, 1900

8. 7. 8. 7. 8. 7. 7. 8. 7. 7.

Lasset uns mit Jesu ziehen
Georg G. Boltze, 1788

1 Let us ev-er walk with Je-sus, Fol-low His ex-am-ple pure,
2 Let us suf-fer here with Je-sus, To His im-age e'er con-form;
3 Let us al-so die with Je-sus. His death from the sec-ond death,
4 Let us glad-ly live with Je-sus; Since He's ris-en from the dead,

Flee the world, which would deceive us And to sin our souls al-lure.
Heav-en's glo-ry soon will please us, Sun-shine fol-low on the storm.
From our soul's de-struc-tion, frees us, Quick-ens us with life's glad breath.
Death and grave must soon re-lease us. Je-sus, Thou art now our Head,

Ev-er in His foot-steps tread-ing, Bod-y here, yet soul a-bove,
Tho' we sow in tears of sor-row, We shall reap in heav'n-ly joy;
Let us mor-ti-fy, while liv-ing, Flesh and blood and die to sin;
We are tru-ly Thine own mem-bers; Where Thou liv-est, there live we.

Full of faith and hope and love, Let us do the Fa-ther's bid-ding.
And the fears that now an-noy Shall be laugh-ter on the mor-row.
And the grave that shuts us in Shall but prove the gate to heav-en.
Take and own us con-stant-ly, Faith-ful Friend, as Thy dear breth-ren.

Let Us Ever Walk with Jesus

Faith-ful Lord, a-bide with me; Sav-ior, lead, I fol-low Thee.
Christ, I suf-fer here with Thee; There, oh, share Thy joy with me!
Je - sus, here I die to Thee There to live e-ter-nal-ly.
Je - sus, here I live to Thee, Al - so there e-ter-nal-ly. A-men.

Jesus, Lead Thou On

410

Luke 5 : 11
Jesu, geh voran
Ludwig von Zinzendorf, 1721
Cento by Christian Gregor, 1778
Tr., Jane Borthwick, 1854, alt.

5. 5. 8. 8. 5. 5.

Seelenbräutigam
Adam Drese, 1697

1 Je - sus, lead Thou on   Till our rest is   won; And al-though the
2 If   the way be drear,   If   the Foe be   near, Let not faith-less
3 When we seek re - lief   From a long-felt grief; When temp-ta-tions
4 Je - sus, lead Thou on   Till our rest is   won. Heav'n-ly Lead-er,

way be cheer-less,   We will fol-low   calm and fear-less.
fears o'er-take us;   Let not faith and   hope for-sake us;
come al - lur-ing,   Make us pa-tient   and en-dur-ing;
still di-rect us,   Still sup-port, con-trol, pro-tect us,

Guide us by   Thy hand   To   our fa-ther-land.
For through man-y a   woe   To   our home we   go.
Show us that bright shore   Where we weep no more.
Till   we safe-ly stand   In   our fa-ther-land. A-men.

411
From Eternity, O God

Acts 8: 15
Gott, du hast in deinem Sohn
Caspar Neumann, 1711, ab.
Tr., August Crull, †1923, alt.

7. 8. 7. 8. 8. 8.

Liebster Jesu
Johann R. Ahle, 1664

1 From e-ter-ni-ty, O God, In Thy Son Thou
2 Though a-live, I'm dead in sin, Lost to all good
3 Drive a-way the gloom-y night Of my heart's per-

didst e-lect me; There-fore, Fa-ther, on life's road
things by na-ture. Ho-ly Ghost, change me with-in,
verse re-flec-tion; Quench all tho'ts that are not right,

Gra-cious-ly to heav'n di-rect me; Send to me Thy
Make of me a new-born crea-ture; For the flesh works
Hold my rea-son in sub-jec-tion; Grant that I from

Ho-ly Spir-it That His gifts I may in-her-it.
ru-i-na-tion And can nev-er gain sal-va-tion.
Thee, with yearn-ing, Wis-dom al-ways may be learn-ing. A-men.

4 Oh, create a heart in me
   That in Thee, my God, believeth
And o'er the iniquity
   Of my sins most truly grieveth.
When dark hours of woe betide me,
In the wounds of Jesus hide me.

5 As a branch upon a vine
   In my blessed Lord implant me;
Ever of my Head divine
   To remain a member grant me.
Oh, let Him, my Lord and Savior,
Be my Life and Love forever!

From Eternity, O God

6 Faith and hope and charity
  Graciously, O Father, give me;
Be my Guardian constantly
  That the devil may not grieve me;
Grant me humbleness and gladness,
Peace and patience in my sadness.

7 Help me speak what's right and good
  And keep silence on occasion;
Help me pray, Lord, as I should,
  Help me bear my tribulation;
Help me die and let my spirit
Everlasting life inherit.

May We Thy Precepts, Lord, Fulfil

412

Matt 6: 10
Edward Osler, 1836, alt.

8. 8. 6. 8. 8. 6.

Meribah
Lowell Mason, 1839

1 May we Thy pre-cepts, Lord, ful-fil And do on earth our Fa-ther's will As an-gels do a-bove; Still walk in Christ, the liv-ing Way, With all Thy chil-dren and o-bey The law of Chris-tian love.

2 So may we join Thy name to bless, Thy grace a-dore, Thy pow'r con-fess, From sin and strife to flee. One is our call-ing, one our name, The end of all our hopes the same, A crown of life with Thee.

3 Spir-it of Life, of Love, and Peace, U-nite our hearts, our joy in-crease, Thy gra-cious help sup-ply. To each of us the bless-ing give In Chris-tian fel-low-ship to live, In joy-ful hope to die. A-men.

413 I Walk in Danger All the Way

1 Pet. 5: 8
Jeg gaar i Fare, hvor jeg gaar
Hans A. Brorson, 1734
Tr., Ditlef G. Ristad, 1909, alt.

8. 7. 8. 7. 6. 6. 8. 8.

Der lieben Sonne Licht und Pracht
"Geistreiches Gesangbuch"
Halle, 1704

1 I walk in dan-ger all the way. The tho't shall nev-er leave me
2 I pass thro' tri-als all the way, With sin and ills con-tend-ing;
3 Death doth pur-sue me all the way, No-where I rest se-cure-ly;
4 I walk with an-gels all the way, They shield me and be-friend me;

That Sa-tan, who has marked his prey, Is plot-ting to de-ceive me.
In pa-tience I must bear each day The cross of God's own send-ing.
He comes by night, he comes by day, And takes his prey most sure-ly.
All Sa-tan's pow'r is held at bay When heav'n-ly hosts at-tend me;

This Foe with hid-den snares May seize me un-a-wares If e'er I
Oft in ad-ver-si-ty I know not where to flee; When storms of
A fail-ing breath, and I In death's strong grasp may lie To face e-
They are my sure de-fense, All fear and sor-row, hence! Un-harmed by

fail to watch and pray. I walk in dan-ger all the way.
woe my soul dis-may, I pass thro' tri-als all the way.
ter-ni-ty for aye. Death doth pur-sue me all the way.
foes, do what they may, I walk with an-gels all the way. A-men.

I Walk in Danger All the Way

5 I walk with Jesus all the way,
   His guidance never fails me;
Within His wounds I find a stay
   When Satan's power assails me;
And by His footsteps led,
My path I safely tread.
In spite of ills that threaten may,
I walk with Jesus all the way.

6 My walk is heavenward all the way;
   Await, my soul, the morrow,
When thou shalt find release for aye
   From all thy sin and sorrow.
All worldly pomp, begone!
To heaven I now press on.
For all the world I would not stay;
My walk is heavenward all the way.

The Man Is Ever Blest   414

Ps. 1   S. M.   St. Michael
Isaac Watts, 1719   "Genevan Psalter," 1551

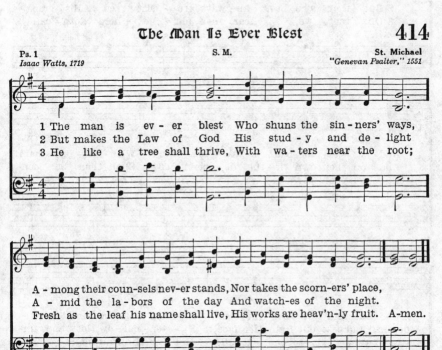

1 The man is ev-er blest Who shuns the sin-ners' ways,
2 But makes the Law of God His stud-y and de-light
3 He like a tree shall thrive, With wa-ters near the root;

A - mong their coun-sels nev-er stands, Nor takes the scorn-ers' place,
A - mid the la-bors of the day And watch-es of the night.
Fresh as the leaf his name shall live, His works are heav'n-ly fruit. A-men.

4 Not so th' ungodly race,
   They no such blessings find;
Their hopes shall flee like empty chaff
   Before the driving wind.

5 How will they bear to stand
   Before that judgment seat
Where all the saints at Christ's right hand
   In full assembly meet?

6 He knows, and He approves,
   The way the righteous go;
But sinners and their works shall meet
   A dreadful overthrow.

415 Lo, Many Shall Come from the East and the West

Matt. 8 : 11, 12
Der mange skal komme fra öst og fra vest
Magnus B. Landstad, 1861
Tr., Peer O. Strömme, 1909

11. 9. 11. 9. 9.

Der mange skal komme
"Then Swenska Psalmboken"
Stockholm, 1695

1 Lo, man - y shall come from the East and the West
2 But they who have al - ways re - sist - ed His grace
3 Oh, may we all hear when our Shep - herd doth call

And sit at the feast of sal - va - tion With A - bra - ham,
And on their own vir - tue de - pend - ed Shall then be con-
In ac-cents per-sua-sive and ten - der, That, while there is

I - saac, and Ja - cob, the blest, O - bey - ing the Lord's in - vi-
demned and cast out from His face, E - ter - nal - ly lost and un-
time, we make haste, one and all, And find Him, our might - y De-

ta - tion. Have mer-cy up - on us, O Je - sus!
friend - ed. Have mer-cy up - on us, O Je - sus!
fend - er! Have mer-cy up - on us, O Je - sus! A - men.

Lo, Many Shall Come from the East and the West

4 Oh, that we the throng of the ransomed may swell,
    To whom He hath granted remission!
God graciously make us in heaven to dwell
    And save us from endless perdition.
       Have mercy upon us, O Jesus!

5 God grant that I may, of His infinite love,
    Remain in His merciful keeping
And sit with the King at His table above
    When here in the grave I am sleeping.
       Have mercy upon us, O Jesus!

6 All trials are then like a dream that is past,
    Forgotten all trouble and sorrow;
All questions and doubts have been answered at last;
    Then dawneth eternity's morrow.
       Have mercy upon us, O Jesus!

7 The heavens shall ring with an anthem more grand
    Than ever on earth was recorded;
The blest of the Lord shall receive at His hand
    The crown to the victors awarded.
       Have mercy upon us, O Jesus!

Oh, that the Lord Would Guide My Ways   416

Ps. 119: 5, 33   C. M.   Evan
Isaac Watts, 1719, cento, alt.   *William H. Havergal, 1846*

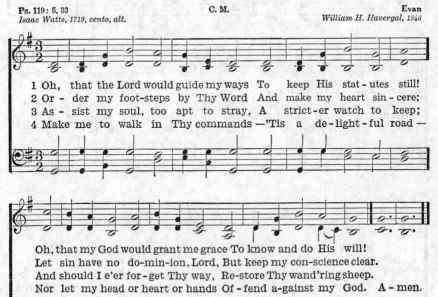

1 Oh, that the Lord would guide my ways To keep His stat-utes still!
2 Or - der my foot-steps by Thy Word And make my heart sin - cere;
3 As - sist my soul, too apt to stray, A strict-er watch to keep;
4 Make me to walk in Thy commands —'Tis a de-light-ful road—

Oh, that my God would grant me grace To know and do His will!
Let sin have no do-min-ion, Lord, But keep my con-science clear.
And should I e'er for - get Thy way, Re-store Thy wand'ring sheep.
Nor let my head or heart or hands Of-fend a-gainst my God. A - men.

417 How Can I Thank Thee, Lord

Ps. 50: 14
6. 7. 6. 7. 6. 6. 6. 6.

Was kann ich doch für Dank
David Denicke, 1648, asc., ab.
St. 6, Johann Heermann, 1630
Tr., August Crull, †1923, alt.

O Gott, du frommer Gott
"Neuvermehrtes Gesangbuch"
Meiningen, 1693

1 How can I thank Thee, Lord, For all Thy lov-ing-kind-ness,
2 It is Thy work a-lone That I am now con-vert-ed;
3 I could but grieve Thee, Lord, And with my sins dis-please Thee;
4 But Thou hast raised me up To joy and ex-ul-ta-tion

That Thou hast pa-tient-ly Borne with me in my blind-ness?
O'er Sa-tan's work in me Thou hast Thy pow'r as-sert-ed.
Yet to a-tone for sin My works could not ap-pease Thee.
And clear-ly shown the way That leads me to sal-va-tion.

When dead in man-y sins And tres-pass-es I lay,
Thy mer-cy and Thy grace That rise a-fresh each morn
Though I could fall from grace And choose the way of sin,
My sins are washed a-way, For this I thank Thee, Lord;

I kin-dled, ho-ly God, Thine an-ger ev-'ry day.
Have turned my ston-y heart In-to a heart new-born.
I had no strength to rise, A new life to be-gin.
And with my heart and soul All dead works are ab-horred. A-men.

How Can I Thank Thee, Lord

5 Grant that Thy Spirit's help
  To me be always given
Lest I should fall again
  And lose the way to heaven;
That He may give me strength
  In mine infirmity
And e'er renew my heart
  To serve Thee willingly.

6 Oh, guide and lead me, Lord,
  While here below I wander
That I may follow Thee
  Till I shall see Thee yonder.

For if I led myself,
  I soon would go astray;
But if Thou leadest me,
  I keep the narrow way.

7 O Father, God of Love,
  Hear Thou my supplication;
O Savior, Son of God,
  Grant me Thy full salvation;
And Thou, O Holy Ghost,
  Be Thou my faithful Guide
That I may serve Thee here
  And there with Thee abide.

My God, My Father, While I Stray — 418

Matt. 26 : 42
Charlotte Elliott, 1834–1839

8. 8. 8. 4.

Es ist kein Tag
Johann D. Meyer, 1692

1 My God, my Fa-ther, while I stray Far from my home on life's rough way,
2 Tho' dark my path and sad my lot, Let me be still and mur-mur not
3 What tho' in lone-ly grief I sigh For friends be-loved, no long-er nigh,
4 Tho' Thou hast called me to re-sign What most I prized, it ne'er was mine;

Oh, teach me from my heart to say, "Thy will be done."
Or breathe the prayer di-vine-ly taught, "Thy will be done."
Sub-mis-sive still would I re-ply— "Thy will be done."
I have but yield-ed what was Thine—"Thy will be done." A-men.

5 Should grief or sickness waste away
  My life in premature decay,
My Father, still I strive to say,
  "Thy will be done."

6 Let but my fainting heart be blest
  With Thy sweet Spirit for its Guest;
My God, to Thee I leave the rest—
  "Thy will be done."

7 Renew my will from day to day;
  Blend it with Thine and take away
All that now makes it hard to say,
  "Thy will be done."

8 Then, when on earth I breathe no more,
  The prayer, oft mixed with tears before,
I'll sing upon a happier shore,
  "Thy will be done."

419 O'er Jerusalem Thou Weepest

Luke 19 : 41
Anna Hoppe, 1919, alt.

8. 7. 8. 7. 7. 7. 8. 8.

Freu dich sehr
"Genevan Psalter," 1551

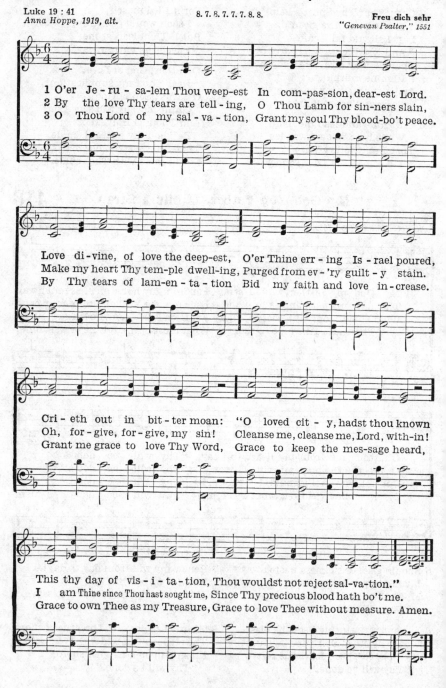

1 O'er Je - ru - sa-lem Thou weep-est In com-pas-sion, dear-est Lord.
2 By the love Thy tears are tell - ing, O Thou Lamb for sin-ners slain,
3 O Thou Lord of my sal - va - tion, Grant my soul Thy blood-bo't peace.

Love di - vine, of love the deep-est, O'er Thine err - ing Is - rael poured,
Make my heart Thy tem-ple dwell-ing, Purged from ev - 'ry guilt - y stain.
By Thy tears of lam-en - ta - tion Bid my faith and love in - crease.

Cri - eth out in bit - ter moan: "O loved cit - y, hadst thou known
Oh, for - give, for - give, my sin! Cleanse me, cleanse me, Lord, with-in!
Grant me grace to love Thy Word, Grace to keep the mes-sage heard,

This thy day of vis - i - ta - tion, Thou wouldst not reject sal-va-tion."
I am Thine since Thou hast sought me, Since Thy precious blood hath bo't me.
Grace to own Thee as my Treasure, Grace to love Thee without measure. Amen.

My Jesus, as Thou Wilt

6. 6. 6. 6. D.

Mark 14: 36
Mein Jesu, wie du willt
Benjamin Schmolck, 1704, cento
Tr., Jane Borthwick, 1854

Denby
Charles J. Dale, 1904

1 My Je-sus, as Thou wilt; Oh, may Thy will be mine!
2 My Je-sus, as Thou wilt. If need-y here and poor,
3 My Je-sus, as Thou wilt. Tho' seen thro' man-y a tear,

In - to Thy hand of love I would my all re - sign.
Give me Thy peo-ple's bread, Thy Word, so rich and sure.
Let not my star of hope Grow dim or dis - ap - pear.

Thro' sor - row or thro' joy Con-duct me as Thine own
This man - na from a - bove Let my soul feed up - on;
Since Thou on earth hast wept And sor-rowed oft a - lone,

And help me still to say, My Lord, Thy will be done.
And if all else should fail, My Lord, Thy will be done.
If I must weep with Thee, My Lord, Thy will be done. A-men.

4 My Jesus, as Thou wilt.
  When death itself draws nigh,
Unto Thy wounded side
  For refuge I would fly
And, clinging to Thee, go
  Where Thou before hast gone.
My times are in Thy hand:
  My Lord, Thy will be done.

5 My Jesus, as Thou wilt.
  All shall be well for me;
Each changing future scene
  I gladly trust with Thee.
Thus to my home above
  I travel calmly on
And sing in life or death,
  My Lord, Thy will be done.

421

Come, Follow Me, the Savior Spake

Matt. 16: 24

Mir nach, spricht Christus, unser Held
Johann Scheffler, 1668, cento
Tr., Charles W. Schaeffer, †1896, alt.

8. 7. 8. 7. 8. 8.

Mach's mit mir, Gott
J. Hermann Schein, 1628

1 Come, fol - low Me, the Sav - ior spake, All in My way a - bid - ing; De - ny your-selves, the world for-sake, O - bey My call and guid - ing. Oh, bear the cross, what-e'er be - tide, Take My ex - am - ple for your guide.

2 I am the Light, I light the way, A god - ly life dis-play - ing; I bid you walk as in the day, I keep your feet from stray - ing. I am the Way, and well I show How you must so - journ here be - low.

3 My heart a - bounds in low - li - ness, My soul with love is glow - ing, And gra-cious words my lips ex - press, With meek-ness o - ver - flow - ing. My heart, My mind, My strength, My all, To God I yield, on Him I call. A-men.

4 I teach you how to shun and flee
   What harms your soul's salvation,
Your heart from every guile to free,
   From sin and its temptation.
I am the Refuge of the soul
And lead you to your heavenly goal.

5 Then let us follow Christ, our Lord,
   And take the cross appointed
And, firmly clinging to His Word,
   In suffering be undaunted.
For who bears not the battle's strain
The crown of life shall not obtain.

Savior, I Follow On

422

Ex. 15: 23
Charles S. Robinson, 1862

6. 4. 6. 4. 6. 6. 6. 4.

Winterton
Joseph Barnby, 1892

1 Sav - ior, I fol - low on, Guid - ed by Thee,
2 Riv - en the rock for me Thirst to re - lieve,
3 Of - ten to Ma - rah's brink Have I been brought;
4 Sav - ior, I long to walk Clos - er with Thee;

See - ing not yet the hand That lead - eth me.
Man - na from heav - en falls Fresh ev - 'ry eve.
Shrink - ing the cup to drink, Help I have sought;
Led by Thy guid - ing hand, Ev - er to be

Hushed be my heart and still, Fear I no fur - ther ill,
Nev - er a want se - vere Caus - eth my eye a tear
And with the prayer's as - cent Je - sus the branch hath rent,
Con - stant - ly near Thy side, Quick-ened and pu - ri - fied,

On - ly to meet Thy will My will shall be.
But Thou dost whis - per near, "On - ly be - lieve."
Quick - ly re - lief hath sent, Sweet-'ning the draught.
Liv - ing for Him who died Free - ly for me. A - men.

423 Jesus, I My Cross Have Taken

Luke 18 : 28
Henry Francis Lyte, 1824

8. 7. 8. 7. D.

Hyfrydol
Rowland H. Prichard, 1855, alt.

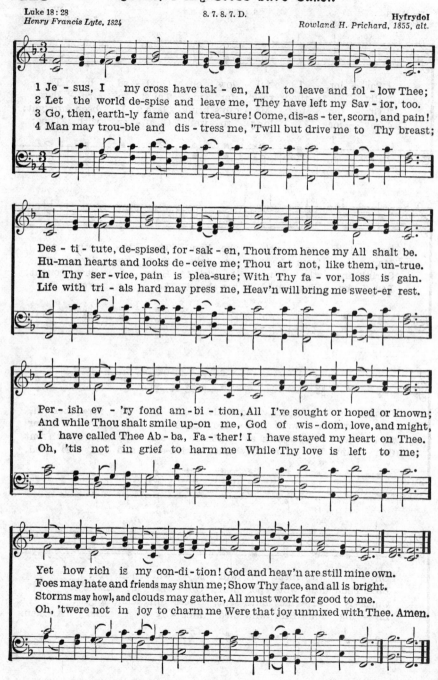

1 Je - sus, I my cross have tak - en, All to leave and fol - low Thee;
2 Let the world de-spise and leave me, They have left my Sav - ior, too.
3 Go, then, earth-ly fame and trea-sure! Come, dis-as - ter, scorn, and pain!
4 Man may trou-ble and dis - tress me, 'Twill but drive me to Thy breast;

Des - ti - tute, de-spised, for - sak - en, Thou from hence my All shalt be.
Hu-man hearts and looks de - ceive me; Thou art not, like them, un-true.
In Thy ser - vice, pain is plea-sure; With Thy fa - vor, loss is gain.
Life with tri - als hard may press me, Heav'n will bring me sweet-er rest.

Per - ish ev - 'ry fond am - bi - tion, All I've sought or hoped or known;
And while Thou shalt smile up - on me, God of wis - dom, love, and might,
I have called Thee Ab - ba, Fa - ther! I have stayed my heart on Thee.
Oh, 'tis not in grief to harm me While Thy love is left to me;

Yet how rich is my con-di-tion! God and heav'n are still mine own.
Foes may hate and friends may shun me; Show Thy face, and all is bright.
Storms may howl, and clouds may gather, All must work for good to me.
Oh, 'twere not in joy to charm me Were that joy unmixed with Thee. Amen.

Jesus, ¶ My Cross have Taken

5 Take, my soul, thy full salvation;
   Rise o'er sin and fear and care;
Joy to find in every station,
   Something still to do or bear.
Think what Spirit dwells within thee,
   What a Father's smile is thine,
What a Savior died to win thee;
   Child of heaven, shouldst thou re-
      pine?

6 Haste, then, on from grace to glory,
   Armed by faith and winged by prayer;
Heaven's eternal day's before thee,
   God's own hand shall guide thee
      there.
Soon shall close the earthly mission,
   Swift shall pass thy pilgrim days,
Hope soon change to glad fruition,
   Faith to sight, and prayer to praise.

My God, My Father, Make Me Strong 424

Ps. 143: 8
Frederick Mann, †1928

8. 8. 8. 4.

Es ist kein Tag
Johann D. Meyer, 1692

1 My God, my Father, make me strong, When tasks of life seem hard and long,
2 Draw from my timid eyes the veil   To show, where earthly forces fail,
3 With confident and humble mind Freedom in service I would find,
4 Things deemed impossible I dare,   Thine is the call and Thine the care;

To greet them with this triumph song: Thy will be done.
Thy pow'r and love must still prevail— Thy will be done.
Praying thro' ev-'ry toil as-signed: Thy will be done.
Thy wisdom shall the way prepare— Thy will be done. A-men.

5 All power is here and round me now;
   Faithful I stand in rule and vow,
   While 'tis not I, but ever Thou:
      Thy will be done.

6 Heaven's music chimes the glad days in;
   Hope soars beyond death, pain, and sin;
   Faith shouts in triumph, Love must win—
      Thy will be done!

425 All Depends on Our Possessing

Prov. 10 : 22
Alles ist an Gottes Segen
Author unknown, c. 1673
Tr., Catherine Winkworth, 1858, alt.

8. 8. 7. 8. 8. 7.

Alles ist an Gottes Segen
Johann B. König, 1738

1 All depends on our possessing God's abundant grace and blessing, Tho' all earthly wealth depart.

He who trusts with faith unshaken In his God is not forsaken And e'er keeps a dauntless heart.

2 He who hitherto hath fed me And to many joys hath led me, Is and ever shall be mine.

He who did so gently school me, He who still doth guide and rule me, Will remain my Help divine.

3 Many spend their lives in fretting Over trifles and in getting Things that have no solid ground.

I shall strive to win a treasure That will bring me lasting pleasure And that now is seldom found.

4 When with sorrow I am stricken, Hope my heart anew will quicken, All my longing shall be stilled.

To His loving-kindness tender Soul and body I surrender; For on Him alone I build. A-men.

All Depends on Our Possessing

5 Well He knows what best to grant me;
  All the longing hopes that haunt me,
    Joy and sorrow, have their day.
  I shall doubt His wisdom never —
  As God wills, so be it ever. —
    I to Him commit my way.

6 If on earth my days He lengthen,
  He my weary soul will strengthen;
    All my trust in Him I place.
  Earthly wealth is not abiding,
  Like a stream away is gliding;
    Safe I anchor in His grace.

The Lord My Shepherd Is
426

S. M.

Ps. 23
Isaac Watts, 1719

Potsdam
"Church Psalter," 1854
Johann S. Bach, †1750, ad.

1 The Lord my Shep-herd is, I shall be well sup-plied.
2 He leads me to the place Where heav'n-ly pas-ture grows,
3 If e'er I go a-stray, He doth my soul re-claim

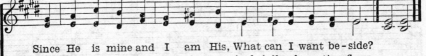

Since He is mine and I am His, What can I want be-side?
Where liv-ing wa-ters gen-tly pass And full sal-va-tion flows.
And guides me in His own right way For His most ho-ly name. A-men.

4 While He affords His aid,
  I cannot yield to fear;
  Though I should walk through death's dark shade,
  My Shepherd's with me there.

5 Amid surrounding foes
  Thou dost my table spread;
  My cup with blessing overflows,
  And joy exalts my head.

6 The bounties of Thy love
  Shall crown my following days,
  Nor from Thy house will I remove
  Nor cease to speak Thy praise.

427 How Firm a Foundation, Ye Saints of the Lord

11. 11. 11. 11.

Is. 43: 1–7
"Keen," 1787, alt.

Firm Foundation
Bernhard Schumacher, 1931

1 How firm a foun - da - tion, ye saints of the Lord,
2 In ev - 'ry con - di - tion — in sick - ness, in health,
3 "Fear not, I am with thee, oh, be not dis - mayed;
4 "When thro' the deep wa - ters I call thee to go,

Is laid for your faith in His ex - cel - lent Word!
In pov - er - ty's vale, or a - bound - ing in wealth,
For I am thy God and will still give thee aid;
The riv - ers of sor - row shall not o - ver - flow;

What more can He say than to you He hath said
At home and a - broad, on the land, on the sea —
I'll strength - en thee, help thee, and cause thee to stand,
For I will be with thee thy trou - bles to bless

Who un - to the Sav - ior for ref - uge have fled?
The Lord, the Al - might - y, thy strength e'er shall be.
Up - held by My right - eous, om - nip - o - tent hand.
And sanc - ti - fy to thee thy deep - est dis - tress. A - men.

How Firm a Foundation, Ye Saints of the Lord

5 "When through fiery trials thy pathway shall lie,
My grace, all-sufficient, shall be thy supply.
The flames shall not hurt thee; I only design
Thy dross to consume and thy gold to refine.

6 "E'en down to old age all My people shall prove
My sovereign, eternal, unchangeable love;
And when hoary hairs shall their temples adorn,
Like lambs they shall still in My bosom be borne.

7 "The soul that on Jesus hath leaned for repose
I will not, I will not, desert to his foes;
That soul, though all hell should endeavor to shake,
I'll never, no never, no never, forsake!"

I Am Trusting Thee, Lord Jesus 428

Acts 2: 33
Frances R. Havergal, 1874

8. 5. 8. 3.

Stephanos
Henry W. Baker, 1868

1 I am trust-ing Thee, Lord Je - sus, Trust-ing on - ly Thee;
2 I am trust-ing Thee for par - don; At Thy feet I bow,
3 I am trust-ing Thee for cleans-ing In the crim-son flood;
4 I am trust-ing Thee to guide me; Thou a - lone shalt lead,

Trust-ing Thee for full sal - va - tion, Great and free.
For Thy grace and ten - der mer - cy Trust-ing now.
Trust-ing Thee to make me ho - ly By Thy blood.
Ev - 'ry day and hour sup-ply - ing All my need. A-men.

5 I am trusting Thee for power;
Thine can never fail.
Words which Thou Thyself shalt give me
Must prevail.

6 I am trusting Thee, Lord Jesus;
Never let me fall.
I am trusting Thee forever
And for all.

429 Lord, Thee I Love with All My Heart

Ps. 18

Herzlich lieb hab' ich dich, o Herr
Martin Schalling, c. 1567
Tr., Catherine Winkworth, 1863, alt.

8. 8. 7. 8. 8. 7. 8. 8. 8. 8. 4. 8. 8.

Herzlich lieb hab' ich dich, o Herr
Bernhard Schmid's "Orgelbuch"
Strassburg, 1577

1 Lord, Thee I love with all my heart; I pray Thee, ne'er from
2 Yea, Lord, 'twas Thy rich boun-ty gave My bod-y, soul, and
3 Lord, let at last Thine an-gels come, To A-bram's bos-om

me de-part, With ten-der mer-cy cheer me.
all I have In this poor life of la - - bor.
bear me home, That I may die un-fear - - ing;

Earth has no plea-sure I would share, Yea, heav'n it - self were
Lord, grant that I in ev-'ry place May glo-ri-fy Thy
And in its nar-row cham-ber keep My bod-y safe in

void and bare If Thou, Lord, wert not near me.
lav-ish grace And serve and help my neigh-bor.
peace-ful sleep Un-til Thy re-ap-pear - - ing.

Lord, Thee I Love with All My Heart

And should my heart for sor-row break, My trust in
Let no false doc-trine me be-guile, Let Sa-tan
And then from death a-wak-en me That these mine

Thee no one could shake. Thou art the Por-tion
not my soul de-file. Give strength and pa-tience
eyes with joy may see, O Son of God, Thy

I have sought; Thy pre-cious blood my soul has bought.
un-to me To bear my cross and fol-low Thee.
glo-rious face, My Sav-ior and my Fount of grace.

Lord Je-sus Christ, My God and Lord, my God and Lord,
Lord Je-sus Christ, My God and Lord, my God and Lord,
Lord Je-sus Christ, My prayer at-tend, my prayer at-tend,

For-sake me not! I trust Thy Word.
In death Thy com-fort still af-ford.
And I will praise Thee with-out end. A-men.

430
What Is the World to Me

1 John 2 : 15–17
Was frag' ich nach der Welt
Georg M. Pfefferkorn, 1667
Tr., August Crull, †1923, alt.

6. 7. 6. 7. 6. 6. 6. 6.

Was frag' ich nach der Welt
Ahasverus Fritsch, 1679

1 What is the world to me With all its vaunt-ed plea-sure
2 The world is like a cloud And like a va-por fleet-ing,
3 The world seeks to be praised And hon-ored by the might-y,
4 The world seeks af-ter wealth And all that Mam-mon of-fers,

When Thou, and Thou a-lone, Lord Je-sus, art my Trea-sure!
A shad-ow that de-clines, Swift to its end re-treat-ing.
Yet nev-er once re-flects That they are frail and flight-y.
Yet nev-er is con-tent Tho' gold should fill its cof-fers.

Thou on-ly, dear-est Lord, My soul's De-light shalt be;
My Je-sus doth a-bide, Tho' all things fade and flee;
But what I tru-ly prize A-bove all things is He,
I have a high-er good, Con-tent with it I'll be:

Thou art my Peace, my Rest —What is the world to me!
My ev-er-last-ing Rock —What is the world to me!
My Je-sus, He a-lone —What is the world to me!
My Je-sus is my Wealth —What is the world to me! A-men.

What Is the World to Me

5 The world is sorely grieved
　　Whenever it is slighted
Or when its hollow fame
　　And honor have been blighted.
Christ, Thy reproach I bear
　　Long as it pleaseth Thee;
I'm honored by my Lord —
　　What is the world to me!

6 The world with wanton pride
　　Exalts its sinful pleasures
And for them foolishly
　　Gives up the heavenly treasures.
Let others love the world
　　With all its vanity;
I love the Lord, my God —
　　What is the world to me!

7 The world abideth not;
　　Lo, like a flash 'twill vanish;
With all its gorgeous pomp
　　Pale death it cannot banish;
Its riches pass away,
　　And all its joys must flee;
But Jesus doth abide —
　　What is the world to me!

8 What is the world to me!
　　My Jesus is my Treasure,
My Life, my Health, my Wealth,
　　My Friend, my Love, my Pleasure,
My Joy, my Crown, my All,
　　My Bliss eternally.
Once more, then, I declare:
　　What is the world to me!

The King of Love My Shepherd Is　　431

Ps. 23
Henry W. Baker, 1868

8. 7. 8. 7. Iambic

Ich dank' dir schon
Michael Prätorius, 1610

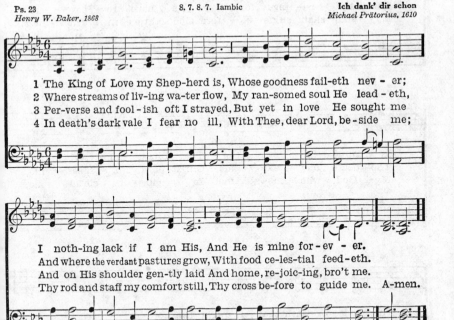

1 The King of Love my Shep-herd is, Whose goodness fail-eth nev-er;
2 Where streams of liv-ing wa-ter flow, My ran-somed soul He lead-eth,
3 Per-verse and fool-ish oft I strayed, But yet in love He sought me
4 In death's dark vale I fear no ill, With Thee, dear Lord, be-side me;

I noth-ing lack if I am His, And He is mine for-ev-er.
And where the verdant pastures grow, With food ce-les-tial feed-eth.
And on His shoulder gen-tly laid And home, re-joic-ing, bro't me.
Thy rod and staff my comfort still, Thy cross be-fore to guide me. A-men.

5 Thou spreadst a table in my sight,
　　Thy unction grace bestoweth;
And, oh! the transport of delight
　　With which my cup o'erfloweth.

6 And so through all the length of days
　　Thy goodness faileth never.
Good Shepherd, may I sing Thy praise
　　Within Thy house forever!

432 In Hope My Soul, Redeemed to Bliss Unending

Rom. 5: 5

11. 11. 5. 5. 11.

I hoppet sig min frälsta själ förnöjer
Elle Andersdatter, 1645
Tr., George H. Trabert, †1931

Norrland
Northern melody, 16th century

1 In hope my soul, re-deemed to bliss un-end-ing,
2 In Him I have sal-va-tion's way dis-cov-ered,
3 More ra-diant there than sun e'er shone in bright-ness,

To heav-en's glo-rious height by faith as-cend-ing,
The her-i-tage for me He hath re-cov-ered.
My soul shall shine be-fore God's throne in white-ness.

Is mind-ful ev-er That Christ did sev-er
Tho' death o'er-takes me, Christ ne'er for-sakes me,
My God, who knows me, In glo-ry clothes me,

The bonds of death that I might live for-ev-er.
To ev-er-last-ing life He sure-ly wakes me.
As He de-clared when for His own He chose me. A-men.

In Hope My Soul, Redeemed to Bliss Unending

4 Oh, may I come where strife and grief are ended,
Where all Thy saints shall meet with peace attended!
    Lord, grant Thy favor
    And mercy ever
And turn my sorrow into joy forever.

5 Lord Jesus Christ, keep me prepared and waking
Till from the vale of tears Thy bride Thou'rt taking
    To dwell in heaven,
    Where joy is given
And clouds of darkness are forever riven.

Jesus, My Truth, My Way   433

S. M.

John 14 : 6
Charles Wesley, 1749, cento

Swabia
Johann M. Spiess, 1745

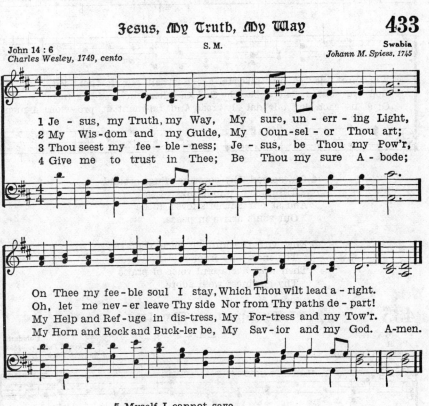

1 Je - sus, my Truth, my Way, My sure, un - err - ing Light,
2 My Wis - dom and my Guide, My Coun - sel - or Thou art;
3 Thou seest my fee - ble - ness; Je - sus, be Thou my Pow'r,
4 Give me to trust in Thee; Be Thou my sure A - bode;

On Thee my fee - ble soul I stay, Which Thou wilt lead a - right.
Oh, let me nev - er leave Thy side Nor from Thy paths de - part!
My Help and Ref - uge in dis - tress, My For - tress and my Tow'r.
My Horn and Rock and Buck - ler be, My Sav - ior and my God. A-men.

5 Myself I cannot save,
    Myself I cannot keep;
But strength in Thee I surely have,
    Whose eyelids never sleep.

6 My soul to Thee alone
    Now, therefore, I commend.
Thou, Jesus, having loved Thine own,
    Wilt love me to the end.

434

O God of Jacob, by Whose Hand

Gen. 28: 20-22
C. M.
St. 1-4, Philip Doddridge, 1737
Recast by John Logan, 1781, and st. 5

St. Savior
Frederick G. Baker, 1872

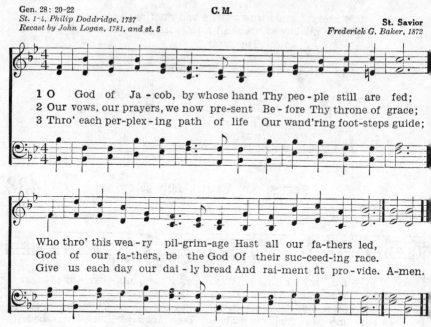

1 O God of Ja - cob, by whose hand Thy peo - ple still are fed;
2 Our vows, our prayers, we now pre-sent Be - fore Thy throne of grace;
3 Thro' each per-plex-ing path of life Our wand'ring foot-steps guide;

Who thro' this wea - ry pil-grim-age Hast all our fa-thers led,
God of our fa-thers, be the God Of their suc-ceed-ing race.
Give us each day our dai - ly bread And rai - ment fit pro-vide. A-men.

4 Oh, spread Thy covering wings around
   Till all our wanderings cease
And at our Father's loved abode
   Our souls arrive in peace.

5 Now with the humble voice of prayer
   Thy mercy we implore;
Then with a grateful voice of praise
   Thy goodness we'll adore.

435

My Spirit on Thy Care

S. M.

Potsdam
"Church Psalter," 1854
Johann S. Bach, 11750, ad.

Ps. 31
Henry F. Lyte, 1834

1 My spir - it on Thy care, Blest Sav - ior, I re - cline;
2 In Thee I place my trust, On Thee I calm - ly rest;
3 What-e'er e - vents be -'tide, Thy will they all per - form;
4 Let good or ill be - fall, It must be good for me;

My Spirit on Thy Care

Thou wilt not leave me to de-spair, For Thou art Love di-vine.
I know Thee good, I know Thee just, And count Thy choice the best.
Safe in Thy breast my head I hide Nor fear the com-ing storm.
Se - cure of hav-ing Thee in all, Of hav-ing all in Thee. A-men.

The Lord's My Shepherd, I'll Not Want **436**

Ps. 23
Francis Rous, et al., 1650

C. M.

Belmont
William Gardiner, 1812

1 The Lord's my Shep-herd, I'll not want; He makes me down to lie
2 My soul He doth re - store a - gain And me to walk doth make
3 Yea, tho' I walk in death's dark vale, Yet will I fear no ill;

In pas-tures green; He lead-eth me The qui - et wa - ters by.
With-in the paths of right-eous-ness, E'en for His own name's sake.
For Thou art with me, and Thy rod And staff me com-fort still. A - men.

4 My table Thou hast furnishèd
   In presence of my foes;
   My head Thou dost with oil anoint,
   And my cup overflows.

5 Goodness and mercy, all my life,
   Shall surely follow me;
   And in God's house forevermore
   My dwelling place shall be.

437 Who Trusts in God, a Strong Abode

Ps. 73 : 25, 26
Wer Gott vertraut, hat wohl gebaut
St. 1, Joachim Magdeburg, 1572
St. 2, 3, author unknown
Tr., Benjamin H. Kennedy, 1863

8. 7. 8. 7. D. Iambic

Was mein Gott will
French melody, 1529
Harm. by Johann S. Bach, †1750

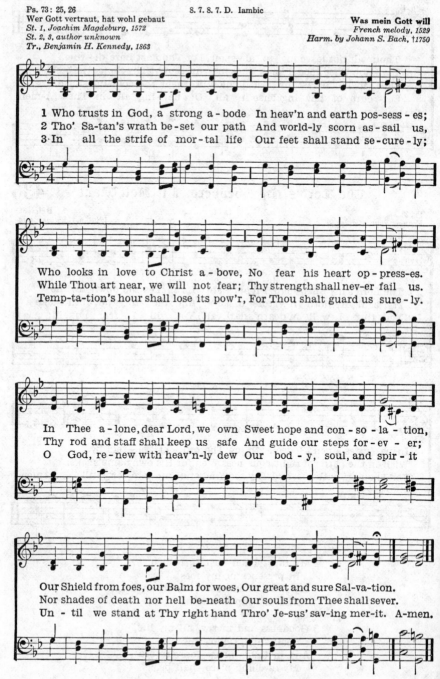

1 Who trusts in God, a strong a-bode In heav'n and earth pos-sess-es;
2 Tho' Sa-tan's wrath be-set our path And world-ly scorn as-sail us,
3 In all the strife of mor-tal life Our feet shall stand se-cure-ly;

Who looks in love to Christ a-bove, No fear his heart op-press-es.
While Thou art near, we will not fear; Thy strength shall nev-er fail us.
Temp-ta-tion's hour shall lose its pow'r, For Thou shalt guard us sure-ly.

In Thee a-lone, dear Lord, we own Sweet hope and con-so-la-tion,
Thy rod and staff shall keep us safe And guide our steps for-ev-er;
O God, re-new with heav'n-ly dew Our bod-y, soul, and spir-it

Our Shield from foes, our Balm for woes, Our great and sure Sal-va-tion.
Nor shades of death nor hell be-neath Our souls from Thee shall sever.
Un-til we stand at Thy right hand Thro' Je-sus' sav-ing mer-it. A-men.

Almighty Father, Heaven and Earth

438

L. M.

1 Pet. 4: 10
Edward A. Dayman, 1867, alt.

O heilige Dreifaltigkeit
Nikolaus Herman, 1560

1 Al - might - y Fa - ther, heav'n and earth With lav - ish
2 The wealth of earth, of sky, of sea, The gold, the
3 To Thee, as ear - ly morn-ing's dew, Our prais - es,

wealth be - fore Thee bow; Those trea-sures owe to Thee their birth,
sil - ver, spar-kling gem, The wav - ing corn, the bend - ing tree,
alms, and prayers shall rise As rose, when joy - ous earth was new,

Cre - a - tor, Rul - er, Giv - er, Thou.
Are Thine; to us Thou lend - est them.
Faith's pa - tri - ar - chal sac - ri - fice. A - men.

4 We, Lord, would lay at Thy behest
   The costliest offerings on Thy shrine;
But when we give, and give our best,
   We give Thee only what is Thine.

5 O Father, whence all blessings come;
   O Son, Dispenser of God's store;
O Spirit, bear our offerings home:
   Lord, make them Thine forevermore.

439 O God of Mercy, God of Might

Luke 10: 36, 37
Godfrey Thring, 1877, alt.

8. 8. 8. 6.

Isleworth
Samuel Howard, †1782

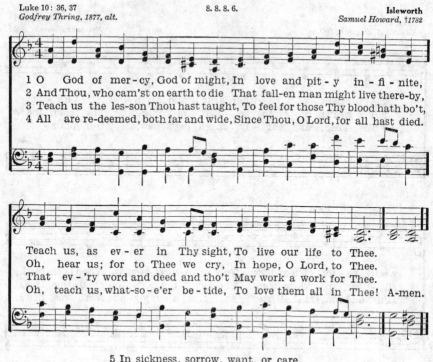

1 O God of mer-cy, God of might, In love and pit-y in-fi-nite,
2 And Thou, who cam'st on earth to die That fall-en man might live there-by,
3 Teach us the les-son Thou hast taught, To feel for those Thy blood hath bo't,
4 All are re-deemed, both far and wide, Since Thou, O Lord, for all hast died.

Teach us, as ev-er in Thy sight, To live our life to Thee.
Oh, hear us; for to Thee we cry, In hope, O Lord, to Thee.
That ev-'ry word and deed and tho't May work a work for Thee.
Oh, teach us, what-so-e'er be-tide, To love them all in Thee! A-men.

5 In sickness, sorrow, want, or care,
   Whate'er it be, 'tis ours to share;
   May we, where help is needed, there
      Give help as unto Thee!

6 And may Thy Holy Spirit move
   All those who live to live in love
   Till Thou shalt greet in heaven above
      All those who live to Thee.

440 Lord, Lead the Way the Savior Went

Matt. 25: 40
William Crosswell, 1831

C. M.

Farrant
Richard Farrant, †1580

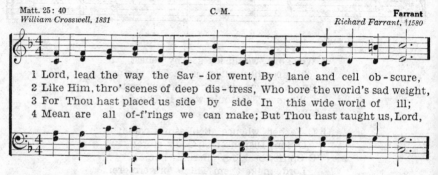

1 Lord, lead the way the Sav-ior went, By lane and cell ob-scure,
2 Like Him, thro' scenes of deep dis-tress, Who bore the world's sad weight,
3 For Thou hast placed us side by side In this wide world of ill;
4 Mean are all of-f'rings we can make; But Thou hast taught us, Lord,

Lord, Lead the Way the Savior Went

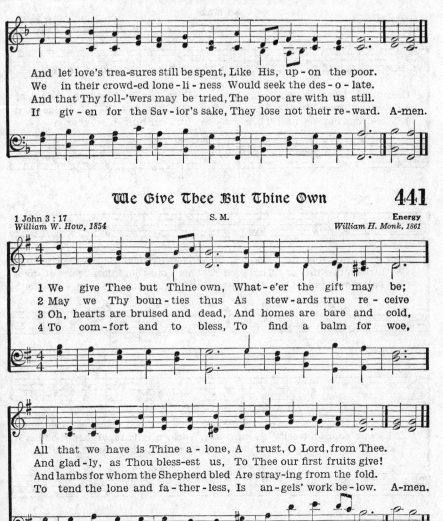

And let love's trea-sures still be spent, Like His, up-on the poor.
We in their crowd-ed lone-li-ness Would seek the des-o-late.
And that Thy foll-'wers may be tried, The poor are with us still.
If giv-en for the Sav-ior's sake, They lose not their re-ward. A-men.

We Give Thee But Thine Own   441

1 John 3 : 17   S. M.   Energy
William W. How, 1854   William H. Monk, 1861

1 We give Thee but Thine own, What-e'er the gift may be;
2 May we Thy boun-ties thus As stew-ards true re-ceive
3 Oh, hearts are bruised and dead, And homes are bare and cold,
4 To com-fort and to bless, To find a balm for woe,

All that we have is Thine a-lone, A trust, O Lord, from Thee.
And glad-ly, as Thou bless-est us, To Thee our first fruits give!
And lambs for whom the Shepherd bled Are stray-ing from the fold.
To tend the lone and fa-ther-less, Is an-gels' work be-low. A-men.

5 The captive to release,
   To God the lost to bring,
   To teach the way of life and peace,
   It is a Christlike thing.

6 And we believe Thy Word,
   Though dim our faith may be:
   Whate'er for Thine we do, O Lord,
   We do it unto Thee.

442 Lord of Glory, Who hast Bought Us

8. 7. 8. 7. D.

Acts 20 : 35
Eliza S. Alderson, 1864

Hyfrydol
Rowland H. Prichard, †1887, alt.

1 Lord of Glo - ry, who hast bo't us With Thy life-blood as the price,
2 Grant us hearts, dear Lord, to yield Thee Glad - ly, free - ly, of Thine own;
3 Won-drous hon-or hast Thou giv - en To our hum-blest char - i - ty

Nev - er grudg-ing for the lost ones That tre-men-dous sac - ri - fice;
With the sun-shine of Thy good-ness Melt our thank-less hearts of stone
In Thine own mys-te - rious sen-tence, "Ye have done it un - to Me."

And with that hast free - ly giv - en Bless-ings count-less as the sand
Till our cold and self - ish na-tures, Warmed by Thee, at length be-lieve
Can it be, O gra-cious Mas-ter, Thou dost deign for alms to sue,

To th' unthankful and the e - vil With Thine own un-spar-ing hand;
That more happy and more bless-ed 'Tis to give than to re-ceive.
Say - ing by Thy poor and need-y, "Give as I have giv'n to you"? A-men.

Lord of Glory, Who hast Bought Us

4 Yes, the sorrow and the sufferings
  Which on every hand we see
Channels are for gifts and offerings
  Due by solemn right to Thee;
Right of which we may not rob Thee,
  Debt we may not choose but pay,
Lest that face of love and pity
  Turn from us another day.

5 Lord of Glory, who hast bought us
  With Thy life-blood as the price,
Never grudging for the lost ones
  That tremendous sacrifice,
Give us faith to trust Thee boldly,
  Hope, to stay our souls on Thee;
But, oh! best of all Thy graces,
  Give us Thine own charity.

O Lord of Heaven and Earth and Sea 443

Matt. 10: 8
Christopher Wordsworth, 1863, ab.

8. 8. 8. 4.

Es ist kein Tag
Johann D. Meyer, 1692

1 O Lord of heav'n and earth and sea, To Thee all praise and glo-ry be.
2 The gold-en sun-shine, ver-nal air, Sweet flow'rs and fruit, Thy love declare.
3 For peaceful homes and healthful days, For all the bless-ings earth dis-plays,
4 Thou didst not spare Thine only Son, But gav'st Him for a world un-done,

How shall we show our love to Thee, Who giv-est all?
When har-vests rip-en, Thou art there, Who giv-est all.
We owe Thee thank-ful-ness and praise, Who giv-est all.
And free-ly with that Bless-ed One Thou giv-est all. A-men.

5 Thou giv'st the Spirit's holy dower,
  Spirit of Life and Love and Power,
  And dost His sevenfold graces shower
    Upon us all.

6 For souls redeemed, for sins forgiven,
  For means of grace and hopes of heaven,
  What can to Thee, O Lord, be given,
    Who givest all?

7 We lose what on ourselves we spend;
  We have as treasure without end
  Whatever, Lord, to Thee we lend,
    Who givest all;

8 To Thee, from whom we all derive
  Our life, our gifts, our power to give.
  Oh, may we ever with Thee live,
    Who givest all!

444 Rise! To Arms! With Prayer Employ You

Eph. 6: 10–18
Rüstet euch, ihr Christenleute
Wilhelm E. Arends, 1714
Tr., John M. Sloan, 1865, alt.

8. 9. 8. 8. 9. 8. 6. 6. 4. 4. 4. 8.

Wachet auf
Philipp Nicolai, 1599

1 Rise! To arms! With prayer em-ploy you, O Chris-tians, lest the
2 Cast a-far this world's vain plea-sures, Aye, bold-ly fight for
3 Wise-ly fight, for time is fleet-ing, The hours of grace are
4 Je-sus, all Thy chil-dren cher-ish And keep them that they

Foe de-stroy you, For Sa-tan has de-signed your fall. Wield God's Word,
heav'n-ly trea-sures, And stead-fast be in Je-sus' might. He will help,
fast re-treat-ing; Short, short, is this our earth-ly way. When the trump
nev-er per-ish Whom Thou hast purchased with Thy blood. Let new life

a weap-on glo-rious! A-gainst each foe you'll be vic-to-rious;
what-e'er be-tide you, And naught will harm with Christ be-side you;
the dead is wak-ing And sin-ners all with fear are quak-ing,
to us be giv-en That we may look to Thee in heav-en

Our God will set you o'er them all. Is Sa-tan strong and fell?
By faith you'll con-quer in the fight. Then shame, thou wea-ry soul!
With joy the saints will greet that Day. Bless God, our tri-umph's sure,
When-ev-er fear-ful is our mood. Thy Spir-it on us pour

Rise! To Arms! With Prayer Employ You

Here is Im-man-u-el. Sing ho-san-na! The strong ones yield,
Look for-ward to the goal: There joy waits thee. The race, then, run;
Tho' long we did en-dure Scorn and tri-al. Thou, Son of God,
That we may love Thee more—Hearts o'er-flow-ing; And then will we

With Christ our Shield, And we as con-qu'rors hold the field.
The com-bat done, Thy crown of glo-ry will be won.
To Thine a-bode Wilt lead the way Thy-self hast trod.
Be true to Thee In death and life e-ter-nal-ly. A-men.

Am I a Soldier of the Cross   445

C. M.

1 Cor. 16: 13
Isaac Watts, 1721, alt.

Winchester Old
"Psalter"
Thomas Este, 1592

1 Am I a sol-dier of the Cross, A foll-'wer of the Lamb,
2 Must I be car-ried to the skies On flow-'ry beds of ease
3 Are there no foes for me to face? Must I not stem the flood?
4 Sure I must fight if I would reign; In-crease my cour-age, Lord!

And shall I fear to own His cause Or blush to speak His name?
While oth-ers fought to win the prize And sailed thro' blood-y seas?
Is this vile world a friend to grace To help me on to God?
I'll bear the toil, en-dure the pain, Sup-port-ed by Thy Word. A-men.

5 Thy saints in all this glorious war
    Shall conquer though they die;
They see the triumph from afar
    With faith's discerning eye.

6 When that illustrious Day shall rise
    And all Thine armies shine
In robes of victory through the skies,
    The glory shall be Thine.

446 Rise, My Soul, to Watch and Pray

Matt. 26 : 41
Mache dich, mein Geist, bereit
Johann B. Freystein, 1697, cento
Tr., Catherine Winkworth, 1863, alt.

7. 6. 7. 6. 3. 3. 6. 6.

Straf mich nicht
"Hundert Arien"
Dresden, 1694

1 Rise, my soul, to watch and pray, From thy sleep a-wak-en;
2 Watch a-gainst the dev-il's snares Lest a-sleep he find thee;
3 Watch! Let not the wick-ed world With its pow'r de-feat thee.
4 Watch a-gainst thy-self, my soul, Lest with grace thou tri-fle;

Be not by the e-vil day Un-a-wares o'er-tak-en.
For in-deed no pains he spares To de-ceive and blind thee.
Watch lest with her pomp un-furled She be-tray and cheat thee.
Let not self thy tho'ts con-trol Nor God's mer-cy sti-fle.

For the Foe, Well we know, Oft his har-vest
Sa-tan's prey Oft are they Who se-cure are
Watch and see Lest there be Faith-less friends to
Pride and sin Lurk with-in All thy hopes to

reap-eth While the Chris-tian sleep-eth.
sleep-ing And no watch are keep-ing.
charm thee, Who but seek to harm thee.
scat-ter; Heed not when they flat-ter. A-men.

Rise, My Soul, to Watch and Pray

5 But while watching, also pray
　To the Lord unceasing.
He will free thee, be thy Stay,
　Strength and faith increasing.
O Lord, bless In distress
And let nothing swerve me
From the will to serve Thee.

6 Therefore let us watch and pray,
　Knowing He will hear us
As we see from day to day
　Dangers ever near us,
And the end Doth impend —
Our redemption neareth
When the Lord appeareth.

Fight the Good Fight with All Thy Might　447

L. M.

Mendon
German melody
Arr. by Samuel Dyer, 1828

1 Tim. 6: 12
John S. B. Monsell, 1863

1 Fight the good fight With all thy might; Christ is thy
2 Run the straight race Thro' God's good grace; Lift up thine
3 Cast care a - side; Up - on thy Guide Lean, and His
4 Faint not nor fear, His arms are near; He chang - eth

Strength and Christ thy Right. Lay hold on life, and it shall be
eyes and seek His face. Life with its way be - fore us lies;
mer - cy will pro - vide; Lean, and the trust - ing soul shall prove
not, and thou art dear. On - ly be - lieve, and thou shalt see

Thy joy and crown e - ter - nal - ly.
Christ is the Path and Christ the Prize.
Christ is its Life and Christ its Love.
That Christ is All in all to thee. A - men.

448 Brief Life Is Here Our Portion

Heb. 13: 14
Hic breve vivitur
Bernard of Morlas, c. 1145, cento
Tr., John M. Neale, 1858

7. 6. 7. 6. D.

Ewing
Alexander Ewing, 1853

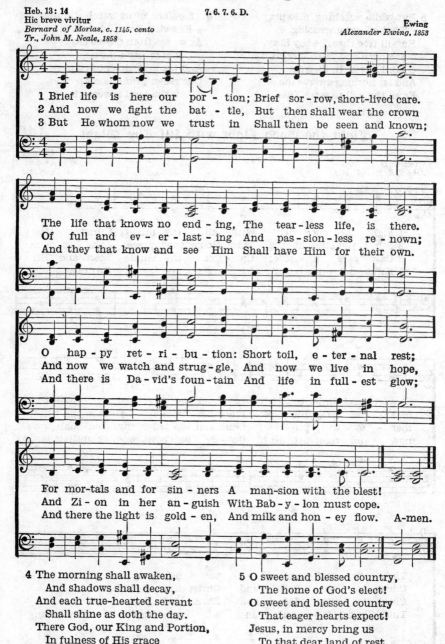

1 Brief life is here our por - tion; Brief sor - row, short-lived care.
2 And now we fight the bat - tle, But then shall wear the crown
3 But He whom now we trust in Shall then be seen and known;

The life that knows no end - ing, The tear - less life, is there.
Of full and ev - er - last - ing And pas - sion - less re - nown;
And they that know and see Him Shall have Him for their own.

O hap - py ret - ri - bu - tion: Short toil, e - ter - nal rest;
And now we watch and strug - gle, And now we live in hope,
And there is Da - vid's foun - tain And life in full - est glow;

For mor - tals and for sin - ners A man-sion with the blest!
And Zi - on in her an - guish With Bab - y - lon must cope.
And there the light is gold - en, And milk and hon - ey flow. A-men.

4 The morning shall awaken,
  And shadows shall decay,
And each true-hearted servant
  Shall shine as doth the day.
There God, our King and Portion,
  In fulness of His grace
Shall we behold forever
  And worship face to face.

5 O sweet and blessed country,
  The home of God's elect!
O sweet and blessed country
  That eager hearts expect!
Jesus, in mercy bring us
  To that dear land of rest,
Who art, with God the Father
  And Spirit, ever blest.

My Soul, Be on Thy Guard

449

S. M.

1 Thess. 5: 6
George Heath, 1781

Schumann
"Cantica Laudis"
Boston, 1850

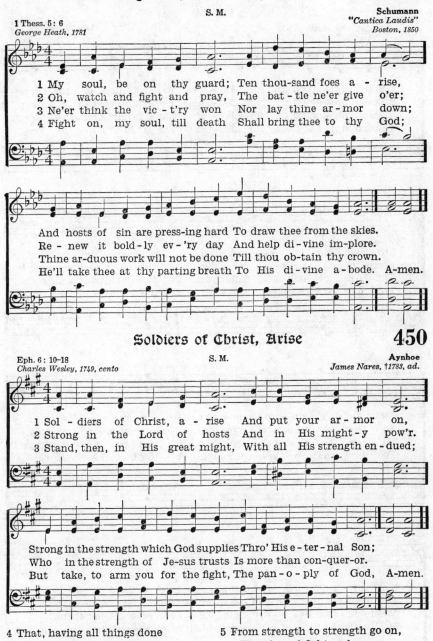

1 My soul, be on thy guard; Ten thou-sand foes a - rise,
2 Oh, watch and fight and pray, The bat - tle ne'er give o'er;
3 Ne'er think the vic - t'ry won Nor lay thine ar - mor down;
4 Fight on, my soul, till death Shall bring thee to thy God;

And hosts of sin are press-ing hard To draw thee from the skies.
Re - new it bold-ly ev - 'ry day And help di - vine im-plore.
Thine ar-duous work will not be done Till thou ob-tain thy crown.
He'll take thee at thy parting breath To His di - vine a-bode. A-men.

Soldiers of Christ, Arise

450

S. M.

Eph. 6: 10–18
Charles Wesley, 1749, cento

Aynhoe
James Nares, †1783, ad.

1 Sol - diers of Christ, a - rise And put your ar - mor on,
2 Strong in the Lord of hosts And in His might - y pow'r.
3 Stand, then, in His great might, With all His strength en - dued;

Strong in the strength which God supplies Thro' His e - ter - nal Son;
Who in the strength of Je-sus trusts Is more than con-quer-or.
But take, to arm you for the fight, The pan - o - ply of God, A-men.

4 That, having all things done
   And all your conflicts past,
Ye may o'ercome through Christ alone
   And stand entire at last.

5 From strength to strength go on,
   Wrestle and fight and pray;
Tread all the powers of darkness down
   And win the well-fought day.

451

Stand Up!—Stand Up for Jesus

7. 6. 7. 6. D.

Luke 12: 8
George Duffield, 1858, cento

Webb
George J. Webb, 1837

1 Stand up!—stand up for Je - sus, Ye sol-diers of the Cross!
2 Stand up!—stand up for Je - sus! The trum-pet - call o - bey;
3 Stand up!—stand up for Je - sus! Stand in His strength a - lone;
4 Stand up!—stand up for Je - sus! The strife will not be long;

Lift high His roy - al ban - ner, It must not suf - fer loss.
Forth to the might - y con - flict In this His glo - rious day!
The arm of flesh will fail you, Ye dare not trust your own.
This day the noise of bat - tle, The next, the vic - tor's song.

From vic - t'ry un - to vic - t'ry His ar - my shall He lead
Ye that are men, now serve Him A - gainst un - num-bered foes;
Put on the Gos - pel ar - mor, Each piece put on with prayer;
To him that o - ver - com - eth A crown of life shall be;

Till ev - 'ry foe is van-quished And Christ is Lord in - deed.
Let cour-age rise with dan - ger And strength to strength oppose.
Where du - ty calls or dan - ger, Be nev - er want-ing there.
He with the King of Glo - ry Shall reign e - ter - nal - ly. A - men.

The Son of God Goes Forth to War

452

C. M. D.

1 Tim. 6: 12
Reginald Heber, 1827

All Saints New
Henry S. Cutler, 1872

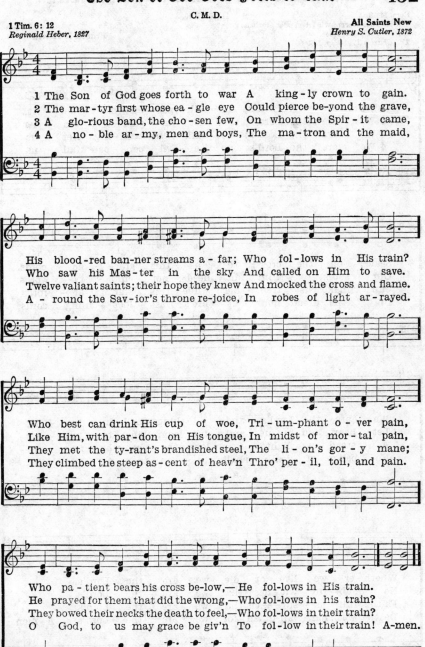

1 The Son of God goes forth to war A king-ly crown to gain.
2 The mar-tyr first whose ea-gle eye Could pierce be-yond the grave,
3 A glo-rious band, the cho-sen few, On whom the Spir-it came,
4 A no-ble ar-my, men and boys, The ma-tron and the maid,

His blood-red ban-ner streams a-far; Who fol-lows in His train?
Who saw his Mas-ter in the sky And called on Him to save.
Twelve valiant saints; their hope they knew And mocked the cross and flame.
A-round the Sav-ior's throne re-joice, In robes of light ar-rayed.

Who best can drink His cup of woe, Tri-um-phant o-ver pain,
Like Him, with par-don on His tongue, In midst of mor-tal pain,
They met the ty-rant's brandished steel, The li-on's gor-y mane;
They climbed the steep as-cent of heav'n Thro' per-il, toil, and pain.

Who pa-tient bears his cross be-low,— He fol-lows in His train.
He prayed for them that did the wrong,—Who fol-lows in his train?
They bowed their necks the death to feel,—Who fol-lows in their train?
O God, to us may grace be giv'n To fol-low in their train! A-men.

453 We Are the Lord's; His All=Sufficient Merit

Rom. 14: 8

Wir sind des Herrn, wir leben oder sterben
Karl J. P. Spitta, 1843
Tr., Charles T. Astley, 1860

11. 10. 11. 10.

Eirene
Frances R. Havergal, 1871

1 We are the Lord's; His all - suf - fi - cient mer - it,
2 We are the Lord's; then let us glad - ly ten - der
3 We are the Lord's; no dark - ness brood - ing o'er us
4 We are the Lord's; no e - vil can be - fall us

Sealed on the cross, to us this grace ac - cords.
Our souls to Him in deeds, not emp - ty words.
Can make us trem - ble while this star af - fords
In the dread hour of life's fast - loos - 'ning cords;

We are the Lord's and all things shall in - her - it;
Let heart and tongue and life com - bine to ren - der
A stead - y light a - long the path be - fore us—
No pangs of death shall e - ven then ap - pal us.

Wheth - er we live or die, we are the Lord's.
No doubt - ful wit - ness that we are the Lord's.
Faith's full as - sur - ance that we are the Lord's.
Death we shall van - quish, for we are the Lord's. A-men.

Prayer

Prayer Is the Soul's Sincere Desire

454

C. M.

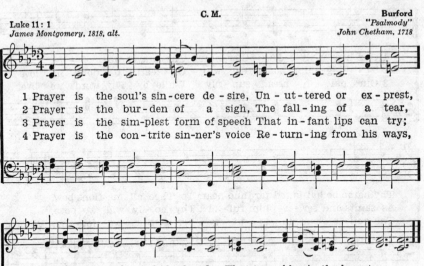

Luke 11: 1
James Montgomery, 1818, alt.

Burford
"Psalmody"
John Chetham, 1718

1 Prayer is the soul's sin-cere de-sire, Un-ut-tered or ex-prest,
2 Prayer is the bur-den of a sigh, The fall-ing of a tear,
3 Prayer is the sim-plest form of speech That in-fant lips can try;
4 Prayer is the con-trite sin-ner's voice Re-turn-ing from his ways,

The mo-tion of a hid-den fire That trem-bles in the breast.
The up-ward glanc-ing of an eye, When none but God is near.
Prayer the sub-lim-est strains that reach The Maj-es-ty on high.
While an-gels in their songs re-joice And cry, "Be-hold, he prays!" A-men.

5 Prayer is the Christian's vital breath,
  The Christian's native air,
His watchword at the gates of death —
  He enters heaven with prayer.

6 The saints in prayer appear as one
  In word and deed and mind,
While with the Father and the Son
  Sweet fellowship they find.

7 Nor prayer is made by man alone —
  The Holy Spirit pleads,
And Jesus on th' eternal throne
  For sinners intercedes.

8 O Thou by whom we come to God,
  The Life, the Truth, the Way,
The path of prayer Thyself hast trod —
  Lord, teach us how to pray.

455 Our Heavenly Father, Hear

Luke 11: 2–4
James Montgomery, 1835

S. M.

St. Bride
Samuel Howard, 1762

1 Our heav'n-ly Fa-ther, hear The prayer we of-fer now.
2 Thy king-dom come; Thy will On earth be done in love
3 Our dai-ly bread sup-ply While by Thy word we live.

Thy name be hal-lowed far and near; To Thee all na-tions bow.
As saints and ser-a-phim ful-fil Thy ho-ly will a-bove.
The guilt of our in-iq-ui-ty For-give as we for-give. A-men.

4 From dark temptation's power,
   From Satan's wiles, defend.
Deliver in the evil hour
   And guide us to the end.

5 Thine shall forever be
   Glory and power divine;
The scepter, throne, and majesty
   Of heaven and earth are Thine.

456 Approach, My Soul, the Mercy Seat

Matt. 11: 28
John Newton, 1779, ab.

C. M.

Spohr
Louis Spohr, 1835, arr.

1 Ap-proach, my soul, the mer-cy seat Where Je-sus an-swers prayer;
2 Thy prom-ise is my on-ly plea, With this I ven-ture nigh;
3 Bowed down be-neath a load of sin, By Sa-tan sore-ly pressed,

There hum-bly fall be-fore His feet, For none can per-ish there.
Thou call-est bur-dened souls to Thee, And such, O Lord, am I.
By wars with-out and fears with-in, I come to Thee for rest. A-men.

Approach, My Soul, the Mercy=Seat

4 Be Thou my Shield and Hiding-place,
   That, sheltered near Thy side,
  I may my fierce Accuser face
   And tell him Thou hast died.

5 O wondrous Love, to bleed and die,
   To bear the cross and shame,
  That guilty sinners such as I
   Might plead Thy gracious name!

What a Friend We Have in Jesus — 457

8. 7. 8. 7. D.

Friend

Matt. 21 : 22
Joseph Scriven, 1865

Charles C. Converse, 1868

1 What a Friend we have in Je - sus,   All   our sins and griefs to bear!
2 Have we tri - als and temp-ta-tions? Is there trou-ble an - y - where?
3 Are we weak and heav - y la - den, Cum-bered with a load of care?

What a priv - i - lege to car - ry   Ev - 'ry-thing to God in prayer!
We should nev - er be dis-cour-aged, Take it to the Lord in prayer.
Pre - cious Sav - ior, still our Ref - uge — Take it to the Lord in prayer.

Oh, what peace we of - ten for - feit, Oh, what need-less pain we bear,
Can we find a Friend so faith - ful Who will all our sor-rows share?
Do thy friends de-spise, for-sake thee? Take it to the Lord in prayer;

All be-cause we do not car - ry   Ev - 'ry-thing to God in prayer!
Je-sus knows our ev-'ry weak-ness —Take it to the Lord in prayer.
In His arms He'll take and shield thee, Thou wilt find a sol-ace there.   A-men.

458 Our Father, Thou in Heaven Above

Matt. 6: 9 ff.
Vater unser im Himmelreich
Martin Luther, 1539
Tr., composite

8. 8. 8. 8. 8. 8.

Vater unser
"Geistliche Lieder"
Leipzig, 1539

1 Our Fa-ther, Thou in heav'n a-bove, Who bid-dest us to
2 Thy name be hal-lowed. Help us, Lord, In pu-ri-ty to
3 Thy king-dom come. Thine let it be In time and in e-

dwell in love, As breth-ren of one fam-i-ly, To
keep Thy Word, That to the glo-ry of Thy name We
ter-ni-ty. Let Thy good Spir-it e'er be nigh Our

cry in ev-'ry need to Thee, Teach us no thought-less words to
walk be-fore Thee free from blame. Let no false doc-trine us per-
hearts with gra-ces to sup-ply. Break Sa-tan's pow'r, de-feat his

say, But from our in-most heart to pray.
vert; All poor, de-lud-ed souls con-vert.
rage; Pre-serve Thy Church from age to age. A-men.

4 Thy gracious will on earth be done
As 'tis in heaven before Thy throne;
Obedience in our weal and woe
And patience in all grief bestow.
Curb flesh and blood and every ill
That sets itself against Thy will.

5 Give us this day our daily bread
And let us all be clothed and fed.
From war and strife be our Defense,
From famine and from pestilence,
That we may live in godly peace,
Free from all care and avarice.

Our Father, Thou in Heaven Above

6 Forgive our sins, Lord, we implore,
Remove from us their burden sore,
As we their trespasses forgive
Who by offenses us do grieve.
Thus let us dwell in charity
And serve our brother willingly.

7 Into temptation lead us not.
When evil foes against us plot
And vex our souls on every hand,
Oh, give us strength that we may stand
Firm in the faith, a well-armed host,
Through comfort of the Holy Ghost!

8 From evil, Lord, deliver us;
The times and days are perilous.
Redeem us from eternal death,
And when we yield our dying breath,
Console us, grant us calm release,
And take our souls to Thee in peace.

9 Amen, that is, So shall it be.
Confirm our faith and hope in Thee
That we may doubt not, but believe
What here we ask we shall receive.
Thus in Thy name and at Thy word
We say: Amen. Oh, hear us, Lord!

Come, My Soul, Thy Suit Prepare 459

1 Kings 3 : 5
John Newton, 1779

7. 7. 7. 7.

Vienna
Justin H. Knecht, 1797

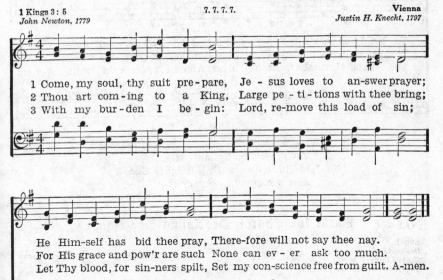

1 Come, my soul, thy suit pre-pare, Je - sus loves to an-swer prayer;
2 Thou art com-ing to a King, Large pe - ti - tions with thee bring;
3 With my bur-den I be-gin: Lord, re-move this load of sin;

He Him-self has bid thee pray, There-fore will not say thee nay.
For His grace and pow'r are such None can ev - er ask too much.
Let Thy blood, for sin-ners spilt, Set my con-science free from guilt. A-men.

4 Lord, I come to Thee for rest,
Take possession of my breast;
There Thy blood-bought right maintain
And without a rival reign.

5 As the image in the glass
Answers the beholder's face,
Thus unto my heart appear;
Print Thine own resemblance there.

6 While I am a pilgrim here,
Let Thy love my spirit cheer;
As my Guide, my Guard, my Friend,
Lead me to my journey's end.

7 Show me what I have to do;
Every hour my strength renew.
Let me live a life of faith;
Let me die Thy people's death.

The Church

460   Behold the Sure Foundation-Stone

Ps. 118: 22
Isaac Watts, 1719

C. M.

St. Anne
William Croft, 1708

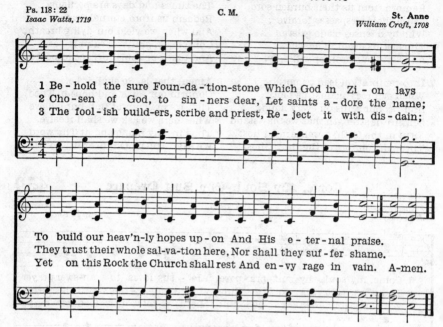

1 Be - hold the sure Foun-da-'tion-stone Which God in Zi - on lays
2 Cho - sen of God, to sin - ners dear, Let saints a - dore the name;
3 The fool - ish build-ers, scribe and priest, Re - ject it with dis - dain;

To build our heav'n-ly hopes up-on And His e - ter - nal praise.
They trust their whole sal-va-tion here, Nor shall they suf - fer shame.
Yet on this Rock the Church shall rest And en - vy rage in vain. A-men.

4 What though the gates of hell withstood,
    Yet must this building rise.
   'Tis Thine own work, Almighty God,
    And wondrous in our eyes.

461   Hark! the Church Proclaims Her Honor

Eph. 1: 4
Das ist der Gemeine Stärke
Samuel Preiswerk, 1844
Tr., Catherine Winkworth, 1858

8. 7. 8. 7.

Lobt den Herrn, die Morgensonne
"Evangelisches Choralbuch"
Halle, 1829

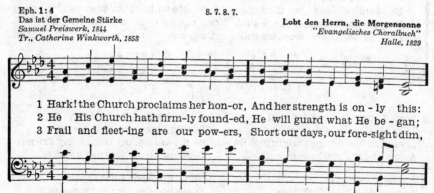

1 Hark! the Church proclaims her hon-or, And her strength is on - ly this:
2 He His Church hath firm-ly found-ed, He will guard what He be - gan;
3 Frail and fleet-ing are our pow-ers, Short our days, our fore-sight dim,

Hark! the Church Proclaims Her Honor

God hath laid His choice up-on her, And the work she doth is His.
We, by sin and foes sur-round-ed, Build her bulwarks as we can.
And we own the choice not ours, We were cho-sen first by Him. A-men.

4 Onward, then! For naught despairing,   5 Tho' we here must strive in weakness,
   Calm we follow at His word,   Though in tears we often bend,
Thus through joy and sorrow bearing   What His might began in meekness
   Faithful witness to our Lord.   Shall achieve a glorious end.

I Love Thy Kingdom, Lord

462

Ps. 137   S. M.   St. Thomas
Timothy Dwight, 1800, ab., alt.   *Aaron Williams, 1770*

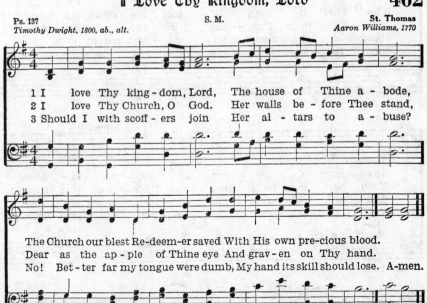

1 I   love Thy king-dom, Lord,   The house of   Thine a - bode,
2 I   love Thy Church, O   God. Her walls be - fore Thee stand,
3 Should I with scoff-ers join   Her al - tars to   a - buse?

The Church our blest Re-deem-er saved With His own pre-cious blood.
Dear as the ap - ple of Thine eye And grav-en on Thy hand.
No! Bet-ter far my tongue were dumb, My hand its skill should lose. A-men.

4 For her my tears shall fall,   6 Jesus, Thou Friend Divine,
   For her my prayers ascend,   Our Savior and our King,
To her my cares and toils be given   Thy hand from every snare and **foe**
   Till toils and cares shall end.   Shall great deliverance bring.

5 Beyond my highest joy   7 Sure as Thy truth shall last,
   I prize her heavenly ways,   To Zion shall be given
Her sweet communion, solemn vows,   The brightest glories earth can **yield**
   Her hymns of love and praise.   And brighter bliss of heaven.

463 For All the Saints Who from Their Labors Rest

Heb. 12: 1
William W. How, 1864, cento

10. 10. 10., with Alleluias

Sine nomine
R. Vaughan Williams, 1906, arr.

1 For all the saints who from their la-bors rest,
2 Thou wast their Rock, their For-tress, and their Might;
3 Oh, may Thy sol-diers, faith-ful, true, and bold,
4 O blest com-mu-nion, fel-low-ship di-vine,

Who Thee by faith be-fore the world con-fest,
Thou, Lord, their Cap-tain in the well-fought fight;
Fight as the saints who no-bly fought of old
We fee-bly strug-gle, they in glo-ry shine;

Thy name, O Je-sus, be for-ev-er blest.
Thou, in the dark-ness drear, their one true Light.
And win with them the vic-tor's crown of gold.
Yet all are one in Thee, for all are Thine.

Al-le-lu-ia!... Al-le-lu-ia!
Al-le-lu-ia!... Al-le-lu-ia!
Al-le-lu-ia!... Al-le-lu-ia!
Al-le-lu-ia!... Al-le-lu-ia! A-men.

For All the Saints Who from Their Labors Rest

5 And when the fight is fierce, the warfare long,
Steals on the ear the distant triumph song,
And hearts are brave again, and arms are strong.
Alleluia! Alleluia!

6 But, lo, there breaks a yet more glorious day;
The saints triumphant rise in bright array;
The King of Glory passes on His way.
Alleluia! Alleluia!

7 From earth's wide bounds, from ocean's farthest coast,
Through gates of pearl, streams in the countless host,
Singing to Father, Son, and Holy Ghost,
Alleluia! Alleluia!

8 The golden evening brightens in the west;
Soon, soon, to faithful warriors cometh rest.
Sweet is the calm of Paradise the blest.
Alleluia! Alleluia!

Blest Be the Tie That Binds 464

Eph. 4: 3
John Fawcett, 1772, alt.

S. M.

Boylston
Lowell Mason, 1832

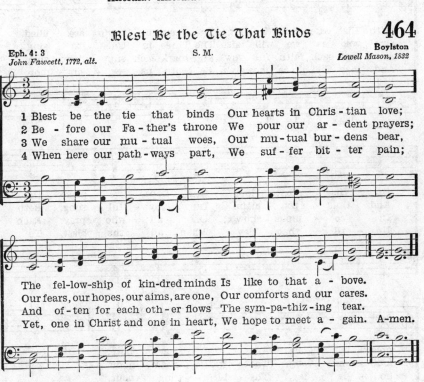

1 Blest be the tie that binds Our hearts in Chris-tian love;
2 Be - fore our Fa-ther's throne We pour our ar - dent prayers;
3 We share our mu - tual woes, Our mu-tual bur - dens bear,
4 When here our path-ways part, We suf - fer bit - ter pain;

The fel-low-ship of kin-dred minds Is like to that a - bove.
Our fears, our hopes, our aims, are one, Our comforts and our cares.
And of-ten for each oth - er flows The sym-pa-thiz-ing tear.
Yet, one in Christ and one in heart, We hope to meet a - gain. A-men.

5 This glorious hope revives
Our courage by the way,
While each in expectation lives
And longs to see the day.

6 From sorrow, toil, and pain,
And sin we shall be free
And perfect love and friendship reign
Through all eternity.

465 Christ Is Our Corner=Stone

1 Kings 9: 3
Angularis fundamentum
Author unknown, c. 700, cento
Tr., John Chandler, 1837

6. 6. 6. 6. 4. 4. 4. 4.

Darwall's 148th
John Darwall, 1770

1 Christ is our Cor - ner - stone, On Him a - lone we build;
2 Oh, then, with hymns of praise These hal-lowed courts shall ring;
3 Here, gra - cious God, do Thou For - ev - er - more draw nigh;
4 Here may we gain from heav'n The grace which we im - plore,

With His true saints a - lone The courts of heav'n are filled.
Our voic - es we will raise The Three in One to sing
Ac - cept each faith - ful vow And mark each sup - pliant sigh.
And may that grace, once giv'n, Be with us ev - er - more

On His great love Our hopes we place Of
And thus pro - claim In joy - ful song, Both
In co - pious show'r On all who pray Each
Un - til that day When all the blest To

pres - ent grace And joys a - bove.
loud and long, That glo - rious name.
ho - ly day, Thy bless - ing pour.
end - less rest Are called a - way! A - men.

Christ, Thou Art the Sure Foundation

466

8. 7. 8. 7. 8. 7.

1 Kings 9: 3
Angularis fundamentum
Author unknown, c. 700, cento
Tr., John M. Neale, 1851, alt.

Regent Square
Henry Smart, 1867

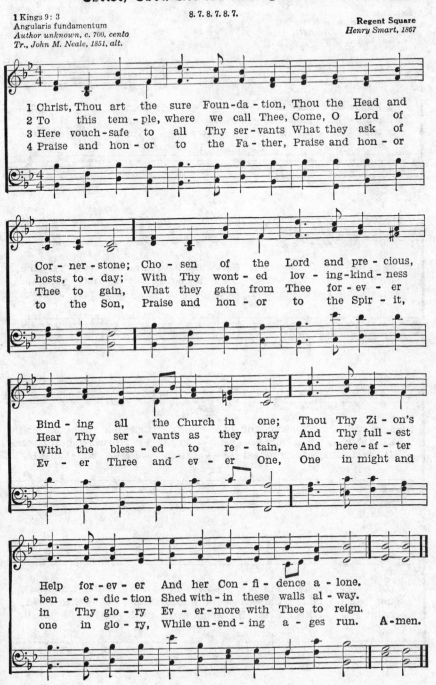

1 Christ, Thou art the sure Foun-da-tion, Thou the Head and
2 To this tem-ple, where we call Thee, Come, O Lord of
3 Here vouch-safe to all Thy ser-vants What they ask of
4 Praise and hon-or to the Fa-ther, Praise and hon-or

Cor-ner-stone; Cho-sen of the Lord and pre-cious,
hosts, to-day; With Thy wont-ed lov-ing-kind-ness
Thee to gain, What they gain from Thee for-ev-er
to the Son, Praise and hon-or to the Spir-it,

Bind-ing all the Church in one; Thou Thy Zi-on's
Hear Thy ser-vants as they pray And Thy full-est
With the bless-ed to re-tain, And here-af-ter
Ev-er Three and ev-er One, One in might and

Help for-ev-er And her Con-fi-dence a-lone.
ben-e-dic-tion Shed with-in these walls al-way.
in Thy glo-ry Ev-er-more with Thee to reign.
one in glo-ry, While un-end-ing a-ges run. A-men.

467 Built on the Rock the Church doth Stand

Eph. 2 : 19–22
Kirken den er et gammelt Hus
Nicolai F. S. Grundtvig, 1837
Tr., Carl Döving, 1909, alt.

8. 8. 8. 8. 8. 8. 8. 8.

Kirken den er et
Ludwig M. Lindeman, 1871

1 Built on the Rock the Church doth stand, E - ven when
2 Sure - ly in tem - ples made with hands, God, the Most
3 We are God's house of liv - ing stones, Build - ed for

stee - ples are fall - ing; Crum-bled have spires in ev - 'ry land,
High, is not dwell - ing; High a - bove earth His tem - ple stands,
His hab - i - ta - tion; He through bap - tis - mal grace us owns

Bells still are chim-ing and call - ing, Call - ing the young and
All earth - ly tem - ples ex - cel - ling. Yet He whom heav'ns can-
Heirs of His won-drous sal - va - tion. Were we but two His

old to rest, But a - bove all the soul dis - trest,
not con - tain Chose to a - bide on earth with men,
name to tell, Yet He would deign with us to dwell,

Built on the Rock the Church doth Stand

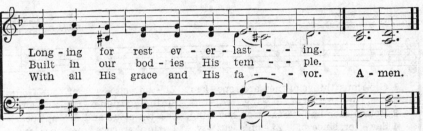

Long - ing for rest ev - er - last - - - ing.
Built in our bod - ies His tem - - ple.
With all His grace and His fa - - - vor. A - men.

4 Now we may gather with our King
  E'en in the lowliest dwelling;
Praises to Him we there may bring,
  His wondrous mercy forthtelling.
Jesus His grace to us accords;
Spirit and life are all His words;
  His truth doth hallow the temple.

5 Still we our earthly temples rear
  That we may herald His praises;
They are the homes where He draws
    near
  And little children embraces.
Beautiful things in them are said;
God there with us His covenant made,
  Making us heirs of His kingdom.

6 Here stands the font before our eyes
  Telling how God did receive us;
Th' altar recalls Christ's sacrifice
  And what His table doth give us;
Here sounds the Word that doth proclaim
Christ yesterday, today, the same,
  Yea, and for aye our Redeemer.

7 Grant, then, O God, where'er men roam,
  That, when the church bells are
    ringing,
Many in saving faith may come
  Where Christ His message is bringing:
"I know Mine own, Mine own know Me;
Ye, not the world, My face shall see.
  My peace I leave with you." Amen.

For All Thy Saints, O Lord   468

Rev. 7: 15   S. M.   Energy
Richard Mant, 1837, cento   *William H. Monk, 1861*

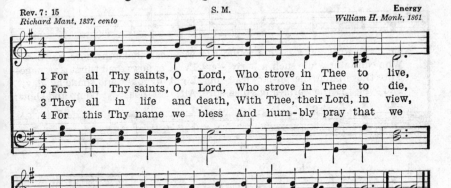

1 For all Thy saints, O Lord, Who strove in Thee to live,
2 For all Thy saints, O Lord, Who strove in Thee to die,
3 They all in life and death, With Thee, their Lord, in view,
4 For this Thy name we bless And hum-bly pray that we

Who fol-lowed Thee, o-beyed, a-dored, Our grate-ful hymn re-ceive.
Who count-ed Thee their great Re-ward, Ac - cept our thank-ful cry.
Learned from Thy Ho-ly Spir-it's breath To suf-fer and to do.
May fol-low them in ho - li - ness And live and die in Thee. A-men.

469 Glorious Things of Thee are Spoken

8. 7. 8. 7. D.

Is. 33 : 20, 21; Ps. 87
John Newton, 1779, ab., alt.

Galilean
Joseph Barnby, 1883

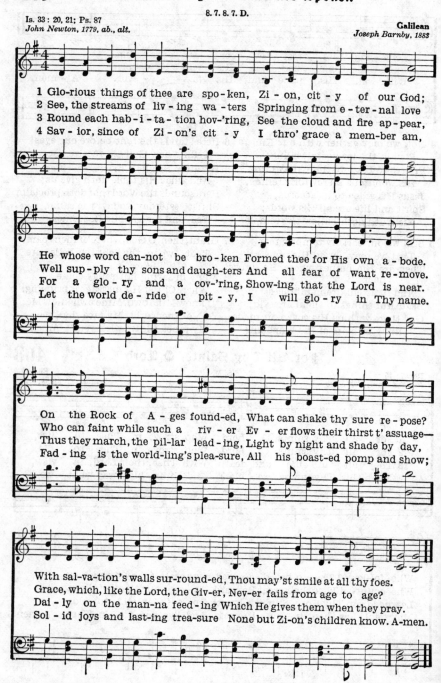

1 Glo-rious things of thee are spo-ken, Zi - on, cit - y of our God;
2 See, the streams of liv-ing wa-ters Springing from e - ter - nal love
3 Round each hab-i - ta-tion hov-'ring, See the cloud and fire ap-pear,
4 Sav - ior, since of Zi-on's cit - y I thro' grace a mem-ber am,

He whose word can-not be bro-ken Formed thee for His own a - bode.
Well sup-ply thy sons and daugh-ters And all fear of want re-move.
For a glo-ry and a cov-'ring, Show-ing that the Lord is near.
Let the world de-ride or pit - y, I will glo-ry in Thy name.

On the Rock of A - ges found-ed, What can shake thy sure re - pose?
Who can faint while such a riv - er Ev - er flows their thirst t' assuage—
Thus they march, the pil-lar lead-ing, Light by night and shade by day,
Fad - ing is the world-ling's plea-sure, All his boast-ed pomp and show;

With sal-va-tion's walls sur-round-ed, Thou may'st smile at all thy foes.
Grace, which, like the Lord, the Giv-er, Nev-er fails from age to age?
Dai - ly on the man-na feed-ing Which He gives them when they pray.
Sol - id joys and last-ing trea-sure None but Zi-on's children know. A-men.

Rise Again, Ye Lion-Hearted

8. 7. 8. 7. 6. 6. 7. 7.

Rev. 2: 10
Löwen, lasst euch wiederfinden
Author unknown, 1712, cento
Tr., Martin Franzmann, 1940

Löwen, lasst euch wiederfinden
Bernhard Klein, 1817

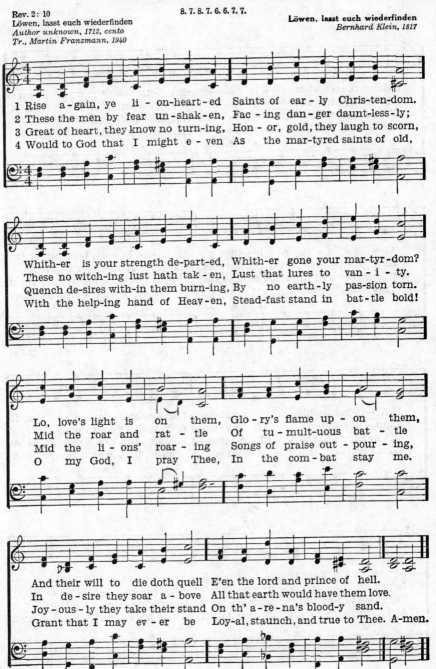

1 Rise a-gain, ye li-on-heart-ed Saints of ear-ly Chris-ten-dom.
2 These the men by fear un-shak-en, Fac-ing dan-ger daunt-less-ly;
3 Great of heart, they know no turn-ing, Hon-or, gold, they laugh to scorn,
4 Would to God that I might e-ven As the mar-tyred saints of old,

Whith-er is your strength de-part-ed, Whith-er gone your mar-tyr-dom?
These no witch-ing lust hath tak-en, Lust that lures to van-i-ty.
Quench de-sires with-in them burn-ing, By no earth-ly pas-sion torn.
With the help-ing hand of Heav-en, Stead-fast stand in bat-tle bold!

Lo, love's light is on them, Glo-ry's flame up-on them,
Mid the roar and rat-tle Of tu-mult-uous bat-tle
Mid the li-ons' roar-ing Songs of praise out-pour-ing,
O my God, I pray Thee, In the com-bat stay me.

And their will to die doth quell E'en the lord and prince of hell.
In de-sire they soar a-bove All that earth would have them love.
Joy-ous-ly they take their stand On th' a-re-na's blood-y sand.
Grant that I may ev-er be Loy-al, staunch, and true to Thee. A-men.

471

Hark! the Sound of Holy Voices

8. 7. 8. 7. D.

Rev. 7: 9, 10
Christopher Wordsworth, 1862

O Durchbrecher
"Neues geistreiches Gesangbuch"
Halle, 1704

1 Hark! the sound of ho-ly voic-es Chant-ing at the crys-tal sea,
2 Pa - tri-arch and ho-ly proph-et, Who pre-pared the way of Christ,
3 They have come from trib-u - la - tion And have washed their robes in blood,
4 March-ing with Thy cross, their ban-ner, They have tri-umphed, fol-low-ing

Al - le - lu - ia, Al - le - lu - ia, Al - le - lu - ia, Lord, to Thee.
King, a - pos - tle, saint, con-fes-sor, Mar - tyr, and e - van-gel-ist,
Washed them in the blood of Je - sus; Tried they were, and firm they stood.
Thee, the Cap-tain of sal - va - tion, Thee, their Sav-ior and their King.

Mul - ti-tudes which none can num-ber Like the stars in glo - ry stand,
Saint - ly maid-en, god - ly ma-tron, Widows who have watched to prayer,
Mocked, imprisoned, stoned, tor-ment-ed, Sawn a - sun-der, slain with sword,
Glad - ly, Lord, with Thee they suf-fered, Glad-ly, Lord, with Thee they died,

Clothed in white ap-par - el, hold-ing Palms of vic-t'ry in their hand.
Joined in ho - ly con-cert, sing-ing To the Lord of all, are there.
They have con-quered death and Sa-tan By the might of Christ the Lord.
And by death to life im-mor-tal They were born and glo-ri-fied. A-men.

Mark! the Sound of Holy Voices

5 Now they reign in heavenly glory,
   Now they walk in golden light,
Now they drink, as from a river,
   Holy bliss and infinite.
Love and peace they taste forever
   And all truth and knowledge see
In the beatific vision
   Of the blessed Trinity.

6 God of God, the One-begotten
   Light of Light, Emmanuel,
In whose body, joined together,
   All the saints forever dwell,
Pour upon us of Thy fulness
   That we may forevermore
God the Father, God the Spirit,
   One with Thee on high, adore.

Rise, Ye Children of Salvation 472

8. 7. 8. 7. 7. 7.

Jude 3
Auf, ihr Christen, Christi Glieder
Justus Falckner, 1697, cento
Tr., Emma F. Bevan, 1858

Neander
Joachim Neander, 1680

1 Rise, ye chil-dren of sal-va-tion, All who cleave to Christ, the Head.
2 Saints and he-roes long be-fore us Firm-ly on this ground have stood;
3 Fight-ing, we shall be vic-to-rious By the blood of Christ, our Lord;
4 When His ser-vants stand be-fore Him, Each re-ceiv-ing his re-ward;

Wake, a-rise, O might-y na-tion, Ere the Foe on Zi-on tread.
See their ban-ner wav-ing o'er us, Con-qu'rors thro' the Sav-ior's blood.
On our fore-heads, bright and glo-rious, Shines the wit-ness of His Word;
When His saints in light a-dore Him, Giv-ing glo-ry to the Lord,

He draws nigh and would de-fy All the hosts of God Most High.
Ground we hold where-on of old Fought the faith-ful and the bold.
Spear and shield on bat-tle-field, His great name we can-not yield.
"Vic-to-ry!" our song shall be Like the thun-der of the sea. A-men.

473 The Church's One Foundation

7. 6. 7. 6. D.

Eph. 2: 20
Samuel J. Stone, 1866, cento

Aurelia
Samuel S. Wesley, 1864

1 The Church's one foun-da-tion Is Je-sus Christ, her Lord;
2 E-lect from ev-'ry na-tion, Yet one o'er all the earth,
3 The Church shall nev-er per-ish! Her dear Lord, to de-fend,

She is His new cre-a-tion By wa-ter and the Word.
Her char-ter of sal-va-tion One Lord, one faith, one birth.
To guide, sus-tain, and cher-ish, Is with her to the end.

From heav'n He came and sought her To be His ho-ly bride;
One ho-ly name she bless-es, Par-takes one ho-ly food,
Tho' there be those that hate her, False sons with-in her pale,

With His own blood He bought her, And for her life He died.
And to one hope she press-es, With ev-'ry grace en-dued.
A-gainst both foe and trai-tor She ev-er shall pre-vail. A-men.

The Church's One Foundation

4 Though with a scornful wonder
  Men see her sore oppressed,
By schisms rent asunder,
  By heresies distressed,
Yet saints their watch are keeping;
  Their cry goes up, "How long?"
And soon the night of weeping
  Shall be the morn of song.

5 Mid toil and tribulation
  And tumult of her war
She waits the consummation
  Of peace forevermore,
Till with the vision glorious
  Her longing eyes are blest
And the great Church victorious
  Shall be the Church at rest.

Zion Stands by Hills Surrounded 474

8. 7. 8. 7. 4. 7.

Ps. 125 : 2
Thomas Kelly, 1806, cento

Zion
Thomas Morely, †1891

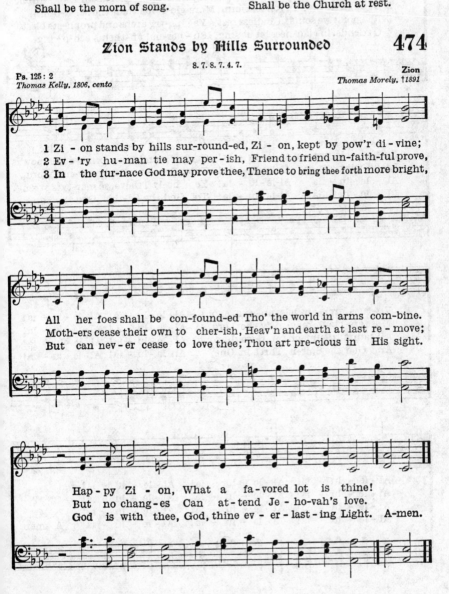

1 Zi - on stands by hills sur-round-ed, Zi - on, kept by pow'r di - vine;
2 Ev - 'ry hu-man tie may per-ish, Friend to friend un-faith-ful prove,
3 In the fur-nace God may prove thee, Thence to bring thee forth more bright,

All her foes shall be con-found-ed Tho' the world in arms com-bine.
Moth-ers cease their own to cher-ish, Heav'n and earth at last re - move;
But can nev - er cease to love thee; Thou art pre-cious in His sight.

Hap - py Zi - on, What a fa-vored lot is thine!
But no chang-es Can at-tend Je - ho-vah's love.
God is with thee, God, thine ev - er - last-ing Light. A-men.

475 Ye Watchers and Ye Holy Ones

L. M., with Alleluias

Ps. 148
John A. L. Riley. 1906

Lasst uns erfreuen
"Geistliche Kirchengesäng"
Cologne, 1623

1 Ye watch-ers and ye ho-ly ones, Bright ser-aphs, cher-u-bim, and thrones,
2 O high-er than the cher-u-bim, More glo-rious than the ser-a-phim,
3 Re-spond, ye souls in endless rest, Ye pa-tri-archs and proph-ets blest,
4 O friends, in glad-ness let us sing, Su - per-nal an-thems ech-o - ing,

Raise the glad strain, Al-le-lu - ia! Cry out, dominions, princedoms, pow'rs,
Lead their prais-es, Al-le-lu - ia! Thou Bear-er of th' e-ter-nal Word,
Al - le-lu-ia, Al-le-lu - ia! Ye ho-ly Twelve, ye mar-tyrs strong,
Al - le-lu-ia, Al-le-lu - ia! To God the Fa-ther, God the Son,

Vir-tues, arch-an-gels, an-gels' choirs, Al-le-lu - ia! Al-le-lu - ia!
Most gra-cious, mag-ni-fy the Lord, Al-le-lu - ia! Al-le-lu - ia!
All saints tri-um-phant, raise the song, Al-le-lu - ia! Al-le-lu - ia!
And God the Spir-it, Three in One, Al-le-lu - ia! Al-le-lu - ia!

Al - le - lu - ia! Al-le - lu - ia! Al-le - lu - ia!
Al - le - lu - ia! Al-le - lu - ia! Al-le - lu - ia!
Al - le - lu - ia! Al-le - lu - ia! Al-le - lu - ia!
Al - le - lu - ia! Al-le - lu - ia! Al-le - lu - ia! A - men.

Ten Thousand Times Ten Thousand

476

7. 6. 8. 6. D.

Rev. 7: 17
Henry Alford, 1867

Alford
John B. Dykes, 1875

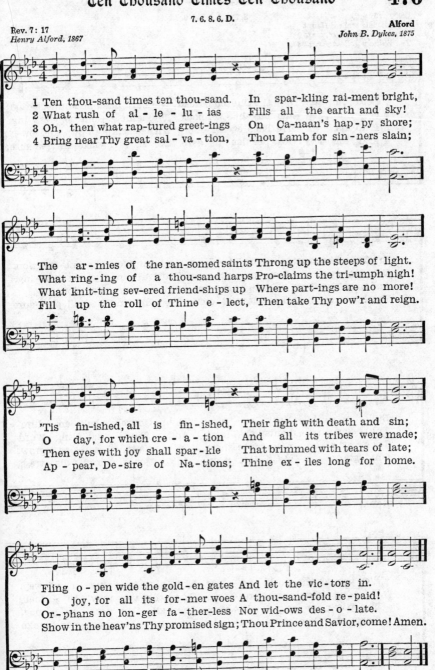

1 Ten thou-sand times ten thou-sand, In spar-kling rai-ment bright,
2 What rush of al - le - lu - ias Fills all the earth and sky!
3 Oh, then what rap-tured greet-ings On Ca-naan's hap-py shore;
4 Bring near Thy great sal - va - tion, Thou Lamb for sin-ners slain;

The ar-mies of the ran-somed saints Throng up the steeps of light.
What ring-ing of a thou-sand harps Pro-claims the tri-umph nigh!
What knit-ting sev-ered friend-ships up Where part-ings are no more!
Fill up the roll of Thine e - lect, Then take Thy pow'r and reign.

'Tis fin-ished, all is fin-ished, Their fight with death and sin;
O day, for which cre - a - tion And all its tribes were made;
Then eyes with joy shall spar-kle That brimmed with tears of late;
Ap - pear, De-sire of Na-tions; Thine ex - iles long for home.

Fling o - pen wide the gold-en gates And let the vic-tors in.
O joy, for all its for-mer woes A thou-sand-fold re-paid!
Or-phans no lon-ger fa-ther-less Nor wid-ows des - o - late.
Show in the heav'ns Thy promised sign; Thou Prince and Savior, come! Amen.

477 Lord Jesus, Thou the Church's Head

Col. 2 : 10
O Jesu, einig wahres Haupt
Johann Mentzer, 1726, cento
Tr., William J. Schaefer, 1933

8. 7. 8. 7. 6. 5. 6. 6. 7.

Reuter
Fritz Reuter, 1916

1 Lord Je-sus, Thou the Church's Head, Thou art her one Foun-da-tion;
2 O Lord, let this Thy lit-tle flock, Thy name a-lone con-fess-ing,
3 Help us to serve Thee ev-er-more With hearts both pure and low-ly;
4 And for Thy Gos-pel let us dare To sac-ri-fice all trea-sure;

In Thee she trusts, be-fore Thee bows, And waits for Thy sal-va-tion.
Con-tin-ue in Thy lov-ing care, True u-ni-ty pos-sess-ing.
And may Thy Word, that light di-vine, Shine on in splen-dor ho-ly
Teach us to bear Thy bless-ed cross, To find in Thee all plea-sure.

Built on this Rock se-cure, Thy Church shall en-dure
Thy Sac-ra-ments, O Lord, And Thy sav-ing Word
That we re-pen-tance show, In faith ev-er grow;
Oh, grant us stead-fast-ness In joy and dis-tress,

E'en though the world de-cay And all things pass a-way.
To us e'er pure re-tain. Grant that they may re-main.
The pow'r of sin de-stroy And all that doth an-noy.
That we Thee ne'er for-sake. Let us by grace par-take

Lord Jesus, Thou the Church's Head

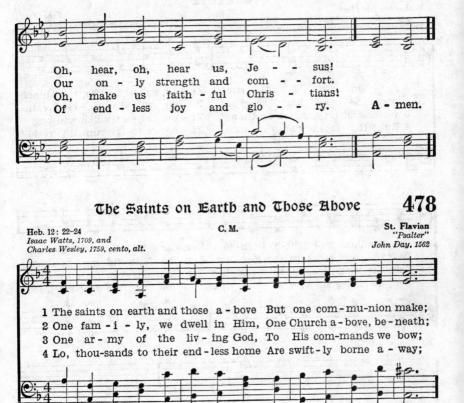

Oh, hear, oh, hear us, Je - sus!
Our on - ly strength and com - fort.
Oh, make us faith - ful Chris - tians!
Of end - less joy and glo - ry. A - men.

The Saints on Earth and Those Above · 478

Heb. 12: 22-24
Isaac Watts, 1709, and
Charles Wesley, 1759, cento, alt.

C. M.

St. Flavian
"Psalter"
John Day, 1562

1 The saints on earth and those a - bove But one com - mu - nion make;
2 One fam - i - ly, we dwell in Him, One Church a - bove, be - neath;
3 One ar - my of the liv - ing God, To His com - mands we bow;
4 Lo, thou - sands to their end - less home Are swift - ly borne a - way;

Joined to their Lord in bonds of love, All of His grace par - take.
Tho' now di - vid - ed by the stream, The narrow stream, of death.
Part of the host have passed the flood, And part are cross - ing now.
And we are to the mar - gin come And soon must launch as they. A - men.

5 Lord Jesus, be our constant Guide;
  Then, when the word is given,
  Bid death's cold flood its waves divide
  And land us safe in heaven.

479 Zion, Rise, Zion, Rise

Rev. 2-3
Fahre fort, fahre fort
Johann E. Schmidt, 1704, cento
Tr., William M. Czamanske, 1938

6. 7. 8. 7. 8. 9. 6.

Fahre fort
"Neues geistreiches Gesangbuch"
Halle, 1704

1 Zi - on, rise, Zi - on, rise, Zi - on, wake, a - rise, and shine!
2 Bear the cross, bear the cross. Zi - on, till thy lat - est breath
3 Watch and pray, watch and pray! Zi - on, ev - er watch and pray
4 Run thy race, run thy race, Zi - on, swift - ly run thy race!

Let thy lamp be bright-ly burn-ing, Nev - er let thy love de-cline,
Bear the cross of scorn and jeer-ing And be faith-ful un - to death;
Lest the wick-ed world mis-guide thee From the nar-row path to stray
Let no lan-guor ev - er find thee I - dle in the mar-ket-place.

For - ward still with hope-ful yearn-ing. Zi - on, yon - der
See the crown of life ap-pear-ing. Zi - on, count all
And thy God re - prove and chide thee. Zi - on, work with
Look not to the things be - hind thee. Zi - on, dai - ly

waits the heav'n-ly prize; Zi - on, rise! Zi - on, rise!
oth - er things as loss. Bear the cross, bear the cross!
zeal while it is day. Watch and pray, watch and pray!
strengthened by His grace, Run thy race, run thy race! A - men.

Lord of the Worlds Above

480

6. 6. 6. 6. 4. 4. 4. 4.

Ps. 84
Isaac Watts, 1719, cento

Darwall's 148th
John Darwall, 1770

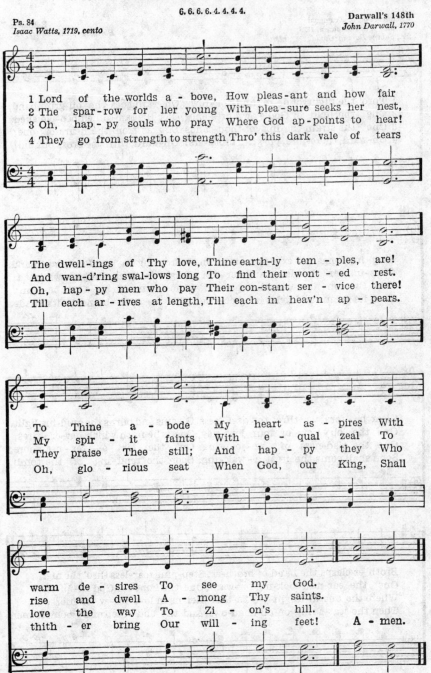

1 Lord of the worlds a-bove, How pleas-ant and how fair
2 The spar-row for her young With plea-sure seeks her nest,
3 Oh, hap-py souls who pray Where God ap-points to hear!
4 They go from strength to strength Thro' this dark vale of tears

The dwell-ings of Thy love, Thine earth-ly tem-ples, are!
And wan-d'ring swal-lows long To find their wont-ed rest.
Oh, hap-py men who pay Their con-stant ser-vice there!
Till each ar-rives at length, Till each in heav'n ap-pears.

To Thine a-bode My heart as-pires With
My spir-it faints With e-qual zeal To
They praise Thee still; And hap-py they Who
Oh, glo-rious seat When God, our King, Shall

warm de-sires To see my God.
rise and dwell A-mong Thy saints.
love the way To Zi-on's hill.
thith-er bring Our will-ing feet! A-men.

481 Through the Night of Doubt and Sorrow

Eph. 4: 5
Igjennem Nat og Trængsal
Bernhardt S. Ingemann, 1825
Tr., Sabine Baring-Gould, 1867, alt.

8. 7. 8. 7. D.

Baltimore
Bernhard Schumacher, 1910

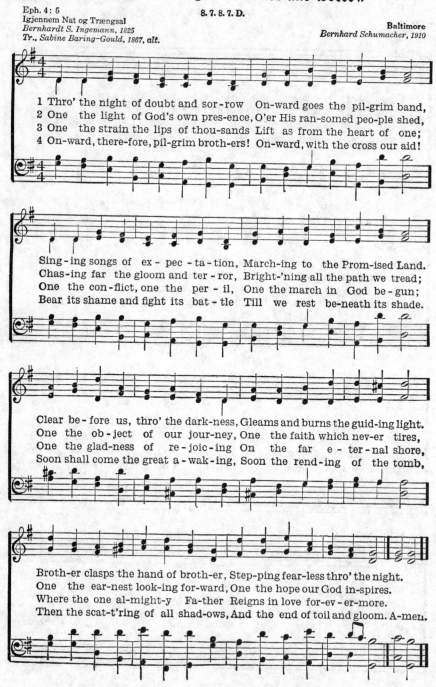

1 Thro' the night of doubt and sor-row On-ward goes the pil-grim band,
2 One the light of God's own pres-ence, O'er His ran-somed peo-ple shed,
3 One the strain the lips of thou-sands Lift as from the heart of one;
4 On-ward, there-fore, pil-grim broth-ers! On-ward, with the cross our aid!

Sing-ing songs of ex-pec-ta-tion, March-ing to the Prom-ised Land.
Chas-ing far the gloom and ter-ror, Bright-'ning all the path we tread;
One the con-flict, one the per-il, One the march in God be-gun;
Bear its shame and fight its bat-tle Till we rest be-neath its shade.

Clear be-fore us, thro' the dark-ness, Gleams and burns the guid-ing light.
One the ob-ject of our jour-ney, One the faith which nev-er tires,
One the glad-ness of re-joic-ing On the far e-ter-nal shore,
Soon shall come the great a-wak-ing, Soon the rend-ing of the tomb,

Broth-er clasps the hand of broth-er, Step-ping fear-less thro' the night.
One the ear-nest look-ing for-ward, One the hope our God in-spires.
Where the one al-might-y Fa-ther Reigns in love for-ev-er-more.
Then the scat-t'ring of all shad-ows, And the end of toil and gloom. A-men.

Dear Lord, to Thy True Servants Give

8. 8. 8. 8. 8. 8.

Is. 61: 1. 2
W. Gustave Polack, 1937

Vater unser
"Geistliche Lieder"
Leipzig, 1539

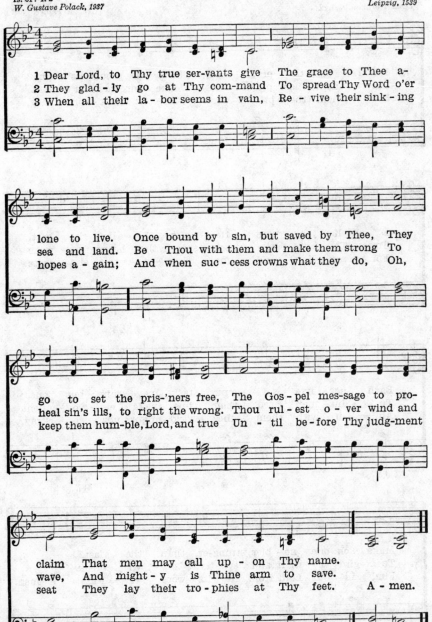

1 Dear Lord, to Thy true ser-vants give The grace to Thee a-lone to live. Once bound by sin, but saved by Thee, They go to set the pris-'ners free, The Gos-pel mes-sage to pro-claim That men may call up-on Thy name.

2 They glad-ly go at Thy com-mand To spread Thy Word o'er sea and land. Be Thou with them and make them strong To heal sin's ills, to right the wrong. Thou rul-est o-ver wind and wave, And might-y is Thine arm to save.

3 When all their la-bor seems in vain, Re-vive their sink-ing hopes a-gain; And when suc-cess crowns what they do, Oh, keep them hum-ble, Lord, and true Un-til be-fore Thy judg-ment seat They lay their tro-phies at Thy feet. A - men.

483 God of the Prophets, Bless the Prophets' Sons

10. 10. 10. 10.

2 Kings 2 : 9 ff.
Denis Wortman, 1884, ab.

Old 124th
"Genevan Psalter," 1551

1 God of the proph - ets, bless the proph-ets' sons;
2 A - noint them proph - ets. Make their ears at - tent
3 A - noint them priests. Strong in - ter - ces - sors, they,

E - li - jah's man - tle o'er E - li - sha cast.
To Thy di - vin - est speech, their hearts a - wake
For par - don and for char - i - ty and peace.

Each age its sol - emn task may claim but once;
To hu - man need, their lips make el - o - quent
Ah, if with them the world might, now a - stray,

Make each one no - bler, strong-er, than the last.
To gird the right and ev - 'ry e - vil break.
Find in our Lord from all its woes re - lease! A - men.

God of the Prophets, Bless the Prophets' Sons

4 Anoint them kings; aye, kingly kings, O Lord.
　　Anoint them with the Spirit of Thy Son.
　　Theirs not a jeweled crown, a blood-stained sword;
　　Theirs, by sweet love, for Christ a kingdom won.

5 Make them apostles, heralds of Thy Cross;
　　Forth may they go to tell all realms Thy grace.
　　Inspired of Thee, may they count all but loss
　　And stand at last with joy before Thy face.

We Bid Thee Welcome in the Name　484

L. M.

1 Cor. 4 : 1, 2
James Montgomery, 1825, cento

Herr Jesu Christ, mein's
"As Hymnodus Sacer"
Leipzig, 1625

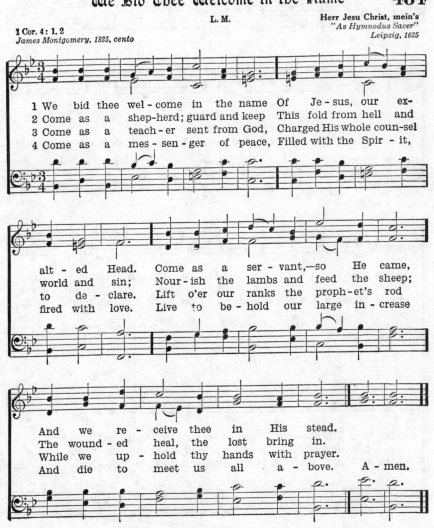

1 We bid thee wel-come in the name Of Je-sus, our ex-
2 Come as a shep-herd; guard and keep This fold from hell and
3 Come as a teach-er sent from God, Charged His whole coun-sel
4 Come as a mes-sen-ger of peace, Filled with the Spir-it,

alt-ed Head. Come as a ser-vant,—so He came,
world and sin; Nour-ish the lambs and feed the sheep;
to de-clare. Lift o'er our ranks the proph-et's rod
fired with love. Live to be-hold our large in-crease

And we re-ceive thee in His stead.
The wound-ed heal, the lost bring in.
While we up-hold thy hands with prayer.
And die to meet us all a-bove. A-men.

485 Lord Jesus, Who art Come

1 Cor. 4: 1
Herr Jesu, der du selbst
Eberhard L. Fischer, 1741, ab.
Tr., composite

6. 7. 6. 7. 6. 6. 6. 6.

O Gott, du frommer Gott
"Neuvermehrtes Gesangbuch"
Meiningen, 1693

1 Lord Je - sus, who art come A Teach - er sent from heav - en
2 Thou hast, O Lord, re-turned, To God's right hand as - cend - ing;
3 O bless - ed min - is - try Of rec - on - cil - i - a - tion,

And by both word and deed God's truth to us hast giv - en,
Yet Thou art in the world, Thy king-dom here ex - tend - ing.
That shows the way to God And brings to us sal - va - tion!

Thou wise - ly hast or - dained The ho - ly min - is - try
Thro' preach-ing of Thy Word In ev - 'ry land and clime
By Thine e - van - gel pure, Lord, Thou pre-serv'st Thy fold,

That we, Thy flock, may know The way to God thro' Thee.
Thy peo-ple's faith is kept Un - til the end of time.
Dost call, en-light-en, keep, Dost com-fort and up - hold. A-men.

Lord Jesus, Who art Come

4 Preserve this ministry
  While harvest-days are keeping;
And since the fields are white
  And hands are few for reaping,
Send workers forth, O Lord,
  The sheaves to gather in
That not a soul be lost
  Which Thou art come to win.

5 The servants Thou hast called
  And to Thy Church art giving
Preserve in doctrine pure
  And holiness of living.
Thy Spirit fill their hearts,
  Endue their tongues with power;
What they should boldly speak,
  Oh, give them in that hour!

6 Yea, bless Thy Word alway,
  Our souls forever feeding;
And may we never lack
  A faithful shepherd's leading!
Seek Thou the wandering sheep,
  Bind up the sore opprest,
Lift up the fallen ones,
  And grant the weary rest.

7 Bring those into Thy fold
  Who still to Thee are strangers;
Guard those who are within
  Against offense and dangers.
Press onward with Thy Word
  Till pastor and his fold
Through faith in Thee, O Christ,
  Thy glory shall behold.

O Thou Whose Feet have Climbed Life's Hill 486
C. M.

1 Cor. 16: 13
Louis F. Benson, 1891

Dundee
"Scottish Psalter," 1615

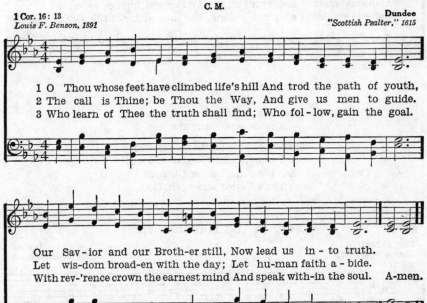

1 O Thou whose feet have climbed life's hill And trod the path of youth,
2 The call is Thine; be Thou the Way, And give us men to guide.
3 Who learn of Thee the truth shall find; Who fol-low, gain the goal.

Our Sav-ior and our Broth-er still, Now lead us in-to truth.
Let wis-dom broad-en with the day; Let hu-man faith a-bide.
With rev-'rence crown the earnest mind And speak with-in the soul.   A-men.

4 Awake the purpose high which strives
  And, falling, stands again;
Conform the will of eager lives
  To quit themselves like men.

5 Thy life the bond of fellowship,
  Thy love the law that rules,
Thy name, proclaimed by every lip,
  The Master of our schools.

487 How Beauteous Are Their Feet

Is. 52: 7
Isaac Watts, 1707

S. M.

St. Michael
"Genevan Psalter," 1551

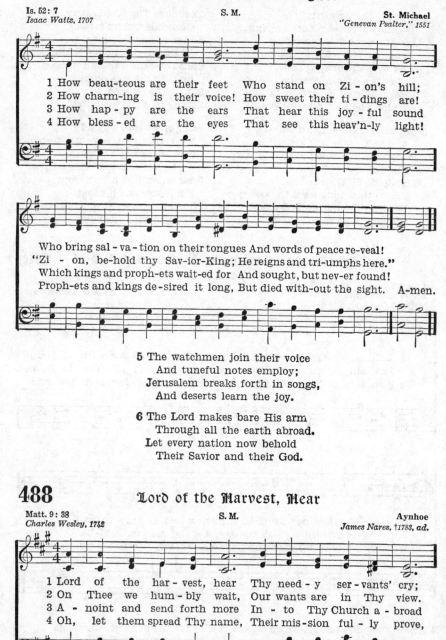

1 How beau-teous are their feet Who stand on Zi - on's hill;
2 How charm-ing is their voice! How sweet their ti - dings are!
3 How hap - py are the ears That hear this joy - ful sound
4 How bless - ed are the eyes That see this heav'n-ly light!

Who bring sal - va - tion on their tongues And words of peace re-veal!
"Zi - on, be-hold thy Sav-ior-King; He reigns and tri-umphs here."
Which kings and proph-ets wait-ed for And sought, but nev-er found!
Proph-ets and kings de-sired it long, But died with-out the sight. A-men.

5 The watchmen join their voice
   And tuneful notes employ;
Jerusalem breaks forth in songs,
   And deserts learn the joy.

6 The Lord makes bare His arm
   Through all the earth abroad.
Let every nation now behold
   Their Savior and their God.

488 Lord of the Harvest, Hear

Matt. 9: 38
Charles Wesley, 1742

S. M.

Aynhoe
James Nares, †1783, ad.

1 Lord of the har - vest, hear Thy need - y ser - vants' cry;
2 On Thee we hum - bly wait, Our wants are in Thy view.
3 A - noint and send forth more In - to Thy Church a - broad
4 Oh, let them spread Thy name, Their mis - sion ful - ly prove,

Lord of the Harvest, Hear

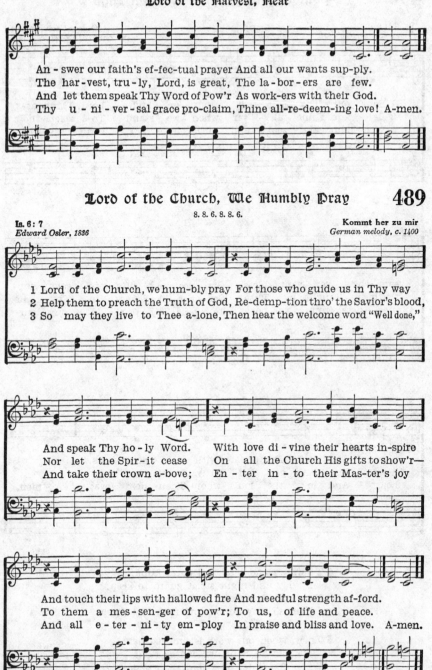

An - swer our faith's ef-fec-tual prayer And all our wants sup-ply.
The har-vest, tru-ly, Lord, is great, The la-bor-ers are few.
And let them speak Thy Word of Pow'r As work-ers with their God.
Thy u - ni - ver-sal grace pro-claim, Thine all-re-deem-ing love! A-men.

Lord of the Church, We Humbly Pray   489

8. 8. 6. 8. 8. 6.

Is. 6: 7
Edward Osler, 1836

Kommt her zu mir
German melody, c. 1400

1 Lord of the Church, we hum-bly pray For those who guide us in Thy way
2 Help them to preach the Truth of God, Re-demp-tion thro' the Savior's blood,
3 So may they live to Thee a-lone, Then hear the welcome word "Well done,"

And speak Thy ho - ly Word.   With love di - vine their hearts in-spire
Nor let the Spir-it cease   On all the Church His gifts to show'r—
And take their crown a-bove;   En - ter in - to their Mas-ter's joy

And touch their lips with hallowed fire And needful strength af-ford.
To them a mes-sen-ger of pow'r; To us, of life and peace.
And all e - ter - ni - ty em-ploy In praise and bliss and love. A-men.

490 Pour Out Thy Spirit from on High

L. M.

Ps. 132: 9
James Montgomery, 1832

O Jesu Christ, mein's
"Nürnbergisches Gesangbuch," 1676

1 Pour out Thy Spir-it from on high, Lord, Thine as-
2 Be-fore Thine al-tar when we stand To teach the
3 Wis-dom and zeal and faith im-part, Firm-ness with

sem-bled ser-vants bless; Gra-ces and gifts to each sup-
truth as taught by Thee, Sav-ior, like stars in Thy right
meek-ness, from a-bove, To bear Thy peo-ple on our

ply And clothe Thy priests with right-eous-ness.
hand The an-gels of Thy church-es be.
heart And love the souls whom Thou dost love; A-men.

4 To watch and pray and never faint
By day and night strict guard to keep,
To warn the sinner, cheer the saint,
Nourish Thy lambs, and feed Thy sheep.

5 Then, when our work is finished here,
We may in hope our charge resign.
When the Chief Shepherd shall appear,
O God, may they and we be Thine!

Send, O Lord, Thy Holy Spirit

491

Acts 11: 24
Segne, Herr, mit deinem Geiste
Author unknown, 19th century
Tr., *Frederick W. Herzberger,* †1930, alt.

8. 7. 8. 7. 7. 7. 8. 8.

Werde munter
Johann Schop, 1642

1 Send, O Lord, Thy Ho - ly Spir - it On Thy ser-vant now, we pray;
2 Thou, O Lord, Thy-self hast called him For Thy pre-cious lambs to care;
3 Help, Lord Je - sus, help him nour - ish Our dear chil-dren with Thy Word

Let him prove a faith - ful shep-herd To Thy lit - tle lambs al - way.
But to pros - per in his call - ing, He the Spir - it's gifts must share.
That in con-stant love they serve Thee Till in heav'n their song is heard.

Thy pure teach-ing to pro-claim, To ex - tol Thy ho - ly name,
Grant him wis - dom from a - bove, Fill his heart with ho - ly love;
Bound-less bless-ings, Lord, be-stow On his faith - ful toil be - low

And to feed Thy lambs, dear Savior, Make his aim and sole en-deav-or.
In all weak-ness be Thou near Him, In his prayers, Good Shepherd, hear him.
Till by grace to him is giv-en His re-ward, the crown of heav-en. A-men.

492 Lord of the Living Harvest

7. 6. 7. 6. D.

Luke 10: 2
John S. B. Monsell, 1866, ab.

Aurelia
Samuel S. Wesley, 1864

1 Lord of the liv-ing har-vest That whit-ens o'er the plain,
2 As la-b'rers in Thy vine-yard, Lord, send them out to be
3 Be with them, God the Fa-ther; Be with them, God the Son;

Where an-gels soon shall gath-er Their sheaves of gold-en grain,
Con-tent to bear the bur-den Of wea-ry days for Thee,
And God the Ho-ly Spir-it, Most bless-ed Three in One.

Ac-cept these hands to la-bor, These hearts to trust and love,
To ask no oth-er wa-ges When Thou shalt call them home
Make them Thy faith-ful ser-vants Thee right-ly to a-dore

And deign with them to hast-en Thy king-dom from a-bove.
Than to have shared the trav-ail Which makes Thy kingdom come.
And fill them with Thy ful-ness Both now and ev-er-more. A-men.

Thou Who the Night in Prayer Didst Spend 493

8. 8. 8. 8. 8. 8.

Luke 6: 12 ff.
Christopher Wordsworth, 1862, cento, alt.

St. Petersburg
Dimitri S. Bortniansky, 1822, ad.

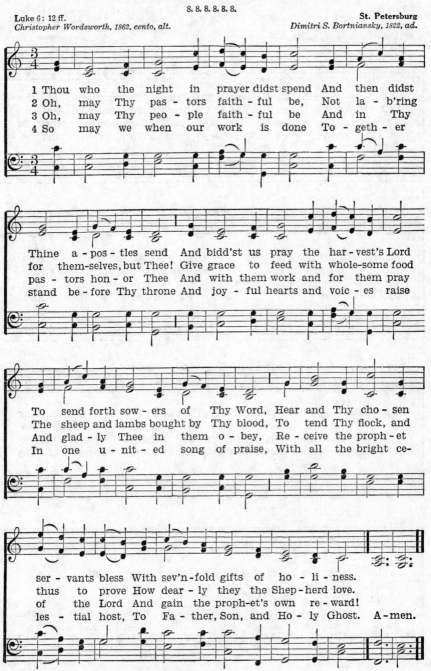

1 Thou who the night in prayer didst spend And then didst Thine a-pos-tles send And bidd'st us pray the har-vest's Lord To send forth sow-ers of Thy Word, Hear and Thy cho-sen ser-vants bless With sev'n-fold gifts of ho-li-ness.

2 Oh, may Thy pas-tors faith-ful be, Not la-b'ring for them-selves, but Thee! Give grace to feed with whole-some food The sheep and lambs bought by Thy blood, To tend Thy flock, and thus to prove How dear-ly they the Shep-herd love.

3 Oh, may Thy peo-ple faith-ful be And in Thy pas-tors hon-or Thee And with them work and for them pray And glad-ly Thee in them o-bey, Re-ceive the proph-et of the Lord And gain the proph-et's own re-ward!

4 So may we when our work is done To-geth-er stand be-fore Thy throne And joy-ful hearts and voic-es raise In one u-nit-ed song of praise, With all the bright ce-les-tial host, To Fa-ther, Son, and Ho-ly Ghost. A-men.

494 Awake, Thou Spirit, Who Didst Fire

2 Thess. 3 : 1

Wach auf, du Geist der ersten Zeugen
Carl H. von Bogatzky, 1750, cento
Tr., Catherine Winkworth, 1855, alt.

8. 8. 8. 8. 8. 8.

All' Ehr' und Lob
"Kirchengesangbuch"
Strassburg, 1541

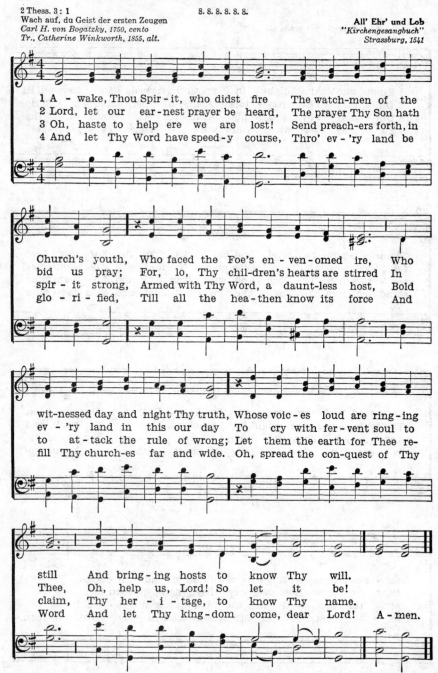

1 A - wake, Thou Spir - it, who didst fire The watch-men of the Church's youth, Who faced the Foe's en - ven - omed ire, Who wit-nessed day and night Thy truth, Whose voic - es loud are ring-ing still And bring-ing hosts to know Thy will.

2 Lord, let our ear-nest prayer be heard, The prayer Thy Son hath bid us pray; For, lo, Thy chil-dren's hearts are stirred In ev - 'ry land in this our day To cry with fer - vent soul to Thee, Oh, help us, Lord! So let it be!

3 Oh, haste to help ere we are lost! Send preach-ers forth, in spir - it strong, Armed with Thy Word, a daunt-less host, Bold to at - tack the rule of wrong; Let them the earth for Thee re-claim, Thy her - i - tage, to know Thy name.

4 And let Thy Word have speed-y course, Thro' ev - 'ry land be glo - ri - fied, Till all the hea - then know its force And fill Thy church-es far and wide. Oh, spread the con-quest of Thy Word And let Thy king-dom come, dear Lord! A - men.

From Greenland's Icy Mountains

7. 6. 7. 6. D.

495

Acts 16 : 9
Reginald Heber, 1819

Missionary Hymn
Lowell Mason, 1824

1 From Green-land's ic - y moun-tains, From In - dia's cor - al strand,
2 What though the spic - y breez - es Blow soft o'er Cey-lon's isle;
3 Can we whose souls are light - ed With wis-dom from on high,
4 Waft, waft, ye winds, His sto - ry, And you, ye wa - ters, roll,

Where Af - ric's sun - ny foun - tains Roll down their gold-en sand;
Though ev - 'ry pros-pect pleas - es And on - ly man is vile;
Can we to men be-night - ed The lamp of life de - ny?
Till like a sea of glo - ry It spreads from pole to pole;

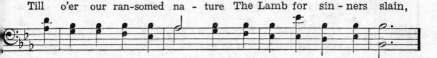

From man-y an an - cient riv - er, From man-y a palm-y plain,
In vain with lav - ish kind - ness The gifts of God are strown;
Sal - va - tion! Oh, Sal - va - tion! The joy - ful sound pro - claim
Till o'er our ran-somed na - ture The Lamb for sin - ners slain,

They call us to de - liv - er Their land from er-ror's chain.
The hea-then in his blind-ness Bows down to wood and stone.
Till each re-mot - est na - tion Has learned Mes-si-ah's name.
Re - deem-er, King, Cre - a - tor, In bliss re-turns to reign. A-men.

496 Hark! the Voice of Jesus Crying

Is. 6: 8
St. 1, 2, 4, Daniel March, 1868
St. 3, author unknown

8. 7. 8. 7. D.

Galilean
Joseph Barnby, 1883

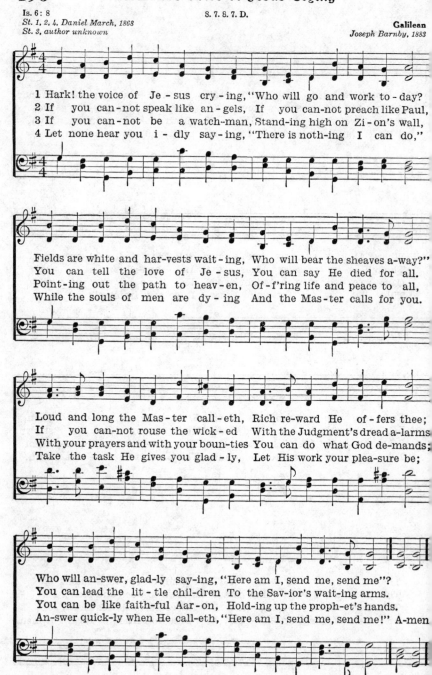

1 Hark! the voice of Je-sus cry-ing, "Who will go and work to-day?
2 If you can-not speak like an-gels, If you can-not preach like Paul,
3 If you can-not be a watch-man, Stand-ing high on Zi-on's wall,
4 Let none hear you i-dly say-ing, "There is noth-ing I can do,"

Fields are white and har-vests wait-ing, Who will bear the sheaves a-way?"
You can tell the love of Je-sus, You can say He died for all.
Point-ing out the path to heav-en, Of-f'ring life and peace to all,
While the souls of men are dy-ing And the Mas-ter calls for you.

Loud and long the Mas-ter call-eth, Rich re-ward He of-fers thee;
If you can-not rouse the wick-ed With the Judgment's dread a-larms,
With your prayers and with your boun-ties You can do what God de-mands;
Take the task He gives you glad-ly, Let His work your plea-sure be;

Who will an-swer, glad-ly say-ing, "Here am I, send me, send me"?
You can lead the lit-tle chil-dren To the Sav-ior's wait-ing arms.
You can be like faith-ful Aar-on, Hold-ing up the proph-et's hands.
An-swer quick-ly when He call-eth, "Here am I, send me, send me!" A-men

The Morning Light is Breaking

7. 6. 7. 6. D.

Matt. 28: 19, 20
Samuel F. Smith, 1832

Webb
George J. Webb, 1837

1 The morn - ing light is break - ing, The dark-ness dis - ap - pears;
2 See hea - then na - tions bend - ing Be - fore the God we love
3 Blest riv - er of sal - va - tion, Pur - sue thine on - ward way;

The sons of earth are wak - ing To pen - i - ten - tial tears.
And thou-sand hearts as - cend - ing In grat - i - tude a - bove,
Flow thou to ev - 'ry na - tion Nor in thy rich - ness stay;

Each breeze that sweeps the o - cean Brings ti - dings from a - far
While sin - ners, now con - fess - ing, The Gos - pel - call o - bey
Stay not till all the low - ly Tri - um-phant reach their home;

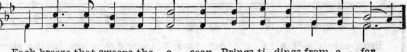

Of na - tions in com - mo - tion, Pre - pared for Zi - on's war.
And seek the Sav-ior's bless - ing, A na - tion in a day.
Stay not till all the ho - ly Pro-claim, "The Lord is come." A-men.

498 Rise, Thou Light of Gentile Nations

Is. 60:1
Gehe auf, du Trost der Heiden
Hermann Fick, †1885
Tr., composite

8. 7. 8. 7. D.

O du Liebe
"Musikalischer Christenschatz"
Basel, 1745

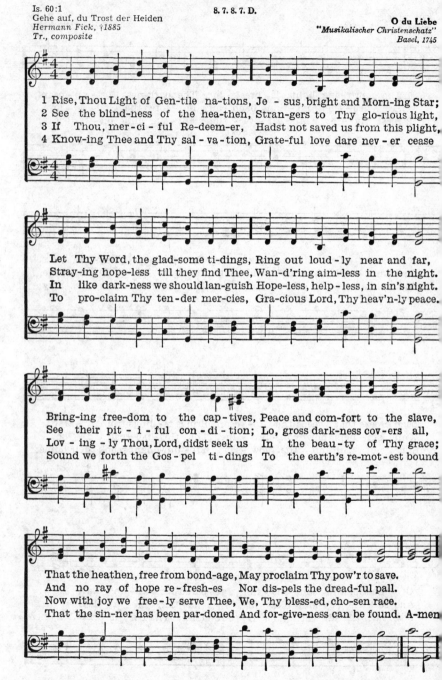

1 Rise, Thou Light of Gen-tile na-tions, Je - sus, bright and Morn-ing Star;
2 See the blind-ness of the hea-then, Stran-gers to Thy glo-rious light,
3 If Thou, mer-ci-ful Re-deem-er, Hadst not saved us from this plight,
4 Know-ing Thee and Thy sal-va-tion, Grate-ful love dare nev-er cease

Let Thy Word, the glad-some ti-dings, Ring out loud-ly near and far,
Stray-ing hope-less till they find Thee, Wan-d'ring aim-less in the night.
In like dark-ness we should lan-guish Hope-less, help-less, in sin's night.
To pro-claim Thy ten-der mer-cies, Gra-cious Lord, Thy heav'n-ly peace.

Bring-ing free-dom to the cap-tives, Peace and com-fort to the slave,
See their pit-i-ful con-di-tion; Lo, gross dark-ness cov-ers all,
Lov-ing-ly Thou, Lord, didst seek us In the beau-ty of Thy grace;
Sound we forth the Gos-pel ti-dings To the earth's re-mot-est bound

That the heathen, free from bond-age, May proclaim Thy pow'r to save.
And no ray of hope re-fresh-es Nor dis-pels the dread-ful pall.
Now with joy we free-ly serve Thee, We, Thy bless-ed, cho-sen race.
That the sin-ner has been par-doned And for-give-ness can be found. A-men

Rise, Thou Light of Gentile Nations

5 May our zeal to help the heathen
　Be increased from day to day
As we plead in true compassion
　And for their conversion pray.
For the many faithful heralds,
　For the Gospel they proclaim,
Let us all be cheerful givers
　To the glory of Thy name.

6 Savior, shine in all Thy glory
　On the nations near and far;
From the highways and the byways
　Call them, O Thou Morning Star.
Guide them whom Thy grace hath chosen
Out of Satan's dreadful thrall
To the mansions of Thy Father—
　There is room for sinners all.

Look from Thy Sphere of Endless Day   499

Is. 35　　　　　　　　　　　　　L. M.　　　　　　　　　　　St. Crispin
William C. Bryant, 1840　　　　　　　　　　　*George J. Elvey, 1862*

1 Look from Thy sphere of end-less day, O God of
mer-cy and of might! In pit-y look on those who stray
Be-night-ed in this land of light.

2 In peo-pled vale, in lone-ly glen, In crowd-ed
mart, by stream or sea, How man-y of the sons of men
Hear not the mes-sage sent from Thee!

3 Send forth Thy her-alds, Lord, to call The thought-less
young, the hard-ened old, A scat-tered, home-less flock, till all
Be gath-ered to Thy peace-ful fold. A-men.

4 Send them Thy mighty Word to speak
　Till faith shall dawn and doubt depart,
To awe the bold, to stay the weak,
　And bind and heal the broken heart.

5 Then all these wastes, a dreary scene
　That makes us sadden as we gaze,
Shall grow with living waters green
　And lift to heaven the voice of praise.

500 May God Bestow on Us His Grace

Ps. 67
Es woll' uns Gott genädig sein
Martin Luther, 1524
Tr., Richard Massie, 1851, alt.

8. 7. 8. 7. 8. 7. 8. 7. 7.

Es woll' uns Gott genädig sein
"Deutsch Kirchenamt"
Strassburg, 1525

1 May God be-stow on us His grace, With bless-ings rich pro-
2 Thine o-ver all shall be the praise And thanks of ev-'ry
3 Oh, let the peo-ple praise Thy worth, In all good works in-

vide us, And may the bright-ness of His face To
na-tion, And all the world with joy shall raise The
creas-ing; The land shall plen-teous fruit bring forth, Thy

life e-ter-nal guide us That we His sav-ing health may know,
voice of ex-ul-ta-tion; For Thou shalt judge the earth, O Lord,
Word is rich in bless-ing. May God the Fa-ther, God the Son,

His gra-cious will and plea-sure, And al-so to the hea-then show
Nor suf-fer sin to flour-ish; Thy peo-ple's pas-ture is Thy Word
And God the Spir-it bless us! Let all the world praise Him a-lone,

May God Bestow on Us His Grace

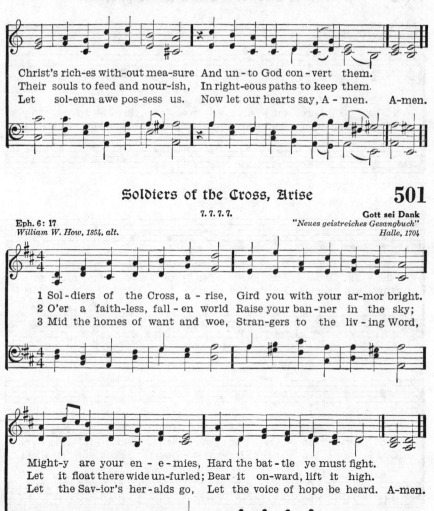

Christ's rich-es with-out mea-sure And un-to God con-vert them.
Their souls to feed and nour-ish, In right-eous paths to keep them.
Let sol-emn awe pos-sess us. Now let our hearts say, A-men. A-men.

Soldiers of the Cross, Arise 501

7. 7. 7. 7.

Eph. 6: 17
William W. How, 1854, alt.

Gott sei Dank
"Neues geistreiches Gesangbuch"
Halle, 1704

1 Sol-diers of the Cross, a-rise, Gird you with your ar-mor bright.
2 O'er a faith-less, fall-en world Raise your ban-ner in the sky;
3 Mid the homes of want and woe, Stran-gers to the liv-ing Word,

Might-y are your en-e-mies, Hard the bat-tle ye must fight.
Let it float there wide un-furled; Bear it on-ward, lift it high.
Let the Sav-ior's her-alds go, Let the voice of hope be heard. A-men.

4 Where the shadows deepest lie,
Carry truth's unsullied ray;
Where are crimes of blackest dye,
There the saving sign display.

5 To the weary and the worn
Tell of realms where sorrows cease;
To the outcast and forlorn
Speak of mercy and of peace.

6 Guard the helpless, seek the strayed,
Comfort troubles, banish grief;
In the might of God arrayed,
Scatter sin and unbelief.

7 Be the banner still unfurled,
Still unsheathed the Spirit's Sword;
Spread Thy Word in all the world;
Let Thy kingdom come, O Lord.

502 Saints of God, the Dawn is Brightening

8. 7. 8. 7. 8. 7.

John 4 : 35
Mary Maxwell, 1849, ab.

Regent Square
Henry Smart, 1867

1 Saints of God, the dawn is bright-'ning, To - ken of our
com - ing Lord; O'er the earth the field is whit - 'ning;
Loud - er rings the Mas - ter's word: Pray for reap - ers,
Pray for reap - ers, In the har - vest of the Lord!

2 Now, O Lord, ful - fil Thy plea - sure, Breathe up - on Thy
cho - sen band, And with Pen - te - cos - tal mea - sure
Send forth reap - ers o'er our land, Faith - ful reap - ers,
Faith - ful reap - ers, Gath - 'ring sheaves for Thy right hand.

3 Soon shall end the time of weep - ing, Soon the reap - ing
time will come, Heav'n and earth to - geth - er keep - ing
God's e - ter - nal Har - vest - home. Saints and an - gels,
Saints and an - gels, Shout the world's great Har - vest - home. A - men.

MISSINGS

Rise, Crowned with Light, Imperial Salem, Rise   503

10. 10. 10. 10.

Is. 60 : 1 ff.
Alexander Pope, 1712, cento, alt.

Old 124th
"Genevan Psalter," 1551

1 Rise, crowned with light, im - pe - rial Sa - lem, rise!
2 See a long race thy spa - cious courts a - dorn;
3 See bar-b'rous na - tions at thy gates at - tend,
4 The seas shall waste, the skies in smoke de - cay,

Ex - alt thy tow - 'ring head and lift thine eyes;
See fu - ture sons and daugh-ters, yet un - born,
Walk in the light, and in thy tem - ple bend;
Rocks fall to dust, and moun-tains melt a - way;

See heav'n its spar - kling por - tals wide dis - play
In crowd-ing ranks on ev - 'ry side a - rise
See thy bright al - tars thronged with pros - trate kings,
But fixed this Word, this sav - ing pow'r, re - mains;

And break up - on thee in a flood of day.
De - mand-ing life, im - pa - tient for the skies.
While ev - 'ry land its joy - ful trib - ute brings.
Thy realms shall last, thine own Mes - si - ah reigns. A - men.

504 O Spirit of the Living God

L. M.

Acts 2: 3
James Montgomery, 1823

Melcombe
Samuel Webbe, 1782

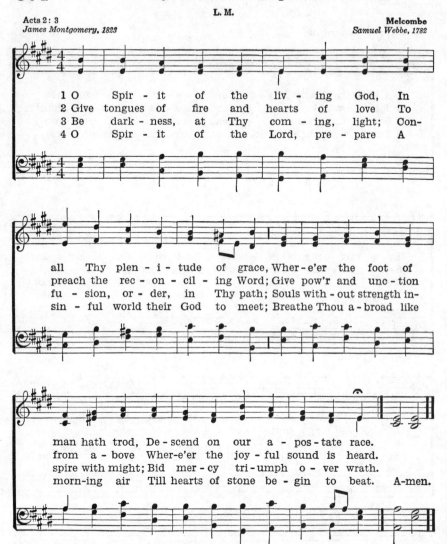

1 O Spir-it of the liv-ing God, In all Thy plen-i-tude of grace, Wher-e'er the foot of man hath trod, De-scend on our a-pos-tate race.

2 Give tongues of fire and hearts of love To preach the rec-on-cil-ing Word; Give pow'r and unc-tion from a-bove Wher-e'er the joy-ful sound is heard.

3 Be dark-ness, at Thy com-ing, light; Con-fu-sion, or-der, in Thy path; Souls with-out strength in-spire with might; Bid mer-cy tri-umph o-ver wrath.

4 O Spir-it of the Lord, pre-pare A sin-ful world their God to meet; Breathe Thou a-broad like morn-ing air Till hearts of stone be-gin to beat.

A-men.

5 Baptize the nations; far and nigh
   The triumphs of the Cross record;
   The name of Jesus glorify
   Till every kindred call Him Lord.

6 God from eternity hath willed
   All flesh shall His salvation see;
   So be the Father's love fulfilled,
   The Savior's sufferings crowned through Thee.

O'er the Gloomy Hills of Darkness

8. 7. 8. 7. 4. 7.

Rev. 14: 6
William Williams, 1772, cento, alt.

Guide Me
George W. Warren, 1884

505

1 O'er the gloom-y hills of dark-ness, Cheered by no ce-
2 King-doms wide that sit in dark-ness, Grant them, Lord, the
3 Fly a-broad, e-ter-nal Gos-pel; Win and con-quer,

les-tial ray, Sun of Right-eous-ness, a-ris-ing,
glo-rious light; And from east-ern coast to west-ern
nev-er cease. May Thy last-ing, wide do-min-ions

Bring the bright, the glo-rious day. Let the morn-ing
May the morn-ing chase the night And re-demp-tion,
Mul-ti-ply and still in-crease! May Thy scep-ter

Of Thy bless-ed Gos-pel dawn.
Free-ly pur-chased, win the day!
Sway th' en-light-ened world a-round! A-men.

506

Send Thou, O Lord, to Every Place

Rom. 8: 37
Mary C. Gates, 1888

8. 8. 8. 6.

Isleworth
Samuel Howard, †1782

1 Send Thou, O Lord, to ev-'ry place Swift mes-sen-gers be-fore Thy face,
2 Send men whose eyes have seen the King, Men in whose ears His sweet words ring;
3 To bring good news to souls in sin, The bruised and broken hearts to win;
4 Thou who hast died, Thy vic-t'ry claim; As-sert, O Christ, Thy glo-ry's name

The her-alds of Thy won-drous grace, Where Thou Thy-self wilt come.
Send such Thy lost ones home to bring; Send them where Thou wilt come,—
In ev-'ry place to bring them in Where Thou Thy-self wilt come.
And far to lands of pa-gan shame Send men where Thou wilt come. Amen.

5 Gird each one with the Spirit's Sword,
    The sword of Thine own deathless Word,
    And make them conquerors, conquering Lord,
        Where Thou Thyself wilt come.

6 Raise up, O Lord the Holy Ghost,
    From this broad land a mighty host;
    Their war cry, "We will seek the lost
        Where Thou, O Christ, wilt come."

507

Spread, Oh, Spread, Thou Mighty Word

Rom. 10: 15
Walte, walte nah und fern
Jonathan F. Bahnmaier, 1827, ab.
Tr., Catherine Winkworth, 1858, alt.

7. 7. 7. 7.

Höchster Priester
"Musikalischer Christenschatz"
Basel, 1745

1 Spread, oh, spread, thou mighty Word, Spread the king-dom of the Lord,
2 Tell them how the Fa-ther's will Made the world and keeps it still,
3 Tell of our Re-deem-er's love, Who for-ev-er doth re-move
4 Tell them of the Spir-it giv'n Now to guide us up to heav'n,

Spread, Oh, Spread, Thou Mighty Word

Where-so-e'er His breath has giv'n Life to be-ings meant for heav'n.
How His on-ly Son He gave Man from sin and death to save.
By His ho-ly sac-ri-fice All the guilt that on us lies.
Strong and ho-ly, just and true, Work-ing both to will and do. A-men.

5 Up! The ripening fields ye see.
   Mighty shall the harvest be;
   But the reapers still are few,
   Great the work they have to do.

6 Lord of Harvest, let there be
   Joy and strength to work for Thee
   Till the nations far and near
   See Thy light and learn Thy fear.

Thou Whose Almighty Word

508

Gen. 1: 8; John 1: 1–14
John Marriott, c. 1813, alt.

6. 6. 4. 6. 6. 6. 4.

Italian Hymn
Felice de Giardini, 1769

1 Thou whose al-might-y word Cha-os and dark-ness heard
2 Thou who didst come to bring, On Thy re-deem-ing wing,
3 Spir-it of Truth and Love, Life-giv-ing, ho-ly Dove,
4 Ho-ly and bless-ed Three, Glo-ri-ous Trin-i-ty,

And took their flight, Hear us, we hum-bly pray, And where the
Heal-ing and sight, Health to the sick in mind, Sight to the
Speed forth Thy flight; Move on the wa-ter's face, Bear-ing the
Wis-dom, Love, Might! Bound-less as o-cean's tide, Roll-ing in

Gos-pel day Sheds not its glo-rious ray, Let there be light!
in-ly blind, Oh, now to all man-kind Let there be light!
lamp of grace, And in earth's dark-est place Let there be light!
full-est pride, Thro' the earth, far and wide, Let there be light! A-men.

509 There Still Is Room

Luke 14: 22, 23
Es ist noch Raum
Author unknown
Tr., William M. Czamanske, 1938

10. 6. 10. 6. 9. 9. 4. 4.

Es ist genug
"Geistliche Arien"
Mühlhausen, 1672

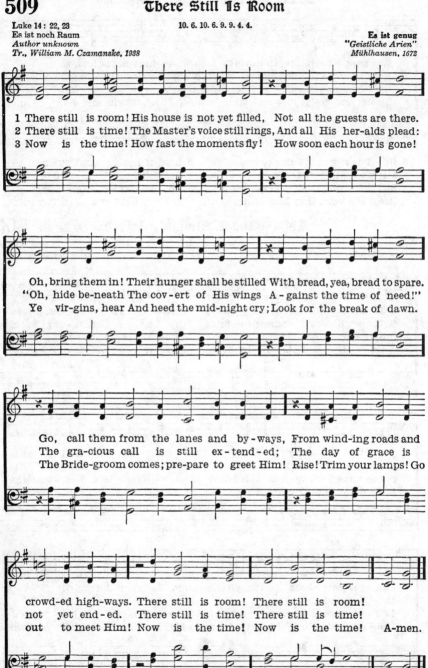

1 There still is room! His house is not yet filled, Not all the guests are there.
2 There still is time! The Master's voice still rings, And all His her-alds plead:
3 Now is the time! How fast the moments fly! How soon each hour is gone!

Oh, bring them in! Their hunger shall be stilled With bread, yea, bread to spare.
"Oh, hide be-neath The cov-ert of His wings A-gainst the time of need!"
Ye vir-gins, hear And heed the mid-night cry; Look for the break of dawn.

Go, call them from the lanes and by-ways, From wind-ing roads and
The gra-cious call is still ex-tend-ed; The day of grace is
The Bride-groom comes; pre-pare to greet Him! Rise! Trim your lamps! Go

crowd-ed high-ways. There still is room! There still is room!
not yet end-ed. There still is time! There still is time!
out to meet Him! Now is the time! Now is the time! A-men.

Savior, Sprinkle Many Nations

510

Is. 54: 2
St. 1, Arthur C. Coxe, 1851
St. 2, 3, W. Gustave Polack, 1927

8. 7. 8. 7. D.

O du Liebe
"Musikalischer Christenschatz"
Basel, 1745

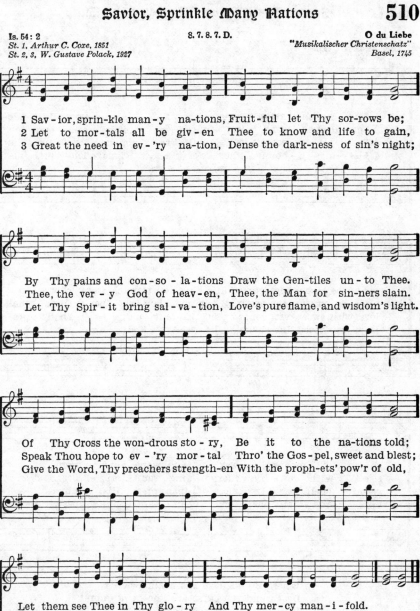

1 Sav-ior, sprin-kle man-y nations, Fruit-ful let Thy sor-rows be;
2 Let to mor-tals all be giv-en Thee to know and life to gain,
3 Great the need in ev-'ry na-tion, Dense the dark-ness of sin's night;

By Thy pains and con-so-la-tions Draw the Gen-tiles un-to Thee.
Thee, the ver-y God of heav-en, Thee, the Man for sin-ners slain.
Let Thy Spir-it bring sal-va-tion, Love's pure flame, and wisdom's light.

Of Thy Cross the won-drous sto-ry, Be it to the na-tions told;
Speak Thou hope to ev-'ry mor-tal Thro' the Gos-pel, sweet and blest;
Give the Word, Thy preachers strength-en With the proph-ets' pow'r of old,

Let them see Thee in Thy glo-ry And Thy mer-cy man-i-fold.
Lead them thro' Thy kingdom's portal To e-ter-nal peace and rest.
Help them Zi-on's cords to length-en, All Thy wand'ring sheep to fold. A-men.

511 Jesus Shall Reign Where'er the Sun

L. M.

Ps. 72
Isaac Watts, 1719, cento

Duke Street
John Hatton, 1793

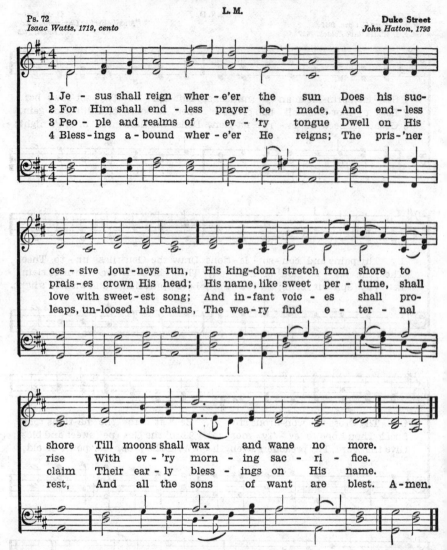

1 Je - sus shall reign wher - e'er the sun Does his suc-
2 For Him shall end - less prayer be made, And end - less
3 Peo - ple and realms of ev - 'ry tongue Dwell on His
4 Bless - ings a - bound wher - e'er He reigns; The pris - 'ner

ces - sive jour - neys run, His king-dom stretch from shore to
prais - es crown His head; His name, like sweet per - fume, shall
love with sweet - est song; And in - fant voic - es shall pro-
leaps, un - loosed his chains, The wea - ry find e - ter - nal

shore Till moons shall wax and wane no more.
rise With ev - 'ry morn - ing sac - ri - fice.
claim Their ear - ly bless - ings on His name.
rest, And all the sons of want are blest. A - men.

5 Where He displays His healing power,
   Death and the curse are known no more;
   In Him the tribes of Adam boast
   More blessings than their father lost.

6 Let every creature rise and bring
   Peculiar honors to our King;
   Angels descend with songs again,
   And earth repeat the loud Amen.

O Christ, Our True and Only Light

512

Luke 1 : 79
O Jesu Christe, wahres Licht
Johann Heermann, 1630
Tr., Catherine Winkworth, 1858, alt.

L. M.

O Jesu Christ, mein's
"Nürnbergisches Gesangbuch," 1676

1 O Christ, our true and on - ly Light, En - light - en those who sit in night; Let those a - far now hear Thy voice And in Thy fold with us re - joice.

2 Fill with the ra - diance of Thy grace The souls now lost in er - ror's maze And all whom in their se - cret minds Some dark de - lu - sion haunts and blinds.

3 Oh, gen - tly call those gone a - stray That they may find the sav - ing way! Let ev - 'ry con - science sore op - prest In Thee find peace and heav'n - ly rest.

4 Oh, make the deaf to hear Thy Word And teach the dumb to speak, dear Lord, Who dare not yet the faith a - vow, Tho' se - cret - ly they hold it now. A - men.

5 Shine on the darkened and the cold,
Recall the wanderers to Thy fold,
Unite all those who walk apart,
Confirm the weak and doubting heart,

6 So they with us may evermore
Such grace with wondering thanks adore
And endless praise to Thee be given
By all Thy Church in earth and heaven.

Cross and Comfort

513   Art Thou Weary, Art Thou Troubled

Matt. 11 : 28
John M. Neale, 1862, cento, alt.

8. 5. 8. 3.

Stephanos
Henry W. Baker, 1868

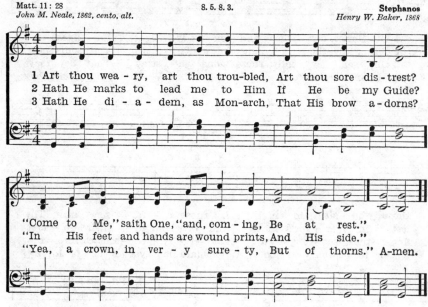

1 Art thou wea-ry, art thou trou-bled, Art thou sore dis-trest?
2 Hath He marks to lead me to Him If He be my Guide?
3 Hath He di-a-dem, as Mon-arch, That His brow a-dorns?

"Come to Me," saith One, "and, com-ing, Be at rest."
"In His feet and hands are wound prints, And His side."
"Yea, a crown, in ver-y sure-ty, But of thorns." A-men.

4 If I find Him, if I follow,
   What His guerdon here?
  "Many a sorrow, many a labor,
   Many a tear."

5 If I still hold closely to Him,
   What hath He at last?
  "Sorrow vanquished, labor ended,
   Jordan passed."

6 If I ask Him to receive me,
   Will He say me nay?
  "Not till earth and not till heaven
   Pass away."

7 Finding, following, keeping, struggling,
   Is He sure to bless?
  "Saints, apostles, prophets, martyrs,
   Answer, Yes."

514   God Moves in a Mysterious Way

John 13 : 7
William Cowper, 1774

C. M.

Dundee
"Scottish Psalter," 1615

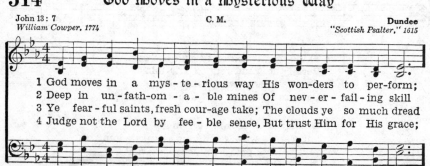

1 God moves in a mys-te-rious way His won-ders to per-form;
2 Deep in un-fath-om-a-ble mines Of nev-er-fail-ing skill
3 Ye fear-ful saints, fresh cour-age take; The clouds ye so much dread
4 Judge not the Lord by fee-ble sense, But trust Him for His grace;

God Moves in a Mysterious Way

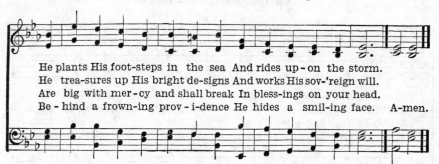

He plants His foot-steps in the sea And rides up-on the storm.
He trea-sures up His bright de-signs And works His sov-'reign will.
Are big with mer-cy and shall break In bless-ings on your head.
Be-hind a frown-ing prov-i-dence He hides a smil-ing face. A-men.

5 His purposes will ripen fast,
   Unfolding every hour;
   The bud may have a bitter taste,
   But sweet will be the flower.

6 Blind unbelief is sure to err
   And scan His work in vain;
   God is His own Interpreter,
   And He will make it plain.

O Thou from Whom All Goodness Flows   515

C. M.

Neh. 13 : 31
Thomas Haweis, c. 1791, alt., ab.

St. Bernard
"Tochter Zion"
Cologne, 1741

1 O Thou from whom all good-ness flows, I lift my heart to Thee;
2 When on my poor and bur-dened heart My sins lie heav-i-ly,
3 When tri-als sore ob-struct my way And ills I can-not flee,
4 If worn with pain, dis-ease, or grief This fee-ble bod-y be,

In all my sor-rows, con-flicts, woes, Dear Lord, re-mem-ber me.
Thy par-don speak, new peace im-part; Dear Lord, re-mem-ber me.
Oh, let my strength be as my day; Dear Lord, re-mem-ber me.
Grant pa-tience, rest, and kind re-lief; Dear Lord, re-mem-ber me. A-men.

5 When in the solemn hour of death
   I wait Thy just decree,
   Be this the prayer of my last breath:
   Dear Lord, remember me.

6 And when before Thy throne I stand
   And lift my soul to Thee,
   Then with the saints at Thy right hand,
   Dear Lord, remember me.

516 In the Hour of Trial

6. 5. 6. 5. D.

Luke 22: 31, 32
James Montgomery, 1834, alt.

St. Mary Magdalene
John B. Dykes, 1862

1 In the hour of tri - al, Je - sus, plead for me
2 With for - bid - den plea - sures Should this vain world charm
3 Should Thy mer - cy send me Sor - row, toil, and woe,
4 When my last hour com - eth, Fraught with strife and pain,

Lest by base de - ni - al I de - part from Thee.
Or its tempt - ing trea - sures Spread to work me harm,
Or should pain at - tend me On my path be - low,
When my dust re - turn - eth To the dust a - gain,

When Thou seest me wa - ver, With a look re - call
Bring to my re - mem - brance Sad Geth - sem - a - ne
Grant that I may nev - er Fail Thy hand to see;
On Thy truth re - ly - ing, Thro' that mor - tal strife,

Nor for fear or fa - vor Suf - fer me to fall.
Or, in dark - er sem - blance, Cross-crowned Cal - va - ry.
Grant that I may ev - er Cast my care on Thee.
Je - sus, take me, dy - ing, To e - ter - nal life. A - men.

The Will of God Is Always Best

Matt. 6: 10
Was mein Gott will, das g'scheh' allzeit
Albrecht von Brandenburg, c. 1554, asc.
Tr., composite

8. 7. 8. 7. D. Iambic

Was mein Gott will
French melody, 1529
Harm. by Johann S. Bach, †1750

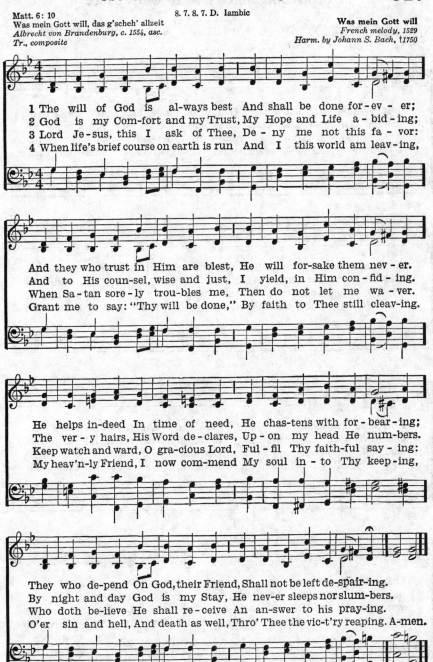

1 The will of God is al-ways best And shall be done for-ev-er;
2 God is my Com-fort and my Trust, My Hope and Life a-bid-ing;
3 Lord Je-sus, this I ask of Thee, De-ny me not this fa-vor:
4 When life's brief course on earth is run And I this world am leav-ing,

And they who trust in Him are blest, He will for-sake them nev-er.
And to His coun-sel, wise and just, I yield, in Him con-fid-ing.
When Sa-tan sore-ly trou-bles me, Then do not let me wa-ver.
Grant me to say: "Thy will be done," By faith to Thee still cleav-ing.

He helps in-deed In time of need, He chas-tens with for-bear-ing;
The ver-y hairs, His Word de-clares, Up-on my head He num-bers.
Keep watch and ward, O gra-cious Lord, Ful-fil Thy faith-ful say-ing:
My heav'n-ly Friend, I now com-mend My soul in-to Thy keep-ing,

They who de-pend On God, their Friend, Shall not be left de-spair-ing.
By night and day God is my Stay, He nev-er sleeps nor slum-bers.
Who doth be-lieve He shall re-ceive An an-swer to his pray-ing.
O'er sin and hell, And death as well, Thro' Thee the vic-t'ry reaping. A-men.

518 If Thou But Suffer God to Guide Thee

Ps. 55 : 22
9. 8. 9. 8. 8. 8.

Wer nur den lieben Gott lässt walten
Georg Neumark, 1640
Tr., Catherine Winkworth, 1863, alt.

Wer nur den lieben Gott
Georg Neumark, 1640

1 If thou but suf - fer God to guide thee And hope in
2 What can these anx - ious cares a - vail thee, These nev - er -
3 Be pa - tient and a - wait His lei - sure In cheer - ful
4 God knows full well when times of glad - ness Shall be the

Him thro' all thy ways, He'll give thee strength, what-e'er be-tide thee,
ceas - ing moans and sighs? What can it help if thou be - wail thee
hope, with heart con - tent To take what-e'er thy Fa-ther's plea-sure
need - ful thing for thee. When He has tried thy soul with sad - ness

And bear thee thro' the e - vil days. Who trusts in God's un-
O'er each dark mo - ment as it flies? Our cross and tri - als
And His dis - cern - ing love hath sent, Nor doubt our in - most
And from all guile has found thee free, He comes to thee all

chang - ing love Builds on the Rock that naught can move.
do but press The heav - ier for our bit - ter - ness.
wants are known To Him who chose us for His own.
un - a - ware And makes thee own His lov - ing care. A - men.

If Thou But Suffer God to Guide Thee

5 Nor think amid the fiery trial
  That God hath cast thee off unheard,
That he whose hopes meet no denial
  Must surely be of God preferred.
Time passes and much change doth bring
And sets a bound to everything.

6 All are alike before the Highest;
  'Tis easy for our God, we know,
To raise thee up, though low thou liest,
  To make the rich man poor and low.
True wonders still by Him are wrought
Who setteth up and brings to naught.

7 Sing, pray, and keep His ways unswerving,
  Perform thy duties faithfully,
And trust His Word; though undeserving,
  Thou yet shalt find it true for thee.
God never yet forsook in need
The soul that trusted Him indeed.

Beloved, "It Is Well!" 519

S. M.

Rom. 11 : 33
George W. Doane, 1833

Cambridge
Ralph Harrison, c. 1784

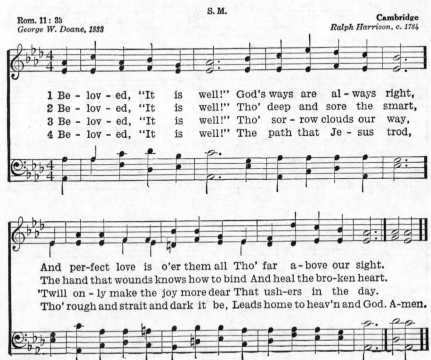

1 Be - lov - ed, "It is well!" God's ways are al - ways right,
2 Be - lov - ed, "It is well!" Tho' deep and sore the smart,
3 Be - lov - ed, "It is well!" Tho' sor - row clouds our way,
4 Be - lov - ed, "It is well!" The path that Je - sus trod,

And per-fect love is o'er them all Tho' far a - bove our sight.
The hand that wounds knows how to bind And heal the bro-ken heart.
'Twill on - ly make the joy more dear That ush-ers in the day.
Tho' rough and strait and dark it be, Leads home to heav'n and God. A-men.

520 Commit Whatever Grieves Thee

Ps. 37 : 5
Befiehl du deine Wege
Paul Gerhardt, 1656
Tr., composite

7. 6. 7. 6. D.

Herzlich tut mich
Hans L. Hassler, 1601

1 Com - mit what - ev - er grieves thee   In - to   the gra-cious hands
2 On   Him place thy   re - li - ance   If   thou wouldst be   se - cure;

Of   Him who nev - er leaves thee,   Who heav'n and earth com-mands.
His   work thou must con-sid - er   If   thine is   to   en - dure.

Who points the clouds their cours - es,   Whom winds and waves o - bey,
By   anx - ious sighs and   griev - ing   And   self - tor-ment-ing care

He   will   di - rect thy foot-steps   And find for thee   a   way.
God   is   not moved to giv - ing;   All   must be gained by prayer. A-men.

Commit Whatever Grieves Thee

3 Thy truth and grace, O Father,
　　Most surely see and know
　Both what is good and evil
　　For mortal man below.
　According to Thy counsel
　　Thou wilt Thy work pursue;
　And what Thy wisdom chooseth
　　Thy might will always do.

4 Thy hand is never shortened,
　　All things must serve Thy might;
　Thine every act is blessing,
　　Thy path is purest light.
　Thy work no man can hinder,
　　Thy purpose none can stay,
　Since Thou to bless Thy children
　　Wilt always find a way.

5 Though all the powers of evil
　　The will of God oppose,
　His purpose will not falter,
　　His pleasure onward goes.
　Whate'er God's will resolveth,
　　Whatever He intends,
　Will always be accomplished
　　True to His aims and ends.

6 Then hope, my feeble spirit,
　　And be thou undismayed;
　God helps in every trial
　　And makes thee unafraid.
　Await His time with patience,
　　Then shall thine eyes behold
　The sun of joy and gladness
　　His brightest beams unfold.

7 Arise, my soul, and banish
　　Thy anguish and thy care.
　Away with thoughts that sadden
　　And heart and mind ensnare!
　Thou art not lord and master
　　Of thine own destiny;
　Enthroned in highest heaven,
　　God rules in equity.

8 Leave all to His direction;
　　In wisdom He doth reign,
　And in a way most wondrous
　　His course He will maintain.
　Soon He, His promise keeping,
　　With wonder-working skill
　Shall put away the sorrows
　　That now thy spirit fill.

9 A while His consolation
　　He may to thee deny,
　And seem as though in trial
　　He far from thee would fly;
　A while distress and anguish
　　May compass thee around,
　Nor to thy supplication
　　An answering voice be found.

10 But if thou perseverest,
　　Thou shalt deliverance find.
　Behold, all unexpected
　　He will thy soul unbind
　And from the heavy burden
　　Thy heart will soon set free;
　And thou wilt see the blessing
　　He had in mind for thee.

11 O faithful child of heaven,
　　How blessèd shalt thou be!
　With songs of glad thanksgiving
　　A crown awaiteth thee.
　Into thy hand thy Maker
　　Will give the victor's palm,
　And thou to thy Deliverer
　　Shalt sing a joyous psalm.

12 Give, Lord, this consummation
　　To all our heart's distress;
　Our hands, our feet, e'er strengthen,
　　In death our spirits bless.
　Thy truth and Thy protection
　　Grant evermore, we pray,
　And in celestial glory
　　Shall end our destined way.

521 What God Ordains Is Always Good

Deut. 32: 4
Was Gott tut, das ist wohlgetan
Samuel Rodigast, 1675
Tr., composite

8. 7. 8. 7. 4. 4. 7. 7.

Was Gott tut
Severus Gastorius, 1681

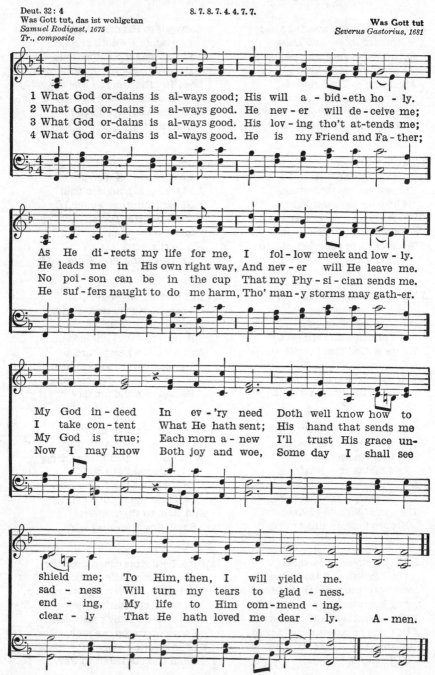

1 What God or-dains is al-ways good; His will a-bid-eth ho-ly.
2 What God or-dains is al-ways good. He nev-er will de-ceive me;
3 What God or-dains is al-ways good. His lov-ing tho't at-tends me;
4 What God or-dains is al-ways good. He is my Friend and Fa-ther;

As He di-rects my life for me, I fol-low meek and low-ly.
He leads me in His own right way, And nev-er will He leave me.
No poi-son can be in the cup That my Phy-si-cian sends me.
He suf-fers naught to do me harm, Tho' man-y storms may gath-er.

My God in-deed In ev-'ry need Doth well know how to
I take con-tent What He hath sent; His hand that sends me
My God is true; Each morn a-new I'll trust His grace un-
Now I may know Both joy and woe, Some day I shall see

shield me; To Him, then, I will yield me.
sad-ness Will turn my tears to glad-ness.
end-ing, My life to Him com-mend-ing.
clear-ly That He hath loved me dear-ly. A-men.

What God Ordains Is Always Good

5 What God ordains is always good.
  Though I the cup am drinking
  Which savors now of bitterness,
  I take it without shrinking.
  For after grief God grants relief,
  My heart with comfort filling
  And all my sorrow stilling.

6 What God ordains is always good.
  This truth remains unshaken.
  Though sorrow, need, or death be mine,
  I shall not be forsaken.
  I fear no harm, For with His arm
  He shall embrace and shield me;
  So to my God I yield me.

When in the Hour of Utmost Need

522

L. M.

2 Chron. 20: 12
Wenn wir in höchsten Nöten sein
Paul Eber, 1560
Tr., Catherine Winkworth, 1858, alt.

Wenn wir in höchsten Nöten
"Genevan Psalter," 1547

1 When in the hour of ut - most need
  We know not where to look for aid;
  When days and nights of anx-ious thought
  Nor help nor coun-sel yet have brought,

2 Then this our com-fort is a - lone,
  That we may meet be-fore Thy throne
  And cry, O faith-ful God, to Thee
  For res-cue from our mis-er - y;

3 To Thee may raise our hearts and eyes,
  Re-pent-ing sore with bit-ter sighs,
  And seek Thy par-don for our sin
  And res-pite from our griefs with-in.
  A - men.

4 For Thou hast promised graciously
  To hear all those who cry to Thee
  Thro' Him whose name alone is great,
  Our Savior and our Advocate.

5 And thus we come, O God, today
  And all our woes before Thee lay;
  For sorely tried, cast down, we stand,
  Perplexed by fears on every hand.

6 Ah! hide not for our sins Thy face,
  Absolve us thro' Thy boundless grace,
  Be with us in our anguish still,
  Free us at last from every ill,

7 That so with all our hearts we may
  To Thee our glad thanksgiving pay,
  Then walk obedient to Thy Word
  And now and ever praise Thee, Lord.

523 Why Should Cross and Trial Grieve Me

Ps. 73 : 23

8. 3. 3. 6. 8. 3. 3. 6.

Warum sollt' ich mich denn grämen
Paul Gerhardt, 1653, cento
Tr., composite, based on John Kelly, 1867

Warum sollt' ich mich denn grämen
Johann G. Ebeling, 1666

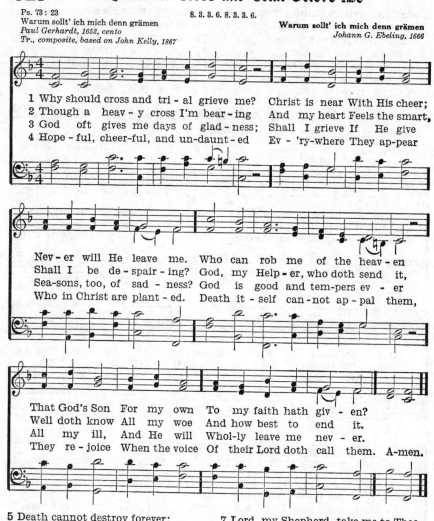

1 Why should cross and tri-al grieve me? Christ is near With His cheer;
2 Though a heav-y cross I'm bear-ing And my heart Feels the smart,
3 God oft gives me days of glad-ness; Shall I grieve If He give
4 Hope-ful, cheer-ful, and un-daunt-ed Ev-'ry-where They ap-pear

Nev-er will He leave me. Who can rob me of the heav-en
Shall I be de-spair-ing? God, my Help-er, who doth send it,
Sea-sons, too, of sad-ness? God is good and tem-pers ev-er
Who in Christ are plant-ed. Death it-self can-not ap-pal them,

That God's Son For my own To my faith hath giv-en?
Well doth know All my woe And how best to end it.
All my ill, And He will Whol-ly leave me nev-er.
They re-joice When the voice Of their Lord doth call them. A-men.

5 Death cannot destroy forever;
    From our fears, Cares, and tears
It will us deliver.
    It will close life's mournful story,
Make a way That we may
    Enter heavenly glory.

6 What is all this life possesses?
    But a hand Full of sand
That the heart distresses.
    Noble gifts that pall me never
Christ, our Lord, Will accord
    To His saints forever.

7 Lord, my Shepherd, take me to Thee.
    Thou art mine; I was Thine,
Even ere I knew Thee.
    I am Thine, for Thou hast bought me;
Lost I stood, But Thy blood
    Free salvation brought me.

8 Thou art mine; I love and own Thee.
    Light of Joy, Ne'er shall I
From my heart dethrone Thee.
    Savior, let me soon behold Thee
Face to face — May Thy grace
    Evermore enfold me!

In Thee, Lord, have I Put My Trust

Ps. 31 : 1-5
In dich hab' ich gehoffet, Herr
Adam Reusner, 1533
Tr., Catherine Winkworth, 1863, alt.

8. 8. 7. 4. 4. 7.

In dich hab' ich gehoffet
"Himmlische Harfen"
Augsburg, 1581

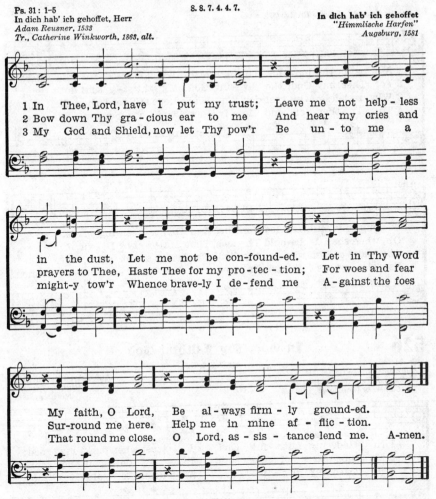

1 In Thee, Lord, have I put my trust; Leave me not help-less
2 Bow down Thy gra-cious ear to me And hear my cries and
3 My God and Shield, now let Thy pow'r Be un-to me a

in the dust, Let me not be con-found-ed. Let in Thy Word
prayers to Thee, Haste Thee for my pro-tec-tion; For woes and fear
might-y tow'r Whence brave-ly I de-fend me A-gainst the foes

My faith, O Lord, Be al-ways firm-ly ground-ed.
Sur-round me here. Help me in mine af-flic-tion.
That round me close. O Lord, as-sis-tance lend me. A-men.

4 Thou art my Strength, my Shield, my Rock,
My Fortress that withstands each shock,
   My Help, my Life, my Treasure.
Whate'er the rod, Thou art my God;
   Naught can resist Thy pleasure.

5 The world for me has falsely set
Full many a secret snare and net
   To tempt me and to harm me.
Lord, make them fail, Do Thou pre-vail,
   Let their disguise not charm me.

6 With Thee, Lord, have I cast my lot;
O faithful God, forsake me not,
   To Thee my soul commending.
Lord, be my Stay, Lead Thou the way
   Now and when life is ending.

7 All honor, praise, and majesty
To Father, Son, and Spirit be,
   Our God forever glorious,
In whose rich grace We'll run our race
   Till we depart victorious.

525 As Pants the Hart for Cooling Streams

Ps. 42
Nahum Tate and Nicholas Brady, 1696, cento

C. M.

Spohr
Louis Spohr, 1835, arr.

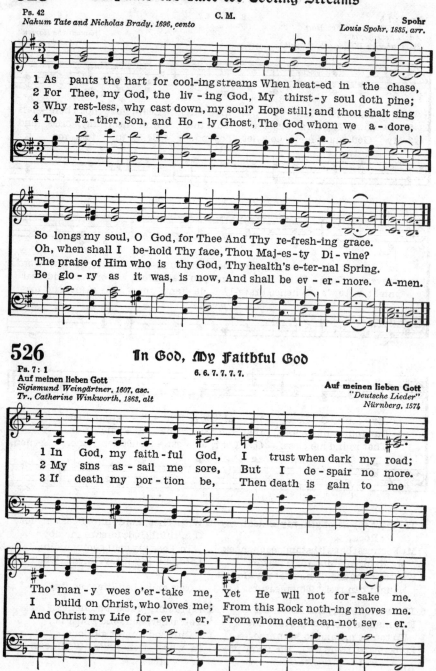

1 As pants the hart for cool-ing streams When heat-ed in the chase,
2 For Thee, my God, the liv-ing God, My thirst-y soul doth pine;
3 Why rest-less, why cast down, my soul? Hope still; and thou shalt sing
4 To Fa-ther, Son, and Ho-ly Ghost, The God whom we a-dore,

So longs my soul, O God, for Thee And Thy re-fresh-ing grace.
Oh, when shall I be-hold Thy face, Thou Maj-es-ty Di-vine?
The praise of Him who is thy God, Thy health's e-ter-nal Spring.
Be glo-ry as it was, is now, And shall be ev-er-more. A-men.

526 In God, My Faithful God

Ps. 7: 1
Auf meinen lieben Gott
Sigismund Weingärtner, 1607, asc.
Tr., Catherine Winkworth, 1863, alt

6. 6. 7. 7. 7. 7.

Auf meinen lieben Gott
"Deutsche Lieder"
Nürnberg, 1574

1 In God, my faith-ful God, I trust when dark my road;
2 My sins as-sail me sore, But I de-spair no more.
3 If death my por-tion be, Then death is gain to me

Tho' man-y woes o'er-take me, Yet He will not for-sake me.
I build on Christ, who loves me; From this Rock noth-ing moves me.
And Christ my Life for-ev-er, From whom death can-not sev-er.

In God, My Faithful God

His love it is doth send them And, when 'tis best, will end them.
To Him I all sur-ren-der, To Him, my soul's De-fend-er.
Come when it may, He'll shield me, To Him I whol-ly yield me. A-men.

4 O Jesus Christ, my Lord,
So meek in deed and word,
Thou once didst die to save us
Because Thy love would have us
Be heirs of heavenly gladness
When ends this life of sadness.

5 "So be it," then I say
With all my heart each day.
We, too, dear Lord, adore Thee,
We sing for joy before Thee.
Guide us while here we wander
Until we praise Thee yonder.

Lord, It Belongs Not to My Care 527

C. M.

Phil. 1: 21
Richard Baxter, 1681, cento, alt.

St. Bernard
"Tochter Zion"
Cologne, 1741

1 Lord, it be-longs not to my care Wheth-er I die or live;
2 If life be long, I will be glad That I may long o-bey;
3 Christ leads me thro' no dark-er rooms Than He went thro' be-fore;
4 Come, Lord, when grace has made me meet Thy bless-ed face to see;

To love and serve Thee is my share, And this Thy grace must give.
If short, no la-bor-er is sad To end his toil-some day.
He that in-to God's kingdom comes Must en-ter by this door.
For if Thy work on earth be sweet, What will Thy glo-ry be? A-men.

5 Then shall I end my sad complaints
And weary, sinful days
And join with all triumphant saints
Who sing my Savior's praise.

6 My knowledge of that life is small,
The eye of faith is dim;
But 'tis enough that Christ knows all,
And I shall be with Him.

528

If God Himself Be For Me

Rom. 8: 31–39
Ist Gott für mich, so trete
Paul Gerhardt, 1656
Tr., based on Richard Massie, 1857

7. 6. 7. 6. D.

Valet will ich dir geben
Melchior Teschner, 1613

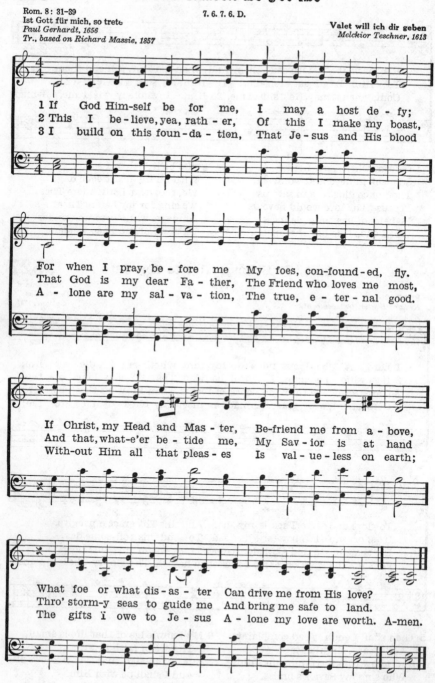

1 If God Him-self be for me, I may a host de-fy;
2 This I be-lieve, yea, rath-er, Of this I make my boast,
3 I build on this foun-da-tion, That Je-sus and His blood

For when I pray, be-fore me My foes, con-found-ed, fly.
That God is my dear Fa-ther, The Friend who loves me most,
A-lone are my sal-va-tion, The true, e-ter-nal good.

If Christ, my Head and Mas-ter, Be-friend me from a-bove,
And that, what-e'er be-tide me, My Sav-ior is at hand
With-out Him all that pleas-es Is val-ue-less on earth;

What foe or what dis-as-ter Can drive me from His love?
Thro' storm-y seas to guide me And bring me safe to land.
The gifts I owe to Je-sus A-lone my love are worth. A-men.

If God Himself Be For Me

4 My Jesus is my Splendor,
   My Sun, my Light, alone;
Were He not my Defender
   Before God's awe-full throne,
I never should find favor
   And mercy in His sight,
But be destroyed forever
   As darkness by the light.

5 He canceled my offenses,
   Delivered me from death;
He is the Lord who cleanses
   My soul from sin through faith.
In Him I can be cheerful,
   Bold, and undaunted aye;
In Him I am not fearful
   Of God's great Judgment Day.

6 Naught, naught, can now condemn me
   Nor set my hope aside;
Now hell no more can claim me,
   Its fury I deride.
No sentence e'er reproves me,
   No ill destroys my peace;
For Christ, my Savior, loves me
   And shields me with His grace.

7 His Spirit in me dwelleth,
   And o'er my mind He reigns.
All sorrow He dispelleth
   And soothes away all pains.
He crowns His work with blessing
   And helpeth me to cry,
"My Father!" without ceasing,
   To Him who dwells on high.

8 And when my soul is lying
   Weak, trembling, and opprest,
He pleads with groans and sighing
   That cannot be exprest;
But God's quick eye discerns them,
   Although they give no sound,
And into language turns them
   E'en in the heart's deep ground.

9 To mine His Spirit speaketh
   Sweet words of holy cheer,
How God to him that seeketh
   For rest is always near
And how He hath erected
   A city fair and new,
Where all that faith expected
   We evermore shall view.

10 In yonder home doth flourish
   My heritage, my lot;
Though here I die and perish,
   My heaven shall fail me not.
Though care my life oft saddens
   And causeth tears to flow,
The light of Jesus gladdens
   And sweetens every woe.

11 Who clings with resolution
   To Him whom Satan hates
Must look for persecution;
   For him the burden waits
Of mockery, shame, and losses,
   Heaped on his blameless head;
A thousand plagues and crosses
   Will be his daily bread.

12 From me this is not hidden,
   Yet I am not afraid;
I leave my cares, as bidden,
   To whom my vows were paid.
Though life and limb it cost me
   And everything I own,
Unshaken shall I trust Thee
   And cleave to Thee alone.

13 Though earth be rent asunder,
   Thou'rt mine eternally;
Not fire nor sword nor thunder
   Shall sever me from Thee;
Not hunger, thirst, nor danger,
   Not pain nor poverty
Nor mighty princes' anger
   Shall ever hinder me.

14 No angel and no gladness,
   No throne, no pomp, no show,
No love, no hate, no sadness,
   No pain, no depth of woe,
No scheme of man's contrivance,
   However small or great,
Shall draw me from Thy guidance
   Nor from Thee separate.

15 My heart for joy is springing
   And can no more be sad,
'Tis full of mirth and singing,
   Sees naught but sunshine glad.
The Sun that cheers my spirit
   Is Jesus Christ, my King;
The heaven I shall inherit
   Makes me rejoice and sing.

529 I Leave All Things to God's Direction

Rom. 8: 23
Ich halte Gott in allem stille
Salomo Franck, 1685
Tr., August Crull, †1923, alt.

9. 8. 9. 8. 8. 8.

Wer nur den lieben Gott
Georg Neumark, 1640

1 I leave all things to God's di - rec - tion, He lov - eth
2 My God hath all things in His keep - ing, He is the
3 The will of God shall be my plea - sure While here on
4 God knows what must be done to save me, His love for

me in weal and woe; His will is good, true His af - fec - tion,
ev - er faith - ful Friend; He grants me laugh - ter af - ter weep - ing,
earth is mine a - bode; My will is wrong be - yond all mea - sure,
me will nev - er cease; Up - on His hands He did en - grave me

With ten - der love His heart doth glow. My For - tress and my
And all His ways in bless - ings end. His love en - dures e -
It doth not will what pleas - eth God. The Chris - tian's mot - to
With pur - est gold of lov - ing grace. His will su - preme must

Rock is He: What pleas-eth God, that pleas-eth me.
ter - nal - ly: What pleas-eth God, that pleas-eth me.
e'er must be: What pleas-eth God, that pleas-eth me.
ev - er be: What pleas-eth God, that pleas-eth me. A - men.

¶ Leave All Things to God's Direction

5 My God desires the soul's salvation,
   Me also He desires to save;
Therefore with Christian resignation
   All earthly troubles I will brave.
His will be done eternally:
What pleaseth God, that pleaseth me.

Thy Ways, O Lord, with Wise Design   530

1 Cor. 13 : 12   **L. M.**   St. Luke
Ambrose Serle, 1786   *Jeremiah Clarke, †1707*

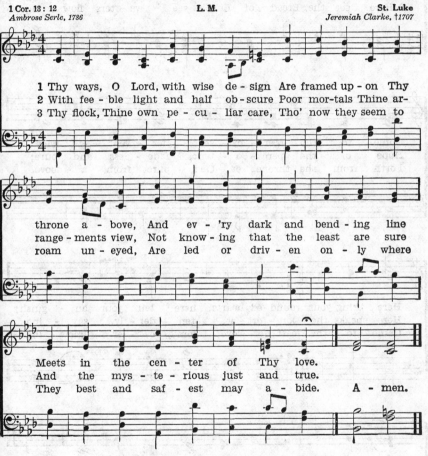

1 Thy ways, O Lord, with wise de-sign Are framed up-on Thy
2 With fee-ble light and half ob-scure Poor mor-tals Thine ar-
3 Thy flock, Thine own pe-cu-liar care, Tho' now they seem to

throne a-bove, And ev-'ry dark and bend-ing line
range-ments view, Not know-ing that the least are sure
roam un-eyed, Are led or driv-en on-ly where

Meets in the cen-ter of Thy love.
And the mys-te-rious just and true.
They best and saf-est may a-bide.   A-men.

4 They neither know nor trace the way;
   But while they trust Thy guardian eye,
Their feet shall ne'er to ruin stray,
   Nor shall the weakest fail or die.

5 My favored soul shall meekly learn
   To lay her reason at Thy throne;
Too weak Thy secrets to discern,
   I'll trust Thee for my Guide alone.

531 Come, Ye Disconsolate

11. 10. 11. 10.

Heb. 4: 16
St. 1, 2, Thomas Moore, 1816, alt.
St. 3, Thomas Hastings, 1832

Alma Redemptoris mater
Samuel Webbe, 1792

1 Come, ye dis - con - so - late, wher - e'er ye lan - guish;
2 Joy of the des - o - late, Light of the stray - ing,
3 Here see the Bread of Life; see wa - ters flow - ing

Come to the Mer - cy - seat, fer - vent - ly kneel.
Hope of the pen - i - tent, fade - less and pure;
Forth from the throne of God, pure from a - bove.

Here bring your wound - ed hearts, here tell your an - guish;
Here speaks the Com - fort - er, ten - der - ly say - ing,
Come to the feast of love; come, ev - er know - ing

Earth has no sor - row that Heav'n can - not heal.
Earth has no sor - row that Heav'n can - not cure.
Earth has no sor - row but Heav'n can re - move. A - men.

Thy Way, Not Mine, O Lord

6. 6. 6. 6. D.

Ps. 25 : 5
Horatius Bonar, 1857, *cento*

Ich halte treulich still
"Musikalisches Gesangbuch"
Leipzig, 1736, ad.

1 Thy way, not mine, O Lord, How - ev - er dark it be.
2 Choose Thou for me my friends, My sick - ness or my health;

Lead me by Thine own hand; Choose Thou the path for me.
Choose Thou my cares for me, My pov - er - ty or wealth.

I dare not choose my lot; I would not if I might.
Not mine, not mine, the choice In things or great or small;

Choose Thou for me, my God; So shall I walk a - right.
Be Thou my Guide, my Strength, My Wis - dom, and my All. A - men.

533 Nearer, My God, to Thee

6. 4. 6. 4. 6. 6. 6. 4.

Gen. 28 : 10–19
Sarah F. Adams, 1841

Bethany
Lowell Mason, 1856

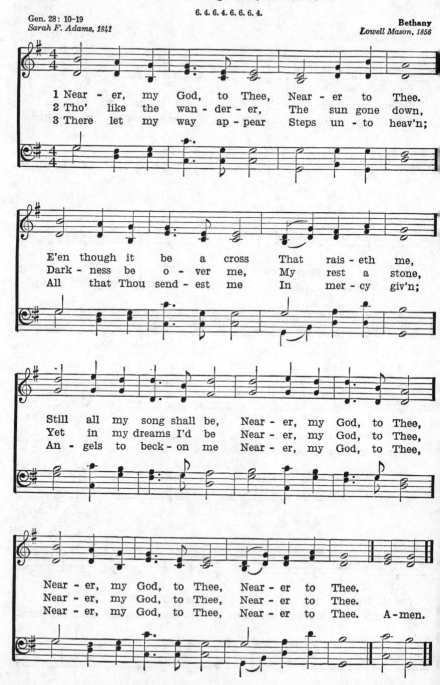

1 Near - er, my God, to Thee, Near - er to Thee.
2 Tho' like the wan - der - er, The sun gone down,
3 There let my way ap - pear Steps un - to heav'n;

E'en though it be a cross That rais - eth me,
Dark - ness be o - ver me, My rest a stone,
All that Thou send - est me In mer - cy giv'n;

Still all my song shall be, Near - er, my God, to Thee,
Yet in my dreams I'd be Near - er, my God, to Thee,
An - gels to beck - on me Near - er, my God, to Thee,

Near - er, my God, to Thee, Near - er to Thee.
Near - er, my God, to Thee, Near - er to Thee.
Near - er, my God, to Thee, Near - er to Thee. A - men.

Nearer, My God, to Thee

4 Then with my waking thoughts
  Bright with Thy praise,
Out of my stony griefs
  Bethel I'll raise,
So by my woes to be
Nearer, my God, to Thee,
  Nearer, my God, to Thee,
  Nearer to Thee.

5 Or if on joyful wing,
  Cleaving the sky,
Sun, moon, and stars forgot,
  Upward I fly,
Still all my song shall be,
Nearer, my God, to Thee,
  Nearer, my God, to Thee,
  Nearer to Thee.

God of My Life, to Thee I Call 534

L. M.

Ps. 46
St. 1–5, *William Cowper, 1779*
St. 6, *author unknown*

Wenn wir in höchsten Nöten
"Genevan Psalter," 1547

1 God of my life, to Thee I call; Af-flict-ed, at Thy feet I fall: When the great wa-ter-floods pre-vail, Leave not my trem-bling heart to fail.

2 Friend of the friend-less and the faint, Where should I lodge my deep com-plaint? Where but with Thee, whose o-pen door In-vites the help-less and the poor?

3 Did ev-er mourn-er plead with Thee And Thou re-fuse that mourn-er's plea? Does not the word still fixed re-main That none shall seek Thy face in vain?

4 Fair is the lot that's cast for me; I have an Ad-vo-cate with Thee. They whom the world ca-ress-es most Have no such priv-i-lege to boast. A-men.

5 Poor though I be, despised, forgot,
Yet God, my God, forgets me not;
And he is safe and must succeed
For whom the Lord vouchsafes to plead.

6 Then hear, O Lord, my humble cry
And bend on me Thy pitying eye.
To Thee their prayer Thy people make:
Hear us for our Redeemer's sake.

535 Rejoice, My Heart, Be Glad and Sing

Ps. 56: 8

C. M.

Ich singe dir mit Herz und Mund
Paul Gerhardt, 1653, cento
Tr., John Kelly, 1867, alt.

Ich singe dir
"Harmonischer Liederschatz"
Frankfurt, 1738

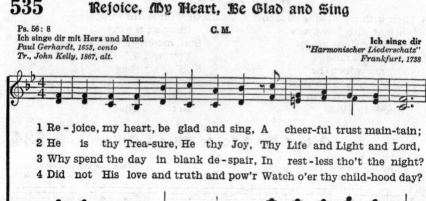

1 Re - joice, my heart, be glad and sing, A   cheer-ful trust main-tain;
2 He   is   thy Trea-sure, He thy Joy, Thy Life and Light and Lord,
3 Why spend the day in blank de-spair, In   rest-less tho't the night?
4 Did not His love and truth and pow'r Watch o'er thy child-hood day?

For God, the Source of ev-'ry-thing, Thy Por-tion shall re-main.
Thy Coun-sel - or when doubts an-noy, Thy Shield and great Re-ward.
On thy Cre - a - tor cast thy care; He makes thy bur-dens light.
Has He not oft in threat'ning hour Turned dreaded ills a - way? A-men.

5 He ever will with patience chide,
  His rod falls gently down,
And all thy sins He casts aside
  And in the sea doth drown.

6 When silent woe thy bosom rends,
  His pity sees thy grief,
Supplies what to His glory tends
  And to thine own relief.

7 He knows how oft a Christian weeps
  And why his tears now fall;
And in the book His mercy keeps
  These things are noted all.

8 His wisdom never plans in vain,
  Ne'er falters or mistakes;
All that His counsels did ordain
  A happy ending makes.

9 Upon thy lips, then, lay thy hand
  And trust His guiding love;
Then like a rock thy peace shall stand
  Here and in heaven above.

Awake, My Soul, and with the Sun

536

Ps. 108: 2

L. M.

Morning Hymn

Thomas Ken, 1695, cento, alt.

François H. Barthélémon, 1785

1 A - wake, my soul, and with the sun Thy
dai - ly stage of du - ty run; Shake off dull sloth and
joy - ful rise To pay thy morn-ing sac - ri - fice.

2 Let all thy con - verse be sin - cere, Thy
con-science as the noon-day clear; Think how th' all-see - ing
God thy ways And all thy se - cret tho'ts sur - veys.

3 All praise to Thee, who safe hast kept And
hast re - freshed me while I slept. Grant, Lord, when I from
death shall wake, I may of end - less light par - take. A - men.

4 Lord, I my vows to Thee renew;
Disperse my sins as morning dew;
Guard my first springs of thought and will
And with Thyself my spirit fill.

5 Direct, control, suggest, this day,
All I design or do or say
That all my powers, with all their might,
In Thy sole glory may unite.

6 Praise God, from whom all blessings flow;
Praise Him, all creatures here below;
Praise Him above, ye heavenly host:
Praise Father, Son, and Holy Ghost.

537 𝕰very 𝕸orning 𝕸ercies 𝕹ew

Lam. 3 : 23
Greville Phillimore, 1863, alt.

7. 7. 7. 7. 7. 7.

Voller Wunder
Johann G. Ebeling, 1666

1 Ev - 'ry morn-ing mer-cies new   Fall as fresh as morn-ing dew;
2 Still the great-ness of Thy love   Dai - ly doth our sins re - move;
3 Let our prayers each morn pre-vail   That these gifts may nev - er   fail;
4 As the morn-ing light re-turns,   As the sun with splen-dor burns,

Ev - 'ry morn-ing let us pay   Trib - ute with the ear - ly day;
Dai - ly, far as east from west,   Lifts the bur-den from the breast;
And as we con - fess the sin   And the Tempt-er's pow'r with-in,
Teach us still to turn to Thee,   Ev - er-bless-ed Trin - i - ty,

For Thy mer-cies, Lord, are sure, Thy com-pas-sion doth en-dure.
Gives un-bought to those who pray Strength to stand in e - vil day.
Feed us with the Bread of Life; Fit us for our dai - ly strife.
With our hands our hearts to raise In un - fail-ing prayer and praise. Amen.

538 𝕹ow the 𝕾hades of 𝕹ight are 𝕲one

Ps. 121
Samson Occom, 1799, asc.

7. 7. 7. 7.

Vienna
Justin H. Knecht, 1797

1 Now the shades of night are gone, Now the morn-ing light is come.
2 Fill   our souls with heav'n-ly light, Ban-ish doubt and cleanse our sight.
3 Keep our haugh-ty pas-sions bound, Save us from our foes a-round;
4 When our work of life is past, Oh, re-ceive us then at last!

Now the Shades of Night are Gone

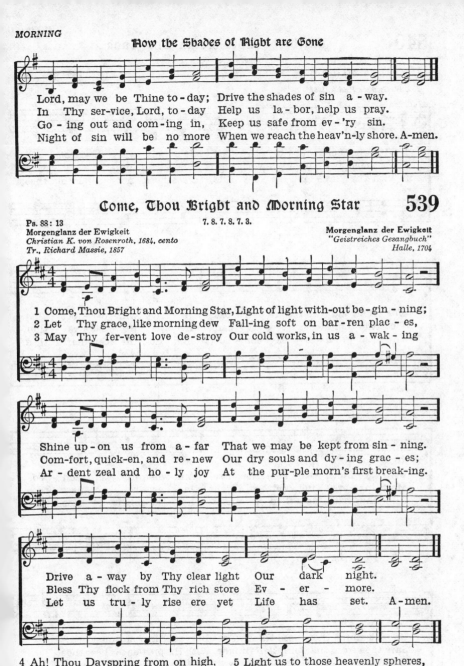

Lord, may we be Thine to-day; Drive the shades of sin a-way.
In Thy ser-vice, Lord, to-day Help us la-bor, help us pray.
Go-ing out and com-ing in, Keep us safe from ev-'ry sin.
Night of sin will be no more When we reach the heav'n-ly shore. A-men.

Come, Thou Bright and Morning Star   539

7. 8. 7. 8. 7. 3.

Ps. 88: 13
Morgenglanz der Ewigkeit
Christian K. von Rosenroth, 1684, cento
Tr., Richard Massie, 1857

Morgenglanz der Ewigkeit
"Geistreiches Gesangbuch"
Halle, 1704

1 Come, Thou Bright and Morning Star, Light of light with-out be-gin-ning;
2 Let Thy grace, like morning dew Fall-ing soft on bar-ren plac-es,
3 May Thy fer-vent love de-stroy Our cold works, in us a-wak-ing

Shine up-on us from a-far That we may be kept from sin-ning.
Com-fort, quick-en, and re-new Our dry souls and dy-ing grac-es;
Ar-dent zeal and ho-ly joy At the pur-ple morn's first break-ing.

Drive a-way by Thy clear light Our dark night.
Bless Thy flock from Thy rich store Ev-er-more.
Let us tru-ly rise ere yet Life has set. A-men.

4 Ah! Thou Dayspring from on high,
Grant that at Thy next appearing
We who in the graves do lie
May arise, Thy summons hearing,
And rejoice in our new life,
Far from strife.

5 Light us to those heavenly spheres,
Sun of grace, in glory shrouded;
Lead us through this vale of tears
To the land where days unclouded,
Purest joy, and perfect peace
Never cease.

540 With the Lord Begin Thy Task

Col. 3: 17

Fang dein Werk mit Jesu an
German author unknown, 1734
Tr., W. Gustave Polack, 1937

7. 6. 7. 6. D. Trochaic

Fang dein Werk
Peter Frank, 1657

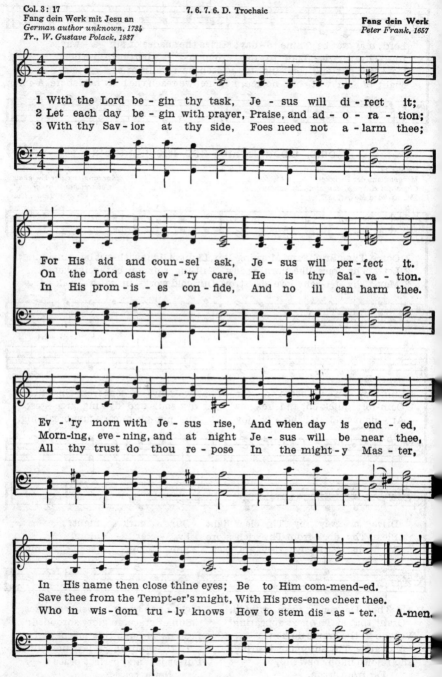

1 With the Lord be - gin thy task, Je - sus will di - rect it;
2 Let each day be - gin with prayer, Praise, and ad - o - ra - tion;
3 With thy Sav - ior at thy side, Foes need not a - larm thee;

For His aid and coun - sel ask, Je - sus will per - fect it.
On the Lord cast ev - 'ry care, He is thy Sal - va - tion.
In His prom - is - es con - fide, And no ill can harm thee.

Ev - 'ry morn with Je - sus rise, And when day is end - ed,
Morn - ing, eve - ning, and at night Je - sus will be near thee,
All thy trust do thou re - pose In the might - y Mas - ter,

In His name then close thine eyes; Be to Him com - mend - ed.
Save thee from the Tempt - er's might, With His pres - ence cheer thee.
Who in wis - dom tru - ly knows How to stem dis - as - ter. A - men.

With the Lord Begin Thy Task

4 If thy task be thus begun
  With the Savior's blessing,
Safely then thy course will run,
  Naught thy soul distressing.
Good will follow everywhere
  While thou here must wander;
Thou at last the joy wilt share
  In the mansions yonder.

5 Thus, Lord Jesus, every task
  Be to Thee commended;
May Thy will be done, I ask,
  Until life is ended.
Jesus, in Thy name begun
  Be the day's endeavor;
Grant that it may well be done
  To Thy praise forever.

O Blessed Holy Trinity

541

Ps. 5 : 3
O heilige Dreifaltigkeit
Martin Behm, 1608, ab.
Tr., Conrad H. L. Schuette, 1880, alt.

L. M.

O heilige Dreifaltigkeit
Nikolaus Herman, 1560

1 O bless-ed Ho-ly Trin-i-ty, Di-vine, e-
2 My soul and bod-y keep from harm, O'er all I
3 The Fa-ther's love shield me this day, The Son's pure
4 My Mak-er, strength-en Thou my heart, O my Re-

ter-nal U-ni-ty, God Fa-ther, Son, and Ho-ly Ghost,
have ex-tend Thine arm, That Sa-tan may not cause dis-tress
wis-dom cheer my way, The Ho-ly Spir-it's light di-vine
deem-er, help im-part, Blest Com-fort-er, keep at my side

Be Thou this day my Guide and Host.
Nor bring me shame and wretch-ed-ness.
Il-lume my heart's be-night-ed shrine.
That faith and love in me a-bide. A-men.

5 Lord, bless and keep Thou me as Thine;
  Lord, make Thy face upon me shine;
  Lord, lift Thy countenance on me
  And give me peace, sweet peace, from Thee.

542 The Sun Arises Now

Ps. 145 : 15
Nu rinder Solen op
Thomas Kingo, 1699, cento
Tr., P. C. Paulsen, c. 1925, alt.

6. 5. 5. 5. 6. 5. 6. 6. 5.

Nu rinder Solen op
"*Koralbog*"
Hartnack O. K. Zinck, 1801

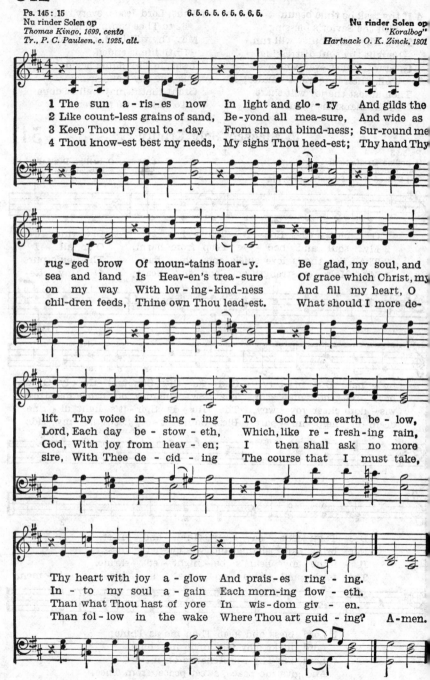

1 The sun a-ris-es now In light and glo-ry And gilds the rug-ged brow Of moun-tains hoar-y. Be glad, my soul, and lift Thy voice in sing-ing To God from earth be-low, Thy heart with joy a-glow And prais-es ring-ing.

2 Like count-less grains of sand, Be-yond all mea-sure, And wide as sea and land Is Heav-en's trea-sure Of grace which Christ, my Lord, Each day be-stow-eth, Which, like re-fresh-ing rain, In-to my soul a-gain Each morn-ing flow-eth.

3 Keep Thou my soul to-day From sin and blind-ness; Sur-round me on my way With lov-ing-kind-ness And fill my heart, O God, With joy from heav-en; I then shall ask no more Than what Thou hast of yore In wis-dom giv-en.

4 Thou know-est best my needs, My sighs Thou heed-est; Thy hand Thy chil-dren feeds, Thine own Thou lead-est. What should I more de-sire, With Thee de-cid-ing The course that I must take, Than fol-low in the wake Where Thou art guid-ing? A-men.

When, Streaming from the Eastern Skies

8. 8. 8. 8. 8. 8.

543

Ps. 55 : 1
William Shrubsole, 1813, cento, alt.

All' Ehr' und Lob
"Kirchengesangbuch"
Strassburg, 1541

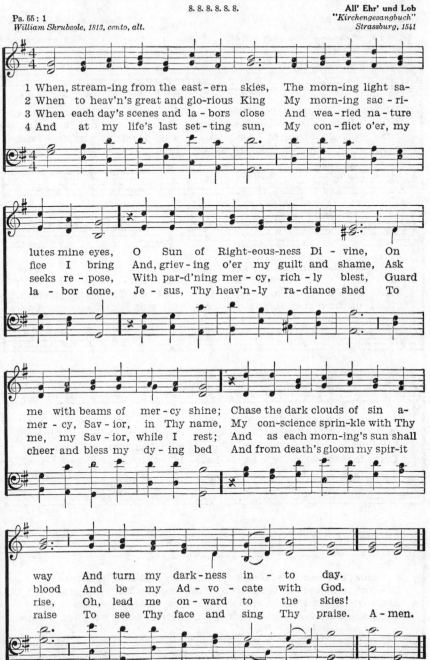

1 When, stream-ing from the east-ern skies, The morn-ing light sa-
2 When to heav'n's great and glo-rious King My morn-ing sac-ri-
3 When each day's scenes and la-bors close And wea-ried na-ture
4 And at my life's last set-ting sun, My con-flict o'er, my

lutes mine eyes, O Sun of Right-eous-ness Di-vine, On
fice I bring And, griev-ing o'er my guilt and shame, Ask
seeks re-pose, With par-d'ning mer-cy, rich-ly blest, Guard
la-bor done, Je-sus, Thy heav'n-ly ra-diance shed To

me with beams of mer-cy shine; Chase the dark clouds of sin a-
mer-cy, Sav-ior, in Thy name, My con-science sprin-kle with Thy
me, my Sav-ior, while I rest; And as each morn-ing's sun shall
cheer and bless my dy-ing bed And from death's gloom my spir-it

way And turn my dark-ness in-to day.
blood And be my Ad-vo-cate with God.
rise, Oh, lead me on-ward to the skies!
raise To see Thy face and sing Thy praise. A-men.

544
While Yet the Morn is Breaking

Ps. 66: 3
Dank sei Gott in der Höhe
Johannes Mühlmann, 1618, ab.
Tr., st. 1, 2, 5, 6, Catherine Winkworth, 1863, alt.
Tr., st. 3 and 4, composite

7. 6. 7. 6. D.

Geduld, die soll'n wir haben
"Geistliche Lieder"
Frankfurt, 1607

1 While yet the morn is break-ing, I thank my God once more,
2 O Is-rael's Guard-ian, hear me, Watch o-ver me this day;
3 O gra-cious Lord, di-rect us, Thy doc-trine pure de-fend,
4 Oh, grant us peace and glad-ness, Give us our dai-ly bread,

Be-neath whose care a-wak-ing, I find the night is o'er.
In all I do be near me. For oth-ers, too, I pray;
From her-e-sies pro-tect us, And for Thy Word con-tend,
Shield us from grief and sad-ness, On us Thy bless-ings shed.

I thank Him that He calls me To life and health a-new;
To Thee I would com-mend them, Our Church, our youth, our land,
That we may praise Thee ev-er, O God, with one ac-cord
Grant that our whole be-hav-ior, In truth and right-eous-ness,

I know, what-e'er be-falls me, His care will still be true.
Di-rect them and de-fend them When dan-gers are at hand.
And say: The Lord, our Sav-ior, Be ev-er-more a-dored.
May praise Thee, Lord, our Sav-ior, Whose ho-ly name we bless. A-men.

While Yet the Morn is Breaking

5 And gently grant Thy blessing
That we may do Thy will,
No more Thy ways transgressing,
Our proper task fulfil,
With Peter's full assurance
Let down our nets again.
Success will crown endurance
If faithful we remain.

6 Thou art the Vine —oh, nourish
The branches graft in Thee
And let them grow and flourish,
A fair and fruitful tree.
Thy Spirit pour within us
And let His gifts of grace
To such good actions win us
As best may show Thy praise.

The Morning Sun is Brightly Beaming 545

1 John 1: 7
Aurinko armas vallolansa
Author unknown, 1836
Tr., Gustaf A. Aho, 1938

9. 8. 9. 8. 8. 8.

O dass ich tausend
Kornelius H. Dretzel, 1731

1 The morn-ing sun is bright-ly beam-ing, And dark-ness deep has
2 Grant un-to me in ten-der mer-cies Thy Ho-ly Spir-it's
3 Dear Je-sus, send Thy mer-cies o'er me Like morn-ing dews to

passed a-way; All earth with life and joy is teem-ing
sav-ing light; The en-trance of Thy Word dis-pers-es
cleanse my soul. Oh, may Thy ho-ly blood re-store me,

In beau-ty of a new-born day. O gra-cious Fa-ther,
From out my mind its sin-ful night. My poor and err-ing
Wash out my sin, and make me whole! Let me be strength-ened

pur-est Light, Thou bring-est day, dis-pel-lest night.
heart in-stil With love to do Thy gra-cious will.
by Thy might To walk in Thy e-ter-nal light. A-men.

546 How Lovely Shines the Morning Star

Lam. 3 : 22, 23
Wie schön leuchtet der Morgenstern
Burkhard Wiesenmeyer, 1640, ad., cento
Tr., Frances E. Cox, 1864, alt.

8. 8. 7. 8. 8. 7. 4. 4. 4. 4. 8.

Wie schön leuchtet
Philipp Nicolai, 1599

1 How love-ly shines the morning star! In twi-light sky it gleams a-far;
2 Then haste, my soul, thy song to raise, De-lay thou not thy Lord to praise,
3 Tho' e-vil spir-its thro' the night With hellish craft and watchful spite
4 Pour down Thy grace in cheering streams And warm my heart with mercy's beams

The reign of night is end - ed.   Cre - a-tion stirs to hail the light
Bow down in ad - o - ra - tion.   For glo - ry, Lord, to Thee be-longs,
Came round me with-out num-ber,   Yet Thou, O Je-sus, with Thy pow'r
From heav'n, Thy throne of beauty;   Thy Spir-it ev - er lead and guide

Whose glo-ries now with radiance bright Stream forth in beau-ty splen-did.
Thy praise re-sounds in grate-ful songs, Thou Lord of all cre - a - tion.
Wast near me in that threat'ning hour, Didst guard me in my slum - ber.
That in my call-ing I a - bide And find my joy in du - ty.

Both far And near All things liv - ing Thanks are giv - ing,
Let all Re - call Hymns of glad-ness With - out sad - ness,
Praise be To Thee, My Con-tend - er And De - fend - er,
Send light And might That each mea-sure, Plan and plea-sure,

How Lovely Shines the Morning Star

Praise out-pour-ing, Earth and sky the Lord a-dor-ing.
For Thy fa-vor And Thy mer-cy nev-er wa-ver.
I'll a-dore Thee While on earth I walk be-fore Thee.
Heav'n-ward tending, E'er in Thee may find its end-ing. A-men.

5 Keep grief, if this may be, away;
 If not, Thy will be done, I pray,
  My choice to Thine resigning.
 Then, O my heart, cast care aside,
 God through the cross His own hath tried;
  Bear loss without repining.
 Hope still Through ill;
  To God cleaving, Grace receiving,
 We shall wonder
 At God's goodness here and yonder.

The Radiant Sun Shines in the Skies 547

Ps. 91: 9–16   L. M.
Die helle Sonn' leucht't jetzt herfür   Die helle Sonn' leucht't
Nikolaus Herman, 1560   *Melchior Vulpius, 1609*
Tr., composite

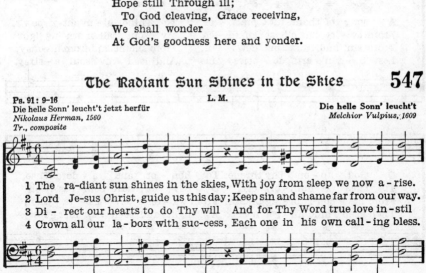

1 The ra-diant sun shines in the skies, With joy from sleep we now a-rise.
2 Lord Je-sus Christ, guide us this day; Keep sin and shame far from our way.
3 Di-rect our hearts to do Thy will And for Thy Word true love in-stil
4 Crown all our la-bors with suc-cess, Each one in his own call-ing bless.

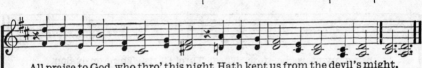

All praise to God, who thro' this night Hath kept us from the devil's might.
Thy guardian an-gels to us send And let them to our wants at-tend.
That we may do what-e'er is right And ev-er pleas-ing in Thy sight.
May all we do or think or say Ex-alt and praise Thee, Lord, this day! Amen.

548   My Inmost Heart Now Raises

7. 6. 7. 6. 6. 7. 7. 6.

Ps. 118:1
Aus meines Herzens Grunde
Georg Nigidius, †1588
Tr., based on Catherine Winkworth, 1863

Aus meines Herzens Grunde
"Neu Catechismus-Gesangbüchlein"
Hamburg, 1598

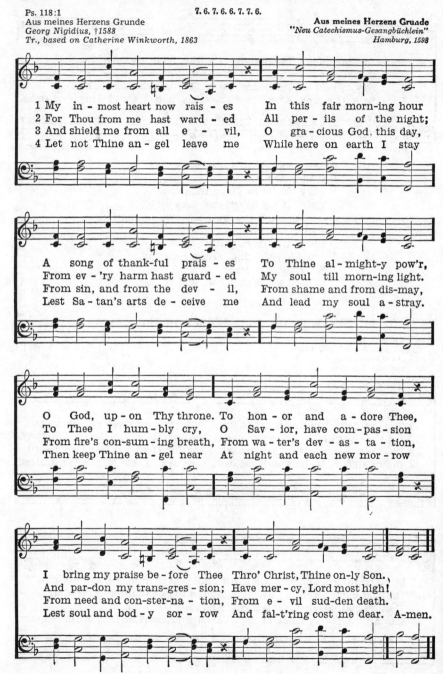

1 My in-most heart now rais-es   In this fair morn-ing hour
2 For Thou from me hast ward-ed   All per-ils of the night;
3 And shield me from all e - vil,   O gra-cious God, this day,
4 Let not Thine an-gel leave me   While here on earth I stay

A song of thank-ful prais-es   To Thine al-might-y pow'r,
From ev-'ry harm hast guard-ed   My soul till morn-ing light.
From sin, and from the dev - il,   From shame and from dis-may,
Lest Sa-tan's arts de - ceive me   And lead my soul a-stray.

O God, up-on Thy throne. To hon - or and a - dore Thee,
To Thee I hum-bly cry,   O Sav - ior, have com-pas-sion
From fire's con-sum-ing breath, From wa - ter's dev - as - ta - tion,
Then keep Thine an-gel near   At night and each new mor - row

I bring my praise be - fore Thee Thro' Christ, Thine on-ly Son.
And par-don my trans-gres - sion; Have mer - cy, Lord most high!
From need and con-ster-na - tion, From e - vil sud-den death.
Lest soul and bod - y sor - row And fal-t'ring cost me dear. A-men.

My Inmost Heart Now Raises

5 God shall do my advising,
   Whose might with wisdom blends;
May He bless rest and rising,
   My efforts, means, and ends!
To God, forever blest,
   Will I with mine confide me,
   And willing let Him guide me
As seemeth to Him best.

6 Amen I say, not fearing
   That God rejects my prayer;
I doubt not He is hearing
   And granting me His care.
Thus I go on my way
   And do not look behind me,
   But ply the task assigned me;
God's help shall be my stay.

God, Who Madest Earth and Heaven   549

8. 7. 8. 7. 7. 7.

Ps. 7: 17
Gott des Himmels und der Erden
Heinrich Albert, 1644, ab.
Tr., Catherine Winkworth, 1855, alt.

Gott des Himmels
Heinrich Albert, 1644

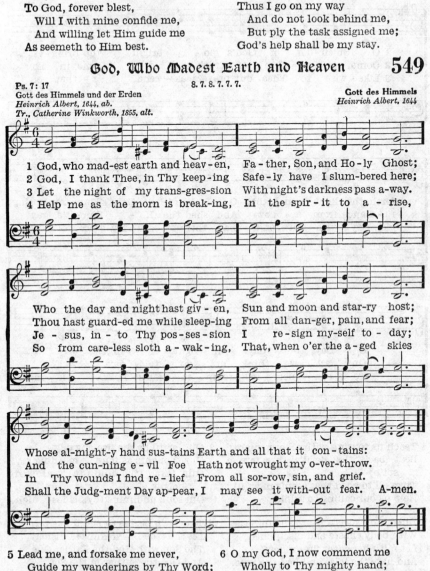

1 God, who mad-est earth and heav-en, Fa-ther, Son, and Ho-ly Ghost;
2 God, I thank Thee, in Thy keep-ing Safe-ly have I slum-bered here;
3 Let the night of my trans-gres-sion With night's darkness pass a-way.
4 Help me as the morn is break-ing, In the spir-it to a-rise,

Who the day and night hast giv-en, Sun and moon and star-ry host;
Thou hast guard-ed me while sleep-ing From all dan-ger, pain, and fear;
Je - sus, in - to Thy pos-ses-sion I re-sign my-self to - day;
So from care-less sloth a - wak-ing, That, when o'er the a-ged skies

Whose al-might-y hand sus-tains Earth and all that it con-tains:
And the cun-ning e - vil Foe Hath not wrought my o-ver-throw.
In Thy wounds I find re - lief From all sor-row, sin, and grief.
Shall the Judg-ment Day ap-pear, I may see it with-out fear. A-men.

5 Lead me, and forsake me never,
   Guide my wanderings by Thy Word;
As Thou hast been, be Thou ever
   My Defense, my Refuge, Lord.
Never safe except with Thee,
Thou my faithful Guardian be.

6 O my God, I now commend me
   Wholly to Thy mighty hand;
All the powers that Thou dost lend me
   Let me use at Thy command.
Lord, my Shield, my Strength divine,
Keep me with Thee — I am Thine.

550 O Splendor of God's Glory Bright

L. M.

John 8 : 12
Splendor paternae gloriae
St. Ambrose, †397
Tr., composite, 1904

O heilige Dreifaltigkeit
Nikolaus Herman, 1560

1 O Splen-dor of God's glo-ry bright, Who bring-est forth the light from Light; O Light of light, light's Foun-tain-spring; O Day, our days en-light-en-ing:

2 Come, ver-y Sun of truth and love, Come in Thy ra-diance from a-bove And shed the Ho-ly Spir-it's ray On all we think or do to-day.

3 Like-wise to Thee our prayers as-cend, Fa-ther of glo-ry with-out end, Fa-ther of sav-ing grace, for pow'r To con-quer in temp-ta-tion's hour. A-men.

4 Teach us to work with all our might;
Beat back the devil's threatening spite;
Turn all to good that seems most ill;
Help us our calling to fulfil.

5 Direct and govern heart and mind,
With body chaste and disciplined;
Let faith her eager fires renew
And hate the false and love the true.

6 On Christ, the true Bread, let us feed,
Let Him to us be drink indeed,
And let us taste with joyfulness
The Holy Spirit's plenteousness.

7 Oh, joyful be the livelong day,
Our thoughts as pure as morning ray,
Our faith like noonday's glowing height,
Our souls undimmed by shades of night.

8 The dawn begins to speed her way,
Let the true Dawn Himself display,
The Son with God the Father One,
And God the Father in the Son.

9 All praise to God the Father be,
All praise, eternal Son, to Thee,
Whom with the Spirit we adore
Forever and forevermore.

Sun of My Soul, Thou Savior Dear

551

L. M.

Luke 24: 29
John Keble, 1820, cento

Hursley
"Allgemeines Gesangbuch"
Vienna, 1775, ad.

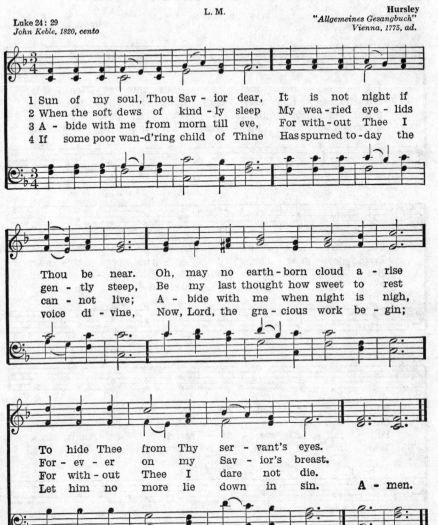

1 Sun of my soul, Thou Sav - ior dear, It is not night if
2 When the soft dews of kind - ly sleep My wea - ried eye - lids
3 A - bide with me from morn till eve, For with - out Thee I
4 If some poor wan-d'ring child of Thine Has spurned to-day the

Thou be near. Oh, may no earth-born cloud a - rise
gen - tly steep, Be my last thought how sweet to rest
can - not live; A - bide with me when night is nigh,
voice di - vine, Now, Lord, the gra - cious work be - gin;

To hide Thee from Thy ser - vant's eyes.
For - ev - er on my Sav - ior's breast.
For with - out Thee I dare not die.
Let him no more lie down in sin.   A - men.

5 Watch by the sick; enrich the poor
 With blessings from Thy boundless store;
 Be every mourner's sleep tonight,
 Like infant's slumbers, pure and light.

6 Come near and bless us when we wake,
 Ere through the world our way we take,
 Till in the ocean of Thy love
 We lose ourselves in heaven above.

552 Abide with Me! Fast Falls the Eventide

Luke 24 : 29
Henry F. Lyte, 1847 (?)

10. 10. 10. 10.

Eventide
William H. Monk, 1861

1 A - bide with me! Fast falls the e - ven - tide;
2 Swift to its close ebbs out life's lit - tle day;
3 Not a brief glance I beg, a pass - ing word,
4 Come not in ter - rors, as the King of kings,

The dark - ness deep - ens; Lord, with me a - bide.
Earth's joys grow dim, its glo - ries pass a - way;
But as Thou dweltst with Thy dis - ci - ples, Lord,
But kind and good, with heal - ing in Thy wings;

When oth - er help - ers fail and com - forts flee,
Change and de - cay in all a - round I see.
Fa - mil - iar, con - de - scend - ing, pa - tient, free.
Tears for all woes, a heart for ev - 'ry plea.

Help of the help - less, oh, a - bide with me!
O Thou, who chang - est not, a - bide with me!
Come not to so - journ, but a - bide with me.
Come, Friend of sin - ners, thus a - bide with me. A - men.

Abide with Me! Fast Falls the Eventide

5 Thou on my head in early youth didst smile,
And though rebellious and perverse meanwhile,
Thou hast not left me, oft as I left Thee.
On to the close, O Lord, abide with me.

6 I need Thy presence every passing hour;
What but Thy grace can foil the Tempter's power?
Who like Thyself my guide and stay can be?
Through cloud and sunshine, oh, abide with me!

7 I fear no foe, with Thee at hand to bless;
Ills have no weight and tears no bitterness.
Where is death's sting? where, grave, thy victory?
I triumph still if Thou abide with me.

8 Hold Thou Thy cross before my closing eyes,
Shine through the gloom, and point me to the skies.
Heaven's morning breaks, and earth's vain shadows flee;
In life, in death, O Lord, abide with me!

Through the Day Thy Love hath Spared Us   553

Ps. 3: 5
Thomas Kelly, 1806

8. 7. 8. 7. 7. 7.

Komm, o komm, du Geist
J. Christoph Bach, 1680

1 Thro' the day Thy love hath spared us, Now we lay us down to rest;
2 Pil - grims here on earth and stran-gers, Dwell-ing in the midst of foes,

Thro' the si - lent watch-es guard us, Let no foe our peace mo-lest.
Us and ours pre-serve from dan-gers; In Tnine arms may we re - pose

Je - sus, Thou our Guard-ian be; Sweet it is to trust in Thee.
And, when life's sad day is past, Rest with Thee in heav'n at last. A-men.

554 Now Rest Beneath Night's Shadow

Ps. 139: 11
Nun ruhen alle Wälder
Paul Gerhardt, 1648, cento
Tr., composite

7. 7. 6. 7. 7. 8.

O Welt, ich muss dich lassen
Heinrich Isaak, c. 1490

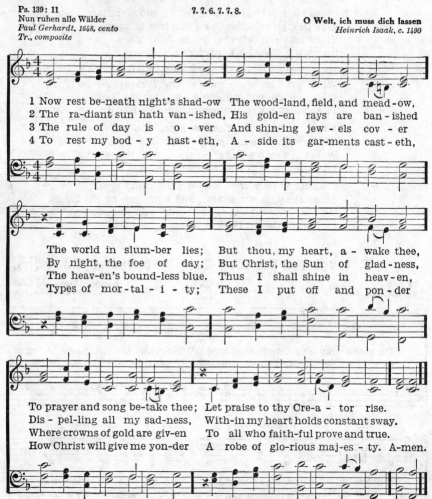

1 Now rest be-neath night's shad-ow The wood-land, field, and mead-ow,
2 The ra-diant sun hath van-ished, His gold-en rays are ban-ished
3 The rule of day is o-ver And shin-ing jew-els cov-er
4 To rest my bod-y hast-eth, A-side its gar-ments cast-eth,

The world in slum-ber lies; But thou, my heart, a-wake thee,
By night, the foe of day; But Christ, the Sun of glad-ness,
The heav-en's bound-less blue. Thus I shall shine in heav-en,
Types of mor-tal-i-ty; These I put off and pon-der

To prayer and song be-take thee; Let praise to thy Cre-a-tor rise.
Dis-pel-ling all my sad-ness, With-in my heart holds constant sway.
Where crowns of gold are giv-en To all who faith-ful prove and true.
How Christ will give me yon-der A robe of glo-rious maj-es-ty. A-men.

5 Lord Jesus, who dost love me,
   Oh, spread Thy wings above me
      And shield me from alarm!
   Though evil would assail me,
   Thy mercy will not fail me:
      I rest in Thy protecting arm.

6 My loved ones, rest securely,
   For God this night will surely
      From peril guard your heads.
   Sweet slumbers may He send you
   And bid His hosts attend you
      And through the night watch o'er your beds.

The Day Is Past and Over

Ps. 13:3

7.6.7.6.8.8.

Τὴν ἡμέραν διελθών
Author unknown, c. 600
Tr., John M. Neale, 1853, alt.

St. Anatolius
Arthur H. Brown, 1862

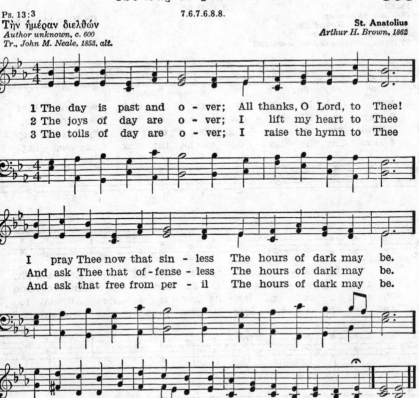

1 The day is past and o - ver; All thanks, O Lord, to Thee!
2 The joys of day are o - ver; I lift my heart to Thee
3 The toils of day are o - ver; I raise the hymn to Thee

I pray Thee now that sin - less The hours of dark may be.
And ask Thee that of - fense - less The hours of dark may be.
And ask that free from per - il The hours of dark may be.

O Je-sus, keep me in Thy sight And save me thro' the coming night.
O Je-sus, keep me in Thy sight And guard me thro' the coming night.
O Je-sus, make their darkness light And guard me thro' the coming night. Amen.

4 Lord, that in death I sleep not,
  And lest my Foe should say,
"I have prevailed against him,"
  Lighten mine eyes, I pray.
O Jesus, keep me in Thy sight
And guard me through the coming night.

5 Be Thou my soul's Preserver,
  O God, for Thou dost know
How many are the perils
  Through which I have to go;
Lover of men, oh, hear my call
And guard and save me from them all!

556

O God, Be with Us

Ps. 121: 3
Die Nacht ist kommen
St. 1-4, 6, Petrus Herbert, 1566
St. 5, author unknown, 1627
Tr., based on Catherine Winkworth, 1863

11. 11. 11. 5.

Die Nacht ist kommen
Petrus Nigidius, 1550

1 O God, be with us, for the night is fall - ing;
2 May e - vil fan - cies flee a - way be - fore us;
3 While we are sleep - ing, keep us in Thy fa - vor;
4 Thro' Thy Be - lov - ed soothe the sick and weep - ing

For Thy pro - tec - tion we to Thee are call - ing; Be-neath Thy
Till morn - ing com - eth, watch, O Fa - ther, o'er us; In soul and
When we a - wak - en, let us nev - er wa - ver All day to
And bid the cap - tive lose his grief in sleep - ing; Wid-ows and

shad - ow to our rest we yield us; Thou, Lord, wilt shield us.
bod - y Thou from harm de-fend us, Thine an - gel send us.
serve Thee, Thy due praise pur-su - ing In all our do - ing.
or - phans, we to Thee commend them, Do Thou be-friend them. A-men.

5 We have no refuge, none on earth to aid us,
Save Thee, O Father, who Thine own hast made us.
But Thy dear presence will not leave them lonely
Who seek Thee only.

6 Thy name be hallowed and Thy kingdom given,
Thy will among us done as 'tis in heaven;
Feed us, forgive us, from all ill deliver
Now and forever.

At Even, When the Sun Did Set
557

L. M.

Mark 1 : 32–34
Henry Twells, 1868

Angelus
"Heilige Seelenlust"
Breslau, 1657, ad.

1 At e - ven, when the sun did set, The sick, O
2 Once more 'tis e - ven - tide, and we, Op-pressed with
3 O Sav - ior Christ, our woes dis - pel; For some are
4 And some are pressed with world - ly care, And some are

Lord, a - round Thee lay. Oh, in what di - vers pains they met!
va - rious ills, draw near. What if Thy form we can - not see,
sick, and some are sad, And some have nev - er loved Thee well,
tried with sin - ful doubt; And some such griev-ous pas - sions tear

Oh, with what joy they went a - way!
We know and feel that Thou art here.
And some have lost the love they had;
That on - ly Thou canst cast them out;   A - men.

5 And some have found the world is vain,
Yet from the world they break not
free;
And some have friends who give them
pain,
Yet have not sought a friend in Thee.

6 And none, O Lord, have perfect rest,
For none are wholly free from sin;
And they who fain would serve Thee
best
Are conscious most of wrong within.

7 O Savior Christ, Thou, too, art man;
Thou hast been troubled, tempted,
tried.
Thy kind but searching glance can scan
The very wounds that shame would
hide.

8 Thy touch has still its ancient power,
No word from Thee can fruitless
fall;
Hear in this solemn evening hour
And in Thy mercy heal us all.

558 All Praise to Thee, My God, This Night

Ps. 91 : 4
Thomas Ken, 1695, cento

L. M.
(FIRST TUNE)

Tallis' Canon
Thomas Tallis, c. 1567

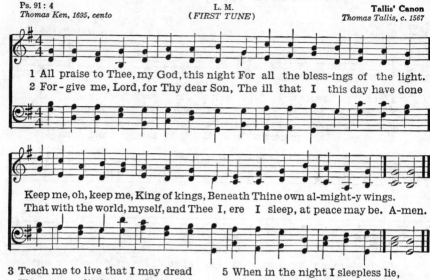

1 All praise to Thee, my God, this night For all the bless-ings of the light.
2 For-give me, Lord, for Thy dear Son, The ill that I this day have done

Keep me, oh, keep me, King of kings, Beneath Thine own al-might-y wings.
That with the world, myself, and Thee I, ere I sleep, at peace may be. A-men.

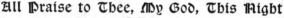

3 Teach me to live that I may dread
The grave as little as my bed.
Teach me to die that so I may
Rise glorious at the awe-full Day.

4 Oh, may my soul on Thee repose,
And may sweet sleep mine eyelids close,
Sleep that shall me more vigorous
make
To serve my God when I awake!

5 When in the night I sleepless lie,
My soul with heavenly thoughts supply;
Let no ill dreams disturb my rest,
No powers of darkness me molest.

6 Praise God, from whom all blessings
flow;
Praise Him, all creatures here below;
Praise him above, ye heavenly host:
Praise Father, Son, and Holy Ghost.

All Praise to Thee, My God, This Night

Ps. 91 : 4
Thomas Ken, 1695, cento

L. M. D.
(SECOND TUNE)

Evening Hymn
Charles F. Gounod, †1893, arr.

St. 1, 3, 5, Congregation and Choir

1 All praise to Thee, my God, this night For all the bless-ings of the light.

Keep me, oh, keep me, King of kings, Beneath Thine own al-might-y wings.

All Praise to Thee, My God, This Night

St. 2, 4, 6, Choir only

2 For-give me, Lord, for Thy dear Son, The ill that I this day have done

All

That with the world, myself, and Thee I, ere I sleep, at peace may be. Amen.

O Christ, Who Art the Light and Day 559

L. M.

John 8: 12
Christe, qui lux es et dies
Author unknown
Tr., William J. Copeland, 1848

Christe, der du bist Tag und Licht
Latin melody, c. 600

1 O Christ, who art the Light and Day, Thou driv-est night and gloom a-way;
2 All - ho - ly Lord, in hum-ble prayer, We ask to-night Thy watch-ful care.
3 Our sleep be pure from sin-ful stain; Let not the Tempt-er van-tage gain

O Light of light, whose Word doth show The light of heav'n to us be - low.
Oh, grant us calm re-pose in Thee, A qui - et night, from per-ils free.
Or our un-guard-ed flesh sur-prise And make us guilt-y in Thine eyes. A-men.

4 Asleep though wearied eyes may be,
Still keep the heart awake to Thee;
Let Thy right hand outstretched above
Guard those who serve the Lord they love.

5 Behold, O God, our Shield, and quell
The crafts and subtleties of hell;
Direct Thy servants in all good,
Whom Thou hast purchased with Thy
blood.

6 O Lord, remember us who bear
The burden of the flesh we wear;
Thou who dost e'er our souls defend,
Be with us even to the end.

7 All praise to God the Father be,
All praise, eternal Son, to Thee,
Whom with the Spirit we adore
Forever and forevermore.

560 Gracious God, Again is Ended

Ps. 121 : 1
Herr, es ist von meinem Leben
Caspar Neumann, 1711
Recast by John T. Mueller, 1938

8. 7. 8. 7. 7. 7. 8. 8.

Werde munter
Johann Schop, 1642

1 Gra-cious God, a-gain is end-ed Of my life an-oth-er day.
2 Faith-ful Fa-ther, thus be-fore Thee Now I come with fer-vent plea;
3 Lov-ing Sav-ior, I will sole-ly Look to Thee for peace-ful sleep;
4 Ho-ly Ghost, Thine eyes for-ev-er Watch tho' darkness hide the view;

Show me where I have of-fend-ed, Where I fal-tered on the way;
Tho' un-wor-thy, I im-plore Thee, Be Thou mer-ci-ful to me;
Sanc-ti-fy my spir-it whol-ly, An-gels send their watch to keep.
Wak-ing al-ways, fail-ing nev-er, They their lov-ing task pur-sue.

Let me by Thy grace di-vine View this sin-ful life of mine.
Let Thy face up-on me shine As the fleet-ing hours de-cline.
Bid all threat-'ning foes be gone, Guard my home and all mine own;
Gen-tle Shep-herd, as Thy sheep Now re-pose in trust-ful sleep,

Calm-ly, as the day now clos-es, In Thy love my soul re-pos-es.
Help me do Thy will and plea-sure Day by day in full-er mea-sure.
Drive a-way all gloom and sor-row, Bless me with a glad to-mor-row.
So with-in Thine arms en-fold me, In Thy care se-cure-ly hold me. A-men.

Gracious God, Again is Ended

5 Gracious God, let me awaken
  To another blessed day
That I may, with faith unshaken,
  Serve Thee as my Strength and Stay.
Should instead death's summons come,
Take me to Thy heavenly home.
To Thy care I thus commend me;
Lord, in life and death attend me.

Now that the Day hath Reached Its Close 561

Ps. 139: 12
C. M.

Nun sich der Tag geendet hat
Johann F. Hertzog, 1670, ab.
St. 9, author unknown, 1693
Tr., composite

Nun sich der Tag geendet hat
Adam Krieger, 1667

1 Now that the day hath reached its close, The sun doth shine no more,
2 But Thou, my God, dost nev-er sleep, For Thou Thy-self art Light;
3 There-fore, O Lord, re-mem-ber me Thro'-out the gloom of night.

In sleep the toil-worn find re-pose And all who wept be-fore.
No dark-ness, how-so-ev-er deep, Can dim Thy per-fect sight.
Pro-tect Thou me most gra-cious-ly And shield me with Thy might. Amen.

4 Keep Satan's fury far from me
  By many an angel arm;
Then shall I be from worry free
  And safe from every harm.

5 I know the evil I have done
  Doth cry aloud to Thee;
But yet in mercy Thy dear Son
  Hath full atoned for me.

6 In Him accepted I shall be
  When suppliant at Thy feet.
He is my Surety and my Plea
  Before Thy judgment seat.

7 And so I close my weary eyes,
  Sweet peace within my breast.
Why toss about in fears or sighs?
  God watches while I rest.

8 Should this night prove the last for me
  In this sad vale of cares,
Then lead me, Lord, to dwell with Thee
  And all Thy chosen heirs.

9 And thus I live and die to Thee,
  Strong Lord of hosts indeed.
In life, in death, deliver me
  From every fear and need.

562

Round Me Falls the Night

Ps. 141: 2
William Romanis, 1903

5. 5. 8. 8. 5. 5.

Seelenbräutigam
Adam Drese, 1697

1 Round me falls the night; Sav-ior, be my Light. Thro' the hours in
2 Earth-ly work is done, Earth-ly sounds are none. Rest in sleep and
3 Bless-ed, heav'n-ly Light, Shining thro' earth's night; Voice, that oft of

dark-ness shroud-ed Let me see Thy face un-cloud-ed;
si-lence seek-ing, Let me hear Thee soft-ly speak-ing;
love hast told me; Arms, so strong to clasp and hold me—

Let Thy glo-ry shine In this heart of mine.
In my spir-it's ear Whis-per, "I am near."
Thou Thy watch wilt keep, Sav-ior, o'er my sleep. A-men.

563

The Sun's Last Beam of Light is Gone

Ps. 91: 11, 12
Hinunter ist der Sonnenschein
Nikolaus Herman, 1560
Tr., composite

L. M.

Wo Gott zum Haus
"Geistliche Lieder"
Wittenberg, 1535

1 The sun's last beam of light is gone, The darksome night comes swiftly on;
2 We thank Thee that thro'-out the day Thine an-gels kept all harm a-way.
3 Lord, if we an-gered Thee to-day, Re-mem-ber not our sins, we pray,
4 Let an-gels guard our sleeping hours And drive a-way all e-vil pow'rs;

The Sun's Last Beam of Light is Gone

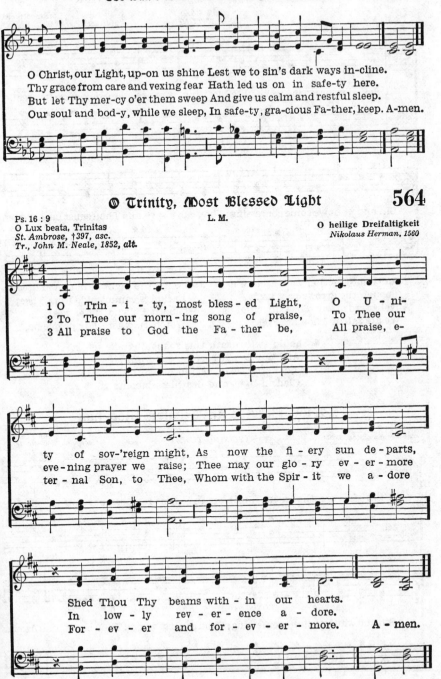

O Christ, our Light, up-on us shine Lest we to sin's dark ways in-cline.
Thy grace from care and vexing fear Hath led us on in safe-ty here.
But let Thy mer-cy o'er them sweep And give us calm and restful sleep.
Our soul and bod-y, while we sleep, In safe-ty, gra-cious Fa-ther, keep. A-men.

O Trinity, Most Blessed Light   564

L. M.

Ps. 16 : 9
O Lux beata, Trinitas
St. Ambrose, †397, asc.
Tr., John M. Neale, 1852, alt.

O heilige Dreifaltigkeit
Nikolaus Herman, 1560

1 O Trin-i-ty, most bless-ed Light, O U-ni-
2 To Thee our morn-ing song of praise, To Thee our
3 All praise to God the Fa-ther be, All praise, e-

ty of sov'reign might, As now the fi-er-y sun de-parts,
eve-ning prayer we raise; Thee may our glo-ry ev-er-more
ter-nal Son, to Thee, Whom with the Spir-it we a-dore

Shed Thou Thy beams with-in our hearts.
In low-ly rev-er-ence a-dore.
For-ev-er and for-ev-er-more. A-men.

565 Savior, Breathe an Evening Blessing

8. 7. 8. 7.
(FIRST TUNE)

Ps. 91: 5
James Edmeston, 1820

Ringe recht
"Musikalischer Christenschatz"
Basel, 1745

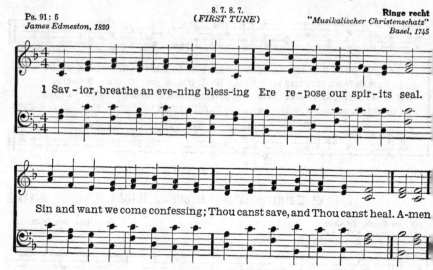

1 Sav-ior, breathe an eve-ning bless-ing Ere re-pose our spir-its seal.

Sin and want we come confessing; Thou canst save, and Thou canst heal. A-men

2 Though destruction walk around us,
  Though the arrows past us fly,
Angel guards from Thee surround us;
  We are safe if Thou art nigh.

3 Though the night be dark and dreary,
  Darkness cannot hide from Thee;
Thou art He who, never weary,
  Watcheth where Thy people be.

4 Should swift death this night o'ertake us
  And our couch become our tomb,
May the morn in heaven awake us,
  Clad in light and deathless bloom.

Savior, Breathe an Evening Blessing

Ps. 91: 5
James Edmeston, 1820

8. 7. 8. 7.
(SECOND TUNE)

Evening Prayer
George C. Stebbins, 1878

1 Sav-ior, breathe an eve-ning bless-ing Ere re-pose our spir-its seal.

Sin and want we come confessing; Thou canst save, and Thou canst heal. Amen.

Christ, by Heavenly Hosts Adored

7. 7. 7. 7. D.

Jer. 29: 7
Henry Harbaugh, 1860, cento, alt.

St. George
George J. Elvey, 1858

1 Christ, by heav'n-ly hosts a-dored, Gra-cious, might-y, sov-'reign Lord,
2 On our fields of grass and grain Send, O Lord, the kind-ly rain;
3 Let our rul-ers ev-er be Men that love and hon-or Thee;

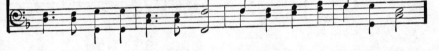

God of na-tions, King of kings, Head of all cre-at-ed things,
O'er our wide and good-ly land Crown the la-bors of each hand.
Let the pow'rs by Thee or-dained Be in right-eous-ness main-tained.

By the Church with joy con-fest, God o'er all, for-ev-er blest.—
Let Thy kind pro-tec-tion be O'er our com-merce on the sea.
In the peo-ple's hearts in-crease Love of pi-e-ty and peace.

Plead-ing at Thy throne we stand, Save Thy peo-ple, bless our land.
O-pen, Lord, Thy bounteous hand; Bless Thy peo-ple, bless our land.
Thus u-nit-ed, we shall stand One wide, free, and hap-py land. A-men.

567 O Lord, Whose Bounteous Hand Again

8. 8. 8. 8. 8. 8.

Ps. 65 : 9
Author unknown

All' Ehr' und Lob
"Kirchengesangbuch"
Strassburg, 1541

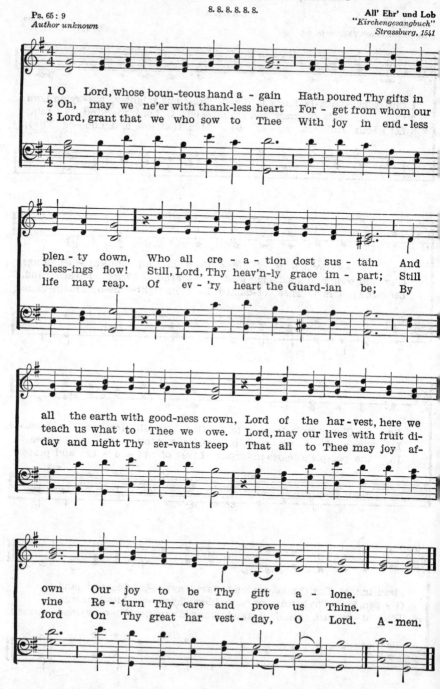

1 O Lord, whose boun-teous hand a - gain
2 Oh, may we ne'er with thank-less heart
3 Lord, grant that we who sow to Thee

Hath poured Thy gifts in
For - get from whom our
With joy in end - less

plen - ty down, Who all cre - a - tion dost sus - tain And
bless-ings flow! Still, Lord, Thy heav'n-ly grace im - part; Still
life may reap. Of ev - 'ry heart the Guard-ian be; By

all the earth with good-ness crown, Lord of the har - vest, here we
teach us what to Thee we owe. Lord, may our lives with fruit di-
day and night Thy ser-vants keep That all to Thee may joy af-

own Our joy to be Thy gift a - lone.
vine Re - turn Thy care and prove us Thine.
ford On Thy great har - vest - day, O Lord. A - men.

We Praise Thee, O God, Our Redeemer, Creator

568

12. 11. 12. 11.

Ps. 26 : 12
Wilt heden nu treden
Author unknown, 1626
Tr., Julia B. Cady Cory, 1882

Kremser
"Nederlandtsch Gedenckclanck"
Haarlem, 1626

1 We praise Thee, O God, our Re-deem-er, Cre-a-tor,
2 We wor-ship Thee, God of our fa-thers, we bless Thee;
3 With voic-es u-nit-ed our prais-es we of-fer,

In grate-ful de-vo-tion our trib-ute we bring;
Thro' life's storm and tem-pest our Guide hast Thou been;
To Thee, great Je-ho-vah, glad an-thems we raise.

We lay it be-fore Thee, we kneel and a-dore Thee,
When per-ils o'er-take us, es-cape Thou wilt make us,
Thy strong arm will guide us, our God is be-side us,

We bless Thy ho-ly name, glad prais-es we sing.
And with Thy help, O Lord, our bat-tles we win.
To Thee, our great Re-deem-er, for-e'er be praise. A-men.

569
O Lord, I Sing with Lips and Heart

Ps. 92:1
Ich singe dir mit Herz und Mund
Paul Gerhardt, 1653, cento
Tr., John Kelly, 1867, alt.

C. M.

Ich singe dir
"Harmonischer Liederschatz"
Frankfurt, 1738

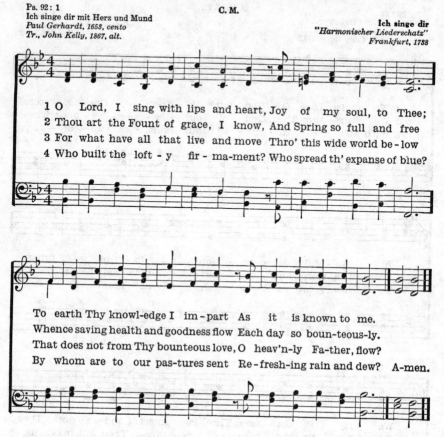

1 O Lord, I sing with lips and heart, Joy of my soul, to Thee;
2 Thou art the Fount of grace, I know, And Spring so full and free
3 For what have all that live and move Thro' this wide world be-low
4 Who built the loft-y fir-ma-ment? Who spread th' expanse of blue?

To earth Thy knowl-edge I im-part As it is known to me.
Whence saving health and goodness flow Each day so boun-teous-ly.
That does not from Thy bounteous love, O heav'n-ly Fa-ther, flow?
By whom are to our pas-tures sent Re-fresh-ing rain and dew? A-men.

5 Who warmeth us in cold and rain?
    Who shields us from the wind?
Who orders it that fruit and grain
    We in their season find?

6 Who is it life and health bestows?
    Who keeps us with His hand
In golden peace, wards off war's woes
    From our dear native land?

7 O Lord, of this and all our store
    Thou art the Author blest;
Thou keepest watch before our door
    While we securely rest.

8 Thou feedest us from year to year
    And constant dost abide;
With ready help in time of fear
    Thou standest at our side.

9 Our deepest need dost Thou supply
    And all that lasts for aye;
Thou leadest to our home on high
    When hence we pass away.

Praise, Oh, Praise, Our God and King

570

Ps. 136
John Milton, 1623
Henry W. Baker, 1861

7. 7. 7. 7.

Monkland
"Hymn Tunes of the United Brethren"
Manchester, 1824

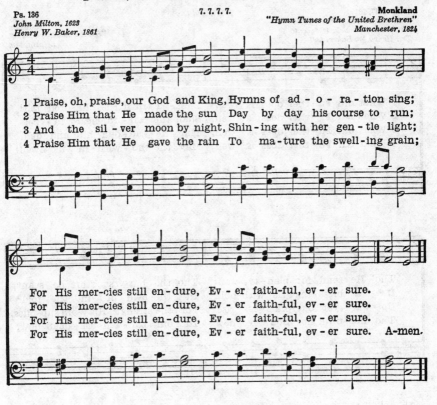

1 Praise, oh, praise, our God and King, Hymns of ad - o - ra - tion sing;
2 Praise Him that He made the sun Day by day his course to run;
3 And the sil - ver moon by night, Shin - ing with her gen - tle light;
4 Praise Him that He gave the rain To ma - ture the swell - ing grain;

For His mer-cies still en-dure, Ev - er faith-ful, ev - er sure.
For His mer-cies still en-dure, Ev - er faith-ful, ev - er sure.
For His mer-cies still en-dure, Ev - er faith-ful, ev - er sure.
For His mer-cies still en-dure, Ev - er faith-ful, ev - er sure. A-men.

5 And hath bid the fruitful field
  Crops of precious increase yield;
  For His mercies still endure,
  Ever faithful, ever sure.

6 Praise Him for our harvest store,
  He hath filled the garner floor;
  For His mercies still endure,
  Ever faithful, ever sure.

7 And for richer food than this,
  Pledge of everlasting bliss;
  For His mercies still endure,
  Ever faithful, ever sure.

8 Glory to our bounteous King,
  Glory let creation sing;
  Glory to the Father, Son,
  And the Spirit, Three in One!

571 What Our Father Does Is Well

7. 7. 7. 7. 7. 7.

Hab. 3: 17, 18
Was Gott tut, das ist wohlgetan
Benjamin Schmolck, 1720, cento
Tr., Henry W. Baker, 1861

Ratisbon
"Sächsisches Choralbuch"
Leipzig, 1815

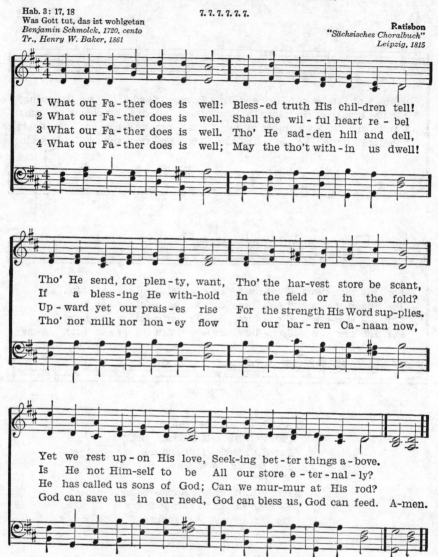

1 What our Fa-ther does is well: Bless-ed truth His chil-dren tell!
2 What our Fa-ther does is well. Shall the wil-ful heart re - bel
3 What our Fa-ther does is well. Tho' He sad-den hill and dell,
4 What our Fa-ther does is well; May the tho't with-in us dwell!

Tho' He send, for plen-ty, want, Tho' the har-vest store be scant,
If a bless-ing He with-hold In the field or in the fold?
Up-ward yet our prais-es rise For the strength His Word sup-plies.
Tho' nor milk nor hon-ey flow In our bar-ren Ca-naan now,

Yet we rest up-on His love, Seek-ing bet-ter things a-bove.
Is He not Him-self to be All our store e - ter-nal - ly?
He has called us sons of God; Can we mur-mur at His rod?
God can save us in our need, God can bless us, God can feed. A-men.

5 Therefore unto Him we raise
Hymns of glory, songs of praise.
To the Father and the Son
And the Spirit, Three in One,
Honor, might, and glory be
Now and through eternity.

Praise to God, Immortal Praise

572

7. 7. 7. 7. 7. 7.

Hab. 3: 17, 18
Anna L. Barbauld, 1772, cento, alt.

Dix
Konrad Kocher, 1838

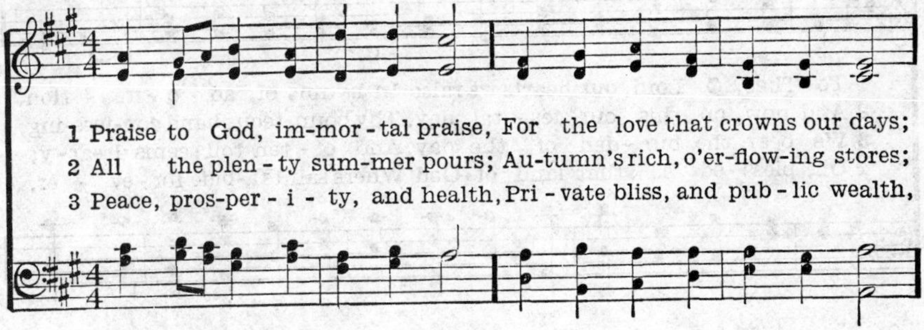

1 Praise to God, im-mor-tal praise, For the love that crowns our days;
2 All the plen-ty sum-mer pours; Au-tumn's rich, o'er-flow-ing stores;
3 Peace, pros-per-i-ty, and health, Pri-vate bliss, and pub-lic wealth,

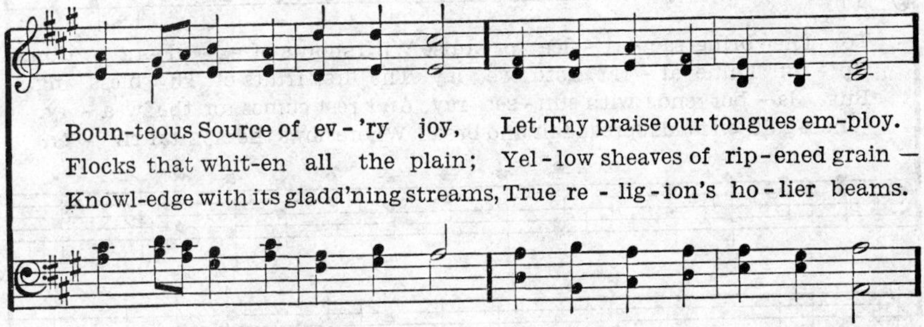

Boun-teous Source of ev-'ry joy, Let Thy praise our tongues em-ploy.
Flocks that whit-en all the plain; Yel-low sheaves of rip-ened grain —
Knowl-edge with its gladd'ning streams, True re-lig-ion's ho-lier beams.

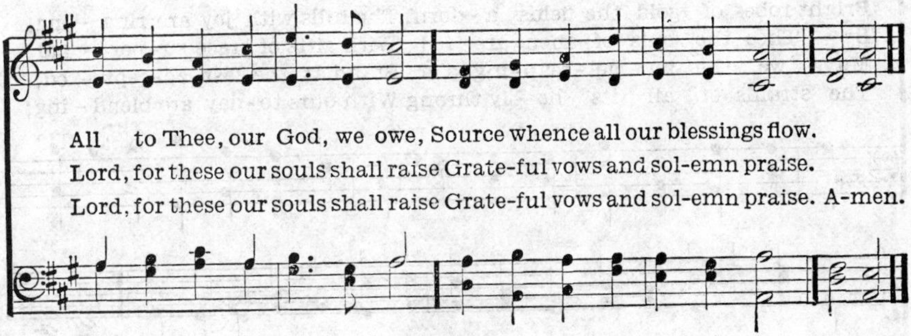

All to Thee, our God, we owe, Source whence all our blessings flow.
Lord, for these our souls shall raise Grate-ful vows and sol-emn praise.
Lord, for these our souls shall raise Grate-ful vows and sol-emn praise. A-men.

4 As Thy prospering hand hath blest,
May we give Thee of our best
And by deeds of kindly love
For Thy mercies grateful prove,
Singing thus through all our days
Praise to God, immortal praise.

573 To Thee, O Lord, Our Hearts We Raise

Ps. 65 : 12
William C. Dix, 1864

8. 7. 8. 7. D. Iambic

Harvest Hymn
"St. Gallen Gesangbuch," 1863, ad.

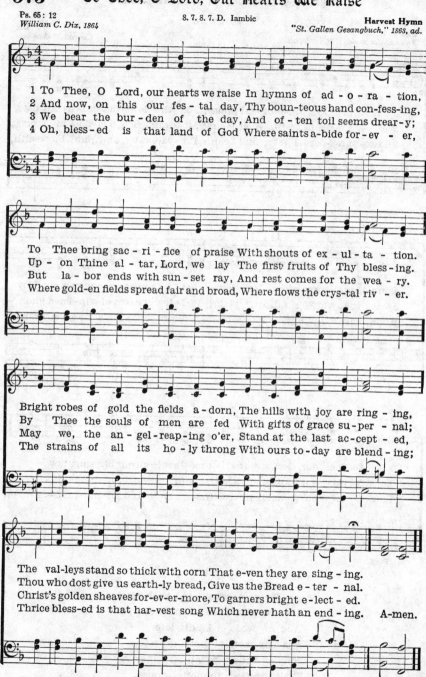

1 To Thee, O Lord, our hearts we raise In hymns of ad - o - ra - tion,
2 And now, on this our fes - tal day, Thy boun-teous hand con-fess-ing,
3 We bear the bur - den of the day, And of - ten toil seems drear-y;
4 Oh, bless - ed is that land of God Where saints a-bide for - ev - er,

To Thee bring sac - ri - fice of praise With shouts of ex - ul - ta - tion.
Up - on Thine al - tar, Lord, we lay The first fruits of Thy bless-ing.
But la - bor ends with sun - set ray, And rest comes for the wea - ry.
Where gold-en fields spread fair and broad, Where flows the crys-tal riv - er.

Bright robes of gold the fields a - dorn, The hills with joy are ring - ing,
By Thee the souls of men are fed With gifts of grace su - per - nal;
May we, the an - gel-reap-ing o'er, Stand at the last ac-cept - ed,
The strains of all its ho - ly throng With ours to - day are blend - ing;

The val-leys stand so thick with corn That e - ven they are sing - ing.
Thou who dost give us earth-ly bread, Give us the Bread e - ter - nal.
Christ's golden sheaves for-ev-er-more, To garners bright e - lect - ed.
Thrice bless-ed is that har-vest song Which never hath an end - ing. A-men.

Come, Ye Thankful People, Come

574

Is. 9 : 3
Henry Alford, 1844, cento, alt.

7. 7. 7. 7. D.

St. George
George J. Elvey, 1858

1 Come, ye thank-ful peo-ple, come; Raise the song of Har-vest-home.
2 All the world is God's own field, Fruit un-to His praise to yield;
3 For the Lord, our God, shall come And shall take His har-vest home;
4 E- ven so, Lord, quick-ly come To Thy fi-nal Har-vest-home;

All be safe-ly gath-ered in Ere the win-ter storms be-gin;
Wheat and tares to-geth-er sown, Un-to joy or sor-row grown;
From His field shall in that day All of-fens-es purge a-way;
Gath-er Thou Thy peo-ple in, Free from sor-row, free from sin,

God, our Mak-er, doth pro-vide For our wants to be sup-plied.
First the blade and then the ear, Then the full corn shall ap-pear.
Give His an-gels charge at last In the fire the tares to cast,
There, for-ev-er pu-ri-fied, In Thy gar-ner to a-bide.

Come to God's own tem-ple, come; Raise the song of Har-vest-home.
Lord of har-vest, grant that we Whole-some grain and pure may be.
But the fruit-ful ears to store In His gar-ner ev-er-more.
Come with all Thine an-gels, come, Raise the glo-rious Har-vest-home. A-men.

575

Before the Lord We Bow

6. 6. 6. 6. 4. 4. 4. 4.

Ps. 145 : 1
Francis S. Key, 1832, alt.

Darwall's 148th
John Darwall, 1770

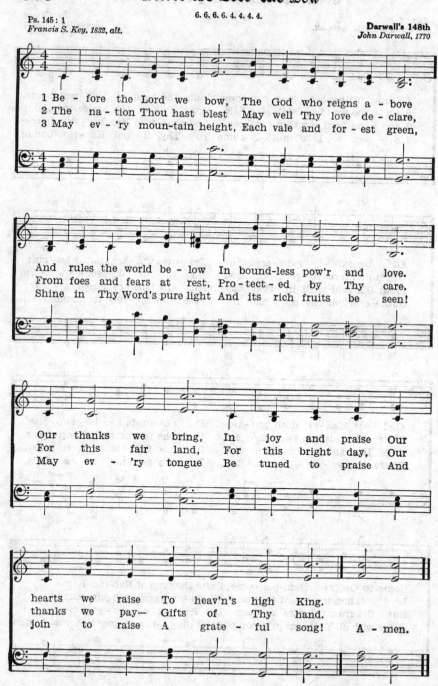

1 Be - fore the Lord we bow, The God who reigns a - bove
2 The na - tion Thou hast blest May well Thy love de - clare,
3 May ev - 'ry moun-tain height, Each vale and for - est green,

And rules the world be - low In bound-less pow'r and love.
From foes and fears at rest, Pro - tect - ed by Thy care.
Shine in Thy Word's pure light And its rich fruits be seen!

Our thanks we bring, In joy and praise Our
For this fair land, For this bright day, Our
May ev - 'ry tongue Be tuned to praise And

hearts we raise To heav'n's high King.
thanks we pay— Gifts of Thy hand.
join to raise A grate - ful song! A - men.

Before the Lord We Bow

4 Earth, hear thy Maker's voice,
  Thy great Redeemer own;
Believe, obey, rejoice,
  And worship Him alone.
Cast down thy pride,
  Thy sin deplore,
  And bow before
The Crucified.

5 And when in power He comes,
  Oh, may our native land
From all its rending tombs
  Send forth a glorious band,
A countless throng,
  For aye to sing
  To heaven's high King
Salvation's song!

Judge Eternal, Throned in Splendor — 576

8. 7. 8. 7. 8. 7.

Ps. 59: 16
Henry S. Holland, 1902

Bis willkommen
J. Christian Kittel, 1790

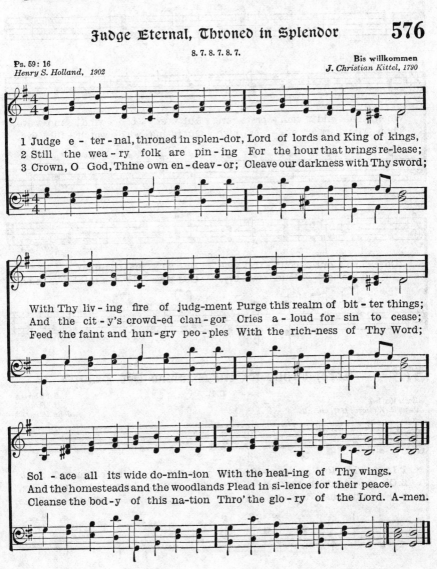

1 Judge e - ter - nal, throned in splen-dor, Lord of lords and King of kings,
2 Still the wea - ry folk are pin-ing For the hour that brings re-lease;
3 Crown, O God, Thine own en - deav - or; Cleave our darkness with Thy sword;

With Thy liv - ing fire of judg-ment Purge this realm of bit - ter things;
And the cit - y's crowd-ed clan-gor Cries a - loud for sin to cease;
Feed the faint and hun-gry peo - ples With the rich-ness of Thy Word;

Sol - ace all its wide do-min-ion With the heal-ing of Thy wings.
And the homesteads and the woodlands Plead in si-lence for their peace.
Cleanse the bod - y of this na-tion Thro' the glo - ry of the Lord. A-men.

577 God Bless Our Native Land

Rom. 13: 1-7
Charles T. Brooks, 1834
John S. Dwight, 1844

6. 6. 4. 6. 6. 6. 4.

America
"Thesaurus Musicus," 1740

1 God bless our na-tive land! Firm may she ev-er stand Thro' storm and night!
2 For her our prayer shall rise To God a-bove the skies; On Him we wait.

When the wild tem-pests rave, Rul-er of wind and wave,
Thou who art ev-er nigh, Guard-ing with watch-ful eye,

Do Thou our coun-try save By Thy great might.
To Thee a-loud we cry, God save the State! A-men.

578 Lord, While for All Mankind We Pray

C. M.

Rom. 13: 1-7
John R. Wreford, 1837, ab., alt.

St. Flavian
"Psalter"
John Day, 1562

1 Lord, while for all man-kind we pray Of ev-'ry clime and coast,
2 Oh, guard our shores from ev-'ry foe, With peace our bor-ders bless,
3 U-nite us in the sa-cred love Of knowl-edge, truth, and Thee;

Lord, While for All Mankind We Pray

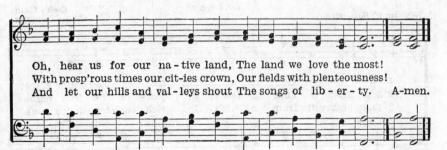

Oh, hear us for our na-tive land, The land we love the most!
With prosp'rous times our cit-ies crown, Our fields with plenteousness!
And let our hills and val-leys shout The songs of lib-er-ty. A-men.

4 Here may Thy Gospel, pure and mild,
   Smile on our Sabbath hours
And piety and virtue bless
   Our fathers' home and ours.

5 Lord of the nations, thus to Thee
   Our country we commend.
Be Thou her Refuge and her Trust,
   Her everlasting Friend.

Almighty Lord, before Thy Throne 579

C. M.

Ps. 59: 16
Anne Steele, 1756, cento, alt.

Burford
"Psalmody"
John Chetham, 1718

1 Al-might-y Lord, be-fore Thy throne Thy mourn-ing peo-ple bend;
2 Dark judg-ments from Thy heav-y hand Thy dread-ful pow'r dis-play;
3 How changed, a-las, are truths di-vine For er-ror, guilt, and shame!

'Tis on Thy grace in Christ a-lone Our fail-ing hopes de-pend.
Yet mer-cy spares our guilt-y land, And still we live to pray.
What im-pious num-bers, bold in sin, Dis-grace the Christian name! A-men.

4 Oh, turn us, turn us, mighty Lord;
   Convert us by Thy grace!
Then shall our hearts obey Thy Word
   And see again Thy face.

5 Then, should oppressing foes invade,
   We will not yield to fear,
Secure of all-sufficient aid
   When God in Christ is near.

580

To Thee, Our God, We Fly

Ex. 34: 6, 7
William W. How, 1871

6. 6. 6. 6. 8. 8.

Croft's 136th
William Croft, 1709

1 To Thee, our God, we fly For mer - cy and for grace;
2 A - rise, O Lord of hosts, Be jeal - ous for Thy name
3 Thy best gifts from on high In rich a - bun-dance pour

Oh, hear our low - ly cry And hide not Thou Thy face!
And drive from out our coasts The sins that put to shame.
That we may mag - ni - fy And praise Thee more and more.

O Lord, stretch forth Thy might - y hand
O Lord, stretch forth Thy might - y hand
O Lord, stretch forth Thy might - y hand

And guard and bless our Fa - ther - land.
And guard and bless our Fa - ther - land.
And guard and bless our Fa - ther - land. A - men.

4 The powers ordained by Thee
    With heavenly wisdom bless;
May they Thy servants be
    And rule in righteousness!
O Lord, stretch forth Thy mighty hand
And guard and bless our Fatherland.

5 The Church of Thy dear Son
    Inflame with love's pure fire;
Bind her once more in one
    And life and truth inspire.
O Lord, stretch forth Thy mighty hand
And guard and bless our Fatherland.

To Thee, Our God, We Fly

6 The pastors of Thy fold
   With grace and power endue
That, faithful, pure, and bold,
   They may be pastors true.
O Lord, stretch forth Thy mighty hand
And guard and bless our Fatherland.

7 Oh, let us love Thy house
   And sanctify Thy day,
Bring unto Thee our vows,
   And loyal homage pay.
O Lord, stretch forth Thy mighty hand
And guard and bless our Fatherland.

8 Give peace, Lord, in our time;
   Oh, let no foe draw nigh
Nor lawless deed of crime
   Insult Thy majesty!
O Lord, stretch forth Thy mighty hand
And guard and bless our Fatherland.

9 Though vile and worthless, still
   Thy people, Lord, are we;
And for our God we will
   None other have but Thee.
O Lord, stretch forth Thy mighty hand
And guard and bless our Fatherland.

All Ye Who on This Earth do Dwell   581

Ecclus. 50: 22–24   C. M.

Nun danket all' und bringet Ehr'
Paul Gerhardt, 1648, cento
Tr., Alfred Ramsey, †1926, alt.

Nun danket all'
Johann Crüger, 1653

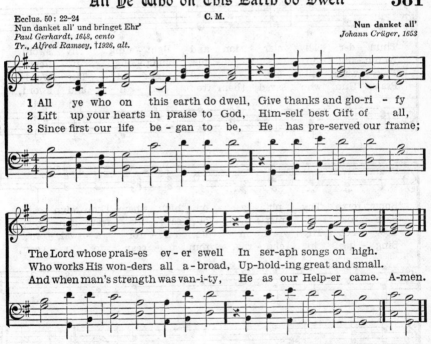

1 All ye who on this earth do dwell, Give thanks and glo-ri - fy
2 Lift up your hearts in praise to God, Him-self best Gift of all,
3 Since first our life be-gan to be, He has pre-served our frame;

The Lord whose prais-es ev-er swell In ser-aph songs on high.
Who works His won-ders all a-broad, Up-hold-ing great and small.
And when man's strength was van-i-ty, He as our Help-er came. A-men.

4 Though often we His patience try
   And well deserve His frown,
In grace He lays His anger by
   And pours new blessings down.

5 'Tis He revives our fainting soul,
   Gives joyful hearts to men;
And when great waves of trouble roll,
   He drives them back again.

6 May He adorn with precious peace
   Our own, our native, land
And crown with joys that never cease
   The labors of our hand!

7 Long as we tarry here below
   Our saving Health is He;
And when from earth to heaven we go,
   May He our Portion be!

582 God, Lord of Sabaoth, Thou Who Ordainest

11. 10. 11. 9.

Ps. 122 : 6
Henry F. Chorley, 1842, alt.

Liebster Immanuel
"Himmelslust"
Leipzig, 1675

1 God, Lord of Sab - a - oth, Thou who or - dain - est
2 God, the om - nip - o - tent, might - y A - veng - er,
3 God, the All - mer - ci - ful, earth hath for - sak - en
4 So shall Thy peo - ple, with thank - ful de - vo - tion,

Thun - der Thy clar - ion and light - ning Thy sword,
Watch - ing in - vis - i - ble, judg - ing un - heard;
Thy ways all ho - ly and slight - ed Thy Word;
Praise Him who saved them from per - il and sword,

Show forth Thy pit - y on high where Thou reign - est;
Save us in mer - cy, oh, save us from dan - ger;
Let not Thy wrath in its ter - ror a - wak - en;
Sing - ing in cho - rus, from o - cean to o - cean,

Give to us peace in our time, O Lord.
Give to us peace in our time, O Lord.
Give to us par - don and peace, O Lord.
Peace to the na - tions and praise to the Lord. A - men.

Great King of Nations, Hear Our Prayer

583

C. M. D.

Ps. 65: 2
John H. Gurney, 1838

Old 137th
"Anglo-Genevan Psalter," 1556

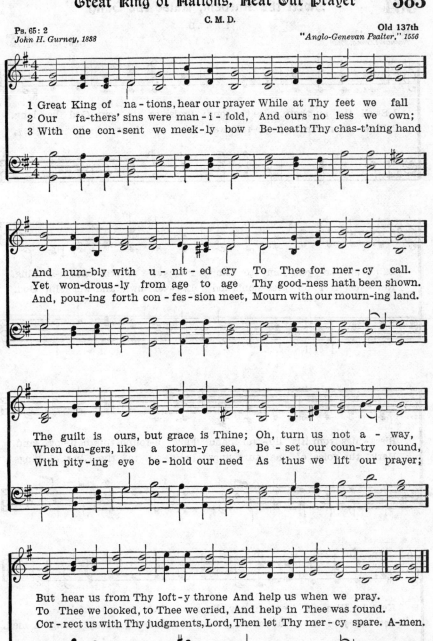

1 Great King of na - tions, hear our prayer While at Thy feet we fall
2 Our fa - thers' sins were man - i - fold, And ours no less we own;
3 With one con - sent we meek - ly bow Be - neath Thy chas - t'ning hand

And hum - bly with u - nit - ed cry To Thee for mer - cy call.
Yet won - drous - ly from age to age Thy good - ness hath been shown.
And, pour - ing forth con - fes - sion meet, Mourn with our mourn - ing land.

The guilt is ours, but grace is Thine; Oh, turn us not a - way,
When dan - gers, like a storm - y sea, Be - set our coun - try round,
With pity - ing eye be - hold our need As thus we lift our prayer;

But hear us from Thy loft - y throne And help us when we pray.
To Thee we looked, to Thee we cried, And help in Thee was found.
Cor - rect us with Thy judgments, Lord, Then let Thy mer - cy spare. A-men.

584 Swell the Anthem, Raise the Song

7. 7. 7. 7. D.

Deut. 8: 10-12
Nathan Strong, 1799

St. George
George J. Elvey, 1858

1 Swell the an-them, raise the song; Prais-es to our God be-long.
2 Here, be-neath a peace-ful sway, May we cheer-ful-ly o - bey,

Saints and an - gels join to sing Prais-es to the heav'n-ly King.
Nev - er feel op-pres-sion's rod, Ev - er own and wor-ship God.

Bless - ings from His lib-'ral hand Flow a-round this hap-py land.
Hark, the voice of na-ture sings Prais-es to the King of kings.

Kept by Him, no foes an-noy; Peace and free-dom we en-joy.
Let us join the cho-ral song And the grate-ful notes pro-long. A-men.

The Last Things

I Fall Asleep in Jesus' Wounds

585

Luke 2: 29
In Christi Wunden schlaf' ich ein
Paul Eber, †1569, asc.
Tr., Catherine Winkworth, 1869, alt.

8. 8. 8. 8. 8. 8.

Vater unser
("Geistliche Lieder"
Leipzig, 1539

1 I fall a-sleep in Je-sus' wounds, There par-don for my sins a-bounds; Yea, Je-sus' blood and right-eous-ness My jew-els are, my glo-rious dress. In these be-fore my God I'll stand When I shall reach the heav'n-ly land.

2 With peace and joy I now de-part; God's child I am with all my heart. I thank thee, Death, thou lead-est me To that true life where I would be. So cleansed by Christ, I fear not death. Lord Je-sus, strength-en Thou my faith. A-men.

586

A Pilgrim and a Stranger

7. 6. 7. 6. D.

Ps. 39 : 12
Ich bin ein Gast auf Erden
Paul Gerhardt, 1666, cento
Tr., Jane Borthwick, 1858 alt.

Herzlich tut mich
Hans L. Hassler, 1601

1 A pil - grim and a stran - ger, I jour - ney here be - low;
2 I've met with storms and dan - ger E'en from my ear - ly years,
3 It is a well-worn path - way; A host has gone be - fore,
4 Who would share Abraham's bless - ing Must Abraham's path pur - sue,

Far dis - tant is my coun - try, The home to which I go.
With en - e - mies and con - flicts, With fight - ings and with fears.
The ho - ly saints and proph - ets, The pa - tri - archs of yore.
A stran - ger and a pil - grim, Like him, must jour - ney thro'.

Here I must toil and trav - ail, Oft wea - ry and op - prest;
There's noth - ing here that tempts me To wish a lon - ger stay,
They trod the toil - some jour - ney In pa - tience and in faith;
The foes must be en - coun - tered, The dan - gers must be passed;

But there my God shall lead me To ev - er - last - ing rest.
So I must hast - en for - ward, No halt - ing or de - lay.
And them I fain would fol - low, Like them in life and death.
A faith - ful sol - dier on - ly Re - ceives the crown at last. A - men.

A Pilgrim and a Stranger

5 So I must hasten forward —
   Thank God, the end will come!
This land of passing shadows
   Is not my destined home.
The everlasting city,
   Jerusalem above,
This evermore abideth,
   The home of light and love.

6 There still my thoughts are dwelling,
   'Tis there I long to be;
Come, Lord, and call Thy servant
   To blessedness with Thee.

Come, bid my toils be ended,
   Let all my wand'rings cease;
Call from the wayside lodging
   To Thy sweet home of peace.

7 There I shall dwell forever,
   No more a parting guest,
With all Thy blood-bought children
   In everlasting rest,
The pilgrim toils forgotten,
   The pilgrim conflicts o'er,
All earthly griefs behind me,
   Eternal joys before.

Asleep in Jesus! Blessed Sleep   587

1 Thess. 4 : 14   L. M.   Rest
Margaret Mackay, 1832, cento   *William B. Bradbury, 1843*

1 A-sleep in Je-sus! Bless-ed sleep, From which none
2 A-sleep in Je-sus! Oh, how sweet To be for
3 A-sleep in Je-sus! Peace-ful rest, Whose wak-ing
4 A-sleep in Je-sus! Oh, for me May such a

ev-er wakes to weep; A calm and un-dis-turbed re-
such a slum-ber meet, With ho-ly con-fi-dence to
is su-preme-ly blest; No fear, no woe, shall dim that
bliss-ful ref-uge be! Se-cure-ly shall my ash-es

pose, Un-bro-ken by the last of foes.
sing That death has lost his ven-omed sting!
hour That man-i-fests the Sav-ior's pow'r.
lie And wait the sum-mons from on high. A-men.

588 I Would Not Live Alway; I Ask Not to Stay

11. 11. 11. 11.

Job 7: 16
William A. Mühlenberg, 1824, cento, alt.

Maldwyn
Welsh melody, c. 1600

1 I would not live al-way; I ask not to stay
2 I would not live al-way; thus fet-tered by sin,
3 I would not live al-way; no, wel-come the tomb;
4 Ah, who would live al-way, a-way from his God,

Where storm af-ter storm ris-es dark o'er the way.
Temp-ta-tion with-out and cor-rup-tion with-in;
Since Je-sus hath lain there, I dread not its gloom.
A-way from yon heav-en, that bliss-ful a-bode,

The few lu-rid morn-ings that dawn on us here
E'en rap-ture of par-don is min-gled with fears,
There sweet be my rest till He bids me a-rise
Where riv-ers of plea-sure flow o'er the bright plains

Suf-fice for life's woes, are e-nough for its cheer.
The cup of thanks-giv-ing with pen-i-tent tears.
To hail Him in tri-umph de-scend-ing the skies.
And noon-tide of glo-ry e-ter-nal-ly reigns; A-men.

I Would Not Live Alway; I Ask Not to Stay

5 Where saints of all ages in harmony meet
   Their Savior and brethren transported to greet,
   While anthems of rapture unceasingly roll,
   The smile of the Lord is the feast of the soul?

Oh, How Blest Are Ye Whose Toils are Ended 589

Rev. 14: 13
O wie selig seid ihr doch, ihr Frommen
Simon Dach, 1635
Tr., Henry W. Longfellow, 1845, alt.

10. 10. 5. 10.

O wie selig
J. Georg Stözel's "Choral-Buch"
Stuttgart, 1744

1 Oh, how blest are ye whose toils are end - ed, Who thro'
2 We are still as in a dun-geon liv - ing, Still op-
3 Ye mean-while are in your cham-bers sleep - ing, Qui - et,
4 Christ has wiped a - way your tears for - ev - er; Ye have

death have un - to God as - cend - ed! Ye have a - ris - en
pressed with sor-row and mis-giv - ing; Our un - der - tak - ings
and set free from all our weep - ing; No cross or sad - ness
that for which we still en - deav - or; To you are chant - ed

From the cares which keep us still in pris - on.
Are but toils and trou - bles and heart-break - ings.
There can hin - der your un - trou - bled glad - ness.
Songs that ne'er to mor - tal ears were grant - ed. A - men.

5 Ah, who would, then, not depart with gladness
   To inherit heaven for earthly sadness?
   Who here would languish
   Longer in bewailing and in anguish?

6 Come, O Christ, and loose the chains that bind us;
   Lead us forth and cast this world behind us.
   With Thee, th' Anointed,
   Finds the soul its joy and rest appointed.

590

In the Midst of Earthly Life

1 Sam. 20: 3   Irregular

Mitten wir im Leben sind   **Mitten wir im Leben sind**

Martin Luther, 1524   *Based on "Media vita," c. 1200*

Tr., composite

1 In the midst of earth-ly life   Snares of death sur-round us;
2 In the midst of death's dark vale   Pow'rs of hell o'er-take us.
3 In the midst of ut-ter woe   When our sins op-press us,

Who shall help us in the strife   Lest the Foe con-found us?
Who will help when they as-sail,   Who se-cure will make us?
Where shall we for ref-uge go,   Where for grace to bless us?

Thou on-ly, Lord, Thou on-ly!   We mourn that we have great-ly erred,
Thou on-ly, Lord, Thou on-ly!   Thy heart is moved with ten-der-ness,
To Thee, Lord Je-sus, on-ly!   Thy pre-cious blood was shed to win

That our sins Thy wrath have stirred.   Ho-ly and right-eous God!
Pit-ies us in our dis-tress.   Ho-ly and right-eous God!
Full a-tone-ment for our sin.   Ho-ly and right-eous God!

Ho-ly and might-y God!   Ho-ly and all-mer-ci-ful Sav-ior!
Ho-ly and might-y God!   Ho-ly and all-mer-ci-ful Sav-ior!
Ho-ly and might-y God!   Ho-ly and all-mer-ci-ful Sav-ior!

In the Midst of Earthly Life

E - ter - nal Lord God! Save us lest we per - ish
E - ter - nal Lord God! Save us from the ter - ror
E - ter - nal Lord God! Lord, pre-serve and keep us

In the bit - ter pangs of death. Have mer-cy, O Lord!
Of the fi - ery pit of hell. Have mer-cy, O Lord!
In the peace that faith can give. Have mer-cy, O Lord! A - men.

Jesus, I Live to Thee   591

Rom. 14: 8   S. M.   Tenbury
Henry Harbaugh, 1850   Frederick A. G. Ousely, 1861

1 Je - sus, I live to Thee, The Love - li - est and Best;
2 Je - sus, I die to Thee When-ev - er death shall come;
3 Wheth-er to live or die I know not which is best;
4 Liv - ing or dy - ing, Lord, I ask but to be Thine;

My life in Thee, Thy life in me, In Thy blest love I rest.
To die in Thee is life to me In my e - ter - nal home.
To live in Thee is bliss to me, To die is end-less rest.
My life in Thee, Thy life in me, Make heav'n for-ev-er mine. A - men.

592 I Know of a Sleep in Jesus' Name

Rev. 14: 13
Jeg ved mig en Sövn i Jesu Navn
Magnus B. Landstad, 1861, ab.
Tr., composite

9. 8. 9. 8. 9. 8.

Den signede Dag
Christoph E. F. Weyse, 1826

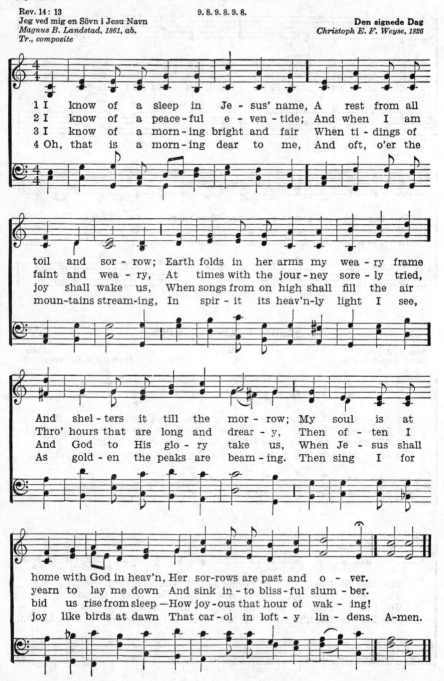

1 I know of a sleep in Je-sus' name, A rest from all toil and sor-row; Earth folds in her arms my wea-ry frame And shel-ters it till the mor-row; My soul is at home with God in heav'n, Her sor-rows are past and o - ver.

2 I know of a peace-ful e-ven-tide; And when I am faint and wea-ry, At times with the jour-ney sore-ly tried, Thro' hours that are long and drear-y, Then of-ten I yearn to lay me down And sink in-to bliss-ful slum-ber.

3 I know of a morn-ing bright and fair When ti-dings of joy shall wake us, When songs from on high shall fill the air And God to His glo-ry take us, When Je-sus shall bid us rise from sleep —How joy-ous that hour of wak-ing!

4 Oh, that is a morn-ing dear to me, And oft, o'er the moun-tains stream-ing, In spir-it its heav'n-ly light I see, As gold-en the peaks are beam-ing. Then sing I for joy like birds at dawn That car-ol in loft-y lin-dens. A-men.

I Know of a Sleep in Jesus' Name

5 God's Son to our graves then takes His way,
   His voice hear all tribes and nations;
The portals are rent that guard our clay,
   And moved are the sea's foundations.
He calls out aloud, "Ye dead, come forth!"
   In glory we rise to meet Him.

6 O Jesus, draw near my dying bed
   And take me into Thy keeping
And say when my spirit hence is fled,
   "This child is not dead, but sleeping."
And leave me not, Savior, till I rise
   To praise Thee in life eternal.

Why do We Mourn Departing Friends 593

C. M.

Mark 5: 39
Isaac Watts, 1707, alt.

Domine, clamavi
Justin H. Knecht, 1797

1 Why do we mourn de-part-ing friends Or shake at death's a-larms?
2 Are we not tend-ing up-ward, too, As fast as time can move?
3 Why should we trem-ble to con-vey Their bod-ies to the tomb?
4 The graves of all the saints He blest And soft-ened ev-'ry bed.

'Tis but the voice that Je-sus sends To call them to His arms.
Nor would we wish the hours more slow To keep us from our Love.
There the dear flesh of Je-sus lay And scattered all the gloom.
Where should the dy-ing members rest But with their dy-ing Head? A-men.

5 Thence He arose, ascending high,
   And showed our feet the way.
Up to the Lord we, too, shall fly
   At the great rising-day.

6 Then let the last loud trumpet sound
   And bid our kindred rise:
Awake, ye nations under ground!
   Ye saints, ascend the skies!

594 When My Last Hour Is Close at Hand

John 15: 5
Wenn mein Stündlein vorhanden ist
St. 1–4, Nikolaus Herman, 1562
St. 5, author unknown, 1575
Tr., Catherine Winkworth, 1869, alt.

8. 7. 8. 7. 8. 8. 7.

Wenn mein Stündlein
"Kirchengesäng"
Frankfurt a. M., 1569

1 When my last hour is close at hand, Lord Je - sus Christ, at-tend me;
2 My sins, dear Lord, dis-turb me sore, My con-science can-not slum-ber;
3 I am a branch in Thee, the Vine, And hence the com-fort bor - row

Be - side me then, O Sav - ior, stand To com-fort and de - fend me.
But tho' as sands up-on the shore My sins may be in num - ber,
That Thou wilt sure-ly keep me Thine Thro' fear and pain and sor - row;

In - to Thy hands I will com-mend My soul at this my
I will not quail, but think of Thee; Thy death, Thy sor - row,
And when I die, I die to Thee, Thy pre-cious death hath

earth-ly end, And Thou wilt keep it safe - ly.
borne for me, Thy suf-f'rings, shall up-hold me.
won for me The life that nev - er end - eth. A - men.

When My Last Hour Is Close at Hand

4 Since Thou the power of death didst rend,
  In death Thou wilt not leave me;
Since Thou didst into heaven ascend,
  No fear of death shall grieve me.
For where Thou art, there shall I be
That I may ever live with Thee;
  That is my hope when dying.

5 My spirit I commend to Thee
  And gladly hence betake me;
Peaceful and calm my sleep shall be,
  No human voice can wake me.
But Christ is with me through the strife,
And He will bear me into life
  And open heaven before me.

Tender Shepherd, Thou hast Stilled 595

Matt. 18: 2
Guter Hirt, du hast gestillt
Johann W. Meinhold, 1833
Tr., Catherine Winkworth, 1858, alt.

7. 8. 7. 8. 7. 7.

Meinen Jesum lass' ich nicht
"Neuverfertigtes Gesangbuch"
Darmstadt, 1699

1 Ten-der Shepherd, Thou hast stilled Now Thy lit-tle lamb's brief weep-ing.
2 In this world of pain and care, Lord, Thou wouldst no longer leave it;
3 O Lord Je-sus, grant that we There may live where it is liv-ing,

Ah, how peace-ful and how mild In its nar-row bed 'tis sleep-ing!
To Thy heav'n-ly mead-ows fair Lov-ing-ly Thou dost re-ceive it.
There the bliss-ful pas-tures see That it heav'n-ly food are giv-ing.

And no sigh of an-guish sore Heaves that lit-tle bos-om more.
Clothed in robes of spot-less white, Now it dwells with Thee in light.
Lost a while our trea-sured love, Gained for-ev-er, safe a-bove. A-men.

596 This Body in the Grave We Lay

L. M.

John 5: 24
Nun lasst uns den Leib begraben
St. 1-7, Michael Weisse, 1531
St. 8, author unknown
Tr., William M. Czamanske, 1933

Nun lasst uns den Leib
"Geistliche Gesänge"
Wittenberg, 1544

1 This bod-y in the grave we lay   There to a-
2 And so to earth we now en-trust   What came from
3 The soul for-ev-er lives with God,   Who free-ly
4 All tri-als and all griefs are past,   A bless-ed

wait that sol-emn Day   When God Him-self shall bid it
dust and turns to dust   And from the dust shall rise that
hath His grace be-stowed   And through His Son re-deemed it
end has come at last.   Christ's yoke was borne with read-y

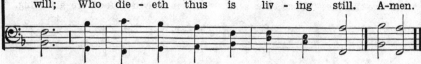

rise To mount tri-um-phant to the skies.
Day In glo-rious tri-umph o'er de-cay.
here From ev-'ry sin, from ev-'ry fear.
will; Who di-eth thus is liv-ing still. A-men.

5 We have no cause to mourn or weep;
  Securely shall this body sleep
  Till Christ Himself shall death destroy
  And raise the blessed dead to joy.

6 For they who with Him suffered here
  Shall there be healed from woe and fear;
  And when eternal bliss is won,
  They'll shine in glory like the sun.

This Body in the Grave We Lay

7 Then let us leave this place of rest
And homeward turn, for they are blest
Who heed God's warning and prepare
Lest death should find them unaware.

8 So help us, Jesus, Ground of faith;
Thou hast redeemed us by Thy death
From endless death and set us free.
We laud and praise and worship Thee.

For Me to Live Is Jesus   597

Phil. 1: 21
Christus, der ist mein Leben
Author unknown, 1609, 1612
Tr., st. 1–7, Catherine Winkworth, 1863, alt.
Tr., st. 8, unknown

7. 6. 7. 6.

Christus, der ist mein
Melchior Vulpius, 1609

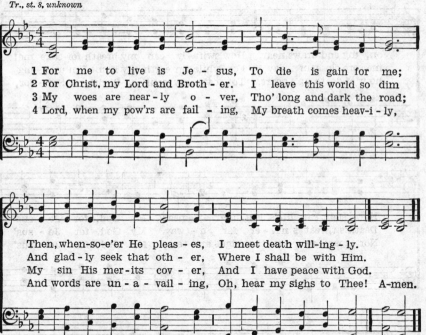

1 For me to live is Je - sus, To die is gain for me;
2 For Christ, my Lord and Broth - er. I leave this world so dim
3 My woes are near - ly o - ver, Tho' long and dark the road;
4 Lord, when my pow'rs are fail - ing, My breath comes heav-i - ly,

Then, when-so-e'er He pleas - es, I meet death will-ing - ly.
And glad - ly seek that oth - er, Where I shall be with Him.
My sin His mer - its cov - er, And I have peace with God.
And words are un - a - vail - ing, Oh, hear my sighs to Thee! A-men.

5 When mind and thought, O Savior,
Are flickering like a light
That to and fro doth waver
Ere 'tis extinguished quite,

6 In that last hour, oh, grant me
To slumber soft and still,
No doubts to vex or haunt me,
Safe anchored on Thy will;

7 And so to Thee still cleaving
Through all death's agony,
To fall asleep believing
And wake in heaven with Thee.

8 Amen! Thou, Christ, my Savior,
Wilt grant this unto me.
Thy Spirit lead me ever
That I fare happily.

598 *Who Knows when Death May Overtake Me*

9. 8. 9. 8. 8. 8.

Ps. 90 : 12
Wer weiss, wie nahe mir mein Ende
Ämilie Juliane, 1686, ab.
Tr., composite

Wer weiss, wie nahe
Christian Möck, 1818

1 Who knows when death may o - ver - take me! Time pass - es on, my end draws near. How swift - ly can my breath for-sake me! How soon can life's last hour ap - pear! My God, for Je - sus' sake I pray Thy peace may bless my dy - ing day.

2 The world that smiled when morn was break - ing May change for me ere close of day For while on earth my home I'm mak - ing Death's threat is nev - er far a - way. My God, for Je - sus' sake I pray Thy peace may bless my dy - ing day.

3 My end to pon - der teach me ev - er And, ere the hour of death ap - pears, To cast my soul on Christ, my Sav - ior, Nor spare re - pen - tant sighs and tears. My God, for Je - sus' sake I pray Thy peace may bless my dy - ing day. A-men.

Who Knows when Death May Overtake Me

4 Help me now set my house in order
   That always ready I may be
To say in meekness on death's border:
   Lord, as Thou wilt, deal Thou with me.
My God, for Jesus' sake I pray
Thy peace may bless my dying day.

5 Reveal the sweetness of Thy heaven,
   Earth's galling bitterness unfold;
May I, amid this turmoil riven,
   Thy blest eternity behold.
My God, for Jesus' sake I pray
Thy peace may bless my dying day.

6 My many sins blot out forever
   Since Jesus has my pardon won;
In mercy robed, I then shall never
   Fear death, but trust in Thee alone.
My God, for Jesus' sake I pray
Thy peace may bless my dying day.

7 Naught shall my soul from Jesus sever;
   In faith I touch His wounded side
And hail Him as my Lord forever,
   Nor life nor death shall us divide.
My God, for Jesus' sake I pray
Thy peace may bless my dying day.

8 Once in the blest baptismal waters
   I put on Christ and made Him mine;
Now numbered with God's sons and daughters,
   I share His peace and love divine.
My God, for Jesus' sake I pray
Thy peace may bless my dying day.

9 His body and His blood I've taken
   In His blest Supper, feast divine;
Now I shall never be forsaken,
   For I am His, and He is mine.
My God, for Jesus' sake I pray
Thy peace may bless my dying day.

10 Then may death come today, tomorrow,
    I know in Christ I perish not;
He grants the peace that stills all sorrow,
    Gives me a robe without a spot.
My God, for Jesus' sake I pray
Thy peace may bless my dying day.

11 And thus I live in God contented
    And die without a thought of fear;
My soul has to God's plans consented,
    For through His Son my faith is clear.
My God, for Jesus' sake I pray
Thy peace may bless my dying day.

599 My Course is Run. Praise God, My Course is Run

2 Tim. 4 : 7
Es ist vollbracht
Andreas Gryphius, 1726, asc., cento
Tr., August Zich, 1937

10. 6. 10. 6. 9. 9. 4. 4.

Es ist genug
"Geistliche Arien"
Mühlhausen, 1672

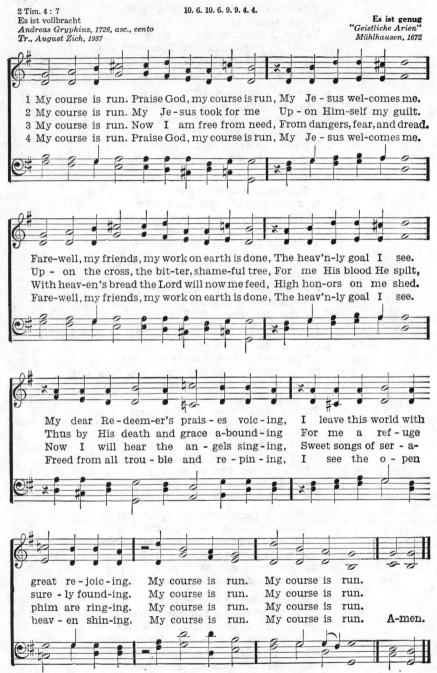

1 My course is run. Praise God, my course is run, My Je-sus wel-comes me.
2 My course is run. My Je-sus took for me Up-on Him-self my guilt.
3 My course is run. Now I am free from need, From dangers, fear, and dread.
4 My course is run. Praise God, my course is run, My Je-sus wel-comes me.

Fare-well, my friends, my work on earth is done, The heav'n-ly goal I see.
Up-on the cross, the bit-ter, shame-ful tree, For me His blood He spilt,
With heav-en's bread the Lord will now me feed, High hon-ors on me shed.
Fare-well, my friends, my work on earth is done, The heav'n-ly goal I see.

My dear Re-deem-er's prais-es voic-ing, I leave this world with
Thus by His death and grace a-bound-ing For me a ref-uge
Now I will hear the an-gels sing-ing, Sweet songs of ser-a-
Freed from all trou-ble and re-pin-ing, I see the o-pen

great re-joic-ing. My course is run. My course is run.
sure-ly found-ing. My course is run. My course is run.
phim are ring-ing. My course is run. My course is run.
heav-en shin-ing. My course is run. My course is run. A-men.

O Lord, My God, I Cry to Thee

8. 8. 8. 8. 8. 8.

Ps. 116 : 9
O Herre Gott, in meiner Not
Nikolaus Selnecker, 1572
Tr., Catherine Winkworth, 1858, alt.

Vater unser
"Geistliche Lieder"
Leipzig, 1539

1 O Lord, my God, I cry to Thee; In my dis-tress Thou help-est me. My soul and bod-y I com-mend In-to Thy hands; Thine an-gel send To guide me home and cheer my heart When Thou dost call me to de-part.

2 O Je-sus Christ, Thou Lamb of God, Once slain to take a-way our load, Now let Thy cross, Thine ag-o-ny, A-vail to save and sol-ace me, Thy death, to o-pen heav'n, and there Bid me the joy of an-gels share.

3 O Ho-ly Spir-it, faith-ful Friend, Grant me Thy com-fort to the end. When death and hell as-sail me sore, Leave me, oh, leave me, nev-er-more, But bear me safe-ly thro' the strife, As Thou hast prom-ised, in-to life. A-men.

601 All Men Living Are But Mortal

Is. 40: 6

Alle Menschen müssen sterben
Johann G. Albinus, 1652
Tr., st. 1-4, 6, 7, Catherine Winkworth, 1863, alt.
Tr., st. 5, unknown

8. 7. 8. 7. 8. 8. 7. 7.

Alle Menschen müssen sterben
"Praxis Pietatis Melica"
Berlin, 1678

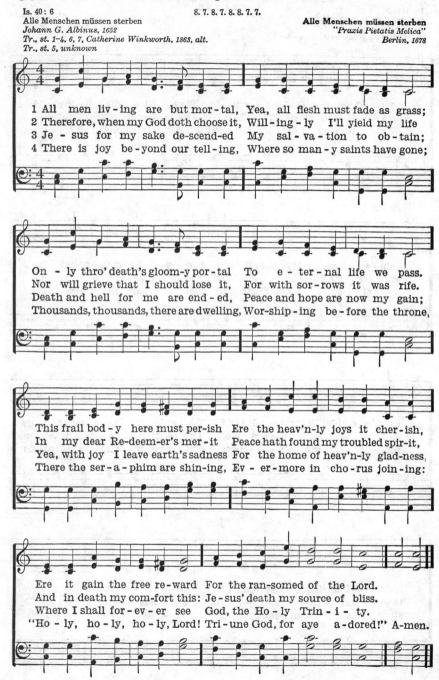

1 All men liv-ing are but mor-tal, Yea, all flesh must fade as grass;
2 Therefore, when my God doth choose it, Will-ing-ly I'll yield my life
3 Je-sus for my sake de-scend-ed My sal-va-tion to ob-tain;
4 There is joy be-yond our tell-ing, Where so man-y saints have gone;

On-ly thro' death's gloom-y por-tal To e-ter-nal life we pass.
Nor will grieve that I should lose it, For with sor-rows it was rife.
Death and hell for me are end-ed, Peace and hope are now my gain;
Thousands, thousands, there are dwelling, Wor-ship-ing be-fore the throne,

This frail bod-y here must per-ish Ere the heav'n-ly joys it cher-ish,
In my dear Re-deem-er's mer-it Peace hath found my troubled spir-it,
Yea, with joy I leave earth's sadness For the home of heav'n-ly glad-ness,
There the ser-a-phim are shin-ing, Ev-er-more in cho-rus join-ing:

Ere it gain the free re-ward For the ran-somed of the Lord.
And in death my com-fort this: Je-sus' death my source of bliss.
Where I shall for-ev-er see God, the Ho-ly Trin-i-ty.
"Ho-ly, ho-ly, ho-ly, Lord! Tri-une God, for aye a-dored!" A-men.

All Men Living Are But Mortal

5 Patriarchs of sacred story
   And the prophets there are found;
The apostles, too, in glory
   On twelve seats are there enthroned.
All the saints that have ascended
Age on age, through time extended,
There in blissful concert sing
Hallelujahs to their King.

6 O Jerusalem, how glorious
   Dost thou shine, thou city fair!
Lo, I hear the tones victorious
   Ever sweetly sounding there.
Oh, the bliss that there surprises!
Lo, the sun of morn now rises,
And the breaking day I see
That shall never end for me.

7 Yea, I see what here was told me,
   See that wondrous glory shine,
Feel the spotless robes enfold me,
   Know a golden crown is mine.
Thus before the throne so glorious
Now I stand a soul victorious,
Gazing on that joy for aye
That shall never pass away.

It Is Not Death to Die   602

John 11: 26   S. M.
Non ce n'est pas mourir   Tenbury
H. A. César Malan, 1832, ab.   Frederick A. G. Ouseley, 1861
German tr., Albert Knapp, 1836
Tr., George W. Bethune, 1847

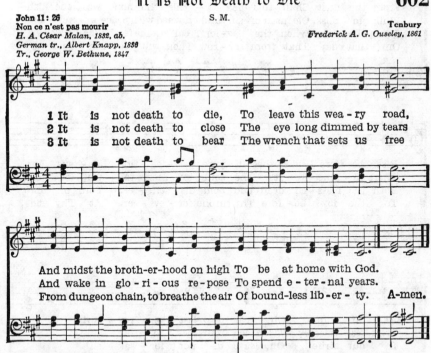

1 It is not death to die, To leave this wea-ry road,
2 It is not death to close The eye long dimmed by tears
3 It is not death to bear The wrench that sets us free

And midst the broth-er-hood on high To be at home with God.
And wake in glo-ri-ous re-pose To spend e-ter-nal years.
From dungeon chain, to breathe the air Of bound-less lib-er-ty. A-men.

4 It is not death to fling
   Aside this sinful dust
And rise, on strong, exulting wing
   To live among the just.

5 Jesus, Thou Prince of Life,
   Thy chosen cannot die;
Like Thee, they conquer in the strife
   To reign with Thee on high.

603
In the Resurrection

Job 19, 25-27
Vzkříšení čekáme
Author unknown, 1660
Tr., John Bajus, 1939

6. 6. 3. 3. 10. 10. 3. 3. 7.

Resurrection
Slovakian melody, c. 1600

1 In the res-ur-rec-tion, In the res-ur-rec-tion, We do trust.
2 Earth re-ceives the mor-tal, Earth re-ceives the mor-tal. Doubt not this,
3 Such rest we shall en-ter, Such rest we shall en-ter, And then rise
4 When we die, dear Sav-ior, When we die, dear Sav-ior, Grant, we pray,

From the dust Shall this bod-y— this the hope we cher-ish—
While in bliss, Cleansed of sin and crowned with peace e-ter-nal,
To the skies When the Sav-ior's call "Come forth" shall wak-en
On that day That from sor-row Thou wilt lead in mer-cy

Rise be-fore God clothed in pure per-fec-tion. Je-sus, Lord,
There se-rene-ly rests the soul im-mor-tal. Oh, re-joice,
Both the bless-ed dead and bold dis-sent-er. Lord of Life,
To the joy be-fore Thy throne for-ev-er. At Thy side,

Help af-ford; Oh, save us lest we per-ish!
Prais-es voice— 'Tis saved from foes in-fer-nal.
In our strife Oh, leave us not for-sak-en!
Glo-ri-fied, Oh, may we ev-er praise Thee! A-men.

Great God, What do I See and Hear?

1 Thess. 4: 16, 17
St. 1, author unknown, 1802
St. 2-4, William B. Collyer, 1812, alt.

8. 7. 8. 7. 8. 8. 7.

Es ist gewisslich
"Geistliche Lieder"
Wittenberg, 1535

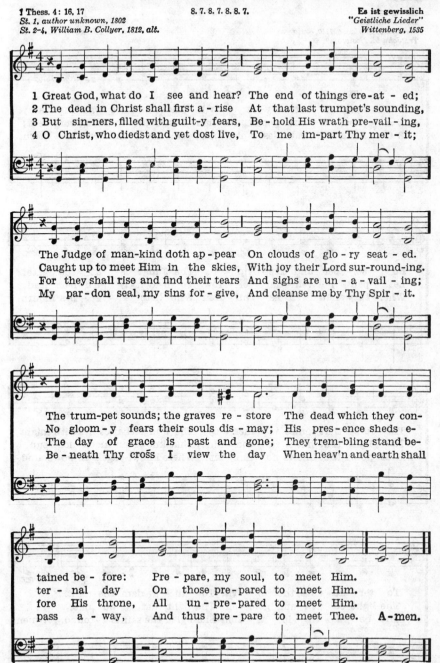

1 Great God, what do I see and hear? The end of things cre-at-ed;
2 The dead in Christ shall first a-rise At that last trumpet's sounding,
3 But sin-ners, filled with guilt-y fears, Be-hold His wrath pre-vail-ing,
4 O Christ, who diedst and yet dost live, To me im-part Thy mer-it;

The Judge of man-kind doth ap-pear On clouds of glo-ry seat-ed.
Caught up to meet Him in the skies, With joy their Lord sur-round-ing.
For they shall rise and find their tears And sighs are un-a-vail-ing;
My par-don seal, my sins for-give, And cleanse me by Thy Spir-it.

The trum-pet sounds; the graves re-store The dead which they con-
No gloom-y fears their souls dis-may; His pres-ence sheds e-
The day of grace is past and gone; They trem-bling stand be-
Be-neath Thy cross I view the day When heav'n and earth shall

tained be-fore: Pre-pare, my soul, to meet Him.
ter-nal day On those pre-pared to meet Him.
fore His throne, All un-pre-pared to meet Him.
pass a-way, And thus pre-pare to meet Thee. A-men.

605 The World Is Very Evil

Rev. 21 : 24
Hora novissima
Bernard of Morlas, c. 1140, cento
Tr., John M. Neale, 1849

7. 6. 7. 6. D.

Ewing
Alexander Ewing, 1853

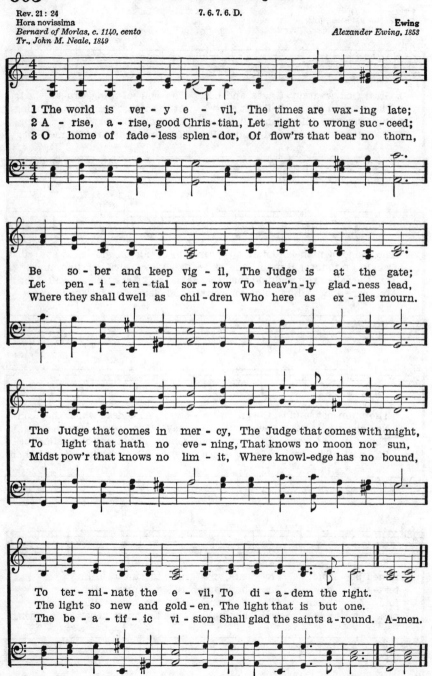

1 The world is ver - y e - vil, The times are wax-ing late;
2 A - rise, a - rise, good Chris - tian, Let right to wrong suc - ceed;
3 O home of fade - less splen - dor, Of flow'rs that bear no thorn,

Be so - ber and keep vig - il, The Judge is at the gate;
Let pen - i - ten - tial sor - row To heav'n - ly glad-ness lead,
Where they shall dwell as chil - dren Who here as ex - iles mourn.

The Judge that comes in mer - cy, The Judge that comes with might,
To light that hath no eve - ning, That knows no moon nor sun,
Midst pow'r that knows no lim - it, Where knowl-edge has no bound,

To ter - mi - nate the e - vil, To di - a - dem the right.
The light so new and gold - en, The light that is but one.
The be - a - tif - ic vi - sion Shall glad the saints a - round. A-men.

The World Is Very Evil

4 Strive, man, to win that glory;
  Toil, man, to gain that light;
Send hope before to grasp it
  Till hope be lost in sight.
Exult, O dust and ashes,
  The Lord shall be thy part;
His only, His forever,
  Thou shalt be and thou art.

5 O sweet and blessed country,
  The home of God's elect!
O sweet and blessed country
  That eager hearts expect!
Jesus, in mercy bring us
  To that dear land of rest,
Who art, with God the Father
  And Spirit, ever blest.

O'er the Distant Mountains Breaking 606

Matt. 24 : 42
John S. B. Monsell, 1863, ab.

8. 7. 8. 7. 4. 4. 7.

O Jerusalem, du Schöne
Johann G. Störl, 1711

1 O'er the dis-tant mountains breaking Comes the redd'ning dawn of day.
2 O Thou Long-ex-pect-ed, wea-ry Waits my anx-ious soul for Thee;
3 Near-er is my soul's sal-va-tion; Spent the night, the day at hand.
4 With my lamp well trimmed and burning, Swift to hear and slow to roam,

Rise, my soul, from sleep a-wak-ing; Rise and sing and watch and pray.
Life is dark, and earth is drear-y, Where Thy light I do not see.
Keep me in my low-ly sta-tion, Watch-ing for Thee till I stand,
Watch-ing for Thy glad re-turn-ing To re-store me to my home.

'Tis thy Sav-ior, 'Tis thy Sav-ior, On His bright re-turn-ing way.
O my Sav-ior, O my Sav-ior, When wilt Thou return to me?
O my Sav-ior, O my Sav-ior, In Thy bright, Thy promised, land.
Come, my Sav-ior, Come, my Sav-ior, O my Sav-ior, quick-ly come. A-men.

607 Day of Wrath, O Day of Mourning

Zeph 1 : 15, 16
Dies irae, dies illa
Thomas de Celano, c. 1250
Tr., William J. Irons, 1848, alt.

8. 8. 8.

Dies irae
Latin melody, c. 1200

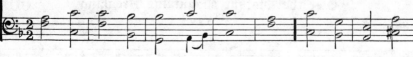

1 Day of wrath, O day of mourn - ing! See ful-filled the
2 Oh, what fear man's bos - om rend - eth When from heav'n the
3 Won-drous sound the trum-pet fling - eth, Thro' earth's sep - ul-

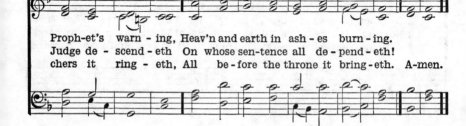

Proph-et's warn - ing, Heav'n and earth in ash - es burn-ing.
Judge de - scend - eth On whose sen-tence all de - pend-eth!
chers it ring - eth, All be-fore the throne it bring-eth. A-men.

4 Death is struck and nature quaking;
All creation is awaking,
To its Judge an answer making.

5 Lo, the book, exactly worded,
Wherein all hath been recorded;
Thence shall judgment be awarded.

6 When the Judge His seat attaineth
And each hidden deed arraigneth,
Nothing unavenged remaineth.

7 What shall I, frail man, be pleading?
Who for me be interceding
When the just are mercy needing?

8 King of majesty tremendous,
Who dost free salvation send us,
Fount of pity, then befriend us!

9 Think, good Jesus, my salvation
Caused Thy wondrous incarnation;
Leave me not to reprobation!

10 Faint and weary Thou hast sought me,
On the cross of suffering bought me;
Shall such grace be vainly brought me?

11 Righteous Judge, for sin's pollution
Grant Thy gift of absolution
Ere that day of retribution!

12 Guilty, now I pour my moaning,
All my shame with anguish owning:
Spare, O God, Thy suppliant groaning!

13 From that sinful woman shriven.
From the dying thief forgiven,
Thou to me a hope hast given.

14 Worthless are my prayers and sighing;
Yet, good Lord, in grace complying,
Rescue me from fires undying.

15 With Thy favored sheep, oh, place me;
Nor among the goats abase me,
But to Thy right hand upraise me.

Day of Wrath, O Day of Mourning

16 While the wicked are confounded,
   Doomed to flames of woe unbounded,
   Call me, with Thy saints surrounded.

17 Low I kneel with heart-submission,
   See, like ashes, my contrition;
   Help me in my last condition!

18 Day of sorrow, day of weeping,
   When, in dust no longer sleeping,
   Man awakes in Thy dread keeping!

19 To the rest Thou didst prepare me
   On Thy cross; O Christ, upbear me!
   Spare, O God, in mercy spare me!

Let Thoughtless Thousands Choose the Road   608

Phil. 1: 21
Joseph Hoskins, 1789

L. M.

Wareham
William Knapp, 1738

1 Let thought-less thou-sands choose the road That leads the
  soul a-way from God; This hap-pi-ness, dear Lord, be
  mine, To live and die en-tire-ly Thine.

2 On Christ, by faith, I fain would live, From Him my
  life, my all, re-ceive, To Him de-vote my fleet-ing
  hours, Serve Him a-lone with all my pow'rs.

3 Christ is my ev-er-last-ing All; To Him I
  look, on Him I call; He will my ev-'ry want sup-
  ply In time and thro' e-ter-ni-ty. A-men.

4 Soon will the Lord, my Life, appear;
  Soon shall I end my trials here,
  Leave sin and sorrow, death and pain.
  To live is Christ, to die is gain.

5 Soon will the saints in glory meet,
  Soon walk through every golden street,
  And sing on every blissful plain:
  To live is Christ, to die is gain.

609 Wake, Awake, for Night is Flying

Matt. 25: 1-13
Wachet auf, ruft uns die Stimme
Philipp Nicolai, 1599
Tr., *Catherine Winkworth, 1863, alt.*

8. 9. 8. 8. 9. 8. 6. 6. 4. 4. 8.

Wachet auf
Philipp Nicolai, 1599

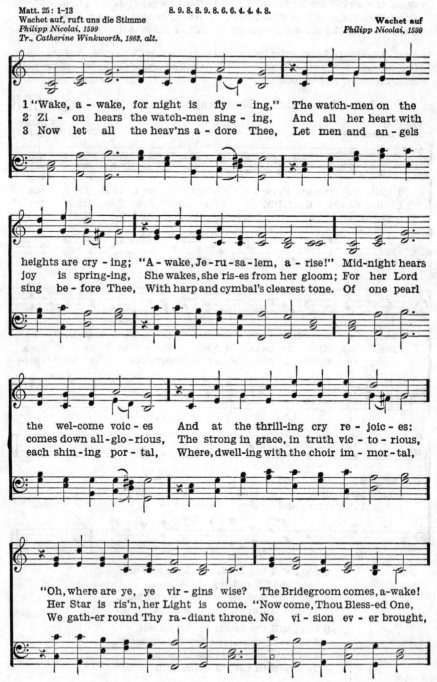

1 "Wake, a - wake, for night is fly - ing," The watch-men on the
2 Zi - on hears the watch-men sing - ing, And all her heart with
3 Now let all the heav'ns a - dore Thee, Let men and an - gels

heights are cry - ing; "A - wake, Je - ru - sa - lem, a - rise!" Mid-night hears
joy is spring-ing, She wakes, she ris-es from her gloom; For her Lord
sing be - fore Thee, With harp and cymbal's clearest tone. Of one pearl

the wel-come voic - es And at the thrill-ing cry re - joic - es:
comes down all-glo - rious, The strong in grace, in truth vic - to - rious,
each shin - ing por - tal, Where, dwell-ing with the choir im - mor-tal,

"Oh, where are ye, ye vir - gins wise? The Bridegroom comes, a-wake!
Her Star is ris'n, her Light is come. "Now come, Thou Bless-ed One,
We gath-er round Thy ra - diant throne. No vi - sion ev - er brought,

Wake, Awake, for Night is Flying

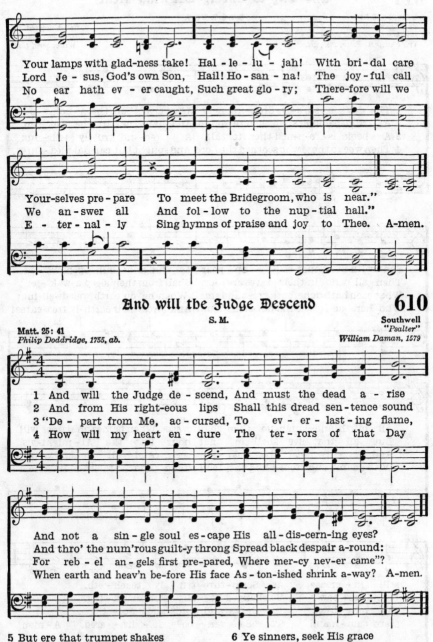

Your lamps with glad-ness take! Hal - le - lu - jah! With bri-dal care
Lord Je - sus, God's own Son, Hail! Ho-san - na! The joy-ful call
No ear hath ev - er caught, Such great glo - ry; There-fore will we

Your-selves pre - pare To meet the Bridegroom, who is near."
We an - swer all And fol - low to the nup-tial hall."
E - ter - nal - ly Sing hymns of praise and joy to Thee. A-men.

And will the Judge Descend 610

S. M.

Matt. 25: 41
Philip Doddridge, 1755, ab.

Southwell
"Psalter"
William Daman, 1579

1 And will the Judge de - scend, And must the dead a - rise
2 And from His right-eous lips Shall this dread sen - tence sound
3 "De - part from Me, ac - cursed, To ev - er - last - ing flame,
4 How will my heart en - dure The ter - rors of that Day

And not a sin - gle soul es - cape His all - dis-cern-ing eyes?
And thro' the num'rous guilt-y throng Spread black despair a-round:
For reb - el an - gels first pre-pared, Where mer-cy nev-er came"?
When earth and heav'n be-fore His face As - ton-ished shrink a-way? A-men.

5 But ere that trumpet shakes
   The mansions of the dead,
Hark from the Gospel's cheering sound
   What joyful tidings spread:

6 Ye sinners, seek His grace
   Whose wrath ye cannot bear;
Fly to the shelter of His cross
   And find salvation there.

611 The Day is Surely Drawing Near

Luke 21: 25–36
Es ist gewisslich an der Zeit
Bartholomäus Ringwaldt, 1586, ad.
Tr., Philip A. Peter, 1880, alt.

8. 7. 8. 7. 8. 8. 7.

Es ist gewisslich
"Geistliche Lieder"
Wittenberg, 1535

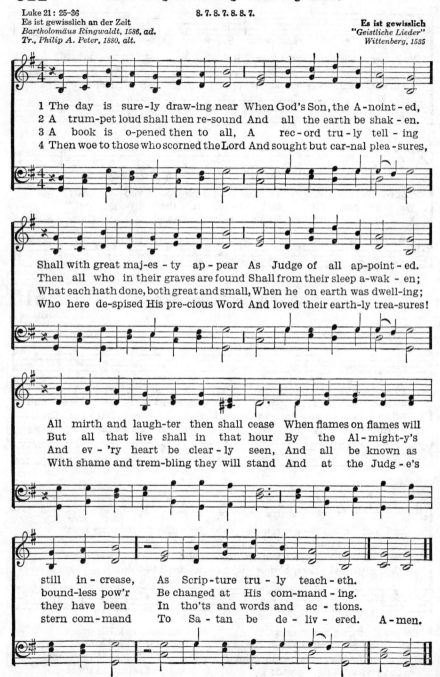

1 The day is sure-ly draw-ing near When God's Son, the A-noint-ed,
2 A trum-pet loud shall then re-sound And all the earth be shak-en.
3 A book is o-pened then to all, A rec-ord tru-ly tell-ing
4 Then woe to those who scorned the Lord And sought but car-nal plea-sures,

Shall with great maj-es-ty ap-pear As Judge of all ap-point-ed.
Then all who in their graves are found Shall from their sleep a-wak-en;
What each hath done, both great and small, When he on earth was dwell-ing;
Who here de-spised His pre-cious Word And loved their earth-ly trea-sures!

All mirth and laugh-ter then shall cease When flames on flames will
But all that live shall in that hour By the Al-might-y's
And ev-'ry heart be clear-ly seen, And all be known as
With shame and trem-bling they will stand And at the Judg-e's

still in-crease, As Scrip-ture tru-ly teach-eth.
bound-less pow'r Be changed at His com-mand-ing.
they have been In tho'ts and words and ac-tions.
stern com-mand To Sa-tan be de-liv-ered. A-men.

The Day is Surely Drawing Near

5 O Jesus, who my debt didst pay
    And for my sin wast smitten,
  Within the Book of Life, oh, may
    My name be also written!
  I will not doubt; I trust in Thee,
  From Satan Thou hast made me free
    And from all condemnation.

6 Therefore my Intercessor be
    And for Thy blood and merit
  Declare my name from judgment free
    With all who life inherit,
  That I may see Thee face to face
  With all Thy saints in that blest place
    Which Thou for us hast purchased.

7 O Jesus Christ, do not delay,
    But hasten our salvation;
  We often tremble on our way
    In fear and tribulation.
  Then hear us when we cry to Thee;
  Come, mighty Judge, and make us free
    From every evil! Amen.

That Day of Wrath, That Dreadful Day   612

2 Pet. 3: 10
Dies irae, dies illa
Thomas de Celano, c. 1250, cento
Tr., Walter Scott, 1805

L. M.

Windham
Daniel Read, 1785

1 That day of wrath, that dread-ful day, When heav'n and earth shall pass a-way! What pow'r shall be the sin-ner's stay? How shall he meet that dread-ful day?

2 When, shriv'l-ing like a parch-ed scroll, The flam-ing heav'ns to-geth-er roll; When loud-er yet, and yet more dread, Swells the high trump that wakes the dead,

3 Lord, on that day, that wrath-ful day, When man to Judg-ment wakes from clay, Be Thou the trem-bling sin-ner's Stay, Tho' heav'n and earth shall pass a-way. A-men.

613 Jerusalem the Golden

Rev. 21: 18
Urbs Sion aurea
Bernard of Morlas, c. 1140, cento
Tr., John M. Neale, 1849

7. 6. 7. 6. D.

Ewing
Alexander Ewing, 1853

1 Je - ru - sa - lem the gold - en, With milk and hon - ey blest,
2 They stand, those halls of Zi - on, All ju - bi - lant with song
3 There is the throne of Da - vid; And there, from care re - leased,
4 O sweet and bless - ed coun - try, The home of God's e - lect!

Be - neath thy con - tem - pla - tion Sink heart and voice op - prest.
And bright with man - y an an - gel And all the mar - tyr throng.
The shout of them that tri - umph, The song of them that feast;
O sweet and bless - ed coun - try That ea - ger hearts ex - pect!

I know not, oh, I know not, What joys a - wait us there,
The Prince is ev - er in them; The day - light is se - rene;
And they who with their Lead - er Have con - quered in the fight
Je - sus, in mer - cy bring us To that dear land of rest,

What ra - dian - cy of glo - ry, What bliss be - yond com - pare.
The pas - tures of the bless - ed Are decked in glo - rious sheen.
For - ev - er and for - ev - er Are clad in robes of white.
Who art, with God the Fa - ther And Spir - it, ev - er blest. A - men.

For Thee, O Dear, Dear Country

614

Heb. 11 : 16
O bona patria
Bernard of Morlas, c. 1140, cento
Tr., John M. Neale, 1849

7, 6, 7, 6, D.

Bona patria
"Sacred Hymns and Tunes"
Bristol, 1876

1 For thee, O dear, dear coun-try, Mine eyes their vig-ils keep;
2 O one, O on-ly man-sion, O Par-a-dise of joy,
3 With jas-per glow thy bul-warks, Thy streets with em-'ralds blaze;

For ver-y love, be-hold-ing Thy hap-py name, they weep.
Where tears are ev-er ban-ished And smiles have no al-loy!
The sar-dius and the to-paz U-nite in thee their rays;

The men-tion of thy glo-ry Is unc-tion to the breast
The Lamb is all thy splen-dor, The Cru-ci-fied thy praise;
Thine age-less walls are bond-ed With am-e-thyst un-priced;

And med-i-cine in sick-ness And love and life and rest.
His laud and ben-e-dic-tion Thy ran-somed peo-ple raise.
The saints build up thy fab-ric, The cor-ner-stone is Christ. A-men.

4 Thou hast no shore, fair ocean;
   Thou hast no time, bright day,
Dear fountain of refreshment
   To pilgrims far away!
Upon the Rock of Ages
   They raise thy holy tower;
Thine is the victor's laurel
   And thine the golden dower.

5 O sweet and blessed country,
   The home of God's elect!
O sweet and blessed country
   That eager hearts expect!
Jesus, in mercy bring us
   To that dear land of rest,
Who art, with God the Father
   And Spirit, ever blest.

615 A Rest Remaineth for the Weary

Heb 4: 9
Es ist noch eine Ruh' vorhanden
Johann S. Kunth, 1730, cento
Tr., composite

9. 8. 9. 8. 9. 8. 9. 8. 9. 8.

Wie wohl ist mir
"Geistreiches Gesangbuch"
Halle, 1704

1 A rest re-main-eth for the wea - ry; A - rise, sad heart, and
2 The Fa-ther's house has man-y a dwell-ing, And there will be a
3 O come, come all, ye weak and wea - ry, Ye souls bowed down with
4 There rest and peace in end-less mea-sure Shall be ours thro' e-

grieve no more; Tho' long the way and dark and drear-y,
place for thee. With per-fect love His heart is well-ing,
man-y a care; A - rise and leave your dun-geons drear-y
ter-ni-ty; No grief, no care, shall mar our plea-sure,

It end-eth on the gold-en shore. Be - fore His throne the
Who loved thee from e - ter-ni-ty. His pre-cious blood the
And lis-ten to His prom-ise fair: "Ye bore your bur-dens
And un-told bliss our lot shall be. Oh, had we wings to

Lamb will lead thee, On heav'n-ly pas-tures He will feed thee.
Lamb hath giv-en That thou might'st share the joys of heav-en,
meek and low-ly, I will ful-fil My pledge most ho-ly,
hast-en yon-der— No more o'er earth-ly ills to pon-der—

A Rest Remaineth for the Weary

Cast off thy bur-den, come with haste; Soon will the toil and
And now He call-eth far and near: "Ye wea-ry souls, cease
I'll be your Sol-ace and your Rest. Ye are Mine own, I
To join the glad, tri-um-phant band! Make haste, my soul, for-

strife be end-ed, The wea-ry way which thou hast wend-
your re-pin-ing, Come while for you My light is shin-
will re-quite you; Tho' sin and Sa-tan seek to smite
get all sad-ness; For peace a-waits thee, joy and glad-

ed. Sweet is the rest which thou shalt taste.
ing; Come, sweet-est rest a-waits you here!"
you, Re-joice! Your home is with the blest."
ness — The per-fect rest is nigh at hand. A-men.

Variant

ed. Sweet is the rest . . . . which thou shalt taste.
ing; Come, sweet-est rest . . . . a-waits you here!"
you, Re-joice! Your home . . . is with the blest."
ness —The per-fect rest . . . . is nigh at hand. A-men.

616

Forever with the Lord

S. M.

1 Thess. 4: 17
James Montgomery, 1835, cento, alt.

Schumann
"Cantica Laudis"
Boston, 1850

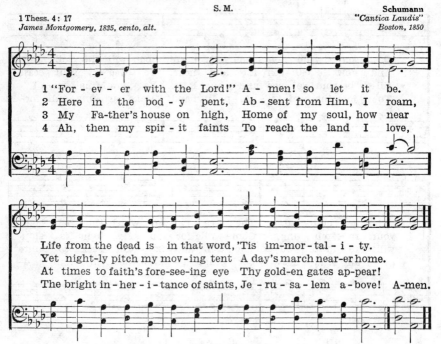

1 "For - ev - er with the Lord!" A - men! so let it be.
2 Here in the bod - y pent, Ab - sent from Him, I roam,
3 My Fa-ther's house on high, Home of my soul, how near
4 Ah, then my spir - it faints To reach the land I love,

Life from the dead is in that word, 'Tis im-mor-tal - i - ty.
Yet night-ly pitch my mov-ing tent A day's march near-er home.
At times to faith's fore-see-ing eye Thy gold-en gates ap-pear!
The bright in - her - i - tance of saints, Je - ru - sa - lem a - bove! A-men.

5 "Forever with the Lord!"
  O Father, 'tis Thy will.
The promise of that faithful word
  E'en here to me fulfil.

6 Be Thou at my right hand,
  Then can I never fail.
Uphold Thou me, and I shall stand;
  Fight Thou, and I'll prevail.

7 So when my dying breath
  Shall rend the veil in twain,
By death I shall escape from death
  And life eternal gain.

8 Knowing as I am known,
  How shall I love that word
And oft repeat before the throne,
  "Forever with the Lord!"

617

There Is an Hour of Peaceful Rest

8. 6. 8. 8. 6.

Heb. 4: 9
William B. Tappan, 1818, ab.

Pax celeste
"Celestial Harps"
Edinburgh, 1824

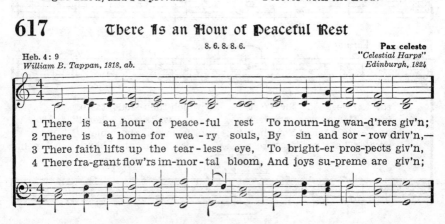

1 There is an hour of peace-ful rest To mourn-ing wan-d'rers giv'n;
2 There is a home for wea - ry souls, By sin and sor - row driv'n,—
3 There faith lifts up the tear - less eye, To bright-er pros-pects giv'n,
4 There fra-grant flow'rs im-mor-tal bloom, And joys su-preme are giv'n;

There Is an Hour of Peaceful Rest

There is a joy for souls dis-trest, A balm for ev-'ry
When tossed on life's tem-pes-tuous shoals, When storms a-rise and
And views the tem-pest pass-ing by, The eve-ning shad-ows
There rays di-vine dis-perse the gloom; Be-yond the con-fines

wound-ed breast: 'Tis found a-bove— in heav'n.
o-cean rolls, And all is drear— but heav'n.
quick-ly fly, And all se-rene— in heav'n.
of the tomb Ap-pears the dawn of heav'n. A-men.

Jerusalem, My Happy Home 618

C. M.

Ps. 42: 2
F. B. P., c. 1580
Cento 1801, alt.

St. Peter
Alexander R. Reinagle, 1836

1 Je - ru - sa - lem, my hap - py home, Name ev - er dear to me,
2 When shall these eyes thy heav'n-built walls And pear - ly gates be-hold,
3 Oh, when, thou cit - y of my God, Shall I thy courts as - cend
4 A - pos - tles, mar-tyrs, proph-ets, there A - round my Sav - ior stand;

When shall my la-bors have an end? Thy joys when shall I see?
Thy bul-warks with sal-va-tion strong, And streets of shin-ing gold?
Where ev - er-more the an-gels sing, Where Sabbaths have no end?
And soon my friends in Christ be-low Will join the glo-rious band. A-men.

5 Jerusalem, my happy home,
   When shall I come to thee?
When shall my labors have an end?
   Thy joys when shall I see?

6 O Christ, do Thou my soul prepare
   For that bright home of love
That I may see Thee and adore
   With all Thy saints above.

619 Jerusalem, Thou City Fair and High

Matt. 17: 1–9
Jerusalem, du hochgebaute Stadt
Johann M. Meyfart, 1626
Tr., Catherine Winkworth, 1858, alt.

10. 6. 10. 6. 7. 6. 7. 6.

Jerusalem, du hochgebaute Stadt
Melchior Franck, 1663

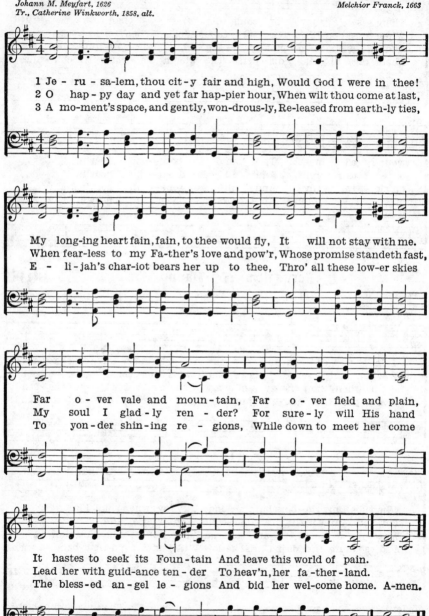

1 Je - ru - sa-lem, thou cit-y fair and high, Would God I were in thee!
2 O hap - py day and yet far hap-pier hour, When wilt thou come at last,
3 A mo-ment's space, and gently, won-drous-ly, Re-leased from earth-ly ties,

My long-ing heart fain, fain, to thee would fly, It will not stay with me.
When fear-less to my Fa-ther's love and pow'r, Whose promise standeth fast,
E - li - jah's char-iot bears her up to thee, Thro' all these low-er skies

Far o - ver vale and moun-tain, Far o - ver field and plain,
My soul I glad - ly ren - der? For sure-ly will His hand
To yon-der shin-ing re - gions, While down to meet her come

It hastes to seek its Foun-tain And leave this world of pain.
Lead her with guid-ance ten - der To heav'n, her fa - ther-land.
The bless-ed an - gel le - gions And bid her wel-come home. A-men.

Jerusalem, Thou City Fair and High

4 O Zion, hail! Bright city, now unfold
   The gates of grace to me.
How many a time I longed for thee of old
   Ere yet I was set free
From yon dark life of sadness,
   Yon world of shadowy naught,
And God had given the gladness,
   The heritage, I sought!

5 What glorious throng and what resplendent host
   Comes sweeping swiftly down?
The chosen ones on earth who wrought the most,
   The Church's brightest crown,
Our Lord hath sent to meet me,
   As in the far-off years
Their words oft came to greet me
   In yonder land of tears.

6 The patriarchs' and prophets' noble train,
   With all Christ's followers true,
Who bore the cross and could the worst disdain
   That tyrants dared to do,
I see them shine forever,
   All-glorious as the sun,
Mid light that fadeth never,
   Their perfect freedom won.

7 And when within that lovely Paradise
   At last I safely dwell,
What songs of bliss shall from my lips arise,
   What joy my tongue shall tell,
While all the saints are singing
   Hosannas o'er and o'er,
Pure hallelujahs ringing
   Around me evermore!

8 Unnumbered choirs before the shining throne
   Their joyful anthems raise
Till heaven's glad halls are echoing with the tone
   Of that great hymn of praise
And all its host rejoices,
   And all its blessed throng
Unite their myriad voices
   In one eternal song.

MARRIAGE

620 Lord, Who at Cana's Wedding=Feast

John 2: 1–11
St. 1, 3, Adelaide Thrupp, 1853
St. 2, Godfrey Thring, 1882

C. M. D.

Bethlehem
Gottfried W. Fink, 1842

1 Lord, who at Ca - na's wed-ding-feast Didst as a Guest ap - pear,
2 This ho - ly vow that man can make, The gold - en thread in life,
3 On those who now be - fore Thee kneel, O Lord, Thy bless-ing pour,

Thou dear - er far than earth - ly guest, Vouch-safe Thy pres-ence here.
The bond that none may dare to break, That bind-eth man and wife,
That each may wake the oth - er's zeal To love Thee more and more.

For ho - ly Thou in - deed dost prove The mar-riage-vow to be,
Which, blest by Thee, what-e'er be - tides, No e - vil shall de - stroy,
Oh, grant them here in peace to live, In pu - ri - ty and love,

Pro - claim-ing it a type of love Be-tween the Church and Thee.
Thro' care-worn days each care di-vides, And dou-bles ev - 'ry joy.
And, this world leav-ing, to re-ceive A crown of life a - bove. A-men.

O Father, All Creating

621

7. 6. 7. 6. D.

Ps. 127 : 1
John Ellerton, 1876

Eden
"Sacred Hymns and Tunes"
Boston, 1880

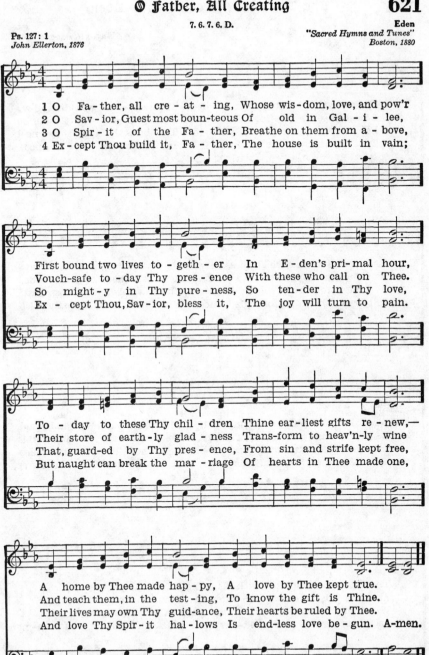

1 O Fa-ther, all cre-at-ing, Whose wis-dom, love, and pow'r
2 O Sav-ior, Guest most boun-teous Of old in Gal-i-lee,
3 O Spir-it of the Fa-ther, Breathe on them from a-bove,
4 Ex-cept Thou build it, Fa-ther, The house is built in vain;

First bound two lives to-geth-er In E-den's pri-mal hour,
Vouch-safe to-day Thy pres-ence With these who call on Thee.
So might-y in Thy pure-ness, So ten-der in Thy love,
Ex-cept Thou, Sav-ior, bless it, The joy will turn to pain.

To-day to these Thy chil-dren Thine ear-liest gifts re-new,—
Their store of earth-ly glad-ness Trans-form to heav'n-ly wine
That, guard-ed by Thy pres-ence, From sin and strife kept free,
But naught can break the mar-riage Of hearts in Thee made one,

A home by Thee made hap-py, A love by Thee kept true.
And teach them, in the test-ing, To know the gift is Thine.
Their lives may own Thy guid-ance, Their hearts be ruled by Thee.
And love Thy Spir-it hal-lows Is end-less love be-gun. A-men.

622 The Voice that Breathed o'er Eden

7. 6. 7. 6. D.

Eccl. 4: 12
John Keble, 1857, ab., alt.

Eden
"Sacred Hymns and Tunes"
Boston, 1880

1 The voice that breathed o'er E - den, That ear - liest wed - ding - day,
2 Be pres - ent, lov - ing Fa - ther, To give a - way this bride
3 Be pres - ent, Ho - ly Spir - it, To bless them as they kneel,
4 To cast their crowns be - fore Thee In hum - ble sac - ri - fice,

The pri - mal mar - riage bless - ing,— It hath not passed a - way.
As Thou gav'st Eve to Ad - am, A help-meet at his side.
As Thou for Christ, the Bride-groom, The heav'n-ly Spouse dost seal.
Till to the home of glad - ness With Christ's own Bride they rise.

Still in the pure es - pou - sal Of Chris-tian man and maid
Be pres - ent, Son of Ma - ry, To join their lov - ing hands
Oh, spread Thy pure wing o'er them, Let no ill pow'r find place
To Fa - ther, Son, and Spir - it, E - ter - nal One and Three,

The Tri - une God is with us, The three-fold grace is said.
As Thou didst bind two na - tures In Thine e - ter - nal bands.
When on - ward to Thine al - tar Their hal-lowed path they trace,
As was and is for - ev - er, All praise and glo - ry be. A-men.

O Perfect Love

11. 10. 11. 10.

Ruth 1: 17
Dorothy F. Gurney, 1884

Caritas perfecta
Frederick C. Atkinson, 1885

1 O per-fect Love, all hu-man tho't tran-scend-ing,
2 O per-fect Life, be Thou their full as-sur-ance
3 Grant them the joy which bright-ens earth-ly sor-row;

Low-ly we kneel in prayer be-fore Thy throne
Of ten-der char-i-ty and stead-fast faith,
Grant them the peace which calms all earth-ly strife

That theirs may be the love which knows no end-ing,
Of pa-tient hope and qui-et, brave en-dur-ance,
And to life's day the glo-rious un-known mor-row

Whom Thou for-ev-er-more dost join in one.
With child-like trust that fears nor pain nor death.
That dawns up-on e-ter-nal love and life. A-men.

624 **O Blessed Home Where Man and Wife**

Ps. 123
I Hus og Hjem, hvor Mand og Viv
Magnus B. Landstad, 1861
Tr., Ole T. Arneson, 1908, alt.

8. 8. 7. 8. 8. 7.

Kommt her zu mir
German melody, c. 1400

1 O bless-ed home where man and wife To-geth-er lead
2 If they have giv-en Him their heart, The place of hon-
3 And if their home be dark and drear, The cruse be emp-
4 O Lord, we come be-fore Thy face; In ev-'ry home

a god-ly life, By deeds their faith con-fess-ing!
or set a-part For Him each night and mor-row,
ty, hun-ger near, All hope with-in them dy-ing,
be-stow Thy grace On chil-dren, fa-ther, moth-er.

There man-y a hap-py day is spent, There Je-sus glad-
Then He the storms of life will calm, Will bring for ev-
Let them de-spair not in dis-tress; Lo, Christ is there
Re-lieve their wants, their bur-dens ease, Let them to-geth-

ly will con-sent To tar-ry with His bless-ing.
'ry wound a balm, And change to joy their sor-row.
the bread to bless, The frag-ments mul-ti-ply-ing.
er dwell in peace And love to one an-oth-er. A-men.

Oh, Blest the House, Whate'er Befall

625

L. M.

Luke 2: 41–52
Wohl einem Haus, da Jesus Christ
Christoph C. L. von Pfeil, 1782, cento
Tr., st. 1, 2, 4, 5, Catherine Winkworth, 1863
Tr., st. 3, unknown

Wo Gott zum Haus
"Geistliche Lieder"
Wittenberg, 1535

1 Oh, blest the house, what-e'er be-fall, Where Je - sus
2 Oh, blest that house where faith ye find And all with-
3 Oh, blest the par - ents who give heed Un - to their

Christ is all in all! Yea, if He were not dwell-ing there,
in have set their mind To trust their God and serve Him still
chil-dren's fore-most need And wea - ry not of care or cost!

How dark and poor and void it were!
And do in all His ho - ly will!
May none to them and heav'n be lost! A - men.

4 Blest such a house, it prospers well,
In peace and joy the parents dwell,
And in their children's lot is shown
How richly God can bless His own.

5 Then here will I and mine today
A solemn covenant make and say:
Though all the world forsake Thy Word,
I and my house will serve the Lord.

626 O Happy Home Where Thou art Loved Most Dearly

Gen. 18: 19

O selig Haus, wo man dich aufgenommen
C. J. Philipp Spitta, 1833, ab.
Tr., Sarah L. Findlater, 1855, alt.

11. 10. 11. 10. D.

O selig Haus
Eduard Niemeyer, 1854

1 O hap-py home where Thou art loved most dear-ly,
2 O hap-py home where two, in heart u-nit-ed,
3 O hap-py home whose lit-tle ones are giv-en
4 O hap-py home where Thou art not for-got-ten

Thou faith-ful Friend and Sav-ior full of grace
In ho-ly faith, are cling-ing un-to Thee;
Ear-ly to Thee in hum-ble faith and prayer,
When joy is o-ver-flow-ing, full, and free!

And where a-mong the guests there nev-er com-eth
Where both, to Thee a joy-ful ser-vice bring-ing,
To Thee, their Friend, who from the heights of heav-en
O hap-py home where ev-'ry wound-ed spir-it

One who can hold such high and hon-ored place!
Hear and o-bey Thy voice most will-ing-ly;
Guides them and guards with more than moth-er's care!
Is brought, O great Phy-si-cian, un-to Thee,

O Happy Home Where Thou art Loved Most Dearly

O hap - py home where all, in heart u - nit - ed,
Where both, to Thee in truth for - ev - er cleav - ing,
O hap - py home where each one serves Thee, low - ly,
Un - til at last, when earth - ly toil is end - ed,

In ho - ly faith and bless - ed hope, are one,
In joy, in grief, make Thee their on - ly Stay
What - ev - er his ap - point - ed work may be,
All meet Thee in the bless - ed home a - bove,

Whom bit - ter death a lit - tle while di - vid - eth,
And fond - ly hope in Thee to be be - liev - ing
Till ev - 'ry com - mon task seems great and ho - ly
From whence Thou cam - est, where Thou hast as - cend - ed,

Yet can - not end the u - nion here be - gun!
Both in the good and in the e - vil day.
When it is done, O Lord, as un - to Thee!
Thine ev - er - last - ing home of peace and love! A - men.

627 Gracious Savior, Gentle Shepherd

Mark 10: 14
Jane E. Leeson, 1842
Jonathan Whittemore, cento, 1850

8. 7. 8. 7. 8. 7.

Sieh, hier bin ich
"Geistreiches Gesangbuch"
Darmstadt, 1698

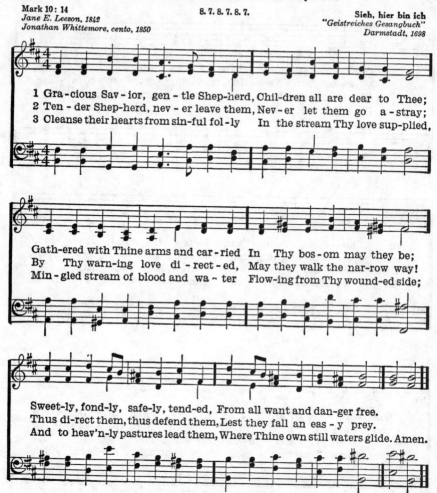

1 Gra-cious Sav-ior, gen-tle Shep-herd, Chil-dren all are dear to Thee;
2 Ten-der Shep-herd, nev-er leave them, Nev-er let them go a-stray;
3 Cleanse their hearts from sin-ful fol-ly In the stream Thy love sup-plied,

Gath-ered with Thine arms and car-ried In Thy bos-om may they be;
By Thy warn-ing love di-rect-ed, May they walk the nar-row way!
Min-gled stream of blood and wa-ter Flow-ing from Thy wound-ed side;

Sweet-ly, fond-ly, safe-ly, tend-ed, From all want and dan-ger free.
Thus di-rect them, thus defend them, Lest they fall an eas-y prey.
And to heav'n-ly pastures lead them, Where Thine own still waters glide. Amen.

4 Let Thy holy Word instruct them;
　　Fill their minds with heavenly light;
Let Thy powerful grace constrain them
　　To approve whate'er is right;
Let them feel Thy yoke is easy,
　　Let them prove Thy burden light.

5 Taught to lisp Thy holy praises
　　Which on earth Thy children sing,
Both with lips and hearts, unfeignèd,
　　Glad thank-offerings may they bring;
Then with all the saints in glory
　　Join to praise their Lord and King.

Shepherd of Tender Youth

628

6. 6. 4. 6. 6. 4.

Is. 40: 11
Στόμιον πώλων ἀδαῶν
Clement of Alexandria, c. 200, asc.
Tr., Henry M. Dexter, 1846

Olivet
Lowell Mason, 1832

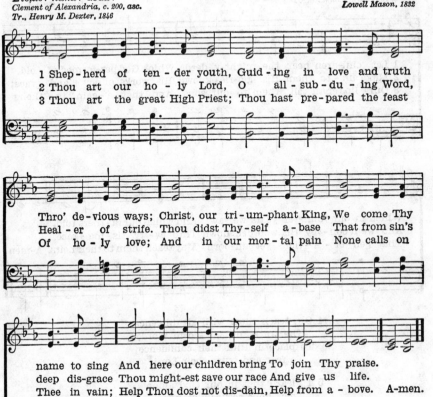

1 Shep - herd of ten - der youth, Guid - ing in love and truth
2 Thou art our ho - ly Lord, O all - sub - du - ing Word,
3 Thou art the great High Priest; Thou hast pre - pared the feast

Thro' de - vious ways; Christ, our tri - um - phant King, We come Thy
Heal - er of strife. Thou didst Thy - self a - base That from sin's
Of ho - ly love; And in our mor - tal pain None calls on

name to sing And here our children bring To join Thy praise.
deep dis - grace Thou might - est save our race And give us life.
Thee in vain; Help Thou dost not dis - dain, Help from a - bove. A - men.

4 Ever be Thou our Guide,
   Our Shepherd and our Pride,
      Our Staff and Song;
   Jesus, Thou Christ of God,
   By Thine enduring Word
   Lead us where Thou hast trod,
      Make our faith strong.

5 So now, and till we die,
   Sound we Thy praises high
      And joyful sing;
   Infants and the glad throng
   Who to Thy Church belong,
   Unite to swell the song
      To Christ, our King.

629 Let Children Hear the Mighty Deeds

Ps. 78
St. 1, 2, 3, 5, Isaac Watts, 1719, alt.
St. 4, Bernhard Schumacher, 1938

C. M.

Nun danket all'
Johann Crüger, 1653

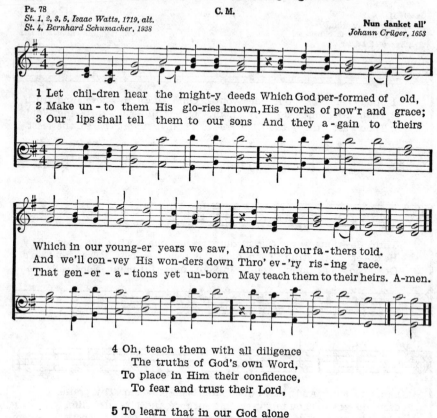

1 Let chil-dren hear the might-y deeds Which God per-formed of old,
2 Make un-to them His glo-ries known, His works of pow'r and grace;
3 Our lips shall tell them to our sons And they a-gain to theirs

Which in our young-er years we saw, And which our fa-thers told.
And we'll con-vey His won-ders down Thro' ev-'ry ris-ing race.
That gen-er-a-tions yet un-born May teach them to their heirs. A-men.

4 Oh, teach them with all diligence
    The truths of God's own Word,
To place in Him their confidence,
    To fear and trust their Lord,

5 To learn that in our God alone
    Their hope securely stands,
That they may ne'er forget His works,
    But walk in His commands.

630 Ye Parents, Hear What Jesus Taught

Mark 10: 14
Höret, ihr Eltern, Christus spricht
Ludwig Helmbold, 1596, cento
Tr., William M. Czamanske, 1939

L. M.

Herr Jesu Christ, dich
"Cantionale Germanicum"
Dresden, 1628

1 Ye par-ents, hear what Je-sus taught When lit-tle ones to
2 O-bey your Lord and let His truth Be taught your chil-dren
3 For if you love them as you ought, To Christ your chil-dren

Ye Parents, Hear What Jesus Taught

Him were brought: For - bid them not, but heed My plea
in their youth That they in church and school may dwell
will be brought. If thus you place them in His care,

And suf - fer them to come to Me.
And learn their Sav - ior's praise to tell.
You and your house - hold well shall fare. A - men.

Savior, Who Thy Flock art Feeding 631

8. 7. 8. 7.

John 10: 11
William A. Mühlenberg, 1826

Ringe recht
"Musikalischer Christenschatz"
Basel, 1745

1 Sav - ior, who Thy flock art feed-ing With the Shepherd's kindest care,
2 Now, these lit - tle ones re - ceiv-ing, Fold them in Thy gra-cious arm;
3 Nev - er, from Thy pas-ture rov-ing, Let them be the Li-on's prey;
4 Then with-in Thy fold e - ter-nal Let them find a rest-ing place,

All the fee - ble gen-tly lead-ing, While the lambs Thy bos-om share,
There, we know, Thy Word believing, On - ly there, se-cure from harm.
Let Thy ten-der-ness, so lov-ing, Keep them thro' life's dang'rous way.
Feed in pas-tures ev - er ver-nal, Drink the riv - ers of Thy grace. A-men.

CORNER-STONE *LAYING*

632 **In the Name which Earth and Heaven**

8. 7. 8. 7. D.

2 Chron. 6: 20
John Ellerton, 1871, alt.

O du Liebe
"Musikalischer Christenschatz"
Basel, 1745

1 In the name which earth and heav-en Ev-er wor-ship, praise, and fear,
2 Here as in their due suc-ces-sion Stone on stone the men did place.
3 Fair shall be Thine earth-ly tem-ple; Here the care-less pass-er-by
4 Yet with tru-er, no-bler beau-ty, Lord, we pray, this house a-dorn,

Fa-ther, Son, and Ho-ly Spir-it, We a house have build-ed here,
Thus, we pray, un-seen, but sure-ly, Je-sus, build us up in grace,
Shall be-think him, in its beau-ty, Of the ho-lier house on high.
Where Thy Bride, Thy Church redeemèd, Robes her for her mar-riage morn;

Here with prayer its deep foun-da-tions, In the faith of Christ, did lay,
Till, as in these walls com-plet-ed, We com-plete in Thee are found
Wea-ry hearts and trou-bled spir-its Here shall find a still re-treat;
Clothed in gar-ments of sal-va-tion, Rich with gems of heav'n-ly grace,

Trust-ing by His help to crown it With the top-stone in its day.
And to Thee, the one Foun-da-tion, Strong and living stones, are bound.
Sin-ful souls shall bring their burden Here to the Ab-solv-er's feet.
Spouse of Christ, arrayed and waiting Till she may be-hold His face. A-men.

In the Name which Earth and Heaven

5 Here in due and solemn order
   Shall her ceaseless prayer arise;
   Here shall strains of holy gladness
   Lift her heart above the skies;
   Here the Word of Life be spoken;
   Here the child of God be sealed;
   Here the Bread of Heaven be broken,
   "Till He come," Himself revealed.

6 Praise to Thee, O Master Builder,
   Maker of the earth and skies;
   Praise to Thee, in whom Thy temple,
   Fitly framed together, lies;
   Praise to Thee, eternal Spirit,
   Binding all that lives in one
   Till our earthly praise be ended
   And th' eternal song begun!

O Lord of Hosts, Whose Glory Fills 633

Is. 60: 13
John M. Neale, 1844, alt.

L. M.

O heilige Dreifaltigkeit
Nikolaus Herman, 1560

1 O Lord of hosts, whose glo-ry fills The bounds of the e-ter-nal hills And yet vouch-saf'st, in Chris-tian lands, To dwell in tem-ples made with hands,

2 Grant that all we who here to-day Re-joic-ing this foun-da-tion lay May be in ver-y deed Thine own, Built on the pre-cious Cor-ner-stone.

3 En-due the crea-tures with Thy grace That shall a-dorn Thy dwell-ing-place. The beau-ty of the oak and pine, The gold and sil-ver, make them Thine.

4 To Thee they all be-long, to Thee, The trea-sures of the earth and sea; And when we bring them to Thy throne, We but pre-sent Thee with Thine own. A-men.

5 The heads that guide endue with skill,
   The hands that work preserve from ill,
   That we who these foundations lay
   May raise the top-stone in its day.

6 Both now and ever, Lord, protect
   The temple of Thine own elect;
   Be Thou in them and they in Thee,
   O ever-blessed Trinity!

634 Come, Jesus, from the Sapphire Throne

L. M.

Gen. 28: 17
Ray Palmer, 1875

Wareham
William Knapp, 1738

1 Come, Je - sus, from the sap - phire throne, Where Thy re-
2 We praise Thee that to - day we see Its sa - cred
3 Oft as re - turns the day of rest, Let heart - felt
4 Here in the dark and sor - r'wing day Bid Thou the

deemed be - hold Thy face; En - ter this tem - ple, now Thine
walls be - fore Thee stand; 'Tis Thine for us, 'tis ours for
wor - ship here as - cend; With Thine own joy fill ev - 'ry
throb - bing heart be still. Oh, wipe the mourn - er's tears a-

own, And let Thy glo - ry fill the place.
Thee, Reared by Thy kind, as - sist - ing hand.
breast, With Thine own pow'r Thy Word at - tend.
way And give new strength to meet Thy will! A - men.

5 Here in baptismal water pure
   We find for sin a gracious cure;
   Our children here to Thee we bring
   To be Thine heirs, O heavenly King.

6 When at Thine altar we shall meet
   And keep the feast of dying love,
   Be our communion ever sweet
   With Thee and with Thy Church above.

Come, Jesus, from the Sapphire Throne

7 Come, faithful Shepherd, feed Thy sheep;
  In Thine own arms the lambs enfold.
Give help to climb the heavenward steep
  Till Thy full glory we behold.

Here in Thy Name, Eternal God 635

L. M.

Mendon
German melody
Arr. by Samuel Dyer, 1823

2 Chron. 6: 20
James Montgomery, 1822, ab., alt.

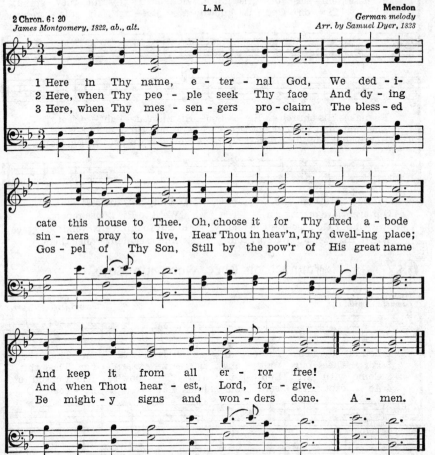

1 Here in Thy name, e-ter-nal God, We ded-i-
2 Here, when Thy peo-ple seek Thy face And dy-ing
3 Here, when Thy mes-sen-gers pro-claim The bless-ed

cate this house to Thee. Oh, choose it for Thy fixed a-bode
sin-ners pray to live, Hear Thou in heav'n, Thy dwell-ing place;
Gos-pel of Thy Son, Still by the pow'r of His great name

And keep it from all er-ror free!
And when Thou hear-est, Lord, for-give.
Be might-y signs and won-ders done. A-men.

4 When children's voices raise the song,
  "Hosanna to the heavenly King!"
Let heaven with earth the strain prolong.
  Hosanna! let the angels sing.

5 Thy glory never hence depart.
  Yet choose not, Lord, this house alone;
Thy kingdom come to every heart,
  In every bosom fix Thy throne.

636 Great Is the Lord, Our God

S. M.

Ps. 48 : 1-8
Isaac Watts, 1719, cento

Schumann
"Cantica Laudis"
Boston, 1850

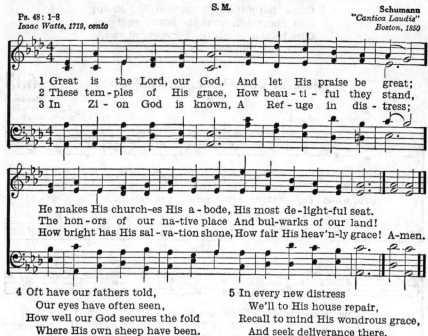

1 Great is the Lord, our God, And let His praise be great;
2 These tem-ples of His grace, How beau-ti-ful they stand,
3 In Zi-on God is known, A Ref-uge in dis-tress;

He makes His church-es His a-bode, His most de-light-ful seat.
The hon-ors of our na-tive place And bul-warks of our land!
How bright has His sal-va-tion shone, How fair His heav'n-ly grace! A-men.

4 Oft have our fathers told,
 Our eyes have often seen,
How well our God secures the fold
Where His own sheep have been.

5 In every new distress
 We'll to His house repair,
Recall to mind His wondrous grace,
And seek deliverance there.

637 Founded on Thee, Our Only Lord

L. M.

Matt. 16 : 18
Samuel F. Smith, 1894

Mendon
German melody
Samuel Dyer, 1828, arr.

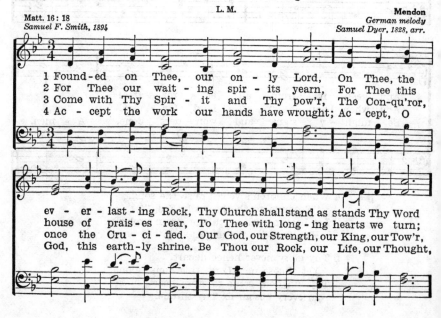

1 Found-ed on Thee, our on-ly Lord, On Thee, the
2 For Thee our wait-ing spir-its yearn, For Thee this
3 Come with Thy Spir-it and Thy pow'r, The Con-qu'ror,
4 Ac-cept the work our hands have wrought; Ac-cept, O

ev-er-last-ing Rock, Thy Church shall stand as stands Thy Word
house of prais-es rear, To Thee with long-ing hearts we turn;
once the Cru-ci-fied. Our God, our Strength, our King, our Tow'r,
God, this earth-ly shrine. Be Thou our Rock, our Life, our Thought,

Founded on Thee, Our Only Lord

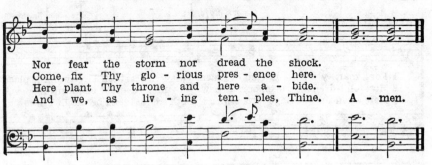

Nor fear the storm nor dread the shock.
Come, fix Thy glo - rious pres - ence here.
Here plant Thy throne and here a - bide.
And we, as liv - ing tem - ples, Thine. A - men.

In Loud, Exalted Strains

638

Gen. 28: 17
Benjamin Francis, 1774, cento, alt.

6. 6. 6. 6. 8. 8.

Darwall's 148th
John Darwall, 1770

1 In loud, ex - alt - ed strains The King of Glo - ry praise. O'er
2 O King of Glo - ry, come And with Thy fa - vor crown This
3 Now let Thine ear at - tend Our sup - pli - cat - ing cries; Now
4 Here may the lis - t'ning throng Re - ceive Thy truth and love; Here

heav'n and earth He reigns Thro' ev - er - last - ing days; But, Zi - on,
tem - ple as Thy home, This peo - ple as Thine own. Be - neath this
let our praise as - cend, Ac - cept - ed, to the skies; Now let Thy
Chris - tians join the song Of ser - a - phim a - bove Till all who

thou, so rich - ly blest, Art His de - light, His cho - sen rest.
roof vouch - safe to show How God can dwell with men be - low.
Word, the Gos - pel, sound, Spread Thy ce - les - tial bless - ing round.
here may seek Thy face Re - joice in Thy a - bound - ing grace. A - men.

639 For Many Years, O God of Grace

Ps. 84: 1
William M. Czamanske, 1934

8. 8. 7. 8. 8. 7. 4. 4. 4. 4. 8.

Wie schön leuchtet
Philipp Nicolai, 1599

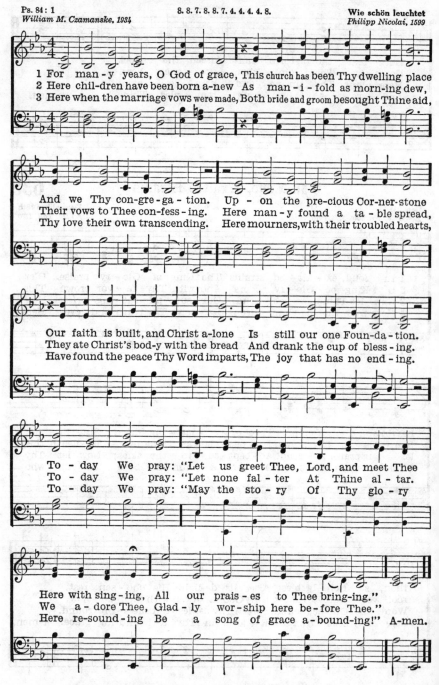

1 For man-y years, O God of grace, This church has been Thy dwelling place
2 Here chil-dren have been born a-new As man-i-fold as morn-ing dew,
3 Here when the marriage vows were made, Both bride and groom besought Thine aid,

And we Thy con-gre-ga-tion. Up-on the pre-cious Cor-ner-stone
Their vows to Thee con-fess-ing. Here man-y found a ta-ble spread,
Thy love their own transcending. Here mourners, with their troubled hearts,

Our faith is built, and Christ a-lone Is still our one Foun-da-tion.
They ate Christ's bod-y with the bread And drank the cup of bless-ing.
Have found the peace Thy Word imparts, The joy that has no end-ing.

To-day We pray: "Let us greet Thee, Lord, and meet Thee
To-day We pray: "Let none fal-ter At Thine al-tar.
To-day We pray: "May the sto-ry Of Thy glo-ry

Here with sing-ing, All our prais-es to Thee bring-ing."
We a-dore Thee, Glad-ly wor-ship here be-fore Thee."
Here re-sound-ing Be a song of grace a-bound-ing!" A-men.

God the Father, Son, and Spirit

640

8. 7. 8. 7. D.

Is. 54: 2, 3
W. Gustave Polack, 1939

St. Hilary
Source unknown

1 God the Fa - ther, Son, and Spir - it, Ev - er - bless-ed Trin - i - ty,
2 Thou didst guide our fa-thers' foot-steps To this land we hold so dear,
3 Grant that we Thy Word may cher-ish And its pu - ri - ty re - tain.
4 God of grace and love and bless-ing, Thine a-lone shall be the praise;

Hum - bly now our thanks we of - fer, All un-wor-thy tho' we be.
Length-en-ing the cords and cur-tains Of their hab - i - ta - tion here;
Lord, un - less Thou art the Build - er, All our la - bor is in vain.
Give us hearts to trust Thee tru - ly, Hands to serve Thee all our days.

Free - ly Thou hast show-ered bless-ings Count-less as the o-cean's sands,
Strength-en-ing Thy tem-ple's pil - lars As Thou hast from age to age;
Keep us from all pride and boast-ing, Van - i - ty and fool-ish trust,
Lord, be-stow Thy fu-ture bless-ing Till we join the heav'n-ly host,

Bless-ings rich and o - ver-flow-ing, On the la-bors of our hands.
Giv - ing us, their sons and daughters, An a - bid-ing her - i - tage.
Know-ing that our work with-out Thee Soon will crumble in-to dust.
There to praise and serve Thee ev - er, Fa-ther, Son, and Ho-ly Ghost. A-men.

641 One Thy Light, the Temple Filling

8. 7. 8. 7. 8. 7.

Is. 6: 8
John Keble, 1856, cento, alt.

Regent Square
Henry Smart, 1867

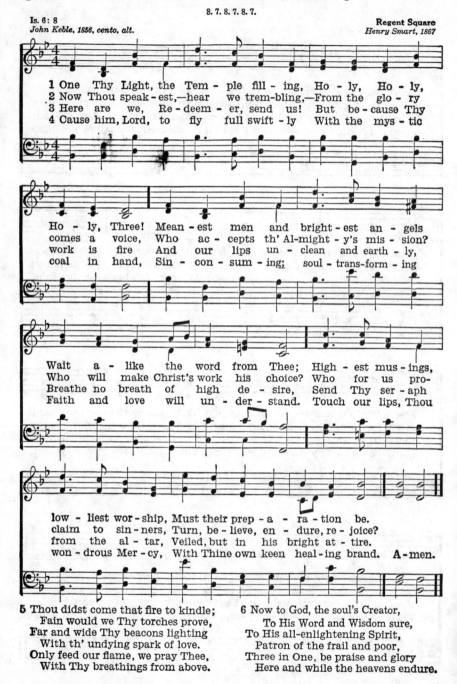

1 One Thy Light, the Tem - ple fill - ing, Ho - ly, Ho - ly,
2 Now Thou speak - est,—hear we trem-bling,—From the glo - ry
3 Here are we, Re - deem - er, send us! But be - cause Thy
4 Cause him, Lord, to fly full swift - ly With the mys - tic

Ho - ly, Three! Mean - est men and bright - est an - gels
comes a voice, Who ac - cepts th' Al-might - y's mis - sion?
work is fire And our lips un - clean and earth - ly,
coal in hand, Sin - con - sum - ing; soul - trans-form - ing

Wait a - like the word from Thee; High - est mus - ings,
Who will make Christ's work his choice? Who for us pro -
Breathe no breath of high de - sire, Send Thy ser - aph
Faith and love will un - der - stand. Touch our lips, Thou

low - liest wor - ship, Must their prep - a - ra - tion be.
claim to sin - ners, Turn, be - lieve, en - dure, re - joice?
from the al - tar, Veiled, but in his bright at - tire.
won - drous Mer - cy, With Thine own keen heal - ing brand. A - men.

5 Thou didst come that fire to kindle;
  Fain would we Thy torches prove,
Far and wide Thy beacons lighting
  With th' undying spark of love.
Only feed our flame, we pray Thee,
  With Thy breathings from above.

6 Now to God, the soul's Creator,
  To His Word and Wisdom sure,
To His all-enlightening Spirit,
  Patron of the frail and poor,
Three in One, be praise and glory
  Here and while the heavens endure.

Arise, O God, and Shine

642

6. 6. 6. 6. 8. 8.

Is. 60: 3
William Hurn, 1813

Darwall's 148th
John Darwall, 1770

1 A - rise, O God, and shine In all Thy sav - ing might
2 Bring dis - tant na - tions near To sing Thy glo - rious praise;
3 Put forth Thy glo - rious pow'r That Gen - tiles all may see
4 To God, the on - ly Wise, The one im - mor - tal King,

And pros - per each de - sign To spread Thy glo - rious light;
Let ev - 'ry peo - ple hear And learn Thy ho - ly ways.
And earth pre - sent her store In con - verts born to Thee.
Let hal - le - lu - jahs rise From ev - 'ry liv - ing thing;

Let heal - ing streams of mer - cy flow That
Reign, might - y God, as - sert Thy cause And
God, our own God, His Church will bless And
Let all that breathe, on ev - 'ry coast, Praise

all the earth Thy truth may know.
gov - ern by Thy right - eous laws.
fill the world with right - eous - ness.
Fa - ther, Son, and Ho - ly Ghost. A - men.

643

Holy Father, in Thy Mercy

Gen. 31: 49
Isabella S. Stephenson, 1889

8. 5. 8. 3.

Stephanos
Henry W. Baker, 1868

1 Ho-ly Fa-ther, in Thy mer-cy Hear our anx-ious prayer;
2 Je-sus, Sav-ior, let Thy pres-ence Be their light and guide;
3 When in sor-row, when in dan-ger, When in lone-li-ness,
4 May the joy of Thy sal-va-tion Be their strength and stay!

Keep our loved ones who are ab-sent 'Neath Thy care.
Keep, oh, keep them in their weak-ness At Thy side.
In Thy love look down and com-fort Their dis-tress.
May they love and may they praise Thee Day by day! A-men.

5 Holy Spirit, let Thy teaching
  Sanctify their life;
 Send Thy grace that they may con-
  quer
 In the strife.

6 Father, Son, and Holy Spirit,
  God the One in Three,
 Bless them, guide them, save them,
  keep them,
 Near to Thee.

THE LONG-METER DOXOLOGY

644

Praise God, from Whom All Blessings Flow

Ps. 150: 1
Thomas Ken, 1695

L. M.

Old Hundredth
"Genevan Psalter," 1551

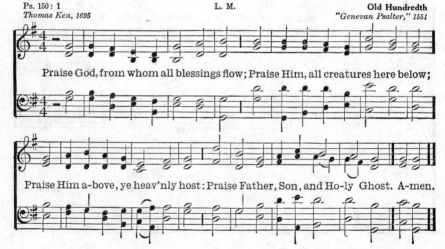

Praise God, from whom all blessings flow; Praise Him, all creatures here below;

Praise Him a-bove, ye heav'nly host: Praise Father, Son, and Ho-ly Ghost. A-men.

Behold, a Branch is Growing

645

Is. 11: 1, 2
Es ist ein' Ros' entsprungen
German author unknown, c. 1500
Tr., st. 1-4, Harriet R. Spaeth, 1875
Tr., st. 5, John C. Mattes, 1914

7. 6. 7. 6. 6. 7. 6.

Es ist ein' Ros'
"Alte geistliche Kirchengesäng"
Cologne, 1599

1 Be - hold, a Branch is grow - ing Of love - liest form and grace,
2 I - sa - iah hath fore - told It In words of prom - ise sure,
3 The shep - herds heard the sto - ry, Pro - claimed by an - gels bright,

As proph - ets sung, fore - know - ing; It springs from Jes - se's race
And Ma - ry's arms en - fold It, A vir - gin meek and pure.
How Christ, the Lord of Glo - ry, Was born on earth this night.

And bears one lit - tle Flow'r In midst of cold - est
Thro' God's e - ter - nal will This Child to her is
To Beth - le - hem they sped And in the man - ger

win - ter, At deep - est mid - night hour.
giv - en, At mid - night calm and still.
found Him, As an - gel her - alds said. A - men.

4 This Flower whose fragrance tender
　With sweetness fills the air,
Dispels with glorious splendor
　The darkness everywhere.
True Man, yet very God;
　From sin and death He saves us
And lightens every load.

5 O Savior, Child of Mary,
　Who felt our human woe;
O Savior, King of Glory,
　Who dost our weakness know,
Bring us at length, we pray,
　To the bright courts of heaven
And to the endless day.

646

Silent Night! Holy Night!

Luke 2: 8
Stille Nacht
Joseph Mohr, 1818
Tr., unknown

Irregular

Stille Nacht
Franz Gruber, 1818

1 Si - lent night! Ho - ly night! All is calm,
2 Si - lent night! Ho - ly night! Shep - herds quake
3 Si - lent night! Ho - ly night! Son of God,

all is bright, Round yon Vir - gin Moth - er and Child.
at the sight; Glo - ries stream from heav - en a - far,
love's pure light Ra - diant beams from Thy ho - ly face,

Ho - ly In - fant, so ten - der and mild, Sleep in
Heav'n - ly hosts sing, Al - le - lu - ia, Christ, the
With the dawn of re - deem - ing grace, Je - sus,

heav - en - ly peace, Sleep in heav - en - ly peace.
Sav - ior, is born! Christ, the Sav - ior, is born!
Lord, at Thy birth, Je - sus, Lord, at Thy birth. A - men.

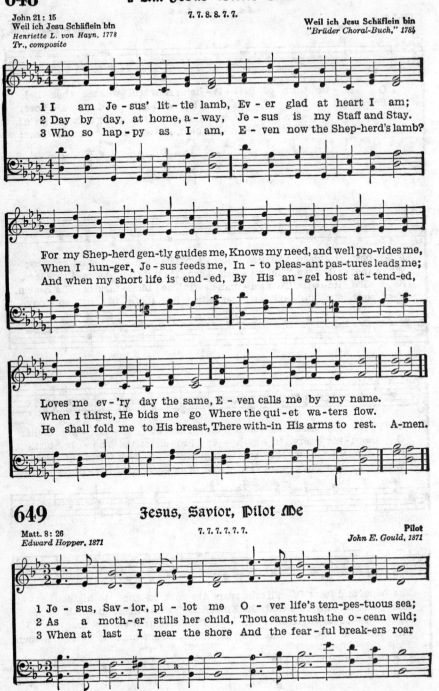

648

I Am Jesus' Little Lamb

John 21: 15
Weil ich Jesu Schäflein bin
Henriette L. von Hayn, 1778
Tr., composite

7. 7. 8. 8. 7. 7.

Weil ich Jesu Schäflein bin
"Brüder Choral-Buch," 1784

1 I am Je-sus' lit-tle lamb, Ev - er glad at heart I am;
2 Day by day, at home, a - way, Je - sus is my Staff and Stay.
3 Who so hap-py as I am, E - ven now the Shep-herd's lamb?

For my Shep-herd gen-tly guides me, Knows my need, and well pro-vides me,
When I hun-ger, Je - sus feeds me, In - to pleas-ant pas-tures leads me;
And when my short life is end-ed, By His an - gel host at - tend-ed,

Loves me ev -'ry day the same, E - ven calls me by my name.
When I thirst, He bids me go Where the qui - et wa-ters flow.
He shall fold me to His breast, There with-in His arms to rest. A-men.

649

Jesus, Savior, Pilot Me

Matt. 8: 26
Edward Hopper, 1871

7. 7. 7. 7. 7. 7.

Pilot
John E. Gould, 1871

1 Je - sus, Sav - ior, pi - lot me O - ver life's tem-pes-tuous sea;
2 As a moth - er stills her child, Thou canst hush the o - cean wild;
3 When at last I near the shore And the fear - ful break-ers roar

O Little Town of Bethlehem

647

8. 6. 4. 4. 6. 7. 6. 4. 4. 6.

Micah 5: 2
Phillips Brooks, 1868, ab.

St. Louis
Lewis H. Redner, 1868

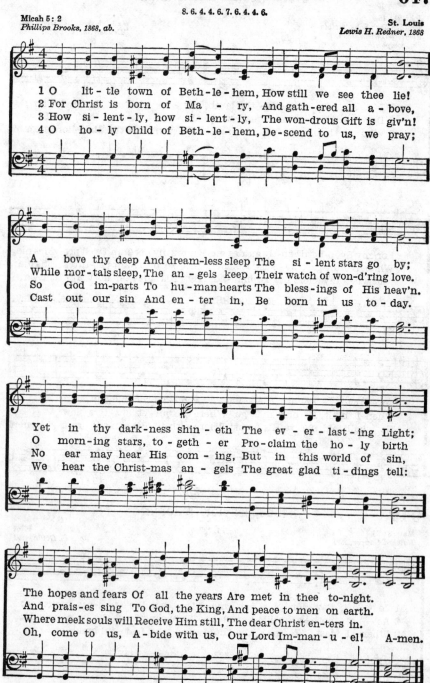

1 O lit-tle town of Beth-le-hem, How still we see thee lie!
2 For Christ is born of Ma - ry, And gath-ered all a - bove,
3 How si-lent-ly, how si-lent-ly, The won-drous Gift is giv'n!
4 O ho - ly Child of Beth-le-hem, De-scend to us, we pray;

A - bove thy deep And dream-less sleep The si - lent stars go by;
While mor-tals sleep, The an - gels keep Their watch of won-d'ring love.
So God im-parts To hu - man hearts The bless-ings of His heav'n.
Cast out our sin And en - ter in, Be born in us to - day.

Yet in thy dark-ness shin-eth The ev - er - last-ing Light;
O morn-ing stars, to - geth - er Pro-claim the ho - ly birth
No ear may hear His com-ing, But in this world of sin,
We hear the Christ-mas an - gels The great glad ti - dings tell:

The hopes and fears Of all the years Are met in thee to-night.
And prais-es sing To God, the King, And peace to men on earth.
Where meek souls will Receive Him still, The dear Christ en-ters in.
Oh, come to us, A - bide with us, Our Lord Im-man-u - el! A-men.

Jesus, Savior, Pilot Me

Un-known waves be-fore me roll, Hid-ing rock and treach-'rous shoal.
Bois-t'rous waves o-bey Thy will When Thou say'st to them, "Be still!"
'Twixt me and the peace-ful rest, Then, while lean-ing on Thy breast,

Chart and com-pass come from Thee: Je-sus, Sav-ior, pi-lot me.
Won-drous Sov-'reign of the sea, Je-sus, Sav-ior, pi-lot me.
May I hear Thee say to me, "Fear not, I will pi-lot thee." A-men.

Behold a Stranger at the Door 650

L. M.

Rev. 3: 20
Joseph Grigg, 1765, cento

Hamburg
Based on First Gregorian Chant
Arr. by Lowell Mason, 1824

1 Be-hold a Stran-ger at the door! He gen-tly knocks, has knocked before,
2 But will He prove a friend in-deed? He will; the ver-y Friend you need;
3 O love-ly at-ti-tude! He stands With melting heart and la-den hands;

Has waited long, is wait-ing still; You treat no other friend so ill.
The Friend of sinners—yes, 'tis He, With garments dyed on Cal-va-ry.
O matchless kindness! And He shows This matchless kindness to His foes. A-men.

4 Admit Him lest His anger burn
And He, departing, ne'er return;
Admit Him, or the hour's at hand
When at His door denied you'll stand.

5 Oh, let the heavenly Stranger in,
Let in thy heart His reign begin.
Admit Him, open wide the door,
And He will bless thee evermore.

651

Be Still, My Soul

Ps. 46: 10
Stille, mein Wille
Catharina von Schlegel, 1752, cento
Tr., Jane Borthwick, 1855

10. 10. 10. 10. 10. 10.

Finlandia
Jean Sibelius, b. 1865, arr.

1 Be still, my soul; the Lord is on thy side; Bear pa-tient-ly the
2 Be still, my soul; thy God doth un-der-take To guide the fu-ture
3 Be still, my soul, tho' dear-est friends de-part And all is dark-ened
4 Be still, my soul; the hour is hast-'ning on When we shall be for-

cross of grief or pain; Leave to thy God to or-der and pro-vide;
as He hath the past. Thy hope, thy con-fi-dence, let noth-ing shake;
in the vale of tears; Then shalt thou bet-ter know His love, His heart,
ev-er with the Lord, When dis-ap-point-ment, grief, and fear are gone,

In ev-'ry change He faith-ful will re-main. Be still, my soul; thy
All now mys-te-rious shall be bright at last. Be still, my soul; the
Who comes to soothe thy sor-rows and thy fears. Be still, my soul; thy
Sor-row for-got, love's pur-est joys re-stored. Be still, my soul; when

best, thy heav'n-ly, Friend Thro' thorn-y ways leads to a joy-ful end.
waves and winds still know His voice who ruled them while He dwelt below.
Je-sus can re-pay From His own ful-ness all He takes a-way.
change and tears are past, All safe and bless-ed we shall meet at last. A-men.

I Lay My Sins on Jesus

652

7. 6. 7. 6. D.

John 1: 29
Horatius Bonar, 1843

Aurelia
Samuel S. Wesley, 1864

1 I lay my sins on Je-sus, The spot-less Lamb of God;
2 I lay my wants on Je-sus, All ful-ness dwells in Him;
3 I rest my soul on Je-sus, This wea-ry soul of mine;
4 I long to be like Je-sus, Meek, lov-ing, low-ly, mild;

He bears them all and frees us From the ac-curs-ed load.
He heal-eth my dis-eas-es, He doth my soul re-deem.
His right hand me em-brac-es, I on His breast re-cline.
I long to be like Je-sus, The Fa-ther's ho-ly Child.

I bring my guilt to Je-sus To wash my crim-son stains
I lay my griefs on Je-sus, My bur-dens and my cares;
I love the name of Je-sus, Im-man-uel, Christ, the Lord;
I long to be with Je-sus A-mid the heav'n-ly throng

White in His blood most pre-cious Till not a spot re-mains.
He from them all re-leas-es, He all my sor-rows shares.
Like fra-grance on the breez-es His name a-broad is poured.
To sing with saints His prais-es, To learn the an-gels' song. A-men.

653 Now the Light has Gone Away

7. 7. 7. 7.

Ps. 3 : 5
Frances R. Havergal, 1869

Müde bin ich
"Liederbuch für Kleinkinder-Schulen"
Kaiserswerth, 1842

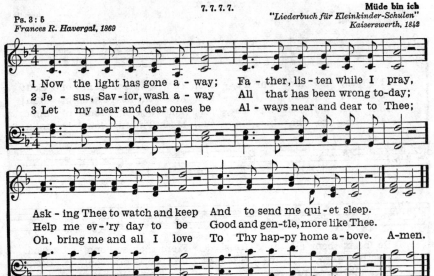

1 Now the light has gone a - way; Fa - ther, lis - ten while I pray,
2 Je - sus, Sav - ior, wash a - way All that has been wrong to-day;
3 Let my near and dear ones be Al - ways near and dear to Thee;

Ask - ing Thee to watch and keep And to send me qui - et sleep.
Help me ev - 'ry day to be Good and gen - tle, more like Thee.
Oh, bring me and all I love To Thy hap - py home a - bove. A - men.

4 Now my evening praise I give;
Thou didst die that I might live.
All my blessings come from Thee;
Oh, how good Thou art to me!

5 Thou, my best and kindest Friend,
Thou wilt love me to the end.
Let me love Thee more and more,
Always better than before.

654 Now the Day Is Over

Prov. 3 : 24
Sabine Baring-Gould, 1865

6. 5. 6. 5.

Eudoxia
Sabine Baring-Gould, 1865

1 Now the day is o - ver, Night is draw - ing nigh;
2 Now the dark - ness gath - ers, Stars be - gin to peep,
3 Je - sus, give the wea - ry Calm and sweet re - pose;
4 Grant to lit - tle chil - dren Vi - sions bright of Thee;

Shad - ows of the eve - ning Steal a - cross the sky.
Birds and beasts and flow - ers Soon will be a - sleep.
With Thy ten - d'rest bless - ing May mine eye - lids close.
Guard the sail - ors toss - ing On the deep - blue sea. A - men.

5 Comfort every sufferer
  Watching late in pain;
Those who plan some evil
  From their sin restrain.

6 Through the long night watches
  May Thine angels spread
Their white wings above me,
  Watching round my bed.

7 When the morning wakens,
  Then may I arise
Pure and fresh and sinless
  In Thy holy eyes.

8 Glory to the Father,
  Glory to the Son,
And to Thee, blest Spirit,
  While all ages run.

I Pray Thee, Dear Lord Jesus 655

7. 6. 7. 6. D.

1 John 3: 23
O Jesu, gid du vilde
Thomas Kingo, 1699
Tr., Norman A. Madson, 1939

Jeg vil mig Herren love
Hartnack Zinck's "Koralbog," 1801

I pray Thee, dear Lord Je - sus, My heart to keep and train
That I Thy ho - ly tem - ple From youth to age re - main.
Turn Thou my tho'ts for - ev - er From world-ly wis-dom's lore;
If I but learn to know Thee, I shall not want for more. A - men.

656 Behold a Host, Arrayed in White

8. 8. 8. 6. 12 lines

Rev. 7: 13-17
Den store hvide Flok vi se
Hans A. Brorson, c. 1760
Tr., composite

Great White Host
Norwegian folk-tune, c. 1600
Arr. *by Edvard H. Grieg,* †1907, ad.

1 Be-hold a host, ar-rayed in white, Like thousand snow-clad mountains bright,
2 Despised and scorned, they sojourned here; But now, how glo-rious they ap-pear!
3 Then hail, ye might-y le-gions, yea, All hail! Now safe and blest for aye,

With palms they stand. Who is this band Be - fore the throne of light?
Those mar-tyrs stand a priest-ly band, God's throne for-ev-er near.
And praise the Lord, who with His Word Sus-tained you on the way.

Lo, these are they of glo-rious fame Who from the great af - flic-tion came
So oft, in trou-bled days gone by, In an-guish they would weep and sigh,
Ye did the joys of earth dis-dain, Ye toiled and sowed in tears and pain.

And in the flood of Je - sus' blood Are cleansed from guilt and blame.
At home a-bove the God of Love For aye their tears shall dry.
Fare-well, now bring your sheaves and sing Sal - va - tion's glad re - frain.

Now gath-ered in the ho - ly place, Their voic-es they in wor-ship raise,
They now en - joy their Sab-bath rest, The pas-chal ban - quet of the blest;
Swing high your palms, lift up your song, Yea, make it myr - iad voic-es strong.

Their anthems swell where God doth dwell, Mid an-gels' songs of praise.
The Lamb, their Lord, at fes-tal board Him-self is Host and Guest.
E - ter - nal-ly shall praise to Thee, God, and the Lamb be-long. A-men.

Beautiful Savior 657

Ps. 45: 2
Schönster Herr Jesu
Author unknown, 1677
Tr., Joseph A. Seiss, 1873

5. 5. 7. 5. 5. 8.

Schönster Herr Jesu
"Schlesische Volkslieder"
Leipzig, 1842

1 Beau - ti - ful Sav - ior, King of Cre - a - tion, Son of
2 Fair are the mead - ows, Fair are the wood-lands, Robed in
3 Fair is the sun - shine, Fair is the moon-light, Bright the
4 Beau - ti - ful Sav - ior, Lord of the na - tions, Son of

God and Son of Man! Tru - ly I'd love Thee, Tru - ly I'd
flow'rs of bloom-ing spring; Je - sus is fair - er, Je - sus is
spar - kling stars on high; Je - sus shines bright-er, Je - sus shines
God and Son of Man! Glo - ry and hon - or, Praise, ad - o -

serve Thee, Light of my soul, my Joy, my Crown.
pur - er; He makes our sor-r'wing spir - it sing.
pur - er, Than all the an - gels in the sky.
ra - tion, Now and for - ev - er-more be Thine! A - men.

658 Onward, Christian Soldiers

6. 5. 6. 5. D., with Refrain

Matt. 16: 18
Sabine Baring-Gould, 1864

St. Gertrude
Arthur S. Sullivan, 1871

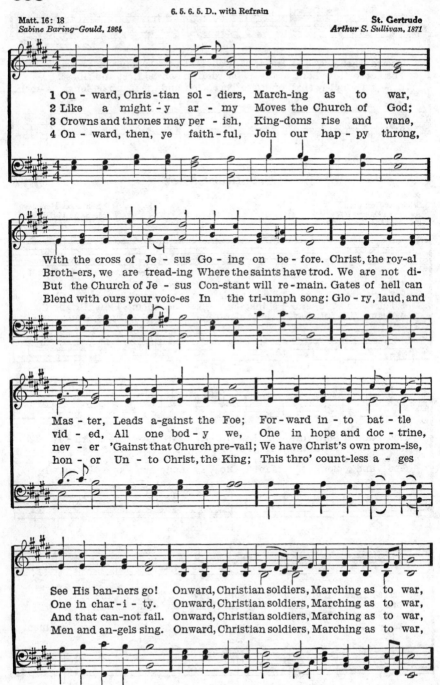

1 On - ward, Chris - tian sol - diers, March - ing as to war,
2 Like a might - y ar - my Moves the Church of God;
3 Crowns and thrones may per - ish, King - doms rise and wane,
4 On - ward, then, ye faith - ful, Join our hap - py throng,

With the cross of Je - sus Go - ing on be - fore. Christ, the roy - al
Broth-ers, we are tread-ing Where the saints have trod. We are not di-
But the Church of Je - sus Con-stant will re - main. Gates of hell can
Blend with ours your voic-es In the tri-umph song: Glo - ry, laud, and

Mas - ter, Leads a-gainst the Foe; For - ward in - to bat - tle
vid - ed, All one bod - y we, One in hope and doc - trine,
nev - er 'Gainst that Church pre-vail; We have Christ's own prom-ise,
hon - or Un - to Christ, the King; This thro' count-less a - ges

See His ban-ners go! Onward, Christian soldiers, Marching as to war,
One in char - i - ty. Onward, Christian soldiers, Marching as to war,
And that can-not fail. Onward, Christian soldiers, Marching as to war,
Men and an-gels sing. Onward, Christian soldiers, Marching as to war,

Onward, Christian Soldiers

With the cross of Je - sus Go - ing on be - fore.
With the cross of Je - sus Go - ing on be - fore.
With the cross of Je - sus Go - ing on be - fore.
With the cross of Je - sus Go - ing on be - fore. A - men.

Feed Thy Children, God Most Holy 659

Ps. 145: 15, 16
Speis uns, o Gott, deine Kinder
Johann Heermann, 1656, alt.
Tr., composite

8. 8. 8. 8. 8. 8. 8. 8. Trochaic

Schmücke dich
Johann Crüger, 1649

Feed Thy chil-dren, God most ho-ly, Com-fort sin-ners poor and low-ly;

O Thou Bread of Life from heav-en, Bless the food Thou here hast giv-en!

As these gifts the bod-y nour-ish, May our souls in gra-ces flour-ish

Till with saints in heav'nly splendor At Thy feast due thanks we render. A-men.

660

I'm But a Stranger Here

6. 4. 6. 4. 6. 6. 6. 4.

Heb. 4: 9
T. R. Taylor, 1836, alt.

Heaven Is My Home
Arthur S. Sullivan, 1872

1 I'm but a stran-ger here, Heav'n is my home;
2 What though the tem-pest rage, Heav'n is my home;
3 There at my Sav-ior's side Heav'n is my home;
4 There-fore I mur-mur not, Heav'n is my home;

Earth is a des-ert drear, Heav'n is my home.
Short is my pil-grim-age, Heav'n is my home;
I shall be glo-ri-fied, Heav'n is my home.
What-e'er my earth-ly lot, Heav'n is my home;

Dan-ger and sor-row stand Round me on ev-'ry hand;
And time's wild win-try blast Soon shall be o-ver-past;
There are the good and blest, Those I love most and best;
And I shall sure-ly stand There at my Lord's right hand.

Heav'n is my fa-ther-land, Heav'n is my home.
I shall reach home at last, Heav'n is my home.
And there I, too, shall rest, Heav'n is my home.
Heav'n is my fa-ther-land, Heav'n is my home. A-men.

Martin Luther, 1529
Tr. unknown

Johann Spangenberg, 1545, ad.

Minister:

Congregation:

1 O Lord,
2 O Christ,
3 O Lord,
4 O Christ,
5 O God the Father in heaven,
6 O God the Son, Redeemer of the world,
7 O God the Holy Ghost,

1 Have mercy up - on us.
2 Have mercy up - on us.
3 Have mercy up - on us.
4 Hear Thou us.
5 Have mercy up - on us.
6 Have mercy up - on us.
7 Have mercy up - on us.

1 Be gracious unto us.
2 Be gracious unto us.

1 Spare us, good Lord.
2 Help us, good Lord.

From all sin;
From all error;
From all evil:

Good Lord, de - liv - er us.

From the crafts and assaults of the devil;
From sudden and evil death;
From pestilence and famine;
From war and bloodshed;
From sedition and rebellion;
From lightning and tempest;
From all calamity by fire and water;
And from everlasting death:

Good Lord, de - liv - er us.

By the mystery of Thy holy Incarnation;
By Thy holy Nativity;
By Thy baptism, fasting, and temptation;
By Thine agony and bloody sweat;
By Thy cross and Passion;
By Thy precious death and burial;
By Thy glorious resurrection and ascension;
And by the coming of the Holy Ghost, the Comforter:

Help us, good Lord.

℣: ℟:

In all time of our tribulation;
In all time of our prosperity;
In the hour of death;
And in the day of Judgment:

Help us, good Lord.

We poor sinners do beseech Thee

To hear us, O Lord God,

And to rule and govern Thy holy Christian Church;
To preserve all pastors and ministers of Thy Church in the true knowledge and understanding of Thy Word and in holiness of life;
To put an end to all schisms and causes of offense;
To bring into the way of truth all such as have erred and are deceived;
To beat down Satan under our feet;
To send faithful laborers into Thy harvest;
To accompany Thy Word with Thy Spirit and grace;
To raise up them that fall and to strengthen such as do stand;
And to comfort and help the weakhearted and the distressed:

We beseech Thee to hear us, good Lord.

To give all nations peace and concord;
To preserve our country from discord and contention;
To give to our nation perpetual victory over all its enemies;
To direct and defend our President and all in authority;
And to bless and keep our magistrates and all our people:

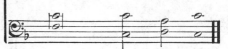

We beseech Thee to hear us, good Lord.

To behold and succor all who are in danger, necessity, and tribulation;
To protect all who travel by land or water;
To preserve all women in the perils of childbirth;
To strengthen and keep all sick persons and young children;
To set free all who are innocently imprisoned;
To defend and provide for all fatherless children and widows;
And to have mercy upon all men:

We beseech Thee to hear us, good Lord.

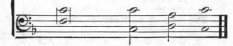

℟:

To forgive our enemies, persecutors, and slanderers and to turn their hearts;
To give and preserve to our use the fruits of the earth;
And graciously to hear our prayers:

We beseech Thee to hear us, good Lord.

O Lord Jesus Christ, Son of God,

We beseech Thee to hear us, good Lord.

O Lamb of God, that takest away the sin of the world,

Have mercy up - on us.

O Lamb of God, that takest away the sin of the world,

Have mercy up - on us.

O Lamb of God, that takest away the sin of the world,

Grant us Thy peace.

O Christ,

Hear Thou us.

O Lord,

Have mercy up - on us.

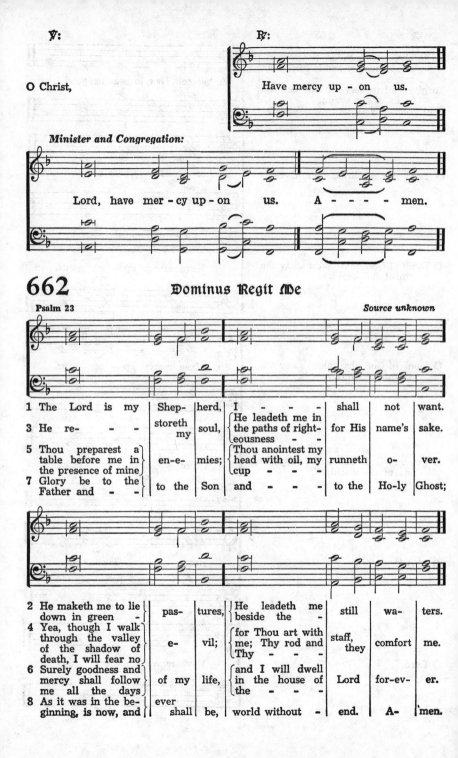

℣:

O Christ,

℟:

Have mercy up - on us.

Minister and Congregation:

Lord, have mer - cy up - on us.   A - - - - men.

662

Dominus Regit Me

Psalm 23

Source unknown

1 The Lord is my | Shep- | herd, | I - - - | shall | not | want.
3 He re- - - | storeth my | soul, | He leadeth me in the paths of right- eousness - - | for His | name's | sake.
5 Thou preparest a table before me in the presence of mine | en-e- mies; | Thou anointest my head with oil, my cup - - - | runneth | o- | ver.
7 Glory be to the Father and - - | to the | Son | and - - - | to the | Ho-ly | Ghost;

2 He maketh me to lie down in green - | pas- | tures, | He leadeth me beside the - | still | wa- | ters.
4 Yea, though I walk through the valley of the shadow of death, I will fear no | e- | vil; | for Thou art with me; Thy rod and Thy - - - | staff, they | comfort | me.
6 Surely goodness and mercy shall follow me all the days | of my | life, | and I will dwell in the house of the - - - | Lord | for-ev- | er.
8 As it was in the be- ginning, is now, and | ever shall | be, | world without - end. | A- | | 'men.

Bonum Est Confiteri

Psalm 92

George A. MacFarren, † 1887

1 It is a good thing to give thanks - -	unto the	Lord	and to sing praises unto - - -	Thy name,	O Most	High;
2 To show forth Thy loving-kindness in the - - -	morn-	ing	and Thy - -	faithful-ness	every	night,
3 Upon an instrument of ten strings and upon the -	psalter-	y,	upon the harp -	with a	solemn	sound.
4 For Thou, O Lord, hast made me glad	through Thy	work:	I will triumph -	in the works	of Thy	hands.
5 Glory be to the Father and - -	to the	Son	and - - -	to the	Holy	Ghost;
6 As it was in the be-ginning, is now, and	ever shall	be,	world without -	end.	A-	men.

De Profundis

Psalm 130

Source unknown

1 Out of the depths have I cried unto Thee, O -	Lord.	Lord, hear my - - -	voice:
3 If Thou, Lord, shouldest mark in- - - -	iquities,	O Lord, who shall - -	stand?
5 I wait for the Lord, my soul doth - - - -	wait,	and in His Word do I -	hope.
7 Let Israel hope in the Lord; for with the Lord there is	mercy,	and with Him is plenteous re- - - - -	demption.
9 Glory be to the Father and to the - - - -	Son	and to the Holy - -	Ghost;

2 Let Thine ears be at- -	tentive	to the voice of my suppli-	cations.
4 But there is forgiveness with	Thee	that Thou mayest be -	feared.
6 My soul waiteth for the Lord more than they that watch for the - -	morning:	I say, more than they that watch for the - - -	morning.
8 And He shall redeem -	Israel	from all his in- - -	iquities.
10 As it was in the beginning, is now, and ever - -	shall be,	world without end. A- -	men.

665
Levavi Oculos
Psalm 121

John F. Burrowes, † 1852

1 I will lift up mine eyes un - - -	to the	hills	from whence -	com-eth	my	help.
2 My help cometh -	from the	Lord,	who hath - -	made	heaven and	earth.
3 He will not suffer thy - - -	foot to be	moved:	{ He that keepeth thee - - -	will not	slum-	ber.
4 Behold, He that keepeth - -	Is-ra-	el	shall - - -	neither	slumber nor	sleep.
5 The Lord is thy -	Keep-	er:	{ the Lord is thy Shade up- -	on thy	right	hand.
6 The sun shall not smite - -	thee by	day	nor the - -	moon	by	night.
7 The Lord shall pre-serve thee - -	from all	evil:	He - - -	shall pre-serve thy	serve thy	soul.
8 The Lord shall pre-serve thy going out and thy - -	coming	in	{ from this time forth and - -	even for-	ev-er-	more.
9 Glory be to the Father and - -	to the	Son	and - - -	to the	Ho-ly	Ghost;
10 As it was in the be-ginning, is now, and	ever shall	be,	world without -	end.	A-	men.

666
Jubilate Deo
Psalm 100

Thomas Kelway, c. 1850

1 Make a joyful noise unto the Lord, -	all ye	lands,	{ 2 Serve the Lord with gladness: come before His	presence	with sing-	ing.
3 Know ye that the Lord, He is God: it is He that hath made us and not - -	we our-	selves;	{ we are His people and the - -	sheep of	His pas-	ture.
4 Enter into His gates with thanksgiving and into His - -	courts with	praise:	be thankful unto	Him and	bless His	name.
5 For the Lord is good; His mercy is ever- -	last-	ing;	{ and His truth en-dureth to all -	gener-	a-	tions.
6 Glory be to the Father and - -	to the	Son	and - - -	to the	Holy	Ghost;
7 As it was in the be-ginning, is now, and	ever shall	be,	world without -	end.	A-	men.

Cantate Domino

667

Psalm 98

James Turle, † 1882

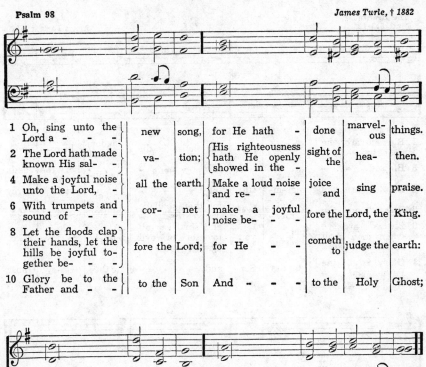

1 Oh, sing unto the Lord a - - - | new | song, | for He hath - done | marvel-ous | things.

2 The Lord hath made known His sal- - | va- | tion; | His righteousness hath He openly showed in the - | sight of the | hea- | then.

4 Make a joyful noise unto the Lord, - | all the | earth. | Make a loud noise and re - - | joice and | sing | praise.

6 With trumpets and sound of - - | cor- | net | make a joyful noise be- - | fore the | Lord, the | King.

8 Let the floods clap their hands, let the hills be joyful together be - - | fore the | Lord; | for He - - | cometh to | judge the | earth:

10 Glory be to the Father and - - | to the | Son | And - - - | to the | Holy | Ghost;

1 His right hand, and His - - - | holy | arm | hath gotten - | Him the | victo- | ry.

3 He hath remembered His mercy and His truth toward the house of - | Isra- | el: | all the ends of the earth have seen the sal- - | vation | of our | God.

5 Sing unto the Lord | with the | harp | and the - - | voice | of a | psalm.

7 Let the sea roar and the ful- - | ness there- | of, | the world and | they that | dwell there- | in.

9 With righteousness shall He - - | judge the | world | and the - - | people with | equi- | ty.

11 As it was in the beginning, is now, and | ever shall | be, | world without - | end. | A- | men.

Beati Pauperes

The Beatitudes
Matt. 5:3-12

James Turle, † 1882

1 Blessed are the | spir- | it: | for theirs is the | kingdom of | heav- | en.
  poor in - -

3 Blessed - - | are the | meek: | for - - - | they shall in- | herit the | earth.

5 Blessed are the | mer-ci- | ful: | for - - - | they shall ob- | tain | mercy.

7 Blessed are the | peace-mak- | ers: | for they shall be called the - | children | of | God.

9 Blessed are ye when men shall revile and - | per-secute | you | and shall say all manner of evil against you - | false-ly | for My | sake.

11 Glory be to the Father and - | to the | Son | and - - - | to the | Ho-ly | Ghost;

2 Blessed are - | they that | mourn: | for they - - | shall be | com-fort- | ed.

4 Blessed are they which do hunger and thirst after | right-eous- | ness: | for - - - | they | shall be | filled.

6 Blessed are the | pure in | heart: | for - - - | they shall | see | God.

8 Blessed are they which are per-secuted for - | right-eousness' | sake: | for theirs is the | kingdom of | heav- | en.

10 Rejoice and be exceeding glad: for great is your reward in - | heav- | en: | for so persecuted they the prophets which - - - | were be- | fore | you.

12 As it was in the beginning, is now, and - | ever shall | be, | world without - | end. | A- | men.

Contents

THE LITURGY

THE HYMNS

General Doxologies

Meter	Hymn Stanzas	Meter	Hymn Stanzas
Short Meter (S. M.)	**68**, 6	7. 7. 7. 7.	**95**, 7
	117, 5		**570**, 8
		7. 7. 7. 7. *with Alleluia*	**199**, 4
Common Meter (C. M.)	**106**, 7		
	360, 7	7. 8. 7. 8. 7. 7.	**250**, 4
	525, 4	7. 8. 7. 8. 8. 8.	**16**, 4
Long Meter (L. M.)	**3**, 4	8. 7. 8. 7.	**60**, 5
	5, 3		
	12, 5	8. 7. 8. 7. D.	**37**, 3
	14, 5		**471**, 6
	63, 5		
	233, 7	8. 7. 8. 7. 4. 7.	**244**, 1
	245, 6		
	331, 8	8. 7. 8. 7. 7. 7.	**257**, 3
	536, 6		
	550, 9	8. 7. 8. 7. 8. 7.	**139**, 4
	558, 6		**466**, 4
	559, 7		
	564, 3	8. 7. 8. 7. 8. 7. 7.	**98**, 5
	644		
		8. 7. 8. 7. 8. 8. 7.	**377**, 10
L. M. with Alleluia	**475**, 4	8. 7. 8. 7. 8. 7. 8. 7. 7.	**500**, 3
6. 6. 4. 6. 6. 6. 4.	**239**, 4	8. 8. 4. 7.	**211**, 7
		8. 8. 7. 4. 4. 7.	**524**, 7
6. 6. 6. 6. 7. 7. 7. 7. 8. 6.	**335**, 4	8. 8. 7. 8. 8. 7. 4. 4. 4. 4. 8.	**23**, 4
6. 6. 8. 4. D.	**40**, 4	8. 8. 8. 8. 8. 8.	**236**, 4
6. 7. 6. 7. 6. 6. 6. 6.	**36**, 3	10. 8. 10. 8. 8. 8. 4. 4.	**26**, 6
7. 6. 7. 6. D.	**9**, 5	11. 11. 11. 5.	**240**, 4

Alphabetical Index of Tunes

Metrical Index of Tunes

Index of First Lines

[848]

Alphabetical Index of Authors

Adam of St. Victor (d. 1172 or 1192).
Adams, Sarah Flower (1805—1848).
Addison, Joseph (1672—1719).
Albert, Heinrich, or Alberti (1604—1651).
Albinus, Johann Georg (1624—1679).
Albrecht von Brandenburg (1522—1557).
Alderson, Eliza Sibbald, nee Dykes (1818 to 1889).
Alexander, Cecil Frances, nee Humphreys (1823—1895).
Alford, Henry (1810—1871).
Allen, Oswald (1816—1878).
Altenburg, Johann Michael (1584—1640).
Ambrose, St. (340—397).
Ämilie Juliane, Countess of Schwarzburg-Rudolstadt (1637—1706).
Andersdatter, Elle (1600—1650?).
Anna Sophia of Hesse Darmstadt (1638 to 1683).
Arends, Wilhelm Erasmus (1677—1721).
Arrebo, Anders Christensen (1587—1637).

Bahnmaier, Jonathan Friedrich (1774—1841).
Baker, Henry Williams (1821—1877).
Barbauld, Anna Letitia, nee Aikin (1743 to 1825).
Baring-Gould, Sabine (1834—1924).
Barton, Bernard (1784—1849).
Bathurst, William Hiley (1796—1877).
Baxter, Richard (1615—1691).
Bede, The Venerable (673—735).
Behm, Martin (1557—1622).
Benson, Louis Fitz-Gerald (1855—1930).
Bernard of Clairvaux (St. Bernard) (1090 to 1153).
Bernard of Morlas (Cluny) (12th century).
Besnault, Abbé Sebastian (d. 1724).
Bienemann, Kaspar (1540—1591).
Birken (Betulius), Sigismund von (1626 to 1681).
Bogatzky, Carl Heinrich von (1690—1774).
Bonar, Horatius (1808—1889).
Böschenstain (Böschenstein), Johann (1472 to 1539?).
Bowring, Sir John (1792—1872).
Boye, Brigitte Katerine (1742—1824).
Boye, Caspar Johannes (1791—1853).
Brady, Nicholas (1659—1726).
Bridges, Matthew (1800—1894).
Brooks, Phillips (1835—1893).
Brorson, Hans Adolf (1694—1764).
Brun, Johan Nordahl (1745—1816).
Bryant, William Cullen (1794—1878).
Byrom, John (1692—1763).

Carlyle, Joseph Dacre (1758—1804).
Cawood, John (1775—1852).
Celano, Thomas de (13th century).
Chorley, Henry Fothergill (1808—1872).
Clausnitzer, Tobias (1619—1684).
Clement of Alexandria, St. (c. 170—c. 220).
Coffin, Charles (1676—1749).
Collyer, William Bengo (1782—1854).
Conder, Josiah (1789—1855).
Cooke, William (1821—1894).
Cooper, Edward (1770—1833).
Cotterill, Thomas (1779—1823).
Cowper, William (1731—1800).
Coxe, Arthur Cleveland (1818—1896).
Crasselius, Bartholomäus (1667—1724).
Cronenwett, Emanuel (1841—1931).
Crosswell, William (1804—1851).
Czamanske, William Martin (1873—1964).

Dach, Simon (1605—1659).
Dayman, Edward Arthur (1807—1890).
Decius, Nikolaus (1490?—1541).
Denicke, David (1603—1680).
Dessler, Wolfgang Christoph (1660—1722).
Dix, William Chatterton (1837—1898).
Doane, George Washington (1799—1859).

Doddridge, Philip (1702—1751).
Downton, Henry (1818—1885).
Duffield, George, Junior (1818—1888).
Dwight, Timothy (1752—1817).

Eber, Paul (1511—1569).
Edmeston, James (1791—1867).
Ellerton, John (1826—1893).
Elliott, Charlotte (1789—1871).
Elliott, Julia Anne, nee Marshall (?—1841).
Elven, Cornelius (1791—1873).
Falckner, Justus (1672—1723).
Fawcett, John (1740—1817).
Fick, Herman (1822—1885).
Fischer (Vischer), Christoph (1520—1597).
Fischer, Eberhard Ludwig (1695—1773).
Fortunatus, Venantius Honorius Clementianus (c. 530—609).
Francis, Benjamin (1734—1799).
Franck, Johann (1618—1677).
Franck, Salomo (1659—1725).
Freystein, Johann Burkhard (1671—1718).
Füger (Fuger, Fugger), Caspar (?) (16th century).
Funcke, Friedrich (1642—1699).

Garve, Karl Bernard (1763—1841).
Gates, Mary Cornelia, nee Bishop (c. 1850).
Gellert, Christian Fürchtegott (1715—1769).
Gerhardt, Paul (1607—1676).
Germanus of Constantinople, St. (634—734).
Gesenius, Justus (1601—1673).
Gramann (Graumann), Johann (Poliander) (1487—1541).
Grant, Sir Robert (1779—1838).
Gregor, Christian (1723—1801).
Grigg, Joseph (c. 1722—1768).
Grodzki, Michal (c. 1550).
Grundtvig, Nicolai Fredrik Severin (1783 to 1872).
Gryphius, Andreas (1616—1664).
Gurney, Dorothy Frances, nee Blomfield (1858—1932).
Gurney, John Hampden (1802—1862).

Hamilton, James (1819—1896).
Hammond, William (1719—1783).
Harbaugh, Henry (1817—1867).
Hart, Joseph (1712—1768).
Hastings, Thomas (1784—1872).
Havergal, Frances Ridley (1836—1879).
Haweis, Thomas (1732—1820).
Hayn, Henriette Luise von (1724—1782).
Heath, George (1745?—1822).
Heber, Reginald (1783—1826).
Heermann, Johann (1585—1647).
Held, Heinrich (?—c. 1659).
Helder, Bartholomäus (?—1635).
Helmbold, Ludwig (1532—1598).
Herberger, Valerius (1562—1627).
Herbert, Petrus (?—1571).
Herman, Nikolaus (c. 1480—1561).
Herrnschmidt, Johann Daniel (1675—1723).
Hertzog, Johann Friedrich (1647—1699).
Heyder (Heider), Friedrich Christian (1677 to 1754).
Holland, Henry Scott (1847—1918).
Homburg, Ernst Christoph (1605—1681).
Hoppe, Anna Bernardine Dorothy (1889 to 1941).
Hopper, Edward (1818—1888).
Hoskins, Joseph (1745—1788).
How, William Walsham (1823—1897).
Humphreys, Joseph (1720—?).
Hurn, William (1754—1829).
Huss (Hus), John (1373?—1415).

Ingemann, Bernhardt Severin (1789—1862).
Irons, Genevieve Mary (1855—?).

Jacobs, Henry Eyster (1844—1932).
John of Damascus, St. (c. 750).
Joseph, the Hymnographer, St. (c. 800—883).
Julian, John (1839—1913).

Keble, John (1792—1866).
Keimann (Keymann), Christian (1607 to 1662).
Kelly, Thomas (1769—1854).
Ken, Thomas (1637—1711).
Kethe, William (?—c. 1593).
Key, Francis Scott (1779—1843).
Kingo, Thomas Hansen (1634—1703).
Kinner, Samuel (1603—1668).
Knapp, Albert (1798—1864).
Koren, Ulrik Vilhelm (1826—1910).
Kunth, Johann Sigismund (1700—1779).

Landstad, Magnus Brostrup (1802—1880).
Laurentius, Laurenti (1660—1722).
Leeson, Jane Eliza (1807—1882).
Lehr, Leopold Franz Friedrich (1709—1744).
Lochner, Karl Friedrich (1634—1697).
Logan, John (1748—1788).
Löwenstern, Matthäus Appeles von (1594 to 1648).
Loy, Matthias (1828—1915).
Ludämilia Elisabeth, Countess of Schwarzburg (1640—1672).
Luther, Martin (1483—1546).
Lyte, Henry Francis (1793—1847).

Mackay, Margaret (1802—1887).
Madan, Martin (1726—1790).
Magdeburg, Joachim (c. 1525—c. 1583).
Major (Gross), Johann (1564—1654).
Malan, Henri Abraham César (1787—1864).
Mann, Frederick (1846—1928).
Mant, Richard (1776—1848).
March, Daniel (1816—1909).
Marriott, John (1780—1825).
Maude, Mary Fawler, nee Hooper (1819 to 1913).
Maxwell, Mary (?).
McComb, William (1793—c. 1870).
Medley, Samuel (1738—1799).
Meinhold, Johann Wilhelm (1797—1851).
Melanchthon, Philipp (Schwarzerd) (1497 to 1560).
Mentzer, Johann (1658—1734).
Messenger, John A. (?).
Meyfart, Johann Matthias (1590—1642).
Milman, Henry Hart (1791—1868).
Milton, John (1608—1674).
Mohr, Joseph (1792—1848).
Molanus, Gerhard Walther (Wolter) (1633 to 1722).
Möller, Johann Joachim (1660—1733).
Monsell, John Samuel Bewley (1811—1875).
Montgomery, James (1771—1854).
Moore, Thomas (1779—1852).
Morison, John (1749—1798).
Mote, Edward (1797—1874).
Mühlenberg, William Augustus (1796—1877).
Mühlmann, Johannes (1573—1613).

Nachtenhöfer, Caspar Friedrich (1624—1685).
Neale, John Mason (1818—1866).
Neander, Joachim (1650—1680).
Neumann, Caspar (1648—1715).
Neumark, Georg (1621—1681).
Neumeister, Erdman (1671—1756).
Newton, John (1725—1807).
Nicolai, Philipp (1556—1608).
Nigidius, G. (1525—1588).

Occom, Samson (1732—1792).
Olearius, Johannes (1611—1684).
Olearius, Johann Gottfried (1635—1711).
Olivers, Thomas (1725—1799).
Omeis, Magnus Daniel (1646—1708).
Onderdonk, Henry Ustic (1789—1858).
Opitz, Martin (1597—1639).
Osler, Edward (1798—1863).

Palmer, Ray (1808—1887).
Perronet, Edward (1726—1792).
Peter, Philip Adam (1832—1917).
Pfefferkorn, Georg Michael (1645—1732).
Pfeil, Christoph Carl Ludwig, Baron von (1712—1784).
Phelps, Sylvanus Dryden, (1816—1895).
Phillimore, Greville (1821—1884).
Pictet, Benedict (1655—1724).
Pisek, Vincent (1859—1930).
Polack, William Gustave (1890—1950).
Pollock, Thomas Benson (1836—1896).
Pope, Alexander (1688—1744).
Preiswerk, Samuel (1799—1871).
Prudentius, Aurelius Clemens (348—c. 413).
Pye, Henry John (c. 1825—1903).

Rambach, Johann Jacob (1693—1735).
Ramsey, Alfred (1860—1926).
Reed, Andrew (1788—1862).
Reusner (Reussner, Reisner, Reissner), Adam (1496—c. 1575).
Rhabanus Maurus (776—856).
Riley, John Athelstan Laurie (1858—1945).
Ringwaldt (Ringwalt, Ringwald), Bartholomäus (1532—c. 1600).
Rinkart (Rinckart), Martin (1586—1649).
Rist, Johann (1607—1667).
Robinson, Charles Seymour, 1829—1899).
Robinson, Joseph Armitage (1858—1933).
Rodigast, Samuel (1649—1708).
Roh (Cornu, Horn), Johann (?—1547).
Romanis, William (1824—1899).
Rosenroth, Christian Knorr, Baron von (1636 to 1689).
Rothe, Johann Andreas (1688—1758).
Rous, Francis (1579—1659).
Ruopp, Johann Friedrich (?—1708).

Sacer, Gottfried Wilhelm (1635—1699).
St. John, Frank B. (?).
Savonarola, Girolamo (1454—1498).
Schalling, Martin (1532—1608).
Scheffler, Johann (Angelus Silesius) (1624 to 1677).
Scheidt, Christian Ludwig (1709—1761).
Schenck (Shenk), Hartmann (1634—1681).
Schirmer, Michael (1606—1673).
Schlegel, Catherina Amalia Dorothea von (1697—?).
Schmidt, Johann Eusebius (1670—1745).
Schmolck, Benjamin (1672—1737).
Schneegass, Cyriacus (1546—1597).
Schneesing (Chiomusus or Chyomusus), Johannes (?—1567).
Schroeder, Johann Heinrich (1667—1699).
Schumacher, Bernard (1886—   ).
Schütz, Johann Jacob (1640—1690).
Scriven, Joseph (1820—1886).
Sedulius, Coelius (c. 450).
Selnecker (Selneccer, Schellenecker), Nikolaus (1532—1592).
Serle, Ambrose (1742—1812).
Shirley, Walter (1725—1786).
Shrubsole, William (1759—1829).
Smith, Samuel Francis (1808—1895).
Spegel, Haquin (1645—1714).
Spengler, Lazarus (1479—1534).
Speratus, Paul (1484—1551).
Spitta, Karl Johann Philipp (1801—1859).
Steele, Anne (1716—1778).
Stegmann, Josua (1588—1632).
Stephenson (Stevenson), Isabella Stephana (1843—1890).
Steuerlein, Johann (1546—1613).
Sthen, Hans Christenson (16th century).
Stone, Samuel John (1839—1900).
Strong, Nathan (1748—1816).
Synesius, of Cyrene (c. 375—430).

Tappan, William Bingham (1794—1849).
Tate, Nahum (1652—1715).
Taylor, Thomas Rawson (1807—1835).
Tersteegen, Gerhard (1697—1769).
Theodulph of Orleans, St. (c. 821).

Thilo, Valentin (1607—1662).
Threlfall, Jeannette (1821—1880).
Thring, Godfrey (1823—1903).
Thrupp, Adelaide (19th century).
Toplady, Augustus Montague (1740—1778).
Tranovsky, Juraj (1591—1637).
Tuttiett, Lawrence (1825—1897).
Twells, Henry (1823—1900).

Walther, Carl Ferdinand Wilhelm (1811 to 1887).
Walther, Johann (1496—1570).
Wandersleben, Martin (1608—1668).
Watts, Isaac (1674—1748).
Wegelin (Wegelein), Josua (1604—1640).
Weisse (Weiss, Wiss, Wegs, Weys, Weyss), Michael (c. 1480—1534).

Weissel, Georg (1590—1635).
Wesley, Charles (1707—1788).
Wesley, John (1703—1791).
Wesley, Samuel, Sr. (1662—1735).
Whittemore, Jonathan (1802—1860).
Wiesenmeyer, Burkhard (17th century).
Williams, William (1717—1791).
Woodd, Basil (1760—1831).
Woodford, James Russell (1820—1885).
Wordsworth, Christopher (1807—1885).
Wortman, Denis (1835—1922).
Wreford, John Reynell (1800—1881).

Ziegler, Casper (1621—1690).
Zinzendorf, Nikolaus Ludwig, Count von (1700—1760).

Alphabetical Index of Composers

Ahle, Johann Rudolph (1625—1673).
Albert, Heinrich, or Alberti (1604—1651).
Anthes, Friedrich Konrad (1812—?).
Atkinson, Frederick Cook (1841—1897).

Bach, Carl Philipp Emanuel (1714—1788).
Bach, Johann Christoph (1642—1703).
Bach, Johann Sebastian (1685—1750).
Baker, Frederick George (1840—?).
Baker, Henry Williams (1821—1877).
Baring-Gould, Sabine (1834—1924).
Barnby, Joseph (1838—1896).
Barthelemon, François Hippolyte (1741 to 1808).
Boltze, Georg Gottfried (c. 1750).
Bortnianski, Dimitris (1752—1825).
Bourgeois, Louis (c. 1510—1561).
Bradbury, William Batchelder (1816—1868).
Brown, Arthur Henry (1830—1926).

Carey, Henry (1692—1743).
Chetham, John (1665—1746).
Clarke, Jeremiah (1670—1707).
Conkey, Ithamar (1815—1867).
Converse, Charles Crozat (1832—1918).
Croft, William (1678—1727).
Crüger, Johann (1598—1662).
Cutler, Henry S. (1824—1902).

Dale, Charles J. (1904).
Daman, William (c. 1580).
Darwall, John (1731—1789).
Day (Daye or Daie), John (1522—1584). (Printer.)
Decius, Nikolaus (1490?—1541).
Drese, Adam (1620—1701).
Dretzel, Kornelius Heinrich (1705—1773).
Dyer, Samuel (1785—1835).
Dykes, John Bacchus (1823—1876).

Ebeling Johann Georg (1620—1676).
Elvey, George Job (1816—1893).
Este (Est, Easte, East), Thomas (1540? to 1608?) (Printer.)
Ewing, Alexander (1830—1895).

Farrant, Richard (c. 1530—1580).
Figulus, Wolfgang (1520—1591).
Filitz, Friedrich (1804—1876).
Fink, Gottfried Wilhelm, (1738—1846).
Franck, Melchior (c. 1575—1639).
Frank, Peter (1616—1675).
Freylinghausen, Johann Anastasius (1670 to 1739).
Friese, Heinrich (18th century).
Fritsch, Ahasverus (1629—1701).

Gardiner, William (1770—1853).
Gastorius, Severus (c. 1650).
Giardini, Felice de (1716—1796).
Gibbons, Orlando (1583—1625).
Gläser, Carl Gotthelf (1784—1829).
Goss, Sir John (1800—1880).
Gould, John Edgar (1822—1875).
Gounod, Charles François (1818—1893).
Grieg, Edvard Hagerup (1843—1907).
Gruber, Franz (1787—1863).

Hammerschmidt, Andreas (c. 1611—1675).
Hampton, John (1834—1922).
Händel, Georg Friedrich (1685—1759).
Harding, John P. (James?) (1850, 1859? to 1911).
Harrison, Ralph (1748—1810).
Hassler, Hans Leo (1564—1612).
Hastings, Thomas (1784—1822).
Hatton, John (?—1793).
Havergal, Frances Ridley (1836—1879).
Havergal, William Henry (1793—1870).

Haweis, Thomas (1732—1820).
Hayne, Leighton George (1836—1883).
Herman, Nikolaus (c. 1480—1561).
Hoff, Erik Christian (1832—?).
Holden, Oliver (1765—1844).
Hopkins, Edward John (1818—1901).
Horsley, William (1774—1858).
Howard, Samuel (1710—1782).

Ilse, Ludwig Herman (1845—1931).
Isaak (Isaac, Izac, Ysack, Yzac), Heinrich (c. 1450—1517).

Kittel, Johann Christian (1732—1809).
Klein, Bernhard (1793—1832).
Knapp, William (1698—1768).
Knecht, Justin Heinrich (1752—1817).
Kocher, Konrad (1786—1872).
König, Johann Balthasar (1691—1758).
Krieger, Adam (1634—1666).

Layriz, Friedrich (1808—1859).
Lemke, August (1820—1913).
Lindeman, Ludwig Mathias (1812—1887).
Luther, Martin (1483—1546).

Mann, Arthur Henry (1850—1929).
Marsh, Simeon Butler (1798—1875).
Mason, Lowell (1792—1872).
Mendelssohn-Bartholdy, Jacob Ludwig Felix (1809—1847).
Meyer, Franz Heinrich Christoph (1705 to 1767).
Meyer (Mayer, Mejer, Meier), Johann David (17th century).
Miller, Edward (1731—1807).
Möck, Christian (1737—1818).
Monk, William Henry (1823—1889).
Morely, Thomas (1842—1891).

Nares, James (1715—1783).
Neander, Joachim (1650—1680).
Neumark, Georg (1621—1681).
Nicolai, Philipp (1556—1608).
Niemeyer, Eduard (1854).
Nigidius (Niege), Georg (1525—1588).
Nigidius, Petrus (1501—1583).

Oakeley, Sir Herbert Stanley (1830—1903).
Oliver, Henry Kemble (1800—1885).
Ouseley, Sir Frederick Arthur Gore (1825 to 1889).

Palestrina, Giovanni Pierluigi Santa da (1525 to 1594).
Polack, Herman Adolph (1862—1930).
Prätorius, Michael (1571—1621).
Prichard, Rowland Hugh (1811—1887).

Read, Daniel (1757—1836).
Redhead, Richard (1820—1901).
Redner, Lewis Henry (1831—1908).
Reinagle, Alexander Robert (1799—1877).
Reuter, Friedrich Otto (Fritz) (1863—1924).

Schein, Johann Hermann (1586—1630).
Schmid, Bernard (c. 1520—c. 1592).
Schop, Johann (?—c. 1664).
Schröter, Leonhart (1540—1602).
Schumacher, Bernhard (1886—   ).
Sibelius, Jean (1865—1957).
Smart, Henry Thomas (1813—1879).
Sohren (Sohr, Sohrer), Peter (c. 1630 to c. 1692).
Spiess, Johann Martin (1715—1772).
Spohr, Louis (1784—1859).
Stainer, John (1840—1901).
Stebbins, George Coles (1846—1945).
Störl (Sterle), Johann Georg Christian (1675 to 1719).

Stobäus, Johann (1580—1646).
Sullivan, Arthur Seymour (1842—1900).

Tallis (Tallys), Thomas (1515—1585).
Teschner, Melchior (c. 1615).
Tye, Christopher (c. 1497—1572).

Vaughan Williams, Ralph (1872—1958).
Vetter, Daniel (18th century).
Vulpius, Melchior (c. 1560—1615).

Wainwright, John (1723—1768).
Walder, Johann Jakob (1750—1817).
Walther, Carl Ferdinand Wilhelm
(1811—1887).

Warren, George William (1828—1902).
Webb, George James (1803—1887).
Webbe, Samuel (1740—1816).
Weingärtner, Sigismund (17th century).
Weisse (Weiss, Wiss, Wegs, Weys, Weyss),
Michael (c. 1480—1534).
Wesley, Samuel Sebastian (1810—1876).
Weyse, Christoph Ernst Friedrich
(1774—1842).
Wheall (Weale), William (d. 1727).
Whinfield, Walter Grenville (1865—1919).
Williams, Aaron (1731—1776).
Williams, Robert (c. 1781—1821).
Wilson, Hugh (c. 1764—1824).

Zinck, Hartnack Otto Konrad (1746—1833).

Alphabetical Index of Translators

A Short Form for Holy Baptism in Cases of Necessity

In urgent cases, in the absence of the Pastor, any Christian may administer Holy Baptism.

Take water, call the child by name, pour or sprinkle the water on the head of the child, saying:

I baptize thee in the name of the Father and of the Son and of the Holy Ghost. Amen.

If there is time, the baptism may be preceded by the following prayer and the Lord's Prayer:

Eternal, merciful God, we pray Thee, extend Thy goodness and mercy unto this child, who now asks; open the door to him (her) who knocks, that he (she) may enjoy the everlasting blessings of Thy heavenly washing and may come to the eternal kingdom which Thou hast prepared through Christ, our Lord. Amen.

Our Father who art in heaven, Hallowed be Thy name; Thy kingdom come; Thy will be done on earth as it is in heaven; Give us this day our daily bread; And forgive us our trespasses, as we forgive those who trespass against us; And lead us not into temptation; But deliver us from evil; For Thine is the kingdom and the power and the glory forever and ever. Amen.